Chapter 2 places the focus on patients' rights, including informed consent, the right to refuse treatment (and the nursing and legal implications when the patient refuses treatment), confidentiality (HIPAA), the right to privacy, and living wills and advanced directives. Chapter 3 advises nurses to be vigilant in their rights and liabilities as employees, as contractors of nursing services, and as participants in grievances, unions, and collective bargaining. Chapter 4 prepares the nurse for her journey through the legal process if she must serve as a fact or expert witness in a medical malpractice lawsuit or as a plaintiff or defendant.

On-the-job legal risks are covered in chapter 5. Included are risks found in high-impact specialty areas: acute care, ambulatory care, community health, long-term care, and academic settings. It presents factors used by a litigious society supported by lawyers, plaintiffs, and systems that seem driven by financial gain: patient safety policies and regulations, staffing, drug administration, triage procedures, sentinel and root cause analysis, and caring for the underrepresented or disabled consumer.

Chapter 6 involves nurses' legal rights off duty, the Good Samaritan Act, giving free advice, and acting during natural or man-made disasters. Chapter 7 covers the aspects of legal documentation, medical record and the law, witnessing and signing documents, and the legal implications of computerized charting.

Part 2, Ethics and nursing practice, includes chapters 8 and 9. Chapter 8 discusses ethics and the law, including moral dilemmas, values, theories, and decision making. Chapter 9 covers ethical conflicts in specialty areas such as those presented in chapter 5. It examines the barriers and facilitators of ethical evidence-based nursing practice embodied in ethics committees, help for the nurse who's a substance user, the patient's right to die, the patient with HIV or AIDS, life-sustaining or life-prolonging interventions, and organ transplantation.

In conclusion, for nurses practicing in today's world, this book serves as a toolkit to legal and professional issues and as a guide toward evidence-based nursing practice.

Rose E. Constantino, RN, PhD, JD, FAAN
Associate Professor
University of Pittsburgh School of Nursing

PART I

Law and nursing practice

Law, nursing, and the legal process

Nurses, as individual citizens, are subject to all the laws of the jurisdiction in which they live. As professional health care providers, nurses are also subject to the laws and regulations established by the board of nursing and nurse practice act in their state or province. These regulations define the scope of practice. Like local, state, and federal laws, these regulations are designed to ensure public safety.

Over the years, nursing practice has expanded dramatically. Technological advances, greater autonomy, increased demand for cost containment, and better educated patients with higher expectations have all contributed to this expansion. As a result, nursing roles and responsibilities have changed. Nurses are being held increasingly accountable and responsible for their actions. Subsequently, more nurses are being named defendants in malpractice lawsuits.[1]

This chapter provides fundamental information on the laws that directly govern nursing. It includes an overview of major concepts that are used to define a nurse's legal responsibilities. It also presents detailed discussions of the nurse practice act—the state law that regulates nursing—and the role of the state board

of nursing. The chapter addresses the legal significance of the nursing license and what to expect when a nurse is disciplined for violating any of the license's provisions. It also describes standards of care, including how such standards are applied and how they may be used as evidence during malpractice litigation. Throughout the chapter, practical advice is presented that reflects legal precedents or expected standards of care.

LAWS

A law is defined as a binding rule of conduct that's established and enforced by an authority to safeguard the public. Public law is associated with direct government involvement. Criminal law involves all federal and state laws that deal with society as a whole. Criminal law deals with felonies and misdemeanors. Private law deals with individuals and the relationships among them. Private law is also known as *civil law*.

Sources of laws

Laws are derived from four major sources: constitutions, statutes, administrative law, and common law. Constitutions dictate how governments are created on the federal and state level. They define authority and identify the specific measures for establishing laws.

Statutes are laws established by legislative bodies. In the United States, these legislative bodies include the Congress or the state legislatures. On the federal level, statutes establish laws and regulatory agencies to oversee health care provisions. On the state level, statutes govern specific health care provisions, such as the content and availability of patient records, living wills, and advance directives; privacy and confidentiality rights and protections; and the definition of child, spousal, and elder abuse.[2]

Additionally, each state is responsible for controlling licensure for institutions and professions. Specific state statutes delineate criteria for licensure of a health care institution. State statutes also are responsible for creating the state board of nursing in each state. Moreover, nurse practice acts are examples of statutes.

Administrative law involves the enforcement of laws via rules and regulations developed by the officers of specific agencies. The state board of nursing is an example of an agency that deals with administrative law. Each board develops specific regulations that define and determine nursing practice.

Common law is associated with the interpretation of legislation in specific situations. The decision is derived by the judiciary system. Common law is also known as *court-made law* or *case law*. The decision derived then becomes the rule to be used when evaluating other similar situations. Common law is typically used in situations involving malpractice.

Civil law

Civil law is administered by individuals rather than by the government. Violations typically are punishable by damages usually in the form of monetary compensation. A judge or jury determines the amount. Civil courts don't impose fines or prison sentences but may rule that a person who violates a civil law must perform a specific action, such as community service.

There are four types of civil law: contract law, labor law, patent law, and tort law. Legal actions involving nursing and health care commonly fall under tort law.

Torts are personal civil injuries or wrongs that reside outside of a contractual relationship. Simply stated, a tort is any action or omission that harms another. Torts result in a civil trial to assess compensation for the plaintiff, the person who files the claim. Torts can be intentional or unintentional.

Intentional torts are a deliberate attempt to violate someone's legal right. Examples include fraud, assault and battery, invasion of privacy, false imprisonment, and defamation of character (slander or libel). Unintentional torts are civil wrongdoings that result from a person's negligence. Examples of unintentional torts include negligence and malpractice. Torts are discussed in greater detail in chapter 4 and chapter 5.

NURSING PRACTICE

The American Nurses Association (ANA) defines nursing as protection, promotion, and optimization of health and abilities, prevention of illness and injury, alleviation of suffering through the diagnosis and treatment of human response, and advocacy in the care of individuals, families, communities, and populations.[3,4] The practice of nursing requires rules and regulations to ensure patient safety and a competent level of behavior in the professional role of the nurse. Nurse practice acts, licensure, and standards of care are key elements in regulating nursing practice.

Levels of nursing practice in the United States

Three levels of nursing practice exist— the advanced practice nurse (APN), the registered nurse (RN), and the licensed practical or licensed vocational nurse (LPN or LVN.) All three levels are designed with special, unique functions in mind. APNs, such as nurse practitioners (NPs), clinical nurse specialists, nurse midwives, and nurse anesthetists, are RNs who have national certification and a master's degree in a clinical specialty. RNs may graduate from diploma (decreasing in numbers), 2-year associate of science in nursing (ASN), or 4-year bachelor of science in nursing (BSN) programs. LPNs, who complete a shorter and less-intensive educational program for entry into practice than RNs, graduate from a 1- or 2-year program.

When licensed, the RN is responsible for developing and managing patient care. The RN must also make professional nursing judgments using the nursing process: patient assessment, planning, nursing diagnosis, implementation, and evaluation.

According to the ANA, the *professional RN* is a graduate of a BSN or higher degree program, and the *technical RN* is a graduate of an ASN program. The function of the professional RN is to develop procedures and protocols and to

set standards for practice; the technical RN implements policies, procedures, and protocols developed by the professional RN. The ANA published its latest *Standards of Nursing Practice* in 2004.

In state law, definitions of the RN's role vary, but basic responsibilities include observing patients' signs and symptoms, recording these observations, notifying the health care provider of changes in a patient's health status, carrying out orders for treatments, and appropriately delegating responsibilities for patient care.

The LPN is commonly referred to as the "bedside nurse" because the role has traditionally centered on the patient's basic physical needs for hygiene and comfort. Many state nurse practice acts define LPN practice as the performance of duties that assist the professional nurse in a team relationship. In some states, the duties of LPNs are more clearly defined in terms of scope of practice; for example, states may prohibit LPNs from inserting I.V. lines.

Because of changes in the workplace, including an emphasis on cutting labor costs, the role of the LPN has expanded over the years. For example, in Pennsylvania, LPNs can now "perform venipuncture and administer and withdraw I.V. fluids" and "administer immunizing agents and do skin testing" if the appropriate requirements are met. Through pressure from long-term care facilities, the Pennsylvania State Board of Nursing now allows the LPN to accept verbal orders from practitioners authorized by law if the appropriate requirements are met (49 Pa Code § 21.145[2] [i] [ii] [iii] [iv] [amended 2003]).

Many states are undertaking measures to deal with unlicensed assistive personnel (UAP). Since 1999, several states passed legislation that defines either the scope of practice or level of accountability of UAPs. The Arizona State Board of Nursing now has the authority to certify nurse assistants and to impose disciplinary measures upon them. In Montana, UAPs are subject to criminal prosecution. North Dakota permits licensed nurses to delegate drug administration to UAPs in specific settings. Virginia allows UAPs to handle insulin administration in the school setting.

Nursing practice in Canada

All Canadian jurisdictions support licensure (commonly known as *registration*) of RNs and nursing auxiliaries (commonly known as LPNs). However, in some jurisdictions, registration isn't mandatory. Some Canadian nursing associations recognize clinical nurse specialists (who usually have master's degrees or doctoral degrees in a specific specialty) and NPs—nurses in expanded roles oriented to primary health care.

In most of Canada's 10 jurisdictions, professional nurses' associations set requirements for graduation from an approved school of nursing, licensing, nurses' professional behavior, and registration fees.

The Canadian RN may receive her education in a diploma school (such as a hospital school of nursing), in a community college, or in a BSN program. One jurisdiction requires a BSN for entry into private practice, and several others may soon have the same requirement. All nurses wishing to practice in Canada must pass the Canadian Nurses Association Test. A nurse also needs to be licensed in the province where she would like to work. Individual provinces issue their own license to practice. A nurse should contact her province board of nursing to confirm the requirement.

Rules and regulations for nursing practice

Each state has a nurse practice act and board of nursing rules and regulations that are designed to protect the public by broadly defining the legal scope of nursing practice. The state legislature enacts the nurse practice act and any amendments. The board of nursing, in accordance with the nurse practice act, publishes its rules and regulations. These rules and regulations, which are generally more specific than what's found in the nurse practice act, establish procedure and carry the same weight as the nurse practice act.

Every nurse is expected to care for patients within these defined practice limits—the most important ones affecting nursing care; if care is given beyond these limits, the nurse becomes vulnerable to charges of violating the law and losing licensure. These laws, rules, and regulations also serve to exclude untrained or unlicensed people from practicing nursing. For a copy of your state's nurse practice act or board of nursing rules and regulations, contact your state nurses' association or the state board of nursing. (See *U.S. and Canadian nurses associations*.)

● NURSE PRACTICE ACTS

The nurse practice act of each state defines the practice of nursing for that state. Nurse practice acts are broadly worded, and the wording varies
(Text continues on page 10.)

U.S. and Canadian nurses associations

This chart lists the name, address, and telephone number, plus the Web site address (when available), of nurses associations in the United States, its territories, and Canada. The American Nurses Association has a Web site (www.nursingworld.org) with links to each state's nurses association Web site.

NATIONAL ASSOCIATIONS

American Nurses Association
8515 Georgia Avenue
Suite 400
Silver Spring, MD 20910-3492
(301) 628-5000
1-800-274-4ANA (4262)
Web site: www.nursingworld.org/

Federal Nurses Association
8515 Georgia Avenue
Suite 400
Silver Spring, MD 20910-3492
(301) 628-5333
Web site: www.fedna.org

STATE ASSOCIATIONS

Alabama State Nurses Association
360 North Hull Street
Montgomery, AL 36104-3658
(334) 262-8321
Web site: www.alabamanurses.org

Alaska Nurses Association
3701 East Tudor Road
Suite 208
Anchorage, AK 99507-1069
(907) 274-0827
Web site: www.aknurse.org

Arizona Nurses Association
1850 E. Southern Ave
Suite #1
Tempe, AZ 85282
(480) 831-0404
Web site: www.aznurse.org

Arkansas Nurses Association
1123 S. University Avenue,
#1015
Little Rock, AR 72204
(501) 244-2363
Web site: www.arna.org

American Nurses Association California
1121 L Street
Suite 409
Sacramento, CA 95814
(916) 447-0225
Web site: www.anacalifornia.org

Colorado Nurses Association
1221 South Clarkson Street
Suite 205
Denver, CO 80210
(303) 757-7483
Web site: www.nurses-co.org

Connecticut Nurses Association
377 Research Parkway
Suite 2D
Meriden, CT 06450
(203) 238-1207
Web site: www.ctnurses.org

Delaware Nurses Association
2644 Capitol Trail
Suite 330
Newark, DE 19711
(302) 368-2333
1-800-381-0939
Web site: www.denurses.org

District of Columbia Nurses Association
5100 Wisconsin Ave, N.W.
Suite 306
Washington, DC 20016
(202) 244-2705
Web site: www.dcna.org

Florida Nurses Association
P.O. Box 536985
Orlando, FL 32853-6985
(407) 896-3261
Web site: www.floridanurse.org

Georgia Nurses Association
3032 Briarcliff Road, NE
Atlanta, GA 30329-2655
(404) 325-5536
Web site: www.georgianurses.org

Guam Nurses Association
P.O. Box CG
Hagatna, GUAM 96932
(671) 477-6877

Hawaii Nurses Association
677 Ala Moana Boulevard
Suite 301
Honolulu, HI 96813
(808) 531-1628
Web site: www.hawaiinurses.org

Idaho Nurses Association
2417 Bank Drive
Suite 111
Boise, ID 83705
(208) 345-0500
Web site: www.nursingworld.org/snas/id

(continued)

U.S. and Canadian nurses associations *(continued)*

Illinois Nurses Association
105 West Adams Street
Suite 2101
Chicago, IL 60603
(312) 419-2900 ext. 229
Web site:
www.illinoisnurses.com

Indiana State Nurses Association
2915 North High School
Road
Indianapolis, IN 46224
(317) 299-4575
Web site:
www.indiananurses.org

Iowa Nurses Association
1501 42nd Street, Suite 471
West Des Moines, IA 50266
(515) 225-0495
Web site:
www.iowanurses.org

Kansas State Nurses Association
1109 SW Topeka Blvd
Topeka, KS 66612
(785) 233-8638
Web site: *www.nursingworld.org/snas/ks*

Kentucky Nurses Association
1400 South First Street
P.O. Box 2616
Louisville, KY 40201-2616
(502) 637-2546
Web site: *www.kentucky-nurses.org*

Louisiana State Nurses Association
5713 Superior Drive
Suite A-6
Baton Rouge, LA 70816
(225) 201-0993
1-800-457-6378
Web site: *www.lsna.org*

American Nurses Association Maine
P.O. Box 3000, PMB #280
York, ME 03909
(207) 799-6350
Web site: *www.anamaine.org*

Maryland Nurses Association
21 Governor's Court
Suite 195
Baltimore, MD 21244
(410) 944-5800
Web site:
www.marylandrn.org

Massachusetts Association for Registered Nurses
P.O. Box 285
Milton, MA 02186
(617) 990-2856
Web site:
www.marnonline.org

Michigan Nurses Association
2310 Jolly Oak Road
Okemos, MI 48864-4599
(517) 349-5640 ext. 14
Web site: *www.minurses.org*

Minnesota Nurses Association
1625 Energy Park Drive
St. Paul, MN 55108
(651) 646-4807
1-800-536-4662
Web site: *www.mnnurses.org*

Mississippi Nurses Association
31 Woodgreen Place
Madison, MS 39110
(601) 898-0670
Web site: *www.msnurses.org*

Missouri Nurses Association
1904 Bubba Lane
P.O. Box 105228
Jefferson City, MO 65110-5228
(573) 636-4623
1-888-662-MONA
Web site:
www.missourinurses.org

Montana Nurses Association
20 Old Montana State
Highway
Clancy, MT 59634
(406) 442-6710
Web site: *www.mtnurses.org*

Nebraska Nurses Association
P.O. Box 82086
Lincoln, NE 68501-2086
(402) 475-3859
Web site: *www.nebraskanurses.org*

New Jersey State Nurses Association
1479 Pennington Road
Trenton, NJ 08618-2661
(609) 883-5335 ext. 10
Web site: *www.njsna.org*

New Mexico Nurses Association
P.O. Box 29658
Santa Fe, NM 87592-965
(505) 471-3324
Web site: *www.nmna.org*

New York State Nurses Association
11 Cornell Road
Latham, NY 12110
Phone: (518) 782-9400
ext. 279
Web site: *www.nysna.org*

U.S. and Canadian nurses associations *(continued)*

North Carolina Nurses Association
103 Enterprise Street
Box 12025
Raleigh, NC 27605
(919) 821-4250
Web site: *www.ncnurses.org*

North Dakota Nurses Association
531 Airport Road
Suite D
Bismarck, ND 58504-6107
(701) 223-1385
Web site: *www.ndna.org*

Ohio Nurses Association
4000 East Main Street
Columbus, OH 43213-2983
(614) 237-5414 ext. 1020
Web site: *www.ohnurses.org*

Oklahoma Nurses Association
6414 North Santa Fe
Suite A
Oklahoma City, OK 73116
(405) 840-3476
Web site: *www.oklahoma nurses.org/*

Oregon Nurses Association
18765 SW Boones Ferry Road
Tualatin, OR 97062
(503) 293-0011
Web site: *www.oregonrn.org*

Pennsylvania State Nurses Association
2578 Interstate Drive
Suite 101
Harrisburg, PA 17110-9601
(717) 657-1222
1-888-707-7762
Web site: *www.panurses.org*

Rhode Island State Nurses Association
67 Park Place
Pawtucket, RI 02860
(401) 305-3330
Web site: *www.risnarn.org*

South Carolina Nurses Association
1821 Gadsden Street
Columbia, SC 29201
(803) 252-4781
Web site: *www.scnurses.org*

South Dakota Nurses Association
P.O. Box 1015
116 N. Euclid
Pierre, SD 57501-1015
(605) 945-4265
Web site: *www.sdnurses association.org*

Tennessee Nurses Association
545 Mainstream Drive
Suite 405
Nashville, TN 37228-1201
(615) 254-0350
Web site: *www.tnaonline.org*

Texas Nurses Association
7600 Burnet Road
Suite 440
Austin, TX 78757-1292
(512) 452-0645
Web site: *www.texasnurses.org*

Utah Nurses Association
4505 South Wasatch Blvd. #290
Salt Lake City, UT 84124
(801) 272-4510
Web site: *www.utahnurses.org*

Vermont State Nurses Association
100 Dorset Street
Suite 13
South Burlington, VT 05403-6241
(802) 651-8886
Web site: *www.vsna-inc.org*

Virgin Islands State Nurses Association
P.O. Box 1794
St. Thomas, VI 00803
(340) 713-0293

Virginia Nurses Association
7113 Three Chopt Road
Suite 204
Richmond, VA 23226
(804) 282-1808/2373
Web site: *www.virginianurses .com*

Washington State Nurses Association
575 Andover Park West
Suite 101
Seattle, WA 98188-3321
(206) 575-7979
Web site: *www.wsna.org*

West Virginia Nurses Association
P.O. 1946
405 Capitol Street
Suite 600
Charleston, WV 25301
(304) 342-1169
1-800-400-1226
Web site: *www.wvnurses.org*

Wisconsin Nurses Association
6117 Monona Drive
Madison, WI 53716
(608) 221-0383
Web site: *www.wisconsin nurses.org*

(continued)

U.S. and Canadian nurses associations (*continued*)

Wyoming Nurses Association
PMB Box 101
501 S Douglas Hwy
Suite A
Gillette, WY 82716
1-800-795-6381
Web site: *www.wyonurse.org*

CANADIAN ASSOCIATIONS
Association of Registered Nurses of Prince Edward Island
17 Pownal Street
Charlottetown, Prince Edward Island C1A 3V7
(902) 368-3764

Association of Registered Nurses of Newfoundland and Labrador
55 Military Road, Box 6116
St. John's, Newfoundland
A1C 5X8
(709) 753-6040
Web site: *www.arnnl.nf.ca/index.shtml*

Canadian Nurses Association
50 Driveway
Ottawa, Ontario
Canada K2P 1E2
(613) 237-2133
1-800-361-8404
Web site: *www.cna-nurses.ca*

College and Association of Registered Nurses of Alberta
11620 - 168 Street
Edmonton, Alberta T5M 4A6
(780) 451-0043
Web site: *www.nurses.ab.ca*

College of Nurses of Ontario
101 Davenport Road
Toronto, Ontario M5R 3P1
(416) 928-0900
1-800-387-5526
Web site: *www.cno.org*

College of Registered Nurses of British Columbia
2855 Arbutus Street
Vancouver, British Columbia
V6J 3Y8
(604) 736-7331
Web site: *www.rnabc.bc.ca*

College of Registered Nurses of Manitoba
647 Broadway Avenue
Winnipeg, Manitoba R3C 0X2
(204) 774-3477
Web site: *www.crnm.mb.ca*

Nurses Association of New Brunswick
165 Regent Street
Fredericton, New Brunswick
E3B 3W5
(506) 458-8731
Web site: *www.nanb.nb.ca*

Registered Nurses Association of Northwest Territories and Nunavut
Box 2757
Yellowknife, Northwest Territories X1A 2R1
(867) 873-2745
Web site: *www.rnantu.ca*

Registered Nurses Association of Nova Scotia
Barrington Tower
1894 Barrington St.
Suite 600
Scotia Square
Halifax, Nova Scotia B3J 2A8
(902) 491-9744
Web site: *www.rnans.ns.ca*

Registered Nurses Association of Ontario
1600 - 438 University Avenue
Toronto, Ontario M5G 2K8
(416) 599-1925
1-800-268-7199
Web site: *www.rnao.org*

Saskatchewan Registered Nurses Association
2066 Retallack Street
Regina, Saskatchewan
S4T 7X5
(306) 359-4200
Web site: *www.srna.org*

Yukon Registered Nurses Association
204 - 4133 - 4th Avenue
Whitehorse, Yukon Y1A 3T3
(867) 667-4062
Web site: *www.yrna.ca*

from state to state. An understanding of a nurse practice act's general provisions is necessary for the nurse to stay within the legal limits of nursing practice. Unfortunately, interpreting a nurse practice act may not be an easy task. Additionally, with the emergence of more autonomous and expanded roles for nurses, many states have started to revise or amend their nurse practice acts to reflect the greater responsibilities associated with current nursing practice. However, nurse practice acts are statutory laws, so any amendments must be accompanied by legislative process, which can be slow and time consuming. Because of the time involved in considering, drafting, and enacting laws, amendments to nurse practice acts may lag well behind the progress of changes in actual practice.

Key definitions

Most nurse practice acts begin by defining important terms, including "the practice of registered nursing" and "the practice of licensed practical nursing." These definitions differentiate between RNs and LPNs, according to their specific scopes of practice and their educational requirements. Some states have separate nurse practice acts for RNs and LPNs.

Scope of practice

Early nurse practice acts contained statements prohibiting nurses from performing tasks considered to be within the scope of medical practice. Nurses couldn't diagnose any patient problem or treat a patient without instructions from a physician. Later, interdisciplinary committees (consisting of nurses, physicians, pharmacists, dentists, and hospital representatives) have helped to ease this restriction on nursing practice. After reviewing some medical procedures that nurses commonly perform, these committees issued joint statements recommending that nurses be permitted legally to perform these procedures in specified circumstances. Some joint statements specifically recommend allowing nurses to perform venipunctures, cardiopulmonary resuscitation, and cardiac defibrillation. Still other joint statements (as well as in-

terpretive statements issued by state boards of nursing and nursing organizations) specifically recommend permitting nurses to perform functions such as nursing assessment and nursing diagnosis. Such joint statements don't have the force of the law—unless state legislatures amend their nurse practice acts to include them. Many state legislatures have incorporated such statements into nurse practice acts. (See *Defining the boundaries of nursing practice,* page 12.)

The nurse practice act also lists violations that can result in disciplinary action against a nurse. Depending on the nature of the violation, a nurse may face state board disciplinary action as well as civil liability for her actions.

Interpretation difficulties

A state's nurse practice act isn't a word-for-word checklist on how the nurse should do the job. Nurses must rely on their own education and knowledge of the hospital's policies and procedures. A nurse may be expected to perform tasks that seem to be within the scope of nursing practice but, in fact, violate the state's nurse practice act.

Nursing diagnoses

Most nurses regularly make nursing diagnoses. A nursing diagnosis is part of a nursing assessment. It's the nurse's professional evaluation of the patient's progress, his responses to treatment, and his nursing care needs. Nurses perform this evaluation to develop and carry out the nursing care plan. It isn't a judgment about a patient's medical disorder. However, in many cases, the state nurse practice acts don't spell out whether nurses can legally make nursing diagnoses.

Defining the boundaries of nursing practice

State nurse practice acts may be characterized as traditional, transitional, or modern, depending on how they define the boundaries of nursing practice.

TRADITIONAL

These nurse practices acts allow only conventional nursing activities. They limit the nurse's responsibilities to traditional patient care, disease prevention, and health maintenance. Traditional nurse practice acts don't allow RNs to participate in expanded nursing activities such as diagnosis, prescription, and treatment. Only a few states continue to have this type of nurse practice act.

TRANSITIONAL

Transitional nurse practice acts have broader boundaries and may include a laundry list of permitted nursing functions. For example, the nurse practice act of Massachusetts allows the following:
• Responsibility for direct and indirect nursing care including providing nursing care

• Health maintenance
• Teaching
• Counseling
• Planning and restoration for optimal functioning and comfort or for the dignified death of those they serve.

Also, Massachusetts broadens the nurse's role by including a separate definition of nurse practitioners. This wording allows nurse practitioners to diagnose and treat patients.

MODERN

States with modern nurse practice acts, such as New York, allow registered nurses to diagnose and treat health problems and to provide traditional nursing care. New York's definition of registered nursing is so broad that it encompasses both current nursing activities and much of what nurses are likely to do in the future.

Some nurse practice acts permit nursing diagnoses but fail to define what the term means. For instance, the Pennsylvania Nurse Practice Act defines the practice of professional nursing as "*diagnosing and treating* human responses to actual or potential health problems through such services as case findings, health teaching, health counseling, and provision of care supportive to or restorative of life and well-being, and executing medical regimens as prescribed by a licensed physician or dentist. The term doesn't include acts of medical diagnosis or prescription of medical therapeutic or corrective measures, except as may be authorized by rules and regulations jointly promulgated by the State Board of Medicine and the Board..."

"Diagnosing" means identification of and discrimination between physical and psychosocial signs and symptoms essential to effective execution and management of the nursing regimen.[5] Unfortunately, this definition and others like it don't distinguish clearly between medical and nursing diagnoses.

Therefore, if the state's nurse practice act permits nurses to make nursing diagnoses, the nurse's sound judgment in applying its provisions should help avoid legal consequences. If the employer's practice and procedures conflict with the nurse practice act, the nurse may be assisted in working out this conflict by going to the state nursing organization to lobby the nursing board for resolution of the conflict.

Procedures and functions

Most nurse practice acts don't specify a nurse's day-to-day legal responsibilities with respect to specific procedures and functions. For instance, along with omitting any reference to nursing diagnosis, some nurse practice acts don't address a nurse's responsibility for patient teaching or the legal limitations on nurse-patient discussions about treatment. However, board of nursing rules and regulations, depending on the state, may provide more guidance.

In a classic case, *Tuma v. Board of Nursing (1979),* the Idaho State Board of Nursing took disciplinary action against a nurse who discussed, at a patient's request, the possibility of using laetrile as alternative therapy. The board suspended her license on the grounds of unprofessional conduct. The Idaho Supreme Court revoked the suspension and ordered the board to reinstate the nurse's license. Why? Because the Idaho Nurse Practice Act contained no provision stating that such a nurse-patient discussion constitutes a violation of the nurse practice act.

Limitations of practice

All nurses must be familiar with the legally permissible scope of their nursing practice, as defined in the state's nurse practice act and board of nursing rules and regulations, and must never exceed those limits. Otherwise, legal problems can develop.

Consider this example. The Pennsylvania Nurse Practice Act forbids a nurse who isn't a certified registered nurse anesthetist to give an anesthetic unless the patient's physician is present. The case of *McCarl v. State Board of Nurse Examiners (1979)* involved a hospital nurse who violated this provision. The Pennsylvania Board of Nursing received a complaint about the incident and conducted a hearing. The nurse admitted to knowing about the law's requirement but argued that the requirement was satisfied by the presence of another physician, although this physician didn't supervise her actions. The board ruled that the nurse had willfully violated a section of the Pennsylvania Nurse Practice Act and issued a reprimand. The nurse appealed, but the court upheld the reprimand.

Independent action

Most nurse practice acts state that you have a legal duty to carry out a primary health care provider's orders. Yet, as a licensed professional, you also have an ethical and legal duty to use your own judgment when providing patient care.

In an effort to deal with this issue, some nurse practice acts give guidance on how to obey orders and still act independently. For example, the Delaware Nurse Practice Act states that the RN practices the profession of nursing by performing certain activities; among these are "executing regimens, as prescribed by a licensed physician, dentist, podiatrist, or advanced practice nurse, including the dispensing and/or administration of medications and treatments." Having said this, the Delaware statute defines the practice of professional nursing as "the performance of professional services by a person who holds a valid license" and "who bears primary responsibility and accountability for nursing practices based on specialized knowledge, judgment, and skill derived from the principles of biological, physical, and behavioral sciences." This wording may be interpreted to mean that a nurse practicing in Delaware is required to follow a physician's or a dentist's orders, unless those orders are clearly wrong or the physician or dentist is unqualified to give them.

When a nurse thinks an order is wrong, she must tell the primary health care provider. If the nurse is confused about an order, then the nurse is to ask the individual to clarify it. If that person fails to correct the error or answer the nurse's questions, it's incumbent upon the nurse to notify her head nurse, nurse manager, or supervisor of these doubts.

A similar problem may arise when dealing with physician assistants (PAs) or APNs. Nurse practice acts in some states specify that nurses may only follow orders given by physicians or dentists, but medical practice acts in those states may allow PAs or APNs to give orders to nurses. Washington and Florida, for example, have decided that PAs and NPs are physicians' agents and may legally transmit the supervising physician's orders to nurses (*Washington State Nurses Ass'n. v. Board of Medical Examiners, [1980];* Fla. Op. Atty. Gen. [077-96, September 1977]).

The State of Delaware permits nurses with advanced credentials to prescribe regimens executed by RNs. Nurses need to know if their health care facility's policy allows PAs or APNs to give nurses orders. If it doesn't, nurses aren't to follow such orders. If facility policy does permit PAs or APNs to give nurses orders, check if such orders must have verification or countersignature of the physician. For further clarification, always check with the state board of nursing.

Conflicts with health care facility policy

Nurse practice acts and health care facility policies don't always agree. For example, hospital licensing laws require each hospital to establish policies and procedures for its operation. The nursing service department develops detailed policies and procedures for staff nurses. These policies and procedures usually specify the allowable scope of nursing practice within the hospital. The scope may be narrower than the scope described in the nurse practice act, but it shouldn't be broader.

A nurse filed suit in federal court after she was fired for not accepting an assignment outside the scope of her nursing practice. She had 9 years of experience in nursing care of adolescents and no training, orientation, or experience in pediatric intensive care, so she refused to accept an assignment floating in the hospital's pediatric intensive care unit. The hospital maintains that the Board's Standards of Nursing Conduct and Administrative Code are intended as guidelines to assist nurses in making day-to-day judgments required by nurses and don't constitute an affirmative duty to refuse an assignment. (*Hudock v. Children's Hospital of Philadelphia*) (filed and pending in federal court.)

Keep in mind that an employer can't legally expand the scope of a nurse's nursing practice to include tasks prohibited by the state's nurse practice act. For example, nurses who measured, weighed, compounded, and mixed ingredients in preparation of parenteral hyperalimentation solutions and I.V. solutions (a long-time hospital practice and procedure) were censured and reprimanded by the New York State Board of Nursing even

Changing a nurse practice act

A nurse practice act can be updated or changed via two mechanisms: amendments or redefinitions.

An *amendment* adds or repeals portions of a nurse practice act or its regulations, thereby giving nurses legal permission to perform certain procedures or functions that have become part of accepted nursing practice. Amendments have the same legal force as the original act. They do, however, have a disadvantage: they represent a piecemeal approach that may allow an outdated nurse practice act to remain in effect.

Redefinition is a rewriting of the fundamental provision of a nurse practice act—the definition of nursing practice. This approach changes the basic premise of the entire act without amending or repealing it. Redefinition might be used, for example, to reverse a definition of nursing practice that prohibits diagnosis. How? By clarifying the term *diagnosis* to allow nurses to make nursing diagnoses. This type of change helps nurses understand exactly what is and isn't prohibited.

When a state legislature changes or expands the state's nurse practice act, it must also repeal sections that conflict with its changes. For example, if a state legislature decides to adopt the nursing board's recommendation for a newly broadened definition of nursing, it must repeal the old definition in the state nurse practice act before it can enact the new definition into law.

though their hospital allowed them to do so. They were placed on 18-month probation and charged with the unlicensed practice of pharmacy in violation of the State of New York's Nurse Practice Act.

Nurses have a legal obligation to practice within their nurse practice act's limits. Except in a life-threatening emergency, nurses can't exceed those limits without risking disciplinary action. To protect yourself, compare the facility's policies with those of the nurse practice act and board of nursing rules and regulations.

Updates to nurse practice acts
To align nurse practice acts with current nursing practice, professional nursing organizations and state boards of nursing generally propose revisions to regulations. Also, the nurse practice act can be changed by amendments or redefinition. (See *Changing a nurse practice act.*)

Nurse practice acts are constantly changed. To ensure the greatest legal pro-

tection, nurses need to thoroughly understand their state's nurse practice act and board of nursing rules and regulations and keep up with any changes. This is easily accomplished by periodically checking the board of nursing's Web site.

State boards of nursing
In every state and Canadian jurisdiction, a nurse practice act creates a state or provincial board of nursing, sometimes called the state board of nurse examiners. The nurse practice act authorizes this board to administer and enforce rules and regulations concerning the nursing profession and specifies the makeup of the board—the number of members as well as their educational and professional requirements. In some states, the nurse practice act requires two nursing boards—one for RNs and one for LPNs. (See *State boards of nursing*, pages 16 to 19.)

(Text continues on page 19.)

State boards of nursing

Alabama Board of Nursing
770 Washington Avenue
RSA Plaza, Suite 250
Montgomery, AL 36104
Phone: (334) 242-4060
Web site: www.abn.state.al.us

Alaska Board of Nursing
Robert B. Atwood Building
550 West 7th Avenue
Suite 1500
Anchorage, AK 99501-3567
Phone: (907) 269-8161
Web site: www.dced.state.
ak.us/occ/pnur.htm

**Arizona State Board of
Nursing**
4747 North 7th Street
Suite 200
Phoenix, AZ 85014-3653
Phone: (602) 889-5150
Web site: www.azbn.gov

**Arkansas State Board of
Nursing**
University Tower Building
1123 South University,
Suite 800
Little Rock, AR 72204-1619
Phone: (501) 686-2700
Web site: www.arsbn.org

**California Board of Registered
Nursing**
1625 North Market Boulevard
Suite N217
Sacramento, CA 95834
Phone: (916) 322-3350
Web site: www.rn.ca.gov

Colorado Board of Nursing
1560 Broadway, Suite 1350
Denver, CO 80202
Phone: (303) 894-2430
Web site:
www.dora.state.co.us/nursing

**Connecticut Board of
Examiners for Nursing**
410 Capitol Avenue, MS#
13PHO
P.O. Box 340308
Hartford, CT 06134-0328
Phone: (860) 509-8389
Web site: www.ct.gov/dph/
cwp/view.asp?a=3143&q=
388910

Delaware Board of Nursing
Cannon Building, Suite 203
861 Silver Lake Boulevard
Dover, DE 19904
Phone: (302) 744-4515
Web site: www.dpr.Delaware.
gov/boards/nursing/index.
shtml

**District of Columbia Board of
Nursing**
Department of Health
825 North Capitol Street,
N.E., 2nd Floor
Washington, DC 20002
Phone: (202) 442-9200
Web site: www.doh.dc.gov

Florida Board of Nursing
4052 Bald Cypress Way, Bin
#C01
Tallahassee, FL 32399-3251
Phone: (850) 488-0595
Web site: www.doh.state.
fl.us/mqa/nursing/

Georgia Board of Nursing
237 Coliseum Drive
Macon, GA 31217-3858
Phone: (478) 207-2440
Web site: www.sos.state.
ga.us/plb/rn

Hawaii Board of Nursing
DCCA-PVL
Att: BON, PO Box 3469
Honolulu, HI 96801
Phone: (808) 586-3000
Web site: www.hawaii.gov/
dcca/areas/pvl/boards/
nursing

Idaho Board of Nursing
280 North 8th Street
Suite 210
PO Box 83720
Boise, ID 83720-0061
Phone: (208) 334-3110
Web site: www2.state.
id.us/ibn/

**Illinois Division of Professional
Regulation**
320 West Washington Street
Springfield, IL 62786
Phone: (217) 785-0800
Web site: www.idfpr.com/
dpr/WHO/nurs.asp

**Indiana State Board of
Nursing**
Professional Licensing Agency
402 West Washington Street,
Room W072
Indianapolis, IN 46204
Phone: (317) 234-2043
Web site: www.ai.org/pla/
bandc/isbn/programs.html

Iowa Board of Nursing
RiverPoint Business Park
400 S.W. 8th Street
Suite B
Des Moines, IA 50309-4685
Phone: (515) 281-3255
Web site: www.state.ia.us/
government/nursing

State boards of nursing *(continued)*

Kansas State Board of Nursing
Landon State Office Bldg.
900 S.W. Jackson Street
Suite 1051
Topeka, KS 66612-1230
Phone: (785) 296-4929
Web site: *www.ksbn.org*

Kentucky Board of Nursing
312 Whittington Parkway
Suite 300
Louisville, KY 40222
Phone: (502) 429-3300
Web site: *www.kbn.ky.gov*

Louisiana State Board of Nursing
5207 Essen Street
Suite 6
Baton Rouge, LA 70809
Phone: (225) 763-3570
Web site: *www.lsbn.state.la.us*

Maine State Board of Nursing
161 Capitol Street
158 State House Station
Augusta, ME 04333-0158
Phone: (207) 287-1133
Web site: *www.state.me.us/ boardofnursing*

Maryland Board of Nursing
4140 Patterson Avenue
Baltimore, MD 21215-2254
Phone: (410) 585-1900
Web site: *www.mbon.org*

Massachusetts Board of Registration in Nursing
Division of Health Professions
Licensure
239 Causeway Street
Second Floor
Boston, MA 02114
Phone: (617) 973-0800
Web site: *www.mass.gov/ dph/boards*

Michigan Board of Nursing
Bureau of Health Professions
Ottawa Building
611 West Ottawa, 1st Floor
Lansing, MI 48933
Phone: (517) 335-0918
Web site: *www.michigan. gov/healthlicense*

Minnesota Board of Nursing
2829 University Avenue SE
Suite 200
Minneapolis, MN 55414
Phone: (612) 617-2270
Web site: *www.nursingboard. state.mn.us*

Mississippi Board of Nursing
1935 Lakeland Drive
Suite B
Jackson, MS 39216-5014
Phone: (601) 987-4188
Web site: *www.msbn.state. ms.us*

Missouri State Board of Nursing
3605 Missouri Boulevard
P.O. Box 656
Jefferson City, MO 65102-0656
Phone: (573) 751-0681
Web site: *www.pr.mo.gov/ nursing.asp*

Montana State Board of Nursing
301 South Park
P.O. Box 200517
Helena, MT 59620-0517
Phone: (406) 841-2300
Web site: *www.mt.gov/dli/ bsd/license/bsd_boards/nur_ board/board_page.asp*

Nebraska Department of Health and Human Services Regulation and Licensure
301 Centennial Mall South
Lincoln, NE 68509-4986
Phone: (402) 471-3121
Web site: *www.hhs.state.ne. us/crl/nursing/nursingindex. htm*

Nevada State Board of Nursing
2500 Sahara Avenue
Suite 207
Las Vegas, NV 89102-4392
Phone: (702) 486-5800
Web site: *www.nursingboard. state.nv.us*

New Hampshire Board of Nursing
21 South Fruit Street
Suite 16
Concord, NH 03301-2431
Phone: (603) 271-2323
Web site: *www.state.nh.us/ nursing*

New Jersey Board of Nursing
P.O. Box 45010
Newark, NJ 07101
Phone: (973) 504-6430
Web site: *www.state.nj.us/ lps/ca/medical/nursing.htm*

New Mexico Board of Nursing
6301 Indian School Road, NE
Suite 710
Albuquerque, NM 87110
Phone: (505) 841-8340
Web site: *www.bon.state. nm.us*

(continued)

State boards of nursing *(continued)*

New York State Board of Nursing
NY State Education Department
Office of the Professions
Division of Professional Licensing Services
Nurse Unit
89 Washington Avenue
Albany, NY 12234-1000
Phone: (518) 474-3817
Web site: *www.nysed.gov/ prof/nurse.htm*

North Carolina Board of Nursing
3724 National Drive
Glenwood Place Office Complex
Camden Building
Suite 201
Raleigh, NC 27612
Phone: (919) 782-3211
Web site: *www.ncbon.com*

North Dakota Board of Nursing
919 South 7th Street
Suite 504
Bismarck, ND 58504-5881
Phone: (701) 328-9777
Web site: *www.ndbon.org*

Ohio Board of Nursing
17 South High Street
Suite 400
Columbus, OH 43215-7410
Phone: (614) 466-3947
Web site: *www.nursing. ohio.gov*

Oklahoma Board of Nursing
2915 North Classen Boulevard
Suite 524
Oklahoma City, OK 73106
Phone: (405) 962-1800
Web site: *www.ok.gov/ nursing*

Oregon State Board of Nursing
17938 S.W. Upper Boones Ferry Road
Portland, OR 97224-7012
Phone: (971) 673-0685
Web site: *www.osbn.state. or.us*

Pennsylvania State Board of Nursing
P.O. Box 2649
Harrisburg, PA 17105-2649
Phone: (717) 787-8503
Web site: *www.dos.state.pa. us/bpoa*

Rhode Island Board of Nurse Registration and Nursing Education
3 Capitol Hill
Room 105
Providence, RI 02908
Phone: (401) 222-5700
Web site: *www.health.ri.gov/ hsr/professions/nurses.php*

South Carolina Board of Nursing
Synergy Business Park
Kingstree Building
110 Centerview Drive
Suite 202
Columbia, SC 29210
Phone: (803) 896-4550
Web site: *www.llr.state.sc.us/ pol/nursing*

South Dakota Board of Nursing
405 South Louise Avenue
Suite 201
Sioux Falls, SD 57106-3115
Phone: (605) 362-2760
Web site: *www.doh.sd.gov/ boards/nursing*

Tennessee State Board of Nursing
227 French Landing
Heritage Place Metro Center
Nashville, TN 37243
Phone: (615) 532-5166
Web site: *www.tennessee. gov/health*

Texas Board of Nursing
333 Guadalupe #3-460
Austin, TX 78701
Phone: (512) 305-7400
Web site: *www.bne.state.tx.us*

Utah State Board of Nursing
160 East 300 South
Salt Lake City, UT 84114
Phone: (801) 530-6628
Web site: *www.dopl.utah. gov/index.html*

Vermont State Board of Nursing
Office of Professional Regulation
National Life Building
North FL2
Montpelier, VT 05620-3402
Phone: (802) 828-1505
Web site: *www.vtprofessionals .org/opr1/nurses*

Virginia Board of Nursing
Perimeter Center
9960 Mayland Drive
Suite 300
Richmond Virginia 23233-1463
Phone: (804) 367-4515
Web site: *www.dhp.state. va.us/nursing/*

State boards of nursing *(continued)*

Washington State Nursing Care Quality Assurance Commission
Health Professions Quality Assurance Customer Service Center
310 Israel Road SE
Tumwater, WA 98501-7864
Phone: (360) 236-4700
Web site: *https://fortress.wa. gov/doh/hpqa1/hps6/Nursi ng/default.htm*

West Virginia Board of Examiners for Registered Professional Nurses
101 Dee Drive
Suite 102
Charleston, WV 25311-1620
Phone: (304) 558-3596
Web site: *www.wvrnboard. com*

Wisconsin Department of Regulation and Licensing
1400 East Washington Avenue
Room 112
Madison, WI 53703
Phone: (608) 266-2112
Web site: *drl.wi.gov/ index.htm*

Wyoming State Board of Nursing
1810 Pioneer Avenue
Cheyenne, WY 82002
Phone: (307) 777-7601
Web site: *http://nursing.state. wy.us*

Virgin Islands Board Nurse Licensure
P.O. Box 304247
Veterans Drive Station
St. Thomas, VI 00803
Phone: (340) 776-7397
Web site: *www.vibnl.org*

The board of nursing is bound by the provisions of the nurse practice act that created it. The nurse practice act is the law; the board of nursing can't grant exemptions to it or waive any of its provisions. Only the state or provincial legislature can change the law. For example, if the nurse practice act specifies that, to be licensed, a nurse must have graduated from an approved school of nursing, then the board of nursing must deny a license to anyone who hasn't done so. This provision applies even to applicants who can provide evidence of equivalency and competency.

In many states and jurisdictions, the board of nursing may grant exemptions and waivers to its own rules and regulations. For example, if a regulation states that all nursing faculty must have master's degrees, the board might be able to waive this requirement temporarily for a faculty member who's in the process of obtaining one.

In most states, the board of nursing consists of practicing RNs. Many boards also include LPNs, health care facility administrators, and consumers—members of the community at large. The state legislature decides on the board's mix; in almost every state, the governor appoints members from a list of nominees submitted by the state nursing association. One state, North Carolina, replaced this appointment process with an elective one, allowing licensed nurses to elect their own board members.

In recent years, there has been some erosion in the concept of the freestanding nursing board. For example, a bill was introduced into the Pennsylvania legislature to eliminate the nursing board and to consolidate all licensing boards and commissions under one bureau, but it wasn't passed into law.

LICENSURE

A state's nurse practice act sets down the requirements for obtaining a license to practice nursing. Entry into the practice of nursing in the U.S. and member board jurisdictions is regulated by the licensing authorities within each jurisdiction. To ensure public protection, each jurisdiction requires candidates for licensure to pass an examination that measures the competencies needed to perform safely and effectively as a newly licensed, entry-level RN.[6] To become licensed as an RN or LPN, an individual must pass the National Council Licensure Examination (NCLEX) and meet certain other qualifications. All states require completion of the basic professional nursing education program. States may have additional requirements; examples include good moral character, good physical and mental health, a minimum age, fluency in English, and no drug or alcohol addiction.

In addition to specifying the conditions for RN and LPN licensure, your state's nurse practice act may specify the rules and regulations for licensure in special areas of nursing practice (usually termed *certification*).

A nursing license entitles an individual to practice as a professionally qualified nurse. However, like most privileges, a nursing license imposes certain responsibilities. A licensed RN or LPN is responsible for providing quality care to patients. To meet this responsibility and to protect one's right to practice, the nurse needs to understand the professional and legal significance of her nursing license.

U.S. licensing laws

Each state's nurse practice act contains licensing laws. They establish qualifications for obtaining and maintaining a nursing license. They also broadly define the legally permissible scope of nursing practice.

Although they vary from state to state, most licensing laws specify:
▶ the qualifications a nurse needs to be granted a license
▶ license application procedures for new licenses and reciprocal (state-to-state) licensing arrangements
▶ application fees
▶ authorization to grant use of the titles *registered nurse, licensed practical nurse,* or *licensed vocational nurse* to applicants who receive their licenses
▶ grounds for license denial, revocation, or suspension
▶ license renewal procedures.

Most state licensing laws don't prohibit nursing students, a patient's friends, or members of his family from caring for him on a routine basis, provided that no fee is involved. They also permit a newly graduated nurse to practice for a specified period while her license application is being processed, and they allow unlicensed people to give care (such as administering cardiopulmonary resuscitation) in an emergency. According to state and federal constitutional requirements, state laws must exempt the following types of nurses from state licensure requirements:
▶ nurses working in federal institutions
▶ nurses practicing in accordance with their religious beliefs
▶ nurses traveling with patients from one state to another.

Canadian licensing laws

Because each jurisdiction in Canada has its own nurse practice act, the laws vary somewhat from one to the next. Licensing laws in all jurisdictions except Ontario require nurses to join jurisdictional nursing associations to obtain their licenses.

Canadian jurisdictions require licensure to practice nursing. Licensing laws establish:

▶ qualifications for membership in the provincial nursing association
▶ examination requirements
▶ applicable fees
▶ conditions for reciprocal licensure
▶ penalties for practicing without a license
▶ grounds for denial, suspension, or revocation of a nurse's license.

Within those jurisdictions that license practical nurses, licensing laws for LPNs are similar to those for RNs.

Federal law and licensure

No federal law has jurisdiction over state boards of nursing. However, federal laws may affect nursing licensure. For example, if a nurse is working in the armed forces and is often subject to transfer, the nurse is required by federal law to hold a current state license but not necessarily in the state to which she is assigned.

A federal public health code requires all state boards that license health care professionals to develop systems for verifying those professionals' continued competence (42 U.S.C. § 13965-2) (2000).

Licensing issues

Before a nurse starts employment, the employer is responsible for checking the nurse's credentials and confirming that she is properly licensed. The nursing li-

What to do if you forget to renew

If you find that you have forgotten to renew your nursing license, use these simple measures to help avoid legal repercussions:
• Notify your employer immediately.
• Find your original license application and immediately notify the state board of nursing of the oversight. Then, ask for a temporary license or authorization to continue nursing until the license is received.

If you can't find the license application, contact the state board of nursing (preferably in writing) for a renewal application and instructions on how to proceed. Then follow the board's instructions exactly.

cense must be current and the nurse must be prepared to furnish proof that she has renewed the license, if necessary.

License renewal

If a nurse fails to renew her license, she can no longer legally practice nursing. (See *What to do if you forget to renew*.) In the United States, an individual can be prosecuted and fined for practicing without a license; fines usually range from as little as $5 to $2,000. The same is true in Canadian jurisdictions that have mandatory registration; in those that don't, the nurse can be fined only for using the initials "RN" after the name.

Fines vary from state to state. For example, Section 223 of the Professional Nursing Law of Pennsylvania states that practicing nursing without a license is a *misdemeanor,* a crime punishable by a jail sentence of 12 months or less. For a first violation, the nurse must pay a fine of up to $1,000 or face a 6-month prison term. For a second violation, the penalty may be a fine of up to $2,000 or 6 months to 1 year in prison, or both. In addition to the criminal penalty, the nurse may be required to pay a civil penalty of up to $1,000.

Some states require active practice in nursing to maintain a license. For example, Maryland requires 1,000 hours of active nursing practice within a 5-year period immediately preceding the date of anticipated renewal *(Title 8 Annotated Code of Maryland, Section 309)*.

The courts have addressed questions concerning license renewal, usually during an appeal of disciplinary action taken by a state board of nursing. The courts don't always agree with the board's decisions. In *Kansas State Board of Nursing v. Burkman (1975),* an RN failed to renew her license and continued to practice nursing. No evidence existed to suggest that she intentionally hadn't renewed her license or knowingly practiced without it. The state board of nursing ruled that her action constituted a violation of state licensing laws and suspended her license for 6 months. After several appeals, a high court ruled that the board had erred, and instructed the board to renew the license.

In *Oliff v. Florida State Board of Nursing (1979),* the court also ruled in a nurse's favor. In this case, the board of nursing refused to renew an LPN's certificate because her application hadn't arrived on time. Evidence indicated that the nurse had mailed her application before the board's specified date. The court ruled that the board's date was a deadline for applications to be mailed, not received.

Change in location
Until the National League for Nursing established the first standardized exami-

nation for nursing licensure, each state had its own qualifications for entry into nursing practice. As a result, arranging to obtain a license in a different state than one's own was usually difficult.

All candidates for licensure currently are required to pass the NCLEX, administered under the auspices of the National Council of State Boards of Nursing. Due to national standards, nurses can now move more freely to new jobs in different states.

When moving to another state to practice nursing, the individual must obtain a license or temporary practice permit from that state before she may legally practice. Most state boards of nursing will license an individual if she is currently licensed to practice nursing in another state or territory. If the person is licensed to practice in Canada, most boards will license the person if her education fulfills the issuing state's requirements; however, some may require the nurse to take the NCLEX examination. The policy of accepting out-of-state licensure is called *endorsement*. Many state boards waive re-examination if the individual is licensed in Canada and wants to practice in the United States. The same usually applies if the person holds a U.S. license and wants to practice in Canada.

When moving to another state, the nurse may be granted a temporary license before its board of nursing has had time to approve the person's application. Nurses need to check both the time limit of the temporary license and the specific nursing functions it authorizes. (See *Nurse licensure compact.*)

When a nurse travels with a patient from one state to another, the nursing license is valid for the duration of the trip

Nurse licensure compact

Nursing licensure compact (NLC), created in 2000, refers to a model for states to mutually recognize nurse licensure. With this law, a nurse can be licensed in one state (usually his or her state of residence) and at the same time can practice in other states. According to this model, a nurse can practice across state lines.

To achieve mutual recognition, each state must pass legislation or regulation that authorizes the use of the NLC. States that do must also adopt the administrative rules and regulations for implementing it (NCSBN, 2007).

In December 2006, the National Council of State Boards of Nursing hosted a summit to announce the receipt of a federal grant from the Health Resources and Services Administration's Office. This grant is to provide money for state boards of nursing to "reduce the licensure barriers impacting telehealth and interstate nursing practice" (Press release, NCSBN, 2007).

Currently 23 states have adopted the NLC law. Of these, 20 states have recognized but not yet implemented the NLC. However, more than 25 boards of nursing haven't adopted the NLC. The NCSBN plans to use this grant to study issues that pose barriers to license portability, such as initial start-up costs for using the NLC, the reasons why some organizations don't support the NLC, and trends associated with licensure portability. The hope is that this information will foster a better understanding of the NLC by all states, ultimately making license portability available in all states.

Source: National Council of State Boards of Nursing. NCSBN Hosts Summit Funded by Federal Grant to Promote Nurse Licensure Portability. 12/4/2006. Available at *https://www.ncsbn.org/1097.htm*.

in most states and Canadian jurisdictions.

If the state board finds that the nurse doesn't have the necessary qualifications to practice nursing in that state, it may reject the application or require that person to complete a written examination, regardless of the education or the laws of the state in which the person lives.

In *Richardson v. Brunelle (1979)*, an LPN who had practiced in Massachusetts for 15 years brought suit after being refused a license to practice in New Hampshire. In her New Hampshire application, she requested a decree of educational equivalency. Although she had originally taken and passed a Massachusetts State licensing examination, she had never graduated from an approved school of practical nursing. At that time, only nursing school graduates were permitted to practice in New Hampshire, so her re-

quest was denied. Her lawsuit was unsuccessful in reversing the New Hampshire decision, and subsequent appeals upheld the original ruling. A similar case, *Snelson v. Culton (1949)*, involved Maine's licensing requirements, which also require a graduation for licensing.

Foreign licensure
If you move to a foreign country, your U.S. nursing license will be reviewed by the appropriate authority, which will either reject or accept it (possibly with conditions). If you're a nurse in the American armed forces working in an American installation, you're exempt from this review.

In a non–English-speaking country, the licensing authority may require you to complete a language proficiency examination.

POLICY & POLITICS

Language proficiency for internationally educated nurses

In December 2005, the National Council of State Boards of Nursing (NCSBN) issued a position statement that recommends new standards of proficiency in the English language for all nurses coming to the United States to practice nursing. According to the NCSBN, these standards are the minimum requirement needed for entry level nurses to practice safely and effectively (NCSBN, 2005).

English language proficiency is a portion of the test used for nurses coming from other countries. Two major tests are used: the International English Language Testing System (IELTS) and the Test of English as a Foreign Language (TOEFL). The TOEFL has three different versions: a written version; a computer-based test (CBT); and most recently, an internet-based test (iBT). The

recommended passing scores for these tests are as follows:
- IELTS – overall score of 6.5 (minimum of 6.0 in all modules)
- TOEFL written – overall score of 560
- TOEFL CBT – overall score of 220
- TOEFL iBT – overall score of 83.

These standards are applicable to registered nurses, licensed practical nurses, and licensed vocational nurses.

The NCSBN is strongly urging state and federal lawmakers to revise and update the section of the Immigration and Nationality Act dealing with English language proficiency for health care workers to meet the standards identified by the NCSBN.

Source: NCSBN. Position Statement NCSBN Recommends English Language Proficiency Standards for Internationally-educated Nurses. December 2005. Available at *https://www.ncsbn.org/positionlangTemplate.pdf*.

If you're an RN or LPN licensed in a foreign country, you can't practice nursing in any state, territory, or province until the appropriate licensing authority has approved your application and issued your nursing license. When you're granted licensure in the United States or Canada, you function at the same legal status as a U.S.- or Canadian-educated RN or LPN. You're also equally accountable for your professional actions.

All states and the federal government require that foreign nurses pass the examination prepared by the Commission on Graduates of Foreign Nursing Schools (the CGFNS examination). A foreign nurse who successfully completes this examination, which includes an English-proficiency segment, may then take the NCLEX. If the nurse passes, she qualifies

for licensure and a work visa. (See *Language proficiency for internationally educated nurses.*)

Legal impact of licensure

Licensing laws help a nurse avoid civil and criminal liabilities by defining the scope of professional nursing practice. If a nurse is named in a malpractice lawsuit, her state licensing laws will be used as partial evidence to determine whether the nurse acted within the legal limits of the profession.

In *Barber v. Reinking (1966)*, the court used the licensing laws in the Washington State Nurse Practice Act to rule against the defendant-nurse. In this case, a 2-year-old boy was taken to a physician's office for a polio booster shot. The physician (also named in the suit) delegated this task to the LPN who worked in his office. While the nurse was administering the shot, the child moved suddenly and the needle broke off in his buttock. Despite attempts to remove it surgically and with a magnet, the needle remained lodged in the child's buttock for 9 months.

During the trial, the licensing law for practical nurses became the crucial factor in the court's decision. The court declared that the nurse had violated the nurse practice act by performing services beyond the legal limit of her practice. (Until the 1970s, the Washington State Nurse Practice Act didn't allow a practical nurse to legally give an injection.) The nurse's attorney attempted to introduce as evidence the fact that LPNs in the local community commonly gave injections. This evidence wasn't allowed. Instead, the judge instructed the jury to consider the violation of the nurse practice act along with other evidence in the case, including the physician's liability under the *respondeat superior* doctrine, to determine if the nurse was negligent.

Standards of nursing care

Standards of care set minimum criteria for a nurse's proficiency on the job, enabling nurses and others to judge the quality of care that they and their nursing colleagues provide. States may refer to standards in their nurse practice acts. Unless included in a nurse practice act, professional standards aren't laws—they're guidelines for sound nursing practice.

Some nurses regard standards of nursing care as pie-in-the-sky ideals that have little bearing on the reality of working life. This is a dangerous misconception. All nurses are expected to meet standards

of nursing care for every nursing task performed.

For example, if the nurse is a medical-surgical nurse, minimal standards require that she develop a nursing care plan for the patient based on the nursing process, including nursing diagnoses, goals, and interventions for implementing the care plan. Standards also call for documentation in the patient's record of the nurse's completion and evaluation of the plan. When documenting patient care, the nurse is actually writing a record of how well she has met these standards. A court may interpret an absence of documentation as an absence of patient care. *Pommier v. ABC Insurance Company et al.*, 715 So. 2d 1270 (La. App. 3d Cir. 1998).

Evolution of nursing standards

Before 1950, nurses had only Florence Nightingale's early treatments, plus reports of court cases, to use as standards. As nursing gradually became recognized as an independent profession, nursing organizations stressed the importance of having recognized standards for all nurses. Then, in 1950, the ANA published the *Code of Ethics for Nursing*, a general mandate stating that nurses should offer nursing care without prejudice and in a confidential and safe manner. Although not specific, this code marked the beginning of written nursing standards.

In 1973, the ANA Congress for Nursing Practice established the first generic standards for the profession—standards that could be applied to all nurses in all settings. (See *ANA standards of nursing practice,* pages 26 to 30.) The Canadian Nurses Association (CNA) has established similar nursing standards.

(Text continues on page 30.)

ANA standards of nursing practice

The standards below are adapted from standards of nursing practice published by the American Nurses Association (ANA). They developed the standards (last revised in 2004) to provide registered nurses with guidelines for determining quality nursing care. Each standard is followed by measurement criteria that give key indicators of competent practice for that standard. This adaptation of the standards doesn't present the standards that are specific to only advance practice nurses.

STANDARDS OF CARE

Standard 1: Assessment
The nurse collects patient health data.

Measurement criteria
1. The priority of data collection is determined by the client's immediate condition or needs.
2. Pertinent data are collected by using appropriate evidence-based assessment techniques, adapted to ensure security and provider safety.
3. Data collection involves the client, significant others, and health care providers.
4. The data collection process is systematic, relevant to the situation and identifies patterns and variances, and is ongoing.
5. Relevant data are documented in a retrievable form.

Standard 2: Diagnosis
The nurse analyzes the assessment data in determining diagnoses.

Measurement criteria
1. Diagnoses are derived from assessment data.
2. Diagnoses are validated with the client, significant others, and health care providers when possible.
3. Diagnoses are documented in a manner that facilitates the determination of expected outcomes and care plan.

Standard 3: Outcome identification
The nurse identifies expected outcomes individualized to the client or situation.

Measurement criteria
1. Outcomes are culturally appropriate and are derived from the diagnoses.

2. Outcomes are documented as measurable goals.
3. Outcomes are mutually formulated with the client, family, and health care providers, when possible and appropriate.
4. Outcomes are realistic in relation to the client's present and potential capabilities and situation.
5. Outcomes include a time estimate for attainment.
6. Outcomes provide direction for continuity of care.
7. Outcomes consider risks, benefits, costs, current evidence, and clinical expertise.

Standard 4: Planning
The nurse develops a care plan that prescribes interventions to attain expected outcomes.

Measurement criteria
1. The plan is individualized to the client's condition or needs.
2. The plan is developed with the client, family, and others.
3. The plan provides direction to other health care workers.
4. The plan provides a timeline.
5. The plan provides for continuity of care.
6. The plan includes strategies that address each diagnosis or issue and prevention of diseases and injury, and promote health.
7. The plan integrates current research and trends.
8. The plan uses standardized terminology in documentation.

Standard 5: Implementation
The nurse implements the care plan.

ANA standards of nursing practice *(continued)*

Measurement criteria

1. Interventions are consistent with the established care plan.
2. Interventions are implemented in a safe and timely manner.
3. Interventions and changes or omissions in the plan are documented.
4. Community resources are utilized within the plan.
5. Nursing colleagues and others use collaboration to implement the plan.

Standard 5A: Coordination of care
The nurse coordinates care.

Measurement criteria

1. The plan is coordinated and implemented.
2. The coordination of the plan is documented.

Standard 5B: Health teaching and promotion
The nurse utilizes strategies to promote health and a safe environment.

Measurement criteria

1. Health teaching provides living a healthy lifestyle, developmental needs, risk-reducing behaviors, activities of daily living and self care that utilizes prevention.
2. Health teaching and promotion strategies are appropriate to the patient's developmental level, learning needs, language preference, readiness and ability to learn, situation, and culture.
3. Feedback and evaluation of the effectiveness of the teaching is included.

Standard 6: Evaluation
The nurse evaluates the client's progress toward attainment of outcomes.

Measurement criteria

1. Evaluation is systematic, criterion-based and ongoing.
2. The effectiveness of interventions is evaluated in relation to outcomes.

3. Ongoing assessment data are used to revise diagnoses, outcomes, and the care plan, as needed.
4. Results are documented.
5. The client, health care providers, and others are involved in the care or situation in the evaluation process, when appropriate.
6. Results are distributed to the patient and others involved in patient care as appropriate according to federal and state laws and regulations.

STANDARDS OF PROFESSIONAL PERFORMANCE
Standard 7: Quality of practice
The nurse systematically evaluates the quality and effectiveness of nursing practice.

Measurement criteria

1. Demonstrates quality by documenting the use of the nursing process in a responsible and ethical manner.
2. The nurse uses the results of quality-of-care activities to initiate changes throughout the health care delivery system, as appropriate.
3. Uses creativity and innovation in nursing practice to improve delivery of care.
4. Utilizes new knowledge to initiate changes in nursing practice if the desired outcome is not achieved.
5. The nurse participates in quality improvement activities. Such activities may include the following:
   a. Identifying aspects of care important for quality monitoring.
   b. Identifying indicators used to monitor the quality and effectiveness of nursing care.
   c. Collecting data to monitor the quality and effectiveness of nursing care.
   d. Analyzing quality data to identify opportunities for improving nursing care.
   e. Formulating recommendations to improve nursing practice or client outcomes.
   f. Implementing activities to enhance the quality of nursing practice.

(continued)

ANA standards of nursing practice *(continued)*

g. Participating in the work of interdisciplinary teams that evaluate clinical practice or health services.

h. Developing, implementing, and evaluating policies and procedures to improve the quality of care.

i. Participating to minimize costs and unnecessary duplication.

j. Analyzing factors related to safety, satisfaction, effectiveness, and cost and benefits options.

k. Analyzing organizational systems for barriers.

l. Implementing processes to decrease or remove barriers within organizational systems.

Standard 8: Education
The nurse attains knowledge and competency that reflects current nursing practice.

Measurement criteria

1. The nurse participates in ongoing educational activities related to clinical knowledge and professional issues.

2. The nurse demonstrates commitment to lifelong learning through self-reflection and inquiry to identify learning needs.

3. The nurse seeks experience that reflects current practice to maintain clinical skills and competence in practice or role performance.

4. The nurse seeks knowledge and skills appropriate to the practice setting, specialty area, role or situation.

5. The nurse maintain professional records that provide evidence of clinical competency and life long learning.

Standard 9: Professional practice evaluation
The nurse evaluates his/her own nursing practice in relation to professional practice standards and relevant statutes and regulations.

Measurement criteria
The nurse's practice reflects the application of knowledge of current practice standards, guidelines, statutes, rules and regulations.

1. The nurse provides age appropriate care in a ethnically and culturally sensitive manner.

2. The nurse regularly engages in performance appraisal, identifying areas of strength as well as areas for professional and practice development.

2. The nurse seeks constructive feedback regarding his/her own practice.

3. The nurse takes action to achieve goals identified during performance appraisal.

4. The nurse participates in peer review as appropriate.

5. The nurse provides rationales for practice beliefs, decisions, and actions as part of the evaluation process.

Standard 10: Collegiality
The nurse contributes to the professional development of peers, colleagues, and others.

Measurement criteria

1. The nurse shares knowledge, skills, and information with peers, colleagues and others as evidenced by informal or formal patient care conferences or presentations.

2. The nurse provides peers with constructive feedback regarding their practice and performance.

3. The nurse interacts with peers and colleagues to enhance professional nursing care and role performance.

4. The nurse contributes to an environment that is conducive to the clinical education of health care professionals.

5. The nurse maintains compassionate and caring relationships with peers and colleagues.

6. The nurse contributes to a supportive and healthy work environment.

Standard 11: Collaboration
The nurse collaborates with the client, family and others in providing patient care.

ANA standards of nursing practice *(continued)*

Measurement criteria
1. The nurse communicates with the client, family and health care providers regarding client care and nursing's role in the provision of such care.
2. The nurse collaborates in creating a documented plan, focuses on outcomes related to client care that reflect collaboration with the client, family and others.
3. The nurse documents referrals, including provisions for continuity of care, as needed.
4. The nurse works with others to effect change and generates positive outcomes through knowledge of the client or situation.

Standard 12: Ethics
The nurse integrates ethical provisions in all areas of care.

Measurement criteria
1. The nurse's uses the Code of Ethics with Interpretive statements (ANA, 2001) to guide practice.
2. The nurse maintains patient confidentiality with legal and regulatory parameters.
3. The nurse acts as a client advocate.
4. The nurse delivers care in a nonjudgmental and nondiscriminatory manner that is sensitive to client diversity.
5. The nurse delivers care in a manner that preserves and protects client autonomy, dignity, and rights.
6. The nurse seeks available resources to help formulate ethical decisions.
7. The nurse demonstrates a commitment to practicing self-care, managing stress and connecting with self and others.
8. The nurse reports incompetent, illegal or impaired practices.

Standard 13: Research
The nurse uses research findings in practice.

Measurement criteria
1. The nurse uses best available evidence, including research findings, to guide practice decisions.
2. The nurse participates in research activities as appropriate to the individual's position, education, and practice environment. Such activities may include the following:
   a. Identifying clinical problems suitable for nursing research.
   b. Participating in data collection.
   c. Participating in a unit, organization, or community research committee or program.
   d. Sharing research activities with others.
   e. Conducting research.
   f. Clinically analyzing and interpreting research for application to practice.
   g. Using research findings in the development of policies, procedures, and guidelines for client care.
   h. Incorporating research as a basis for learning.

Standard 14: Resource utilization
The nurse considers factors related to safety, effectiveness, and cost in planning and delivering client care.

Measurement criteria
1. The nurse evaluates factors related to safety, effectiveness, efficiency, and cost when two or more practice options would result in the same expected client outcome.
2. The nurse assigns tasks or delegates care based on the needs of the client and on the knowledge and skill of the provider selected.
3. The nurse assists the client and family in identifying and securing appropriate, available services to address health-related needs.
4. The nurse assists the client and family to be informed consumers about the costs, options, risk and benefits or treatment and care.

(continued)

ANA standards of nursing practice *(continued)*

Standard 15: Leadership
The nurse provides leadership in the professional practice setting and the profession.

Measurement criteria:
1. The nurse is a team player and a team builder.
2. The nurse creates and maintains a healthy work environment in the regional, national, or international community.
3. The nurse displays a clear vision, goals, and plans to implement and measure progress.
4. The nurse displays creativity and flexibility through change.

5. The nurse shows a commitment to continuous lifelong learning.
6. The nurse teaches others to succeed by mentoring.
7. The nurse demonstrates energy, excitement and passion about quality work.
8. The nurse is loyal and values others in the organization.
9. The nurse coordinates care across settings and among caregivers including licensed and unlicensed personnel.
10. The nurse participates in committees, councils and administrative teams.
11. The nurse participates in professional organizations.

Reprinted with permission from American Nurses Association, *Nursing: Scope and Standards of Practice*, © 2004 nursesbooks.org, Silver Spring, Md.

Some states and jurisdictions have incorporated ANA and CNA standards into their nurse practice acts.

By 1974, each of the ANA divisions of nursing practice (such as nursing administration, community health, geriatrics, maternal-child, mental health, and medical-surgical) had established distinct standards for its specialty. The ANA Congress called these *specialty standards*. State nursing associations also helped develop specialty standards. (See *ANA standards for nursing administration*.)

Federal regulations for staffing Medicare and Medicaid services have influenced the development of standards, especially nursing home standards. By suggesting ethical approaches to nursing practice, ethics codes written by the ANA, the CNA, and the International Council of Nurses also influence how nursing care standards are developed.

Other standards affecting nursing

Other organizations have contributed to the development of nursing standards. The Joint Commission, a private, nongovernmental agency that's responsible for evaluating and accrediting more than 17,000 health care organizations in the United States, such as hospitals, nursing homes, health care networks, health care providers, and long-term care facilities, has also developed nursing standards to be used in hospital audit systems. In some states, Joint Commission standards have been incorporated into law, resulting in broadly applicable standards of patient care. In addition, state nursing associations and the specialty nursing organizations actively work with hospital nursing administrators for adoption of standards.

(Text continues on page 35.)

ANA standards for nursing administration

The standards below are adapted from standards for nursing administration published by the American Nurses Association (ANA). They were last revised in 2003. In the original document, the ANA referred to nursing administration as "organized nursing services."

STANDARDS OF PRACTICE
Standard 1: Assessment
The nurse administrator develops, maintains, and evaluates patients and data collection systems to support the nursing practice and the delivery of patient care.

Measurement criteria
1. Identifies assessment elements, including nursing-sensitive indicators appropriate to a given organizational context.
2. Utilizes current research findings and current practice guidelines and standards to modify data collection elements.
3. Monitors and evaluates assessment processes that are sensitive to the unique and diverse needs of individuals and target populations.
4. Identifies and documents the necessary resources to support data collection, and advocates for appropriate resources.
5. Analyzes the workflow related to effectiveness and efficiency of assessment processes in the target environment.
6. Develops, maintains, and evaluates systems for efficient data collection as part of the overall institutional data collection system.
7. Promotes, maintains, and evaluates a data collection system in an accessible and retrievable format.
8. Initiates processes to modify information systems as needed to meet changing data requirements and needs.
9. Develops criteria and establishes procedures to assure confidentiality of data.
10. Facilitates integration of unified assessment processes developed in collaboration with other health care disciplines and across the continuum of care.

11. Evaluates assessment practices to assure timely, reliable, valid, and comprehensive data collection.
12. Collaborates with appropriate departments.

Standard 2: Diagnosis and problem identification
The nurse administrator supports the professional nurse in analysis of assessment data and in making decisions based on that information.

Measurement criteria
1. Identifies and advocates for adequate resources for decision analysis in conjunction with appropriate departments.
2. Assists and supports staff in developing and maintaining competency in the diagnostic process.
3. Facilitates interdisciplinary collaboration in data analysis and decision-making processes.
4. Promotes an organizational climate that supports validation of diagnoses.
5. Assures a system for documentation of diagnoses that facilitates development of a patient-centered plan of care and determination of desired outcomes.
6. Conducts and formulates a diagnosis of the organization's context of care.

Standard 3: Identification of outcomes
The nurse administrator develops, maintains, and evaluates information processes that promote desired, client-centered, and organizational outcomes.

Measurement criteria
1. Participates in the design and development of multidisciplinary processes to establish and maintain standards consistent with the identified outcomes.

(continued)

ANA standards for nursing administration *(continued)*

2. Facilitates nurse, client, and other staff member participation in interdisciplinary identification of desired outcomes.
3. Assists in identification, development, and utilization of databases that include nursing measures and desired outcomes.
4. Facilitates nurse participation in the monitoring and evaluating of nursing care in accordance with established professional, regulatory, and organizational standards of practice.
5. Fosters establishment and continuous improvement of clinical guidelines linked to client outcomes that provide direction for continuity of care and are attainable with available resources.
6. Collaborates with appropriate departments.
7. Integrates clinical, human resource, and financial data to support decision-making.

Standard 4: Planning
The nurse administrator develops, maintains, and evaluates organizational planning systems to facilitate the delivery of nursing care.

Measurement criteria
1. Contributes to the development and continuous improvement of organizational systems in which plans related to the delivery of nursing services can be developed, modified, documented, and evaluated.
2. Contributes to the development and continuous improvement of organizational systems that support prioritization of activities within plans related to the delivery of nursing services and patient care.
3. Contributes to the development and continuous improvement of mechanisms for plans to be recorded, retrieved, and updated across the continuum of care.
4. Advocates organizational processes that allow for creativity in the development of alternative plans for achieving desired, client-centered, cost-effective outcomes.
5. Fosters interdisciplinary planning and collaboration that focuses on the individuals and populations served.

6. Promotes the integration of applicable contemporary management and organizational theories, nursing and related research findings, and practice standards and guidelines into the planning process.
7. Assists and supports staff in developing and maintaining competency in the planning and change process.
8. Advocates integration of policies into action plans for achieving desired client-centered outcomes.
9. Participates in the development, implementation, and use of a system for preventing and reporting abuse of client's rights, and incompetent, unethical, or illegal practices by health care providers.
10. Reviews and evaluates plans for appropriate utilization of staff at all levels of practice in accordance with the provision of the state's nurse practice act and the professional standards of practice.
11. Integrates clinical, human resource, and financial data to appropriately plan standards of nursing and patient care, facilitating continuity across a continuum.
12. Collaborates with appropriate departments.

Standard 5: Implementation
The nurse administrator develops, maintains, and evaluates organizational systems that support implementation of plans and delivery of care.

Measurement criteria
1. Participates in the development, evaluation, and maintenance of organizational systems that integrate policies and procedures with regulations, practice standards, and clinical guidelines.
2. Designs and improves systems and identifies resources that support interventions that are consistent with the established plans.
3. Facilitates staff participation in decision-making regarding the development and implementation of organizational systems,

ANA standards for nursing administration *(continued)*

and the specification of resources necessary for implementation of the plan.

4. Collaborates with appropriate departments.
5. Collaborates in the design and improvement of systems and the identification of resources that ensure that interventions are safe, effective, efficient, and culturally sensitive.
6. Collaborates in the design and improvement of systems and processes, which ensures that the most appropriate personnel implement interventions.
7. Collaborates in the design and improvement of systems to ensure appropriate and efficient documentation of interventions.

Standard 6: Evaluation
The nurse administrator evaluates the plan and its progress in relation to the attainment of outcomes.

Measurement criteria
1. Promotes implementation of processes and resources that deliver data and information to empower staff to participate meaningfully in clinical decision-making.
2. Ensures educational opportunities for staff specific to current interventions, available technologies, or other skills to enhance ability to promote quality in health care delivery.
3. Utilizes appropriate research methods and findings to improve care processes, structures, and measurement of desired outcomes.
4. Facilitates staff participation in the systematic, interdisciplinary, and ongoing evaluation of programs, processes, and desired client-centered outcomes.
5. Sets priorities for allocation of resources.
6. Advocates for resources sufficient to provide time for critical assessment and evaluation of desired outcomes.
7. Fosters participation and recognition of staff in formal and informal organizational committees, teams, and task forces.

8. Advocates for and supports a process of governance that includes participation of nurses.
9. Participates in the peer review, credentialing, certification, and privileging process for all appropriate health care providers.
10. Supports effective information handling processes and technologies that facilitate evaluation of effectiveness and efficiency of decisions, plans, and activities in relation to desired outcomes.
11. Promotes the development of policies, procedures, and guidelines based on research findings and institutional measurement of quality outcomes.
12. Utilizes data generated from outcome research to develop innovative changes in patient care delivery.

STANDARDS OF PROFESSIONAL PERFORMANCE
Standard 1: Quality of care and administrative practice
The nurse administrator systematically evaluates the quality and effectiveness of nursing practice and nursing services administration.

Measurement criteria
1. Leads the development, implementation, and performance improvement of care delivery models and services that meet or exceed customer expectation.
2. Identifies key indicators including measures of quality of nursing practice and customer needs and expectations.
3. Advocates for and participates in the development of clinical, operational, and financial databases upon which nurse-sensitive outcomes can be derived, reported, and used for improvement.
4. Leads in creating and evaluating systems, processes, and programs that support institutional and nursing core values and objectives.
5. Evaluates and ensures safe care delivery.

(continued)

ANA standards for nursing administration *(continued)*

Standard 2: Performance appraisal

The nurse administrator evaluates personal performance based on professional practice standards, relevant statutes, regulations, and organizational criteria.

Measurement criteria

1. Systematically identifies industry trends and competencies in nursing administration and nursing practice.
2. Engages in self-assessment of role accountabilities on a regular basis, identifying areas of strength, as well as areas for professional development.
3. Evaluates efficacy of the plan and the vision for professional nursing.
4. Seeks constructive feedback regarding own practice.
5. Takes action to achieve plans for performance improvement.
6. Participates in peer review as appropriate.

Standard 3: Education

The nurse administrator maintains and demonstrates current knowledge in the administration of health care organizations to advance clinical practice.

Measurement criteria

1. Seeks experiences to advance skills and knowledge base in areas of responsibilities.
2. Seeks formal education and certification for career path.
3. Networks with peers to share ideas and conduct mutual problem solving.

Standard 4: Professional environment

The nurse administrator must provide a professional environment.

Measurement criteria

1. Creates a professional practice environment that fosters excellence in nursing services.
2. Creates a climate of effective communication.
3. Fosters professional nurse empowered decision-making, accountability, and autonomy in nursing practice.
4. Leads through a well-established nursing leadership structure and as a formal authority participant in organizational senior leadership.
5. Establishes and promotes a framework for professional nursing practice built on core ideology which includes vision, mission, philosophy, core values, evidence-based practice, and standards of practice.
6. Assures mutual respect for individuals and the profession at work.
7. Develops strategies to recruit and retain, mentor, assure quality education and training, and ensure meaningful work to maximize job satisfaction of nursing staff.
8. Promotes understanding and effective use of organization, management, and nursing theories and research.
9. Contributes to nursing management education and professional development of staff, students, and colleagues.
10. Adheres to the Bill of Rights for Registered Nurses (ANA, 2001).
11. Shares knowledge and skills with students, colleagues, and others, and acts as a role model and mentor.

Standard 5: Ethics

The nurse administrator's decisions and actions are ethical.

Measurement criteria

1. Advocates for recipients of services and personnel.
2. Maintains privacy, confidentiality, and security of patient, client, staff, and organization data.
3. Adheres to the Code of Ethics for Nurses with Interpretive Statements (ANA, 2001).
4. Assures compliance with regulatory and professional standards, as well as integrity in business practices.
5. Assures that nursing care is given in a nondiscriminatory and socioculturally sensitive manner.
6. Assures a system to identify and address ethical issues within nursing and the organization.

ANA standards for nursing administration *(continued)*

Standard 6: Collaboration
The nurse administrator collaborates with all nursing staff, interdisciplinary teams, executive leaders, and other stakeholders.

Measurement criteria
1. Facilitates and models collaboration within nursing services and the organization.
2. Collaborates with nursing staff and other disciplines at all levels in the development, implementation, and evaluation of programs and services.
3. Collaborates with administrative peers in determining the acquisition, allocation, and utilization of fiscal and human resources.
4. Fosters relationships that support the continuous enhancement of care delivery and patient, client, and employee satisfaction.

Standard 7: Research
The nurse administrator supports research and integrates it into nursing administration and the delivery of nursing care.

Measurement criteria
1. Creates the environment and advocates for resources supportive of nursing research and scholarly inquiry.
2. Assures nursing research priorities align with plan and objectives.
3. Supports research that promotes evidence-based, clinically effective and efficient, nurse-sensitive patient outcomes.
4. Facilitates the dissemination of research findings and the integration of evidence-based guidelines and practices into health care.

5. Supports procedures for review of proposed research studies, including protection of the rights of human subjects.
6. Identifies areas of clinical and administrative inquiry suitable for nurse researchers.

Standard 8: Resource utilization
The nurse administrator evaluates and administers the resources of nursing services.

Measurement criteria
1. Assures nursing workload is measured and resources are allocated based upon patient or client need.
2. Develops systems to continuously monitor and measure the quality, safety, and outcomes of nursing services.
3. Develops, values, and expands the intellectual capital of the organization.
4. Assures and optimizes fiscal resource allocation to support current and potential nursing objectives and initiatives.
5. Provides fiscal oversight of allocated resources to optimize the provision of quality, cost-effective care.
6. Guides the delegation of responsibilities appropriate to the licensure, education, and experience of staff.
7. Designs and negotiates organizational acceptance of appropriate roles for the utilization of all staff.
8. Monitors and evaluates appropriate utilization of staff.

Reprinted with permission from American Nurses Association, *Scope and Standards for Nurse Administrators*, 2nd edition, © 2004 nursesbooks.org, Silver Spring, Md.

The Joint Commission continuously creates and publishes new standards to improve patient safety. Hospitals and other health care organizations must comply with these standards to receive Joint Commission accreditation. The Joint Commission has implemented the new "Patient Safety Standards" for hospitals, which became effective in July 2001, requiring hospitals to create an environment of safety. It also issues National Patient Safety Goals each year, which focus on the prevention of health

The Joint Commission's National Patient Safety Goals

The Joint Commission's National Patient Safety Goals were created to improve patient safety. The goals are followed by evidence- and expert-based solutions for achieving the goal. The goals listed below are those published by The Joint Commission for 2008, which are solutions to:

GOAL 1
Improve the accuracy of patient identification
- Use at least two patient identifiers when providing care, treatment, or services.
- Perform a final verification process to confirm the correct patient, procedure, and site using active, not passive communication before the start of any invasive or surgical procedure.

GOAL 2
Improve the effectiveness of communication among caregivers
- Verify the complete order test result (for verbal or telephone orders or for telephonic reporting of critical test results) by having the person receiving the information record and "read back" the complete order or test result.
- Develop a standardized list of abbreviations, acronyms, symbols, and dose designations that are **not** to be used throughout the organization.
- Measure and assess, and if appropriate, take action to improve the timeliness of reporting, and the timeliness of receipt by the responsible licensed caregiver, of critical test results and values.
- Implement a standardized approach to "hand off" communications, including an opportunity to ask and respond to questions.

GOAL 3
Improve the safety of using medications
- Identify and, at a minimum, annually review a list of look-alike/sound-alike drugs used by the organization, and take action to prevent errors involving the interchange of these drugs.
- Label all medications, medication containers (for example, syringes, medicine cups, basins), or other solutions on and off the sterile field.
- Reduce the likelihood of patient harm associated with the use of anticoagulation therapy.

*GOAL 7
Reduce the risk of health care-associated infections.
- Comply with current World Health Organization (WHO) Hand Hygiene Guidelines or Centers for Disease Control and Prevention (CDC) hand hygiene guidelines.
- Manage as sentinel events all identified cases of unanticipated death or major permanent loss of function associated with a health care-associated infection.

GOAL 8
Reconcile medications across the continuum of care accurately and completely
- Ensure that there is a process for comparing the patient's current medications with those ordered while the patient is under the care of the organization.
- Make sure that a complete list of the patient's medications is communicated to the next provider of service when a patient is referred or transferred to another setting, service, practitioner, or level of care within or outside the organization. The complete list of medications is also provided to the patient on discharge from the facility.

GOAL 9
Reduce the risk of [patient] harm resulting from falls
- Implement a fall reduction program, including an evaluation of the effectiveness of the program.

GOAL 10
Reduce the risk of influenza and pneumococcal disease in institutionalized older adults
- Develop and implement a protocol for administration and documentation of the flu vaccine.

The Joint Commission's National Patient Safety Goals
(continued)

- Develop and implement a protocol for administration and documentation of the pneumococcal vaccine.
- Develop and implement a protocol to identify new cases of influenza and to manage an outbreak.

GOAL 11
Reduce the risk of surgical fires
- Educate staff, including operating licensed independent practitioners and anesthesia providers, on how to control heat sources and manage fuels with enough time for [patient] preparation, and establish guidelines to minimize oxygen concentration under drapes.

GOAL 12
Implement applicable National Patient Safety Goals and associated requirements by components and practitioner sites
- Inform and encourage components and practitioner sites to implement the applicable National Patient Safety Goals and associated requirements.

GOAL 13
Encourage patients' active involvement in their own care as a patient safety strategy
- Define and communicate the means for patients and their families to report concerns about safety and encourage them to do so.

GOAL 14
Prevent health care-associated pressure ulcers (decubitus ulcers)
- Assess and periodically reassess each [patient's] risk for developing a pressure ulcer (decubitus ulcer), and take action to address any identified risks

GOAL 15
The organization identifies safety risks inherent in its patient population
- The organization identifies patients at risk for suicide. (Applicable to psychiatric hospitals and patients being treated for emotional or behavioral disorders in general hospitals—NOT APPLICABLE TO CRITICAL ACCESS HOSPITALS.)
- The organization identifies risks associated with long-term oxygen therapy, such as home fires

GOAL 16
Improve recognition and response to changes in a patient's condition
- The organization selects a suitable method that enables health care staff members to directly request additional assistance from a specially trained individual(s) when the patient's condition appears to be worsening. [Critical Access Hospital, Hospital]

---

*Gaps in numbering reflect that the goal is not applicable or has been "retired." This most often occurs when a goal has been incorporated into the standards.

Source: JCAHO. 2008 National Patient Safety Goals Hospital Program. Available at: *http://www.jointcommission.org/PatientSafety/NationalPatientSafetyGoals/08_hap_npsgs.htm.* Reprinted with permission.

care errors. (See *Joint Commission's National Patient Safety Goals.*)

Local or national standards
The courts once used local standards—reflecting a community's accepted, common nursing practices—to judge the quality of nursing care. This practice has been eroded in recognition of national standards applied by accreditation agencies. Now, nurses are held to a national standard.

Local standards were established in two ways: by individual health care facilities, through their policies and procedures, and by expert witnesses who testified in court cases that involves nurses. Every facility established standards to fit its own community's needs. An expert witness interprets local standards by testifying about how nursing is commonly practiced in the community. Today, expert witnesses testify to the appropriate national standard of care. Additionally, facility policy and procedure manuals conform to the standards as published by the Joint Commission.

Legal significance of standards

Nursing standards aren't laws. However, they have important legal significance. The allegation that a nurse failed to meet appropriate standards of care, and that breach of these standards caused harm (proximate cause) to the patient, is the basic premise of every nursing malpractice lawsuit.

During a malpractice trial, the court will measure the defendant-nurse's action against the answer it obtains to the following question: *What would a reasonably prudent nurse, with like training and experience, do under these circumstances?*

To answer this question, the plaintiff-patient, through his attorney, has the burden to show that certain standards of care exist and that the defendant-nurse failed to meet those standards in her treatment of him. He must also show the appropriateness of those standards, show how the nurse failed to meet them, and how that failure caused him injury.

When the standard of care is at issue, the plaintiff-patient presents expert witness testimony to support his claims. The defendant-nurse and attorney will also produce expert witness testimony to support the claim that the nurse's actions

didn't fall below accepted standards of care and that the nurse acted in a reasonable and prudent manner.

The court may consider written standards when considering the standards of care involved in a nursing malpractice lawsuit. The court seeks information about all the national and state standards applicable to the defendant-nurse's actions. The court may also seek applicable information about the policies of the defendant-nurse's employer.

Because of two trends—uniform nursing educational requirements and standardized medical treatment regimens—national standards have gained favor with the courts. These trends have made the ANA's standards more influential than local standards or the standards of other organizations. For example, in the case of *Planned Parenthood of Northwest Indiana v. Vines (1980),* an NP who inserted an intrauterine device was held to the minimum standard of care that was uniform throughout the country.

As the role of nurses expands across the country, so does the standard of care. Nurses who perform the same medical services are subject to the same standard of care and liability as physicians. *Pommier v. ABC Insurance Company,* 715 So. 2d 1270, 1297-1342 (La. App. 3d Cir. 1998).

Application of nursing standards in court

In (*Weiner v. Kwait,* 2003 Ohio 3409 [Ohio App. 2003]), the patient's next of kin sued the physician and a skilled nursing home for a patient's untimely death due to sepsis. Weiner, an 86-year-old whose primary diagnosis included hypothyroidism, depression, and prostate cancer was admitted to the skilled nursing facility. The standard of care, as dictated in the home's policy and procedure manual, was for vital signs to be taken and recorded twice daily and for the patient to be seen by his physician at least every 30 days unless the nursing staff detected a problem that required the patient to be seen immediately.

The court noted in their findings that the nursing staff did take and record the patient's vital signs twice daily. When the nursing staff noted a low-grade fever and a lowering of the patient's blood pressure, the physician was called early in the day and blood was drawn to verify if there was a possible overdosage of the patient's thyroid medication. That evening, the patient's blood pressure remained low and his temperature was higher than it had been earlier in the day and the physician was again notified of the change in the patient's condition. Following the physician's order, the patient was transported to the emergency center of the local acute care facility where he died the next morning. In dismissing the case in favor of the defendant physician and skilled nursing home nursing staff members, the court noted that the institution's policies and procedures had been appropriately followed in the care of this patient (*Weiner*).

In *Hodges v. Effingham County Hospital (1987)*, a woman entered the emergency department (ED) and complained to the nurses of chest pains. No physician was present. After conferring with the nurses by telephone, the physician on call decided to discharge the patient. The nurses didn't tell the physician that the patient had a history of heart disease and had recently taken a nitroglycerin tablet. The patient later died.

The plaintiff alleged that the nurses in the ED demonstrated negligence because they failed to obtain an accurate medical history and to "fully report known and observable symptoms to the physician on call." The physician wasn't sued: The plaintiff thought that the physician had treated the patient appropriately based on the information given to him.

Although the nurses won the trial court decision, on appeal, the higher court found the nurses liable. The higher court stated that because the nursing action in question involved nursing judgment rather than the adequacy of services or facility, the question was whether the nurses followed general standards of nursing care.

Issues with physicians

Consider the case of a nurse found negligent for not recognizing and reporting inconsistent intentions of the attending physician and the first-year resident.

In *St. Germain v. Pfeifer*, 637 N.E. 2d 848 (Mass. 1994), a first-year orthopedic resident ordered the plaintiff-patient, who underwent a midlumbar osteotomy, out of bed on the second postoperative day, whereas the attending orthopedic surgeon's postoperative plan was for the patient to be confined to bed for 4 or 5 days after surgery. The charge nurse noted the resident's order without question and without considering the patient's care plan, of which she should have been aware. Therefore, she should have known and reported the inconsistent intentions of both physicians regarding the movement of the patient. The nurse got the patient out of bed and, as he moved, he heard a loud snapping sound in the back of his neck and fell backward, screaming in pain. The hooks and rods in his back snapped out of position, and he was severely injured. The nurse's motion to dismiss the case against her was granted, but later the grant was overturned because there was expert opinion that her acts fell below the standard of care.

Issues with nonnursing professionals

During a malpractice trial, nonnursing professionals who are trained and educated in medicine, are familiar with standards of nursing care, and delegate nursing orders may provide expert witness testimony with regard to standards of nursing care. For example, in *Hiatt v. Groce (1974),* a patient sued an obstetric nurse for failing to notify a physician when the patient was about to deliver a baby. The court permitted a physician to testify about the adequacy of the nurse's care. In *Gugino v. Harvard Community Health Plan (1980),* the court allowed a physician to testify about the standards for a nurse practitioner.

However, the prevailing standard isn't to allow nonnurses to testify to the standards of nursing care for RNs and LPNs. Two precedent court cases in 1980, *Maloney v. Wake Hospital Systems* and *Avet v. McCormick,* individually held that nurses must serve as expert witnesses regarding the standards of nursing care. In *Maloney,* the court held that "the role of the nurse is critical to providing a high standard of health care .... Her expertise is different from, but no less exalted, than that of the physician (at 683). Other courts have also concluded that physicians may not establish the nursing

standards of care, including *Young v. Board of Hospital Directors, Lee County (1984),* where the court held that a psychiatrist wasn't familiar with the daily practices of psychiatric nursing and therefore couldn't testify to a deviation from nursing standards (*Maloney* v. *Wake Hospital Systems,* 262 S. E. 2d 680 [North Carolina, 1980]; *Avet v. McCormick,* 271 S. E. 2d 833 [Georgia, 1980]; *Young v. Board of Hospital Directors, Lee County,* #82-429 [Florida, 1984]).

In cases in which the act of negligence is within the common knowledge and experience of a lay person, it may not be necessary to produce expert testimony. In *Jones v. Hawkes Hospital (1964),* the court instructed jurors to rely on their own common sense to judge whether a nurse met standards of practice instead of relying on expert testimony. In this case, a nurse left a sedated patient in labor to assist a physician with another patient in labor. She did this because the hospital had a rule that no physician could attend a woman in labor unless a nurse was present. Left alone, the plaintiff-patient got out of bed, fell, and suffered serious injuries. The nurse wanted the court to allow expert testimony to establish what standard of care should have been applied. However, the court ruled that any reasonably prudent person could determine this case on the basis of ordinary experience and knowledge and that the jurors could decide on their own whether the defendant-nurse's nontechnical nursing tasks met reasonable standards of care. The jury found the nurse negligent.

In a similar case, *Larrimore v. Homeopathic Hospital Association*, a nurse was found liable for failing to read a new order or for reading it negligently. The court stated that the jury could apply ordinary common sense, without an expert witness, to establish the applicable standard of care because the standard of care applied depends upon the given circumstances. (176 A.2d 362, 367-68 [Del. Supr. 1961], *off'd* 181 A.2d 573, 576-77 [Del. Supr. 1962].)

VIOLATIONS AND DISCIPLINARY ACTION

The state board of nursing can take disciplinary action against a nurse for any violation of the state's nurse practice act. In all states and in Canadian jurisdictions, a nurse faces discipline if she endangers a patient's health, safety, or welfare. Depending on the severity of the violation, a state board may formally reprimand the nurse, place the nurse on probation, suspend or refuse to renew her license, or even revoke the license. Other types of disciplinary action include imposing a probationary period, imposing a fine, and restricting the nurse's scope of practice. Some boards may require a nurse to take courses in the legal aspects of nursing.

The list of punishable violations varies from state to state. The most common ones include:

▶ conviction of a crime involving moral turpitude, if the offense bears directly on whether the person is fit to be licensed
▶ use of fraud or deceit in obtaining or attempting to obtain a nursing license
▶ incompetence because of negligence or because of physical or psychological impairments

▶ habitual use of or addiction to drugs or alcohol
▶ unprofessional conduct, including (but not limited to) falsifying, inaccurately recording, or improperly altering patient records
– negligently administering medications or treatments
– performing tasks beyond the limits of the state's nurse practice act
– failing to take appropriate action to safeguard the patient from incompetent health care
– violating the patient's confidentiality
– taking on nursing duties that require skills and education beyond one's competence
– violating the patient's dignity and human rights by basing nursing care on prejudice
– abandoning a patient
– abusing a patient verbally or physically. The Pennsylvania Board of Nursing also has sexual misconduct regulations.

Administrative review process

When a nurse is accused of professional misconduct, the state board of nursing usually conducts an investigation. This is followed by an administrative review if the investigation warrants it.

Usually, the board's actions are "complaint driven," meaning that the board investigates complaints about licensees rather than actively looking for infractions of the nurse practice act to prosecute.

As an administrative body, the state board of nursing wields broad discretionary powers and can issue a decision or ruling. As a result, court proceedings, and possibly legal penalties, may result from the board's administrative review findings. A nurse has the right to appeal through the court system for reversal of the nursing board's decision. (See *Disciplinary proceedings for nurse misconduct.*) It's important to remember that administrative proceedings are civil proceedings that are intended to be remedial in nature; they have no criminal bearing.

Steps in administrative review

In most states and jurisdictions, the nurse practice act and board of nursing rules and regulations specify the steps that the board of nursing must follow during an administrative review. In some states, a general administrative procedure act (separate from the nurse practice act) specifies the steps; in still other states, the board of nursing determines protocol.

An administrative review begins when a person, a health care facility (the nurse's employer), or a professional organization files a signed complaint against a nurse with the state board of nursing, or when the board itself initiates such action.

The board then reviews the complaint to decide if the nurse's action appears to violate the state's nurse practice act. It may begin the process by requesting a meeting with the nurse to discuss the allegations or ask the nurse to submit a statement about the specific incident that led to the complaint. (The nurse should consult with a nurse-attorney, who has experience in disciplinary matters, before submitting any information to the board of nursing.) If the board decides that the nurse's actions were in violation of the state's nurse practice act, it prepares for a formal hearing, including subpoenaing

witnesses. When these preparations begin, the accused nurse's due process rights include the right to receive timely notice of both the charge and the hearing date.

At the hearing, the nurse has the following due process rights:
▶ to be represented by an attorney
▶ to present evidence and cross-examine witnesses
▶ to appeal the board's decision to a court.

At the formal hearing, an impartial attorney may act as a hearing officer (in lieu of a judge), or the board itself may hear the case. A court reporter documents the entire proceeding, or it may be taped. Members of the board act as the plaintiffs bringing the claim against the defendant-nurse. Witnesses, including coworkers, testify for the board and the nurse.

It's advisable to buy a medical insurance liability policy to cover legal expenses to defend against a complaint filed. Although nurses may be protected by their health care employer's insurance liability policy, these employer policies only protect the nurse in the event of a civil nursing negligence or medical malpractice action. They don't protect the nurse in the event of an administrative board of nursing disciplinary investigation or hearing. Buying a personal professional liability insurance policy provides you with protection against civil and administrative actions. Nurses should check with their malpractice carrier and expand insurance coverage, if necessary. Chapters 3 and 4 provide a more in-depth discussion of professional liability insurance.

Disciplinary proceedings for nurse misconduct

This flow chart shows what happens when the state board of nursing takes disciplinary action against a nurse for violation of the state's nurse practice act.

SWORN COMPLAINT FILED

A sworn complaint is brought before a state board by:
- a health care agency
- a professional organization
- an individual.

If the board finds sufficient evidence, it will conduct a formal review.

STATE BOARD OF NURSING REVIEW

The board:
- reviews the evidence
- calls witnesses
- determines if the nurse is guilty of misconduct.

If the board finds the nurse guilty of misconduct, it can take disciplinary action.

DISCIPLINARY ACTION

The board can:
- issue a reprimand
- place the nurse on probation
- refuse to renew her license
- suspend her license
- revoke her license.

If the nurse wants to challenge the board's decision or disciplinary action, she can file an appeal in court.

COURT REVIEW

The court will do one of two things, depending on the jurisdiction:
- reexamine the board's decision and decide if the board conducted the hearing properly
- conduct a trial.

If the nurse wants to challenge the court's ruling, she can appeal to a higher court. If the board wants to appeal the court's ruling, it, too, can appeal to a higher court.

APPELLATE REVIEW

The nurse or the board can appeal for a reversal of the lower court's ruling.

Canadian administrative review

In Canada, the process for administrative review of complaints against nurses is similar to that in the United States. In some jurisdictions, a complaints committee of the jurisdictional nursing board hears the complaint first and either dismisses or endorses it. If the complaints committee endorses it, the complaint is sent to a discipline committee for a full hearing. In other jurisdictions, only a discipline committee hears the complaint.

Note that in many jurisdictions, an employer who terminates a nurse's employment for incompetence, misconduct, or incapacity must report the termination to the board of nursing in writing (this rule doesn't apply if the nurse's employer is a patient). If the employer fails to do this, the board may impose a fine.

Judicial review process

In every state, nurses have the right to challenge the board's disciplinary decisions by the process of appeal through the courts. This basic right can't be revoked by any means; in many states, this right is spelled out in the nurse practice act.

Each state and court jurisdiction sets its own rules on how to file this type of appeal. In some jurisdictions, the nurse, through an attorney, must appeal to a special court that handles only cases from state agencies. In other states, the nurse must appeal to the lowest level court.

In an appeal, the court reviews the legality of the state board's original decision against the nurse, not the nurse's allegedly improper conduct. The court attempts only to determine whether the board of nursing exceeded its legal powers or conducted the hearing improperly. It decides if the state board's decision is unlawful, arbitrary, or unreasonable according to law, or whether it constitutes "abuse of discretion" (meaning the board didn't have enough evidence to determine unprofessional conduct, and so made a decision without proper foundation). The

court may also review the original evidence before deciding whether to sustain or reverse the board's decision.

Consider the following case. In *Colorado State Board of Nurse Examiners v. Hohu (1954),* a physician filed a complaint of incompetence against a nurse, claiming that her failure to admit a patient quickly and to contact the physician caused the patient's injury. The board of nursing ordered the nurse's license revoked. However, when the nurse appealed, the court reversed the board's revocation order. This court ruled that the board of nursing had abused its discretionary powers because the evidence didn't support the physician's charges.

The court also may allow a *trial de novo,* in which the court hears the board's complete case against the nurse as though the administrative review had never happened. New evidence, if it exists, may be introduced by the plaintiff (the board) or by the defendant-nurse, through her attorney. The court hears the case and then either sustains or reverses the board's original decision.

If the defendant-nurse loses this appeal, she may, depending on the jurisdiction, appeal to a higher court. (If the nurse wins, the board of nursing can appeal to a higher court.) To begin the new appeal, the nurse's attorney must file it with the lower court that ruled against the nurse; this court will send the trial transcript and the appeal to the higher court. All states have rules and regulations governing appeals, and abiding by them is an attorney's legal responsibility.

The higher court decides whether to hear the appeal, based on its merits. The appeal usually must establish that the lower court made an error of law. The higher court won't hear the case a second time or reconsider facts, but the defendant-nurse and attorney may continue to appeal through all higher courts up to the state's highest court. Exceptional cases may reach the U.S. Supreme Court.

In a Connecticut case, *Leib v. Board of Examiners for Nursing (1979),* a nurse was accused of improper conduct: charting the administration of meperidine to her patient but using the drug herself. After voluntarily admitting to this action, she testified on her own behalf at the board hearing. The board issued an order revoking her nursing license. The nurse appealed the revocation order to the court of common pleas. When this court dismissed her appeal, she appealed to the Supreme Court of Connecticut. This higher court also ruled that the evidence supported the board's findings of unprofessional conduct. The nurse's license was revoked. Other cases in which courts have upheld boards' decisions include *Tighe v. State Board of Nurse Examiners (1979)* and *Ullo v. State Board of Nurse Examiners (1979).*

Canadian nurses may also challenge disciplinary action through the court system. An appeal involves a written application to a superior court. The application states that the disciplinary tribunal made an error and requests that the superior court correct or modify the tribunal's decision.

License revocation and reinstatement

License revocation, if sustained despite all appeal efforts, is usually permanent. Each state's nurse practice act identifies whether a revoked license can be reinstated.

If a nurse's license is suspended, she may petition for reinstatement. Every nurse practice act contains a provision allowing reinstatement of a suspended license, and some license-suspension orders specify a date when the nurse may apply. In most states, after a suspension has been in effect for more than a year, the board of nursing will consider reinstatement. For example, in Alabama, nurses must wait a minimum of 1 year before applying for reinstatement.

As the first step, the nurse would probably need to petition the board for reinstatement. Then the board would have to decide whether the nurse is qualified to practice nursing again. In some states, nurses have the right to another hearing before the board makes this decision.

The board usually bases its decision on current evidence of the nurse's fitness to practice. For example, in a drug violation case, the board may consider whether a nurse has successfully completed a drug rehabilitation program. In some cases, the nurse may be required to demonstrate ongoing participation in a rehabilitation program with periodic reports of the nurse's participation by those supervising the rehabilitation.

REFERENCES

1. Croke, E.M. "Nurses, Negligence, and Malpractice," *AJN* 103(9):54-63, September 2003.
2. Nurses Service Organization. *What to do if you're sued for malpractice. Nurse's Guide to Malpractice: Module 3.* March 2003. Available at *www.nursingcenter.com/upload/Journals/Documents/20030 3nsoce3sued.htm.* Accessed 7/1/09.
3. American Nurses Association. *Nursing's Social Policy Statement,* 2nd ed.

Washington, DC: American Nurses Association, 2003, p. 6.

4. American Nurses Association. *Nursing: Scope and Standards of Practice.* Washington, DC: American Nurses Association, 2004, p. 7.

5. Pennsylvania Department of State. RN Law. PA State Board of Nursing. (1) amended Dec. 9, 2002, P.L.1567, No. 206). Available at *www.dos.state.pa.us/ bpoa/lib/bpoa/20/nurs_board/nurseact.p df.* Accessed 7/1/07.

6. National Council of State Boards of Nursing. *2007 NCLEX-RN Detailed Test Plan.* Chicago: National Council of State Boards of Nursing, 2007, p. 2.

Patients' rights

At one time, nurses were forbidden to give patients even the most basic information about their care or health. Only physicians could answer questions about a patient's condition. However, during the 1960s, attitudes began to change and patients began demanding more information about their care. Subsequently, patients turned to nurses to assist them in getting the information.

This chapter describes the fundamental concepts associated with patients' rights. It also includes an overview of important historical milestones in the development of patients' rights. In addition, the chapter describes key patients' rights, implications for violating these rights, and guidelines for how nurses can ensure that these rights are upheld.

PATIENTS' RIGHTS

Under the constitution, all people have basic rights, such as equal protection, religious freedom, freedom of expression, and freedom from cruel and inhuman punishment. When a person becomes a patient or receives health care, additional rights are afforded by state and federal regulators of health care facilities. All health care facilities are required to have established policies that address patients' rights and how they'll be upheld by those working with the patient or in the facility.

Over the years, major health care groups and consumer and professional organizations have developed and endorsed various patients' bills of rights. The bill of rights defines a person's rights while receiving health care. These bills have helped to reinforce the public's expectation of quality of care.

Historical evolution of patients' rights

The concept of a formal document setting forth patients' rights has been around since 1959, when the National League for Nursing (NLN) issued its position paper, which outlined seven key points to help patients better understand nursing care. It was titled "What People Can Expect of Modern Nursing Practice" and referred to the patient as a partner in health care, whose ultimate goal was self-care. This document was further expanded and updated in 1977 with the development of the NLN's Patients' Bill of

NLN Patients' Bill of Rights

In 1977, the National League for Nursing (NLN) published its *Patients' Bill of Rights*, which states that the NLN believes that nurses are responsible for upholding these rights of patients:

- People have the right to health care that is accessible and that meets professional standards, regardless of the setting.
- Patients have the right to courteous and individualized health care that is equitable, humane, and given without discrimination as to race, color, creed, sex, national origin, source of payment, or ethical or political beliefs.
- Patients have the right to information about their diagnosis, prognosis, and treatment, including alternatives to care and risks involved, in terms they and their families can readily understand, so that they can give their informed consent.
- Patients have the legal right to informed participation in all decisions concerning their health care.
- Patients have the right to information about the qualifications, names, and titles of personnel responsible for providing their health care.
- Patients have the right to refuse observation by those not directly involved in their care.
- Patients have the right to privacy during interview, examination, and treatment.
- Patients have the right to privacy in communicating and visiting with persons of their choice.

- Patients have the right to refuse treatments, medications, or participation in research and experimentation, without punitive action being taken against them.
- Patients have the right to coordination and continuity of health care.
- Patients have the right to appropriate instruction or education from health care personnel so that they can achieve an optimal level of wellness and an understanding of their basic health needs.
- Patients have the right to confidentiality of all records (except as otherwise provided for by law or third-party payer contracts) and all communications, written or oral, between patients and health care providers.
- Patients have the right of access to all health records pertaining to them, to challenge and have their records corrected for accuracy, and to the transfer of all such records in the case of continuing care.
- Patients have the right to information on the charges for services, including the right to challenge these.
- Above all, patients have the right to be fully informed of all their rights in all health care settings.

Reprinted with permission from the National League for Nursing.

Rights. (See *NLN Patients' Bill of Rights*.)

Patients' rights received increasing public support during the 1960s as more people became aware of their rights as consumers. In a 1962 message to Congress, President John F. Kennedy further heightened this awareness when he outlined four basic consumer rights: the right to safety, the right to be informed, the right to choose, and the right to be heard.

The American Hospital Association (AHA), in 1973, issued its "Statement on a Patient's Bill of Rights." The statement—the result of a study the AHA had conducted with consumer groups—listed 12 patient rights. This statement was revised in 1992. In 2003, the AHA replaced this Bill of Rights with its brochure, "The Patient Care Partnership." This brochure, written in simple language and given to patients on admission to a hospital, informs them about what

they should expect during their hospital stay. These expectations include:
▶ High quality hospital care
▶ A clean and safe environment
▶ Involvement in care
▶ Protection of privacy
▶ Help and preparation for leaving the hospital
▶ Help with billing and insurance claims.

In addition, the brochure also explains what's needed from the patient, as well as his rights and responsibilities.[1]

Also, in 1973, Minnesota became the first state to enact a law protecting a patient's rights. That law requires all state health care facilities to post Minnesota's patient's bill of rights conspicuously and to distribute it to their patients.

Since these early milestones, all states, many advocacy groups, and health care organizations such as hospitals and extended-care facilities have developed their own published patients' bills of rights to inform consumers of some of their rights in the health care setting. For example, in 1990, the Advisory Board of Directors of the Hospice Association of America approved a bill of rights for hospice patients. (See *Hospice Patient's Bill of Rights,* pages 50 and 51.)

These privately drafted bills of rights are designed to protect such basic rights as human dignity, privacy, confidentiality, and refusal of treatment. They also assert the patient's right to receive a full explanation of the cost of medical care, to be fully informed, and to be required to give consent before participating in experimental treatments because the patient exercises control over his own health care. These bills emphasize the patient's right to acquire information about *all* aspects of his care.

Federal legislative impact on patients' rights

Various governmental legislation has had a direct impact on the issue of patients' rights. (See *Landmarks in the evolution of patients' rights,* page 52.)

In 1973, Congress passed the Rehabilitation Act. This Act guaranteed the physically or mentally disabled person the right to any service available to a nondisabled person. In 1990, an expanded version of this act, called the Americans with Disabilities Act, was passed.[2] The Act prohibited discrimination on the basis of disability by employers with 15 or more employees, and restricted employers' medical testing of employees and job applicants.

Other laws passed by Congress to protect the rights of the disabled included the Community Mental Health Amendment of 1975, the Rehabilitation Comprehensive Services and Development Disability Amendment of 1978, the Personal Responsibility and Work Opportunity Reconciliation Act of 1996, and the Individuals with Disabilities Education Act of 1997.

In 1980, Congress enacted the Mental Health Systems Act (MHSA), a comprehensive federal law on mental health services. Although much of this statute was later repealed, the MHSA Patient's Bill of Rights, which recommended that states review their mental health laws in light of patients' rights, survived. Since then, several states have used the bill as a model when revising their laws concerning the rights of patients suffering from mental illness.

In 1987, Congress enacted the Omnibus Budget Reconciliation Act, which included provisions that imposed dozens of new requirements on extended-care facil-

Hospice Patient's Bill of Rights

In 1990, the Hospice Association of America issued a bill of rights for hospice patients.

Patients have a right to be notified in writing of their rights and obligations before their hospice care begins. Consistent with state laws, the patient's family or guardian may exercise the patient's rights when the patient is unable to do so. Hospice organizations have an obligation to protect and promote the rights of their patients, including the following:

DIGNITY AND RESPECT

Patients and their hospice caregivers have the right to mutual respect and dignity. Caregivers are prohibited from accepting personal gifts and borrowing from patients, families, or primary caregivers.

Patients have the right:
• to have relationships with hospice organizations that are based on honesty and ethical standards of conduct
• to be informed of the procedure they can follow to lodge complaints with the hospice organization about the care that is, or fails to be,

furnished and regarding a lack of respect for property (to lodge complaints with us, call _____)
• to know about the disposition of such complaints
• to voice their grievances without fear of discrimination or reprisal for having done so.

DECISION-MAKING

Patients have the right:
• to be notified in writing of the care that is to be furnished, the types (disciplines) of caregivers who'll furnish the care, and the frequency of the services that are proposed to be furnished
• to be advised of any change in the plan of care before the change is made
• to participate in the planning of care and in planning the changes in the care, and to be advised that they have the right to do so
• to refuse services and to be advised of the consequences of refusing care
• to request a change in caregiver without fear of reprisal or discrimination.

ities and home health agencies, to protect the rights of residents receiving long-term care. This law established minimum standards for the presence of registered nurses and the training of nursing assistants. Under the law, nursing homes can be fined up to $10,000 a day for violating a patient's rights.

In 1991, Congress enacted the Patient Self-Determination Act. This act required facilities that received reimbursement for services from Medicare and Medicaid to inform patients of their right to be involved in their health care decisions. This law requires that every patient on admission be given information about advance directives, such as living wills and durable powers of attorney for health

care. In addition, each patient must be asked at that time if he has an advance directive document, and this information must be recorded in the patient's medical record. If the patient doesn't have a document, he must be given information about it, including how to execute or initiate such a document.

Patient privacy is another area of health care that was affected by federal legislation. The Federal Privacy Act of 1974 protected the confidential medical information of patients in veterans' hospitals. In 1996, the Health Insurance Portability and Accountability Act (HIPAA) was passed but didn't go into effect until the Spring of 2003.[3] This act was designed to strengthen and protect

PRIVACY

Patients have the right:

- to be informed of the extent to which payment may be expected from Medicare, Medicaid, or any other payer known to the hospice organization
- to be informed of any charges that won't be covered by Medicare
- to be informed of the charges for which the patient may be liable
- to receive this information, orally and in writing, within 15 working days of the date the hospice organization becomes aware of any changes in charges
- to have access, upon request, to all bills for the service the patient has received, regardless of whether they are paid out-of-pocket or by another party
- to be informed of the hospice's ownership status and its affiliation with any entities to whom the patient is referred.

QUALITY OF CARE

Patients have the right:

- to receive care of the highest quality

- in general, to be admitted by a hospice organization only if it's assured that all necessary palliative and supportive services will be provided that are necessary to promote the physical, psychological, social, and spiritual well-being of the dying patient; however, an organization with less than optimal resources may nevertheless admit the patient if a more appropriate hospice organization isn't available, but only after fully informing the patient of its limitations and the lack of suitable alternative arrangements
- to be told what to do in case of an emergency. The hospice organization will assure that:
- all medically related hospice care is provided in accordance with physicians' orders, and that a plan of care developed by the patient's physician and the hospice interdisciplinary group specifies the services to be provided and their frequency and duration
- all medically related personal care is provided by an appropriately trained homemaker-home health aide who is supervised by a nurse or other qualified hospice professional.

patient privacy. Recently, a new bill, The Health Information Privacy and Security Act (HIPSA) of 2007, was introduced in the Senate. This legislation focuses on revising HIPAA and reducing areas of uncertainty.

Legal status and patients' rights

Bills of rights that have become laws or state regulations carry the most authority because they give the patient specific legal recourse. If a patient believes a health care facility has violated his legal rights, he can report the violation to the appropriate legal authority, usually the state health or licensing department. If an investigation shows that the facility violated the patient's rights, the state will demand that the facility modify its practices to conform to state law.

Bills of rights issued by health care facilities and professional associations aren't legally binding. However, facilities may jeopardize federal funding, such as Medicare and Medicaid reimbursement or research funding, if they violate federal regulations or the standards of The Joint Commission.

Nurses need to regard bills of rights for patients as professionally binding where they exist as a facility's stated policy, and nurses are required to uphold those rights. Nurses are also expected to uphold the bills of rights published by professional organizations.

Landmarks in the evolution of patients' rights

A spirit of paternalism dominated health care until the 1970s and severely limited the rights of patients. Due in part to the growth in consumer activism, more attention is being paid to the rights of consumers of health care. It's interesting to note that despite the progress that has been made, nowhere in the United States is a person guaranteed an absolute right to health care.

1950s
1959: National League for Nursing issued the first patients' bill of rights outlining seven points to help patients understand nursing care

1960s
1962: President John F. Kennedy's message to Congress outlining four basic consumer rights: right to safety, right to be informed, right to choose, and right to be heard

1970s
1973: Rehabilitation Act of 1973
1975: Community Mental Health Amendment of 1975
1975: Education for Handicapped Children Act
1976: New Jersey Supreme Court decision in the Quinlan case granting the parents of Karen Ann Quinlan (in a persistent vegetative state) permission to remove her ventilator—first case to use the constitutional right to privacy as a basis for withdrawing life support
1978: Rehabilitation Comprehensive Services and Development Disability Amendment passage

1980s
1980: Mental Health Systems Act
1987: Omnibus Budget Reconciliation Act

1990s
1990: U.S. Supreme Court ruling in Cruzan case (parents requested removal of daughter Nancy's feeding tube after several years in a persistent vegetative state; court refused, citing that under the Constitution, a state has the right to require clear and convincing evidence that the patient wanted life-sustaining treatment withheld [implying that when such evidence exists, the patient's desires will be respected])
1991: Patient Self-Determination Act effective
1992: Revision of American Hospital Association's (AHA's) Patient's Bill of Rights
1996: Passage of the Health Insurance Portability and Accountability Act (HIPAA)

2000s
2003: Replacement of AHA's Patient's Bill of Rights with The Patient Care Partnership
2003: Enactment of Health Insurance Portability and Accountability Act (HIPAA) as mandatory
2007: Introduction of Health Information Privacy and Security Act to Congress to revise HIPAA

Interpretation of patients' rights

The theory of patients' rights is clear, but the practice is inherently full of conflict. What happens if defending a patient's rights requires that the nurse exceed the bounds of nursing practice?

Consider the case of *Tuma v. Board of Nursing (1979)*. A patient with myelogenous leukemia was admitted to a hospital in Idaho for chemotherapy. Although she had agreed to this treatment, she was openly distressed about it. Instead of asking her physician about alternative treatment, she asked Jolene Tuma, RN, MSN, a nursing instructor at the College of Southern Idaho who supervised nursing students at the hospital. Ms. Tuma had asked to be assigned to the patient because of her interest in the needs of dying patients.

Ms. Tuma told the patient, in detail, about alternative treatments. She discussed laetrile therapy and various natural food and herbal remedies, comparing their adverse effects with those of chemotherapy. She also gave the patient the name of a therapist who practiced alternative treatments and offered to arrange an appointment.

Ms. Tuma didn't encourage the patient to alter her treatment plan or indicate that alternative treatments were better than the prescribed therapy or would cure her.

At the patient's request, Ms. Tuma also discussed the alternative treatments with the patient's son and daughter-in-law. They told the patient's physician and, as a result, he interrupted the chemotherapy until he could discuss the situation with the patient. The next day the patient again agreed to undergo chemotherapy. Two weeks later, she went into a coma and died.

The patient's physician demanded that the hospital remove Ms. Tuma from her position as clinical instructor at the College of Southern Idaho.

At the hospital's request, the board of nursing conducted an investigation and hearing. The board interpreted Ms. Tuma's behavior as unprofessional. They agreed that she had interfered with the physician-patient relationship and suspended her nursing license for 6 months.

Ms. Tuma appealed, lost the appeal, and appealed again. This time, 3 years after the incident, the Idaho State Supreme Court declared her not guilty of unprofessional conduct. The Court ruled that the Idaho Nurse Practice Act neither clearly defined unprofessional conduct nor provided guidelines for avoiding it.

The decision failed to define the nurse's specific role in upholding a patient's right to information. This leaves several troubling questions unanswered.

For example, Ms. Tuma's patient asked her, not the physician, for information about alternative therapies. The physician testified that he wasn't knowledgeable about these therapies, so what recourse did his patient have? If a physician can't or won't answer such questions, does a patient have the right to obtain answers from a nurse? Unfortunately, there are no easy answers unless the courts or legislatures address such questions.

Guidelines for upholding patients' rights

The best guideline to follow in protecting a patient's interests is to become familiar with the employer's stated policy on patients' rights. If no such policy exists, consider the NLN's position statement on the role of nursing in patients' rights.

The NLN encourages nurses to view patients as partners in the health care process. In planning a patient's care, recognize his right to participate in decisions. Help him set realistic goals for his health care, and teach him the various approaches he can use to achieve them.

Throughout the decision-making process, keep assessing the patient's understanding of his illness. When he needs and wants more information, first determine who should provide it—the nurse or the physician. Then let the patient participate in the development of his plan of care, which must address that patient's unique needs as well as his rights.

Upholding patients' rights provides additional benefits, such as opening health care to new ideas. For example, nurse-

midwives and other maternity nurses have acted as advocates for patients who challenge traditional childbirth practices. As a result, many health care facilities have introduced changes, such as:
▶ using birthing rooms as an alternative to traditional delivery rooms
▶ using less intervention and medication during delivery
▶ allowing patients to use a birthing chair or walk at will during labor
▶ encouraging the company and support of a "coach"—husband, other relative, or friend—during labor and delivery
▶ allowing families, including other children and grandparents, to participate in or attend the delivery.

Hospitals employ full-time patient advocates, or ombudsmen, to mediate between the patient and the hospital when a patient is dissatisfied with care. Patient advocates may help nurses uphold their responsibilities to patients. However, advocates don't diminish those responsibilities. Respecting and safeguarding a patient's rights is mandatory and the law.

INFORMED CONSENT

Being adequately informed about proposed treatment, procedures, surgery, or research to properly consent is a patient's legal right. So, it isn't surprising that the topic of informed consent appears in all current medical and nursing texts and must be evidenced in the patient's records when invasive or experimental procedures, treatment, or surgery are contemplated.

In the 1960s, physicians were primarily responsible for obtaining the patient's consent. Since then, nurses also have come to play a role in obtaining in-

formed consent. It's a basic rule that the responsibility for obtaining a patient's informed consent rests with the person who will carry out the procedure. This procedure may be delegated to an appropriate person under certain circumstances (for example, to another physician who will participate in the procedure).

Informed consent basically involves the patient, or someone acting on his behalf, having enough information to know what the patient is risking should he decide to undergo the proposed treatment or surgery or the anticipated consequences should consent to the treatment be refused or withdrawn. Nurses may provide patients and their families with information that's within a nurse's scope of practice and knowledge base. However, a nurse can't substitute personal knowledge for a physician's input.

Under certain circumstances, people with mental disorders may be held competent to consent. When there's a question about an individual's capacity to give consent, a legal determination may be sought from the appropriate court (for example, probate court) or an ethics committee of the facility.

The bottom line in determining capacity must be whether the person giving consent is impaired in his capacity or judgment so as not to know what he's getting into before the treatment begins.

To assess capacity to consent, a nurse may need to rely on instincts as well as professional judgment. If the nurse believes the patient doesn't understand, the nurse must reassess and discuss the consent issue with the patient, his guardian if applicable, and the physician before the treatment begins.

Elements of informed consent

Informed consent must be obtained whenever a patient needs information to make an informed decision when faced with choices about treatment.[4] Informed consent should include:

▶ a description of the treatment or procedure

▶ a description of inherent risks and benefits that occur with frequency or regularity or specific consequences known by the health care practitioner to be particularly significant to this patient or his designated decision maker

▶ an explanation of the potential for death or serious harm (such as brain damage, stroke, paralysis, or disfiguring scars) or for discomforting adverse effects during or after the treatment or procedure

▶ an explanation and description of alternative treatments or procedures

▶ the name and qualifications of the person who will perform the treatment or procedure

▶ a discussion of the possible effects of not having the treatment or procedure.

Patients must also be told that they have a right to refuse the treatment or procedures without having other care or support withdrawn, and that they can withdraw consent after giving it. (See *Informed consent: A landmark ruling*, page 56.)

A health care professional such as a physician or nurse must ensure that the patient understands the purpose, benefits, risks, and alternatives of an invasive test or treatment. Once this is determined, the patient can provide informed consent and sign the consent form.[5]

When a nurse witnesses a patient's signature on a consent form, she is attesting to three things:

▶ The patient voluntarily consented.

▶ The signature of the patient or the patient's designated decision maker is authentic.

▶ The patient appears to be competent to give consent.

However, consent and privacy issues are more plentiful now, particularly because of such procedures as human immunodeficiency virus (HIV) testing, drug and alcohol treatment, and sterilization. The facility's risk manager should define nurses' responsibilities, the employer's policies, and the state's legal requirements. Each state has specific statutes governing informed consent issues that are subject to change as tort reform evolves and as case law interprets existing statutes or legal concepts.

Informed consent is a process, not a document. Hospitals generally address informed consent in policy and procedure manuals to ensure consistency and thorough implementation and documentation. Current Joint Commission "hot spots" include issues of restraints, informed consent (especially for participating in research), advance directives, and confidentiality. Regarding informed consent issues, evidence is required that the consent is voluntary and that sufficient information regarding the treatment was given. This includes an explanation of alternatives, differences in effectiveness of alternatives, consequences of not having the proposed treatment, risk and benefits, impact on daily living, likelihood of success, responsible practitioners, and any possible conflicts of interest. In addition, this information must be presented in a manner that the patient understands, including appropriate language, reading level, cognitive ability, and ethnic orien-

Informed consent: A landmark ruling

The right of informed consent didn't exist at the beginning of the century. A patient had no legal right to information about his medical treatment. If a physician performed surgery without the patient's consent, the patient could sue for battery—legally defined as one person touching another without consent. A patient could claim battery only if he had refused consent or wasn't asked to give it, but not if he didn't have enough information to make an appropriate decision.

RARE EXCEPTIONS
Most battery lawsuits were unsuccessful because courts usually took the physician's word over the patient's. Two cases in which patients did win were *Mohr v. Williams (1905)*, in which the patient consented to surgery on one ear but the physician performed it on both, and *Schloendorff v. Society of New York Hospitals (1914)*, in which the patient consented to an abdominal examination, but the physician performed abdominal surgery.

ESTABLISHING A PATIENT RIGHT
The right to receive informed consent wasn't expressed legally until 1957, when the California Supreme Court introduced the theory in the case of *Salgo v. Leland Stanford, Jr., University Board of Trustees*. This case involved a patient who had acute arterial insufficiency in his legs. The physician recommended diagnostic tests but failed to describe the tests or their risks. The day after the patient underwent aortography, his legs became permanently paralyzed. The court found the physician negligent for failing to explain the potential risks of aortography.

This decision established a basic rule: a physician violates "his duty to his patient and subjects himself to liability if he withholds any facts that are necessary to form the basis of an intelligent consent by the patient to the proposed treatment."

Since this landmark ruling, a patient can sue for negligent nondisclosure if his physician fails to provide enough information to enable him to make an informed decision.

---

tation. Lastly, the appropriate documentation must be completed properly.

Standards of informed consent
Legally, informed consent can be viewed generally from two different perspectives. The first, from the physician's standpoint, is known as the majority rule, or malpractice model: what a reasonable physician would have disclosed to his patient regarding proposed treatment under the same or similar circumstances as the case in question (*Karp v. Cooley [1974]*). See also *Nathanson v. Kline (1960)*, in which the physician allegedly failed to inform the patient of the adverse effects of cobalt radiation therapy. The court ruled that the physician had a duty to disclose information that "a reasonable medical practitioner would disclose under the same or similar circumstances." Therefore, under the majority rule, the information is viewed from what a reasonable health care professional would tell a patient or patient's family about the procedure.

The second perspective, known as the minority rule, looks at disclosure of the material information that a *reasonable patient* in the situation *would deem significant to know* in making a decision to undergo the proposed treatment.

Reasonable disclosure
Consider *Canterbury v. Spence (1972)*. In this case, a patient had a laminectomy and then fell and developed paralysis. The patient sued the physician for failing to warn him of the inherent risks. The court ruled that the physician had a duty

to disclose as much information as he knew, or should have known, a reasonable patient would need to make an informed decision.

The question then arises, what should the patient be told? It's well accepted that a duty of reasonable disclosure of risks, incident to the medical diagnosis and treatment, is required. The patient must be given an opportunity to evaluate the options, alternatives, and risks, and then exercise his choice. In medical malpractice cases that involve consent issues, expert testimony is usually required to establish whether the information given to the patient was reasonable, understandable, presented at a time when the patient was functionally able to process the information (as opposed to being sedated or medicated), and complete enough to allow the patient to knowledgeably agree to proceed. However, not every remote risk or benefit must be raised or addressed. It's generally agreed that only the risks and benefits that arise frequently or regularly need to be discussed with the patient or the decision maker for the patient. Alternatively, if the health care practitioner knows that specific consequences are particularly significant to this patient, those must be discussed before true informed consent may be obtained. Professional judgment must be exercised by all health care practitioners involved at this point.

Negligent nondisclosure

Negligent nondisclosure refers to the failure to fully inform a patient about treatment. Consider this landmark case from Texas, *Karp v. Cooley*. It's a good example of how nondisclosure and informed consents are raised and added to other allegations in malpractice cases.

Mr. Karp was offered a mechanical heart transplant when it was obvious that his medical condition was deteriorating and he was near death. Many consultants evaluated Mr. Karp. One, Dr. Beasley, wrote in Mr. Karp's chart that he didn't recommend the procedure because he thought the patient wasn't a suitable candidate for the surgery. Dr. Cooley, the surgeon, admitted at trial that he didn't tell Mr. Karp of Dr. Beasley's note, which was made during initial workups and was actually directed and related to Beasley's reservation about the patient's psychological or emotional acceptance of a less-than-perfect outcome.

Mrs. Karp testified to what Mr. Karp's physicians said in her presence. However, Mr. Karp also spoke with his physicians on several occasions about the proposed treatment when his wife wasn't present, and it was Mr. Karp who signed the consent form. The consent form matched the details Dr. Cooley testified to as being the basis of discussions with Mr. Karp before he signed the form.

No expert testimony was offered to indicate that what Dr. Cooley discussed with Mr. Karp was inadequate or breached Dr. Cooley's duty to obtain informed consent.

The court dismissed the informed consent issue on that basis and also raised the issue that the plaintiff, the estate of Mr. Karp, didn't present substantial evidence that there was any causal connection between their claimed lack of informed consent and Mr. Karp's death. To address this proximate cause relationship, the court looked at Texas case law (previous cases on this issue) and noted that for a finding of proximate causation between the alleged omissions of in-

When a patient doesn't understand

Suppose you're caring for a patient scheduled for surgery. He has talked to his physician and signed the consent form. However, the night before surgery, he doesn't seem to understand the implications of the procedure. What should you do?

As the nurse assigned to the patient, you should page the physician who's scheduled to perform the surgery and express your concern that the patient isn't properly informed. Also, if your facility provides institutionally approved guidelines or pamphlets on the procedure, you may review these with the patient before the patient talks to the physician.

formed consent and injury (in this case, death), certain factors must be present:

▶ A hidden risk that should have been made known, and wasn't, must materialize.

▶ The hidden risk must be harmful to the patient.

▶ Causality exists only when disclosures of significant risks incidental to treatment would have resulted in the patient's decision against the treatment.

What the court relied upon, then, in discussing the case on the proximate cause issue was testimony that Mr. Karp was near death before the wedge excision operation to which he gave consent. Mrs. Karp didn't dispute the validity of that consent. After the excision, Mr. Karp was also near death. Therefore, no one testified that to a reasonable degree of medical certainty the mechanical heart caused Mr. Karp's death. Finally, no proof was offered at trial that Mr. Karp wouldn't have agreed to proceed with the mechanical-heart surgery had alleged undisclosed

material risks been disclosed. On appeal, the dismissal on the informed consent issue was upheld.

State laws and informed consent

Many state legislatures have passed laws supporting the standards of informed consent set by the courts. States have procedural laws on informed consent—laws that describe, for example, the tort of negligent nondisclosure. A few states have laws that are *substantive*, meaning they actually define what must be present for informed consent to have been established. These laws define who can give consent and for what, and what type of documentation is required. These laws define exemptions to documented consent and when consent becomes invalid. Although the physician or practitioner is primarily involved with explaining the treatment, the nurse plays an important role in documenting the patient's decision. (See *When a patient doesn't understand.*)

Invalidation of informed consent

Informed consent can become invalid if a change in the patient's medical status alters the risks and benefits of treatment. In such situations, the practitioner must explain the new risks and benefits to make sure the patient will consent to the treatment.

Inability to consent

Informed consent relies on an individual's capacity, or ability, to make decisions at a particular time under specific circumstances. To make medical decisions, people must possess both the capacity to make such decisions and the

competence to make decisions. Consider these three elements of decision making:
▶ The ability to understand and communicate information relevant to the decision
▶ The ability to reason and deliberate concerning the decision
▶ The ability to apply a set of values to the decision.

If there's any reason to believe that a patient is incompetent to participate in giving consent because of medication or sedation, nurses are obligated to call that to the practitioner's attention immediately. If a nurse learns that the practitioner discussed consent issues with the patient at a time when the patient was heavily sedated or medicated, the nurse needs to bring these concerns to the attention of the practitioner. If the practitioner isn't available, the nurse should discuss these concerns with the nursing supervisor. In addition, the nurse needs to document attempts to reach the practitioner and attending physician in the medical record before allowing the patient to proceed with the surgery or invasive procedure.

Along with discussing the matter with the practitioner and the supervisor, the nurse must assess the patient's understanding of the information provided by the practitioner. Nurses are trained to make professional assessments about patient understanding, and this is the proper time and place to use those professional skills, without, of course, interfering with the practitioner-patient relationship in the process. However, if the nurse does nothing, and the patient undergoes the procedure without giving proper consent, the nurse may be named as a codefendant in a battery lawsuit. The patient's attorneys, judges, and juries will look closely at the medication records to see

when, in relation to the signing of the consent form, the patient was last medicated, and the patient's response to the medication as documented in the record. The nurse could be held jointly responsible for the patient undergoing a procedure that he didn't consent to, if the nurse:
▶ took part in the battery by assisting with the treatment
▶ knew it was taking place and didn't try to stop it.

If the practitioner fails to provide adequate information for consent because of the patient's medicated status, the patient may sue the practitioner for lack of informed consent due to temporary incapacitation. The courts might hold the nurse responsible if, knowing the practitioner hadn't provided adequate information to a patient, she failed to try to stop the procedure until proper consent could be obtained.

The nurse is always obligated to notify the practitioner in a timely manner if a patient is confused or medicated, the nurse can't provide the information the patient needs, or the nurse assesses that the patient wasn't competent to provide consent when speaking with the practitioner because of medication or sedation. All observations must be documented in the patient's chart and the nurse must ensure that the patient gets information from his practitioner or another appropriate source. These actions and documentation will be key evidence in case of a lawsuit. Moreover, by briefly delaying the surgery, the nurse may be saving the practitioner from a battery claim, as well.

Discrepancies involving consent
How far does the nurse's duty to protect the patient's interest in informed consent

cases extend? Consider the following two cases.

In a Georgia case, Charlotte Butler sought relief for chronic pain, which she believed to be caused by breast cancer treatments. Her oncologist referred her to an anesthesiologist, who was working as an independent contractor at the South Fulton Medical Center in East Point, Georgia. The anesthesiologist, Dr. Kim, used epidural steroid injections on several occasions. Because the patient failed to obtain long-term relief, he administered a neurolytic block injection. At one point, the medication was injected too close to the spinal cord, and the patient became quadriplegic.

The patient sued and settled with Dr. Kim, but the patient also pursued litigation against South Fulton Medical Center, alleging that the nursing staff was negligent for filling out the consent form incorrectly and not noticing the error—that the procedure listed on the form was an epidural steroid injection, not a neurolytic block.

The court found in favor of the hospital (and its staff nurses) in a 6-to-3 decision, holding that the direct cause of her injury was the physician's negligence, not the nurses'. The patient's deposition testimony played a key role. She acknowledged that she didn't understand the difference between the treatments she received. Further, although she had signed consent forms for the steroid injections and for a prior neurolytic block, *she had never read any of them.*" The court reasoned that she probably would have signed no matter what procedure had been listed. The court also held the physician solely responsible for failing to tell the patient what he was doing and what risks were involved. The dissenting

judges felt the nurses had violated their duties to the patient because they violated their own policies, which required them to check that the consent form was complete and accurate and, if it wasn't, to notify the physician or administration, before the procedure was administered. This case (*Butler v. South Fulton Medical Center* [1994]) highlights the importance of communicating with the patient. A few simple questions to the patient would have revealed that she didn't understand the complicated procedure or its risks.

In a Wisconsin case (*Mathias v. St. Catherine's Hospital* [1997]), the court held that simply notifying the physician that there was no signed consent form was enough for the nurses to fulfill their duty. In that case, a physician performed a postdelivery tubal ligation on a patient after being told by the nurses that there was no signed consent form in the patient's chart. The physician reportedly replied, "Oh, okay," then performed the surgery. A few days after the tubal ligation had been performed, one nurse approached the patient with a consent form for the procedure and told the patient that the form was "just to close up our records." The nurse with the form then signed another nurse's name and backdated the form to the date of the procedure.

When the patient sued the physician and the hospital, claiming that the nurses should have stopped the physician from performing the surgery, the appeals court disagreed. It held that the nurses' only duty under these circumstances was to make the physician aware that there was no signed consent. The reason behind the decision apparently was that the court believed the nurses had no way of knowing the physician hadn't obtained the patient's consent and had no reason to think the absence of a signed form in the chart was anything more than a clerical error. The court wasn't swayed by the nurse's forging of another's signature, by the backdating of the form, or by the circulating nurse's testimony that she was an "advocate" for the patient.

Not all courts, however, would have reasoned as the Wisconsin Appeals Court did. Some courts would have taken the actions of the nurses in obtaining the patient's signature on the consent form several days after the procedure as evidence of "consciousness of guilt," fraud, or as a betrayal of the patient's trust. Some courts would have considered the nurse's conduct unethical, illegal, and unconscionable.

Even in cases in which the patient says he understands, this must be documented because it could save the nurse from assault and battery charges for violating the patient's rights, should the nurse participate in the procedure without consent being properly obtained. Nurses also must document any teaching done in conjunction with answering questions the patient asks. Based on the American Nurses Association's (ANA's) *Code of Ethics with Interpretive Statements,* nurses are responsible for identifying and responding to situations that suggest or indicate inadequate preparation or understanding on the part of the patient.[6]

Special circumstances, such as a patient speaking a different language or being unable to read (and the form was read to the patient), should be documented as well. If the patient doesn't speak English, a translator must be involved in the process and he should also sign the consent form.[7] If the patient can't sign his name, have him make an X on the form and note on it by whom the mark was made. Also, record the patient's verbal consent in the chart.

Competence vs. Incompetence

A patient is deemed mentally incompetent if he can't understand the explanations or can't comprehend the results of his decisions. When the patient is incompetent, the practitioner has two alternatives: one is to seek consent from the patient's next of kin, usually a spouse. (Legal definition of next of kin varies from state to state.)

Alternatively, other interested family members or people, the physician, or the hospital may petition the court to appoint a legal guardian for the patient. Sometimes, a Probate Court may decide who the proper legal guardian should be after reviewing petitions and taking testimony. This works well if there's time to appoint a proper guardian.

However, that isn't always possible in the case of a potentially dangerous or deadly medical condition. Under those circumstances, the courts will look to the reasonableness of the actions by the health care providers, before proceeding with the treatment, in determining if there was informed consent by a proper party, or whether the informed consent requirement was properly waived.

Mental illness doesn't imply or denote incompetence. People suffering from mental illness have been found competent to consent because they're alert and, above all, can understand the proposed treatment, risks, benefits, and alternatives as well as the consequences of refusing treatment. Consider a patient who has been hospitalized involuntarily but remains alert and oriented. His mental

IN THE NEWS

Mandatory reporting and adolescents

An attorney general in the state of Kansas issued an opinion about the mandatory reporting of child abuse, including sexual abuse. In this opinion, sexual abuse is assumed to include any sexual activity involving anyone younger than age 16. Numerous groups have responded to this opinion, including the American Nurses Association and the Kansas State Nurses Association, citing that the Kansas state law definition of sexual abuse is too broad. They state that those obligated to report cases of suspected abuse, such as nurses, would be forced to notify authorities when adolescents engage in a range of sexual activities from intercourse to touching with the intent to arouse. The underlying issue involves trust and the nurse-patient relationship. According to those opposed, this opinion would undermine the development of trust with an adolescent and the professional's ability to make judgments about what is normal sexual activity, what is consensual activity, and what is sexual abuse. The groups fear that this opinion would compromise the care of the adolescent, for example, leading the adolescent to avoid seeking needed care or delay care. In addition, they feel that this opinion would interfere with their ability to provide adolescents with the information needed to treat them. Moreover, the groups fear that fewer resources would be available to pursue actual cases of abuse due to the enforced mandatory reporting of all adolescent sexual activities.

Source: Troussman, S. "Mandatory Reporting Law Gone Awry," *AJN* 105(6):73-75, 2005.

status and education enable him to understand the information presented by the practitioner, but he lacks freedom from incarceration. Should this patient be allowed to make medical decisions that will affect his life or future health? Why should a court-appointed person assume this authority? On the other hand, shouldn't the patient have the right to refuse treatment even if it might ease his mental illness (for example, electroconvulsive therapy)?

Since the late 1980s, practitioners have had to reexamine medical restraint issues that involve elderly, confused, and infirm patients. It's now well established that a confined patient, mentally or physically disabled, may be forcibly medicated only in an emergency when he may cause harm to himself or others. In such cases, documentation in the patient record regarding the actual mental status of the

patient and competency to give consent is critical.

Minors

Over the past 25 years, great social and legal challenges have arisen that involve the rights of minors, especially their right to seek health care. As concerns for the rights of minors regarding consent to health care have developed, all states have looked at the issue of just who can give consent for minors to receive what care and what information a minor may keep confidential in regard to that care. (See *Mandatory reporting and adolescents*.) Certain rules have evolved.

Usually, the person giving consent for care and treatment of a minor is a parent or other designated adult. This isn't always the case, however. The practitioner must disclose all relevant information to the person giving consent to ensure that the consent is informed.

The patchwork of rights and limitations of the various state laws governing when minors can and can't consent provides alternating perceptions of teenagers. They're viewed as adultlike and childlike, and there's a desire to protect and respect both these qualities.

For example, a teenage mother must give consent before her baby can receive treatment but in general isn't permitted to determine the course of her own health care. Under federal law, adolescents can be tested and treated for HIV without parental involvement. However, parental consent is required to set an adolescent's broken arm in most cases.

Every state will allow an emancipated minor to consent to his own medical care and treatment. So far, state definitions of emancipation vary, but it's generally recognized that to be emancipated, the individual must be a minor by state definition (less than the legal age of majority in that state) and must have obtained a legal declaration of freedom from the custody, care, and control of his parents. In doing so, emancipated minors forgo the right to financial support from their parents and any protection from lawsuits. When declared emancipated, minors gain the right to enter binding contracts; to sue; and to consent to medical, dental, or psychiatric care without parental approval. They also assume all the financial obligations for this care, just as an adult would if he entered into such contracts. In granting emancipated status to minors, the courts look for employment, demonstrated fiscal responsibility, and other evidence of support systems the minor has available, as well as the individual circumstances that underlie the request for legal determination of emancipation.

Most states allow teenagers to consent to treatment, even though they haven't been determined emancipated, in cases involving pregnancy and sexually transmitted diseases. Privacy issues are involved as well, so the nurse must understand the specific circumstances allowing a minor to consent and when to contact the parent or legal guardian. A risk manager should be able to help. Contact with a parent or legal guardian and disclosure of confidential information has resulted in lawsuits for breach of confidentiality.

An unemancipated minor in mid to late teens who shows signs of intellectual and emotional maturity is considered a "mature minor." In some cases, a mature minor is allowed to exercise health care rights that are generally reserved for adults. Because there's no consensus about when maturity occurs and, thus, no clear guidelines for those who must make such assessments, the issue of maturity must be decided on a case-by-case basis.

It's an accepted practice to allow children, to the extent they may participate, to be involved in the decision-making process regarding life-sustaining medical treatment. In making the ultimate decisions, there must be a weighing of "the best interests" standard, which involves considering the benefits and the burdens to the child. Some benefits to be considered are prolonging life and improving quality of life after treatment. Burdens of the proposed treatment may include intractable pain, irremediable disability or helplessness, emotional suffering, and invasiveness of the procedure, which could severely detract from the quality of life. Keep in mind that the quality of life to be considered is from the child's perspective, not that of the parent, the decision maker, or even the health care providers. However, the assumption, without evidence to the contrary, is that life-sustaining medical treatment will be provided in accordance with existing medical, ethical, and legal norms.

Evidence of consent

Consent can be demonstrated by a signed, witnessed document; a note in the medical record detailing communications between the physician and patient; or the patient willfully undergoing the procedure by appearing at the appointed time and place. Some states (such as Georgia) have statutes stating that a signed consent form disclosing the treatment in general terms is deemed conclusive proof of a valid consent. Of course, the validity of the signature may be challenged. However, if the patient is legally competent to sign the form and does so, he waives the right to a later claim that he didn't. He also waives the right to a later claim that he didn't understand the medical treatment or that the physician didn't explain to him information in the consent form.

Other states take the position that a signed consent form is evidence of informed consent, but that may be refutable if the patient offers sufficient evidence to the contrary. The patient may challenge his consent by attacking the substance of the consent form. He may claim the practitioner didn't explain the medical terms in a manner that a patient could understand or (given the medical diagnosis, the patient's condition, or the surgery contemplated) that relevant information significant to the patient wasn't provided.

A signed consent form may not be required in one's own state. However, there must still be evidence that the patient has

been provided with the required information and that he has evidenced his consent to proceed. This may be done by a physician's notation in the progress notes indicating that the patient has been told of specific risks, benefits, and alternatives; has had an opportunity to have questions answered; and understands and agrees to the procedure. The evidence of informed consent is further enhanced if the medical record documents other family members who were present with the patient when the consent was obtained, such as "Wife present and concurs with patient's decision to proceed with the surgery."

If the nurse works in a facility that uses investigational drugs or engages in research (RI.1.2.1.1), the facility's policies and procedures must state that the patient or surrogate receives a clear explanation of experimental treatment. This includes the procedures to be followed (RI.1.2.1.4), a clear description of potential discomforts and risks (RI.1.2.1.2), a list of alternative treatments (RI.1.2.1.3), and a clear explanation that patients may refuse to participate in the research project without compromising their access to care and treatment (RI.1.2.1.5). (See *Informed consent guidelines for research*.)

Most Joint Commission type 1 recommendations given after the site visit involve informed consent and result from inadequate or incomplete documentation. (Health care organizations must resolve insufficient or unsatisfactory compliance with standards in a specific performance area within a specific time to maintain accreditation.) It's easier to comply with Joint Commission standards if forms are user-friendly and include the required criteria, if an audit system is in

Informed consent guidelines for research

The U.S. Office for Human Research Protections (OHRP) has established a Code of Federal Regulations (CFR) that addresses specific information that must be given to individuals before they agree to participate in a research study.[10] These include the following:

- A statement that the study involves research
  – an explanation of the purposes
  – expected duration of participation
  – description of procedures to be followed
  – identification of any procedures considered experimental
- Description of any reasonably foreseeable risks or discomforts to the subject
- Description of any benefits to the subject or others that may reasonably be expected from the research
- Disclosure of appropriate alternative procedures or courses of treatment, if any, that might be advantageous to the subject
- Statement describing the extent, if any, to which confidentiality of records identifying the subject will be maintained

- If more than minimal risk, an explanation as to whether there are any treatments or compensation if injury occurs, and if so, what they consist of, or where further information may be obtained
- Explanation of whom to contact for answers to pertinent questions about the research and research subjects' rights and whom to contact in the event of a research-related injury to the subject
- Statement that participation is voluntary and refusal to participate will involve no penalty or loss of benefits to which subject is otherwise entitled, and that subject may discontinue participation at any time without penalty or loss of benefits to which the subject is otherwise entitled.

Source: United States Department of Health and Human Services: Part 46 Protection of Human Subjects, Subpart A: Basic HHS Policy for Protection of Human Research Subjects. Revised 6/23/2005. Available at: www.hhs.gov/ohrp/humansubjects.

place to validate that forms are consistently completed appropriately, and if the forms are included in the medical records. The nurses' notes or progress notes must also include an entry that the health care practitioner has discussed these issues with the patient or surrogate decision maker and that he understands and gives consent or refuses it.

The controversy over informed consent typically centers on medical and surgical treatments and procedures that are invasive, risky, experimental, or have low likelihood for a successful outcome. Much time has passed since the concept of silence, or therapeutic privilege. In that situation, the physician was allowed to withhold information from a patient at the sole discretion of the physician and

the patient's family, who believed that the information would jeopardize the patient's health. In some instances, patients weren't told that they were dying or that the treatment would have no benefit. Now, therapeutic privilege is viewed narrowly because withholding significant information from patients or their designated decision makers is frowned upon by the courts as a violation of a patient's right to self-determination, a right that the nurse is charged with protecting. (See *Right to consent: From birth to adulthood,* page 66.)

Exceptions to informed consent

Emergency treatment (to save a patient's life or to prevent loss of organ, limb, or a

Right to consent: From birth to adulthood

From birth, everyone has medical rights to:
• confidentiality concerning medical records
• privacy during treatment
• reasonable and prudent medical care.
   A person attains more medical rights as he reaches the age of majority, defined as the age when a person is considered legally responsible for his activities and becomes entitled to the legal rights held by citizens generally.

MINORS

Anyone younger than the age of majority (18 or 21, depending on the state in which he lives) has the right to consent to treatment for sexually transmitted diseases, serious communicable diseases, and drug or alcohol abuse (although state law may require that the minor's parents be notified).

MATURE MINORS

In certain instances, a physician or judge may decide that a minor is sufficiently mature—has a sufficiently developed awareness and mental capacity—to consent to medical treatment. If so, the minor has the right to make decisions about medical care.

ADULTS

Anyone who has reached majority or who's a legally emancipated minor has the right to:
• consent to or refuse medical treatment
• consent to or refuse medical treatment for his children (in most circumstances).

has been held to be appropriate even if no one is available to consent to the procedure.

Children brought to the emergency department after serious injury in school whose parents can't be located in time may be provided with emergency medical care without consent while attempts are made to locate the parents. Even though consent can be legally presumed in these cases, health care facilities may still face lawsuits. For example, if blood is given to a severely injured, unconscious person, the patient or family could still sue if such an action were against their religious convictions. Courts will uphold emergency medical treatment as long as reasonable effort was made to obtain consent and no alternative treatments were available to save life or limb. The courts won't uphold treatment in the absence of informed consent if the practitioner has had prior contact and has been told that such treatment would be refused. If the practitioner has time to locate family members or to obtain proper consent from the patient, the courts will require the practitioner to do so.

Before proceeding, a prudent nurse will make certain that the medical emergency, the assumptions to obtain proper consent, and any information that has been conveyed to the patient is documented in the medical record. If the practitioner wants to provide care to the patient without consent, but the nurse feels that the care could wait, the nurse should discuss this with the practitioner. If the practitioner insists on proceeding anyway, the nurse should evaluate the situation. If refusal to help would harm the patient or create an unsafe situation (a practitioner caring for a patient without assistance), the nurse should assist. If the

function) may be done without first obtaining consent in specific circumstances. If the patient is unconscious or a minor who can't give consent, emergency treatment may be performed. The presumption is that the patient would have consented had he been able, unless there's reason to believe otherwise. For example, to sustain the life of unconscious patients in the emergency department, intubation

When a patient says no

A patient must give his consent before you can perform any treatment. If the patient refuses, take these steps:

1. Explain the risks involved in not having the treatment performed.
2. If the patient understands the risks but still refuses, notify your supervisor and the physician.
3. Record the patient's refusal in the nurses' notes.
4. Ask the patient to complete a refusal of treatment form, like the one shown below. The signed form indicates that appropriate treatment would have been given had the patient consented.
5. If the patient refuses to sign the release form, document this in your nurses' notes and write "refused to sign" on the patient's signature line. Initial it with your own initials and date it.
6. For additional protection, facility policy may require you to get the patient's spouse or closest relative to sign a refusal of treatment form. Document in the same manner as above whether the spouse or relative does this.

REFUSAL OF TREATMENT RELEASE FORM

I, [patient's name], refuse to allow anyone to [insert treatment].
The risks attendant to my refusal have been fully explained to me, and I fully understand the results for this treatment and that if the same isn't done, my chances for regaining my normal health are seriously reduced and that, in all probability, my refusal for such treatment or procedure will seriously affect my health or recovery.

I hereby release [name of hospital], its nurses and employees, together with all physicians in any way connected with me as a patient, from liability for respecting and following my expressed wishes and direction.

_____	_____
Witness	Patient or Legal Guardian
_____	_____
Date	Patient's Date of Birth

---

nurse refuses to participate, she should notify the nursing supervisor. The incident should also be reported to hospital administration.

Patients may also waive their rights to additional information by appointing someone else as their medical decision maker. Advance directives are one way to have another person participate and be responsible for one's medical care and treatment. If this has been decided beforehand, proper documentation must appear in the medical record.

● REFUSAL OF TREATMENT

Any mentally competent adult may legally refuse treatment if he's fully informed about his medical condition and about the likely consequences of his refusal. As a professional, the nurse must respect that decision.

When a patient refuses treatment, nurses must understand more than his rights and their responsibilities. (See *When a patient says no*.)

The right to refuse

Also inherent in the right to consent to treatment is the right to refuse treatment. According to AHA's "The Patient Care Partnership," discussing the treatment plan with the health care provider is a major component of the patient's involvement in care. This discussion serves to protect the patient's right to consent to or refuse a treatment. Along with this discussion, the health care provider is obligated to explain the medical consequences of refusing the recommended treatment.[11]

Most court cases related to the right to refuse treatment have involved patients with a terminal illness, or their families, who want to discontinue life support. In one of the best known cases, Karen Ann Quinlan's parents argued that unwanted treatment violated their comatose daughter's constitutional right to privacy. In 1976, the Quinlans successfully petitioned the New Jersey Supreme Court to stop her life support (*In re Quinlan*).

In another landmark case, *Cruzan v. Director, Missouri Department of Health (1990)*, Nancy Cruzan's parents petitioned to have their comatose daughter's tube feedings stopped. In 1990, the U.S. Supreme Court held that the state of Missouri has the constitutional right to refuse to permit termination of life-sustaining treatment *unless "clear and convincing evidence" exists about a patient's wishes*. Because this standard wasn't met, the Court didn't allow removal of the feeding and hydration tube. Significantly, the Court implied that when clear and convincing evidence exists, the patient's wishes will be respected.

Two months after the Supreme Court ruling, the Cruzans petitioned the local court with new evidence. A Missouri judge granted them the right to remove Nancy's feeding and hydration tube. She died shortly thereafter. Publicity about Nancy Cruzan's legal ordeal heightened the awareness of millions of Americans to the need to prepare ahead for critical medical decisions.

Religious considerations

Certain religious beliefs may impact a patient's right to refuse. Jehovah's Witnesses may refuse treatment on the grounds of freedom of religion. Members of this sect oppose blood transfusions, based on their interpretation of a biblical passage that forbids "drinking" blood. Some sect members believe that even a lifesaving transfusion given against their will deprives them of everlasting life. The courts usually uphold their right to refuse treatment because of the constitutionally protected right to religious freedom. In the case of *In re Osborne (1972)*, for example, the court respected a Jehovah's Witness' right to refuse consent.

Most other religious freedom court cases involve Christian Scientists, who oppose many medical interventions, including medicines. For example, in *Winters v. Miller (1971)*, a psychiatric patient claimed she involuntarily received treatment and medications at a New York state hospital. After her discharge, she sued for damages based on a violation of her religious freedom as a Christian Scientist. The trial court dismissed her complaint, but an appeals court ordered a new trial on the grounds that the unwanted treatment might have violated her rights.

Besides court rulings, most patients' bills of rights support the right to refuse treatment, starting with the bill of rights adopted by the AHA in 1973, revised in

1992, and replaced in 2003 with "The Patient Care Partnership."

When a Jehovah's Witness refuses blood because of religious beliefs, health care professionals are challenged to provide optimal care without using standard medical treatment. Health care, legal, ethical, and management issues of how to treat blood loss when it occurs must be carefully considered. Some strategies are currently available that minimize blood loss during cardiac surgeries, for example, as well as methods to increase endogenous production. With more than 3.9 million Jehovah's Witnesses worldwide and about 1 million in the United States, more health care providers are facing situations in which blood transfusion isn't a treatment option.

The use of blood-conserving techniques during surgery has been validated by several investigations and allows patients to adhere to their religious beliefs while resolving the dilemmas associated with the unacceptability of standard, accepted treatments. Of course, physicians would have the ethical and legal rights to refuse to care for any patient in a non-emergency situation when standard medical care isn't acceptable to the patient. Court orders can also be obtained, requiring the patient to undergo the standard treatment against the patient's wishes. Health care providers could also honor the patient's request under all circumstances. By looking at the available alternatives and trying to honor the patient's wishes, nurses may be able to comply with the Code of Nurses of the ANA, which specifies that nurses are obligated to support and protect each patient's right of self-determination, to respect the patient's individuality, to adhere

to standards of care, and to maintain the patient's safety.

Age-related considerations

It's generally held that parents have the right to refuse life-sustaining medical treatment for unemancipated children who lack the capacity or statutory criteria for maturity to make such decisions for themselves.

Decisions to limit, withhold, stop, or forgo treatment must be carefully documented and must be specific in nature. The collaborative process must occur between patient, parent (or legal guardian), and practitioner. Young children deserve to hear the general conclusions of a decision that will affect their survival, especially when the clinician believes treatment will no longer benefit the patient and should be withdrawn.

Emancipated or mature minors are presumed to have the capacity to give consent. Regarding younger children, however, it might be helpful to consider what the Tennessee State Supreme Court did in a 1987 case. It used the "Rule of Sevens." The court presumed that up to age 7, the child lacked capacity to consent. From ages 7 to 14, the presumption of incapacity can be rebutted (by evidence demonstrating that the child, in fact, possesses maturity); at age 14 and older, the individual should be presumed to have capacity.

Conflict between autonomy and beneficence

A patient may refuse any treatment, whether ordinary or extraordinary. However, the decision to refuse ordinary treatment presents an especially complex ethical dilemma, which hinges on the conflict between beneficence and autono-

Saying "no" to rehabilitation

One reward of rehabilitation nursing is watching a patient with severe injuries come to terms with an altered body image and eventually go on to live a fulfilling life with a disability. But what happens when a patient turns down the help that nurses and therapists offer? Nurses may experience a bitter ethical conflict between the principle of patient autonomy, which includes the right to refuse treatment, and the principle of beneficence. Consider the case of Philip Munson, a young quadriplegic who refused rehabilitative treatment, deciding that he preferred to die.

WANTING TO DIE

Mr. Munson, age 30, was left a C3 quadriplegic after he broke his neck in an automobile accident. First admitted to the intensive care unit (ICU), Mr. Munson was totally dependent on others for all activities and all aspects of his care. His only relatives were a brother and a sister-in-law, who visited regularly and planned to have him live with them after rehabilitation.

During his month in the ICU, Philip told the nurses that he wanted to live. Shortly after being transferred to the rehabilitation unit, however, he changed his mind. He wanted to die and insisted on stopping his rehabilitation program. His brother made it clear that he wanted Mr. Munson's wishes respected. A psychiatrist evaluated Mr. Munson and concluded that he was competent and showed no evidence of psychosis or thought disorder.

Mr. Munson understood his condition and his prognosis; he was aware that after rehabilitation he would be able to operate a wheelchair and a computer. He also understood that he would be paralyzed from the neck down and would always need assistance with activities of daily living. Mr. Munson said that he wasn't afraid of death and wanted no heroic measures taken. His brother helped him draft an extensive legal statement establishing the right to refuse specific treatments, including antibiotic and I.V. therapy. Plans were made to discharge him to a nursing home.

ETHICAL CONSIDERATIONS

Many of the nurses and therapists on the rehabilitation unit were distressed by the decision to stop Mr. Munson's program. Depression, anger, and refusal of treatment are common among young accident victims, and these health care professionals were skilled at encouraging, bargaining with, and even coercing patients to comply. They argued that Mr.

Munson's decision was misguided and that there was justification for intervention based on the principles of paternalism and beneficence.

Jim DiFrancesco, RN, a nurse on the rehabilitation team, pointed out that there was a significant difference between a young, recently injured quadriplegic and a terminal cancer patient who finally decides to "pull the plug." He believed that Mr. Munson was under too much stress from the initial impact of the injury and would probably later change his mind and view life as worth living once again. He pointed out to members of the health care team that there are many examples of patients reversing their decision to die. Elizabeth Bouvia, a young woman incapacitated by cerebral palsy, received national publicity when she requested that the hospital stop her tube feedings and allow her to starve herself to death, but she later changed her mind and stated that she wanted to live.

Mr. DiFrancesco pointed out that many factors, such as depression, fear of treatment, hidden family dynamics, and ambivalence, complicated Mr. Munson's ability to make an autonomous decision. Furthermore, Mr. Munson was clearly ambivalent about his desire to die. His behavior wasn't always consistent with his expressed wish for death. For example, he was cheerful on many days and took great interest in the positioning of his joints and measures taken to prevent joint contractures.

In fact, for a brief period, Mr. Munson reneged on his wish to die. His best friend from high school learned about the accident and decided to devote a long visit to helping Philip. When he learned his friend would be arriving soon, Mr. Munson asked to start full therapy again. Although his high school buddy helped out tirelessly and offered to stay even longer, Mr. Munson quickly became overwhelmed by the pain and hardship of his existence and re-

Saying "no" to rehabilitation (continued)

quested that his previous statement outlining his wish to die be reactivated.

RESPECTING PATIENT AUTONOMY
Another nurse on the unit, Christina Walsh, RN, pointed out that the rehabilitation unit's mission was to serve the patient's best interest, not meet the emotional needs of the staff. She believed that members of the health care team had their own vested interest in keeping Mr. Munson alive. For example, the occupational therapist was excited about experimenting with the latest wheelchair control devices. Many of her coworkers, accustomed to seeing their patients readjust to life, couldn't accept that they would inevitably fail some of their patients. It wasn't right, asserted Ms. Walsh, to pursue every technological intervention regardless of the cost or burden to the patient.

AN ETHICAL STRUGGLE
During the time Mr. Munson remained on the rehabilitation unit, the nurses who cared for

him experienced an intense ethical struggle. It was difficult to agree not to perform routine tracheostomy care or range-of-motion exercises or to care for the pressure ulcer that developed on the back of Mr. Munson's head. It also was difficult, however, to do these things in good conscience for a patient who asked that they not be done. It seemed like a total usurpation of what little power and control Mr. Munson still had. Each nurse had to struggle with questions about the rights of a patient who doesn't have the ability to leave the hospital against medical advice, protest his treatment, or even complain without the assistance of another person.

Mr. Munson's ordeal finally came to an end when he was transported to a nursing home near the residence of his brother's family. After 2 months, he slipped into a coma and died. His existence was a lesson to the rehabilitation team: most patients are grateful for the opportunity for a second chance at life; for some, however, the pain is too great. Ultimately, the decision to accept treatment belongs to the patient.

my. If a patient can make an informed decision, he has a right to refuse treatment. But what if his decision doesn't serve his best interests? Which moral principle, autonomy or beneficence, should take precedence? (See *Saying "no" to rehabilitation.*)

Autonomy
One of the cornerstones of ethical decision making, autonomy refers to the right to make decisions about one's health care. It's the right to self-determination and independence when individuals consider and act upon decisions that they believe serve their interests.[12] However, external and internal pressures can limit the patient's autonomy.

Family members and health professionals can exert appreciable external in-

fluence over the patient. Typically, this influence takes the form of persuasion or encouragement. Infrequently, it takes the form of coercion, in which the patient comes to believe he has no free choice.

Physician-patient relationships are inherently imbalanced. The physician possesses knowledge and skill; the patient, a need for care. Because the patient has a need, he assumes a dependent and potentially vulnerable position. He must trust the caregiver. In doing so, he may think that assertiveness is inappropriate. Nurses, however, can counteract this thinking by encouraging the patient to be informed and to ask questions.

Internal pressures involve the patient. Doubt and illness itself can sap autonomy. For instance, the patient may see himself as too ignorant to make crucial decisions about his health. If he does, bolster his self-esteem; encourage him to take an active role in decision making, and support him in his efforts. The patient's signs and symptoms, such as dyspnea and pain, may distract him. If they do, try to relieve them so that the patient can make thoughtful decisions.

Beneficence

Beneficence refers to the duty to protect the patient from harm and to provide treatment that promotes the good of the individual.[13] When dealing with children or patients who can't make informed decisions, beneficence outweighs autonomy. Young children, for instance, don't understand the implications of not being vaccinated for measles or mumps and would simply prefer to avoid the pain of an injection.

For patients who can make an informed decision, though, the burden of proof for beneficence lies with the health care provider. Typically, a health care provider can advance these arguments in support of beneficence:

▶ The patient is under excessive stress and can't think rationally.

▶ The patient may change his mind later, when little or nothing can be done to restore his health.

▶ The patient needs to be protected from acting irrationally.

Underlying all these arguments is a spirit of paternalism, of possessing superior or clearer knowledge than the patient. Of course, the patient could and might change his decision, but this uncertainty doesn't constitute grounds for overruling a competent patient's decision.

Futility

Medical futility refers to treatment that can't benefit a patient, not necessarily because the treatment itself has no merit, but more commonly because the condition of the patient makes the medical action futile. A futile intervention differs from one that's harmful, ineffective, or impossible, and it shouldn't be equated with hopelessness. Hope may be maintained by patients even in impossible situations.

A futile treatment differs from an ineffective or a highly improbable treatment in that it may achieve a short-term gain (such as improving carbon dioxide excretion in a ventilated patient who has chronic obstructive pulmonary disease), but it remains fruitless because it doesn't lead to a true personal benefit (restoration of health).

Usually, health care teams don't render care they deem futile, but with the growing importance of patient autonomy and self-determination, such choices aren't so readily made. Patients believe that they have a right to determine what constitutes a "benefit" to them. At the same time, nurses and physicians should be able to decide when a treatment is futile based on their knowledge of the treatment and its probable effect on the patient's quality of life. The patient's right to choose is limited by the nurses and physicians whose duty it is to provide quality care and practice medicine responsibly.

Ethicists argue that patient self-determination offers a right to refuse treatment or to choose from medically justifiable options. It isn't, they argue, a right to demand treatment. Furthermore, with growing emphasis on cost containment, it's probable that futile treatment won't even be a patient option in the future. Treatment options may become a function of statistical measurement of probable benefits to a patient.

Helga Wanglie represents a classic case in futility. This 85-year-old woman was unconscious and ventilated at a hospital after suffering a heart attack at the nursing home where she resided. The physicians wanted to withdraw the life-sustaining support they deemed to be futile, but her husband objected and had her transferred to another medical center, where she was diagnosed as being in a persistent vegetative state. The physician at the second facility concurred and suggested that the ventilator be removed.

The family ultimately asked the courts to decide if the physicians should be compelled to provide treatment they believed to be nonbeneficial and inappropriate. The courts appointed the husband conservator and decided in his favor. The judge's decision wasn't based on medical values and principles but, rather, on the fact that the husband was the proper surrogate and the surrogate's decisions about the patient's wishes were reliable.

Society's values of freedom to choose and autonomy held precedence over the physicians' professional judgment of futility. "Self-benefit," as determined by a patient or his decision maker, is subjective and can be decidedly different from the medical view of benefit, which consists of restoration of health, cure, pain relief, improved well-being, and quality of life.

Grounds to challenge treatment refusal

There are two grounds for challenging a patient's right to refuse treatment: One is to claim that the patient is incompetent. The courts consider a patient incompetent when he lacks the mental ability to make a reasoned decision, such as when he's delirious. The other is to claim that compelling reasons exist to overrule his wishes. (See *Overruling the patient*, page 74.)

The courts also recognize several compelling circumstances that justify overruling a patient's refusal of treatment. These include:

▶ when refusing treatment endangers the life of another—for example, a court may overrule a pregnant woman's objection to treatment if it endangers her unborn child's life.

▶ when a parent's decision to withhold treatment threatens a child's life—for example, a court may overrule the parents' religious objections to their child's treatment when the child's life is endangered. When the child's life isn't in danger, the courts are more likely to respect the parents' religious convictions.

▶ when, despite refusing treatment, the patient makes statements indicating that he wants to live—for example, some Jehovah's Witnesses who oppose blood transfusions say or imply that they won't prevent the transfusions if a court takes responsibility for the decision. In *Powell v. Columbia-Presbyterian Medical Center (1965)*, the court authorized transfusions when a Jehovah's Witness indicated that she wouldn't object to receiving blood, although she refused to give written consent.

Overruling the patient

Even when a patient's decision to refuse treatment rests on constitutionally protected grounds, such as religious beliefs, the court will intervene in certain circumstances. Becoming familiar with court rulings in this area will help you better cope if you're ever caught between a patient and his family and a court. Here are some delicate legal situations the courts have ruled on. Keep in mind that each case is binding only in its own jurisdiction. A court where you practice may hold differently.

INCAPACITATED PATIENT
If an adult patient becomes physically or mentally incapacitated, a relative can't always refuse treatment for him. The court reserves the right to overrule even a spouse on the patient's behalf if the decision seems to be medically unreasonable. For example, in *Collins v. Davis* (1964), the court overruled a wife's refusal of surgery for her unconscious husband.

PATIENT RESPONSIBLE FOR CHILD
If a patient who's responsible for the care of a child refuses lifesaving treatment, the court may reverse the patient's decision. In Application of the *President and Directors of Georgetown College, Inc.* (1964), the New York Supreme Court ordered a blood transfusion for a Jehovah's Witness who was the mother of an infant and who refused to give consent for her own transfusion. In the case of *In re Melideo* (1976), the court said that it might have or-

dered a lifesaving transfusion for the patient if she had had a child.

PREGNANT PATIENT
If a patient who's pregnant refuses treatment, thereby threatening not only her own health but also that of her unborn child, the courts can reverse the patient's decision. In *Jefferson v. Griffin Spalding County Hospital Authority* (1981), the court awarded temporary custody of an unborn child to a state agency. The mother had a complete placenta previa but had refused to consent to a cesarean birth. The court's custody award included full authority to give consent for a surgical delivery.

PATIENT WHO'S A MINOR
If a patient is a minor, the court will allow his parents or legal guardian to consent to medical treatment, but it won't allow them to deny him lifesaving treatment. *In re Sampson* (1972) was such a case.

▶ when the public interest outweighs the patient's right—for example, the law requires school-age children (with few exceptions) to receive a polio vaccine before they can attend classes.

Responses to patient refusal of treatment
When a patient plans to refuse treatment, the nurse may be the person he tells first. Whether he states that he's going to refuse treatment or he simply refuses to give consent, all preparations for treatment must be stopped at once. Immediately notify the physician and report the patient's decision to the nursing supervi-

sor. Never delay informing the supervisor, especially if a delay could be life-threatening. Any delay that the nurse is responsible for will greatly increase her legal risks.

The physician and hospital have the responsibility to take action, such as trying to convince the patient to accept treatment or asking him to sign a release form. This form relieves the hospital and the health care team of liability for any consequences the patient suffers by refusing treatment. It doesn't, however, release the health care team from its obligation to continue providing other forms of care.

Never ignore a patient's request to refuse treatment. A patient can sue you for battery—intentionally touching another person without authorization to do so—for simply following physician's orders.

To overrule the patient's decision, the physician or the facility must obtain a court order. Only then is the nurse legally authorized to administer the treatment.

If the physician or facility tries to convince the court to overrule the patient on the grounds that he's incompetent, they'll need proof that he lacks the mental ability to make a reasoned decision. Documented observations about the patient's mental status may be used as evidence.

No matter how serious the patient's condition, refusing treatment doesn't constitute evidence of incompetence. In *Lane v. Candura (1978),* for example, a patient with diabetes first agreed to have her leg amputated and then changed her mind and refused the surgery. After attempting to persuade the patient that the amputation was necessary, the physicians applied for a court order, arguing that by changing her mind, the patient had shown incompetence. The court disagreed, and upheld the patient's right to withdraw her consent.

Refusal of emergency treatment

In an emergency situation, a competent adult has the right to refuse emergency treatment. Her family can't overrule her decision, and her physician may not give the expressly refused treatment, even if the patient becomes unconscious.

If there are no grounds for overruling the patient's decision, nurses have an ethical duty to defend the patient's right to refuse treatment in the face of all opposition, even that of the family. Try to explain the patient's choice to family members. Emphasize that the decision is his as long as he's competent.

Discharge against medical advice

The patient's bill of rights and the laws and regulations based on it give a competent adult the right to refuse treatment for any reason without being punished or having his liberty restricted. Some states have turned these rights into law. And the courts have cited the bill of rights in their decisions.

The right to refuse treatment provides patients with the right to leave the hospital against medical advice (AMA) any time, for any reason. All nurses can do is try to talk the patient out of it.

Nurses have more contact with patients than any other health care professional. Therefore, they're likely to be the first persons to suspect that a patient is contemplating leaving AMA. For example, complaints or hostile behavior may indicate the patient's extreme dissatisfaction with hospital routine or with the care he's receiving. By carefully observing, listening, and talking with him, the nurse may be able to help resolve the problems (if it's within the nurse's scope of practice), offer a fresh perspective, and perhaps change his mind about leaving. If the problem lies outside the scope of the nurse's practice, the nurse should call the patient's physician.

A patient may tell the nurse that he has changed his mind about leaving just to divert the nurse's attention. Frequent checks, staying with the patient, and accompanying him to other areas of the facility can be helpful in reducing the risk of leaving.

Patient who leaves AMA

If a patient still insists on leaving AMA and the hospital has a policy on managing the patient who wants to leave, follow it exactly. Adherence to the policy helps to protect the hospital, coworkers, and nurse from charges of unlawful restraint or false imprisonment. If no policy exists, take these steps:

▶ Contact the patient's family (if he hasn't already called them), and explain that the patient is getting ready to leave. If unable to reach the family, contact the person listed in the patient's records as responsible for him or for his body and valuables if he should die.

▶ Explain the AMA procedures to the patient if the facility's policy delegates this responsibility to nurses.

▶ Give the patient the AMA form to sign. (See *Documenting a patient's decision to leave AMA.*) His decision to leave is the same as a refusal of treatment. Inform the patient of his medical risks if he leaves the hospital, and explain the alternatives available at the hospital and at other locations, such as regular visits to the hospital's outpatient clinic or admission to another facility. His signature on the AMA form is evidence of his refusal of treatment. The nurse should witness the signature.

▶ Provide routine discharge care. Even though the patient is leaving AMA, his rights to discharge planning and care are the same as those for a patient who's signed out with medical advice. So if the patient agrees, escort him to the door (in a wheelchair, if necessary), arrange for medical or nursing follow-up care, and offer other routine health care measures. These procedures will protect the hospital as well as the patient.

If the patient refuses to sign the AMA form, document his refusal in a note stating that all risks have been explained to the patient. One innovative nurse routinely told emergency department patients that she would like them to indicate their refusal to sign by signing the back of the form. Most patients complied with her request.

Patient who escapes

If a nurse discovers that a patient is missing from the hospital, notify the nursing supervisor and security immediately. If the patient was in police custody or poses a threat to anyone outside the hospital, the administration should contact the police. The hospital administration subsequently may ask the nurse to notify the patient's family or friends, collect the patient's belongings, and document the escape in the patient's medical chart and incident report.

False imprisonment

A competent adult has a right to leave and should never be detained. Any attempt to detain or restrain him may be interpreted as unlawful restraint or false imprisonment, for which legal action can be taken.

The facility's policy should reflect state law. It should specifically answer such questions as:

▶ How long and for what reasons may a patient be detained?

▶ When can personnel use forcible restraints?

▶ Who may order the use of restraints?

▶ Who may apply the restraints?

Knowledge of these policies will help to reduce liability exposure.

Most courts disapprove of detaining a patient arbitrarily or for an unreasonably

Documenting a patient's decision to leave AMA

An against-medical-advice (AMA) form is a medical record as well as a legal document. It's designed to protect you, your coworkers, and your facility from liability resulting from the patient's unapproved discharge or escape.

To document an AMA incident, begin by getting your facility's AMA form. The form may look like the one shown below. The form clearly states that the patient:
- knows he's leaving AMA
- has been advised of, and understands, the risks of leaving
- knows he can come back.

Discuss this form with the patient and ask him to sign it. Don't try to force the patient to sign if he's unwilling to do so. You should sign as a witness.

Add the AMA form to the patient's medical chart. Then write a detailed description of how you first learned of the patient's plan to leave AMA, what you and the patient said to each other, and what alternatives to the patient's action were discussed.

Also, check facility policy concerning incident reports. If the patient leaves without anyone's knowledge or if he refuses to sign the AMA form, you'll probably be required to file an incident report. Be sure to include the names of any other employees involved in the discovery of the patient's absence. The administration or your nurse-manager may want to solicit corroborating reports from other employees, including other registered nurses, licensed practical nurses, nurses' aides, orderlies, and clerical staff.

RESPONSIBILITY RELEASE

This is to certify that I, _____,

a patient in _____,

am being discharged against the advice of my doctor and the hospital administration. I acknowledge that I have been informed of the risk involved and hereby release my physician and the hospital from all responsibility for any ill effects that may result from such a discharge. I also understand that I may return to the hospital at any time and have treatment resumed.

_____	_____
[Patient's signature]	[Date]
_____	_____
[Witness' signature]	[Date]

RE: _____   _____
[Name of patient]   Patient #

---

long time, which may be ruled false imprisonment. (See *Patient or prisoner?* page 78.)

Court cases that involve false imprisonment charges have occurred when facilities threatened to hold patients or their personal belongings until bills were paid. In most cases, the courts ruled against the facilities.

A hospital or nursing home can delay a patient's discharge, for a reasonable period, until routine paperwork is complete. *Bailie v. Miami Valley Hospital*

Patient or prisoner?

The case of *Big Town Nursing Home v. Newman (1970)* provides a good example of how a health care facility can become vulnerable to charges of false imprisonment.

Mr. Newman, age 67, had Parkinson's disease, arthritis, heart trouble, hiatal hernia, a speech impediment, and a history of alcoholism. Four days after his nephew signed him into a nursing home, Mr. Newman decided to leave.

NO EXIT

Employees at the nursing home stopped Mr. Newman, locked away his suitcase and clothes, restricted his use of the phone, and restricted his right to visitors. When Mr. Newman tried to walk off the grounds, employees locked him in a wing with severely emotionally disturbed patients and patients addicted to drugs and alcohol. He made other unsuccessful escape attempts, so the staff tied Mr. Newman to a chair for long periods. Twenty-two days after his admission, Mr. Newman escaped. Eventually, he sued.

The court ruled in favor of Mr. Newman. Despite his physical infirmities, Mr. Newman hadn't legally been declared incompetent and was, therefore, legally entitled to exercise his rights.

(1966) was a case in which the court ruled in favor of a hospital.

In a few cases, because of extenuating circumstances, the courts have ruled against patients who sued on grounds of false imprisonment. The case of *Pounders v. Trinity Court Nursing Home (1979)* is one such example.

Mrs. Pounders, age 75, was a disabled widow. When her niece and nephew no longer wanted her to live with them, the niece arranged for her to move to Trinity Court Nursing Home. Mrs. Pounders didn't object.

During her 2 months at Trinity Court, Mrs. Pounders complained only once to a nurses' aide that she wanted to leave. Unfortunately, the aide failed to report the complaint to anyone in authority at the home.

Mrs. Pounders was finally released, through the aid of an attorney, into another niece's care. She eventually sued the nursing home.

However, because Mrs. Pounders couldn't prove she had been involuntarily detained, the court absolved the nursing home of the false imprisonment charges.

Lawful detention

The right to leave the hospital AMA isn't absolute. Certain patients who pose a threat to themselves or to others can't legally leave the hospital. Restraint through the use of physical means or medication, when necessary, is lawful with psychiatric patients, prisoners, and violent patients.

If a patient transferred to the facility for medical care from a prison or psychiatric hospital threatens to escape, notify the custodial facility immediately. They're responsible for sending personnel to guard the patient and for making new arrangements for his care. Restrain the patient only if his medical condition warrants it or if the police or psychiatric hospital authorities instruct one to do so.

If the prisoner or psychiatric patient escapes, the nurse or facility or nursing administration should call the authorities at the custodial facility or the police.

If the nurse suspects that a patient with a history of violence or violent threats is planning to leave AMA, notify hospital and nursing administrators immediately. If state law allows it, the facility administrators may decide to get police assistance to restrain the patient.

If the violent patient has escaped, notify nursing or facility administration immediately. They'll contact the police and mental health authorities. If the patient ever expressed an intention to harm a known person, the administration also should contact that person.

CONFIDENTIALITY AND PRIVACY

The ANA's Code for Nurses states that nurses must safeguard the patient's right to privacy "by judiciously protecting information of a confidential nature." Maintaining confidentiality is essential to preserving the trust necessary to provide effective nursing care. A patient typically must reveal sensitive or embarrassing information during his assessment if an accurate diagnosis is to be made. The patient must have confidence that this information will be shared in a professional manner only with those who require it for his care.

Commonly the terms *confidentiality* and *privacy* are used interchangeably. However, there's a slight difference between the two. *Confidentiality* primarily refers to the protection of information. When nurses learn personal information about a patient, they have an ethical and legal obligation not to disclose it to any person or any agency other than those involved in the patient's care or other designated people or agencies.[14] Confidentiality, as such, is integrated into the broader concept of privacy. *Privacy* is defined as the freedom from unwanted intrusions into one's life and violations of one's bodily integrity and to keep secret

one's personal information.[15] A patient's right to privacy is identified in the AHA's Patient Care Partnership and in the codes of ethics for many professional organizations.

Ethical foundations
Underlying confidentiality are two key ethical principles: autonomy and fidelity. *Autonomy* includes the patient's right to maintain control over his life; this extends to the right to maintain control over personal information. *Fidelity* refers to one's faithfulness to agreements that one has accepted. The temptation to gossip is strong. To maintain confidentiality, the nurse's ethical belief in the patient's right to maintain autonomy must outweigh the temptation to gossip. If a nurse pledges to keep a confidence, she must recognize the seriousness of this obligation. After all, it's normal to share confidential information in the course of developing a therapeutic relationship. Without fidelity and respect for confidentiality, meaningful nurse-patient relationships can't survive.

Breaches of confidentiality
Confidential information can ethically be disclosed in certain circumstances, such as when failure to disclose information could cause serious physical harm to the patient, his family, facility staff, or another third party. However, knowing when confidentiality may be appropriately breached isn't always easy. (See *Should confidentiality be breached?* pages 80 and 81.)

Privilege doctrine
The state courts have been strong in protecting a patient's right to have information kept confidential. Even in court, the

ETHICAL DILEMMA

Should confidentiality be breached?

Consider the three clinical scenarios here. For each case, decide whether you agree with the ethical decision made by the nurse.

PREVENTING PATIENT HARM

Kitisha Jefferson, RN, was caring for Will Cooke, a 33-year-old electrician who fractured his femur in a fall at a construction site. She had established a good nurse-patient relationship with him. However, Mr. Cooke had seemed bored and edgy for the past day or so. When Ms. Jefferson checked his room, she found his curtain drawn halfway around his bed. She walked to the open side and saw Mr. Cooke hurriedly closing a plastic bag that contained white powder. "What are you doing?" she asked him.

"All right," Mr. Cooke replied. "Because you're a good nurse, I'll level with you. I was doing cocaine. I know I shouldn't, but it gets boring when you're in traction with nothing to do but watch the tube. Please, don't tell anybody. If my wife finds out, I'm finished."

Ms. Jefferson patiently explained that cocaine can have severe effects, especially when taken with other drugs. She advised Mr. Cooke to stop using cocaine—at least while he's hospitalized.

After taking these measures, Ms. Jefferson still faced ethical dilemmas. What should she write in the patient's chart? Should she tell Mr. Cooke's physician? Should she recommend that Mr. Cooke tell the physician?

After careful consideration, Ms. Jefferson decided to tell Mr. Cooke that she had an obligation to let the physician know about his cocaine use—unless Mr. Cooke wanted to tell the physician himself. Her decision was based on the ethical principle of beneficence; she believed that the risk of cardiac arrest caused by the combination of cocaine and other medications was an overriding factor.

PROTECTING THE STAFF

Steve Walcott, RN, was reviewing Tamara Smith's chart before giving her a preoperative sedative when he realized that one of his colleagues had been discussing her at lunch the day before. This colleague, who worked in the laboratory, didn't mention Ms. Smith by name, but the age and admission date gave away the patient's identity. She had said that Ms. Smith tested positive for human immunodeficiency virus (HIV) infection but that the results weren't being noted on the chart. Should Mr. Walcott inform the surgical team of Ms. Smith's test results?

Mr. Walcott felt a strong temptation to protect his coworkers as the first consideration. However, he also realized that his colleague was remiss in discussing Ms. Smith's test results. Therefore, he reasoned that he would be remiss in further violating the confidentiality of this information. He also feared stigmatizing the patient. He further reasoned that the surgical team should use standard precautions for all patients, not just those who test positive for HIV. After all, patients who haven't had the test can also carry the antibody.

patient is protected by the privilege doctrine. People who have a protected relationship, such as a physician and patient, can't be forced (even during legal proceedings) to reveal communication between them, unless the person who benefits from the protection agrees to it. This means that the patient must agree before confidential information is revealed in court. The purpose of the privilege doctrine is to encourage the patient to reveal confidential information that may be essential to his treatment. State law determines which relationships are protected by the privilege doctrine. Most states include husband-wife, lawyer-client, and physician-patient relationships.

PROTECTING THE PATIENT'S FAMILY

Jenny Chu, RN, was caring for Susan Schaffer, a 32-year-old mother of five scheduled for a tubal ligation. She wanted to make sure her patient understood the effects of this surgery, so she asked Mrs. Schaffer to explain the procedure. Mrs. Schaffer did so eagerly and added, "I'm so happy I won't have to worry about getting pregnant again. Five kids is more than I can handle as it is."

Satisfied, Ms. Chu left Mrs. Schaffer and continued her rounds. Later that day, she met Mrs. Schaffer's husband, Matt, at the nurses' station. He asked for a box of tissues and said, "I hope the surgery fixes Susan's problem. Did she tell you we've been trying to have another baby for over 1 year? I really want to have a few more kids."

What should Ms. Chu do: protect Mrs. Schaffer's confidentiality or tell Mr. Schaffer the truth? Ms. Chu believed that her first obligation was to protect Mrs. Schaffer's confidentiality. The urge to tell Mr. Schaffer about his wife's deception was compelling, but he wasn't in danger of physical harm from her action. Ms. Chu felt badly that Mr. and Mrs. Schaffer couldn't talk to each other frankly, but she also believed that this wasn't an excuse for breaching confidentiality. Nonetheless, Ms. Chu decided to discuss the matter with the surgeon, especially because hospital policy required a spouse's signature on the consent form for a sterilization procedure.

Only a few states (including New York, Arkansas, Oregon, and Vermont) recognize the nurse-patient relationship as protected. However, some courts have said that the privilege exists when a nurse s following a physician's orders. Whether the privilege applies to licensed practical nurses and licensed vocational nurses as well is uncertain.

State laws also determine the extent of privilege in protected relationships. In *Hammonds v. Aetna Casualty and Surety Co. (1965)*, the court reinforced the privilege doctrine by declaring that protecting a patient's privacy is a physician's legal duty. It further ruled that a patient could sue for damages any unauthorized person who disclosed confidential medical information about him. Similarly, a patient can sue for invasion of privacy any unauthorized personnel, such as student nurses, who observe him without his permission. The only hospital personnel who have a right to observe a patient are those involved in his diagnosis, treatment, and related care.

Exceptions to privilege

In some states, a patient automatically waives his right to physician-patient privilege when he files a personal injury or workers' compensation lawsuit.

A hospital or physician can't invoke the privilege doctrine if the motive is self-protection. In *People v. Doe (1978)*, a nursing home was being investigated for allegedly mistreating its patients. The court ruled that the nursing home's attempt to invoke patient privilege was unjust because the issue at hand was the patients' welfare.

Canadian law and privilege

In all Canadian jurisdictions, privilege doctrine applies only to solicitor-client communications. Physicians and nurses are bound by codes of ethics as well as legislation concerning confidentiality. Cases that suggest the physician-patient privilege include *Dembie (1963)*, *Re SAS (1977)*, and *Geransy (1977)*. The Canadian Nurses Association has its own code of ethics, which has been largely adopted

in nurse practice acts in Canadian jurisdictions. The code requires nurses to
keep confidential any personal information they receive from a patient during
nursing care. Consequently, although
violation of a patient's right to privacy
isn't subject to criminal prosecution in
Canada, it's deemed professional misconduct. A nurse who violates a patient's
right to privacy could lose her nursing
license.

Right to privacy

Obtaining highly personal information
from a patient can be uncomfortable and
embarrassing. Reassuring the patient that
the nurse will keep information confidential may help to put the patient and nurse
at ease. But stop to think about the legal
complexities of this responsibility. Ethical
issues also arise. What should a nurse do
when a patient's spouse, other health
care professionals, the media, or public
health agencies ask the nurse to disclose
confidential information? (See *Right to
privacy.*)

Privacy and confidentiality were first
proposed as basic legal rights in 1890 in
a *Harvard Law Review* article titled
"The Right to Privacy."

The U.S. Constitution doesn't explicitly sanction a right to privacy. But in several court cases, including *Roe (1973),*
the U.S. Supreme Court cited several constitutional amendments that imply the
right.

The right to privacy essentially is the
right to make personal choices without
outside interference. In the landmark
case of *Griswold v. Connecticut (1965),*
for example, the Supreme Court recognized a married couple's right to privacy
in contraceptive use. In *Eisenstadt v.*

Baird (1972), the Supreme Court extended the right to privacy in contraceptive
use to include unmarried people. In
*Carey v. Population Services Internat-
ional (1977),* the Supreme Court said a
state law that prohibited the sale of contraceptives to anyone younger than age
16 was unconstitutional.

The U.S. Department of Health and
Human Services tried to modify the
Carey ruling by publishing a regulation,
"Parental Notification Requirements
Applicable to Projects for Family Planning Services." Also known as the
"squeal rule," this regulation proposed
that any federally funded clinic or health
agency giving contraceptives to a minor
be required to inform the minor's parents
or guardian. A New York federal district
court, however, declared that divulging
such confidential information invades the
minor's privacy and is unconstitutional.

Health Insurance Portability and Accountability Act

HIPAA was first enacted by Congress in
1996 as a means to prevent employers
from denying individuals health insurance coverage due to preexisting medical
conditions. As part of this legislation, it
directed the Department of Health and
Human Services to develop privacy rules
for health information, termed *protected
health information,* or PHI. In 2003, a
security rule was published to provide a
uniform level of protection for all health
information that's housed or transmitted
electronically and that pertains to an individual.[16] Commonly called *the privacy
rule,* it identifies those to which the rule
applies, termed "covered entities," which
includes nurses, other employees in
health care facilities or other agencies,

ETHICAL DILEMMA

Right to privacy

When entering the hospital, most patients tacitly agree to sacrifice a considerable amount of privacy to enable physicians and nurses to plan and provide care. Occasionally, however, a patient refuses to cooperate. If his resistance hampers your ability to give good care, you may face an ethical dilemma, as the following clinical scenario shows.

HIDDEN MEDICINE BOTTLE

John Gordon is admitted to the hospital with chronic diarrhea. All diagnostic test results have come back normal. His physician, Marvin Stein, suspects that Mr. Gordon is causing the diarrhea by taking laxatives—a charge Mr. Gordon vehemently denies.

Mr. Gordon's nurse, Susan Morrison, is starting to think that Dr. Stein may be right. Yesterday, Mr. Gordon put a medicine bottle in his satchel as she walked into his room. When she asked him what was in the bottle, he became defensive and refused to answer.

Dr. Stein asks Ms. Morrison to "do a little detective work" by searching Mr. Gordon's room for laxatives the next time he receives visitors in the lounge. "After all," he tells her, "we can't help Mr. Gordon until we know for sure what's going on."

ETHICAL CONSIDERATIONS

At first, Ms. Morrison is willing to conduct a search of Mr. Gordon's room. Later, she begins to have doubts about whether such a search would be ethical. She decides to write down her concerns.

• Do we know Mr. Gordon is lying when he denies taking laxatives? Several possible explanations exist for his defensive behavior. Perhaps he doesn't know what a laxative is and is reluctant to reveal his ignorance. Why did he hide the medicine bottle? He might be embarrassed to admit that he's taking a home remedy. There may be several other reasons. What appears to be a medicine bottle could contain any number of things.

• Even if Mr. Gordon is lying, is a search justified? Can one person's unethical behavior justify another's? Dr. Stein, after all, is a medical authority, not a moral authority.

• Even if conducting an investigation is necessary, wouldn't openly searching Mr. Gordon's room without his permission be more ethical than conducting a search behind his back?

• What about Dr. Stein's role in this incident? Should I allow him to delegate this distasteful duty to me?

• Even if Mr. Gordon is indeed lying and is taking laxatives, who—besides himself—is he harming? Doesn't he have the right to treat himself with an over-the-counter medication against his physician's advice?

• How would a search affect my nurse-patient relationship with Mr. Gordon? If he thinks that I violated his trust, it will probably destroy it forever.

• Will the search really help us to accomplish our goal—to help Mr. Gordon get better? Unless we find out why he's taking a laxative, he'll probably continue taking it.

PRESENTING ALTERNATIVES

Ms. Morrison decides that she has too many ethical misgivings to cooperate with the search. Before telling Dr. Stein her decision, she outlines the ways in which she's willing to help. Her first recommendation is to call a conference with the patient. She's willing to discuss with Mr. Gordon the need for the health care team to know about all of his medications, including over-the-counter medications and home remedies, and to again ask him to identify the medication he takes. If Mr. Gordon still refuses to discuss the problem, she'll make it clear that she's willing to listen if he should change his mind.

She's also willing to arrange to be in Mr. Gordon's room during morning care. If, for example, she opens his drawer to get his toothbrush and finds a medicine bottle, she can then ask about it. However, that's as far as she'll go. She won't participate in a search without the patient's consent, even in his presence. She realizes that, as Dr. Stein said, this might limit the ability of the health care team to help Mr. Gordon, but a competent patient has the right to forgo help.

health insurance companies, and medical-billing or data collection companies.[17]

Health care providers, health insurance plans, and government programs must notify patients about their rights to privacy and how their health information will be used and shared. This health information includes information in the patient's medical record, conversations about the patient's care between health care providers, billing information, and the health insurer's computerized records.

HIPAA established minimum privacy standards for the nation as a whole.[18] Under HIPAA, the patient has the right to access his medical information, know when health information is shared, and make changes or corrections to his medical record. Patients also have the right to decide if they want to allow their information to be used for certain purposes, such as marketing or research. In addition, only those who have a need to know patient information for the care of the patient and those authorized by the patient to have access to his medical information can lawfully view a patient's medical record. (See *Summarizing the patient's rights under HIPAA*.)[19]

When a patient receives health care, he must sign an authorization form before protected health information can be used for purposes other than routine treatment or billing. This form is placed in the patient's medical record.

Unfortunately, there's much confusion involving the implementation of this legislation. Although health care professionals are more conscientious about disclosing a patient's private information, many mistakenly believe that they must have the patient's permission to disclose any information. The issues aren't clearly delineated and are subject to much interpretation. Additionally, many view this legislation as unnecessary, as many state laws or professional practice standards have more stringent standards.[20] As patient advocates, nurses have the duty to protect the well-being of patients entrusted to their care, protect the integrity of the nurse-patient relationship, protect patients' rights and provide the accurate information and appropriate reassurances to ensure continuity of care and compliance with HIPAA standards.[21,22]

As a result of difficulties with HIPAA, Senator Patrick Leahy from Vermont and Senator Edward Kennedy from Massachusetts sponsored a bill in the Senate (S.1814) in July 2007 to help clarify HIPAA. The bill, the Health Information Privacy and Security Act of 2007 (HIPSA) is to "provide individuals with access to health information of which they're a subject, ensure personal privacy with respect for health-related information, promote the use of non-identifiable information for health research, impose criminal and civil penalties for unauthorized use of protected health information, to provide for the strong enforcement of these rights, and to protect States' rights."[23]

Privacy and abortion law

The Supreme Court ruling in *Roe* protects a woman's right to privacy in a first-trimester abortion. After the first trimester, a state may regulate abortion to protect the mother's health and prohibit an abortion if the fetus is judged viable. However, state legislators have complicated access to abortion services in different ways. In 1999 alone, President

Summarizing the patient's rights under HIPAA

The HIPAA act ensures that the patient has certain rights regarding their health information.

A patient has the right to:
• Ask to see and get a copy of his health records (medical record and other health information); copies must be given to the patient within 30 days, but this can be extended for another 30 days if a reason is given. The patient may have to pay for the cost of copying and mailing if he requests these.
• Have corrections added to his health information; for example, ask to change any wrong information or add information if it's incomplete; file should be changed within 60 days, but the hospital can take an extra 30 days if a reason is given.
• Receive a notice that tells him how his health information is used and shared; patient must receive a notice that tells him how the provider or insurer may use and share his health information and how the patient can exercise his rights. This notice is usually given on the patient's first visit to a provider or in the mail from his health insurer; patient can ask for a copy at any time.
• Decide whether to give permission before information can be used or shared for certain purposes; in general, health information can't be given to patient's employer, used or shared for things like sales calls or advertising, or used or shared for many other purposes unless permission is obtained by signing an authorization form. This authorization form must identify who will get the information and what the information will be used for.
• Get a report on when and why the patient's health information was shared.

Under the law, the patient's health information may be used and shared for particular reasons, such as making sure doctors give good care, making sure nursing homes are clean and safe, reporting when the flu is in the area, or making required reports to the police, such as reporting gunshot wounds. In many cases, patients can ask for and get a list of those with whom health information has been shared for these reasons. This report is free once per year. In most cases, the report should be available within 60 days, but it can take an extra 30 days if a reason is given.
• Ask to be reached somewhere other than home, reasonably requesting to be contacted at different places or in a different way. For example, contacting the patient at his office instead of home, or sending mail in an envelope instead of on a postcard. If sending information to the patient at home might put the patient in danger, the health insurer must talk, call, or write to the patient where requested and in the way that the patient requested, if the request is reasonable.
• Ask that his information not be shared with certain people, groups, or companies. However, they don't have to agree to do what he asks.
• File complaints with the provider or health insurer if the patient believes information was used or shared in a way that isn't allowed under the privacy law, or if the patient was not able to exercise his rights; the patient also may file a complaint with the U.S. Government.

Source: Department of Health and Human Services. *Your Health Information Privacy Rights.* Available at http://www.hhs.gov/ocr/hipaa/consumer_rights.pdf

George W. Bush, then governor of Texas, passed several laws affecting abortion rights. One law mandates parental notification and a 48-hour waiting period for minors. Another prohibits licensed medical professionals from performing third-trimester abortions. Another law excludes organizations that offer abortion procedures from receiving family planning funding and mandates that funds for prescription contraceptives for minors be given only with parental consent; another denies tax-exemption to non-profit organizations that perform, refer for, or assist other organizations that perform or refer for abortion. Yet another law prohibits the state Child Health Plan from covering any services that prevent conception or birth. Another prohibits school-based health centers from providing reproductive services, counseling, or referrals if they receive certain grants. Other states have passed similar laws, including Virginia, Arizona, Iowa, and Florida.

Restrictions on abortion rights

Since *Roe,* the Supreme Court has handed down more than 20 major opinions related to the abortion issue. A 1989 Supreme Court decision, *Webster v. Reproductive Health Services*, placed certain aspects of *Roe* into doubt. Although viability of the fetus remains the guideline, the Supreme Court now appears more willing to allow states to regulate abortion. For example, in 1992, in *Planned Parenthood of Southeastern Pennsylvania v. Casey*, the Supreme Court let stand Pennsylvania's Abortion Control Act of 1989. This Act requires that a woman wait 24 hours between consenting to and receiving an abortion, except in narrowly defined medical emergencies, and that a woman seeking an abortion be given state-mandated abortion information and offered state-authored materials on fetal development. The Supreme Court struck down the requirement that a married woman inform her husband of her intent to have an abortion. Overall, the decision reaffirmed a woman's right to abortion, but suggest-

ed that the Court had revised its long-standing definition of that right as fundamental.

In May 1991, antiabortion groups won a victory on another front. In *Rust v. Sullivan (1991),* the Supreme Court upheld federal regulations prohibiting health care workers at more than 4,000 government-subsidized family planning clinics from providing any information about abortion. Under the regulations, if a nurse works in a subsidized clinic, the nurse may not advise a pregnant woman that abortion is a possibility, nor may the nurse help her find a private abortion clinic. The nurse is obligated to refer pregnant women for prenatal care.

Privacy and abortion rights for minors

Roe played an important role in extending abortion rights to minors. In *Planned Parenthood of Central Missouri v. Danforth (1976),* the Supreme Court overruled a law that prevented first-trimester abortions for minors without parental consent. This decision was based on *Roe.*

In *Bellotti v. Baird II (1979),* the Supreme Court acknowledged that the privacy rights of a minor aren't equal to those of an adult. The Court held, however, that a state law requiring a minor to obtain parental consent for an abortion infringed on the minor's rights.

In *H.L. v. Matheson (1981),* the Supreme Court upheld a Utah law requiring a physician to notify the parents of an unemancipated minor before an abortion. However, in *Hodgson v. Minnesota (1990),* a Minnesota statute that required notification of both biological parents before a minor's abortion, after a wait of at least 48 hours, was held unconstitutional. The chief difference between the two cases is that the Utah law required notification of only one parent, where feasible; the Minnesota law required notification of both parents, even if they were divorced or separated. In *Hodgson*, the Supreme Court decreed that the rule requiring notification of both parents was too burdensome on the right to abortion because it could create exceptional difficulties for one-parent families. The Court also stated that the 48-hour waiting period required under the Minnesota law would not, by itself, render the statute unconstitutional.

By letting stand Pennsylvania's Abortion Control Act in 1992, the Supreme Court allowed the state to require that one parent or guardian give consent in person for a minor seeking an abortion, unless the minor obtains a judicial waiver.

In *Hodgson* and *Ohio v. Akron Center for Reproductive Health (1990)*, the Supreme Court set forth its position on judicial bypass statutes. Judicial bypass statutes allow a minor to avoid notifying parents or obtaining consent for an abortion by going before a judge. The Court stated that judicial bypass satisfies the requirement that parents or other third parties can't have an absolute veto over the minor's abortion decision.

Disclosure of confidential information

Under certain circumstances, nurses may lawfully disclose confidential information about a patient. For example, the courts allow disclosure when the welfare of a person or a group of people is at stake. Consider the patient who's diagnosed as an epileptic and asks the nurse not to tell his family. Depending on the circumstances, the nurse may decide that this isn't in the patient's and his family's best interest, particularly in terms of safety. In that situation, inform the patient's physician; he may then decide to inform the patient's family to protect the patient's well-being. In most states, the physician is required to inform the Department of Motor Vehicles of uncontrolled epilepsy.

Nurses are also protected by law if they disclose confidential information about a patient that's necessary for his continued care or if the patient consents to the disclosure.

Nurses need to be careful not to exceed the specified limit of a patient's consent. Taking pictures is the largest single cause of invasion of privacy lawsuits. In *Feeney v. Young (1920)*, a woman consented to the filming of her cesarean birth for viewing by medical societies, but the physician incorporated the film into a generally released movie titled *Birth*. The court awarded damages to the woman under the state's privacy law.

Prevention of public harm

The courts have granted immunity to health care professionals who, in good faith, have disclosed confidential information to prevent public harm. In *Simonsen v. Swenson (1920)*, a physician who thought that his patient had syphilis told the owner of the hotel in which the patient was staying about the patient's contagious disease. The court ruled that physicians are privileged to make disclosures that will prevent the spread of disease.

A controversial California case established a physician's right to disclose information that would protect any person whom a patient threatened to harm. In *Tarasoff v. Regents of the University of California (1976),* a woman was murdered by a mentally ill patient who had told his psychotherapist that he intended to kill her. The victim's parents sued the physician for failing to warn their daughter. The Supreme Court found the physician liable because he didn't warn the intended victim. The Court ruled similarly in *McIntosh v. Milano (1979).*

Child abuse

All 50 states and the District of Columbia have disclosure laws for child abuse cases. Except for Maine and Montana, all states also grant immunity from legal action for a good faith report on suspected child abuse. In fact, there may be a criminal penalty for failure to disclose such information.

Courts may also order health care professionals to disclose confidential information in cases of child custody and child neglect. One case involving such an order was *D. v. D. (1969).* Despite the physician-patient privilege, the court ordered the physician to turn the mother's medical records over to the court for a private inspection. The mother had a history of illness, and the court said that the inspection would help to decide which parent should be granted custody. The courts made a similar ruling in *In re Doe Children (1978).* The court stated that the children's welfare outweighed the parents' right to keep their medical records private.

Criminal cases

Some laws create an exemption to the privilege doctrine in criminal cases so that the courts can have access to all essential information. In states where neither a law nor an exemption to the law exists, the court may find an exemption to the doctrine in criminal cases.

Government requests

Certain government agencies can order nurses to reveal confidential information, including federal agencies such as the Internal Revenue Service, the Environmental Protection Agency, the Department of Labor, and the Department of Health and Human Services. State agencies that may order disclosure of confidential information include revenue or tax bureaus and public health departments. For example, most state public health departments require reports of all communicable diseases, births and deaths, and gunshot wounds.

Public's right to know

The newsworthiness of an event or person can make disclosure acceptable. In such circumstances, the public's need for information may outweigh a person's right to keep his medical condition private. For example, newspapers routinely publish the findings of the President's annual physical examination in response to the public's demand for information. Even the First Lady's health may become a matter of public record.

Other events for which the public's right to know may outweigh the patient's right to privacy include breakthroughs in medical technology (the first successful hand transplant) and product-tampering cases, for example. In 1999, the national media gave wide exposure to an incident in New York State in which nine people died after being bitten by a mosquito that transmitted a flavivirus that causes St. Louis encephalitis.

Even when the public has a right to know about a confidential matter, the courts won't allow public disclosure to undermine a person's dignity. In *Barber v. Time, Inc. (1942)*, *TIME* magazine was sued by a woman whose name and photograph were published in an article that revealed she suffered from an illness that caused her to eat as much food as 10 people could eat. The court ruled that publishing the patient's name and picture was an unnecessary invasion of her privacy, and that ethics required keeping such information confidential.

Doe v. Roe (1977) is a similar case. A patient sued his psychiatrist for publishing the patient's biography and thoughts verbatim. Even though the physician didn't use the patient's name, the court stated that the patient was readily identifiable by the article. It found the physician liable for violating the physician-patient privilege.

● SELF-DETERMINATION

The Patient Self-Determination Act of 1990 ensured the rights of patients to author or execute *advance directives*—written or verbal instructions by the patient about his wishes for medical treatment in the event he becomes "incapacitated." Examples include living wills, durable powers of attorney for health care, and any document that states the patient's wishes. (See *Living will,* pages 90 and 91 and *Durable power of attorney for health care,* page 92.) Joint Commission standard RI.1.2.4 mandates that each hospital assure patients older than age 18 the opportunity to initiate an advance directive. The hospital must also honor the directives within the limits of the law and their capabilities.

Requirements of the law

The Patient Self-Determination Act includes the following requirements:
▶ Each patient must be given written information about his rights under state law to make decisions concerning medical care, including the right to accept or refuse medical or surgical treatment and to formulate advance directives.
▶ The patient's decision whether to execute an advance directive must be documented in the medical record.
▶ The facility must ensure that the patient's decision about the execution of an advance directive doesn't influence the provision of care. Furthermore, health care providers can't discriminate against a patient in any way based on his decision.
▶ The health care facility must provide education for the staff and community on issues concerning advance directives.

Information about the patient's rights and the opportunity to draft an advance directive should be initiated during the admission process and documented on the admission form. Regular chart audits should ensure that an advance directive or a statement that a patient was told about his right to draft such an advance directive is included in the medical record. All employees of the facility must be told, during orientation and annual updates, that patients have rights to an advance directive. Policy and procedures must be drafted to include procedures in which conflicts regarding advance direc-

Living will

The living will is an advance care document that specifies a person's wishes with regard to medical care, should he become terminally ill, incompetent, or unable to communicate. The will is commonly used in combination with the patient's durable power of attorney.

All states and the District of Columbia have living will laws that outline the documentation requirements for living wills. The sample document below is from Ohio.

LIVING WILL

If my attending doctor and one other doctor who examines me determine, to a reasonable degree of medical certainty and in accordance with reasonable medical standards, that I am in a terminal condition or in a permanently unconscious state, and if my attending doctor determines that at that time I no longer am able to make informed decisions regarding the administration of life-sustaining treatment, and that, to a reasonable degree of medical certainty and in accordance with reasonable medical standards, there is no reasonable possibility that I will regain the capacity to make informed decisions regarding the administration of life-sustaining treatment, then I direct my attending doctor to withhold or withdraw medical procedures, treatment, interventions, or other measures that serve principally to prolong the process of my dying, rather than diminish my pain or discomfort.

I have used the term "terminal condition" in this declaration to mean an irreversible, incurable, and untreatable condition caused by disease, illness, or injury from which, to a reasonable degree of medical certainty as determined in accordance with reasonable medical standards of my attending doctor and one other doctor who has examined me, both of the following apply:

1. There can be no recovery.
2. Death is likely to occur within a relatively short time if life-sustaining treatment is not administered.

I have used the term "permanently unconscious state" in this declaration to mean a state of permanent unconsciousness that, to a reasonable degree of medical certainty, is determined in accordance with reasonable medical standards by my attending doctor and one other doctor who has examined me, as characterized by both of the following:

1. I am irreversibly unaware of myself and my environment.
2. There is a total loss of cerebral cortical functioning, resulting in my having no capacity to experience pain or suffering.

Nutrition and hydration

I hereby authorize my attending doctor to withhold or withdraw nutrition and hydration from me when I am in a permanent unconscious state if my attending doctor and at least one other doctor who has examined me determine, to a reasonable degree of medical certainty and in accordance with reasonable medical standards, that nutrition or hydration will not, or no longer will serve to provide comfort to me or alleviate my pain.

_____

[Sign here for withdrawal of nutrition or hydration]

Living will (continued)

I hereby designate [Print name of person to decide] as the person whom I wish my attending doctor to notify at any time that life-sustaining treatment is to be withdrawn or withheld pursuant to this Declaration.

_____   _____
            [Sign your name here]   [Today's date]

Witness by: _____

[Living will person's name] voluntarily signed or directed another individual to sign this Living Will in the presence of the following who each attests that the Declarant appears to be of sound mind and not under or subject to duress, fraud, or undue influence.

[First witness signs here] _____

[Second witness signs here] _____

---

tives will be resolved such as by referral to the bioethics committee.

Not all advance directives are black and white and may not address all contingencies or medical situations that a patient may encounter. For example, the patient may not realize that advanced life support may only be necessary for a brief time to help him regain sufficient strength or to support breathing during surgery. (See _Advance directives_, page 93.)

Although the health care proxy (that is, one authorized to act for another) is supposed to be the ultimate decision maker, the physician has a legitimate role in the decision-making process and may refuse to comply with any decision that he believes is contrary to the patient's wishes or best interests. If that happens, the proxy may ask that the patient be transferred to a physician who will honor the patient's or the proxy's requests. Alternatively, the proxy may request the ethics committee of the hospital to mediate. As a last resort, the proxy may seek a court order to stop the unwanted care or treatment.

Right to die laws

Most states have enacted right-to-die laws (also called _natural death laws_ or _living will laws_). These laws recognize the patient's right to choose death by refusing extraordinary treatment when he has no hope of recovery.

Whenever a competent patient expresses his wishes concerning extraordinary treatment, health care providers should attempt to follow them. If the patient is incompetent or unconscious, the decision becomes more difficult.

In some cases, the next of kin may express the patient's desires for him, but whether this is an honest interpretation of the patient's wishes is sometimes uncertain.

Durable power of attorney for health care

The sample document below is an example of a durable power of attorney, which allows a competent patient to delegate to another person the authority to consent to or refuse health care treatment. This helps the patient ensure that his wishes will be carried out if he should become incompetent.

Each state with a durable power of attorney for health care law has specific requirements for executing the document. The sample form below is from Nebraska.

POWER OF ATTORNEY FOR HEALTH CARE

I appoint _____

whose address is _____

and whose telephone number is _____

as my attorney in fact for health care. _____

I appoint _____

whose address is _____

and whose telephone number is _____

as my successor attorney in fact for health care.

I authorize my attorney in fact appointed by this document to make health care decisions for me when I am determined to be incapable of making my own health care decisions. I have read the warning which accompanies this document and understand the consequences of executing a power of attorney for health care.

I direct that my attorney in fact comply with the following instructions or limitations (optional):

I direct that my attorney in fact comply with the following instructions on life-sustaining treatment (optional):

I direct that my attorney in fact comply with the following instructions on artificially administered nutrition and hydration (optional):

I have read this power of attorney for health care. I understand that it allows another person to make life and death decisions for me if I am incapable of making such decisions. I also understand that I can revoke this power of attorney for health care at any time by notifying my attorney in fact, my physician, or the facility in which I am a patient or resident. I also understand that I can require in this power of attorney for health care that the fact of my incapacity in the future be confirmed by a second physician.

_____   _____
[Signature of person making designation]   [Date]

EVIDENCE-BASED PRACTICE

 Advance directives

Question: *How useful are advance directives to members of the health care team in determining treatment and end-of-life decisions in patients who received cardiopulmonary resuscitation (CPR)?*

Research: Adults who are competent have the right to choose their own resuscitative measures and can do so by making sure they have living wills or advanced directives in place to convey their wishes. The Patient Self-Determination Act of 1991 requires health care providers to honor the wishes of patients as expressed in their advance directives. State and federal regulations as well as hospital policy mandate that individuals at the age of 18 or older must be asked if they have an advanced directive and should be provided information about advance directives or given the opportunity to complete one which is then kept on file with their medical records.

In this study the medical records of 135 patients who had received cardiopulmonary resuscitation within the previous year were evaluated. The medical records were studied to determine if the advance directives were useful in directing the end-of-life care that the patient received and to what extent they were useful. The advance directives were categorized as "vague and required more clarification," "independently directive," and "nondirective."

Conclusion: Regardless of the type of advance directive, the health care provider should always discuss and clarify the patient's wishes and end-of-life care decisions. Consumer education about the importance, nature and intent of the advance directives should be a priority.

Application: This study can also be used to clarify treatment options for end-of-life care to ensure that the advance directives are useful and meaningful documents.

Source: Gilbert, M., et al., "Determining the relationship between end-of-life decisions expressed in advance directives and resuscitative efforts during cardiopulmonary resuscitation," *Outcomes Management for Nursing Practice* 5(2):87-92, April-June 2001.

Written evidence of the patient's wishes provides the best indication of what treatment he would consent to if he could still communicate. This information may be provided through:

▶ a living will—specifies a person's wishes with regard to medical care if he should become unable to communicate. In some states, living wills don't address the issue of stopping artificial nutrition and hydration.

▶ a durable power of attorney for health care—the patient designates a person who will make medical decisions for him if he can't do so. This differs from the usual power of attorney, which requires the patient's ongoing consent and deals only with financial issues.

Most states recognize living wills as legally valid and have laws authorizing durable powers of attorney for initiating or terminating life-sustaining medical treatment.

REFERENCES

1. American Hospital Association. *The Patient Care Partnership.* Chicago: American Hospital Association, 2003. Available at *www.aha.org/aha/issues/ Communicating-With-Patients/pt-care- partnership.html.*

2. U.S. Department of Justice. *A Guide to Disability Rights Laws. U. S. Department of Justice Civil Rights Division Disability Rights Section.* Washington, D.C.: U.S. Department of Justice, September 2005. Available at *www.usdoj.gov/crt/ada/cguide.pdf.*

3. Anderson, F. "Finding HIPAA in Your Soup," *AJN* 107(2):66-71, February 2007.

4. Iyer, P.W. *Legal Nurse Consulting Principles and Practices,* 2nd ed. Boca Raton, Fla.: AALNC/CRC Press, 2003, p. 95.

5. American Cancer Society. *Making Treatment Decisions—Informed Consent.* Information revised 3/19/2007. Available at *www.cancer.org/docroot/ ETO/content/ETO_1_2X_Informed_ Consent.asp?*

6. Grace, P.J., and McLaughlin, M. "When Consent Isn't Informed Enough: What's the Nurse's Role when a Patient has given Consent but Doesn't Fully Understand the Risks?" *AJN* 105(4):79-84, April 2005.

7. Iyer, p. 98.

8. Troussman, S. "Mandatory Reporting Law Gone Awry: The ANA and KSNA Fight to Protect Adolescents' Access to Confidential Care," *AJN* 105(6):73, June 2005.

9. Troussman, p. 75.

10. United States Department of Health and Human Services: Code of Federal Regulations, Title 45, Public Welfare. Part 46, Protection of Human Subjects, Subpart A: Basic HHS Policy for Protection of Human Research Subjects. Revised 6/23/2005. Available at *www.hhs.gov /ohrp/humansubjects/guidance/45cfr46. htm.*

11. AHA, p. 3.

12. Iyer, p. 226.

13 Iyer, p. 226.

14. Levine, C. "HIPAA and Talking with Family Caregivers: What Does the Law Really Say?" *AJN* 106(8):52, August 2006.

15. Levine, p. 51.

16. HIPAAdvisory. HIPAA Primer. Washington, D.C.: U.S. Department of Labor, 2005. Available at *www.hipaadvisory.com/REGS/HIPAAprimer.htm. Updated 7/2005.*

17. Anderson, p. 67

18. Anderson, p. 67.

19. Department of Health and Human Services. *Your Health Information Privacy Rights.* Available at *http://www.hhs.gov/ocr/hipaa/ consumer_rights.pdf.* Washington, D.C.: Department of Health and Human Services.

20. Anderson, p. 68.

21. Flores, J.A., and Dodier, A. "HIPAA: Past, Present, and Future Implications for Nurses," *Online Journal of Issues in Nursing* 10(2), May 2005. Available at *http://nursingworld.org/ MainMenu Categories/ANAMarketplace/ANAPerio dicals/OJIN/TableofContents/Volume10 2005/No2May31/tpc27_416020.aspx.* Assessed 9/17/07.

22. Erickson, J.I., and Millar, S. "Caring for Patients While Respecting Their Privacy: Renewing our Commitment," *Online Journal of Issues in Nursing* 10(2), May 2005. Available at *http://nursingworld. org/MainMenuCategories/ANAMarketpl ace/ANAPeriodicals/OJIN/Tableof Contents/Volume102005/No2May31/ tpc27_116017.aspx.* Assessed 9/17/07.

23. Leahy, P., and Kennedy, E. S. *1814.* Washington, D.C.: 110th Congress, 1st session. Library of Congress, 2007. Available at *http://thomas.loc.gov/cgi-bin/query/D?c110:1:./temp/~c110X59Q Na::* Assessed 9/17/07.

ADDITIONAL RESOURCES

American Medical Association. *HIPAA Privacy Standards.* Available at *www.ama-assn.org/ama/pub/category/11434.html.* Chicago: American Medical Association. Updated 1/12/07.

Health Privacy Project (2007). *Myths and Facts about the HIPAA Privacy Rule.* Available at *www.healthprivacy.org/info-url_nocat2303/info-url_nocat_show.htm?doc_id=173435.*

U.S. Department of Health and Human Services. National Institutes of Health. What health information is protected by the privacy rule? Available at *http://privacyruleandresearch.nih.gov/pr_07.asp.* Updated 2/2/07.

3

Nurses' rights

All nurses, as individuals, have the basic rights afforded to them by the constitution. Additionally, nurses have specific rights associated with their role and employment. In 2001, the American Nurses Association (ANA) established a Nurses' Bill of Rights to protect the dignity and autonomy of nurses in the workplace.[1] Although this isn't a legal document, it can be used as a guide in developing policies and procedures and workplace agreements and contracts. The Bill of Rights remains in effect today. (See *Nurses' Bill of Rights,* page 98.)

Nurses need to have a firm understanding of their rights. For example, decent wages means financial security. Optimal working conditions can mean improved job security, enhanced job satisfaction, and the opportunity to deliver the best possible care to patients. However, to achieve the wages, benefits, and working conditions that nurses deserve, they need to understand their rights as employees. Nurses also need to be prepared to take appropriate action if employee rights are violated.

This chapter describes the major issues that can affect nurses' rights. These issues include employment contracts, work-place safety, unions, collective bargaining, and grievances. This chapter also presents important legislation and policies directly affecting nurses' rights.

EMPLOYMENT CONTRACTS

Most nurses are hired without benefit of a written employment contract. Usually, an application or a résumé is submitted and an agreement is reached as to the start date, position, benefits, and starting pay. This arrangement is no less legal than a written contract. It does, however, present certain problems if, at a later date, some portion of the employment agreement is disputed by either party.

When signing an employment contract, read it carefully to make sure it adequately defines duties, authority, and benefits. Knowing what to look for in a contract will help in deciding if a particular job is right for that person. Learning to interpret contract terms will help the nurse function within the contract's specified limits. Also, make sure to carefully read the procedure for terminating the contract.

Nurses' Bill of Rights

The ANA has identified the following rights to be afforded to all nurses to protect their dignity and autonomy:

• Nurses have the right to practice in a manner that fulfills their obligations to society and to those who receive nursing care
• Nurses have the right to practice in environments that allow them to act in accordance with professional standards and legally authorized scopes of practice
• Nurses have the right to a work environment that supports and facilitates ethical practice in accordance with the *Code of Ethics for Nurses with Interpretive Statements*
• Nurses have the right to freely and openly advocate for themselves and their patients without fear of retribution
• Nurses have the right to fair compensation for their work, consistent with their knowledge, experience, and professional responsibilities
• Nurses have the right to a work environment that is safe for themselves and for their patients
• Nurses have the right to negotiate the conditions of their employment, either as individuals or collectively, in all practice settings.

Source: American Nurses Association. *Nurses' Bill of Rights*. Silver Spring, Md.: American Nurses Association. Available at *http://www.nursingworld.org/MainMenuCategories/ThePracticeof ProfessionalNursing/workplace/RightsofNurses/ BillofRights.aspx.*
Reprinted with permission © 2001 nursesbooks.org, Silver Spring, Md.

Types of contracts

A *contract* is a legally binding promise between two parties that can be enforced in court. According to U.S. and Canadian law, an employment contract is legally binding if all of these provisions apply:

▶ The person accepted an offer, verbally or in writing, to perform in a certain capacity.

▶ The individual and the other person are legally competent, of legal age, and without mental impairment.
▶ Both understand the agreement.
▶ The terms of the agreement are lawful.
▶ The individual receives something of value, such as money, for fulfilling the agreement or, in some cases, he gives up something of value.

In general, agreements about conscience, morals, and social activities aren't legally binding. For example, if a person breaks a lunch date, he can't be fined or taken to court. However, if that person violates any term in a legally binding contract, he may face consequences.

Written contract

Sometimes an employment contract is a formal, written contract. It may be an individual contract, which the person negotiates, or a collectively bargained contract that was negotiated by a nurse negotiation committee and a labor organization or union. In either contract, wage increases may be awarded automatically or may be linked to merit or experience.

Oral express contract

Contracts need not be in writing to be legally binding. An employment agreement can be and is usually an oral contract, offered and accepted orally. Most states allow parties to agree orally to employment relationships, and those contracts are legal and enforceable in court (assuming state law allows them). However, because the judge and jury won't have a written contract to consider if a dispute about the terms of employment arises, other documents (such as an employee handbook, a notice of a physical examination, a welcoming letter, or pay stubs) would play a major role in proving that such an oral contract existed and outlining its terms.

Finally, witnesses who may have overheard the offer extended to the nurse and the nurse's acceptance may be called to testify at a hearing, deposition, or trial to prove the existence of an oral employment agreement.

An oral contract can be problematic if the parties involved disagree about its terms. Memories fail and witnesses move away or may become otherwise unavailable. Consequently, if the original agreement isn't in writing, the subjective and fallible memories of the parties may have to reconstruct it. If the matter must be litigated, more time and money will be spent to prove what simply could have been put into writing.

If an employer doesn't offer the nurse a written contract, he can write a letter to the person with whom he spoke, confirming acceptance of the offer and repeating the terms heard. The start date is confirmed and a statement is included to say that the nurse is looking forward to working with that person. All important, agreed-to terms and conditions should be stated in the letter. At the end, the nurse should include a statement indicating that if the employing person has anything to add or disagrees with the matters stated in the letter, she should contact the nurse in writing at her earliest convenience. The nurse should make a copy of the letter for his personal file and then send it.

At-will contracts

Labor attorneys try to draft most employment agreements as *at-will contracts,* meaning that either party can end the agreement for any reason or for no rea-

son. These contracts are in contrast to the less common just cause agreements, in which the employer must have just cause to fire the individual or risk penalties if a court finds that the individual was wrongfully terminated. Although the at-will contract has benefits for the employer, the employer risks having the employee quit at any time, without a reason.

There are some important restrictions on an employer's ability to terminate an employee at will. Primarily, these restrictions arise if an employer's decision to terminate an employee violates a law—for example, firing someone based on race, religion, sex, or other factors addressed by antidiscrimination laws. (The scope of these laws differs depending on the state. Firing based on race, for example, is illegal in all states as well as under federal law. Firing based on sexual orientation, on the other hand, is illegal in some states, but not in others, and it isn't prohibited by federal law.)

In some states, legislation has recently been enacted that prohibits health care employers from firing nurses (and, in many cases, other employees) who act as whistle-blowers by reporting unsafe conditions or illegal activities to state or federal agencies. Employers also can't fire someone for exercising her legal right to join a union or to engage in collective bargaining.

In addition to situations in which terminating an employee violates an existing law, most states (except Alabama, Florida, Georgia, Louisiana, Maine, Nebraska, New York, and Rhode Island) recognize a "public-policy" exemption to at-will employment. Under the public-policy exemption, an employer wrongfully terminates an employee when said termination violates a state's well–established public policy, which can be found in the state's constitution, statutes, administrative rules, common laws, and any expansion thereof. For example, it would be against public policy if an employer fired an employee for filing a worker's compensation claim after being injured on the job or for refusing to break the law at the employer's request. However, states differ in terms of how they define public policy.

Some states also recognize an *implied covenant of good faith and fair dealing*, meaning that an employer can't fire an employee maliciously or in bad faith. Even among those states that recognize this exception to at-will employment, there are differences in how far it extends and how to apply it.

Implied conditions

Most contracts contain *implied conditions*—elements that aren't explicitly stated but are assumed to be part of the contract. For example, an employer assumes that the nurse will practice nursing in a safe, competent manner as defined by the nurse practice act and the health care facility's standards and policies. The nurse assumes, based on implied conditions, that the employer will provide the necessary resources, supplies, and equipment to perform the work and that the employer will ensure a safe working environment.

Offer and acceptance

In any contract, there must be an offer and an acceptance. An offer must be definite and communicated by words or actions. The employer can't interpret silence (a failure to respond) as acceptance, but can withdraw the offer without penalty at any time before it has been accepted. Although a nurse may orally accept an offer or simply report for duty, a written acceptance is generally best. The employment contract should be as specific as possible about wages, hours, and the terms and conditions of the relationship. (See *Components of an employment contract*.)

Breach of contract

Unjustified failure to perform all or part of one's contractual duty is considered a breach of contract. If the breach is substantial, the entire agreement may have been broken and legal damages may result. (In the case of at-will employment, a likely consequence is that the employment relationship will terminate.) If only part of the agreement has been breached, the remaining contract may still be effective and both parties may want to continue the relationship, with some clarification. Breaches can be avoided if both parties carefully consider the terms and conditions of the contract and know what they're promising each other. Because Canadian law varies by jurisdiction, it's best to check with local legal counsel about procedures and deadlines.

Employee breach

When a person agrees to do (or not to do) something in an employment contract, and then doesn't perform as promised, he may be in breach of the contract and subject to litigation forcing him to perform as promised. The person may even be required to reimburse the employer for the cost of hiring someone else to do the job that he was supposed to do.

It's rare, except in unusual circumstances, for a court to order an employee to perform services against his will. If the employment relationship is at-will, failure to perform may simply terminate the agreement. However, in other employment contracts, especially those involving specialized services, failure to perform as agreed may result in legal consequences, which may require the person to perform as agreed in the contract.

Of course, the terms and conditions of a contract can be changed or modified by oral or written agreement; certainly, it's far better to change a contract than to breach it. Good communication may prevent a perceived breach, and renegotiation is cheaper than litigation.

Employer breach

An employer may also breach a contract. If, for example, he fails to give the employee the vacation time agreed to, he has breached the contract. If the employee discovers a breach, he must follow procedures outlined in the employee handbook.

Commonly, misunderstandings can be cleared up by talking with the proper people in the chain of command (always in a professional and unemotional manner). If documents are involved, they're important proof. If a union contract is in place, the representative should be told as soon as the employee becomes aware of a breach.

If all channels of appeal are exhausted, the employee may need to discuss the problem with an attorney with contract and employment law expertise, using a written log of attempts to rectify the situation, including statements made, with dates and times.

Invalid contracts

A nursing employment contract is considered invalid when the agreement con-

Components of an employment contract

For an employment contract to be legally binding, it must include the following components:

A PROMISE
Two or more legally competent parties must promise each other to do or not do something.

MUTUAL UNDERSTANDING
The parties involved must clearly understand the terms and obligations the contract imposes on them.

COMPENSATION
The parties involved must agree that, to fulfill the contract, lawful actions will be performed in exchange for something of value.

cerns actions that are illegal or impossible to carry out, or when any of the following applies:
▶ An applicant has lied about qualifications.
▶ A nurse is forced into signing a contract.
▶ The agreement involves unlawful activity; for example, it requires you to bill for services that weren't actually performed.
▶ A minor or mentally incompetent person signs the contract.

Physical or mental inability to carry out the agreement may be a basis to set the agreement aside but not always. Both parties *expect*, from the start, that the nurse will be able to physically carry out the agreement.

If the employee's health status changes, he may feel that the agreement no longer stands. If litigated, the employee's obligation will be determined on an individual basis by the judge. Mere physical or mental disability won't void the contract. However, the employee may be protected under the Americans with Disabilities Act, which requires reasonable accommodations in certain instances.

Contract termination

When an employee terminates a contract, he has fulfilled or absolved himself of all obligations. Because most employment contracts don't specify termination dates, the individual can end them at any time, if he follows proper notification procedures. The employee can also end contracts with termination dates if the employer agrees to the date. Follow the contract's procedures for giving written notice (most require 2 to 4 weeks) or, if the contract has an automatic expiration date, don't renew it.

An employer can terminate a contract if he determines that the employee has been incompetent or has behaved unprofessionally on the job. Before discharging the employee, he'll probably give the individual several warnings about the quality of his work. Then he might confront the employee with several examples of shortcomings from previous written evaluations of the employee's performance. If the employee doesn't want to lose the job, he should discuss areas of improvement with the employer.

If the employee disagrees with the employer's complaints, he can request an evaluation by someone else who supervised the employee's work, or he can request a transfer to another unit where he would be reevaluated after an agreed-upon length of time. However, an employer isn't obligated to agree to either request unless these steps are part of a disciplinary process stated in an employment contract or an employee manual. If the employer doesn't agree, the employee may seek written support from coworkers who will refute the employer's complaints. He can also seek support from the union, if one is present. The union may file a grievance on the employee's behalf.

Most hospitals operate on an employment-at-will basis, in which there's either no employment contract or the existing contract fails to specify the job's duration. However, the hospital can't violate a union bargaining agreement that mandates proof of just cause for discipline or discharge.

WORKPLACE SAFETY

Health care workers are entitled to work in a safe environment. The ethical principle of justice or fairness supports the position that employers should provide security measures, whether in an institution or in the community. Without those safeguards, an ethical dilemma arises. Although nurses must provide care to patients (nonabandonment and fidelity), they also need to protect themselves.

According to the ANA, "nurses have a right to a safe and secure workplace in which to provide quality patient care...Improving the health and safety of the health care workplace is key to solving the growing nursing shortage."[2] Policies that address appropriate staffing levels, adequate training, and security escorts minimize the ethical conflicts between providing care and ensuring safety. Federal safety and health standards require that all employers develop injury and illness prevention programs for hazards unique to their facility or program. However, it remains up to the individual nurse to recognize and protect herself from on-the-job hazards, such as the following:

▶ *Infection:* A particularly serious threat to nurses is the patient whose infection hasn't yet been diagnosed. In many cases, the infections of patients with obviously noninfective conditions, such as heart failure, aren't guarded against or detected for several days. Nurses in high-contact areas, such as emergency departments, are particularly at risk for diseases such as tuberculosis. In addition, HIV has triggered a new era in the care of patients with communicable diseases. The Centers for Disease Control and Prevention has mandated the use of standard precautions to prevent the spread of HIV. Although it's up to the nurse to follow the precautions, employers must provide the gloves, eye covers, sharps containers, and other equipment for this form of protection.

▶ *Hazardous chemicals:* Many potentially hazardous chemicals are routinely used in health care. For example, anesthetic gases increase the risk of birth defects and spontaneous abortions. New standards attempt to control the anesthetic in the operating room, but many hospitals move pregnant nurses out of areas in which these gases are used. Chemotherapeutic drugs, radiation, and powerful cleaning solutions and disinfectants are common hazards for health care workers. They all require knowledge and vigilance from the nurse and strict supervision by the facility.

▶ *Musculoskeletal injuries:* Musculoskeletal injuries involving direct-care nurses rank as the 10th leading cause of injury for all occupations.[3] The most common physical reason nurses lose time from work is back injuries. Additionally, chronic back pain and severe back pain are a major reason for nurses leaving the workforce. Many of these nurses don't return. (See *Safe patient handling legislation,* page 104.)

▶ *Latex allergies:* As the use of latex gloves has increased, more nurses are becoming sensitized to the allergenic proteins in the latex. This growing problem is compounded by the lack of knowledge many nurses have about latex allergies. These nurses tend to dismiss the symptoms as a simple rash or hay fever and treat it with lotion or creams.

Latex allergy follows a predictable progression of symptoms that continue as long as the person is in contact with the allergen. The initial allergy-producing culprit seems to be the latex-laden powder in the glove rather than the glove itself. After there has been a primary immune reaction to the powder, further exposure to any type of latex triggers an ever-increasing immune response that can eventually produce a massive release of histamine, causing anaphylactic shock.

A secondary problem is that after a person develops a latex allergy, exposure to even the microscopic particles of latex powder that become airborne whenever a coworker puts on or takes off a pair of powdered gloves can trigger a severe reaction. The powder can be carried through the ventilation system in the hospital and circulate to parts of the building in which gloves aren't being used. Sensitized people working in these areas, although away from the actual glove use, can suffer severe reactions.

An associated problem is the development of latex allergies by patients. The allergy development process is identical

Safe patient handling legislation

Activities that involve lifting, moving, and repositioning patients can lead to serious injury for nurses. On January 10, 2007, Congressman Jon Conyers introduced the "Nurse and Patient Safety and Protection Act" (H.R. 378) to address the establishment of safe patient handling standards for direct-care nurses as a means to increase patient safety, protect nurses, and address the nursing shortage.[3]

KEY POINTS OF THIS LEGISLATION INCLUDE:
- establishment of a federal safe patient handling standard to ensure the use of mechanical devices to eliminate manual lifting of patients

except during a declared emergency; this standard would be applicable to direct care nurses and other health care personnel
- hospital development of a safe patient handling plan with input from registered nurses (RNs), experts on ergonomics, and RN organizations
- posting of a notice about the standard in each unit
- protection for nurses for refusal of assignment and whistle-blowing
- development of a grant program for financial assistance to facilities to cover the cost of purchasing the necessary handling equipment

Source: United American Nurses, AFL-CIO (2007). *Legislative Issue Brief H.R. 378 – Safe Patient Handling Legislation.* Available at http://uannurse.org/legislative/pdfs/Conyers_Safe_Patient_Handling_Issue_Brief_110_Congress.pdf.

to what happens to the health care provider and can be triggered by one of the large number of latex products used in patient care today, such as surgical drains, catheters, tourniquets, and gloves. Consider latex allergy whenever unexplained rashes develop in hospitalized patients.

Understaffing and overtime

With the current focus on the nursing shortage, concerns about understaffing have received increased attention from the public and health care providers. For nurses, understaffing is a professional concern because inadequate staffing can compromise patient safety. In addition, if staffing is inadequate, nurses must work extended hours, usually with increased numbers of patients to care for and possibly increased patient acuity. All these factors can lead to increased stress and fatigue, which can negatively affect patients as well as nurses. Continued understaffing also can lead to nurses leaving the institutions and the profession, further exacerbating the nursing shortage. Unfortunately, what's considered safe nurse-patient ratio, safe staffing, or appropriate staffing has yet to be specifically delineated. (See *Healthy workplace environments.*)

Understaffing commonly leads to overtime. According to the Institutes of Medicine (IOM), nurses should work no more than 12 hours in 24-hour period and no more than 60 hours in a 7-day period.[4] However, various research studies have shown that actual work times exceed that recommended by the IOM, resulting in several negative effects including:
- chronic stress, which can adversely impact the neurologic, immune, and cardiovascular systems

Healthy workplace environments

Question: *Does the nurse-patient ratio affect patient mortality, deaths following complications, emotional exhaustion and job satisfaction of nurses?*

Research: It has long been debated that the nurse-patient ratio affects, job satisfaction, patient outcomes and increases the rate of medical errors due to exhaustion.

This study examined the relationship between nurse-staffing levels and patient and nurse outcomes at an acute care hospital licensed for 572 beds. It studied 2,709 patients and 140 staff RNs.

Conclusion: This study concluded that staffing and nurse-patient ratios were not a significant predictor of mortality or death after complications. In addition, the clinical specialty did not predict emotional exhaustion or job dissatisfaction. It was also found that emotional exhaustion was not increased by the clinical specialty or the nurse-patient ration, however, emotional exhaustion and job satisfaction was found to be increased by the number of years a nurse worked at the institution.

Application: Although these findings reinforce adequate staffing ratios at this institution, programs that support nurses in their daily practice and positively impact job satisfaction need to be explored. For instance, although job satisfaction and emotional exhaustion was not affected by nurse-patient ratios but the number of years a nurse worked in the facility did affect the job satisfaction, the facility should consider instituting low-lift teams or purchasing equipment to ease the stress and the physical demands of older nurses. Some facilities have also instituted critical incident stress debriefing teams.

Source: Halm, M., et al., "Hospital Nurse Staffing and Patient Mortality, Emotional Exhaustion, and Job Dissatisfaction," *Clinical Nurse Specialist: The Journal for Advanced Nursing Practice* 19(5):241-51, September-October 2005.

▶ injuries due to chronic exposure to highly demanding work
▶ fatigue, pain, performance deficits and slowed reaction time due to increased physical demands and little time for recovery
▶ physiologic depletion and exhaustion due to reduction in rest and recovery
▶ unhealthy behaviors such as smoking, excessive caffeine ingestion, alcohol consumption, poor diet, and lack of exercise
▶ errors related to fatigue
▶ conflicts related to family, social, and leisure activities.[5]

Studies involving other occupations, such as airline pilots and interstate truck drivers, have shown similar results—that fatigue impacts an individual's ability to make decisions, attend to details, and

solve problems.[6] Federal legislation is in effect to limit the amount of time an individual in these occupations can work. Currently, legislation is being proposed to ban unsafe mandatory overtime and establish standards for safe nurse staffing.[7,8] (See *Legislation for nurse staffing and mandatory overtime,* page 106.)

Workplace violence

Workplace violence is a serious problem in the United States. How serious? A 2002 survey reported that workplace violence accounts for 1000 deaths and more than 1.5 million nonfatal injuries each year. Unfortunately, hospitals, long-term care facilities, hospices, and other health care facilities aren't immune from this

Legislation for nurse staffing and mandatory overtime

Two pieces of legislation have been proposed to improve workplace safety for nurses.

THE SAFE NURSE STAFFING FOR PATIENT SAFETY AND QUALITY CARE ACT OF 2007 (H.R. 2123)

This legislation, introduced by Representative Jan Schakowsky from Illinois, calls for the establishment of minimum direct care registered nurse-to-patient ratios for each shift. With this legislation, one nurse would be assigned to no more than:

1. patient in the operating room and trauma emergency unit
2. patients in all critical care units, intensive care, labor and delivery, and postanesthesia units
3. patients in antepartum, emergency, pediatrics, step-down and telemetry units
4. patients in intermediate care nursery, medical surgical, and acute care psychiatric units
5. patients in rehabilitation units
6. patients in postpartum and well-baby units (three couplets)

In addition, the bill also safeguards nurses from discrimination and recrimination if they report violations. Moreover, this bill also provides protection to nurses who refuse an assignment when a patient's health and safety would be threatened because of a violation of the standard ratios.

THE SAFE NURSING AND PATIENT CARE ACT (H.R. 2122)

This legislation, introduced in May 2007 by Representative Peter Stark from California, sets strict federal limits on facilities and their requirements for mandatory overtime unless an official state of emergency is declared by the federal, state or local government. A nurse is free to use his or her judgment about volunteering for overtime.

United American Nurses, AFL-CIO (2007). *Legislative Summary. The Safe Nurse Staffing for Patient Safety and Quality Care Act of 2007 (H.R. 2123).* Available at http://www.uannurse.org/legislative/pdfs/RNratioIssueBrief110Congress.pdf.

United American Nurses, AFL-CIO (2007). *Legislative Issue Brief. Safe Nursing and Patient Care Act (H.R. 2122). Legislation to Strictly Limit Mandatory Overtime.* Available at: http://ww.uannurse.org/legislative/pfs/MoT100thCongress.pdf.

growing trend. The violent behaviors occurring in health care facilities today simply mirror those of the larger society.

Nurses are particularly vulnerable to workplace violence. On average, 30% of nurses report experiencing assault, abusive language, emotional or mental abuse, or sexual harassment. Patients and physicians are the most common perpetrators of physical violence against nurses; physicians, nurse managers, or other supervisors are the most common perpetrators of verbal and emotional abuse.

Studies indicate that drugs, poor staffing, hospital type and location, gangs, easy access to a hospital emergency department, long hours worked, inadequate training, power and control issues, and stress contribute to violence in health care settings. A history of abuse can also be a contributing factor: more than 50% of all abused nurses report being victims of childhood or adult abuse.

Initiatives to promote safety

Health care officials and nursing leaders have an ethical and legal responsibility to create and maintain a safe, healthy work environment. To do this, they need to develop policies and procedures detailing behavioral expectations, reporting mechanisms that don't further victimize victims of workplace violence, and effective security policies and systems. Some of the initiatives that they can take include:

▶ documenting required employee safety and self-protection training provided for all employees by the organization

▶ teaching proven strategies of intervention for situations of escalating violence

▶ teaching caregivers to work as a team when responding to violence

▶ clearly stating behavioral expectations for employees, medical staff, patients, and visitors

▶ stating the organization's expectations for reporting instances of violence or abuse and describing appropriate documentation

▶ establishing a mechanism (such as the organizational ethics committee) for investigating, negotiating, and resolving conflicts and disputes.

In addition, The Joint Commission issued a report identifying three recommendations to address the evolving nursing crisis. This report can be found at: *http://www.jointcommission.org/NR/ rdonlyres/5C138711-ED76-4D6F-909F-B06E0309F36D/0/health_care_at_the_ crossroads.pdf.*

Interventions and employees' rights

Interventions should be immediate and appropriate to the level of violence. Ignoring the angry or belligerent patient, physician, or coworker can heighten violence by increasing the violent individ-

ual's suspicions, paranoia, fear, anxiety, and feelings of being out of control.

When violence occurs in the workplace, employees may have claims against their employer under federal or state law. Employees may have additional legal remedies against their abusers and their employer under legal principles involving tort or contract issues. Tort cases may occur if an employer or manager intentionally or negligently violates an employee right. Cases involving contract issues may occur if the employer was negligent in providing contracted security safeguards.

Needle-stick injuries

Needle sticks are among the most commonly reported occupational hazards nurses face. With an estimated 600,000 to 1 million needle-stick injuries occurring each year, it's important that nurses take every precaution when handling sharps and using needle delivery systems. One careless moment can lead to infection with human immunodeficiency virus, acquired immunodeficiency syndrome, hepatitis C, or any of the other deadly diseases that can be transmitted by needle stick.

According to the American Hospital Association, the cost for an infection due to a needle stick with a blood-borne organism can reach as high as $1 million or more when considering testing, treatment, follow-up, lost time, and disability expenditures. When no infection occurs, one needle-stick injury can cost as much as $3,000. These amounts are incredible because the cost of a safe needle device is approximately 28 cents more than a standard device.[9]

Although safer needle delivery devices have been available for many years, many employers have failed to provide them until recently. However, the Needlestick Safety and Prevention Act, which took effect in April 2001, strengthened the requirement for employers to provide safer needle delivery devices. It also required employers to maintain a sharps injury log of all needle sticks and to consult employees when reviewing, evaluating, and selecting devices.

Nurses who work in settings in which needle sticks are a risk need to understand their rights. Nurses can demand that the employer provide safer equipment by requesting a meeting with the employer to discuss this issue or by getting coworkers to sign a petition demanding safer needles. Another alternative is to contact the union representative if the nurse is a member of the union.

Sexual harassment

Sexual harassment in the workplace isn't new, nor is it unique to health care facilities. Anecdotal evidence suggests that the problem is related in part to the nurse's traditionally subservient role to that of the physician in health care and the sexism underlying this problem. However, sexism and sexual harassment can and do involve same-sex advances as well as female-male situations.

From coworkers, sexual harassment is best understood as a form of violence in the workplace. It's much less about sex than about abuse and control issues. For this reason, sexual harassment is experienced in two forms: *quid pro quo* and *hostile workplace.*

The Latin term *quid pro quo* means "this for that." *Quid pro quo* sexism occurs when a manager, supervisor, or individual in a "dominant" role (such as a physician) indicates or hints to an em-

ployee or person in a "nondominant" position that he'll trade job advancement, job benefits, or other special considerations for sexual favors.

Sexual harassment may also be defined as any form of sexual hostility in the workplace. Sexual hostility can include sexually offensive jokes, pictures, innuendoes, or behaviors. Although this type of sexual harassment is commonly repeated in the work environment, with the intent to shock, annoy, and degrade the recipient, it may sometimes take only one incident to provoke a charge of sexual harassment. For example, a vice president for nursing, the hospital's only female senior manager, brought suit against the hospital when the other senior manager hired a male stripper to "perform" at a management birthday party for her.

Harassment may also include any unwelcome or offensive verbal or physical conduct from a patient or visitor. Such acts may intimidate or threaten the nurse, be offensive, or undermine the therapeutic relationship. Such acts may be gestures or physical acts, slurs, taunting, verbal abuse or epithets, comments or jokes, or the displaying of derogatory objects, cartoons, posters, drawings, or pictures.

Sexual harassment is a violation of Title VII of the 1964 Federal Civil Rights Act, which was amended by the Civil Rights Act of 1991. Over time, it has become a bit easier for employees to prove discrimination and receive higher awards in damages.

Hospitals and other health care organizations should establish fair policies and procedures that clearly define sexual harassment. Nurses should receive consistent education about sexual harassment in the workplace, including how to recognize it and how to avoid causing it. Some of the ways to protect one's self from becoming a victim of sexual harassment include:

▶ refraining from talking or joking with employees about sex, including remarks that seem innocent

▶ stopping sexually oriented conduct among employees, such as joke telling and gestures

▶ keeping sexually oriented materials (such as posters, cartoons, or E-mails) from being posted in the workplace

▶ calling employees by their name or title

▶ refraining from expressing sexual interest or feelings for another employee.

Whistle-blowing

Whistle-blowing refers to an employee's disclosure of illegal, immoral, or illegitimate practices under an employer's control. The American Nurses Association's (ANA's) Code for Nurses outlines the nurse's obligation to report acts of negligence and incompetence by other health care providers. It states that "the nurse acts to safeguard the patient and public when health care and safety are affected by incompetent, unethical, or illegal practice by any person."

The ANA guidelines on reporting incompetent, unethical, or illegal practices identify helpful parameters for judging problematic conduct. Incompetent nursing practice is measured by nursing standards, unethical practice is evaluated in light of the Code for Nurses, and illegal practice is identified in terms of violations of the law. As a patient advocate, a nurse must be willing to take appropriate action—in short, to blow the whistle.

The Canadian Nurses Association also has a Code for Nurses that conveys the same message: "The nurse, as a member of the health care team, is obliged to take steps to ensure that the patient receives competent and ethical care."

Nurses are, by their professional code of ethics and licensure standards, required to act as patient advocates. (See *Patient advocacy and medical malpractice,* page 110.) Whenever nurses see other health care providers acting in a way that could endanger a patient's health or safety, they should make a report of what they witnessed. (In many states, state law *requires* nurses to report patient endangerment.)

The concept of moral agency should guide nurses, not only in situations of whistle-blowing, but also in reporting witnessed or suspected malpractice. Some states have regulations and case law that protect nurses who speak up in cases of suspected or confirmed medical malpractice.

Implications of whistle-blowing

Many nurses equate whistle-blowing with heroic self-sacrifice: a moral victory in the midst of a professional defeat. In fact, some nurses have had their reputations tarnished, lost their jobs, or been named in libel suits after reporting professional misconduct. Fortunately, such bitter retaliation isn't the norm. Keep in mind, however, that the higher the professional standing of the health care professional who commits misconduct, the greater the risk you face when blowing the whistle. (See *Whistle-blowing: A systematic approach,* page 111.)

Situations evolving to whistle-blowing

A health care professional who makes a mistake usually wants to ensure that it

Patient advocacy and medical malpractice

Nursing policies and procedures must clarify the circumstances under which nurses, as advocates for their patients, are required to report suspected or witnessed malpractice. Nurses must know the method by which such reports are to be made, to whom they should be made, and whether they can be considered discoverable and are protected under quality assurance protocols.

Of course, there can be problems with reporting instances of witnessed or suspected malpractice. Nurses may confuse issues of malpractice with other ethical or legal issues. For example, a nurse sees a physician lose his temper and slap a patient. Is this an instance of medical malpractice? No. But it's an example of violence in the workplace and the nurse's reporting procedure should be addressed in the facility's policy on managing violence in the hospital. Suppose a nurse witnesses a physician giving a dying patient an excessive dose of morphine? Is this an instance of medical malpractice? Possibly, but it's also an ethical issue and should be reported to and addressed by the facility's ethics committee.

won't happen again. Correcting an error usually involves admitting the mistake, expressing honest regret, and completing an incident report. At times, though, you may encounter a health care professional who makes repeated mistakes, attempts to cover them up or minimize them, and engages in suspect or misleading behavior. To uphold the ethical standards of your profession, you need to blow the whistle. (See *Is whistle-blowing warranted?* page 112.) Legally, 18 states provide some type of protection for nurses and health care employees related to whistle-blowing. This extent and degree of protection varies among the states. Twenty-six more states have proposed legislation in 2007, with three of these states passing legislation.[10]

Report of nurse misconduct

Usually, institutional channels exist through which an individual can report the misconduct of another nurse or nursing assistant without fear of reprisal. Typically, a nurse-manager and the personnel office assume joint responsibility for investigating allegations of misconduct. For the nurse, the only drawback is animosity from the affected staff member—and possibly from her acquaintances or sympathizers. The benefits, though, include correcting an injustice, preventing future harm, and strengthening your sense of moral integrity.

Report of medical or management misconduct

If a nurse reports the misconduct of a physician, a nursing supervisor, a nurse-manager, or a member of the institution's administration, expect stiffer resistance and, possibly, more severe retaliation, especially if management has cooperated in concealing the misconduct. Be prepared for a lengthy and hard-fought battle. That's because the accused professional may attempt to discredit the nurse, or have the nurse fired, rather than face the allegations honestly.

Consider the case of Barry Adams, a registered nurse (RN) in Boston, who was fired after reporting allegedly unsafe working conditions to the administration of the now-closed Youville Health Care Center in Cambridge. The National Labor Relations Board validated his complaints of retaliation, and now he has a complaint pending with the Massachusetts Board of Nursing against one of the

Whistle-blowing: A systematic approach

As with other nursing actions, whistle-blowing can be carried out successfully if it's planned, systematic, and purposeful.

GATHERING FACTS

Begin by gathering all the facts. Then put in writing the misconduct you want to report. Be sure to include the incident's date and time, the person or people involved, and the source of your information. Above all, avoid accusations and personal opinions.

STATING THE PROBLEM

Clearly state the problem and identify causative factors. Was incompetence or negligence involved? Were supplies adequate? Did equipment malfunction? Was facility policy at fault?

When answering these questions, try to eliminate your personal biases. If possible, review the problem with a trusted colleague.

DETERMINING YOUR OBJECTIVE

State your objective in confronting the problem. For example, you may want to eliminate threats to patient safety; eliminate illegal, immoral, or illegitimate practices; uphold professional ethical standards; or put into effect changes in facility policy.

CONFRONTING THE PROBLEM

Confront the person who committed the misconduct in a constructive, nonthreatening way. Express your concerns and ask for an explanation of the incident. Seek reassurance that the problem will be addressed.

MAKING YOUR DECISION

After a reasonable duration, determine if the problem has been corrected. If it hasn't, identify the pros and cons of whistle-blowing. The pros include correction of a harmful or potentially harmful situation, retained moral integrity, and an enhanced sense of moral accountability. The cons include alienation, stress and, possibly, loss of reputation, professional standing, and job. After you weigh the pros and cons, talk over the issue of whistle-blowing with your lawyer or another knowledgeable person.

Next, realistically appraise your situation. Will you be able to cope if you blow the whistle? Are you secure professionally and financially? Do you have the support of your family, colleagues, or administration? How much help can you count on?

Now make your decision based on your analysis of the severity of the incident, the consequences of whistle-blowing, and your resources. If you elect to blow the whistle, carefully devise a strategy that follows facility channels.

If you're fearful of losing your job as a result of your actions, consider taking a position in another facility before you blow the whistle. If you fail to get satisfaction through facility channels, consider consulting professional organizations, regulatory agencies and, as a last resort, the media. Be sure to document each step you take.

center's executives, Ann Poster, alleging unprofessional and unethical conduct in connection with allegedly unsafe patient conditions at the center. If a nurse risks significant personal losses, she may want to make a thorough moral assessment before taking action. If these losses extend to the nurse's dependents, consider the situation carefully. The nurse may have moral grounds for not blowing the whistle if dependents could be harmed emotionally, financially, or even physically.

Methods of whistle-blowing

Whistle-blowing can be pursued one of two ways: by going public or proceeding through the institution's chain of command. The nurse should make every effort to correct the situation internally before going public. Working through the

Is whistle-blowing warranted?

The scenarios below describe two types of whistle-blowing.

HABITUALLY LATE COLLEAGUE

An hour after her shift began, Sylvia Myers, RN, can't locate her coworker Mary Calvo, RN. She checks Ms. Calvo's time card; it shows that she punched in on time. A few minutes later, Ms. Myers sees Ms. Calvo with her coat and gloves on, getting off the elevator.

Ms. Myers approaches Ms. Calvo and asks where she has been. Ms. Calvo impatiently tells her to mind her own business and adds, "You have no idea how hard it is to raise three kids and have to work."

Upset and confused, Ms. Myers decides that she had better find out what's going on. After some investigation, she realizes that Allison Henkel, RN, a mutual friend, has been punching in Ms. Calvo. Ms. Henkel tells her that Ms. Calvo arrives up to an hour late two to three times per week. She goes on to say, "Don't worry. I'll keep covering for Ms. Calvo. What's important is that we're helping Ms. Calvo out and no one's getting hurt."

Ms. Myers is faced with an ethical dilemma: Should she report Ms. Calvo's lateness and Ms. Henkel's cover-up? Or should she remain quiet; after all, Ms. Calvo's lateness hasn't affected patient care thus far, and blowing the whistle might undermine her friendship with Ms. Henkel.

After careful consideration, Ms. Myers decides that there's no getting around the fact that Ms. Calvo is jeopardizing her patients' well-being and that Ms. Henkel shares partial responsibility. Although sympathetic to Ms. Calvo's child-care problems, Ms. Myers recognizes her overriding obligations to ensure the health and safety of patients.

Ms. Myers decides that her first step is to talk directly to Ms. Calvo about the situation. If Ms. Calvo's behavior persists, Ms. Myers will explain that she's ethically obligated to report Ms. Calvo to the nurse-manager. Before taking action, Ms. Myers is careful to document specific circumstances of Ms. Calvo's lateness.

QUESTIONING MEDICAL PROTOCOL

Rachel Kirkwood, RN, is the nurse-manager of a small oncology unit that develops treatment protocols for the National Cancer Institute. She has worked for several years on the unit, finds her position rewarding, and enjoys a good relationship with the medical staff. However, the latest protocol of the chief oncologist troubles her. None of the patients are improving with the experimental therapy. Ms. Kirkwood knows from her own extensive clinical experience that patients with the same condition fare much better with conventional therapy.

Ms. Kirkwood decides to share her concerns with the oncologist. He responds curtly, saying only that his research brings a large grant for the unit. He makes it clear that he doesn't want to discuss the matter with her further.

Ms. Kirkwood is faced with a choice: Should she defer to the oncologist's knowledge and trust his sense of professional responsibility? Or should she pursue her concerns?

Ms. Kirkwood realizes that her options are limited: she's in no position to make charges against the chief oncologist, but she can still take steps to correct the situation. She decides to discuss the matter confidentially with another oncologist and see what insight he can provide. In addition, she begins keeping accurate records of each patient's treatment and its results. If the evidence she gathers indicates that the patients are suffering harm and the chief oncologist continues to ignore her, Ms. Kirkwood is ready to blow the whistle.

Ms. Kirkwood is committed to preparing herself for the long haul. She gathers numerous articles on whistle-blowing and arranges to meet with a lawyer experienced in representing whistle-blowers. Aware that her actions may jeopardize her job, she has begun to search for alternative employment, and she also realizes that she must emotionally prepare to deal with the wrath of coworkers, especially those who disagree with her conclusions.

chain of command successfully can help accomplish the goals with a minimum of exposure. Ethically, the nurse owes management an opportunity to change the situation before going public. For personal legal protection, she should maintain a record of efforts to work through channels before considering more drastic measures.

When failing to get satisfaction from the institution's chain of command, contact the appropriate regulatory agencies. Contact the media only as a last resort.

Documentation

Document the disclosure carefully. Write a clear, objective summary of the relevant facts. Explain why the information is significant and what needs to be done. Avoid focusing on personalities. Personal accusations detract from the disclosure and may invite a lawsuit for libel or slander. Have other professionals verify the information if possible. This will lend objectivity to the information and may shield you from retaliation.

Aftermath survival

The nurse needs to prepare herself for possible retaliation. Management may find it more convenient to attack the whistle-blower than to address the problem. Colleagues may start giving the nurse the cold shoulder, or the nurse may experience overt harassment. Rumors of dishonesty or incompetence may spread through the institution. For self-protection and to maintain pressure on management, the nurse should meticulously document everything, including continued incidents of incompetence or negligence. She should consider photocopying all the incident reports filed. The nurse must be especially vigilant in prac-

tice, and document personal nursing actions carefully. The employer may try to distract attention from the disclosure by portraying the nurse as a troublemaker; to counter this tactic, the nurse should maintain diplomatic relations with as many colleagues as possible.

If the nurse anticipates that whistle-blowing will cause severe personal hardship, she should consider mapping out a self-protection strategy. She should find new employment before blowing the whistle and retain a lawyer who will provide competent legal advice throughout the ordeal. She should seek out friends and colleagues who have the moral integrity to provide support.

UNIONS

Although individual contracts provide significant legal protection, employees in many areas—from farm workers, laborers, and truck drivers to actors, teachers, and musicians—have found that they're better off signing a contract negotiated for them as a group. Their union representatives engage in collective bargaining for contract conditions. When necessary, they use arbitration, strikes, and threats of strikes to enhance their terms of employment and enforce contracts.

Before 1974, nurses' rights to form labor unions were limited primarily to employees of nursing homes, for-profit hospitals, and many public hospitals and health care agencies. Also, some state laws allowed for labor unions in nonprofit hospitals, and some private nonprofit hospitals voluntarily recognized nurses' unions. In 1974, Congress extended the National Labor Relations Act

(NLRA) to cover private, nonprofit health care facilities and agencies. Since then, the number of unionized nurses has increased dramatically.

The NLRA now applies to employees of hospitals and other health care facilities with annual revenues of at least $250,000 and to nursing homes, visiting nurses' associations, and related nursing facilities with annual revenues of at least $100,000. Also, many states now have collective bargaining laws patterned after the NLRA that control public sector bargaining in the state.

A new window of opportunity for nurses to unionize was opened in 1991, when the U.S. Supreme Court decided, in *American Hospital Association v. National Labor Relations Board* (NLRB), that the NLRB had acted properly in defining eight bargaining units in acute-care hospitals, including one unit composed of only RNs. After the 1991 decision, unions stepped up campaign efforts to organize nurses.

The supervisory issue

Two U.S. Supreme Court cases—*NLRB v. Health Care & Retirement Corporation (1994)* and *NLRB v. Kentucky River Community Care (2001)*—have addressed the issue of whether and when nurses who direct the work of others should be considered "supervisors" within the meaning of the NLRA. This is an extremely important issue because supervisors aren't covered by the NLRA, and thus they aren't protected by it—meaning, among other things, that they have no right to form or join unions or to bargain collectively. Furthermore, because many RNs may "direct" the work of others (for example, licensed practical nurses, licensed vocational nurses, unit clerks,

and nurses aides) in the course of performing their own professional duties, the issue of where and how to draw the line in determining who's a "supervisor" has tremendous implications for the nursing community as a whole.

Before 1994, the NLRB generally found that nurses weren't considered supervisors because, when they direct the work of others as an incidental aspect of providing patient care, they're acting in the interests of the patient and not of the employer. However, in *Health Care & Retirement Corporation,* the U.S. Supreme Court rejected this distinction, even though it didn't make a blanket decision as to whether nurses were supervisors. Instead, the Court found that the NLRB couldn't use this distinction to determine whether a nurse or a group of nurses worked in a supervisory role. After this case, the NLRB continued to examine each case individually, and RNs continued to organize despite disputes as to whether charge nurses (sometimes including nurses who are assigned charge duties on a rotating basis) were supervisors.

In 2001, the Supreme Court revisited the issue of nurses as supervisors in the case of *NLRB v. Kentucky River Community Care.* It rejected the NLRB's argument that nurses who direct other employees as part of their patient care duties are exercising professional judgment, and that this differs from exercising independent judgment as supervisors. However, the Court didn't specifically rule that all RNs who direct the work of others are supervisors. It left open other avenues for finding that nurses who direct the work of others aren't supervisors and, once again, the NLRB continued to evaluate each case individually. The

Court also ruled that employers and not employees have the burden of proof in demonstrating that a nurse is a supervisor.

Nurses' unions objected to the Supreme Court's decision but emphasized that it didn't eliminate nurses' rights to organize, whereas employer groups supported the decision. (See *Nurses' unions and collective bargaining,* page 116.)

In September 2006, the NLRB issued a decision involving Oakwood HealthCare, Inc. that revisited the issue of what it meant to be a "supervisor." This decision expanded the definition of "supervisory" to include such duties as work assignments, responsibility to direct, and use of independent judgment. According to this decision, workers are supervisors if they have a regular responsibility to assign an employee to a particular unit or location, to work at a certain time, or to do a significant task. Also, they would be supervisors if they were held accountable for job tasks they assigned. This decision was met with concern. According to the ANA, this decision would "effectively deprive hundreds of thousands of registered nurses and licensed practical nurses of their right to choose to impact their work environment through collective bargaining." The ANA found issue with the wide-ranging scope of key terms as defined by the NLRB.[11] In response, a bill was submitted in Congress to reverse the decision[12]. (See *The RESPECT Act,* page 117.)

Advantages and disadvantages

Union officials have targeted the hospital field as one of the last large industries ripe for organizing. Unionization continues to spark debate within the hospital setting and the nursing profession.

Union proponents argue that unionization gives nurses a strong voice in such issues as wages, benefits, and pensions. Unionization, they argue, assures fair grievance procedures and provides nurses with more influence in patient care decisions. Unionization also gives nurses more control over working conditions, such as staffing and overtime, and equalizes bargaining power between employer and employee.

Critics argue that unionization tarnishes the image of the nursing profession by shifting emphasis away from patient care to economic advancement. Many nurses are reluctant to depend on an organization for their economic and professional well-being. Some nurses fear the potential disruption of picketing and strikes. Others argue that unionization creates antagonism between nurses and their employers, preventing effective cooperation.

Considerations for joining a union

Before deciding whether to participate in collective bargaining, ask yourself these questions:

▶ Am I eligible? (A nurse who works as an employee can join a labor union; some nurses, such as managers or supervisors, may be excluded.)

▶ Can I be forced to join a union? (If eligible and the nurse works under a "union shop," she must join the union within a specified time to remain employed; if an "open shop," the nurse may choose not to join and still keep her job.)

▶ Can the hospital fire me for helping to organize a union? (Federal regulations strictly forbid such action.)

▶ Will collective bargaining help my professional and economic status?

Nurses' unions and collective bargaining

The question of whom nurses should choose as their collective bargaining representative has been a hot-button issue for years. In July 2001, the American Nurses Association (ANA) addressed this issue when it published its *Code of Ethics for Nurses with Interpretive Statements*, which addressed collective bargaining in Provision 6. It states that nurses "participate in establishing, maintaining, and improving health care environments and conditions of employment conducive to the provision of quality health care and consistent with the values of the professional through individual and collective action." It also recommends that nurses address their concerns about the health care environment through the proper channels, preferably through a professional association, such as their state nurses' association.

STATE NURSES' ASSOCIATIONS

Many registered nurses choose their ANA-affiliated state nurses' association as their collective bargaining representative because they believe that their association can best advocate for them on practice and professional issues, as well as wages and working conditions. Organizing through a state nurses' association also means that nurses are part of the ANA and, by extension, of the International Council of Nurses.

However, not all state nurses' associations have chosen to engage in collective bargaining. Reasons for this vary. Association leadership may not want the association to get involved with collective bargaining activity, or the association may not possess the expertise or resources to engage effectively in collective bargaining.

UNIONIZATION

In 1999, the ANA formed the United American Nurses (UAN), a union composed of state nurses' associations that engage in collective bargaining, those associations' labor programs, or both. The following year, UAN joined AFL-CIO, the federation to which most labor unions belong. The UAN also provides a mechanism for organizing nurses in states where the state nurses' association doesn't engage in collective bargaining

In addition to the UAN, several large unions that represent a wide range of workers in different industries have been active in organizing nurses. These include the Service Employees International Union; the American Federation of State, County, and Municipal Employees; and the American Federation of Teachers. In some instances, nurses are represented by independent unions, which operate only at one or two hospitals. There are also state-specific nursing unions. For example, the California Nurses Association and the Massachusetts Nurses Association are statewide labor unions that were affiliated with the ANA but decided to become independent.

▶ Can I address my professional concerns through collective bargaining?
▶ Can I change my working conditions as an individual, or do I need to organize with other nurses?

If one believes that organizing a union is necessary to improve the professional or economic status of the nurses in the facility, the full force of the law will protect these efforts.

Protection of the right to unionize

In the United States, regulations governing union organizing among nurses in private-sector employment come under the jurisdiction of the NLRB, the agency that enforces federal labor laws.

The NLRB protects eligible employees' rights to organize a union, join a union, or decertify a union (vote the union out), and may defend you against unfair labor practices. The NLRB also helps employ-

POLICY & POLITICS

The RESPECT Act

The Re-Empowerment of Skilled and Professional Employees and Construction Tradesworkers (RESPECT) Act was submitted to Congress to reverse the National Labor Relations Board's (NLRB's) attempt in 2006 to expand the definition of "supervisor." This bill would narrow the definition of supervisor back to what Congress had identified in 1947 with passage of the Taft-Hartley Act. This act expressly excluded supervisors from coverage under the National Labor Relations Act.

Nurses practicing within the scope of practice routinely exercise critical judgment and delegate tasks to other health care workers. However, under NLRB's broad definition, these nurses would be considered supervisors even though they did not engage in any managerial activities. Thus thousands of nurses would be unable to participate in unions and collective bargaining if they so chose. The RESPECT Act would prevent these nurses from being classified as supervisors, thus retaining their collective bargaining rights.[12]

ers by enforcing regulations that control picketing and strikes, and by providing remedies for any unfair union practices.

If a nonsupervisor decides to organize a union, the NLRB supervises procedures for elections. These procedures enforce rules that both the union and management must follow. The NLRB works to investigate unfair labor practices that may arise during the election process. (See *Recognizing unfair labor practices,* page 118.)

Unionization

To organize a collective bargaining unit at a facility, begin by contacting the state nurses' association, if it engages in collective bargaining, or the union of choice (See *The right to choose a union,* page 119.)[13]

The union will assign a union staff member to help organize the campaign. The union may support the efforts by supplying stationery, printing, legal advice, organizational guidance, and encouragement. The union can also arrange for meeting halls and publicity, and can file the proper election petitions with the NLRB.

Management's rights and limitations

During a union drive, the NLRB also protects the rights of management. Under the law, management is allowed to:
► tell you the disadvantages of belonging to a union
► explain to you your election rights, such as your right to refuse to sign an authorization card
► encourage you to vote "no" in a union election (provided they don't use threats or coercion of any kind).

However, to protect the right to organize and belong to a union, the NLRB places the following limitations on management:
► Management can't interfere with your organizing activities.
► Management can't discriminate against you for participating in union activities, for testifying against management, or for filing a grievance.
► Management can't dominate a union by gaining undue influence over it, such as by paying union expenses or giving union leaders special benefits.
► Management can't refuse to bargain in *good faith* (an honest desire to reach an agreement).

Recognizing unfair labor practices

If eligible, you have a legal right to participate in union activities. If your work involves supervising others, you may be ineligible to join the union. However, you still have some protection under Sections 7 and 8 of the National Labor Relations Act regarding the organization of a union in your facility and management's practice. If your employer infringes on that right, through interference, domination, discrimination, or refusal to bargain, you can charge unfair labor practices.

INTERFERENCE

Employers may interfere with a union election by unilaterally improving wages or benefits to encourage votes against the union. This is considered an unfair labor practice. Other unfair practices include:
* helping employees withdraw from union membership
* making coercive statements about participation in union activities
* libeling or slandering union officials
* threatening to close down the facility
* questioning employees about union activities or organizers
* spying on—or implying the possibility of spying on—union meetings
* creating an atmosphere of fear.

DOMINATION

The National Labor Relations Board (NLRB) doesn't allow management to dominate a union by paying a union's expenses, giving union leaders special benefits, or taking an active part in organizing a union.

DISCRIMINATION

Discrimination is an unfair labor practice that can involve discharging, disciplining, or threatening an employee for joining a union or for encouraging others to join. Other types of discrimination include:
* refusing to hire anyone who belongs to a union
* refusing to reinstate or promote an employee because she testified at an NLRB hearing
* enforcing rules unequally between employees who are involved in union activities and those who aren't.

REFUSAL TO BARGAIN

To weaken union participation, management may refuse to take part in collective bargaining. It's an unfair labor practice to take unilateral action to alter employment conditions that either are covered in an existing contract or are included among legally mandated areas of bargaining. Other unfair labor practices include:
* refusing to meet with a union representative
* refusing to negotiate a mandatory issue
* demanding to negotiate a voluntary issue.

▶ Management must assume responsibility for any unfair labor practice committed by a supervisor. (See *The NLRB: Protecting your right to organize a union,* page 120.)

Union's rights and limitations

Neither management nor the union can interfere with an individual's rights as guaranteed by federal or state law. Federal laws that help protect employee rights include the Fair Labor Standards Act, the Civil Rights Act, and the Age Discrimination in Employment Act. States also enact protective legislation, such as so-called whistle-blower statutes, equal employment opportunity acts, and public employee collective bargaining laws.

However, just like management, the union must also comply with certain limitations. The NLRB ensures that the union:
▶ bargains in good faith

POLICY & **POLITICS**

The right to choose a union

According to United American Nurses (UAN), AFL-CIO, nurses experience harassment, coercion, and intimidation, with the possibility of termination when they attempt to form a union. As a result, the UAN supports the Employee Free Choice Act, reintroduced by Senator Edward Kennedy of Massachusetts and Representative George Miller of California. This act is designed to allow workers to unionize freely without the threat of barriers from their employers. Key aspects of this legislation include:

• development of a simple, fair, and direct method to form a union such that when a majority of employees (50% + 1) sign authorization cards, a petition can be filed with the National Labor Relations Board for investigation
• provision of monetary payment, three times the amount of actual back pay, if an employee is terminated during the time the union is being organized or during first-contract negotiations
• establishment of set time limits for bargaining a first contract.

Source: United American Nurses, AFL-CIO. *Legislative Issue Brief: The Employee Free Act (H.R.800/S. 1041)— Legislation to Protect Americans' Right to Choose a Union.* Silver Spring, Md.: United American Nurses, 2007. Available at http://www.uannurse.org/legislative/pdfs/EFCA110Congress.pdf.

▶ assumes responsibility for any unfair labor practice committed by union officials
▶ doesn't threaten or force a person to support the union
▶ doesn't demand that the employer do business only with companies that have unions.

Union election

In the initial step toward a union election, eligible nurses or union representatives distribute authorization cards. Nurses who want a union election sign an authorization card. In the United States, if at least 30% of eligible nurses sign the cards, the nurses or the union can ask the NLRB to authorize and supervise an election. If 50% or more of eligible nurses sign the cards, U.S. law allows the employer to forgo the election process and simply recognize the union, but this rarely occurs. In Canada, more than 50% of nurses must sign the cards to authorize an election. (See *What hap-*

pens when nurses decide to unionize, page 121.)

Union and management may disagree about which nurses are eligible to vote. Either side can challenge a nurse's eligibility. In the United States, the NLRB will settle an eligibility dispute by reviewing the individual nurse's job description, her duties and responsibilities, and her supervisory functions, if any.

To win the election, the union must get a majority of the votes of those nurses who actually voted, not those who are eligible to vote.

In some cases, more than one union may be on the ballot. This can happen when, after the first petitioning, the union demonstrates that 30% or more of the eligible nurses want an election. If this occurs, other unions can get on the ballot provided they can obtain a show of interest from 10% of the nurse-employees.

If elected, the union will negotiate a contract addressing mutually agreeable wages, benefits, and work rules and oth-

The NLRB: Protecting your right to organize a union

If your hospital punishes you solely because you're involved in organizing a union, the National Labor Relations Board (NLRB) will protect you. This board enforces the National Labor Relations Act, the federal labor laws that explicitly set forth your rights to form and join a union.

AN EXAMPLE

Suppose you're working as a hospital pediatrics nurse, and you support unionization of the hospital's nurses. Union organizers ask you to distribute prounion pamphlets to your colleagues. You begin giving out pamphlets in the nurses' lounge, but a hospital administrator orders you to stop. He says the hospital solicitation policy prohibits anyone from distributing literature inside the hospital. You remind him that the hospital has allowed nurses to distribute other information, such as literature to solicit volunteers for the local cancer society. You ignore the administrator's order and resume handing out pamphlets. You are suspended or intimidated by management staff.

You file an unfair labor practice charge with the NLRB. After a hearing, the board concludes that the hospital can't prevent you from distributing the pamphlets on your own time in a nonwork area. The board also concludes that the hospital was discriminatory in applying the nonsolicitation policy.

A LIKELY RULING

In this situation, the board would most likely order the hospital to reinstate you, pay your back wages, and refrain from punishing you or any other nurse who was active in the union drive.

When making a commitment to a unionization drive, be prepared to continue to nurture good relations with supervisors and coworkers who oppose the union. Keep in mind that, regardless of the election's outcome, everyone will need to continue to work together. If the union wins, both management and labor will have to adjust to new rules spelled out in the contract. If the union loses, management should optimally correct the problems that led to the organizing campaign; otherwise, the same problems will resurface.

● COLLECTIVE BARGAINING

In collective bargaining, the employer and the employees' representatives meet to confer about employment issues and put their agreements into writing. According to the NLRB, two or more people who share employment interests and conditions may constitute a bargaining unit.

Agency roles

In the United States, the laws governing collective bargaining are outlined in the NLRA and the Labor Management Relations Act (LMRA), also known as the *Taft-Hartley Act*. The NLRB is the federal agency authorized to administer and enforce these laws. (See *Appealing to the NLRB*, page 122.)

NLRB

The NLRB's responsibilities include determining appropriate bargaining units for employee groups, resolving disputes between labor and management, and conducting elections for employee bargaining representatives. The NLRB won't

er professional issues. The contract will be devised by the negotiators and ratified by members of the bargaining unit.

What happens when nurses decide to unionize

The decision to unionize initiates a step-by-step process. First, organizers distribute leaflets and authorization cards. At least 30% of all proposed union employees must sign those cards to authorize a union election.

STEPS IN THE ELECTION PROCESS

After the employees sign the authorization cards, the following occurs:

1. The union notifies the National Labor Relations Board (NLRB), and an NLRB representative steps in to referee and organize the election.
2. The NLRB holds a hearing to decide who's eligible to join the bargaining unit. The employer may challenge any employee's eligibility. For example, the employer may argue that one or more employees are supervisors and are therefore ineligible.
3. The NLRB determines the place and election date. The employer and the union can then begin campaigning.
4. Within 7 days of the NLRB announcement of the election date and place, the employer provides the NLRB the names and addresses of all eligible employees. The NLRB gives this list to the union.
5. On election day, employees vote by secret ballot to accept or reject the union. If more than one union is on the ballot, employees can select one of the unions or vote for no representation at all.
6. The NLRB representative tallies the votes. The results depend on the majority of ballots cast, regardless of the percentage of eligible employees who actually vote. (If only a minority of eligible employees vote, those few employees will decide the question of unionization for all.)

THE OUTCOME

If most of the voting employees choose the union, that union is legally required to represent all eligible employees, even those who didn't vote. The NLRB will certify the union as the employees' collective bargaining representative.

If most of the voting employees reject the union, the law prohibits another election involving a union for 1 year.

---

assert jurisdiction over labor laws for minimum wages, overtime pay, termination, or discrimination unless those issues have been written into the employees' labor contract and the contract doesn't provide for binding arbitration of alleged violations. If arbitration is provided for, the NLRB usually declines its jurisdiction and defers to the arbitrator.

Along with rule making, the NLRB also resolves disputes by interpreting provisions of the LMRA. The NLRB hears cases on the supervisor's role and the employee's right to solicit new members or picket. The NLRB also determines whether labor or management has committed unfair acts during a campaign or the term of a contract. For example, in *NLRB v. Baptist Hospital (1979),* the NLRB upheld its rule against soliciting new members in upper-floor hospital halls and sitting rooms near patients, but upheld the employees' right to talk about the union in first-floor lobbies and other areas away from patients. If a hospital or bargaining unit disagrees with an NLRB decision, either can appeal in a federal appellate court.

Canadian labor relations

In Canada, the provincial or territorial labor relations boards handle local labor

Appealing to the NLRB

If you feel that management is engaging in unfair labor practices, begin by telling your union representative. If she believes your charges are valid, either you or the union can appeal to the National Labor Relations Board (NLRB.)

NLRB RESPONSE
The board will ask you for a sworn statement concerning the dates and times of the alleged events, the names and positions of management staff involved, and the names and addresses of other employee witnesses. Your statement will serve as a legal affidavit that will supply the NLRB with the information it needs to carry out an investigation.

Should the NLRB investigate and find that management is engaging in unfair labor practices, it will issue a formal complaint against your employer. The employer may appeal the NLRB's complaint, but if the court upholds it, the employer must comply with the NLRB's penalty, usually reinstating employees, issuing back pay, or restoring other benefits.

AN EXAMPLE
While nurses at Good Faith Hospital were organizing a union campaign, supervisors asked them for the names of nurses who attended meetings the organizers sponsored. Also, one supervisor suggested to her staff that if a nurses' union was organized, the union might try to force management to increase wages, which because of the hospital's precarious financial position, could result in layoffs. Several nurses complained about the supervisor's remarks at a subsequent union meeting. The union organizers agreed that management was interfering with union organization—an unfair labor practice—and consequently filed a complaint against the employer with the NLRB.

issues, and the Canada Labour Relations Board deals with labor issues at the federal level, as in the case of military hospitals. Canada's courts are unlikely to interfere with a provincial labor relations board decision unless that board acted outside its jurisdiction or violated common law.

Bargaining
Bargaining units usually represent different groups of workers in the same hospital. The NLRA empowers the NLRB to decide what's an appropriate bargaining unit. This gives the NLRB considerable power. It's much easier to unionize employees if there's a bargaining unit for each kind of job classification; employees in each bargaining unit typically have more shared interests.

In 1987, the NLRB issued rules permitting eight bargaining units for acute-care hospitals. Since its establishment in 1935, this was the first time the NLRB had drafted rules defining permissible bargaining units for an entire industry. These bargaining units include:
▶ RNs in nonsupervisory positions
▶ physicians
▶ professionals other than RNs and physicians
▶ technical employees
▶ skilled maintenance employees
▶ business office clerical employees
▶ guards
▶ all other nonprofessional employees.

In response to these 1987 rules, the American Hospital Association (AHA) filed suit. In *AHA v. NLRB (1991)*, the AHA claimed that the NLRB rules were illegal, arguing that the Taft-Hartley Act requires determination of appropriate bargaining units in each individual hospital.

The U.S. Supreme Court unanimously rejected the AHA's interpretation and ruled that the NLRB has the power to promulgate rules for all hospitals, not just on a hospital-by-hospital basis. This ruling made it easier for unions to organize nurses and was considered a blow to management's efforts to resist.

Mandatory bargaining issues

The NLRB has interpreted the *mandatory bargaining issues* (issues an employer must address during bargaining) broadly to include wages and hours; seniority; leaves of absence; work schedules and assignments; benefits; promotion and layoff policies; grievance and discipline procedures; and breaks, holidays, and vacations. (See *Perils of not bargaining.*)

Voluntary issues

Bargaining on other issues may occur if both parties voluntarily agree. The NLRB considers voluntary bargaining issues to include all other possible legal employment issues. It excludes illegal issues, such as requiring new employees to join a union in less than 30 days, or job discrimination. Because nurses can't force an employer to bargain over voluntary issues, negotiating or not negotiating with the employer usually depends on how committed nurses are to their professional concerns and on management's willingness to be flexible.

Negotiations

Before bargaining begins, union negotiators should prepare for the procedure by understanding the beliefs and attitudes of the people they represent and developing a system of communication between negotiators and the bargaining unit. They should also consider in advance how management might respond to various issues.

Perils of not bargaining

A hospital can't avoid collective bargaining by refusing to recognize its nurses' union. The law, strengthened by court decisions, requires a hospital to bargain in good faith with duly elected unions. A key court case, *Eastern Maine Medical Center v. NLRB (1981)*, illustrates this principle.

AN ANTIUNION STAND

Nurses at Eastern Maine Medical Center voted 114 to 110 to be represented by the Maine State Nurses Association, the state's largest nurses' union. In response, the hospital administration adopted a strong antiunion stand, refusing to meet with the nurses for collective bargaining talks. Moreover, the administration gave substantial wage-and-benefit increases to nonunion employees and withheld the increases from the unionized nurses.

The administration's policy of not bargaining with the union made the union nurses bitter and frustrated. The union filed unfair labor practice charges against the hospital administration.

NLRB RULING

The National Labor Relations Board (NLRB) concluded that the hospital had violated the National Labor Relations Act by refusing to bargain in good faith and by discriminating against the unionized nurses. The board directed the hospital administration to negotiate with the union and to pay the wage-and-benefit increases withheld from members of the bargaining unit.

APPEALS COURT RULING

In upholding the actions of the NLRB, an appeals court ruled that the hospital's refusal to negotiate violated the nurses' collective bargaining rights.

The actual bargaining involves good-faith negotiations (an honest desire to reach an agreement) between the union's and the management's negotiating teams. Proposals may be exchanged for study before the first session. Each proposal and counterproposal is discussed, and disagreements are debated in detail, sometimes with teams taking time-outs to privately reconsider positions. When disagreements persist and outside mediation fails, the union members may decide to strike. If all issues are resolved, however, the written agreement is taken to the union members with a recommendation that they ratify the terms.

Decision to strike

Collective bargaining doesn't guarantee that the bargaining parties will reach an agreement. If the parties arrive at a stalemate, employees may decide to strike in hopes of forcing the employer to make concessions. A strike decision is an extreme measure, so labor laws have established provisions that require any curtailment of services to be orderly.

In the United States, negotiating parties must follow this timetable—and series of steps—before a strike can be called:

▶ The side wanting to modify or terminate the contract must notify the other side 90 days before the contract expires (or labor or management proposes that changes take place).

▶ If, 30 days later, the two sides don't agree, they must notify the Federal Mediation and Conciliation Service (FMCS) and the corresponding state agency of the dispute.

▶ Within 30 days, the FMCS will appoint a mediator and, in rare cases, an inquiry board. Within 15 days, the mediator or inquiry board will give both sides its recommendations.

▶ If, after 15 more days, the parties don't agree, the employees may plan to strike. If the union didn't have employees vote earlier, a vote will be held to decide whether to send a strike notice.

▶ If most employees vote to send a strike notice, the union must send management the strike notice at least 10 days before the scheduled strike, specifying the exact date, time, and place of the strike. The strike can't be scheduled before the contract expires.

In most cases, union and management representatives, with the assistance of a mediator, schedule additional negotiations during this period. A strike vote is held before the walkout is scheduled to begin.

Note that, in many states, public sector employees are prohibited from striking. If an impasse occurs, labor and management must resolve their differences through binding arbitration.

Some Canadian jurisdictions prohibit health care employees from striking. In these jurisdictions, compulsory arbitration is imposed when employees and employer fail to reach an agreement. The arbitrator can then draft and impose contract terms.

Wildcat strikes

Employees who ignore the strike provisions and engage in illegal strikes lose the protection of the NLRA. They may be discharged by their employer. Unions that sanction or encourage illegal strikes may have their certification revoked by the NLRB.

Strike delay

Employees may delay a strike for up to 72 hours if they feel the extra time would enable them to come to terms with management.

To delay the strike, they must give management written notice at least 12 hours before the time the strike was scheduled to start. If the initial strike date passes during the negotiations, the union must issue another 10-day strike notice. If the contract expires during the negotiations, the employer and employees remain bound by the contract.

GRIEVANCES

When an employee's dispute isn't resolved, tempers flare, morale declines, and apparent injustices smolder. That's why union and management officials give grievance and arbitration procedures high priority when they negotiate collective bargaining agreements. Even if your workplace isn't unionized, understanding these procedures can help you create fair work rules and grievance procedures in your workplace.

When unionized employees and management sign a labor contract, they agree to abide by certain rules and policies. A contract can't cite every potential dispute, so it includes grievance procedures—specific steps that both sides agree to follow. Usually, the process moves from discussions to formal hearings and written statements of times, dates, details, and even witnesses. If the matter can't be resolved, the aggrieved party requests arbitration.

Types of grievances

The definition of *grievance* depends on the contract. Some contracts define the term as any complaint that reflects dissatisfaction with union or management policies. However, most contracts define it as a complaint that involves contract violations.

A nurse or union representative can file a grievance against an employer. A union can file a grievance against management. Management can file a grievance, usually called a disciplinary action, against any employee. Most grievances are filed against management because of management's decision-making role.

Differentiation from gripes

Smooth labor relations require both sides to honor the contract's terms and to show good faith in using the grievance procedures. Both parties need to know when to compromise and when to retreat on a disputed issue.

Union representatives must typically defuse complaints before they become formal grievances. An effective union representative can distinguish between a legitimate grievance and a gripe. A grievance is a substantive complaint that involves a contract violation; a gripe is a personal problem unrelated to the contract.

Sometimes union or management representatives pursue a groundless grievance (that is, a gripe) for political or harassment purposes. A nurse's self-interest or her resentment of authority can lead to a groundless grievance. So can a supervisor's poor decision or misuse of her authority.

Legitimate grievances

Most grievances fall into one of two classifications:

▶ unfair labor practices
▶ violations of a contract, a precedent, or a past practice. (See *Legitimate grievances.*)

Unfair labor practices are tactics prohibited by state and federal labor laws. For example, under federal law, an employer who discriminates against you because you're involved in union activities commits an unfair labor practice. Violations of a contract, precedent, or past practice are actions that break mutually accepted work rules. For example, suppose a contract says a supervisor must give a nurse 2 weeks' notice before making her rotate to another shift. If a supervisor assigns the nurse to another shift without giving notice, the nurse can file a grievance.

Common grievances

Grievances can involve an almost infinite number of complaints, but some are more common than others. Management usually takes disciplinary action against employees who:

▶ allow personal problems to interfere with their jobs
▶ fail to perform their assigned duties
▶ show poor work habits, such as tardiness or unreliability
▶ take an antagonistic attitude toward management in labor relations when serving in union positions.

Employees commonly file grievances against supervisors who dispense discipline inconsistently, show favoritism, or treat employees unfairly. Other common sources of grievances include management's selection policies for promotions, favored shift assignments, disciplinary actions, and merit salary raises. Staff nurses sometimes file grievances when they're temporarily assigned nurse-manager responsibilities without getting commensurate pay.

Many grievances result from unwitting contract violations (such as poorly thought-out workload decisions) by first-level or midlevel managers. Personnel and labor relations departments can resolve many actions that would otherwise lead to grievances by answering labor questions and offering advice.

Grievance procedures

The elements of a grievance procedure vary from contract to contract. Key elements always include:

▶ reasonable time limits for filing a grievance and making a decision
▶ procedures to appeal a grievance to higher union-management levels if the grievance is unresolved
▶ assigning priority to crucial grievances (such as worker suspensions or dismissals)
▶ an opportunity for both sides to investigate the complaint.

The first step is usually an informal discussion between the nurse and her supervisor. The nurse may then submit her complaint in writing. If the supervisor doesn't or can't resolve the grievance, the nurse can ask for a union representative, or *steward*, to assist her. The representative will meet with the supervisor to discuss the grievance's merits. If the supervisor stands firm, the nurse can then file a written complaint within a contract-specified time period. Subsequent hearings move to higher levels of management. The number of steps in a grievance procedure varies with each contract's provisions.

Legitimate grievances

Not all complaints against an employer meet the definition of a "legitimate grievance." If your complaint fits into one of the following categories, chances are it's a legitimate grievance upon which your union can act.

CONTRACT VIOLATIONS

Your employment contract is binding between you and your employer. If your employer violates it, you have a valid grievance. The following examples describe violations that would likely be prohibited by an employment contract:
• You're performing the charge nurse's job 2 to 3 days per week but still receiving the same pay as other staff nurses.
• You've had to work undesirable shifts or on Sundays more often than other nurses.
• Your supervisor doesn't post time schedules in advance.
• Your employer fires you without just cause.

FEDERAL AND STATE LAW VIOLATIONS

An action by your employer that violates a federal or state law would be the basis of a grievance, even if the employment contract permits the action. For example:
• You receive less pay for performing the same work as a male nurse.
• You don't receive the overtime pay to which you're entitled.
• Your employer doesn't promote you because of your race.

PAST PRACTICE VIOLATIONS

A past practice—one that has been accepted by both parties for an extended time but that's suddenly stopped by the employer without notification—may be the basis for a grievance. The past practice need not be specified in the contract. If the practice violates the contract, either party can demand that the contract be enforced. If the practice is unsafe, an arbitrator may simply abolish it. Examples of past practice violations might include:
• Your employer charges you for breaking equipment when others haven't been charged.
• Your employer revokes parking lot privileges.
• Your employer eliminates a rotation system for float assignments.

HEALTH AND SAFETY VIOLATIONS

Grievances pertaining to health and safety violations usually involve working conditions for which the employer is responsible. Legitimate grievances may be recognized even if the contract doesn't address the specific complaint. For example:
• You're required to hold patients during X-rays.
• You have no hand-washing facilities near patient rooms.

EMPLOYER POLICY VIOLATIONS

Employers have the right to establish *reasonable* work rules and policies. These rules and policies aren't usually specified in the employment contract. Your employer can't violate its own rules without being guilty of a grievance. (Note, however, that an employer can change rules unilaterally.) For example:
• You haven't received a performance evaluation in 2 years, though your employee handbook states that such evaluations will be done annually.
• Your employer assigns you a vacation period without your consent, contrary to personnel policies.

Arbitration

When neither side can work out a settlement on a substantive issue, arbitration is indicated. During arbitration, the parties present evidence to a neutral labor relations expert. Parties who have negotiated a collective bargaining agreement or are covered by one with an arbitration clause are required to arbitrate contract disputes. Parties with no bargaining agreement (nonunionized) may agree to independent arbitration, hoping to resolve a matter short of litigation or termination of the relationship.

The side requesting arbitration gives a written notice to the other party. The requesting party then contacts one of several national agencies that supply arbitrators, such as the FMCS or the American Arbitration Association. Both sides must agree on a specific arbitrator; the date, time, and place of the hearing; and the finality of the arbitrator's decision.

Arbitration hearing

An arbitration hearing resembles a courtroom proceeding, except that it's less formal. The party requesting arbitration has the burden of proof and must present evidence that the contract has been violated. (However, when a nurse challenges disciplinary action, management must prove its case first by presenting supporting evidence.) In an arbitration hearing, both sides may call and cross-examine witnesses. The requesting side makes a closing summary, followed by one from the opposing side. Each side can submit written briefs instead of making summary statements.

The arbitrator usually renders a written decision weeks or even months after the hearing. If both sides request an immediate response, the arbitrator can issue an oral decision and withhold a written explanation of the decision unless both parties request it.

In most cases, both sides prefer arbitration to a lengthy court fight because arbitration is speedier and less expensive, and may be conducted without attorneys. When a dispute goes to arbitration, both sides lose control of the outcome because, in the United States, the arbitrator's decision is binding. Although the losing party can challenge the decision in court, the court rarely overturns an arbitrator's decision.

In Canada, arbitrators' decisions are binding, and courts don't interfere with decisions unless there's a question of jurisdiction or the decision is patently unreasonable.

Resolution of unfair labor practices

Most grievances arising from contract violations follow contract-stipulated grievance and arbitration procedures. The NLRB addresses allegations of unfair labor practices. If a nurse who isn't a member of a collective bargaining unit brings an allegation to the NLRB, the NLRB must determine if she's engaged in concerted action—that is, if her action is part of (or in concert with) a group effort. The NLRB will conduct a hearing to review evidence and then issue a decision. Either side can challenge an NLRB decision in court.

If a nurse has a complaint involving discrimination on the basis of race, religion, national origin, age, disability, or sex, she can file a charge of discrimination with the U.S. Equal Employment Opportunity Commission (EEOC) or a comparable state agency in addition to filing a grievance.

The EEOC handles violations of:
▶ the Equal Pay Act of 1963, which forbids wage discrimination based on an employee's sex
▶ the Civil Rights Act of 1964, which forbids job and wage discrimination based on an employee's religion, race, sex, or ethnic background
▶ the Age Discrimination in Employment Act of 1967, which forbids discrimination based on an employee's age

▶ the Americans with Disabilities Act of 1990, which states that "no individual shall be discriminated against on the basis of disability in the full and equal enjoyment of the goods, services, facilities, privileges, advantages, or accommodations of any place of public accommodation...."

The EEOC will also prosecute disputes involving sexual harassment. Employees don't have to be union members to file a complaint with the EEOC.

Disciplinary hearings

A disciplinary hearing can be initiated by the complaint of an employer or a patient. The hearing may be based on allegations of incompetence or alleged violation of state law pertaining to nursing practice.

If you're ever served with notice that a state's licensing board is investigating you, seek legal counsel, plus emotional and professional support. Don't approach these proceedings lightly or unprepared. The hearing process and the outcome can have a major impact on your view of yourself, nursing practice and the profession.

Before the hearing, do homework, be aware of recent state laws, muster witnesses and evidence, and be prepared to stand up for your rights and nursing license. Learn everything possible from the experience. Finally, be prepared to support colleagues who may also go through a disciplinary hearing.

REFERENCES

1. American Nurses Association. *Nurses' Bill of Rights.* Silver Spring, Md.: American Nurses Association, 2001. Available at *www.nursingworld.org/ MainMenuCategories/ThePracticeofProf essionalNursing/workplace/Rightsof Nurses/BillofRights.aspx.*
2. American Nurses Association. *Health Care Worker Safety. Nursing's Legislative and Regulatory Initiatives for the 110th Congress: Workplace Health and Safety.* Silver Spring, Md.: American Nurses Association, 2007. Available at *www.nursingworld.org/MainMenu Categories/ThePracticeofProfessional Nursing/workplace/workersafety.aspx.*
3. United American Nurses, AFL-CIO. *Legislative Issue Brief H.R. 378 – Safe Patient Handling Legislation.* Available at *http://uannurse.org/legislative/pdfs/ Conyers_Safe_Patient_Handling_Issue_ Brief_110_Congress.pdf.*
4. Institute of Medicine. *Keeping Patients Safe: Transforming the Work Environment of Nurses.* Washington, D.C.: National Academies Press, 2004.
5. Trinkoff, A., et al. "How Long and How Much are Nurses Working Now?" *AJN* 106(4):60-71, April 2006.
6. American Nurses Association. *Acute Care Staffing: Mandatory Overtime. Nursing's Legislative and Regulatory Initiatives for the 110th Congress: Workplace Health and Safety.* Silver Spring, Md.: American Nurses Association, 2007. Available at *www.nursingworld.org/MainMenuCateg ories/ThePracticeofProfessionalNursing/ workplace/workforce/ShortageStaffing/ Staffing/Appropriatestaffing.aspx.*
7. United American Nurses, AFL-CIO. *Legislative Summary. The Safe Nurse Staffing for Patient Safety and Quality Care Act of 2007 (H.R. 2123),* 2007. Available at *www.uannurse.org/ legislative/pdfs/RNratioIssueBrief110 Congress.pdf.*
8. United American Nurses, AFL-CIO. *Legislative Issue Brief. Safe Nursing and Patient Care Act (H.R. 2122). Legislation to Strictly Limit Mandatory Overtime,* 2007. Available at *www. uannurse.org/legislative/pfs/MoT100th Congress.pdf.*

9. American Nurses Association. *Facts about needlestick injury.* Silver Spring, Md.: American Nurses Association, 2007, Available at *www.nursingworld. org/MainMenuCategories/Occupationala ndEnvironmental/occupationalhealth/Saf eNeedles/NeedlestickInjuryFacts.aspx.*

10. American Nurses Association. *Whistle-blower Protection.* Silver Spring, Md.: American Nurses Association, 2007. Available at *www.nursingworld.org/ MainMenuCategories/ANAPoliticalPow er/State/StateLegislativeAgenda/whistle-blower_1.aspx.*

11. American Nurses Association. *ANA Rejects NLRB Decision to Block Nurses' Freedom to Unionize.* Silver Spring, Md.: American Nurses Association, 2006. Available at *www.nursingworld.org/ FunctionalMenuCategories/MediaResour ces/PressRelease/2006/PR1003068567. aspx.*

12. American Nurses Association. *ANA Statement on H.R. 1644/S. 969: The Re-Empowerment of Skilled and Profes-sional Employees and Construction Tradeworkers (RESPECT) Act.* Silver Spring, Md.: American Nurses Association, 2007. Available at *http://www.nursingworld.org/MainMenu Categories/ThePracticeofProfessional Nursing/workplace/RightsofNurses/The RESPECTAct/ReEmpowermentofSkilled andProfessionalEmployees_1.aspx.*

13. United American Nurses, AFL-CIO. *Legislative Issue Brief: The Employee Free Act (H.R. 800/S. 1041)—Legis-lation to Protect Americans' Right to Choose a Union.* Silver Spring, Md.: American Nurses Association, 2007. Available at *www.uannurse.org/ legislative/pdfs/EFCA110Congress.pdf.*

ADDITIONAL RESOURCES

Johnson, C.L. "Stopping Verbal Abuse in the Workplace," *AJN* 107(4):32-34, April 2007.

Welton, J.M. "Occupational Mix Adjustment: A Risky Plan," *AJN* 107(7):70-72, July 2007.

Welton, J.M. "Paying for Nursing Care in Hospitals," *AJN* 106(11):67-69, November 2006.

4

Lawsuits and the legal process

No legal issue sparks as much anxiety among nurses as malpractice, which can be emotionally harrowing and financially devastating. Unfortunately, more nurses are being named in lawsuits, and this trend shows no sign of changing. Several reasons for this phenomenon exist:

▶ With easier access to the internet, patients are more knowledgeable about health care, and their expectations are higher.

▶ The health care system relies more on nurses and providers than on physicians to help contain costs.

▶ Nurses are more autonomous in their practice.

▶ The courts are expanding the definition of liability, holding all types of medical professionals to higher standards of accountability.

Losing a malpractice lawsuit can jeopardize one's nursing career. Prospective employers and insurance companies will ask a prospective employee if she has been found liable for nursing malpractice, been named a defendant in a lawsuit, or been disciplined by the state's board of nursing. If the individual answers "yes" to any of these queries, she may find job hunting more difficult or have an extended probation period or restrictions placed on her nursing practice. The National Practitioner Data Bank (NPDB) provides prospective employers with such information. The NPDB is a "resource to assist State licensing boards, hospitals, and other health care entities in conducting investigations of the qualifications of the health care practitioners they seek to license or hire, or to whom they wish to grant membership or clinical privileges."[1] (See *National Practitioner Data Bank,* pages 132 and 133.) Also, one's insurance company may refuse to renew professional liability coverage. Other insurance carriers may refuse to insure the individual or require that person to pay higher premiums for coverage.

Fortunately, nurses can take steps to help limit their risk of malpractice litigation. The best protection against malpractice litigation is giving patients the best possible nursing care, according to the highest professional standards. To do this, nurses must be familiar with and follow the standards of care that apply to the specific area of nursing, as well as state and federal regulations, accreditation standards promulgated by The Joint

National Practitioner Data Bank

In 1990, the National Practitioner Data Bank (NPDB) began operation. As a result, physicians, dentists, nurses, and other health care practitioners who are forced to pay malpractice judgments are going to have a much harder time concealing their professional histories from potential employers. The data bank, which stores malpractice data on a nationwide scale, was created under the Health Care Quality Improvement Act of 1986 and the Medicare and Medicaid Patient and Program Protection Act of 1987.

REPORTING REQUIREMENTS

The NPDB collects information about practitioners who have paid judgments, entered into settlements, or have adverse action against their license or privileges to practice. All hospitals and health care facilities, professional health care societies, state licensure boards, and insurance companies are now required to report the following information about nurses to the data bank:
- a nurse's malpractice payments (including judgments, arbitration decisions, and out-of-court settlements)
- actions taken against a nurse's clinical privileges
- adverse licensure actions, including revocations, suspensions, reprimands, censure, or probation.

Failure to report a nurse's malpractice payment of any amount—no matter how small—carries a $10,000 fine. However, the filing of a suit isn't, by itself, reportable; only the making of a payment is. Adverse clinical privilege actions against nurses may be reported at the discretion of the reviewing health care agency.

FEDERAL AGENCIES

Under the law, federal agencies aren't required to report to the NPDB. However, the Department of Defense, the Drug Enforcement Administration, and the Department of Health and Human Services have voluntarily agreed to observe the regulations.

AVAILABILITY OF INFORMATION

The information in the data bank isn't available to the general public, nor is it available to attorneys, except in a specific context. If a practitioner is sued and it's determined that the employer

Commission or the Community Health Accreditation Program, standards adapted by the American Nurses Association (ANA), standards of clinical specialty nursing organizations, and policies set forth by the employer.

Becoming familiar with malpractice law provides another means of protection. This chapter describes malpractice law, defines key legal terms, and explains legal doctrines that may be used as a defense during a malpractice lawsuit. It also provides extensive information on steps to take to avoid malpractice suits and important considerations for professional liability insurance.

MALPRACTICE LAW

Our legal system's view of malpractice evolved from the premise that each person is responsible, or *liable,* for the consequences of his actions. Malpractice law deals with a professional's liability for negligent acts, omissions, and intentional harms. (See *Understanding tort law,* pages 134 and 135.)

didn't check the data bank, the attorney can send verification that the employing institution didn't check, along with the pending charges. If a similar case is in the data bank, notification will be sent. State licensing boards, hospitals, professional societies, and health care facilities involved in peer review may access the data bank. Individual nurses have access to records that pertain to themselves.

All hospitals must check the data bank when a nurse applies for clinical privileges. The hospital must request information on the nurse again every 2 years. The courts will presume that the hospital is aware of any information the data bank contains on any nurse or other practitioner in its employ. If knowledge of the information contained in the data bank would have resulted in denial of clinical privileges, the hospital could be held vicariously liable in a malpractice lawsuit for the nurse's negligence, as well as for negligence in hiring the nurse.

INFORMATION IN THE DATA BANK
Reports made to the data bank typically include:
- the nurse's full name, home address, date of birth, professional schools attended and graduation dates, place of employment, Social Security number, and license number and state
- name, title, and phone number of the official submitting the report
- relationship of the reporting official to the practitioner
- dates of judgment or settlement or amount paid
- description of judgment, settlement, or action.

DISPUTING A REPORT
If a report about you is submitted to the data bank, you'll receive a copy for your review. If you believe the report is in error, ask the official submitting the report to correct it. The official making the report must submit corrections to the data bank.

If you fail to get satisfaction from the reporting official, you'll have to follow a detailed procedure for disputing the report. This must be done within 60 days of the initial processing of the report. Ultimately, you may request review from the Secretary of Health and Human Services.

CASE LAW

Case law, or *judicial precedent,* may set a standard of care in nursing or may impact the outcome of a specific malpractice case. Case law arises when a lawsuit has gone to trial and someone, either the plaintiff or defendant, has been unhappy with the verdict and filed an appeal. After the appeals court has rendered a decision about the issues raised in the appeal, the written decision of the court is published and becomes case law.

Generally, the case law that applies to an individual nurse's practice is the case law for the state in which she practices and any applicable federal case law. A seminal case from another state may also establish a standard of care because of the national acceptance of its ruling.

Hospital and corporate liability
Employers have the overall responsibility and liability for the actions of their employees under the doctrine of vicarious liability or *respondeat superior.* This means that an employer may be responsible for an employee's actions, even if that employee wasn't following its policies and procedures.

Understanding tort law

Most lawsuits against nurses fall into the tort category. If you're ever a defendant in a lawsuit, understanding the distinctions in this broad category may prove especially important.

A tort is a civil wrong or injury resulting from a breach of a legal duty that exists by virtue of society's expectations regarding interpersonal conduct or by the assumption of a duty inherent in a professional relationship (as opposed to a legal duty that exists by virtue of a contractual relationship). More generally, you may define a *tort* as "any action or omission that harms somebody." Malpractice refers to a tort committed by a professional acting in his professional capacity.

UNINTENTIONAL VS. INTENTIONAL TORTS

The law broadly divides torts into two categories: unintentional and intentional. An *unin-*

tentional tort is a civil wrong resulting from the defendant's negligence. If someone sues you for negligence, he must prove four things in order to win:
* You owed him a specific duty. (In nursing malpractice cases, this duty is equivalent to the standard of care.)
* You breached this duty.
* The plaintiff was harmed. (The harm can be physical, mental, emotional, or financial.)
* Your breach of duty caused the harm.

An *intentional tort* is a deliberate invasion of someone's legal right. In a malpractice case involving an intentional tort, the plaintiff doesn't need to prove that you owed him a duty. The duty at issue (for example, not to touch people without their permission) is defined by law, and you're presumed to owe him this duty. The plaintiff must still prove that you breached this duty and that this breach caused him harm.

TORT CLAIM	ACTIONS THAT LEAD TO CLAIM
Unintentional tort	
Negligence	• Leaving foreign objects inside a patient after surgery • Failing to observe a patient as the physician ordered • Failing to obtain informed consent before a treatment or procedure • Failing to report a change in a patient's vital signs or status • Failing to report a staff member's negligence that you witnessed • Failing to provide for a patient's safety • Failing to provide the patient with appropriate teaching before discharge
Intentional tort	
Assault	• Threatening a patient
Battery	• Assisting in nonemergency surgery performed without the consent of the patient • Forcing a patient to ambulate against his wishes • Forcing a patient to submit to injections • Striking a patient • Inappropriately restraining a patient
False imprisonment	• Confining a patient in a psychiatric unit without a physician's order • Refusing to let a patient return home

Understanding tort law *(continued)*

TORT CLAIM	ACTIONS THAT LEAD TO CLAIM
Intentional tort (continued)	
Invasion of privacy	• Releasing private information about a patient to third parties • Allowing unauthorized persons to read a patient's medical records • Allowing unauthorized persons to observe a procedure • Taking pictures of the patient without his consent
Slander reputation	• Making false statements about a patient to a third person, which causes damage to the patient's reputation

Because of the potential for corporate liability, health care facilities and agencies must be especially diligent in their hiring processes. They have to verify identity, training (including certificates, diplomas, transcripts, and licensure), and references, and they have to perform a background check (with the applicant's permission). Employers also have to thoroughly interview applicants, test basic nursing skills that are applicable to the open position, and check driving records. Then they must make sure that their findings are properly documented.

Physician liability
A nurse is responsible for following the nursing process in the care and treatment of patients and for recognizing deviations from the standard of care. Furthermore, as a patient advocate, a nurse is expected to question the appropriateness of every order received. For orders that a nurse knows to be potentially detrimental to a patient, the nurse must question the order, seek alternative treatment, and seek advice or intervention from the nursing supervisor, in addition to documenting the actions taken. For example, if a physician orders a drug that a patient is allergic to, the nurse must question the physician's order and obtain an order for a different drug, one that the patient isn't allergic to. Doing otherwise puts the nurse and the physician at risk for liability. This is known as *joint responsibility.*

A classic example of joint responsibility would be that of a foreign object (such as a sponge) being left in a patient during surgery. The surgeon is responsible for not leaving a foreign object in the patient during surgery; the nurses assisting in the operating room are responsible for making sure that all equipment, supplies, and sponges used are accounted for before the surgeon closes. If the surgeon and the nurses fail in their responsibilities and the patient is harmed, then the surgeon and the nurses are responsible for their negligence. (Keep in mind that there have been a few cases in which only the nurses doing the surgical counts were held liable for a foreign object being left in the patient.)

Nurse liability
Educational and licensing requirements for nurses increased after World War II.

Nursing tasks became more complex, which led to specialization.

These changes meant that nurses began to make independent judgments. Although this increased responsibility provides a sense of autonomy and a more rewarding working environment, it also makes nurses more liable for errors and increases their likelihood of being sued.

Causes of lawsuits against nurses

Patient falls and drug errors are the two most common causes of lawsuits against nurses. Other problems that prompt lawsuits include:

▶ operating room errors, such as a foreign object (for example, a sponge or an instrument) being left inside a patient because counts weren't performed or were performed inaccurately before the surgeon closed
▶ communication breakdown between nurses and physicians or between nurses on different shifts
▶ inadequate observation or assessment of patients leading to a delay in diagnosis or treatment, permanent injury, or death
▶ failure to know and follow a facility's or agency's chain of command policy, thus causing injury to a patient because of a lack of appropriate intervention.

In addition to the above-mentioned areas of liability, nurses who work in special practice areas may be vulnerable to other areas of liability. (See Chapter 5 for a more in-depth discussion of these areas.)

Negligence versus malpractice

The court's view of nursing liability has changed significantly over the years. At one time, nurses were charged only with negligence. Today, however, all courts recognize nursing negligence as a form of malpractice.

The Joint Commission defines *negligence* as failure to use such care as a reasonably prudent and careful person would use under similar circumstances. A claim of negligence requires that there be a duty owed by one person to another, that the duty be breached, and that the breach of duty results in injury.[2] Although nurses always have a duty to their patients, *malpractice* is a more restricted, specialized kind of negligence, defined as a violation of professional duty or a failure to meet a standard of care or failure to use the skills and knowledge of other professionals (nurses) in similar circumstances. The Joint Commission defines malpractice as the improper or unethical conduct or unreasonable lack of skill by a holder of a professional or official position. This definition is usually applied to physicians, dentists, lawyers, and public officers to denote negligent or unskillful performance of duties when professional skills are obligatory. Malpractice is a cause of action for which damages are allowed.[3]

The distinction shows that the courts recognize nursing as its own profession. This professional status may affect the statute of limitations applicable in a particular case. The *statute of limitations* defines the time period in which a lawsuit may be filed. Many states have statutes of limitations specifically pertaining to medical malpractice claims, which may be shorter than those for ordinary negligence actions. Generally, one statute of limitations applies to adults (usually 2 to 3 years) and one applies to minors (up to 21 years depending on the state). However, additional statutes may limit or extend the statute of limitations, depending on the claim, the entity being sued, and the state where the harm was done.

Criminal liability

Although most legal actions arising out of nursing practice are civil actions, nurses occasionally face criminal charges. When this happens, prosecutors need to prove criminal intent. Showing such intent involves proving that the nurse knew or should have known that what she was doing or failing to do would cause the patient harm and that she intentionally failed to take the necessary actions. A nurse can also be held criminally liable if she intentionally harms a patient.

An example of failing to take the necessary actions might involve a registered nurse (RN) ignoring the observations of a licensed practical nurse (LPN) regarding the severity of a patient's condition and failing to appropriately observe and assess the patient, ensure the necessary intervention, and follow up. If the RN's inaction leads to a severe worsening of the patient's condition, she could face criminal action.

An example of intentionally acting to harm the patient would include a violent act that caused either physical or mental harm to a patient, such as wrongfully restraining him in a way that caused injury. Another example is abuse that causes the patient physical or mental harm.

Statute of limitations

The statute of limitations specifies the number of years within which one person can sue another. For malpractice lawsuits, the statute of limitations is specified in each state's medical malpractice law. These limits vary widely from state to state, so nurses need to know the limits in their state. Contact the attorney,

lobbyist, or legislative committee members of the state nurses' association for information about the statute of limitations in your state. (For a list of state nurses' associations, see pages 6 to 10.) Statutes of limitations also vary widely from jurisdiction to jurisdiction in Canada, and even within a jurisdiction.

Purpose

As time passes, evidence vanishes, witnesses' memories fail, and witnesses die. A time limit for bringing a lawsuit ensures that enough relevant evidence exists for a judge or jury to decide a case fairly.

The statute of limitations for general negligence usually gives a person 3 years to sue another for damages. Defendants may invoke these limits as a defense in general personal-injury lawsuits. However, in response to pressure from medical and insurance groups, states have established shorter statutes of limitations for professions that require independent judgments and frequent risks. The statutes of limitations of medical malpractice laws, for example, usually give the patient 2 years or less to sue for damages.

Application of statutes

In many states, only physicians and dentists are expressly subject to medical malpractice statutes of limitations. These states view the nurse as someone carrying out orders, not making independent, risk-taking judgments.

If a nurse alleges a patient's claim is invalid because he didn't file suit until after the statute of limitations expired, the court must determine whether the statute of limitations for state medical malpractice law or the statute of limitations for general personal-injury lawsuits applies. (The statute of limitations for malpractice law is usually shorter.) The court bases its decision on two considerations:

▶ *The amount of limitation protection the court believes the defendant-nurse's job warrants.* If the nurse's job forces her to make many independent patient-care judgments, the court may apply a strict, or short, statute of limitations. A short time limit offers more protection for the nurse because the patient has less time to seek damages.

▶ *The type of negligent act the plaintiff-patient claims the nurse committed.* An injured patient may sue a nurse for one or several charges that constitute negligence or malpractice. The patient's attorney determines which charge has the best chance of winning the most damages for his client and structures his case accordingly. Then, if a statute of limitations is used as part of the nurse's defense, the court decides which statute of limitations to apply in relation to the patient's charges.

Consider this example. In an Alaska case, *Pedersen v. Zielski (1991),* the plaintiff-patient argued that a 6-year statute of limitations for controlled claims applied to a physician's negligence because the physician had a contract to provide care to that patient. The Alaska court disagreed and held that the 2-year statute of limitations for medical malpractice claims was applicable because the plaintiff's claims arose in tort (personal injury) law, not in contract law. The Alaska Supreme Court reaffirmed this holding in 1993 in a related case, *Pederson v. Flannery (1993).*[4]

Even if a patient files suit long after the statute of limitations has expired, that statute may not necessarily protect a nurse from liability. Remember that the patient's attorney knows about the statute of limitations, and the suit is being filed anyway. That means he believes the court may set aside the statute of limitations because of the case's special circumstances.

However, what happens if the plaintiff doesn't know he was injured or doesn't find out he has grounds for a suit until after the normal limitation period expires? Determining when the applicable statute begins to run has become the pivotal question whenever a defense attorney invokes the statute of limitations. Legislatures and the courts, which are continually struggling with this question, have devised a series of rules to help decide, in individual malpractice cases, when a statute should begin to run. A court can apply these rules, when a plaintiff-patient's attorney requests that it do so, to extend the applicable statute of limitations beyond the limit written in the law. That means that the nurse's use of a statute of limitations as a defense may be invalidated, and the plaintiff-patient would still be allowed to sue. (See *Rules and the statute of limitations.*)

Proof of fraud

Courts, in most states, will extend the limitation period indefinitely if a plaintiff-patient can prove that a nurse or physician used fraud or falsehood to conceal from the patient information about his injury or its cause. In most cases, the law says that the concealment must be an overt act, not just the omission of an act. The most flagrant frauds involve concealing facts to prevent an inquiry, elude an investigation, or mislead a patient. (See *Extending the statute of limitations,* page 141.)

Rules and the statute of limitations

RULE	DESCRIPTION/ TIME LIMIT	LEGAL IMPLICATIONS
Occurrence rule	• Statute of limitations begins to run on the day the patient is injured. • This rule generally leads to the shortest time limit.	• Statute of limitations begins to run on the day the patient is injured. • This rule generally leads to the shortest time limit. • The courts in several states have interpreted the occurrence rule strictly, so even badly injured patients have been prevented from bringing suit after the applicable statute of limitations had expired.
Termination-of-treatment rule	• Statute of limitations begins on the date of the last treatment. • Rule is applied when a patient's injury results from a series of treatments extended over time, rather than from a single treatment. • The courts reasoned that for the patient, a series of treatments could obscure just how and when the injury occurred.	• Statute of limitations begins on the date of the last treatment. • Rule is applied when a patient's injury results from a series of treatments extended over time, rather than from a single treatment. • The courts reasoned that for the patient, a series of treatments could obscure just how and when the injury occurred. • The Supreme Court of Virginia applied this rule in *Justice v. Natvig (1989)*. In this case, a patient filed a lawsuit 8 years after an allegedly negligent operation. The patient had continued to receive treatment during this interval. The defendant-physicians argued that the statute of limitations had lapsed. The court ruled, however, that the statute didn't begin to run until the treatment had ended, so the patient's lawsuit was allowed.
Constructive-continuing-treatment rule	• This rule is essentially the same as the termination-of-treatment rule, but it applies even after the patient leaves a nurse's or a physician's care.	• This rule is essentially the same as the termination-of-treatment rule, but it applies even after the patient leaves a nurse's or a physician's care. • A patient previously cared for is injured later in someone else's care and files a lawsuit. • If a subsequent health care provider relied on decisions a nurse or physician made earlier in caring for the patient, the court may extend the statute of limitations in malpractice cases.
Discovery rule	• Statute of limitations begins to run when a patient discovers the injury. • This may take place many years after the injury occurred. • The rule considerably extends the time a patient has to file a malpractice lawsuit. • This rule is usually applied in cases involving foreign objects and sterilization; the applicable statute of limitations wouldn't begin until the patient found out about the error.	• Statute of limitations begins to run when a patient discovers the injury. • This may take place many years after the injury occurred. • The rule considerably extends the time a patient has to file a malpractice lawsuit. • This rule is usually applied in cases involving foreign objects and sterilization; the applicable statute of limitations wouldn't begin until the patient found out about the error. • A court's decision to apply the discovery rule depends on whether it believes the patient could have discovered the error earlier. If evidence indicates the patient should have recognized that something was wrong (for example, if he had chronic pain for months after the surgery but didn't take legal action until long afterward), the court could apply the termination-of-treatment rule instead. • Time limits for applying the discovery rule in foreign-object cases vary from state to state.

(continued)

Rules and the statute of limitations *(continued)*

RULE	DESCRIPTION/ TIME LIMIT	LEGAL IMPLICATIONS
Discovery rule *(continued)*		• In lawsuits involving tubal ligations or vasectomies, the courts have sometimes allowed the discovery rule to apply when a subsequent pregnancy occurs. In these cases, the courts' reasoning is that a patient can't discover the negligence until the procedure proves unsuccessful, no matter how long after the surgery this proof appears. • A number of states have adopted separate statutes of limitations, one for readily detected injuries and one for injuries discovered later. Other states permit statute of limitations extensions only in foreign-object cases.

Consider, for example, *Garcia v. Presbyterian Hospital Center (1979).* In this case, a patient who sued was operated on for cancer of the prostate gland twice in 1972 and once again in 1973. He had repeatedly asked his physician and attending nurses why the third operation was needed, but he hadn't received any explanation. He later learned that the third operation had resulted from retention of a catheter in his body during the second operation. The court held that the applicable statute of limitations didn't prevent the patient from bringing suit.

Patients who are minors or mentally incompetent

In most states, laws give special consideration to patients who are minors and those who are mentally incompetent because they lack the legal capacity to sue. Some states postpone applying the statute of limitations to an injured minor until he reaches the age of majority, which may be age 18 or 21, depending on the state. Some states have specific rules about how statutes of limitations apply to minors.

Cases involving mentally incompetent patients who file after the statute of limitations has expired usually follow the discovery rule or a special law. Most special laws state that a statute of limitation doesn't begin until the patient recovers from his mental incompetence.

Statutes as a defense

When a defendant-nurse and attorney use a statute of limitations as a defense, they're making, in legal terms, an affirmative defense. The defendant must prove that the statute of limitations has run out. If the court decides the statutory time limit has expired, the plaintiff-patient's case is dismissed.

For example, in the Wisconsin case *Claypool v. Levin (1997),* the 3-year statute of limitations covering malpractice actions was determined to begin running when a plaintiff obtains actual or constructive notice of injury and its cause, even though the first attorney they went to for legal advice said they didn't have a viable claim. Because a separate cause or the delay in bringing a lawsuit may exist doesn't toll (or pause) the statute. Thus, a patient can't argue that because he sought legal advice that indicated no viable claim, the statute is tolled.

Certain states require that the party bringing the action "use reasonable diligence in discovering the acts or omissions complained of."[5] For example, in the case of *Trudeau v. Dupre (1994)*, the plaintiffs had argued that they had no knowledge of wrongful conduct on the defendant's part until several years later, when a newspaper article revealed that the defendant's medical license had been recently revoked as a result of malpractice in connection with the death of another infant. The plaintiffs also argued that their complaint was filed in a timely manner, within 3 years of that article. The Rhode Island Supreme Court upheld a finding by the lower court that had the plaintiffs exercised reasonable diligence at the time of their son's death, any act of alleged negligence on the defendant's part could have been discovered, and dismissed the case.

Medical records

Because a patient may file a malpractice suit years after he claims his injury occurred—and because a nurse may be called on to recall specific clinical facts and procedures—accurate medical records should be kept on file for several years. Complete documentation of care is usually found only in these medical records. These records provide a nurse's best defense. Without them, the nurse is legally vulnerable.

Few states have laws setting precise time periods, but many legal experts urge

Extending the statute of limitations

If a plaintiff-patient can prove that a nurse or physician willfully deceived him, the court may lengthen the statute of limitations for filing a lawsuit.

PAINFUL OVERTREATMENT
Consider the case of *Lopez v. Swyer (1971)*. Mary Lopez, age 32, underwent a radical mastectomy after discovering a lump in her breast. Several physicians prescribed postsurgical radiation treatments, which a radiologist performed.

These treatments occurred six times per week for more than a month, and left painful radiation burns over most of her body. When Mrs. Lopez asked why the complications were so severe, her physician assured her that the burns weren't unusual. He never suggested that the treatments could have been too numerous or too long.

Mrs. Lopez's condition worsened. Over the next several years, she was hospitalized 15 times, including twice for reconstructive surgery made necessary by the radiation treatment. She didn't file a malpractice suit until she heard a consulting physician tell other physicians, gathered near her hospital bed, that she was a victim of negligence.

EXTRA TIME FOR THE PLAINTIFF
A lower court dismissed the suit because the 2-year statute of limitations for malpractice had expired. The New Jersey Supreme Court ruled that the statute of limitations didn't begin to run until Mrs. Lopez learned that her physicians had concealed the truth from her. This effectively lengthened the statute of limitations by nearly 10 years. The Supreme Court ruling allowed Mrs. Lopez to bring the facts of her case before a jury.

hospitals and other health care facilities to maintain medical records long after patients are discharged. New Jersey, for example, requires hospitals to keep medical records for at least 7 years.

Some states have adopted the Uniform Business Records Act. This act calls for keeping records for no less than 3 years. Some states allow microfilm copies of medical records to be admitted as evidence in malpractice cases, but other states insist that only the original records can be used in court.

MEDICAL MALPRACTICE LAWSUITS

Before the early 1970s, health care providers seldom thought about their potential for being sued for medical malpractice because patients and their families were generally unaware of their rights within the health care system. Patients didn't know their options when dealing with less-than-satisfactory outcomes. However, the malpractice crisis that erupted in the late 1970s, spurred on by greater patient awareness of disorders (and their specific treatments) and higher patient awards, quickly taught all health care providers that patients now expect higher quality of care and will sue if they feel they don't receive it. Today, specialization, daily advances in technology, and extensive media coverage coupled with the consumers' expanding knowledge of medical techniques and therapies, have culminated in a glut of medical malpractice lawsuits that's threatening the foundation of the entire health care system.

Most malpractice lawsuits against nurses are filed under the auspices of tort law. Patients typically file malpractice lawsuits against nurses when they perceive their nursing care to be substandard or the cause of foreseeable injuries. Keep in mind, however, that malpractice is more than an undesired outcome: in order for a patient to *successfully* file a malpractice lawsuit against a nurse, there must be evidence that some action or inaction that the nurse was obligated to perform resulted in harm to the patient. If the patient doesn't have compelling evidence, he may still file suit, but the court may find the suit to be frivolous and the suit will generally be unsuccessful.

Every patient can sue, but not every patient can win a lawsuit.

Elements of malpractice
In court, four elements must be shown before a nurse is said to be liable for malpractice: duty owed the patient, breach of duty owed the patient, causation, and injury and damages.

Duty owed the patient
The patient-plaintiff must show that the nurse-defendant owed him a specific duty and to what level the duty was owed. The nurse-patient relationship, showing that the patient was relying on the professional judgment of the nurse to deliver safe and competent care, forms the basis for this element. Standards of care become the main issue. The patient's attorney and the nurse's attorney will both present their views of what a reasonably prudent nurse, with like training and experience, would have done under similar circumstances.

Breach of duty owed the patient
Attorneys for the patient-plaintiff will present testimony concerning the nurse-defendant's failure to competently deliver

quality nursing care. Attorneys for the nurse will present contradictory testimony. This portion of the lawsuit can be lengthy and usually involves the use of expert witnesses. (See *Courtroom controversy: Nurses as expert witnesses,* pages 144 and 145.)

Causation

Causation, the concept that certain events may reasonably be expected to cause specific results, is usually the most difficult element to prove at trial. The law states that the specific outcome must be foreseeable before there can be liability.

Causation may be further divided into cause-in-fact (also called *direct cause*) and proximate cause. Cause-in-fact involves the concept that what the nurse does or fails to do must be directly attributable to the harm that the patient incurs. It isn't enough that a patient is harmed; there must be a direct relationship to the harm and what the nurse did or failed to do. This element, like breach of duty owed the patient, is commonly argued at court through the use of expert witnesses.

Finally, there can be proximate cause for which nurses are held liable. Proximate cause actually builds on foreseeability and attempts to determine how far the liability of the individual extends for consequences following negligent actions. If a nurse gives an overdose of a known nephrotoxic medication and the patient develops renal failure 2 years later, is the nurse liable for the renal failure? Under the concept of proximate causation, the answer could be *yes.* However, if a patient is deemed partially responsible for her injury, proximate causation may not

apply. (See *Proximate causation,* page 146.)

The "cause" is an essential component of malpractice. Health care today is filled with complexities and is ever-changing. Numerous factors, including the patient's actions or condition, as well as the actions or lack of actions by other health care providers. can impact the damage that occurred regardless of the nurse's action or inaction.[6]

Injury and damages

For a nurse to be held liable for malpractice, the patient must prove physical injury and significant monetary damages. Although courts allow some award of damages for pain and suffering, damages are generally awarded to compensate the patient for expenses incurred (actual and projected) as a direct or indirect result of the injury sustained. These damages may be apportioned among the various health care providers that are named as defendants in the case.

Sometimes the court awards punitive damages, which are meant to punish the nurse or other health care providers for harms that were the result of malicious or wanton disregard for the patient's safety. For example, in *Manning v. Twin Falls Clinic and Hospital (1992),* a decision was made to move a terminally ill patient to another room on the same unit. The patient, who was projected to have less than 24 hours to live, was on oxygen. His family requested that supplemental oxygen be given during the transfer. His nurses declined the request because "the patient was a no-code." The patient went into cardiac arrest about 15 feet from his original room and was pronounced dead by the attending physician.

Courtroom controversy: Nurses as expert witnesses

Testimony by experts is an essential ingredient in malpractice cases for both plaintiff and defendant. In lawsuits against nurses, the court's position is that a nurse is the appropriate expert witness when dealing with the actions or decisions of a nurse. Before 1980, it was common for physicians to testify about the standards for nursing care.

NO DOUBLE STANDARD
In the case of *Young v. Board of Hospital Directors, Lee County (1984)*, the court concluded that physicians may not determine nursing standards of care. The physician, being unfamiliar with the daily practices of nurses, can't set a standard or testify as to deviation from common nursing practice. The expert witness nurse can explain technology or nursing care in the language jurors can understand. This type of testimony is crucial to dispel common misconceptions or to explain scientific facts as they pertain to nursing care and the care at hand.

QUALIFICATIONS OF AN EXPERT
A nurse expert witness testifying for the plaintiff in a malpractice case must be able to describe the relevant standard of care, describe how the nurse deviated from the acceptable standard, and explain how failure to meet acceptable nursing standards caused or contributed to the patient's injury. Defense counsel will also provide a nurse expert who will testify to the standard and whether the defendant nurse met the standard.

A nurse must meet certain criteria to be considered an expert witness. The first and only absolute criterion is current licensure to practice

nursing. Also, the expert witness' credentials must match or exceed the defendant's. This includes clinical expertise in that specialty area, certification in the clinical specialty, and recent education relevant to the nursing specialty at issue. However, the expert witness may hold licensure in another state. Another criterion is a lack of bias; the expert witness must not have any relationship, professional or personal, with any parties involved in the suit.

EXPERT WITNESS OR LEGAL CONSULTANT?
There's a difference between being a legal consultant and an expert witness. A legal consultant may be an expert, but her name and the information and opinions she gives aren't disclosed to the opposition. However, when a nurse agrees to become an expert witness, her name is given to opposing counsel and she may have to testify in court. Also, any comments, notes, or reports she makes may be discovered and reviewed by opposing counsel.

The nurse expert witness faces two dilemmas: the changing standard of care, and being trapped into saying that only one opinion is correct. As the nurse expert witness, she must con-

In the subsequent malpractice court case, the court allowed punitive damages because the nurses' action was an extreme deviation from standards of care.

Burden of proof
The plaintiff in a medical malpractice lawsuit has to meet a burden of proof to collect damages. This means that he must not only prove the four above-mentioned elements exist but also that they meet an

evidentiary standard called the *preponderance of the evidence*. The preponderance of the evidence standard (the least stringent of the evidentiary standards) requires that the fact finder—the judge or jury—believes that the evidence presented to prove each of the four elements is more than 50% likely to be true. If the fact finder believes that the plaintiff's attorney has proved the four required elements to be true by a preponderance of that the evidence is true for each required element for him to prevail at trial.

A third standard of evidence, *beyond a reasonable doubt,* is used in criminal cases and requires the fact finder to believe that each element of the prosecution's case has a 90% or greater chance of being true.

In a malpractice case, the only time that the plaintiff doesn't have the burden of proof is when evidence important to the plaintiff's case has been destroyed (or *spoliated*). For example, if a malpractice case involved issues related to the appropriate management of a patient in labor, and it was shown that the fetal monitor strips taken during labor were missing from the medical record, this would be considered a spoliation of evidence; the burden of proof would then shift from the plaintiff to the defendant. Although this situation doesn't occur often, it underscores the rationale for carefully preserving the medical record.

Doctrines applied to malpractice

Over the years, the law has developed special doctrines, or theories, to apply to cases involving subordinate-superior relationships. These doctrines may be used in a nurse's defense during a lawsuit. Exactly how much protection they offer, however, depends on the circumstances of the case and the development of the law in the nurse's state or province.

Respondeat superior

One of the most important doctrines used in malpractice defenses is the doctrine of *respondeat superior* (Latin for "let the master answer"), also called *the theory of vicarious liability*. This doctrine holds that when an employee is found

sider the possibility that the standard of care may have changed by the time the case goes to trial, and thus it's crucial to know what was acceptable at the time of the incident. Furthermore, when there's more than one acceptable choice, the expert witness must repeatedly emphasize that more than one approach could have been selected and still be appropriate.

On occasion, a nurse may testify as an expert about a physician's care, when the physician performs an act that's also a nursing function, such as drawing blood or inserting a nasogastric tube.

CASE STUDY

In *Prairie v. University of Chicago Hospitals (1998),* an Illinois appellate court held that expert testimony wasn't needed to establish that a nurse acted negligently. A patient underwent a laminectomy; 2 days later a nurse forced the patient out of bed in spite of complaints of severe pain. The patient sued. The trial court ruled in favor of the nurse because of the plaintiff's failure to present expert testimony on the standard of care. However, the appellate court overturned the ruling. It said the fact existed that the nurse had acted negligently and that it was unnecessary for expert testimony to establish the standard because the propriety of the nurse's conduct could be evaluated by the jury on the basis of common knowledge.

the evidence, then the fact finder should rule in favor of the plaintiff.

Another evidentiary standard that's used in civil litigation is *clear and convincing evidence,* which requires that there be substantial proof that the evidence presented is true. In states that require this level of evidence, a plaintiff's attorney would have to convince the fact finder that there's about a 75% chance

Proximate causation

In *Moore v. Willis-Knighton Medical Center (1998)*, a patient was discharged to her home after hip replacement surgery. She was ordered to use a walker after discharge and to have an elevated toilet seat installed in her home. Part of the discharge planning included teaching the patient how to use a walker.

About 70 days after her discharge, the patient fell off the elevated toilet seat and reinjured her hip. She sued the health care facility for failure to provide adequate discharge planning instructions for using an elevated toilet seat with a walker, under the theory of proximate causation. The court found on behalf of the nurses. Its conclusion? The longer a patient has been living independently, with limitations but without problems, the more she's responsible for her own safety.

Whether the court would have made the same conclusion if the patient had fallen within the first few days after discharge is uncertain.

negligent, the employer must accept responsibility if the employee was acting within the scope of his employment. The doctrine applies to all occupations, not just health care—a utility company, for instance, is liable for injuries that result if one of its on-duty truck drivers negligently hits a pedestrian.

To the extent that a nurse is working as the hospital's functionary, she can claim some protection under this theory. This doctrine is attractive to plaintiffs as well as employees because hospitals usually have much more money available to pay claims than nurses do (a reality facetiously known as the "deep pocket" doctrine).

Consider, for example, *Nelson v. Trinity Medical Center (1988)*. A nurse delayed placing a woman who was in labor on a continuous fetal heart rate monitor, despite standing orders to do so. The child was born severely brain damaged, a condition that might have been prevented if the monitor had been operating to alert the physician to the need for a cesarean delivery. It was the hospital, not the nurse, who was found liable for the actions of its employee. (The physician settled out of court before the trial.) The parents were awarded $5.5 million.

In another case, *Crowe v. Provost (1963)*, a mother returned with her child to her pediatrician's office one afternoon after having been there earlier that morning. She said her child was convulsing. The physician was at lunch, so the office nurse briefly examined the child. The nurse then called the physician, told him that she didn't feel the child's condition had changed since he had examined her, and advised that he need not rush back. After the nurse left the office, the child vomited violently, stopped breathing, and died before the receptionist could contact the physician.

The mother filed negligence charges against the nurse. At the trial, the court found the nurse's negligence was indeed the proximate cause of the child's death. However, the physician was also liable, according to the doctrine of *respondeat superior,* because the nurse was working as his employee.

Borrowed servant

A concept closely related to *respondeat superior* is the borrowed-servant or captain-of-the-ship doctrine. It's still applied in malpractice lawsuits, but not as commonly as it was in the past. The borrowed-servant doctrine might apply when a person, as a hospital employee, commits a negligent act while under the direction or control of someone other than a supervisor, such as a physician in the operating room. Because the physician is an independent contractor and the individual is responsible to him during surgery, that person is considered his borrowed servant at the time. If the individual is sued for malpractice, his liability is vicarious, meaning that even though the physician didn't direct this person negligently, he's responsible because he was in control.

Many states have moved away from strict application of the borrowed-servant theory. One reason for this shift is that operating room procedures are becoming so complex that they're beyond the direct control of any one person, thus making it too difficult for courts to determine responsibility under the borrowed-servant doctrine.

Res ipsa loquitur

In some cases, injured parties who can't fully meet the element of causation may still be successful in a subsequent lawsuit. *Res ipsa loquitur,* literally "the thing speaks for itself," is a rule of evidence that's applied when patients are injured in such a way that they can't show how the injury occurred or who was responsible for the injury. Malpractice may be inferred from the fact that the injury occurred. The principle underlying this doctrine is that the injury wouldn't have occurred in the absence of malpractice. The importance of applying the doctrine lies in the fact that expert witnesses aren't needed to assist the jury in understanding the facts of the case. Essentially, the rule of *res ipsa loquitur* allows a plaintiff to prove negligence with circumstantial evidence, when the defendant has the primary, and sometimes the only,

knowledge of what happened to cause the plaintiff's injury.

Res ipsa loquitur derives from a 19th-century English case, *Byrne v. Boadle (1863).* In this case, the injured person had been struck by a flour barrel that fell from a second-floor window of a warehouse, but the plaintiff couldn't show which warehouse employee had been negligent in allowing the barrel to fall. The court applied the concept of *res ipsa loquitur* to the warehouse owners, who were found liable in the absence of proof that the employees weren't responsible for the plaintiff's injury.

Application of res ipsa loquitur

In most medical malpractice cases, the plaintiff has the responsibility for proving every element of his case against the defendant; until he does, the court presumes that the defendant has met the applicable standard of care. However, when a court applies the *res ipsa loquitur* rule, the burden of proof shifts from the plaintiff to the defendant. The plaintiff doesn't have to prove that the defendant was negligent. Rather, the defendant must prove that he wasn't.[7] The defendant must prove that the injury was caused by something other than his negligence.

The case that set the precedent for this doctrine, *Ybarra v. Spangard (1944),* concerned a patient who suffered a permanent loss of neuromuscular control in his right shoulder and arm after an appendectomy. At trial, the patient's attorney was able to show that this wasn't the type of injury that normally occurs during an appendectomy but couldn't show how the injury occurred or who was responsible for it. The court in that case established three criteria that must be shown for *res ipsa loquitur* to apply:

▶ The injury must be the kind that ordinarily doesn't occur in the absence of some type of negligence.

▶ The injury must be caused by an action within the exclusive control of the defendant.

▶ The injury must not be the result of any voluntary action or contribution on the part of the plaintiff.

Usually, *res ipsa loquitur* is applied in lawsuits where the patient was unconscious and had no means of asserting any level of control in the situation, such as a case involving an anesthetized surgical patient. Examples of court cases where *res ipsa loquitur* was successfully applied include those in which a foreign object was left in a surgical patient, infection was caused by unsterile instruments, surgical burns occurred, or a surgical operation was performed on the wrong part of a patient's body.

A case allowing for the application of *res ipsa loquitur* was *Babits v. Vassar Brothers Hospital (2001)*. In that case, a patient awoke from surgery with third-degree burns on the back of her thighs. Although it wasn't clear how the burns got there, an expert witness gave two different hypothetical explanations. The court, acknowledging that the expert witness' theories were speculative, ruled that such an injury wouldn't have happened in the absence of negligence and applied the doctrine of *res ipsa loquitur*.

For and against res ipsa loquitur

Not all states that allow *res ipsa loquitur* apply this doctrine in the same manner. Some states limit its application, especially in cases in which more detail is needed to ensure the jury's understanding of the issues of the case, such as in instances of secondary infection. Other states have to-

tally rejected the doctrine on the premise that negligence and malpractice must be proven, not presumed. *Garcia v. Bronx Lebanon Hospital (2001)* illustrates this point. In that case, a patient awoke in the emergency department (ED) with bruises over his entire body. He testified that he had been drinking, went to the ED because of chest pain, sat down to rest, and woke to find bruises over his body. The hospital security guards testified that the patient had come in highly intoxicated, picked up and swung a chair, and had to be physically restrained for the safety of staff and patients. The court refused to apply the doctrine of *res ipsa loquitur*, stating that the patient's injuries, in and of themselves, didn't prove that the hospital was negligent and that it would have to be shown that the security guards had used excessive force when the patient was restrained.

Application in Canada

Canadian courts have allowed for the application of the *res ipsa loquitur* doctrine, though its application varies from province to province. Court cases indicate that although the doctrine is still in use, *res ipsa loquitur* may be less favored in the future (*Farrell v. Snell, 1990; McInnes, 1998*). The courts seem to want to ensure that the rule doesn't place too heavy a burden on the defendant.

Mitigation

Nurses and other health care providers aren't the only people who may have accountability for injuries that befall patients. Various circumstances may help to mitigate a health care providers' negligence and malpractice liability. (See *Challenging a malpractice suit*.) The three most commonly known mitigating

Challenging a malpractice suit

If your attorney can establish one of the following malpractice defenses, the court will either dismiss the allegations or reduce the damages for which you're liable.

DEFENSE	RATIONALE
False allegations	Does the plaintiff have legally sufficient proof that your actions caused his injuries? If he doesn't, the court may rule that the allegations against you are false and dismiss the case.
Contributory negligence	Did the plaintiff, through carelessness, contribute to his injury? If he did, some states permit the court to charge the plaintiff with failing to meet the standards of a reasonably prudent patient. Such a ruling may prevent the plaintiff from recovering damages. Many states permit the court to apportion liability, which prevents the plaintiff from recovering some, but not all, of the damages he claims.
Comparative negligence	Does the patient share a percentage of the blame for his injuries? If so, damages may be proportionately reduced.
Assumption of risk	Did the plaintiff understand the risk involved in the treatment, procedure, or action that allegedly caused his injury? Did he give proper informed consent and so voluntarily expose himself to that risk? If so, the court may rule that the plaintiff assumed some of the risk by knowingly disregarding the danger, thus relieving you of some or all the liability, depending on your state's laws.

defenses are contributory negligence, comparative negligence, and assumption of risk.

Contributory and comparative negligence

Contributory negligence and comparative negligence are essentially variations of the same concept. Both hold injured parties responsible for their own actions in creating or augmenting an injury. Examples of how patients contribute to injuries include failure to take prescribed medications, failure to keep follow-up appointments with health care providers, and giving misinformation to health care providers.

Contributory negligence, which is the older of the two doctrines, states that a patient who had any part in the adverse consequences of his medical or nursing care is barred from receiving compensa-

tion. Today, more states follow the comparative negligence concept, which reduces monetary awards by the percentage of harm that the injured party caused. For example, in a case in which $750,000 is the total monetary award and the patient's actions account for 20% of the harm, the final settlement to the patient would be $600,000. Some states disallow compensation for the injured party if he's found more than 50% accountable for the ultimate injury.

Assumption of risk

Assumption of risk states that patients are partially responsible for consequences if they understood the risks involved at the time they proceeded with the action. Many medical therapies, surgical interventions, and drug protocols have risks involved, and patients are made aware of these risks during the informed consent process. The doctrine of assumption of risk assists in allocating liability if untoward outcomes result.

AVOIDANCE OF MALPRACTICE LIABILITY

Tort liability can be avoided by using caution and common sense and by being aware of legal responsibilities. Follow the guidelines described here. (See *Everyday situations that can trigger lawsuits.*)

First impressions
The patient's first impression of a nurse is lasting and can set the tone for the nurse-patient relationship. Because a patient is less likely to sue someone he likes and trusts, a favorable first impression can help prevent a malpractice suit. A common element in malpractice lawsuits involves patients and their families feeling ignored, manipulated, or dehumanized.[8] Convey a caring attitude, give your full attention to the patient, demonstrate respect for the patient and his dignity and desire for privacy, try to avoid interruptions, and create a trusting relationship.

Baseline information
Nurses commonly find themselves in trouble because they fail to obtain adequate information about a patient before attempting to care for him. To avoid problems caused by lack of knowledge, each nurse should establish her own baseline for each of her patients by:
▶ reviewing each patient's medical records and noting significant information

▶ reading all pertinent information contained in the care plan
▶ discussing the care plan and past and current problems with the patient
▶ revising the care plan as needed
▶ appropriately reporting and documenting the patient's condition.

Knowledge of strengths and weaknesses
Never accept responsibilities for which you aren't prepared. For example, if a nurse hasn't worked in pediatrics for 10 years, accepting an assignment to a pediatric unit without orientation only increases her chances of making an error. If the nurse does make an error, claiming lack of familiarity with the unit's procedures won't protect her against liability.

As a professional, nurses shouldn't accept a position if they can't perform as a reasonably prudent nurse would in a similar setting. Courts may, however, be more lenient when dealing with nurses who work in emergency settings, such as in a fire or a flood. However, simply being told "We need you here today" doesn't constitute an emergency.

Assignment evaluation
A nurse may be assigned to work on a specialized unit, which is reasonable, as long as the nurse is assigned duties she can perform competently and as long as an experienced nurse on the unit assumes responsibility for the specialized duties. Assigning a nurse to perform total patient care on the unit is unsafe if that nurse doesn't have the skills to plan and deliver that care.

Therefore, before accepting an assignment, the nurse must make sure that she's competent to complete the assignment. If the nurse is in the process of be-

Everyday situations that can trigger lawsuits

Everyday nursing situations can present legal hazards. These examples of nursing liability, based on actual court decisions, show how deviating from accepted standards can harm a patient and result in lawsuits. By being aware of how certain common situations can cause you legal entanglements, you can avoid making similar mistakes.

FAILING TO PERFORM A PROPER ASSESSMENT

When a man traveling between cities began having chest pain and numbness in his left shoulder and arm, he and his companion stopped at a small hospital for help. The nurse on duty advised him to travel to a larger hospital 24 miles away. She failed to perform a physical assessment or to obtain a formal history. On his way to the other hospital, the man had a massive myocardial infarction and died.

Clearly, the nurse failed to accurately assess her patient. Her mistake cost the patient his life and resulted in a landmark decision that established a nurse's independent relationship with her patient.

The court held the nurse responsible and accountable for her omissions, stating that she had failed to meet her duty to protect the patient from harm.

Federal law (Emergency Medical Treatment and Active Labor Act) also prohibits an emergency department from refusing treatment or discharging a patient without medical screening and stabilization. Hospitals are subject to fines and liability for failure to comply. Moreover, the plaintiff-patient may file suit under federal law as well as state negligence law for any injury that occurred as a result of the nurse's failure to screen him and stabilize his condition.

FAILING TO TAKE APPROPRIATE PRECAUTIONS

An elderly senile patient with a history of falling down was left in bed with the side rails down. She fell out of bed and hurt herself.

Another patient, an alert 28-year-old, was instructed by a nurse to call for help before getting out of bed. After the nurse left the room, the patient got herself out of bed and fell.

In the first case, the nurse was found liable for failing to raise the side rails. When a patient is at clear risk for injury, the nurse must take extra measures to protect her.

In the second case, the nurse wasn't held liable for the patient's injuries. Her patient, a competent adult, had received appropriate instructions and chose to ignore them. In such circumstances, a court will hold the patient responsible.

NEGLECTING TO DOCUMENT AND COMMUNICATE INFORMATION

A mother took her two sons to an emergency department because they had head and chest rashes and high fevers. The mother gave the nurse an accurate history, which included the recent removal of two ticks from one of the boys.

The nurse didn't tell the physician about the ticks or record the information in the chart. The physician diagnosed measles in both boys and sent them home.

Two days later, one boy died of Rocky Mountain spotted fever, which is transmitted by ticks.

Although neither the hospital nor the physician was held responsible for the boy's death, the nurse's omission was found to be a contributing cause of death.

PERFORMING NURSING PROCEDURES INCORRECTLY

A nurse gave an I.M. injection in the wrong quadrant of a patient's buttocks. He later developed footdrop from sciatic nerve damage.

In this case, both the nurse and the hospital were found negligent. The law expects a nurse to give drugs and treatments without injuring patients by following set standards of care. (Drug errors are one of the most common sources of negligence claims against nurses.)

The hospital's liability was established under the legal doctrine *respondeat superior,* which

(continued)

Everyday situations that can trigger lawsuits *(continued)*

holds an employer responsible for an employee's errors.

FAILING TO REPORT ANOTHER'S MISTAKES
While delivering a patient's baby, an obstetrician made an incision in the patient's cervix to relieve a constrictive band of muscle. After delivery, he failed to suture the incision.

The patient was sent to the postpartum unit for care and observation. The patient's nurse, noticing that the patient was bleeding heavily, called the obstetrician three times. He assured the nurse that the bleeding was normal. Within 2 hours, the patient went into shock and died.

Even though the nurse contacted the patient's physician, the court held the nurse negligent for failing to intervene further. The courts expect nurses to exercise professional, independent judgment and to object when a physician's orders are inappropriate. In this case, the nurse should have reported the facts to her manager or the unit's medical director, insisting that the patient receive proper care.

BEING INVOLVED IN A SURGICAL TEAM'S ERROR
During a cholecystectomy, the surgical team accidentally left a sponge in the patient's body. When the sponge was discovered later, the patient needed another operation to remove it.

When the court awarded damages, both the surgeon and the nurse paid. At one time, the surgeon would have been fully responsible under the captain-of-the-ship doctrine. Today, all members of the surgical team are responsible for their actions.

---

ing oriented to a new unit or a new facility, she shouldn't accept an assignment that's above her skill level. Whenever an assignment requires skills that the nurse doesn't have, another nurse with the necessary skills should be available to help with that portion of the care.

Nurses working in acute-care facilities are sometimes asked to float to units on which they aren't qualified to work. For example, a medical-surgical nurse might be asked to float to an orthopedic unit. If the nurse knows nothing about orthopedic nursing, she should insist on being paired with an experienced orthopedic nurse and work alongside that experienced nurse in caring for orthopedic patients. However, if a nurse is asked to work in a critical-care area or an ED, it may not be feasible to pair her with another nurse in that type of setting; therefore, the nurse should refuse to be floated to that unit.

Delegation
An RN may delegate patient-care responsibilities to another RN, an LPN, or unlicensed assistive personnel (UAP), such as a nursing assistant or a medical technician. However, before delegating a given responsibility, the nurse must know the skills and abilities of the delegatee and which patient-care needs may be met by LPNs and UAPs and which require the intervention of an RN.

Proper delegation of tasks involves adhering to six rights:
▶ right task
▶ right person
▶ right time
▶ right information (clear concise instructions, including goal, limitations, and expectations)
▶ right supervision (appropriate monitoring, evaluation, interventions, and feedback as needed)
▶ right follow up[9]

For example, if a nurse wants a nursing assistant to take a blood pressure reading on a patient who has an arteriovenous fistula, the state's nursing practice act must allow it. The nurse must also make sure that the assistant knows how to properly take and record the blood pressure reading and understands special considerations that must be observed.

Nurses can be held liable if they fail to delegate responsibilities appropriately. It's important for every delegating nurse to remember to:
▶ make sure staff members are competent
▶ teach and direct staff members
▶ evaluate staff members on an ongoing basis
▶ rectify any incompetent actions
▶ reassess patients
▶ take responsibility for all delegated tasks
▶ ensure accurate documentation.

A delegating nurse should check her state's nurse practice act to learn which tasks may and may not be delegated. However, tasks involving health assessment analysis, teaching, or nursing judgment about care should never be delegated to another person unless that person is another RN.[10] Report incompetent health care personnel to superiors through the facility's chain of command.

Implementation of orders

Never treat any patient without orders from his physician, except in an emergency. Don't prescribe or dispense any drug without authorization. In most cases, only physicians and pharmacists may perform these functions legally.

Don't carry out an order from a physician if there's any doubt about its accuracy or appropriateness. Follow the facility's policy for clarifying ambiguous orders. Document efforts to clarify the order, and whether the order was carried out.

If, after you carry out an order, the treatment adversely affects the patient, stop it. Report all unfavorable signs and symptoms to the patient's physician. Resume treatment only after discussing the situation with the physician and clarifying the orders. Document all actions.

Keep in mind that a physician can change his orders at any time, including while the nurse isn't on duty. A patient may know something about his prescribed care that no one has told the nurse. If a patient protests a procedure, drug dosage, or drug administration route—saying that it's different from "the usual" or that it has been changed—give him the benefit of the doubt. Question the physician's orders, following the facility's policy.

Be sure to clarify all standing orders. Contact the prescribing physician for guidance, or tell the supervisor about any uncertainties with following the order, and let the supervisor decide whether to delegate the responsibility to a more experienced nurse.

Drug administration

Drug errors are the most common type of nursing error. They typically occur because nurses fail to check the drug order appropriately or are unfamiliar with the drug they're giving.

Nurses can avoid drug errors by adhering to the six "rights" of medication administration: right medication, right patient, right dosage, right route, right time, right documentation.[11] Two additional rights also have been suggested: the right to be educated and the right to refuse. Also, when a nurse is unfamiliar with a drug to be given, she has the duty to look up the drug to understand its intended effects, any contraindications, and potential adverse effects or drug interactions. Finally, the nurse needs to be able to evaluate and document the patient's response to the drug being given.

Mistakes in dosage, patient identification, or drug selection by nurses have led to vision loss, brain damage, cardiac arrest, and death. In *Norton v. Argonaut Insurance Company (1962)*, an infant died after a nurse gave injectable digoxin at a dosage level appropriate for elixir of Lanoxin, an oral form of the drug. The nurse was unaware that digoxin was available in an oral form. The nurse questioned two physicians who weren't treating the infant about the order, but failed to mention that the order was written for elixir of Lanoxin. She also failed to clarify the order with the physician who wrote it. The nurse, the physician who originally ordered the drug, and the hospital were all found liable.

Patient rapport

Trial attorneys have a saying: "If you don't want to be sued, don't be rude." Failing to communicate with patients is the cause of many legal problems. A relationship exists between the patient and the nurse and the quality of that relationship usually is important in the patient's decision to file a lawsuit.[12]

Always remain calm when a patient or his family becomes difficult. Patients must be told the truth about adverse outcomes, but this information should be communicated with discretion and sensitivity. (See *Who's looking for litigation?*)

Communication

Avoid offering an opinion when a patient asks you what you think is the matter with him. If you do, you could be accused of making a medical diagnosis, which would be practicing medicine without a license. Don't volunteer information about possible treatments for the patient's condition or about possible choices of physicians, either.

Avoid making any statement that could be perceived by the patient as an admission of fault or error. Don't criticize other nurses or health care practitioners, or the care they provide, if the patient can hear you. Don't discuss with the patient or visitors which members of the health care team are covered by malpractice insurance.

Be careful not to discuss a patient's confidential information with anyone except when doing so is consistent with proper nursing care. Also, avoid such discussions in public areas, such as waiting areas, elevators, or cafeterias.

Documentation

From a legal standpoint, documented care is as important as the actual care. If a procedure wasn't documented, the courts assume it wasn't performed. Documentation of observations, decisions, and actions is considered to be more solid evidence than oral testimony. Chapter 7 describes the legal aspects of documentation in detail.

The patient's medical record, when taken into the jury room, is a nurse's "best evidence" of the care given. The chart should follow the FACT rule—that is, it should be factual, accurate, complete, and timely.

Use incident reports to identify and report accidents, errors, or injuries to a pa-

Who's looking for litigation?

Patients who are more likely to file lawsuits against nurses share certain personality traits and behaviors. Furthermore, nurses who are more likely to be named as defendants also have certain common characteristics.

BEWARE OF THESE PATIENTS

Although not all persons displaying the behaviors listed here will file a lawsuit, a little extra caution in your dealings with them won't hurt. Providing professional and competent care to such patients will lessen their tendency to sue.

A patient who's likely to file a lawsuit may:
- persistently criticize all aspects of the nursing care provided
- purposefully not follow the care plan
- overreact to any perceived slight or negative comment, real or imagined
- unjustifiably depend on nurses for all aspects of care and refuse to accept any responsibility for his own care
- openly express hostility to nurses and other health care personnel
- project his anxiety or anger onto the nursing staff, attributing blame for all negative events to health care providers
- have filed lawsuits previously.

NURSES AT RISK

Nurses who are more likely to be named as defendants in a lawsuit display certain characteristic behaviors. If you recognize these attributes in yourself, changing your behavior will reduce your risk of liability.

A nurse who's likely to be a defendant in a lawsuit may:
- be insensitive to the patient's complaints or fail to take them seriously
- fail to identify and meet the patient's emotional and physical needs
- refuse to recognize the limits of her nursing skills and personal competency
- lack sufficient education for the tasks and responsibilities associated with a specific practice setting
- display an authoritarian and inflexible attitude when providing care
- inappropriately delegate responsibilities to subordinates
- fail to advocate for the patient.

tient. A long period may elapse between an incident and subsequent court proceedings, and this documentation may contain pertinent facts of the incident that may have been left out of the patient's medical record.

Don't ever correct or revise a patient's medical record after he has filed a lawsuit. The case of *Carr v. St. Paul Fire and Marine Insurance Company (1974)* illustrates the liability a hospital can incur when nurses or other employees alter or destroy patient records. In this case, the patient came to the hospital ED suffering severe pain. One nurse on duty refused to call a physician for the patient, so he returned home and died a short time later.

The nurses on duty in the ED that night testified that they had taken the patient's vital signs, but this couldn't be proved or disproved because the patient's records had been destroyed. When instructing the jury, the judge indicated that they could find the hospital negligent.

In the case of *Sweet v. Providence Hospital (1995)*, the court held that a rebuttable presumption of negligence arises if a health care facility's records are unavailable to a plaintiff and the plaintiff can demonstrate that the missing records are necessary to prove his negligence claim.

Procedures

Never assist with a surgical procedure unless you're satisfied the patient has given proper informed consent. Never force a patient to accept treatment he has expressly refused. Don't use equipment that you're unfamiliar with or aren't trained to use or that seems to be functioning improperly. And, if you're an operating room nurse, always check and double-check to ensure that no surgical equipment, such as sponges or instruments, is unaccounted for after an operation is completed.

Restraints

Restraints need to be applied correctly and checked according to your facility's policy. Documentation must be exact about the reason for restraint, the need for restraint, the amount and kind of restraint used, and the status of the restrained patient. Generally, there must be a physician's order for restraints to be used. Restraining patients without a proper order may be a claim for patient abuse or false imprisonment. An omission or failure to properly monitor a restrained patient may also result in a malpractice claim.

Patient falls and environmental safety

Patient falls are a common area of nursing liability. Patients who are elderly, infirm, sedated, confused, agitated, or mentally incapacitated are the most likely to fall. Commonly, there's no way to predict if and when a patient is going to fall. However, if the nurse has any reason to suspect that a patient is at an increased risk for falling, she must take appropriate measures to safeguard the patient. The case of *Stevenson v. Alta Bates (1937)* in-

volved a patient who had a stroke and was learning to walk again. As two nurses, each holding one of the patient's arms, assisted her into the hospital's sunroom, one nurse let go of the patient and stepped forward to get a chair for her. The patient fell and sustained a fracture. The nurse was found negligent. The court reasoned that the nurse should have anticipated the patient's need for a chair and made the appropriate arrangements before bringing the patient into the sunroom.

Knowledge about the safety features, capabilities, and limitations of any equipment used by nurses is a critical responsibility. When providing care, nurses must follow the manufacturer's directions for safe usage and not change or adapt the equipment.[13] Additionally, nurses must avoid using faulty equipment. Clearly mark the equipment as defective and unusable. Even after repairs are done, don't use the repaired equipment until technicians demonstrate that the equipment is operating properly. Document steps taken to handle problems with faulty equipment to show adherence to the proper procedure.

Advance directives

The Patient's Self-Determination Act, a federal law, requires that every patient, upon admission to a hospital, be given information about living wills and durable power of attorney. Follow the facility's policy for providing the required information. A nurse, as one of the patient's health care providers, should never become a witness to a living will or a durable power of attorney. Nurses also must be aware of state laws concerning living wills and advance directives.

Facility policies

Nurses have a responsibility to adhere to their facility's policies. If policies are sound and followed carefully, they can protect a nurse against a malpractice claim. The court in *Roach v. Springfield Clinic (1992)* held that "hospital policies are admissible as standards of care for the treatment of patients within that hospital."

Inexperienced nurses are at high risk for liability. The RN must be able to recognize her limitations and admit to them, especially if the patient's safety is at issue. If the nurse doesn't know how to perform a nursing function or doesn't understand the reason for a particular treatment, it's her duty to obtain timely and appropriate assistance.

As the nursing profession changes, so should a health care facility's policies. The nurse, as a professional, is responsible for keeping these policies up to date. For example, does the facility have a written policy on dealing with emergency situations? "We've always done it this way" isn't an adequate substitute for a clearly written, officially accepted policy.

If administrators are reluctant to make policy changes based on one nurse's suggestion, join with colleagues to address the legal implications.

PROFESSIONAL LIABILITY INSURANCE

In any work setting, nurses are at risk for malpractice suits, and the risk may increase when working in an area that requires a high level of skill, specialized knowledge, or independent functioning. Because of this risk, owning a personal nursing malpractice policy

is important. (See *Choosing liability insurance,* pages 158 and 159.) It can provide the nurse with an extra layer of security should the nurse find herself or himself on the wrong end of a lawsuit and alleviates the stress of having to worry whether the employer is making a change in its coverage or failing to maintain adequate coverage.

Many nurses mistakenly believe that purchasing an individual malpractice policy invites lawsuits. Unfortunately, this false belief deters some nurses from obtaining individual insurance coverage. The reality? A plaintiff's attorney won't know if a nurse has malpractice insurance unless he has begun a lawsuit and asked questions about insurance coverage via interrogatories or at a deposition.

Policy provisions

Professional liability insurance protects the nurse via a contract for a designated period from the financial consequences of certain professional errors. The type of insurance policy bought determines the amount that the insurance company will pay if the judgment goes against the individual in a lawsuit.

Single versus double limits

A policy may be designated with "single limits" or "double limits." In a single-limits policy, an individual buys protection in set dollar increments—for example, $100,000; $300,000; or $1,000,000. The stipulated amount will shield that person if a judgment, arising out of a single nursing malpractice occurrence, goes against him or her.

In the double-limits policy, protection is provided in a combination package, such as $100,000/$300,000; $300,000/$500,000; or $1,000,000/$3,000,000.

Choosing liability insurance

To find professional liability coverage that fits your needs, compare the coverage of several different policies. Make sure your policy provides coverage for in-court and out-of-court malpractice suits and expenses and for defense of a complaint or disciplinary action made to or by your board of nursing. Understanding insurance policy basics will enable you to shop more aggressively and intelligently for the coverage you need. You should work with an insurance agent who's experienced in this type of insurance. If you already have professional liability insurance, the information below may help you better evaluate your coverage.

TYPE OF COVERAGE

Ask your insurance agent if the policy covers only claims made before the policy expires (claims-made coverage), or if it covers any negligent act committed during the policy period, regardless of when it's reported (occurrence coverage). Keep in mind that the latter type offers better coverage.

COVERAGE LIMITS

All malpractice insurance policies cover professional liability. Some also cover representation before your board of nursing, general personal liability, medical payments, assault-related bodily injury, and property damage.

The amount of coverage varies, as does your premium. Remember that professional liability coverage is limited to acts and practice settings specified in the policy. Make sure your policy covers your nursing role, whether you're a student, a graduate nurse, or a working nurse with advanced education and specialized skills.

OPTIONS

Check whether the policy would provide coverage for these incidents:
• negligence on the part of nurses under your supervision
• misuse of equipment
• errors in reporting or recording care
• failure to properly teach patients
• errors in administering medication
• mistakes made while providing care in an emergency, outside your employment setting.

Also, ask if the policy provides protection if your employer sues you.

DEFINITION OF TERMS

Definition of terms can vary from policy to policy. If your policy includes restrictive definitions,
you won't be covered for actions outside those guidelines. Therefore, for the best protection, seek the broadest definitions possible and ask the insurance company for examples of actions the company hasn't covered.

DURATION OF COVERAGE

Insurance is an annual contract that can be renewed or canceled each year. Most policies specify how they can be canceled—for example, in writing by either you or the insurance company. Some contracts require a 30-day notice for cancellation. If the company is canceling the policy, you'll probably be given at least 10 days' notice.

EXCLUSIONS

Ask the insurer about exclusions—areas not covered by the insurance policy. For example, "This policy doesn't apply to injury arising out of performance of the insured of a criminal act" or "This policy doesn't apply to nurse anesthetists."

OTHER INSURANCE CLAUSES

All professional liability insurance policies contain "other insurance" clauses that address payment obligations when a nurse is covered by more than one insurance policy, such as the employer's policy and the nurse's personal liability policy:
• The *pro rata* clause states that two or more policies in effect at the same time will pay any claims in accordance with a proportion established in the individual policies.
• The *in excess* clause states that the primary policy will pay all fees and damages up to its limits, at which point the secondary policy will pay any additional fees or damages up to its limits.

Choosing liability insurance *(continued)*

● The *escape clause* relieves an insurance company of all liability for fees or damages if another insurance policy is in effect at the same time; the clause essentially states that the other company is responsible for all liability.

If you're covered by more than one policy, be alert for "other insurance" clauses and avoid purchasing a policy with an escape clause for liability.

ADDITIONAL TIPS

Here's some additional information that will guide you in the purchase of professional liability insurance.

● The insurance application is a legal document. If you provide false information, it may void the policy.

● If you're involved in nursing administration, education, research, or advanced or nontraditional nursing practice, be especially careful in selecting a policy because many policies don't cover these activities.

● After selecting a policy that ensures adequate coverage, stay with the same policy and insurer, if possible, to avoid potential lapses in coverage that could occur when changing insurers.

● No insurance policy will cover you for acts outside of your scope of practice or licensure, nor will insurance cover you for intentional acts that you know will cause harm.

● Be prepared to uphold all obligations specified in the policy; failure to do so may void the policy and cause personal liability for any damages. Remember that an act of willful wrongdoing on your part renders the policy null and void and may lead to a breach of contract lawsuit.

● Check out the insurance company by calling your state division of insurance to inquire about the company's financial stability.

The smaller sum is what the insurance company will make available to protect the nurse from any one injury arising out of a single nursing malpractice occurrence. The larger sum is the maximum amount that will be paid for all claims under that policy in a given year. Although the single-limits policy will also protect nurses against injuries to more than one patient, the double-limits policy makes considerably more money available to protect the nurse who's involved in multiple lawsuits.

Occurrence versus claims-made policies

The two main types of insurance policies available to nurses are occurrence policies and claims-made policies. If a nurse purchases an occurrence policy that begins on January 1, 2008, and ends on December 31, 2008, she's covered for

any incident that occurs in this period that later results in a malpractice suit or board of nursing complaint, regardless of when it's reported. When the nurse ceases to practice nursing for any reason, she doesn't have to purchase additional coverage.

If the nurse purchases a claims-made policy that begins on January 1, 2008, and goes through December 31, 2008, she's covered only for the incidents that both occur and are reported during the indicated time period. However, if the nurse continues the claims-made coverage with a new policy the following year and in the subsequent years during which she's practicing, she'll be covered for any incident that occurs and is reported during any consecutive policy period. If the nurse retires from nursing or if she doesn't renew a claims-made policy, she'll need to purchase a reporting endorsement, commonly referred to as "tail" coverage, so that she can later report and have coverage for an incident that occurred when the policy was in effect. If a nurse changes insurance carriers and goes from one claims-made policy to another, she'll need to obtain prior-acts coverage, which allows her to report incidents that occurred during a previous policy period and have resulted in a lawsuit or board of nursing complaint during the new policy period with the new insurance carrier.

Excess judgment

A judgment that exceeds policy limits is known as *excess judgment*. However, if a nurse has purchased her own policy to supplement the coverage the employer is providing, it's unlikely that there will be an excess judgment. Also, if the insurance carrier or carriers providing coverage think that a verdict in excess of the nurse's policy limits is possible, they're obligated to try to get the case settled within the policy limits.

If an attorney has told the nurse that the case might result in an excess judgment and the insurance company isn't moving to get it settled, the attorney should write a letter demanding that the case be settled within the nurse's policy limits. Once such a letter is written, the insurance carrier may become responsible for any excess judgment if it fails to make a good faith effort to settle the case. If a good faith effort to settle the case is unsuccessful and there's an excess judgment, then the nurse may end up being personally responsible for the excess judgment.

Depending on the laws in your state, almost everything you own, except for a limited portion of your equity in your home and the clothes on your back, can be taken to satisfy the uninsured portion of a judgment.

Subrogation

Subrogation is defined as the act of substituting another (that is, a second creditor) with regard to a legal right or claim. Employers (or other defendants, such as physicians) who have been found liable for damages can subsequently sue another involved in the incident to recoup their losses.

In a Pennsylvania case, *Mutual Insurance Company of Arizona v. American Casualty Company of Reading (1997)*, a patient underwent angioplasty and had a complication, which was treated. However, during nurse-to-nurse report, the incident wasn't mentioned. The patient went into cardiac arrest and died within 12 hours. The patient's family sued the hospital and the physician, but the nurses weren't named in the lawsuit. After the hospital was found liable, the hospital's insurer filed suit against the nurses involved, saying the patient would have been more closely monitored if the staff had known it hadn't been a routine angioplasty. The court ruled that the suit was permissible.

Insurance costs

Fortunately, premiums for insurance coverage of $1 million aren't much more than they are for smaller limits. The reason is a substantial part of the premium pays for the insurance company's assumption of risk; higher limits don't increase the premium disproportionately.

General duty RNs usually pay less for coverage than critical care nurses, operating room nurses, ED nurses, postanesthesia care nurses, and advanced practice nurses. In recent years, nurses specializing in obstetrics have typically paid the highest insurance premium rates, in part because of the large number of lawsuits filed against obstetricians.

Insurance companies offer various liability insurance policies. If possible, choose an agent who's experienced in professional liability coverage. Organizations such as the ANA and the state nurses' association offer group plans at attractive premiums. Nurses need to review the extent of coverage with an agent to make sure it's adequate for their needs.

Insurer's role in a lawsuit

Professional liability insurance can supply a nurse with more than just financial protection. The insurance company may also provide a defense counsel to represent the nurse for the entire course of litigation if it's included in the insurance contract. Remember: insurance companies aren't in business to lose money; they'll retain highly experienced attorneys with considerable experience in defending malpractice lawsuits.

When preparing the defense, attorneys will investigate the subject of the lawsuit, obtain expert witnesses, handle motions throughout the case, and prepare medical models, transparencies, photographs, and other court exhibits, if necessary. The cost incurred in preparing a defense and defending the nurse through trial and appeals will be covered by the insurance policy.

Out-of-court settlements

During litigation, and even before a lawsuit is filed in court, an insurance company may seek an out-of-court settlement from the plaintiff's attorneys. Although this saves time and money, it may not be

in the nurse's best interest professionally. In the United States, if a nurse believes that her professional reputation is at stake, she may be able to refuse to agree to an out-of-court settlement. If the policy contains a threshold limit, the insurer can't settle a case out of court for an amount greater than the threshold limit without the nurse's permission. Without a threshold limit, the insurer has control over out-of-court settlements.

If the lawsuit against the nurse goes to court and the insurance company is defending the nurse, the insurer has the right to control how the defense is conducted. The insurer's attorney, however, makes all decisions regarding the case's legal tactics and strategy.

The nurse has a right to be kept informed about every step in the case because the nurse, not the insurance company, is the client, so the attorney must perform his legal duties according to what's in the nurse's best interest, not the insurance company's. After all, the insurer knows that a successful defense depends in part on the defendant's cooperation. Also, the nurse can sue the insurance agency if it fails to provide a competent defense.

If a nurse loses a malpractice lawsuit, the insurance company will cover the nurse for jury-awarded general and special damages. Basic damages that can be verified in terms of past, present, and future expenses include but aren't limited to:
▶ medical expenses
▶ lost wages
▶ loss of earning potential
▶ other related expenses, such as:
  – modifications that need to be made to a home or vehicle

– equipment that needs to be purchased or leased

– homemaker or housekeeping services.

Other monetary damages that also may be added to the settlement or verdict value of a case include damages awarded for pain and suffering, loss of consortium, or emotional harm, now and in the future. Such damages can't be defined in verifiable monetary terms but are given values by those negotiating a settlement or by a judge or jury before rendering a verdict.

In states where tort law has undergone tort reform, there may be caps on the amount of recovery legally allowable for such things as pain and suffering or loss of consortium.

Punitive damages

Some states allow a plaintiff-patient to recover punitive damages from a defendant-nurse (or other health care provider) if that defendant did something to intentionally harm the patient or knowingly failed to take steps to prevent harm to the patient.

Some insurance carriers have provisions in their policies that specifically state they won't indemnify a policy holder for punitive damages if the policy holder is shown to have acted with malice or reckless disregard. Why? Punitive damages are meant to punish the defendant, and the defendant isn't really being punished if such damages are paid. However, many insurance carriers have decided to indemnify their insured health care provider for punitive damages that have been included in a settlement or verdict. Such decisions are generally made on a case-by-case basis. Additionally, if an insurance carrier doesn't have a specific ex-

clusion in the policy for punitive damages, it's clear that the insurance carrier will be responsible for payment of any and all damages up to the limits of liability in any given policy.

Multiple insurers

If a nurse has more than one insurance policy—for example, malpractice coverage through an employer as well as a personal individual insurance policy—both insurance companies might well become involved in defending or settling a patient's claim. Determining who pays is complex. Generally, the coverage provided by the employer would be the primary policy if the lawsuit involves actions performed at the place of employment within the nurse's scope of practice. The coverage provided by an individual policy would be secondary and would take effect only after the primary policy was exhausted.

A secondary policy would cover the nurse up to its policy limits for any excess verdicts or settlements that weren't covered by the primary policy. However, the nurse must promptly notify each insurance company with which she has a policy when she's the target of a malpractice lawsuit. If the nurse fails to notify the insurance companies of this or if she delays in notifying the insurance company, they can use such policy defenses to avoid responsibility for providing coverage.

Indemnification suits

If several insurance companies are representing different parties in a malpractice lawsuit, they'll typically file counteractions against the other parties, seeking compensation, or *indemnification*, for all or part of any damages the jury awards.

Many states now permit damages to be apportioned among multiple defendants, the extent of liability depending on the jury's determination of each defendant's relative contribution to the harm done. This is called *comparative negligence*. For example, suppose the nurse was responsible for the instrument count during surgery in a foreign-object case, and the court found the nurse to be 75% responsible. The nurse's insurance company would pay 75% of the total award. The other insurance companies would be held liable for the remaining 25%, in proportion to the percentage of harm attributed to each remaining defendant.

Also, a plaintiff's acts or omissions (for example, failure to follow a physician's order) may be considered by a jury in determining where liability lies. A judgment would be reduced by the plaintiff's own negligence. If one codefendant, such as the surgeon, decided that he had been judged negligent only because of the nurse's negligence, he could instruct his insurance attorneys to file a new, separate lawsuit in his name against that nurse.

Indemnification suits are becoming more common. The hospital, a fellow nurse, or a laboratory technician, as long as each has individual professional liability insurance, can file an indemnification suit against another person, such as a nurse. This possibility strengthens the argument for having personal professional liability insurance.

Liability cost containment

Many states are taking steps to decrease malpractice litigation and the size of potential jury verdicts. Besides establishing special statutes of limitations, some states

More physicians coming to Texas

Four years ago, Texas passed a constitutional amendment to limit the amount of awards dispersed with malpractice claims. Currently, there's an influx of physicians applying for licensure to practice in the state. According to officials, there has been an increase of 18% since the legislation was imposed, and an increase of 30% in just the last year. The executive director of the Texas Medical Board believes that this increase is the result of a "friendlier malpractice climate." However, others are somewhat skeptical about the increase, stating that although there are more physicians, the question remains if the increased numbers will actually improve patient safety.[14]

have imposed a maximum limit on the monetary sums a jury can award for certain damages, such as loss of consortium, wrongful death, and pain and suffering. The federal government has also been debating a proposed award cap of $250,000 for pain and suffering, but the proposal has met stiff resistance; it has been called unconstitutional by certain members of Congress and various special-interest groups. Some states, such as Texas, have instituted caps on medical malpractice awards. (See *More physicians coming to Texas*)

Medical associations and insurance companies are trying to limit malpractice awards by forcing malpractice claims into arbitration, thus removing them from the province of lay juries, and by requiring that claims be screened by a medical malpractice screening panel. A few states, such as Ohio, provide for submission to nonbinding arbitration panels if all parties agree. State laws may also provide for binding arbitration if specified by a written contract between a patient and the physician or hospital.

If a malpractice screening panel decides the plaintiff's claim is invalid, the plaintiff can't file suit unless he posts a bond to cover his defense costs in advance. Although more than half the states have set up screening panels, these panels have been criticized by consumer groups and plaintiffs' attorneys and challenged in court as being unconstitutional. In *Keyes v. Humana Hospital, Alaska, Inc. (1988),* Alaska courts upheld the constitutionality of the panels.

Employer's insurance

Virtually all health care facilities carry insurance to protect against their liability for an employee's mistakes. Without professional liability insurance, the facility would have to pay damages awarded in a lawsuit out of its own funds, which could lead it to bankruptcy.

To help in assessing personal professional liability insurance needs more wisely, find out the degree of professional and financial protection provided under the employer's liability insurance. To do this, consider obtaining and reviewing a copy of the employer's insurance policy. If you don't understand something in the policy, contact the insurer.

Coverage limits

Although each health care facility's professional liability insurance policy has a maximum dollar coverage limit, an employer can purchase coverage that exceeds the basic limit. Many hospitals do so for extra protection.

Deductible limit

Most hospitals also have a deductible provision that makes them responsible for damages under a certain figure. The higher the deductible limit, the lower the premium the insurer charges. Pay careful attention to the deductible limit because an employer may be able to settle a claim against a nurse, for which they may be held financially responsible, under that figure without ever consulting the nurse or the insurer. Because the nurse won't have a chance to defend herself, and because many people interpret a settlement as an admission of guilt, such an action could tarnish a nurse's professional reputation. A tarnished reputation, in turn, could jeopardize one's ability to obtain personal professional liability insurance or a new job. Therefore, in the event of a lawsuit, maintain close contact with the employer's legal staff and insist on being informed about every step in the case.

Provisions for defense

If a nurse is sued and the employer's insurance provides coverage, the insurer may have a duty to provide a complete defense, including assigning an attorney to handle the entire case. The insurer will pay attorney fees as well as any investigation costs and expert witness fees.

Keep in mind that the nurse is a player in the lawsuit, but the defense counsel is for the hospital first and the nurse incidentally. If there's ever a conflict between the nurse's best interest and the employer's best interest, the nurse should obtain her own attorney who will be concerned with her defense. This attorney may work closely with hospital counsel, but his loyalty is to the nurse. He'll provide the nurse with an opportunity to confer with him and give her side of the story.

If the employer grants written consent to settle the case, the insurer may do so or it may decide to try the case in court if its legal advisors overrule the employer. If the plaintiff wins the lawsuit, the insurer is obliged to pay damages awarded to the patient up to the insurance policy's coverage limit.

Stipulations for denying coverage

Insurance companies that provide professional liability coverage for hospitals and other health care facilities reduce the risk they assume under *respondeat superior* in several ways. One way is by stipulating a precise coverage period, typically 1 year. Another way is by defining the type of coverage they provide, whether, for example, it's an occurrence policy or a claims-made policy. A third way is by putting exclusions into malpractice policies. These exclusions vary considerably from policy to policy, but all list specific acts, situations, or personnel that the insurance doesn't cover.

Besides exclusions, insurers may deny coverage to nurses or the employer because of other circumstances, including:
▶ The insurance policy lapses because the employer failed to pay the premiums.
▶ The employer refuses to cooperate with the insurance company, for whatever reason.
▶ The insurer discovers that the employer made misstatements on the insurance application.

In some malpractice situations, an insurer could agree to provide the nurse with a defense but refuse to pay damages awarded to a patient. The insurer agrees to defend the nurse in this situation because he doesn't want to be accused of breach of contract. However, he must notify the nurse of his intention not to pay damages in a reservation-of-rights letter. This letter informs the nurse and the employer that the insurer believes the case falls outside what's covered by the insurance policy.

When the employer and the insurer disagree about whether insurance coverage exists, the dispute may have to be resolved through separate legal action. Similarly, the nurse has the right to bring such action against the employer's insurance company if it refuses to cover the nurse.

Additional considerations

Keep in mind a few more concerns when reviewing the employer's policy. First, is the policy purchased for the nurse as an employee benefit? In that case, the insurer protects the nurse and not the hospital. Second, the policy may provide coverage only for incidents that occur while the nurse is on the job. The nurse may be held liable for nursing actions off the job, unless those actions are covered under a Good Samaritan act, a state law that protects health care professionals who act in an emergency.

Third, many employers provide only a claims-made policy. If a suit is filed against a nurse for work she performed while working for a *former* employer, the nurse probably won't be covered by the former employer's insurance plan.

Fourth, if the nurse is an independent contractor, such as a private-duty nurse, the court likely won't consider her to be under the hospital's direct supervision and control. Consequently, the hospital won't be considered responsible for her actions, and its insurance probably won't cover her. However, if the policy is the nurse's with the hospital paying the premiums as an employee benefit, the nurse is still covered.

Finally, with regard to intentional acts of harm, such as striking a patient, the nurse would be responsible for any criminal or civil penalties levied against him or her. Simply keep in mind that intentional acts of harm usually aren't covered by any professional liability policy.

DEFENSE IN A MALPRACTICE LAWSUIT

Imagine being named in a lawsuit for nursing malpractice. When and how should you respond? The best bet is to act immediately. Failing to respond to the complaint could result in a default judgment against you. However, how you respond depends on whether you have professional liability insurance. (See *Responding to a malpractice summons.*)

Notification of appropriate personnel

If a nurse is covered by an employer's insurance, she should immediately contact the legal services administrators at work. They'll tell her how to proceed.

If the nurse has personal professional liability insurance, she should consult the policy and read the section that describes what to do when a lawsuit is filed. Every policy describes the person to notify and the amount of time in which to do so. Immediately telephone this representative, and tell him that you're being sued. Document the time, his name, and his instructions. Then hand-deliver the lawsuit papers to him, if possible, and get a signed, dated receipt. Alternatively, send lawsuit papers by certified mail, return receipt requested, to ensure that the person has received them.

Failure to contact the appropriate representative within the specified time can result in the insurance company's refusal for coverage. Act quickly, document actions, and get a receipt.

In addition, contact the National Nurses Claims Data Bank established by the ANA. Provide a full report of the incident in question, including the date, time, and persons involved. This contact will give you access to national data that may support your case, and your data will, in turn, help other nurses who are involved in lawsuits. Your name and address will be kept confidential.

Upon notifying the insurance company about the lawsuit, it will first consider whether it must cover you at all. The insurer does this by checking for policy violations you may have committed. For example, your insurance company will check whether you gave late notice of the lawsuit, gave false information on your insurance application, or failed to pay a premium on time. If the company is sure you've committed such a violation, it will use this violation as a policy defense, and it can simply refuse to cover you. If the company thinks you've committed such a violation but isn't sure it has evidence to support a policy defense, it will probably send you a letter by certified mail informing you that the company may not have to defend you, but that it will do so while reserving the right to deny coverage later, withdraw from the case, or take other actions. Meanwhile, the company will seek a declaration of its rights from the court. If the court decides the company doesn't have to defend you, the company will withdraw from the case.

Usually, however, an insurance company takes this action only after careful consideration because denying coverage may provide you with grounds for suing

Responding to a malpractice summons

If you receive a summons notifying you that you're being sued, your immediate response can significantly affect the suit's outcome.

If you're contacted by the plaintiff, family members, or friends of the plaintiff, or by his attorney, don't speak to them. They should speak only through your attorney. If you're insured, you should politely insist to the insurer that your claim be handled by an attentive, experienced claims adjuster (the insurance company representative who investigates your claim and makes estimates for settlement) and a qualified attorney.

Be prepared to maintain your separate file on the case. Ask for copies of all relevant documents and reports from the claims adjuster, your attorney, and reports your attorney gets from the patient's attorney. Check the status of your case regularly with your attorney.

SELECTING A DEFENSE ATTORNEY

One of your first concerns will be finding a qualified attorney to represent you.

If the patient names your hospital in the lawsuit, the hospital's insurance company may supply an attorney to defend you as the hospital's employee. If the hospital's attorney is representing the hospital's interest in the lawsuit, you should have a separate attorney to represent your interest. If you're sued alone, your insurance carrier may appoint a defense attorney to represent you. If you're uninsured, you'll have to find an attorney on your own.

If the dollar amount for which you're being sued exceeds your insurance coverage, consider hiring a private lawyer. This attorney will work exclusively for you. He'll notify your primary defense attorney and your insurer that, should the judgment exceed your coverage, the carrier may be held liable.

SHOPPING AROUND

When seeking a qualified attorney, consider:
● consulting with your hospital's legal services department
● consulting with your state nurses' association or other appropriate professional organization
● asking friends or relatives with legal experience whose judgments you can trust
● calling your local bar association.

When you meet with a prospective attorney, ask him about his experience with malpractice cases. If he has little experience or if too many of his cases were decided for the plaintiff, you have the right to ask your insurance carrier for another attorney.

WORKING WITH YOUR ATTORNEY

Establishing a good working relationship with your attorney is crucial. It's your job to educate the attorney about the medical information he needs to defend you. Be prepared to spend many hours reviewing charts, licensing requirements, hospital policies and procedures, journals, and texts as well as your professional qualifications and the details of the case. Here are some pointers:
● Provide your attorney and claims adjuster with all the information you can about the case, including anything relevant you remember that may not appear in the record.
● Supply your attorney with the nursing practice standards for your specialty.
● Discuss with your attorney how you feel about settling out of court.
● Develop a list of experts qualified to testify on the standards of care in your specialty, and present it to your attorney. Avoid recommending friends, because the jury may believe them to be less objective.
● Review all available records, including those obtained by your attorney that are normally inaccessible to you, such as the records of the patient's private physician.

the company. If you receive such a letter, find your own attorney to defend you in the lawsuit and to advise you in your dealings with the insurance company. If

your case against the insurance company is sound, the attorney may suggest that you sue the insurer.

Your employer will almost certainly be named as a codefendant in the lawsuit. Even if that isn't the case, notify your employer that you're being sued. Your insurance company may try to involve your employer as a defendant.

Attorney assignment or selection

If your insurance company doesn't assert a policy defense, your company representative will select and retain an attorney or a law firm specializing in medical malpractice cases as your attorney of record in the lawsuit. When so designated, this attorney is legally bound to do all that's necessary to defend you.

If you don't have insurance—either your own or your employer's—you'll have to find your own attorney. Don't even consider defending yourself. You need an attorney who's experienced in medical malpractice because the case will be complex and experienced attorneys will be the opposition.

Make appointments with a few attorneys who seem qualified to defend you. In most cases, you won't be charged for this initial consultation. When you meet with each one, ask how long he thinks the lawsuit will take and how much money he'll charge. Also, try to get a feel for the attorney's understanding of the issues in your case. Then choose one as your attorney of record. Do this as soon as possible.

Defense preparation

Your attorney will file the appropriate legal documents in response to the papers you were served. He'll ask you for help in preparing your defense. He should give you a chance to present your position in detail. Remember that all discus-

sions between you and your attorney are *privileged communication,* meaning that your attorney can't disclose this information without your permission. Your attorney will also obtain complete copies of the pertinent medical records and other documents he or you feel are important in your defense.

Interrogatories, depositions, and examinations

Your attorney will use discovery tools to uncover every pertinent detail about the case against you. *Discovery tools* are legal procedures for obtaining information and may include:

▶ *interrogatories*—questions written to the other party that require answers under oath

▶ *depositions*—oral cross-examination of the other party under oath, either taken before a court reporter or recorded on videotape

▶ *defense medical examination*—a medical examination of the injured party by a physician selected by your attorney or insurance company.

The plaintiff-patient's attorney will also use discovery tools, so you may have to answer interrogatories and appear for a deposition as well. Your attorney will carefully prepare you for these procedures.

Neither the interrogatories nor the deposition should be taken lightly. Don't speculate when answering a question. Work closely with your attorney in preparing your written answers to the interrogatories, and never submit interrogatories or other documents directly to the plaintiff's attorney. Your attorney must review everything and submit the final copies to the opposing counsel.

That doesn't mean, however, that you must say or do anything your attorney asks. If you feel he's asking you to do or say things that aren't in your best interest, tell him so. You have the right to change attorneys at any time. If you believe an attorney selected by your insurance company is more interested in protecting the company than in protecting you, discuss the problem with a company representative. Then, if you still feel that he isn't properly defending you, hire your own attorney. You may have grounds for subsequently suing the insurance company and the company-appointed attorney.

Preparation for court

Plan on spending a considerable amount of time preparing your case before you appear in the courtroom. Make sure you dress nicely and present yourself professionally. This time can be stressful, and you need to be prepared.

Don't try to placate the person suing you by calling him and discussing the case. Every word you say to him can be used against you in court. In fact, before the trial, don't discuss the lawsuit with anyone except your attorney. That will help prevent information leaks that could compromise your case. To protect your professional reputation, don't even mention to your colleagues that you've been sued.

Review of medical records

Your attorney will ask you to study relevant medical records as soon as possible. Examine the complete medical chart, including nurses' notes, laboratory reports, and physicians' orders. If you must, on a separate sheet of paper, make appropriate notes on key entries or omissions about the records, but don't make any changes on the records. Such an action will undermine your credibility and hurt your case. Remember that you aren't the only person with a copy of these records. Also remember that once the plaintiff acquires your notes, they may be used as evidence against you. Only your attorney's notes are safe from discovery.

Personal legal file

Ask your attorney to send you copies of all documents and correspondence pertaining to the case. Try to maintain a file that's as complete as your attorney's. Also, make sure you understand all the items in your file. If you receive a document you don't understand, ask your attorney to explain it. Maintaining such a file should keep you current on the status of your case and prevent unpleasant surprises in court.

Protection of property

Many states have homestead laws that protect a substantial part of the equity in your house, as well as other property, from any judgment against you. Ask your attorney about the law in your state or province. If you don't have malpractice or professional liability insurance or if damages awarded to the plaintiff exceed your insurance coverage, you'll probably want to mount as aggressive a defense as possible.

Pretrial events

While your attorney prepares your defense, he'll also explore the desirability of reaching an out-of-court settlement. If he decides an out-of-court settlement is in your best interest, he'll try to achieve it before your trial date. (See *Settling out of court,* page 170.)

Settling out of court

Only a small number of malpractice suits that are filed actually go to court; of those that do go to court, even fewer end with a final judgment. The rest are settled out of court.

MAKING A COMPROMISE

Settling your case out of court isn't an admission of wrongdoing. The law regards settlement as a compromise between two parties to end a lawsuit and to avoid further expense. You may choose to pay a settlement rather than incur the possibly greater expense, financial and emotional, of defending yourself at trial.

DETERMINING YOUR SETTLEMENT RIGHTS

If you're covered by professional liability insurance, the terms of your policy will determine whether you and your attorney or the insurance company can control the settlement. Most policies don't permit the nurse to settle a case without the consent of the insurance company. In fact, many policies, especially those provided by employers, permit the insurance company to settle without the consent of the nurse involved.

Review your policy to determine your settlement rights. If the policy isn't clear on this point, call the insurance company representative and ask for clarification.

EVALUATING A POSSIBLE SETTLEMENT

Offer your attorney and your insurance company's representative all the information you can about the case so they can evaluate your liabilities, as well as a possible settlement with the plaintiff.

If your case goes to trial, your attorney will participate in selecting the jury. During this process, attorneys for both sides will question prospective jurors, and your attorney will ask your opinion on their suitability. Either attorney may reject a small number of prospective jurors without reason (a peremptory challenge). Either attorney may reject an unlimited number of jurors for specific reasons. For example, an attorney may reject someone who knows the plaintiff or someone who has a personal interest in the lawsuit (*challenge for cause*).

To help prepare you to testify, your attorney will ask you to review the complete medical record, your interrogatory answers, and your deposition. You should also review the entire legal file you've been keeping, to make sure you understand all aspects of the case.

Before the trial, you'll probably be called to testify at a deposition. (If you're called to testify as an expert witness at another defendant's trial, you should be aware that some states don't permit expert witnesses to give pretrial depositions.) The deposition can take place in an attorney's office or in a special room in the courthouse set aside for that purpose. Although the deposition takes place in a less formal atmosphere than a courtroom, don't forget that every word you and the attorneys say will be recorded. In a way, it's a rehearsal for the actual trial. At the trial, the plaintiff's and the defendant's attorneys have the right to use your pretrial testimony to bolster their respective cases, which is why you should work with your attorney to thoroughly prepare for your deposition.

Trial process

Keep in mind that your trial may last several days or even weeks. After all witnesses have given their testimony, the jury, not the judge, will decide if you're liable unless both sides agree not to have a jury trial. If the jury finds you liable, it will also assess damages against you. (See *The trial process: Step-by-step.*) In some

The trial process: Step-by-step

This list summarizes the basic trial process from complaint to execution of judgment. If you're ever involved in a lawsuit, your attorney will explain the specific procedures that your case requires.

PRETRIAL PREPARATION

1. *Complaint*
   Plaintiff files a complaint stating his charges against the named defendants, injuries sustained, and demand for award.
2. *Service*
   Court issues defendant a service of the complaint stating plaintiff's charges.
3. *Answer or counterclaim*
   Defendant files an answer and may add a counterclaim to plaintiff's allegations or those of other defendants. A motion for judgment may also be filed.
4. *Discovery*
   Plaintiff's and defendant's attorneys develop their cases by gathering information by means of depositions and interrogatories and by reviewing documents and other evidence.
5. *Pretrial hearing*
   Court hears statements from both parties and tries to narrow the issues.
6. *Negotiation by settlement*
   Both parties meet to try to resolve the case outside the court and try to reach settlement.
7. *Jury selection*
   Attorneys from both sides question prospective jurors and select a final panel of jurors.
8. *Opening statements*
   Plaintiff's and defendant's attorneys outline for the jury what they intend to show during the trial.
9. *Plaintiff presents case*
   Plaintiff's witnesses testify, explaining what they saw, heard, and know. Expert witnesses review any documentation and give their opinions about specific aspects of the case.
10. *Cross-examination*
    Defendant's attorney questions plaintiff's witnesses.

11. *Plaintiff closes case*
    Defendant's attorney may make a motion to dismiss the case, claiming plaintiff's evidence is insufficient.
12. *Defendant presents case*
    Defendant's witnesses testify, explaining what they saw, heard, and know. Expert witnesses review any documentation and give their opinions about specific aspects of the case.
13. *Cross-examination*
    Plaintiff's attorney questions defendant's witnesses.
14. *Defendant closes case*
    Defendant's attorney may claim the plaintiff hasn't presented an issue for the jury to decide. Either side may move for a direct verdict.
15. *Closing statements*
    Each attorney summarizes his case for the jury, making a final argument for the jury to consider.
16. *Jury instruction*
    Judge instructs the jury in points of law that apply in this particular case and the specific charges.
17. *Jury deliberation and verdict*
    Jury reviews facts and votes on verdict. Jury announces verdict before the judge and both parties. After the verdict is known, the losing side may request a new trial.
18. *Appeal (optional)*
    Attorneys review transcripts. The party against whom the court ruled may appeal if he feels the judge didn't interpret the law properly, instruct the jury properly, or conduct the trial properly.
19. *Execution of judgment*
    Appeals process is completed, and the case is settled.

instances, an arbitration proceeding is used instead of a jury trial, but that's the exception and not the rule.

Testimony

When you're called to testify in a malpractice lawsuit, as a defendant or as an expert witness in another defendant's trial, you may be expected to respond quickly to a confusing presentation of claims, counterclaims, allegations, and contradictory evidence. You can use various techniques to help reduce stress and enhance the value of your testimony.

How you present yourself from the witness stand is very important. The jury may form its first, and sometimes lasting, impression of your credibility while you're testifying.

Your attorney will help prepare you to testify at the trial. He'll tell you how to dress—conservatively, as if you were going to an important job interview—and how to act. Your attorney may recommend, for example, that you sit with both feet on the floor with your hands folded in front of you and pay polite attention to other speakers. He'll also tell you to look at the jurors while you testify to help you appear more credible to them. Keep in mind that the purpose of these instructions is to help you win the case. Remember also that if you fail to cooperate with an attorney provided by an insurance company, the insurance company can use that information to deny coverage.

Malpractice lawsuits are notoriously slow moving. Interruptions occur in the form of recesses, attorneys' lengthy arguments in the judge's chambers, and the calling of witnesses out of turn. Be patient regardless of what happens. When you're asked to appear, be prompt. You may not score points with your punctuality, but you'll definitely lose a few if you aren't in court when you're called to testify.

When you testify, the jury doesn't expect you to be letter-perfect or to have instant or total recall. If you don't know the answer, say so. You may also refer to your prior deposition for answers that are specific, such as what was the patient's blood pressure at the time of the incident or how many milliliters of a drug you gave to the patient. Listen closely to questions, and answer only what the questioner has asked. Always answer the questions simply and in lay terms, and never elaborate or volunteer information. If you're going to be describing a piece of equipment that's unfamiliar to a lay audience, get your attorney's approval to bring it to the courtroom and show it to the jury.

Above all, be honest. When your testimony must be critical of a colleague or of your hospital's policies, you may be tempted to bend the truth a little—but don't.

During the trial, your professional reputation will be at stake. Project a positive attitude at all times, suggesting that you feel confident about the trial's outcome. Never disparage the plaintiff inside or outside the courtroom. Characterizing him as a gold digger, for example, can only generate bad feelings that may interfere with a possible settlement. If you happen to speak to him during the trial, make sure you're polite and dignified.

Cross-examination

During cross-examination, the opposing attorney will try to discredit your testimony. This may take the form of an attack on your credentials, experience, or education—especially if you're testifying as an expert witness. Don't take the attacks personally or allow them to fluster you.

Another way of discrediting expert testimony is the "hired gun" insinuation. The cross-examining attorney may imply that because you accept payment for your testimony, you're being unethical and biased. Remember that as an expert witness you have the right to expect compensation for the time you spend on behalf of the case in and out of the courtroom, just as the attorney does. Say so if necessary.

Another ploy the opposing attorney can use to discredit your testimony is the "hedge." He may try to get you to change or qualify an answer you gave previously on direct examination or at the deposition. He may also try to confuse the issue by asking you a similar, but hypothetical, question with a slightly different, but significant, slant. Just remember that a simple but sincere "I don't know" can reinforce a jury's belief in your honesty and competence. You may also state that you don't understand a question and ask the attorney to clarify it. Your best protection against cross-examination jitters is adequate preparation and honest answers.

The judgment

The final stage of a lawsuit is the execution of the judgment, which occurs after all appeals have been exhausted. Two conclusions are possible: monetary damages are awarded to the injured party, or all causes of action are dismissed against the defendant-nurse. If the injured party has prevailed, the individual will request that the award of damages be executed. This request is necessary because it gives legal relief if a losing defendant chooses to ignore the court order. In certain states, such a request allows for the garnishing of wages or for property to be confiscated and sold to pay the amount of the award. Because states vary greatly with regard to such measures, attorneys guide their clients at this stage of the trial process.

RES JUDICATA

Nurses may wonder, because there are different courts in which a lawsuit may be filed, if an injured party may attempt to bring a second lawsuit based on the same facts as an unsuccessful lawsuit. The doctrine of *res judicata*, literally "a thing or matter settled by judgment," prevents the same parties in a lawsuit from retrying the same issues as were involved in the original lawsuit, thus preventing duplication of litigation and the possibility of contradicting decisions. However, a word of caution about this doctrine: it doesn't apply to appeals, to parties not named in the original lawsuit, or to issues that weren't part of the original lawsuit. Therefore, it's possible for a losing party to file a second lawsuit if the issues at hand weren't part of the original trial.

REFERENCES

1. National Practitioner Data Bank and Healthcare Integrity and Protection Data Bank (May 2006). "Fact Sheet on the National Practitioner Data Bank." [Online]. Available at *www.npdb-hipdb.hrsa.gov/pubs/fs/Fact_Sheet-National_Practitioner_Data_Bank.pdf*.
2. The Joint Commission (2007). "Sentinel Event Glossary of Terms." [Online]

Available at *www.jointcommission.org/ SentinelEvents/se_glossary.htm.*

3. The Joint Commission (2007).

4. *Pederson v. Flannery,* 863 P.2d 856, 1993 Alas. LEXIS 120, Alaska Adv. 4033 (Alaska 1993).

5. *Trudeau v. Dupree,* 6430 A.2d 534: 1994 R.I. LEXIS 126 (Rhode Island, 1994).

6. Nurses Service Organization (2003). "Nurse's Guide to Malpractice: Module 3: What to Do if You're Sued for Malpractice." [Online] Available at *www. nursingcenter.com/upload/Journals/Docu ments/200303nsoce3sued.htm.*

7. Nurses Service Organization (2003), "Module 3."

8. Nurses Service Organization (2003). "Nurse's Guide to Malpractice: Module 2: How to Protect Yourself from Malpractice." [Online] Available at *www.nursingcenter.com/upload/Journals/ Documents/200303nsoce2protect.htm.*

9. Reising, D.L., and Allen, P.N. "Protecting Yourself from Malpractice Claims." *American Nurse Today* 2(2), February 2007.

10. Reising and Allen, 2007.

11. Lynn, P. *Taylor's Clinical Nursing Skills,* 2nd ed. Philadelphia: Lippincott Williams & Wilkins, 2008.

12. Brous, E.A. "7 Tips on Avoiding Malpractice Claims: Careful Practice and Documentation Help Keep You Out of Court," *Nursing* 34(6):16-18, June 2004.

13. Croke, E.M. "Nurses, Negligence, and Malpractice," *AJN* 103(9):54-63, September 2003.

14. Blumenthal, R. "After Texas Caps Malpractice Awards, Doctors Rush to Practice There," *New York Times* October 10, 2008.

ADDITIONAL RESOURCES

Nurses Service Organization (2003). "Nurse's Guide to Malpractice: Module 1: Nursing Malpractice: Understanding the Risks." [Online] Available at *www.nursingcenter.com/upload/Journals/ Documents/200303nsoce1risks.htm.*

Ferrel, K.G. "Documentation, Part 2: The Best Evidence of Care," *AJN* 107(7):61-64, July 2007.

Miracle, V.A. "A Closing Word: What Every Nurse Should Know About Malpractice," *Dimensions of Critical Care Nursing* 23(2):99-100, March-April 2004.

Monarch, K. "Documentation, Part 1: Principles for Self-protection. Preserve the Medical Record—and Defend Yourself," *AJN* 107(7):58-60, July 2007.

Legal risks on the job

At one time, most nurses were employed in the hospital setting. Over time, employment opportunities have changed such that nurses now practice in a wide variety of settings. In addition, nurses have achieved advanced education, training, certification, and specialization, allowing them to practice with greater independence and autonomy. With the increase in independence and autonomy, nurses also assume a greater responsibility and, subsequently, greater risks.

This chapter describes the legal implications associated with working in various clinical practice areas and settings. It also addresses important issues associated with legal risk such as hospital policies, staffing, patient safety, and drug administration. In addition, the chapter describes the legal risks and responsibilities when caring for specific patient populations, such as minors, victims of abuse, and those who are mentally ill, developmentally disabled, or suspected of a crime.

DIVERSE CLINICAL PRACTICE AREAS AND SETTINGS

Nurses work in a wide range of clinical settings. Although most nurses work in the hospital setting, many others work as private-duty nurses or in long-term care facilities, home health care, schools, or freestanding clinics. The law affects these nurses in different ways, which is why it's important to know the subtleties of one's particular field.

Specialty areas

In specialty care areas, such as the emergency department (ED), operating room, postanesthesia care unit (PACU), intensive care unit (ICU), and cardiac care unit (CCU), nurses regularly perform tasks that only physicians used to perform. Here, patient care offers exciting nursing challenges, increased nursing responsibilities—and extra risk of liability. (See *Liability in special practice settings*, pages 176 and 177.)

For example, ED nurses employ triage—classifying patients according to the seriousness of their medical problems. If the nurse makes a mistake and a

(Text continues on page 178.)

Liability in special practice settings

Although errors can be made in virtually any practice setting, nurses who work in certain specialty areas are more vulnerable to malpractice charges because their errors usually prove more costly for patients. Also, the courts may expect a higher standard from a nurse who practices a specialty.

CRITICAL CARE NURSING

Compared with nurses in other units, critical care nurses spend more time in direct contact with their patients, thus increasing the opportunity for errors and the number of potential lawsuits. Because of the many invasive and potentially harmful procedures performed in this setting, critical care nurses are especially vulnerable to charges of negligence and battery. Furthermore, if they perform duties or procedures that are outside their scope of practice, they may be accused of practicing without a license.

Additional tort claims that may be filed against critical care nurses include:
• abandonment—the unilateral severance of a professional relationship with a patient without adequate notice and while the patient still needs attention (a critical care nurse who fails in her duty to observe the patient closely for any subtle changes in condition is vulnerable to this charge)
• invasion of privacy, intentional infliction of emotional distress, or battery—such cases usually involve a patient who was placed on or removed from life support
• failure to obtain informed consent—this is more likely to occur in a critical care setting because of the inherent pressure and urgency for immediate treatment (a critical care nurse who denies a competent patient the right to refuse treatment, even if lack of treatment results in the patient's death, exposes herself to charges of various intentional torts).

EMERGENCY DEPARTMENT NURSING

Many day-to-day practices of emergency department (ED) nurses fall into a legal gray area because the law's definition of a true emergency is open to interpretation; for example, health care workers who treat a patient for what they regard as a true emergency may be liable for battery or failure to obtain informed consent if the court ultimately concludes that the situation wasn't a true emergency.

One of the most common charges filed against ED nurses is failure to assess and report a patient's condition. Inadequate triage may be considered negligence. All too commonly, the use of high-tech equipment combined with a hectic daily pace increases the potential for lawsuits.

Other tort claims made against ED nurses include:
• failure to instruct a patient adequately before discharge
• discounting complaints of pain from a patient who's mentally impaired by alcohol, medication, or injury
• failure to obtain informed consent, giving rise to claims of battery, false imprisonment, and invasion of privacy.

PSYCHIATRIC NURSING

Malpractice cases involving psychiatric care usually involve failure to obtain informed consent. A nurse may wrongly assume she doesn't need informed consent, especially if the patient's condition interferes with his awareness or understanding of the proposed treatment or procedure. Violation of a patient's right to refuse treatment may stem from the mistaken belief that all mentally ill patients are incompetent. The right to refuse treatment isn't absolute, however, and can be abrogated if a drug or treatment is required to prevent serious harm to the patient or others. Generally, a physician, not a nurse, makes this decision, and in many cases, a court makes the decision.

A nurse who reveals personal information about a patient to someone not directly involved in the patient's care also is vulnerable to malpractice charges. Violation of a patient's right to privacy and confidentiality is a common complaint in lawsuits against psychiatric health care workers, probably because of the stigma associated with mental illness.

Malpractice allegations may also stem from failing to protect a patient from inflicting foreseeable harm to himself or others. Protecting a patient or his potential victims from harm may include a duty to warn the patient's family that he's a threat to himself or a duty to warn a potential victim. This duty to warn is a standard of care in mental health practice that has been incorporated as either case law, statutory law, or both in many states.

If a nurse fails to report information given by the patient, even in confidence, that could have prevented the harm, she may be held liable for breaching her duty to appropriately assess the patient and for failing to comply with her duty to warn.

However, in a recent case example, a nurse and hospital were found to be liable for breaching patient confidentiality involving a situation in which a psychiatric patient of Middle Eastern descent who was involuntarily committed began verbalizing threats about the U.S. President and government facilities and property. The nurse informed the Secret Service. While the court acknowledged that the nurse had the right to speak up on a sensitive subject of public concern, the patient also had a right to medical confidentiality and the nurse should have gone through the proper channels.[1]

OBSTETRIC NURSING

Cases involving labor and delivery may have at least two plaintiffs: mother and infant. Monetary damages may be substantial, especially if the neonate sustained permanent and long-term injuries and is expected to live a long or near-normal life expectancy despite the injuries. An obstetric nurse may be held liable for:
● negligence through participation in transfusion of incompatible blood, especially in relation to Rhesus factor incompatibility
● failure to attend to or monitor the mother or the fetus during labor and delivery

● failure to recognize labor symptoms and to provide adequate support and care
● failure to monitor contractions and fetal heart rate, particularly in obstetric units that have internal monitoring capabilities
● failure to recognize high-risk labor patients who show signs of preeclampsia or other labor complications
● failure to warn parents of the risks of diagnostic tests—or the consequences of refusing such tests—if the failure contributes to maternal or fetal injury
● abandonment of a patient in active labor
● failure to exercise independent judgment, such as knowingly carrying out medical orders that will harm the patient
● failure to ensure that a patient has given informed consent for various procedures or treatments, including physical examinations, administration of a medication, type of delivery method, sterilization, and postdelivery surgical procedures.

Other common sources of malpractice suits filed against obstetric and neonatal nurses include failure to attend to the infant in distress, failure to monitor equipment, use of defective equipment, failure to monitor oxygen levels, and failure to recognize and report neonatal jaundice during the immediate postnatal period.

In some states, parents can file a wrongful birth lawsuit if a nurse failed to advise them of contraceptive methods or the methods' potential for failure, potential genetic defects, the availability of amniocentesis to detect defects, or the option of abortion to prevent birth of a defective child. A child with a genetic defect can file a wrongful birth lawsuit if a nurse failed to inform the parents of amniocentesis and the option of abortion. Failure to provide adequate genetic counseling and prenatal testing when the mother has a history of Down syndrome can also result in a wrongful birth or wrongful life lawsuit. (Keep in mind that many states don't allow recovery for wrongful birth.)

Self-protection for nurses on special care units

If you're working on a special care unit of a hospital—the emergency department, intensive care unit, operating room, or postanesthesia care unit—your expanded responsibilities make you especially vulnerable to malpractice lawsuits. To protect yourself, follow these precautions.

KNOW YOUR ROLE

Request a clear, written definition of your role in the hospital. Your hospital should have an overall policy and an individual, written job description for you that specifies the limits of your nursing role. You'll be better protected if guidelines for advanced nursing competencies are formally established.

DOCUMENT THOROUGHLY

Document everything you do, so there's no question later about your actions. Your nurse's notes, of course, should reflect the nursing process: document your assessment of the patient, your care plan, your actual care, and your evaluation of the plan's effectiveness. Be sure to accurately document the date and time.

MAINTAIN SKILLS

Make sure of your own competence. If your role expands, your skills have to grow, too. If that requires advanced courses and supervised clinical experience, make sure you get both.

INSURE YOURSELF

Damages awarded to patients can be very high, and high legal fees may mean you can't afford even to defend yourself in a lawsuit. If you don't have your own professional liability insurance, and your hospital doesn't help defend you against a lawsuit, you could face a startling bill even after all claims against you are proved groundless and dropped. (You might never even get to court, but you could still find yourself with a large bill for legal consultation.)

patient's treatment is needlessly delayed, the nurse may be liable.

If the PACU, ICU, or CCU is the area of practice, nurses must be ever vigilant for signs and symptoms of adverse anesthetic effects, of postoperative cardiac and pulmonary complications, and of shock caused by hypoxia, hemorrhage, or infection. On these units, nurses may also have to give drugs associated with a high risk of injury or perform complex procedures, such as operating an intra-aortic balloon pump. On these special care units, the patient's survival may depend on nursing judgment.

Legal liability

When working in a specialty care area, nurses must take their increased liability seriously. Remember, even though hospital policy requires the performance of certain tasks, or performance under a physician's orders as a physician's borrowed servant or ostensible agent, individual liability continues. If a patient sues for malpractice, all the persons involved can be held separately and jointly liable. That suggests that nurses must carefully evaluate the tasks and interventions they're asked to do. If a task is beyond the nurse's training and expertise, she shouldn't attempt it. Even if the nurse can do it, she's responsible for making sure that she's permitted to do it according to hospital policy and the state or jurisdictional nurse practice act. (See *Self-protection for nurses on special care units.*)

Role expansion and the law

In general, a nurse can't legally make a medical diagnosis or prescribe medical, therapeutic, or corrective measures, except as authorized by the facility or agency and the state in which she's working. This means that if a nurse intubates a patient with an endotracheal tube while working on a postoperative orthopedic floor, she may be liable for performing a medical function, especially if she could have called a physician. However, the nurse probably wouldn't be liable if she had been trained in Advanced Cardiac Life Support and performed endotracheal intubation in the ED during a disaster.

In Canada, several jurisdictions, including Ontario and Quebec, have passed medical practice acts that permit the delegation of specific medical functions to nurses. Some jurisdictions require that a nurse obtain special training or certification to perform these functions. In the United States, however, current laws provide little guidance for nurses who regularly face situations such as these, unless they're licensed as advanced practice nurses (APNs).

Suppose, for example, a nurse is working on an ICU and so must usually act on standing orders and without a physician's supervision. How can the nurse be sure when performing quasi-medical functions, even with standing orders, that she isn't violating the nurse practice act?

The nurse can't be sure, of course, because nurse practice acts don't provide specific guidelines. They were written in general terms, probably to give discretion to the practitioner. The hospital needs to write specific, practical policies that comply with the nurse practice act while providing the necessary supervision and instruction to nurses performing these advanced interventions.

Treating patients based on standing orders is a matter of judgment. In such situations, the nurse must be qualified to rec-ognize the problem and then follow established medical and nursing protocol.

Application of nursing standards

In general, a nurse working in a specialty care area is subject to the same general rule of law as other staff nurse colleagues: that is, the nurse must meet the standard of care that a reasonably well-qualified and prudent nurse would meet in the same or similar circumstances. However, in a malpractice lawsuit, when deciding whether a specialty nurse has acted reasonably, the court won't consider what the average licensed practical nurse (LPN), licensed vocational nurse (LVN), registered nurse (RN), or APN would have done. Instead, the court will seek to determine the standard of care that an LPN, LVN, RN, or APN specifically trained to work in the specialty care area would have met. Thus, the law imposes a higher standard of conduct on persons with superior knowledge, skill, or training.

Courts' view of standards

Hunt v. Palm Springs General Hospital (1977) illustrates how the courts evaluate the reasonable nurse standard in light of prevailing practices.

The patient, Mr. Hunt, was rushed to the ED with seizures. When he was examined, his physician concluded that Mr. Hunt, a known drug addict, was experiencing seizures because he had gone without drugs for several days. The physician advised the hospital administration that the patient's condition wasn't critical, but he nevertheless requested hospitalization.

The hospital refused to admit Mr. Hunt because of a history of unpaid bills. During the next 4 hours, Mr. Hunt waited in the ED while the physician tried to find hospitalization for him elsewhere in the city. Eventually, Mr. Hunt was admitted to a neighboring hospital. He lived for 26 hours before dying of brain damage caused by prolonged seizures.

During the lawsuit that followed, the court examined the practice of ED nurses elsewhere and found that the Palm Springs General Hospital nurses had acted unreasonably. Their duty was to monitor Mr. Hunt's condition periodically while he awaited transfer to another hospital. If this duty had been carried out, the court concluded, the nurses would have noted his elevated temperature—a clear indication that he needed immediate hospitalization.

Similarly, in *Cline v. Lund (1973)*, the patient, Ms. Cline, was sent to a coronary care step-down unit when problems developed after she underwent a hysterectomy on July 10. Except for one bout with nausea, she appeared to be making satisfactory progress. At about 2:30 p.m. on July 11, a nurse dangled Ms. Cline's legs from the side of her bed. The nurse charted that the patient tolerated the dangling well. By 3:30 p.m., Ms. Cline was unresponsive, her blood pressure was rising, and she was vomiting.

At 9 p.m., when Ms. Cline's blood pressure reached 142/90 mm Hg, the attending nurse notified her supervisor, who at 9:40 p.m. notified the attending physician. He came to the hospital, examined the patient, and, suspecting an internal hemorrhage, ordered blood work and vital signs taken every 30 minutes. At 11:45 p.m., the patient's blood pressure was 160/90 mm Hg. Her arms and legs were stiff and her fists were clenched.

Instead of summoning the physician again, the attending nurse once more notified her supervisor. At 12:15 a.m. on July 12, when Ms. Cline's blood pressure had reached 230/130 mm Hg, the physician was called. The patient stopped breathing at 12:40 a.m., suffered a cardiac arrest at 12:45 a.m., and died at 4:45 a.m.

In the ensuing lawsuit, the court found the nurse liable, stating that her care had fallen below that of a reasonably prudent nurse in the same or similar circumstances. "Nurses," the court decision said, "should notify the physician of any significant change or unresponsiveness."

Canadian nursing standards

A Canadian nurse's performance is also measured against the appropriate standard of care. For example, in *Laidlaw v. Lions Gate Hospital (1969)*, the court held that both the PACU nurse who left for a coffee break and the supervisor who permitted her to leave should have anticipated an influx of patients from the operating room.

When the nurse left on her break, only two patients and the nurse supervisor were in the PACU. In a short time, however, three more patients arrived, including the plaintiff, Mrs. Laidlaw. Because only one nurse was on duty to care for five patients, Mrs. Laidlaw didn't receive appropriate care and suffered extensive, permanent brain damage as a result of anesthesia-related hypoxia.

When the resulting lawsuit came to trial, another nursing supervisor testified that usually two nurses were present in the PACU and that nurses weren't permitted to take breaks after new patients arrived. Other testimony revealed that PACU nurses should know the operating room schedule and should anticipate when new patients will arrive.

The court found the nurse who left and her supervisor negligent in leaving only one nurse on duty in the PACU.

Limits of nursing practice

When working in specialty care areas, nurses must not presume that increased training and broadened authority permit them to exceed nursing's legal limits. That's especially important in an area such as medical diagnosis, in which you can easily cross the legal boundary separating nursing from medicine.

One place where this sometimes happens is in the ED, where an on-call physician may refuse to see a patient himself, instead ordering care based on a nurse's observations of the patient. In another common ED situation, a patient asks an ED nurse for advice over the telephone. In such a case, she should respond carefully, telling the patient to come to the ED or see his physician if he has questions or his symptoms persist. Similar situations may occur in the PACU, ICU, and CCU, where split-second patient care decisions are sometimes made based on nurses' phone calls to attending physicians.

Keep in mind that all state and jurisdictional nurse practice acts prohibit nurses from medically diagnosing a patient's condition. The nurse can tell the physician about signs and symptoms observed but she can't decide which medical treatments to administer. If she does so, she'll be practicing medicine without a license and will be held at least partly liable for any harm to the patient that results.

Caution is necessary when advising patients about when to seek treatment or what course to follow when presented with patient symptoms. In *Starkey v. St. Rita's Medical Center (1997)*, an RN was answering telephone calls for the defendant's "The Professionals," a call-in and general referral service for the public, when the patient's wife called and reported his symptoms of sweating, belching, and feeling pressure in his chest. The patient had taken an anti-gas medication and fallen asleep before his wife made the call. According to Mrs. Starkey, the nurse told her to wait until he woke up to determine whether he should be brought to the hospital. Several hours later the patient awoke, was having the same symptoms, and was taken to the ED, where it was determined that he was having a heart attack. The patient contended that the delay in his treatment, based on this negligent advice, worsened his condition and injury, ultimately leading to his inability to resume his former employment.

The nurse testified that she didn't remember the conversation with the patient's wife and documentation of the phone conversation related to the fact that the nurse discussed symptoms of a heart attack, sent literature about heart attacks, and didn't make any recommendation about how to treat Mr. Starkey. But because the content of the conversation was in dispute, the nurse's conduct could have been found negligent in regard to giving improper advice, even in giving inappropriate medical advice. Although the plaintiff-patient lost his case on the issue of proving that this advice was the proximate cause of his injuries under the traditional burden of proof standard, he was given an opportunity to amend his complaint under a newly enacted cause of action, allowing

Should you practice as an independent contractor?

Thousands of nurses in the United States have chosen to become independent contractors. They work directly for patients (or patients' families) and bill their patients (or third-party insurers) on a fee-for-service basis. If you're considering practicing on an independent contractor basis, first weigh the pros and cons.

PROS
- You can schedule your work hours to suit your lifestyle.
- You can put your nursing philosophy into practice by independently planning each patient's nursing care.
- You'll be relatively free from institutional politics and bureaucracy.
- You can negotiate your own contract with each patient and set your own fee.
- You'll assume a more prestigious role in the health care community, and your working relations with other professionals may improve.
- You'll keep more of your earnings because tax laws favor self-employment.
- You can tailor your benefits package to your own personal needs.
- You can become more involved in the total care of your patient.

CONS
- You'll lose the security that continuous employment provides.
- You may experience strained working relations with professionals who feel threatened by your autonomy.
- You'll have to compete for work with other nurses who also are independent contractors.
- Your patients may be admitted to hospitals or other health care facilities where you don't have privileges.
- You'll have to educate yourself about the financial and legal aspects of running a business.
- You'll have to deal with getting patients to pay their bills.
- You'll carry the full responsibility for your liability and, if named in a lawsuit, be obligated to pay the entire cost of any damages awarded to a plaintiff.

recovery if the health care provider's negligence increased the risk of harm to the patient.[2]

Giving advice over the phone or other electronic devices should be done with caution. Recommendations include the use and following of standard questions, scripts, and protocols with accurate recording of the conversation or advice in a retrievable document or hard copy.

Private duty nursing
A private-duty nurse is any authorized RN or LPN that a patient or his family hires for skilled, direct, and comprehensive nursing care. (Some states, such as Maine, don't allow LPNs to become private-duty nurses.) Working as a private-duty nurse allows you to devote all your nursing skills to the care of one patient. Other advantages of working as a private-duty nurse include choosing where you work, when you work, and what type of patient you care for, as well as setting your own fee.

Employment status is the major factor that distinguishes a private-duty nurse from an agency nurse. A private-duty nurse is an independent contractor. She bills her patient or a third-party insurer directly. (See *Should you practice as an independent contractor?*) An agency may indirectly provide authorized private-duty nursing services, but in that instance the nurse works for the agency. (For more information, see Agency nursing discussed later in this chapter.)

A hospital or other health care facility may also hire a private-duty nurse. If that's the case, the private-duty nurse will bill the hospital for reimbursement directly.

Patients are referred to a private-duty nurse through nurse registries and referrals from other nurses and physicians who are familiar with the nurse's practice. Many hospitals maintain referral lists of private-duty nurses. If you work as a private-duty nurse long enough, you'll build up a clientele of hospitals, other health care facilities, nurses, physicians, and families.

Scope and limits of private duty nursing

A private-duty nurse performs most tasks a hospital staff nurse performs, and she's expected to have the same degree of knowledge and skill. The private duty nurse plans a patient's care, observes and evaluates his condition, reports signs and symptoms, carries out treatments under a physician's direction, and keeps accurate records so that the patient's physician has the data he needs to diagnose and prescribe. It's a private-duty nurse's obligation to perform her job within the scope of the state nurse practice act—the same as a staff nurse. A private-duty nurse working in a hospital setting can expect the hospital to provide her with adequate equipment and support services for proper patient care.

Private-duty nurses should be aware of the various states' laws on reimbursement, because they vary from state-to-state. Depending on the state, certain services may not be reimbursable under a state's Medicaid Administrative Code be-

cause they may not fall under the category of "skilled nursing."

Legal risks

A private-duty nurse faces legal risks not encountered by the hospital staff nurse. For example, a private-duty nurse doesn't retain professional liability insurance through an employer. As an independent contractor, she's solely liable for any damages assessed as the result of a lawsuit, although a court may decide that a hospital shares liability for her actions if the malpractice or injury occurred within the hospital. When working as a private-duty nurse, the nurse must purchase professional liability insurance. In addition, the private-duty nurse should have valid car insurance if she's using a personal vehicle for transportation.

Home health care

As an independent contractor, a private-duty nurse's legal risks are highest when caring for a patient in the patient's home. The nurse is responsible not only for providing proper care but also for obtaining and correctly using any equipment the patient requires, and for recognizing and acting on the need for appropriate referral. These added responsibilities naturally increase the chances of making a mistake. What's more, because the nurse is self-employed, legally she's solely responsible for paying court-ordered damages if sued and found negligent.

Making written contracts with the patient can help to reduce legal risks. Although a contract spells out the conditions of employment, having a contract doesn't prevent a lawsuit, nor can it provide evidence that will exonerate the nurse if sued.

Hospital care

The case of *Emory University v. Shadburn (1933)* set a precedent for a hospital's liability for a private-duty nurse's wrongful conduct. A patient jumped out a window after the assigned private-duty nurse, who had reason to know that his condition warranted continuous watching, left him unattended. The court ruled that the hospital was liable for the nurse's negligence because the hospital had hired and paid the nurse on a private-duty basis.

A hospital usually insists on tight control of a private-duty nurse's practice, both to protect patients and to demonstrate "reasonable supervision" in case of a lawsuit. Because of the trend to make hospitals share liability, a nurse will probably face liability alone only if she commits a negligent act despite the hospital's reasonable supervision.

Hospital controls include checking every private-duty nurse's credentials and approving her nursing qualifications. The case of *Ashley v. Nyack Hospital (1979)* ruled that a hospital has the right to refuse practice privileges to a nurse if the hospital doesn't approve her qualifications. Most hospitals also establish policies to govern how private-duty nursing relates to hospital nursing practice. Hospitals are obligated to inform all health care team members about private-duty nurses' responsibilities and rights in the hospital.

Financial challenges

A private-duty nurse working as an independent contractor must manage certain financial areas. For example, the nurse is responsible for making Social Security payments and paying federal, state, and local taxes on schedule. If injured on the job, the nurse isn't eligible for workers' compensation benefits. The courts have repeatedly rejected private-duty nurses' claims for workers' compensation. For example, in a Maryland case, *Edith Anderson Nursing Homes, Inc. v. Bettie Walker (1963),* a private-duty nurse was hurt caring for a nursing home patient who was in a wheelchair. The nurse attempted to collect workers' compensation benefits from the nursing home because her injury occurred there. At that time, however, the nurse was an independent contractor who was paid by the patient's family, didn't work for the nursing home, and took her orders only from the patient's physician. As an independent contractor, the court ruled, she wasn't entitled to the benefits available to the nursing home's employees. A subsequent appellate court decision upheld the denial of the nurse's claim. Therefore, the private-duty nurse should obtain her own insurance for such situations.

Professional challenges

Working *as* a private-duty nurse and working *with* a private-duty nurse each present their own unique challenges.

Working as a private-duty nurse requires the nurse to conform to the state's laws. Many states impose a laundry list of regulations on private-duty nurses (such as the minimum number of hours they must work for each patient), and it's important to follow them and keep up with any changes. The nurse is also responsible for knowing how the patient is paying for the service. If the patient is insured by a health maintenance organization, Medicare, or Medicaid, the nurse must meet the requirements listed in order to obtain reimbursement.

Other professional challenges include building a clientele; collaborating with physicians, health care prescribers, and patients and their families; and keeping up on medical research and clinical techniques.

When working on a unit on which a private-duty nurse is working, the unit nurse is responsible for seeing that the private-duty nurse receives the help needed. However, the unit nurse's responsibility doesn't end there; she's still responsible for the patient.

Monitor the private-duty nurse's care. If the unit nurse sees the private-duty nurse negligently performing care, she must inform the charge nurse. The charge nurse must intervene immediately. Regardless of the nurse's staff position, if she observes that the private-duty nurse is negligently performing emergency care when the patient's life is in danger, she must intervene immediately. Ignoring the private-duty nurse's negligence makes the unit nurse and the hospital liable if the patient or his family files a malpractice lawsuit.

If acting as the charge nurse, remember that the private-duty nurse's contract outlines her responsibilities. Read over the contract and keep its provisions in mind when making assignments. Never assign a private-duty nurse a job that involves responsibilities not included in the contract.

Long-term care
According to the American Association of Retired Persons compiling data from the U.S. Census Bureau, more than 15% of the population in the states of Florida, West Virginia, and Pennsylvania was older than age 65 in 2005. However, they project that by the year 2020, 42 states will exceed this percentage.[3] For those older than age 65, the increase is most likely due to the aging of the baby boomer population (those born between 1946 and 1964), whereas the increase in those age 85 or more is largely due to longevity.[4] This trend means that more patients will be cared for in long-term care facilities, such as nursing homes.

The rapid growth in the number of nursing homes and nursing home patients began in 1965, when Congress passed the Medicare and Medicaid amendments to the Social Security Act. These amendments provided government reimbursement for long-term care of elderly and disabled patients.

The Medicare and Medicaid amendments also provided reimbursement for skilled nursing care in extended-care facilities. These facilities were initially planned to deliver short-term nursing care to elderly patients who no longer needed intensive medical and nursing care in a hospital. Today, most patients admitted to long-term care facilities come directly from hospitals or other health care facilities. In 2005, 45% of nursing facility residents had dementia and approximately 20% had other psychological diagnoses.[5]

Scope and limits of long-term care nursing
Nurses in long-term care facilities provide skilled nursing, such as giving medications and patient teaching. They must be familiar with geriatric and rehabilitative medicine. Most of the long-term care workforce includes nursing assistants, home health care aides, personal care workers, and personal care attendants. It's important for the nurse to work with

Helping your patient select a long-term care facility

Your elderly or disabled patient may need the care provided at a long-term care facility. Help the patient and his family choose a facility by explaining the three types of long-term care facilities available and what type of care each offers.

RESIDENTIAL CARE FACILITY

Best for a patient who needs minimal medical attention, a residential care facility provides meals, modest medical care, and assistance with housekeeping responsibilities. Some offer recreational and social programs as well.

INTERMEDIATE-CARE FACILITY

Best for a patient who can't manage independently, an intermediate-care facility provides room, board, and daily nursing care. The cost may be covered by government subsidy programs. Some offer rehabilitation programs as well as recreational programs.

SKILLED NURSING FACILITY

Best for a patient who needs constant medical attention, a skilled nursing facility provides 24-hour nursing care, medical care when needed, and rehabilitation services such as physical and occupational therapies. Depending on the patient's eligibility, Medicare or Medicaid may subsidize the cost.

these health care workers effectively and delegate responsibilities efficiently.

Liability

Although the focus of long-term care nursing is on caring for those who are recovering from an illness (short-term) and providing supervision and medical care for those who have chronic medical problems (long-term), all patients in such facilities must be under the care of a physician. However, the fact that a patient is under a physician's care doesn't absolve the nurse from sharing in the responsibility for his care. If a patient's medical condition becomes emergent and goes unnoticed or if a patient's care doesn't meet reasonable standards, the nurse may be held liable.

Substandard care

Many long-term care facilities come under attack by state licensing and certification agencies for providing substandard care. (See *Helping your patient select a long-term care facility.*)

One major problem is that long-term care facilities employ only a small number of RNs. In 1996, the Institute of Medicine, which was chartered in 1970 by the National Academy of Sciences, released the results of a study that found that, although sickness and disability have increased among nursing home patients, employers' demands for nursing services haven't kept pace. In 2005, direct care nursing hours averaged about 3.7 hours per patient per day, out of which certified nursing assistants provided approximately 2.3 hours of direct care.[6] Medicare and Medicaid payments aren't sufficient to pay for adequate nursing staff. Ironically, Medicare and Medicaid payments, intended by Congress to help elderly and disabled patients, have inadvertently resulted in substandard care by subsidizing unsafe and understaffed facilities.

Aware of these trying circumstances, many RNs and LPNs working in long-term care facilities are greatly concerned about their legal rights and responsibilities. Areas of concern include staffing patterns, quality of care, and patients' rights.

Staffing patterns

In most long-term care facilities, RNs hold administrative positions, shouldering supervisory responsibility for the quality of care. According to the American Nurses Association (ANA), RNs provided approximately 20 minutes of care per day to residents in long-term care facilities.[7] LPNs in many facilities work as charge nurses, performing most nursing procedures and supervising nursing assistants. Patients may depend on nursing assistants for a substantial amount of care. This arrangement, created by minimal licensed personnel staffing, may lead to legal problems concerning both supervision and the scope of nursing practice. (See *Minimal licensed personnel staffing*.)

Legally, a supervisor is responsible for her supervisory acts and decisions. Suppose a supervisor knows—or should know—that a subordinate is inexperienced, untrained, or unable to perform a task safely. A court may indeed find that supervisor liable in a malpractice lawsuit for delegating such a task to the subordinate. To limit liability, a supervisor must determine that the individual to whom tasks are delegated is competent to perform the tasks. Even then, the supervisor must evaluate the outcomes of the performance of the tasks. (See six rights of delegation in Chapter 4.)

If the subordinate performs a task negligently, she will also be liable. Furthermore, if the court finds that the supervisor and the subordinate were working within the scope of their employment, the nursing home may share liability under the doctrine of *respondeat superior.*

Minimal licensed personnel staffing

Health care professionals use the term *minimal licensed personnel staffing* to describe the staffing situation in many long-term care facilities. Consider the following statistics:
- Only about 1 of every 20 nursing home employees is a registered nurse.
- Only about 1 licensed health care professional is employed for every 100 nursing home patients.
- Physicians spend only about 2 hours per month with their nursing home patients.
- In some extended-care facilities, about 6 of 10 charge nurses on the 3 p.m. to 11 p.m. shift and about 7 of 10 charge nurses on the 11 p.m. to 7 a.m. shift are licensed practical nurses.

In determining whether the defendant-nurse's actions met professional standards for the position, the courts may review details of the staffing situation. For example, a New York court found that nurses were negligent when an unsupervised patient jumped from a balcony (*Horton v. Niagara Falls Memorial Medical Center [1976]*). The court reached this conclusion after reviewing evidence detailing how many patients were on the unit, how many staff members were there, and what each staff member was doing. During this review, the court discovered that a charge nurse had permitted the only available nursing assistant to go to supper when she had the authority to prevent it, leaving the disoriented patient unsupervised.

An RN or LPN working in a long-term care facility must practice within the legal limits set by the state's nurse practice act, meet professional standards for the position, and be familiar with state regulations for the type of facility in which the nurse works.

An RN must possess the management and supervisory skills required by the job. If sued for malpractice, the nurse will be judged according to how a reasonably prudent nursing supervisor would act in similar circumstances. Defending one's self by claiming lack of training to supervise isn't valid.

An LPN working in a long-term care facility must remember that no person or facility can force her to practice beyond the limits outlined in the state's nurse practice act. Exceeding the legally permissible scope of nursing practice in the state can lead to license suspension or revocation by the state board of nursing. The nurse couldn't use the employer's expectations to excuse the actions.

Under the law, an LPN who performs a nursing function legally restricted to RNs will be held to the RN standard if she's sued for malpractice. *Barber v. Reinking (1966)* involved an LPN who had performed an RN function. The court stated, "In accordance with public policy of this state, one who undertakes to perform the services of a trained or graduate nurse must have the knowledge and skill possessed by the registered nurse."

Quality of care

Many nurses working in long-term care facilities are particularly concerned about the fragmentation of the nursing process. Although an RN remains responsible for overall patient assessment and evaluation, an LPN commonly decides on the daily assessments, planning, and evaluation, and a nursing assistant implements the assessment plan.

Fragmenting the nursing process can greatly reduce the quality of patient care. It can also have legal consequences if nursing actions are performed improperly—or not performed at all. This list describes poor nursing practices that plague long-term care facilities:

▶ Failing to make a nursing diagnosis
▶ Being careless in the observation of a patient's condition
▶ Failing to document
▶ Writing illegibly when documenting
▶ Failing to keep up with current nursing knowledge required to care for elderly and disabled patients
▶ Failing to use nursing consultants
▶ Delegating improperly
▶ Failing to insist on clear facility policies
▶ Failing to question an order
▶ Taking a dangerous patient care shortcut
▶ Excluding the patient's family from patient care
▶ Failing to call the physician whenever nursing judgment indicates that a patient needs medical attention.

Consider the case of an RN named Adams who reported unsafe staffing levels at his facility in Massachusetts. He was harassed by management and then fired in 1996. Mr. Adams filed a lawsuit and a complaint with the National Labor Relations Board (NLRB), and both a judge and the NLRB ruled that he was wrongfully terminated and his firing was "illegal" and "an attempt to silence and retaliate against him." (NLRB case 1-CA-34663[1-2] and 1-CA-34699). Mr. Adams then filed a complaint with the Massachusetts Board of Nursing against his former nursing supervisor alleging unprofessional and unethical conduct. The complaint stated that, based on her actions, she condoned the unsafe staffing levels that may have contributed to a patient's death. Massachusetts Board of Nursing members said the allegations were either lacking in sufficient evidence or had been resolved.

Patients' rights

Many states have enacted patients' rights legislation patterned after the Patient's Bill of Rights published by the American Hospital Association. Most of these states have passed laws that make reporting maltreatment of patients a legal responsibility. Some states have even established an ombudsman's office that has the authority to investigate complaints of abuse and the obligation to post complaint procedures in all geriatric facilities.

On the federal level, the Omnibus Budget Reconciliation Act of 1987 dramatically strengthens the rights of nursing home residents. The law says that nursing home residents have the right to choose a personal attending physician, to participate in planning their own care and treatment, and to be free from physical or mental abuse, corporal punishment, and physical or chemical restraints imposed for purposes of discipline or convenience. The law also imposes new requirements for additional nursing staff. In 1989, the Department of Health and Human Services, in an effort to carry out the 1987 law, issued new rules governing Medicare and Medicaid reimbursement for nursing homes.

The Omnibus Budget Reconciliation Act of 1990 brought about the Patient Self-Determination Act. This legislation covers all long-term care facilities that participate in Medicare or Medicaid funding. It requires that the facility or agency must provide the patient with written information about the patient's rights under the state law at the time of admission to any hospital or nursing home or enrollment with a health maintenance organization, hospice, or home health agency. In addition, the facility must document if the patient has an advance directive and comply with all state laws regarding advance directives, including providing staff and community education on advance directive issues.

If you work in a long-term care facility, you should request that your facility:

▶ require a patient's signature for any release of information

▶ ask if the patient has an advance directive, living will, or durable health care power of attorney

▶ clearly specify who has access to medical records and impose penalties for unauthorized disclosure of patient information

▶ foster a patient's right to know about his condition and provide for informed consent for his treatment

▶ help combat drug abuse and misuse by requiring nurses who give drugs to know their effects and how to assess each patient's changing needs

▶ ensure prompt, effective communication between physicians and nurses

▶ acknowledge and respect a patient's right to refuse treatment

▶ encourage nurses to evaluate the quality of nursing services

▶ encourage nurses to work cooperatively with patient representatives and accreditation agencies

▶ restrict the use of chemical and physical restraints; restraints should be used only when the patient's physical or mental status gives evidence that restraints are necessary (and even then only with a physician's order) and solely for the patient's safety.

Most health care professionals are patients' rights advocates, but advocating for patient's rights may lead to conflicts with coworkers and employers. This is one paradox of nursing practice: Nurses have a professional obligation to protect their patients' rights, but doing so could end up costing the nurse her job. Unfortunately, the nurse's legal protection in this situation is limited. If the nurse is an employee working without a contract, also known as *employee-at-will,* he can be dismissed for any reason the employer wants to give. Nurses do have legal grounds to protest their dismissal if:

▶ the contract clearly states that the nurse can't be fired on these grounds
▶ the facility guarantees the nurse the right to notice and a hearing before dismissal
▶ the state's laws prevent the employer from retaliating if the nurse reports violations to the appropriate agency
▶ the nurse is a government employee and can claim the First Amendment right to free speech.

Financial challenges
Because many long-term care patients are Medicare or Medicaid recipients, the nurse must be familiar with the strict federal medical coding for billing. She should ensure that the long-term care facility follows strict billing procedures.

Professional challenges
Working in a long-term care facility can present many professional challenges, including those related to time management, a patient's quality of life, declining functional and cognitive status, chronic health conditions, interactions with a patient and his family over an extended period, and end-of-life issues. It's important to handle these challenges with care that's based on the nurse practice act and board of nursing rules and regulations; doing so ensures solid legal standing.

Opportunities
In a long-term care facility in which physicians' involvement with patients is limited, RNs and LPNs have an opportunity to grow professionally and to influence the quality of patient care. RNs can learn about geriatric nursing and management. An LPN may have the chance to fill a charge nurse position and to expand nursing skills. Depending on the nurse practice act, the LPN may also learn how to perform nursing assessment and patient teaching. However, keep in mind that along with opportunity comes responsibility—for practicing within legal limits and for continuing one's education to meet professional standards.

Alternative practice settings
Practicing nursing outside of traditional settings, such as hospitals, clinics, and nursing homes, dates back to the 19th century. Back then, most nurses worked outside hospitals: in physicians' offices, in patients' homes, and on battlefields. Today, many nurses practice in alternative settings. Their employers include factories, schools, the military, insurance companies, and claims review agencies. (See *Providing nursing care in alternative settings.*)

When working in an alternative setting, a nurse may not have the legal services of a hospital's administration to provide assistance during a dispute. The nurse must take on the special challenge of knowing her legal responsibilities.

Providing nursing care in alternative settings

Nurses choose to practice in alternative settings for many reasons: to take on greater challenges and achieve more responsibility, for a change of pace, to increase their earning power, or to make an impact on public health policy.

The list below describes some of the important options for nurses today: school nursing, occupational health nursing, air rescue nursing, and hospice nursing. You'll also find descriptions of nursing opportunities in the business world: working as a case coordinator for an insurance company, making it on your own as an entrepreneur, or working in the legal arena.

SCHOOL NURSE

As a school nurse, your responsibilities include providing nursing care for sick or injured students and giving first aid in emergencies. When authorized, you also give medications to students. Other tasks include:
● assisting in examinations
● giving annual screening tests, for example, vision, audiometry, and scoliosis tests, and referring students for further testing or treatment when appropriate
● counseling parents and students
● meeting with teachers and other staff members about health problems and health education programs
● enforcing state immunization policies for school-age children
● visiting sick or injured students at home when necessary
● helping identify and meet special needs of disabled students.

OCCUPATIONAL HEALTH NURSE

As an occupational health nurse, your primary responsibility is to provide nursing care for sick or injured employees. Other responsibilities include:
● giving first aid in emergencies
● performing medical screening tests or helping the physician perform them
● referring sick or injured employees for appropriate treatment
● counseling employees on health matters
● meeting with management regarding health-related issues
● developing and maintaining employee medical records
● maintaining records for government agencies, such as workers' compensation agencies, the Occupational Safety and Health Administration, and state or federal labor and health departments
● alerting management to potential health and safety hazards.

AIR RESCUE NURSE

As an air rescue nurse, you have a job that's glamorous, challenging, and hazardous. Many of the dilemmas that you and your fellow air rescue nurses face are unique and, as a small group, you don't have much power to exact change. Dilemmas include:
● scheduled 24-hour shifts for nurses and pilots, which cause concerns for quality work and safety for everyone on board the helicopter
● right to refuse an assigned flight because of personal safety concerns
● applying patient restraints unnecessarily or risking patients with borderline behavior becoming violent during flight and jeopardizing all on board
● safety concerns related to loading and unloading while rotor blades are in motion
● protective equipment for the helicopter and protective gear for crew members, which is lacking in most helicopters
● air rescue nurse familiarity with aircraft-specific emergency procedures and equipment.

HOSPICE NURSE

As a hospice nurse, your most important responsibility is to provide skilled nursing care to the terminally ill patient. Expect to focus on providing pain relief and symptom control. Patients and their families rely heavily on you for emotional and psychosocial support. Professional satisfaction typically comes from knowing that you've helped the dying patient maintain dignity and make the most of the time he has left. The most significant means of limiting your lia-

(continued)

Providing nursing care in alternative settings *(continued)*

bility is to review advance directives and living wills that have been prepared on behalf of the patient. If these documents haven't been drafted, you need to consider reviewing these issues with the patient to prepare for the ultimate care and treatment. Before your patient becomes unconscious, review options with him so his wishes are carried out.

NURSING CASE COORDINATOR FOR AN INSURANCE COMPANY

When working for an insurance company, your responsibilities may include reviewing records and assessing insurance claims by talking with the patient, his physician, his family, and his employer. You may be asked to help design patient care plans. These care plans typically include medical, nursing, social service, and payment goals. You may also monitor the patient's progress and prognosis by talking with the patient and his physicians. Other tasks include:

● helping to coordinate medical, rehabilitation, and other services
● supervising other nursing case reviewers
● developing and maintaining insurance company records.

NURSE ENTREPRENEUR

As an entrepreneur, you must organize and manage your own business undertaking. You take on the risk of failure for the sake of potential profit. Your opportunity to apply nursing skills as an entrepreneur is limited only by your own imagination. For example, nurses have established successful businesses providing such services as reviewing medical records and performing research for insurance companies and

personal injury lawyers; finding medical experts for testimony in medical malpractice actions, personal injury litigation, and workers' compensation matters; and developing educational programs for use inside hospitals.

In Canada, self-employed nurses are permitted to offer any service that falls within the practice of nursing and doesn't infringe upon the exclusive practice of another health discipline. The service requires applying professional nursing knowledge. Services offered include direct patient care such as patient teaching about breast-feeding for new mothers; family counseling; health promotion services, such as stress management or occupational health nursing services; and administrative services such as quality assurance monitoring in health care facilities and agencies.

NURSING IN THE LEGAL ARENA

As a legal nurse consultant, you provide valuable support during the investigation and litigation of claims, serve as an expert witness, and review medical records. Many nurses work as independent contractors to provide these services to law firms.

Nurse expert witnesses provide advice during litigation and testify in court about nursing issues. Although there's no special training for the witness role, an attorney will consider nursing experience and credentials when choosing an expert witness.

Nurses who pursue additional education may become attorneys or paralegals. Nurse paralegals primarily research law and write as well as organize and examine medical records in a medical negligence case.

Scope and limits of alternative practice nursing

Most states' nurse practice acts don't discuss professional standards for nurses working in alternative settings. However, the nurse still must meet the same practice standards as a hospital nurse. Any violation can result in license suspension or

revocation by the state board of nursing, just as it would for hospital nursing. In addition, the patient may sue the nurse for malpractice.

Historically, courts have held nurses who work in alternative settings to state standards for nursing practice. A California malpractice case, *Cooper v.*

National Motor Bearing Co. (1955), concerned an occupational health nurse who failed to diagnose suspected cancer and didn't refer the patient for further evaluation and treatment. At the trial, the court ruled that the only point of law to be considered in deciding the case was whether the nurse met the standards of nursing practice in her area. When expert testimony showed that she had breached those standards, the court found her negligent. Her occupational setting was irrelevant to the court's decision. Similar court cases illustrating this principle include *Planned Parenthood of Northwest Ind. v. Vines (1989)*, *Barber v. Reinking (1966)*, and *Stahlin v. Hilton Hotels Corp. (1973)*.

The Canadian approach to such cases is similar to the American approach. In *Dowey v. Rothwell (1974)*, a nurse who worked in a physician's office knew that an epileptic patient was about to have a seizure, yet she failed to stay with the patient. This patient did have a seizure, fell, and fractured an arm. The court found that the nurse failed "to provide that minimum standard of care which a patient has a right to expect in an office setting." The court based its findings on testimony about the expected performance standards of experienced RNs in many settings.

Liability

In certain cases, when working in an alternative setting, the nurse may be protected from a liability suit. For example, working for a government agency may protect the nurse from lawsuits because of the doctrine of sovereign immunity. Depending on the state in which you're working, this immunity may be complete or partial. To determine the extent of the

Understanding sovereign immunity

The doctrine of sovereign immunity goes back to the days when a person couldn't sue a sovereign or his agents unless the sovereign consented. In the United States, the courts transferred this privilege, applicable in most circumstances, to the elected government and its appointed agents—government employees. So government employees ordinarily can't be sued for their on-the-job mistakes.

UNFAIR RESULTS

In the past, this immunity has had some unfair results. A patient harmed in a private hospital could sue the hospital and its employees, but a patient harmed in a municipal or state hospital couldn't.

Perhaps because of this immunity, public hospitals gained a reputation for substandard practice; the public suspected that because public hospitals couldn't be sued for malpractice, their standards of care were lax.

LEGISLATIVE ACTION

In recent decades, most state legislatures have recognized the unfairness of this system. Many have passed laws that allow patients to sue public hospitals and other government agencies on a full or limited basis. In some states, legislatures have created special courts, usually called *courts of claims,* in which such lawsuits must be heard. Many state legislatures have set dollar limits on the amount a patient can recover from a government agency if he wins his suit.

immunity, check with the personnel office or agency attorney. (See *Understanding sovereign immunity*.)

Even if she's working for a privately owned business, such as an insurance company or a small medical practice group, the nurse is still vulnerable to malpractice suits. In some states, however, the nurse can't be sued by a fellow employee she has treated for a job-related injury. State workers' compensation laws, which protect the employer from excessive business costs, also protect the nurse.

Financial challenges

Employee benefits is an important area to evaluate when choosing a nursing career in an alternative setting. Benefits and liability coverage may be somewhat different from that provided in a hospital setting.

Professional liability insurance

Most private medical employers have coverage that includes the nurses they employ, but private industrial employers, especially small companies, may not. Check the employer's coverage thoroughly. If there's any doubt about protection, consider purchasing personal liability insurance.

Personal professional liability insurance also may be necessary when working for a peer-review organization or a state or federal government agency, unless the law grants the nurse complete immunity from job-related lawsuits.

Union eligibility

A nurse usually retains the right to join a union. In fact, when working as an occupational health nurse in a factory with a closed shop, the nurse may be required to join a union.

When working for a state or local government, state laws may permit the nurse to join a union but may forbid the union to strike. Remember that the National Labor Relations Act exempts state and local governments and doesn't protect government nurses, such as community health nurses and public school nurses, in unionization disputes.

Termination of employment

Regardless of the setting, nothing but a contract clause, a union agreement, or a civil service law can legally protect a nurse from being fired. Even with such protection, the nurse may be vulnerable to discretionary firing until the end of an initial probationary period. After this period, any of these forms of protection guarantees the nurse the right to appeal the employer's decision.

Workers' compensation

When working in an alternative setting, nurses need to know what coverage the employer and the state, federal, or Canadian jurisdictional government provide for on-the-job injuries. Workers' compensation will usually cover the nurse, but not always.

Most states and jurisdictions require many privately owned businesses to participate in workers' compensation plans. Employment for such a business usually means that the individual will probably receive workers' compensation for job-related injuries. However, nurses need to be aware that, if the money received from this fund is inadequate, workers' compensation laws prevent the nurse from suing the employer for additional compensation.

Some states don't require employers with few employees or limited income (for example, a physician with a small practice) to participate in the workers' compensation plan. So nurses working in such a setting need to be aware that they may not be covered by workers' compensation for job-related injuries. In the event of a job-related injury, the nurse can sue the employer directly.

Most small employers buy their own insurance to cover workers' injuries. If the employer doesn't have such insurance, nurses can buy their own insurance.

When working for a state or federal government agency, a nurse may receive compensation from the state workers' compensation plan or by filing a claim under a state or federal tort claims act, depending on the applicable laws. However, if the sovereign immunity doctrine applies, the nurse may not be eligible for compensation.

If a nurse is eligible for workers' compensation, it usually covers any on-the-job injury. For example, if a student kicks a school nurse, workers' compensation will normally cover the nurse. The nurse also usually has the legal right to sue the person who caused the injury. If the nurse wins the lawsuit, the court, depending on state or territory statute, may consider any money the nurse has already received, either from workers' compensation or from other insurance, in deciding the amount of damages to be awarded. Because lawsuits are costly and can take years to resolve, most nurses don't sue.

Professional challenges

Nurses working in an alternative health care setting will face many challenges unlike those faced in the traditional hospital setting. Depending upon the setting the nurse has chosen, he'll have to meet and overcome these challenges. The nurse will have to understand and meet the needs of culturally and ethnically diverse clients, stay current with emerging trends, and be responsible in continuing her professional education.

Home health care nursing

More patients are receiving nursing care in their homes. From 1993 to 2006, the number of persons working in home health care increased by an average of 5.4 % with the largest numbers being home health aides and RNs.[8] What's more, nursing care measures implemented in the patient's home are becoming more sophisticated. Whereas every hospital has similar characteristics, every home is unique. Each represents a different pattern of legal risks and an unknown constellation of interpersonal relationships.

Scope and limits of home health care nursing

Home health care nursing makes it possible for patients to obtain nursing care in their own homes. Unlike what patients receive with home health care aide service, RNs can provide skilled nursing care for all patients, regardless of their age or disease state. However, it's important for the home health care nurse to follow the federal and state laws that regulate home health care nursing as well as her state's nurse practice act.

Liability

One factor that clearly affects a nurse's potential liability as a home health care nurse is the degree of control over the home environment, which is much less controlled than the hospital environment. For example, situations such as safety hazards that result in liability in the hospital may have a different outcome in home health care litigation because the health care provider has little control over the home setting. One of the greatest hazards for home health care is related to the amount of lifting, which can lead to severe muscle injuries.

If a nurse works for a home health care agency and her responsibilities include managing other home health care workers, keep in mind that it's more difficult to evaluate personnel who work in the patient's home. Negligent training of a home health care worker may form the basis for a legal action. In *Loton v. Massachusetts Paramedical Inc. (1989),* a personal care worker employed by a home health care company left the patient unattended in a shower. The worker left the apartment to go to another part of the building to do laundry. While the patient was alone, the temperature of the water became very hot. As the patient tried to readjust the water, she fell from the shower seat and inadvertently moved the temperature control to the hot zone. Because of her underlying disability, she couldn't move away from the scalding water. When the worker returned, she couldn't reach her supervisor. She then applied ice to the burns and waited before calling an ambulance. The patient suffered third-degree burns over a large portion of her body, requiring numerous operations and skin grafting.

The plaintiff alleged that the home health care agency was negligent in failing to educate personnel in managing patients with disabilities and also in not training staff for the appropriate response in emergency situations. The jury rejected the agency's defense and awarded the plaintiff $1 million.

Along with civil claims for malpractice and negligence, a home health care provider or agency may be held liable for criminal actions in cases of serious neglect. In one case involving neglect, a patient had been receiving home health care service. She was admitted to the hospital with numerous pressure ulcers, some of which extended to the bone. The woman looked unwashed and had a necrotic odor. An indictment was brought against the home health care agency, the administrator of one of its offices, a visiting nurse employed by the company, and an LPN in the agency's nursing and supportive care program. The charge involved knowingly and willfully neglecting the patient, causing serious mental and physical injury. After a jury trial, the company was convicted of a Class A misdemeanor and fined more than $8,000.

Financial challenges

Most home health care nurses must own their own vehicle or provide their own transportation to their clients' homes; however, most home health care agencies reimburse nurses for gas and mileage.

Professional challenges

Over the past several years, home health care has had many setbacks. The industry's main obstacles have been increased government regulation and the cuts in Medicare reimbursement. For example, Medicare will pay for skilled services such as wound care in the home, but not for long-term care for the chronically ill, which is tragic for this aging population. Home health care nurses must also continually prove the "cost-effectiveness" of their services and care to the government and to the insurers. Much of a nurse's time is spent on paperwork, proper billing and coding, and reimbursement for supplies and services.

The challenges for home health care nurses aren't all financial. When the nurse enters a patient's home, she must assess the patient's living situation, the physical environment, and family support, and figure how it affects the care and the patient's activities of daily living. The nurse alone must assess the patient's status at home, his well-being, and his ability to stay at home or his need for acute care, and she is usually the first person to assess a patient following discharge from a hospital or after a surgical procedure.

The home health care nurse is also required to keep up with technological advances in nursing care and provide the patient with appropriate patient teaching.

Agency nursing

Temporary nursing service agencies represent an innovative approach to the delivery of nursing services—one response to the constant demand for practical, efficient, and cost-effective nursing care. Many nurses decide to work for a temporary nursing service agency to achieve greater work schedule flexibility and the right to choose their own hours. What's more, most agencies pay higher salaries than hospitals. In addition, travel nursing agencies are available which provide nurses with an opportunity to travel to different states or regions.

When working for an agency, the nurse has an employee-employer relationship with that agency. The agency charges a fee for the nurse's services from which it pays the nurse's salary. It may also provide such benefits as Social Security and other tax deductions, workers' compensation, sick pay, and professional liability insurance. Traditional nursing registries don't enter into employee-employer relationships with private-duty nurses when they provide client referrals.

Scope and limits of agency nursing

Agency nurses work for a health care agency. The agency contracts with a health care facility to provide RN coverage in a capacity that fulfills the facility's needs. An agency nurse may work in a hospital as a staff nurse, in a home as a home health care nurse, in a clinical research study for a university or pharmaceutical company, or wherever else the agency places the individual. The scope is that of an RN, and the agency can't contract the nurse for a job that's beyond her credentials. For example, if the nurse hasn't been certified in telemetry, then that nurse can't work on a telemetry floor. The agency nurse is obligated by her state's nurse practice act and the contractual agreement between the nurse and the employer-agency. For the travel nurse, she must obtain the necessary licensure of the state in which the assignment is located. In such situations, the agency typically works with the nurse to obtain the necessary information. In addition, most travel agencies suggest that the nurse contact individual state boards of nursing from the states in which the nurse is planning to work to get the most up-to-date information.

A nurse's professional responsibilities as an agency worker are typically vague. No set of uniform policies and procedures has been formally identified or administratively defined. For example, if an RN and an LPN are assigned to care for the same patient in his home but on different shifts, what responsibility does the RN have for the LPN's work? Is the RN responsible for supervising home health care aides? Also, should communication between the RN and the patient's physician be direct or channeled through an agency supervisor?

Large agencies, especially those with nationwide placement, may have specific policies to deal with situations like these. But smaller, more regional agencies may not. Without clear-cut guidelines, nurses need to rely heavily on their professional nursing judgment. However, remember that the courts apply the same legal principles governing staff nurse malpractice cases to agency nurse malpractice cases.

Liability

A nurse is liable for her own wrongful conduct. However, if an agency nurse is judged to have been working within the legally permissible scope of employment, then the agency may be held vicariously liable and may be required to pay any damages awarded to the plaintiff. The court may use the doctrine of *respondeat superior* to interpret the nurse's legal status. This doctrine makes an employer responsible for the negligent acts of the employees, so the agency is responsible for the actions of the nurses it employs. If the court finds that the nurse exceeded the scope of employment, she may be solely responsible for any damages.

An agency employee may be assigned to work in a patient's home, to care for a single patient in a hospital or other health care facility, or to temporarily supplement a facility's staff. These different practice circumstances can influence how a court determines liability. A malpractice lawsuit that involves an agency nurse will probably name as defendants the nurse, the temporary nursing service agency and, if applicable, the health care facility in which the alleged malpractice happened. When working as an agency nurse in a patient's home, the agency-employee status is usually clear-cut. The

same is true when caring for a single patient in a health care facility.

The courts have more difficulty assigning legal liability in cases that involve agency nurses working as supplemental facility staff. In this situation, the nurse is an agency employee, but she's also in the "special service" of another "employer"—the facility.

Courts may apply the borrowed servant (or *ostensible agent*) doctrine, holding that the regular employer (the agency) isn't liable for injury negligently caused by the nurse-employee (the "servant") while in the special service of another employer (the hospital). Although the legal liability shifts from the agency to the hospital or facility when a court interprets a case this way, the nurse may be held to be the agent of both the agency and the hospital, under the doctrine of dual agency, making both potentially liable.

Professional guidelines

To help protect against a lawsuit, a nurse needs to be sure to fully understand what's expected when accepting an agency job. Be prepared to adjust to different policies and procedures. This requires review of policy manuals and a clear understanding of what they contain. When working in a patient's home, for example, the agency's policies and procedures govern the nurse's actions. Be sure to understand them thoroughly and follow them carefully. How competently the nurse follows a procedure may affect such matters as whether a claim for workers' compensation is allowed or whether the agency will be included as a defendant with the nurse in a malpractice suit. Don't perform any nonnursing functions when working in a patient's home or arbitrarily change his nursing regimen policies and procedures from what the agency has specified. If the nurse does so and the patient or his family decides to sue, the nurse may be found solely liable.

ANA guidelines

The ANA has issued guidelines outlining the responsibilities of temporary-nursing agencies and agency nurses. These guidelines say that an agency has a duty to select, orient, evaluate, and assign nurses and to provide them with professional development. According to these guidelines, agency nurses should:
▶ keep their licenses current
▶ select reputable employers
▶ maintain their nursing skills
▶ observe the standards of professional nursing practice
▶ document their nursing practice
▶ adhere to the policies and procedures of their agencies and clients.

The last point is particularly important if an agency assigns a nurse to work in a hospital or other health care facility. As always, the nurse must be sure to understand the policies and procedures of the facility for the nursing tasks she's expected to perform.

The hospital or facility, in turn, is obligated to supply any equipment that may be needed for patient care and to keep its premises and equipment in safe condition.

Financial challenges

Although agency nurses are paid a higher salary because of the flexibility and skill they're willing to offer, agencies don't have to offer benefits (such as health, pension, and savings plans) because these nurses are temporary employees. To obtain such benefits, agency nurses must ei-

ther bear the cost on their own (for example, by purchasing private health insurance) or seek additional, part-time employment with an employer that offers such benefits.

Professional challenges

Agency nurses must have years of acute care experience and be comfortable and confident with their acute care skills. Flexibility in where to work and willingness to travel or work in different areas or in different capacities (such as a home health care nurse, a staff nurse, or a critical care nurse) and in different settings are important considerations. An agency nurse is expected to keep up with the most current information and technology. Although the employing agency may offer additional classes, the nurse is ultimately responsible for maintaining certifications and continuing education.

Agency nurses must learn quickly and adjust to the working environment and be able to work well with others. Additionally, because of the nursing shortage crisis, many health care facilities are turning to agency nurses to help solve their staffing problem. In this situation, an agency nurse will have to be prepared for whatever challenges may arise, such as heavy patient loads, the absence of more experienced nurses to whom the nurse may turn for support, and low morale.

Despite the challenges that agency nursing presents, many agency nurses find their role fulfilling because it offers them flexibility as well as the opportunity to put their wide range of nursing skills to use.

If you're a hospital staff nurse and an agency nurse is assigned to your unit, your responsibilities as a coworker are the same as those when you're working with a nonagency nurse. For example, if you see the agency nurse performing a procedure in a way that may harm the patient, you have a responsibility to stop the procedure, just as you would if you saw a nonagency nurse performing that same procedure. If you see an agency nurse performing a procedure incorrectly but without potential harm to the patient, simply report your observation to your nursing supervisor.

Controversy over agency nursing
When a nursing shortage exists, many health care facilities suffer imbalances in the number of nurses available to work regularly scheduled shifts. Temporary nursing service agencies provide a valuable service by supplying skilled nurses on short notice. However, use of agency-provided RNs and LPNs as supplemental staff in hospitals, nursing homes, and extended-care facilities can be controversial.

On the one hand, critics point out that inequities in salaries between hospital and agency nurses performing the same functions can lead to morale problems. Proponents of agency-based supplemental staffing, on the other hand, stress the cost-effectiveness of the practice and believe that its flexibility helps to keep nurses working and prevents nurse burnout. Proponents and critics urge that nursing administrations plan supplemental staffing programs instead of bringing in agency nurses on a few hours' notice before a shift begins. Adequate planning helps to maintain quality and continuity of patient care.

Potential for legal precedent
Although no plaintiff has ever charged a hospital with inadequate staffing caused by a failure to obtain available supplemental staff from an agency, observers of the nursing profession believe that this may happen soon. In a Louisiana case, *McCutchon v. Mutual of Omaha Insurance Co. (1978),* a court required an insurance company to pay the agency fees of two LPNs recruited to care for a critically ill patient whose physician had ordered RNs (and whose insurance policy allowed payment for only RNs). The court reached its decision after reviewing evidence that the temporary nursing service agency, the hospital, and the insurance company could locate no available RNs at the time the LPNs were assigned. The court also considered the fact that the assigned LPNs were closely supervised by an RN at all times.

JOB-RELATED ISSUES ASSOCIATED WITH LEGAL RISK

Consider this. You're struggling through your shift in an ICU. You're already caring for more patients than one nurse can possibly handle, when the ED calls and says two more patients will be arriving soon. You know there's no way you can provide safe care. Your supervisor turns down your pleas for additional staff. Your first impulse is to walk out. How can you remedy this situation?

You're caring for a patient with a criminal record and a reputation for narcotics dealing. You're nervous enough as it is, but the situation gets worse when a stranger stops you in the hallway, flashes a detective's badge, and asks for articles of the patient's clothing and a blood sample. He says you're legally obligated to turn over this evidence. Should you do what he tells you?

A prestigious civic leader who's a candidate for local political office recently has made several trips to the ED. She has brought her daughter, whom she calls "Miss Clumsy." The child has had multiple hematomas. You think it *might* be child abuse. Fearful of wrongfully damaging the woman's reputation, you hesitate to make a report. What should you do?

Your patient has told you repeatedly that he doesn't want any "heroic measures" taken or "means" used to preserve his life if there's no reasonable chance of recovery. However, one evening after the patient has experienced a massive stroke, five members of his family march into your office demanding that everything be done to preserve his life. Should you fight to have the patient's wishes respected?

The situations described above are examples of the complex legal dilemmas you may encounter in daily practice. As the nursing profession grows and you take on greater responsibilities, you'll inevitably face increased legal vulnerability. Hardly any aspect of nursing practice is untouched by legal risk. It's important that you know how to avoid possible litigious or legally damaging situations. (See *Taking steps to prevent lawsuits,* pages 202 and 203.)

Regardless of educational background, a nurse is always legally accountable for her nursing actions. In any practice setting, a nurse's care must meet minimum legal standards. In addition, care should:
▶ reflect the scope of the state's nurse practice act

▶ measure up to established practice standards
▶ consistently protect the patient.

Upholding these standards should provide a base for sound legal practice no matter where the nurse practices.

Hospital policies

Every hospital and health care facility has *policies*—a set of general guidelines and principles by which it manages its affairs. Nurses are obligated to know these policies and to follow the established procedures that flow from them.

However, never do this blindly. A nurse is also obligated to maintain professional standards, and these standards may sometimes conflict with the employer's policies and procedures. At times, a nurse may be forced to make decisions and take actions that risk violating those policies and procedures. A nurse must do what's best for her patient. If it's unsafe to follow the policy, then don't. Document the reasons for not following policy and inform the nurse-manager and the nursing supervisor of your actions.

At times such as these, a nurse may need help in balancing duty to the patient with responsibility to the employer. The best help is a nursing department policy manual that states relevant, clear guidelines based on up-to-date standards of care that are generally accepted by the profession. A typical problem with policies is that they aren't practical, are too restrictive, or involve standards too difficult to meet. In addition, there may be so many policies that nurses aren't familiar with all of them.

A policy manual that states relevant, clear guidelines based on the most up-to-date standards of care is the mark of a successful nursing department—one

Taking steps to prevent lawsuits

Any time you provide care that falls short of current legal and nursing standards, you make yourself a target for a malpractice suit.

In most situations, you can prevent this from happening by following these guidelines in your daily practice.

DEFEND THE PATIENT

Your first duty is to protect your patient, not his physician. If your judgment says your patient's condition warrants a call to his physician, don't hesitate, in the middle of the day or in the middle of the night, to fully communicate your concerns to the physician. If your judgment says to question a physician's order because you can't read it, don't understand it, think it's incomplete, or think it may harm your patient, don't hesitate.

If your hospital doesn't already have a policy covering nurse-physician communications, ask for one and keep asking until you get one. Meanwhile, for your own protection, carefully record all contacts with physicians, including the date, time, and the substance of the communication.

STAY CURRENT

Here are some effective ways to stay up-to-date on nursing practices: read nursing journals, attend clinical programs, attend in-service programs, and seek advice from nurse specialists. If your hospital doesn't offer needed in-service programs, ask for them. Check the Internet for online continuing education courses.

Remember, ignorance of new techniques is no excuse for substandard care. If you're ever sued for malpractice, your patient care will be judged against current nursing standards, regardless of whether your employer has offered you the nec-

essary training. This is especially true if you're certified in a specialty area.

USE THE ENTIRE NURSING PROCESS

Taking shortcuts increases risks to your patient's well-being and your own. If you're charged with malpractice, and the court finds that you took a dangerous patient-care shortcut, the court may hold you liable for causing harm to your patient.

DOCUMENT THOROUGHLY

Document every step of the nursing process for every patient. Chart your observations as soon as possible, while facts are fresh in your mind; express yourself clearly; and always write legibly. When using charting forms, make certain they're complete and leave no omissions or blank spaces. If you're ever involved in a lawsuit, a complete patient care record could be your best defense.

AUDIT YOUR NURSING RECORDS

Audit your records consistently and comprehensively, using specific criteria to evaluate the effectiveness of patient care. Ask for a charting class—or start one yourself—to encourage staff nurses to chart patient care correctly, uniformly, and legibly. Use problem-oriented charting (to make sure you're documenting all parts of the nursing process) and flow sheets (to record large volumes of data). Encourage other nurses to use these documenting aids. If certain charting

whose first concern is delivering safe, high-quality patient care.

Nursing department manuals

Although nursing department manuals will differ, they should:
▶ show how general policies apply to the nursing department

▶ outline the nursing department's roles and responsibilities, internally and in relation to other departments
▶ identify the expected limits of nursing action and practice
▶ offer guidelines for handling emergency situations

forms, such as admission or evaluation forms, need the counter-signature of a supervisor or physician, be sure to have the form signed.

USE WHAT YOU KNOW

Use your nursing knowledge to make nursing diagnoses and give clinical opinions. You have a legal duty to your patient not only to make a nursing diagnosis, but also to take appropriate action to meet his nursing needs. Doing so helps protect your patient from harm and you from malpractice charges.

DELEGATE PATIENT CARE WISELY

Know the legal practice limits of the people you supervise, and caution them to act only within those limits. If your delegation of skilled tasks to an unskilled person harms a patient, you can be held liable for violating your nurse practice act.

KNOW YOUR NURSING DEPARTMENT POLICY MANUAL

Review the policies at least yearly. If you think policies need to be added, amended, or omitted, ask for them. If you're ever involved in a malpractice lawsuit, a well-prepared manual and your knowledge of nursing policies could be important in your defense.

SHOW KINDNESS AND RESPECT

Treat your patient and his family with kindness and respect. When you help relatives cope with the stress of the patient's illness and teach them the basics of home care, they'll more likely remember you with a thank-you card than with a legal summons.

▶ contain procedures that show compliance with state and federal laws, such as patient antidumping laws
▶ give standing orders for nurses in special areas, such as ICU and CCU
▶ show the steps to be taken before— and after—arriving at nursing care decisions. These steps provide the basis for

the facility's nursing care standards. The manual itself will be used as evidence in malpractice cases.

However, policies typically aren't helpful when they're:
▶ too specific
▶ too restrictive
▶ too idealistic
▶ irrelevant
▶ so voluminous that nurses don't know them
▶ not reviewed or discussed in regular staff meetings
▶ not updated or reviewed on a regular basis
▶ not communicated to the staff when changes are made.

Today, hospitals are rapidly revising and expanding their basic policies and procedures. Any good nursing department manual should undergo regular revision. Some of these procedure and policy changes result from efforts to streamline and standardize patient care. Others result from efforts to comply with new state, jurisdictional, territorial, and federal regulations or to implement recommendations of The Joint Commission or the Canadian Council on Health Services.

Effect of policies on court decisions

Policies aren't laws, but courts generally have ruled against nurses who violated their employers' policies. Courts have also held hospitals liable for poorly formulated, or poorly implemented policies. As discussed in previous chapters, nurses' duties are commonly described in nurse practice acts, licensing board regulations, state and federal laws, case law, and professional organization standards.

Legally, if a nurse practices within the scope of her job description and is sued for malpractice, the hospital typically assumes secondary responsibility under the theory of *respondeat superior.* Whether the nurse has acted properly is determined, in court, by the patient's condition, the hospital's nursing service policies, and the standard of care reasonably expected in the community.

In *Utter v. United Health Center (1977),* nurses failed to report a patient's deteriorating condition to the department chairman after the physicians they notified failed to act, causing a critical 24-hour delay in the patient's treatment. A provision in the hospital's nursing manual said that if ever a physician in charge—after being notified—did nothing about adverse changes in a patient's condition or acted ineffectively, the nurse was to "call this to the attention of the Department Chairman."

The judge told the jury that it could label the nurses' failure to follow this provision as the proximate cause of the patient's injury. Because they failed to follow hospital policy, the nurses shared blame for the physicians' inaction.

Laws and hospital policies

Many hospital policies and procedures are mandated by state or jurisdictional licensing laws or by such federal regulations that are the conditions for participation in Medicare or Medicaid.

Many such mandatory requirements exist. In the United States, for instance, the Patient Self-Determination Act, 42 U.S.C. Section 1395 cc(f), is a federal law that requires hospitals, nursing homes, home health care agencies, and health maintenance organizations (HMOs) that are Medicare providers to inform patients about their rights to execute living wills. The Freedom of Information Act requires hospitals to give consumers and patients access to certain data previously considered privileged. In addition, U.S. Department of Health and Human Services regulations require that hospitals observe strict guidelines when using patients in research studies.

Canadian law and policies

In Canada, each jurisdiction has its own laws governing hospitals. Although health care is the responsibility of the jurisdictions, the federal government outlines requirements for receiving federal funding. Since passage of the Canada Health Act of 1984, health care facilities are considered public institutions in Canada.

The jurisdictional legislatures also pass laws governing hospitalization in psychiatric facilities. Matters of criminal law, however, are in the hands of the federal parliament, so hospital policy makers look there for guidance on such issues as opioids and abortions.

U.S. versus Canadian policies

Hospital policies in the United States and Canada are similar in many ways; however, the differences are sometimes important. Always check the laws that prevail in your region.

Under English common law, people usually aren't obligated to help each other, not even in emergencies. However, where hospitals are concerned, Canadian jurisdictional legislatures have departed from this tradition. For example, the Public Hospitals Act of Nova Scotia states that if a qualified medical practitioner makes application for a patient and the hospital has room, it must admit the patient, even if he can't pay for his care.

In 1986, the U.S. Congress amended the Social Security Act to prevent hospitals from turning away uninsured or financially strapped patients. Called *patient antidumping laws,* the amendments require that hospitals participating in Medicare provide screening and stabilizing treatment for anyone who has an emergency condition or is in labor. Furthermore, the Act gives guidelines and requires documentation for transfers or for hospital discharge.

Failure to comply can lead to fines, loss of Medicare provider status, or both. This legislation has expanded regularly since 1989 and currently is known as the Emergency Treatment and Active Labor Act, or EMTALA.

Policies and employment

Hospital administrators write policies to guide workers in the hospital's daily operations. These policies stem from the hospital's philosophy and objectives and are part of the hospital's planning process, so they affect a nurse's job directly.

When considering employment at a hospital or other health care agency, ask to see its policies. Study its policies carefully; if they're well defined, they can provide an indication of how satisfied and secure a nurse can expect to be in her job.

When working in a specialized nursing area, such as the ICU or CCU, give special attention to any policies that directly or indirectly apply. Ensure that the specialty is clearly defined in keeping with the state or jurisdictional nurse practice act and with the standards recommended

by accrediting agencies and professional medical and nursing associations.

Besides reading policies—the general principles by which a hospital is guided in its management—read the hospital's rules too. These are usually written in an employee manual and describe the actions that employees should or shouldn't take in specific situations.

Feeling reasonably comfortable with the hospital's philosophy, objectives, policies, rules, and quality of care usually translates into feeling comfortable on the job. However, if the hospital's policy calls for nursing procedures that conflict with personal nursing standards or ethics, then the nurse needs to consider looking elsewhere for employment.

Conflicts between policy and nurse practice acts

A nurse must refuse to follow hospital policy when it conflicts with her nurse practice act. A willful violation of rulings passed by the board of nursing, even with the hospital's knowledge and encouragement, could result in disciplinary action such as suspension or revocation of one's nursing license.

The case of *Lama v. Borras (1994)* illustrates the risk that nurses face when following hospital policy without using nursing judgment. A jury found nurses negligent for following a hospital policy for charting "by exception" rather than recording qualitative nurses' notes for each shift. A patient who had had spinal surgery developed a serious infection and discitis that was difficult to treat and required a prolonged hospitalization. Nurses didn't record his ongoing symptoms of severe pain, presence of "very bloody" drainage and other symptoms that would have alerted physicians to this developing wound infection. The nurses' failure to document these qualitative findings by instead following the hospital's "charting by exception" policy was negligent and contributed to the patient's delay in treatment. Even though the hospital was found liable in this case, it was the negligent conduct of the nurses that was the basis for the liability.[9] The case illustrates the importance of always looking at policies as guidelines for the standard of care, while recognizing that a particular situation may require judgment to go beyond what's required by an agency policy.

Policies and LPNs and LVNs

LPNs and LVNs shouldn't be coerced to exceed limits that the law places on their practice, although practice may extend beyond the nurse's academic training. State law and national health commissions have recognized the rights of LPNs and LVNs to perform in an expanded role—for example, to give drugs and I.V. fluids—if the LPN or LVN is properly trained for the task and it's one that other LPNs and LVNs perform in the hospital.

Safeguards

Always protect yourself. Make sure that the conditions for job performance are included in the hospital's written policies and that the policies have been established by a committee representing the medical staff, the nursing department, and the administration. The written version should be available to all medical and nursing staff members. If, for example, the policy that allows LPNs and LVNs to give I.V. drugs isn't stated in writing, then it shouldn't occur. If a nurse is sued on this basis and can't back up her actions with written hospital policy or state regulation, the nurse may be found liable.

Policy change

When seeking to bring nursing policy problems to the hospital or agency administration's attention, involve your health-team colleagues by discussing policy problems at committee meetings, conferences, and interdepartmental meetings. Many health care facilities require policy implementation to follow the chain of command. A charge nurse or manager should be able to provide direction on where to start on a particular issue. Alternatively, nurses can communicate directly with the administration via the grievance procedure, counseling, attitude questionnaires, and formal and informal unit management committees.

Understaffing

Understaffing occurs when the hospital administration fails to provide enough professionally trained personnel to meet the patient population's needs. Most nurses are familiar with understaffing and the problems it can cause.

Plaintiffs' attorneys typically argue that understaffing is widespread and that it results in substandard bedside care, increased mistakes and omissions, and hasty documentation—all of which increase nurses' (and their employers') liability. For example, if during hospitalization a patient is harmed and can demonstrate that the harm resulted from the hospital's failure to provide sufficient qualified personnel, the hospital may be held liable.

POLICY & POLITICS

Nursing-sensitive quality indicators for acute-care settings

Since the development of quality indicators, various indicators have been identified for measurement. Here is a list of indicators currently in use, as well as ones that are being developed.

CURRENTLY IN USE
- Nursing hours per patient day
- Skill mix (% of RNs)
- RN education and certification
- Fall rate
  Injury fall rate and level
  Fall assessment
  Fall prevention
- Hospital-acquired pressure ulcer rate (including stages, assessment, and prevention)
- Pediatric I.V. Infiltration
- Pediatric pain assessment cycle
- Psychiatric injury assault rate

IN DEVELOPMENT
- Restraint use
- Voluntary turnover
- Nursing musculoskeletal injuries
- Smoking cessation for acute myocardial infarction, pneumonia, and heart failure
- Obstetric/newborn indicators

Source: Schumann, M.J. "ANA Coming to You 2006," 2006. [Online] Available at http://www.nursingworld.org/MainMenuCategories/ThePracticeofProfessionalNursing/workplace/Workforce/ShortageStaffing/UtilizationGuide.aspx.

Criteria for adequate staffing

Few legal guidelines are available to identify what exactly is meant by adequate staffing. Over the years, various studies have been done to correlate RN staffing and patient outcomes. These studies addressed staffing effects on sentinel events, adverse outcomes such as complications and patient mortality, length of stay, operational costs, and health care costs.[10] One study involving long-term care showed that higher RN staffing led to improved patient functional status, lower mortality rates, increased discharges from the facility, fewer pressure ulcers, decreased use of restraints, decreased numbers of urinary catheterizations and urinary tract infections, and decreased antibiotic use.[11] As a result, the ANA in 1994 funded the Nursing Safety and Quality Initiative to identify nursing-sensitive indicators to evaluate the relationship between nurse staffing and patient outcomes. The National Database of Nursing Quality Indicators was established to "promote and facilitate the standardization of information submitted by facilities across the United States on nursing quality and patient outcomes."[12] (See *Nursing-sensitive quality indicators for acute care settings*.)

Lawmakers have taken note of this issue. In October 1999, California passed a bill that requires hospitals to meet minimum nurse-patient ratios on all units, mandates additional staffing based on patient acuity, and prohibits nurses from being assigned to areas for which they lack adequate orientation or clinical training. In September 2002, the California Department of Health Services also announced nurse-patient ratios.

The courts have had no reliable standard for ruling on cases of alleged understaffing. Each case has been decided on an individual basis.

Recently a bill was introduced in Congress to address nurse-patient ratios. It's designed to improve patient safety and quality of care and address the nursing shortage. The Safe Nurse Staffing for Patient Safety and Quality Care Act of 2007 (H.R. 2123), introduced by Representative Jan Schakowsky from Illinois, calls for the establishment of minimum direct care RN-to-patient ratios for each shift.[13] (See Chapter 3 for more information.)

Court rulings

The decision in the landmark case *Darling v. Charleston Community Memorial Hospital (1965)* was based partly on the issue of understaffing. A young man broke his leg while playing football and was taken to Charleston's ED, where the on-call physician set and cast his leg. The patient began to complain of pain almost immediately. Later, his toes became swollen and dark, then cold and insensitive, and a stench pervaded his room. Nurses checked the leg only a few times per day, and they failed to report its worsening condition. When the cast was removed 3 days later, the necrotic condition of the leg was apparent. After making several surgical attempts to save the leg, the surgeon had to amputate below the knee.

After an out-of-court settlement with the physician who had applied the cast, the court found the hospital liable for failing to have enough specially trained nurses available at all times to recognize the patient's serious condition and to alert the medical staff.

Since the Darling case, several similar cases have been tried—for example,

Cline v. Lun (1973), Sanchez v. Bay General Hospital (1981), and *Harrell v. Louis Smith Memorial Hospital (1990).* Almost every case involved a nurse who failed to continuously monitor her patient's condition, especially his vital signs, and to report significant changes to the attending physician. In each case, the courts have emphasized:
▶ the need for sufficient numbers of nurses to continuously monitor a patient's condition
▶ the need for nurses who are specially trained to recognize signs and symptoms that require a physician's immediate intervention.

Facility liability

Courts have held hospitals primarily liable in lawsuits in which nursing understaffing is the key issue. A hospital can be found liable for patient injuries if it accepts more patients than its facilities or nursing staff can accommodate. The hospital controls the financial resources and, in the courts' view, is the only party that can resolve the problem.

Defense of understaffing

Hospitals accused of failing to maintain adequate nursing staffs have offered various defenses. Some have argued they acted reasonably because their nurse-patient ratio was comparable to other area hospitals. This argument fails if any applicable rules and regulations contradict it.

Other hospitals have defended understaffing by arguing that no extra nurses were available. The courts have hesitated to accept this defense, however, especially when hospitals have knowingly permitted an unsafe condition to continue for a long period. One possible future scenario—a hospital may be held liable for failing to use the nursing personnel available from temporary-nursing service agencies or nurses' registries.

Still other hospitals have excused understaffing by pleading lack of funds. The courts have repeatedly rejected this defense.

Emergency defense

Hospital liability for understaffing isn't automatic. If the hospital couldn't have provided adequate staff by any reasonable means—because, for example, a nurse suddenly called in sick and no substitute could be found quickly—the hospital may escape liability. This is known as the *sudden emergency exception* when used as a defense during a trial. The emergency couldn't have been anticipated, in contrast to chronic understaffing.

Except for the sudden emergency exception defense, a hospital has only two alternatives for avoiding liability for understaffing: either hire sufficient personnel to staff an area adequately or else close the area (or restrict the number of beds) until adequate staff can be found.

Charge nurse's liability

A nurse put in charge of a unit, even temporarily, may find himself or herself personally liable in understaffing situations, including these examples, when the nurse:

▶ knows understaffing exists but fails to notify the hospital administration about it

▶ fails to assign staff properly and then also fails to supervise their actions continuously (see *When coworkers put you at risk*)

▶ tries to perform a nursing task for which she lacks the necessary training and skills.

When coworkers put you at risk

To help you avoid legal dangers when working with a health care team, here are some questions and answers to clarify legal responsibilities.

Can I be held liable for mistakes made by a student nurse under my supervision?

Yes, if you have primary responsibility for instructing the student and correcting her mistakes.

If a student performs tasks that only a licensed nurse should perform and does so with my knowledge but without my supervision, am I guilty of breach of duty?

Yes, because as a staff nurse, you should know that a student nurse can perform nursing tasks only under the direct supervision of a nurse licensed to perform those tasks.

What should I do if I see another health team member perform a clinical procedure incorrectly?

If the incorrect procedure can harm the patient, you have a legal duty to stop the procedure—tactfully, when possible—and immediately report your action to your nursing supervisor. If the incorrect procedure doesn't threaten to harm the patient, don't stop the procedure, but report your observation to your supervisor.

Can I face legal action if I ask a hospital volunteer to help me give patient care and she does something wrong?

Yes. Don't ask a volunteer to participate in a task she isn't trained and professionally qualified to perform.

Legal cases

In *Horton v. Niagara Falls Memorial Medical Center (1976)*, the charge nurse, one LPN, and one nursing assistant were responsible for 19 patients on a unit. During their shift, one patient became delirious and tried to climb down from a balcony off his room. The attending physician, when notified, ordered that someone stay with the patient at all times to keep him from going out on the balcony again.

The charge nurse, instead of calling for additional help from within the hospital or notifying the administration, called the patient's wife and summoned her to the hospital. The wife agreed to send her mother but said it would take time before her mother could arrive. During the interim, the charge nurse provided no supervision of the patient, who went out on the balcony again, jumped, and sustained injuries. In the lawsuit that followed, the court held the charge nurse liable.

In *Norton v. Argonaut Insurance Co. (1962),* a temporary staff shortage led the assistant director of nurses to volunteer her nursing services on a pediatric floor. Because she had been an administrator for several years and was unfamiliar with pediatric care, she proceeded to give a neonate 3 ml of digoxin in injectable, rather than elixir, form. The infant died of cardiac arrest, and the court held the assistant director liable.

Viable defenses

A charge nurse isn't automatically liable for mistakes made by a nurse on her staff. Most courts won't hold the charge nurse liable unless she knew, or should have known, that the nurse who made the mistake:

▶ had previously made similar mistakes
▶ wasn't competent to perform the task
▶ had acted on the charge nurse's erroneous orders.

Remember, the plaintiff-patient has to prove two things: that the charge nurse failed to follow customary practices,

thereby contributing to the mistake, and that the mistake actually caused the patient's injuries.

Sudden patient overload

Like other nurses, you're probably all too familiar with understaffing. You begin your shift and suddenly find yourself assigned more patients than you can reasonably care for. What can you do to protect yourself?

First, make every effort to protest the overload and get it reduced. Begin by asking your supervisor or director of nursing services to supply relief. If they can't or won't, notify the hospital administration. If no one there will help either, write a memorandum detailing exactly what you did and said and the answers you received. Don't walk off the job (you could be held liable for abandonment); instead, do the best you can. After your shift is over, prepare a written report of the facts and file it with the director of nursing.

Keep in mind that filing a written report isn't guaranteed to absolve you from liability if a patient is injured during your shift. You may still be found liable, especially if you could have foreseen and prevented the patient's injury; however, a written report will impress a jury as a sincere attempt to protect your patients. The report could also provide you with a defense if the alleged malpractice involves something you should have done but didn't because of understaffing.

Refusing to work

If conditions become intolerable and a nurse refuses to work, she may be suspended from duty without pay. Consider the Canadian case, *In re Mount Sinai*

Hospital and Ontario Nurses Association (1978).

This case involved three nurses in the hospital's ICU. Because they were already caring for many critically ill patients, they refused to accept still another from the ED. The nurses argued that admitting the new patient would endanger the patients already under their care. The hospital disagreed and suspended them for three shifts without pay.

The case was settled in favor of the hospital, on the premise that a hospital is legally obligated to provide care for patients it admits and can insist that certain instructions be carried out. If the hospital had to defer to its employees' opinions, the decision stated, it would be placed in an intolerable legal position.

Floating

The hospital or agency is required by The Joint Commission and other regulators to provide adequate numbers of competent staff to care for patients. In order to do this, it's sometimes necessary to have staff "float" to another workplace area or assignment. As long as the staff member is adequately trained for and competent to undertake the new assignment, employers can generally require floating to meet staffing needs.

The case of *Francis v. Memorial General Hospital (1986)* illustrates some factors that must be considered with a floating request.[14] Nurse Francis brought a suit against his employer claiming wrongful discharge and breach of contract when he was fired for refusing to float from his primary assigned area of the ICU to the orthopedics unit. He refused to float because he was unfamiliar with the new floor and felt incompetent to be the charge nurse on that unit. The

hospital had offered to orient Francis to all the floors so that he would feel more comfortable "floating" as the need arose, but he declined this offer. Nurse Francis was aware of the hospital's valid administrative floating policy.

Francis asserted that the nurse practice act protected him because it required nurses to be competent in their area of practice, as otherwise it would jeopardize the health and safety of patients. The court disagreed because he wouldn't allow the hospital to orient him to see if he could overcome his feeling of incompetence. In fact, the public policy of providing adequate staff to all patients in a cost-effective manner was persuasive to the court in finding against Nurse Francis and denying his claims.

The ANA has a position statement on "The Right to Accept or Reject an Assignment" (1995) and provides guidance to nurses who are considering this option. Permitted refusal is based on very narrow circumstances in which the nurse caring for the patient would put the patient at a substantial risk for his health and safety. (See *Floating: Understanding your legal responsibility,* page 212.)

Suggestions for both employees and employers in situations that include both short staffing and floating include:
▶ orienting and assigning staff to more than one area but with some limitation, such as to all pediatric floors
▶ limiting assignments of floated personnel to more routine and less specialized procedures, assessments, and patient care activities
▶ using a "buddy system" with experienced staff on the unit to serve as a resource for the floated staff

Floating: Understanding your legal responsibility

For many nurses, an order to float to an unfamiliar unit triggers worry and frustration. It may cause worry about using skills that have grown rusty since nursing school or frustration at being pulled away from familiar or enjoyable work.

UNAVOIDABLE
Unfortunately, floating is necessary. Hospitals must use it to help solve their understaffing problems. The courts sanction it as being in the public's best interest.

EXCEPTIONS
Legally, you can't refuse to float simply because you fear that the skills you need for the assignment have diminished or because you're concerned about legal risks in the assigned unit. You'll have to go along with an order to float unless:
• you have a union contract that guarantees you'll always work in your specialty
• you can prove you haven't been taught to do the assigned task.
  Tell your supervisor if you haven't been taught a task she has assigned you. Usually, she'll accommodate you by changing your assignment. However, if she insists that you perform the task that you don't know how to do, refuse the assignment. If the hospital reprimands or fires you, you may be able to appeal the action taken against you in a court of law.

▶ trying to fill extra shifts from within the regular staff from the unit or from a float pool of cross-trained workers
▶ using agency or temporary staff.
  In some instances, employers may have to close units or restrict services offered, such as elective surgeries, if enough competent staff can't be provided for safe and effective patient care.

Chronic understaffing
Chronic understaffing, if it occurs on a unit, presents nurses with a dilemma. On the one hand, a nurse's conscience tells her to try her best to help every patient. On the other hand, the nurse feels compelled to protect herself from liability.

The best protection is prevention—action taken to remedy the understaffing situation. Try to work with the institution to develop creative, workable solutions. The law will protect the nurse in several important ways, as long as the nurse and colleagues act responsibly and collectively to try to bring about institutional change.

A case in point is *Misericordia Hospital Medical Center v. N.L.R.B. (1980)*, which involved a charge nurse who was discharged from her job because her employer found her activities "disloyal."

She belonged to a group of hospital employees called the Ad Hoc Patient Care Committee. The committee was formed after The Joint Commission, which intended to survey the hospital, had invited interested parties, including hospital staff, to submit at a public meeting information on whether accreditation standards were being met. One complaint lodged by the nurse and her committee was insufficient coverage on many shifts—a situation the hospital had failed to remedy.

Even though Joint Commission examiners approved the hospital, the nurse was fired shortly afterward. When the NLRB ordered the hospital to reinstate the nurse, the hospital appealed. The appeals court upheld the NLRB order, citing a U.S. Supreme Court ruling that employees don't lose protection "when they seek to improve terms and conditions of employment or otherwise improve their lot as employees through channels outside the immediate employee-employer relationship."

Although this decision offers nurses some protection in conflicts with employers, especially those in which working conditions directly affect the care given to patients, persons involved in the hiring, firing, scheduling, disciplining, or evaluation of employees are considered management and may not be included in the collective bargaining unit. Therefore, a nurse may not be covered, depending on the court's interpretation of whether she's management.

Be sure to follow the appropriate channels of communication. If help isn't available to remedy a dangerous understaffing situation, first go through all hospital channels. Simply report what the problem is, the number of hours forced to work without relief, the number of consecutive days forced to work, and any other relevant facts. Then if the nurse still can't get help and the complaint involves an alleged unfair labor practice, consider contacting the NLRB. (See Chapter 3 for more information about nurses' rights and whistle-blowing.)

Patient safety

One of a nurse's most important responsibilities is the patient's physical safety. Raised bed rails, assistance with ambulation, proper transfer techniques, and immobilizing devices may be necessary to prevent falls.

In the interest of patient safety, nurses also have to keep an eye on the hospital's facilities and equipment. Loose or improperly functioning side rails, water or some other substance on the unit floor, or an improperly functioning ventilator

need to be reported for repairs or housekeeping assistance. Failure to do so may not only endanger patients, but also make the nurse—and the hospital—liable if injuries occur.

Patient-safety standards of care

In a malpractice lawsuit, the nurse's conduct is judged by comparing what was done against the appropriate standards of care. The court will analyze whether the defendant-nurse gave the plaintiff-patient care equal to that given by a reasonably well-qualified and prudent nurse in the same or similar circumstances.

With regard to patient safety, a nurse's duty includes anticipating foreseeable risks. For example, if the nurse is aware that the floor in a patient's room is dangerously slippery, she must report the condition to the appropriate hospital department and place caution signs on the floor to warn of the dangers. If this isn't done and a patient falls and is injured, the nurse could be held liable.

In fact, the nurse may be held liable even if she didn't know the floor was slippery. Using accepted standards of care, a court might reason that part of the nurse's duty as a reasonable and prudent nurse was to check the floor of the unit regularly and report any patient hazard immediately.

The standards of care that nurses meet will vary with the job and the nurse's training. A staff nurse's actions, for example, will be measured against staff nurse standards, and a gerontologic nurse's actions will be measured against standards that gerontologic nurses must meet.

National Patient Safety Goals

In July 2002, The Joint Commission approved its first set of National Patient Safety Goals, which are reviewed and updated yearly. The Joint Commission established these goals to help accredited organizations better address patient safety. Current goals include:

▶ improving the accuracy of patient identification

▶ improving the effectiveness of communication among caregivers

▶ improving the safety of using medications

▶ reducing the risk of health-care associated infections

▶ reconciling accurately and completely mediations across the continuum of care

▶ reducing the risk of (patient) harm from falls

▶ reducing the risk of influenza and pneumococcal disease in institutionalized older adults

▶ reducing the risk of surgical fires

▶ implementing applicable National Patient Safety Goals and associated requirements by components and practitioner sites

▶ encouraging active patient involvement in their own care

▶ preventing health care-associated pressure ulcers

▶ identifying safety risks inherent in the patient population by the organization

▶ improving recognition and response to changes in a patient's condition.[15]

Failure to implement these safety goals will result in a special Type I recommendation.

Special safety concerns

In practice, nurses need to recognize special safety concerns, such as patient falls, the use of restraints, the prospect of suicide attempts, the safety of equipment, and the risk of transmitting disease.

Patient falls

Almost anything can cause a patient to fall, particularly if he's elderly or receiving medication. Elderly patients may be, in many instances, confused, disoriented, and weak. Medications can cause or increase confusion and lessen a patient's ability to react in situations in which he might fall. Here are some ways to protect a patient from falls:

▶ Assess the patient's risk of falls.

▶ Make sure the bed's side rails are kept up, when indicated.

▶ Orient him to where he is and what time it is, especially if he's elderly.

▶ Monitor him regularly—continually, if his condition makes this necessary.

▶ Offer a bedpan or commode regularly.

▶ Provide adequate lighting and a clean, clutter-free environment.

▶ Make sure that someone helps and supports him whenever he gets out of bed and that he wears proper shoes when walking.

▶ Make sure adequate staff are available to transfer him, if necessary.

▶ Make sure the call bell is within his reach and in working order.

Elderly patients and patients taking medications that cause orthostatic hypotension, central nervous system depression, or vestibular toxicity need special nursing care when physicians' orders require them to be "up in chair for 15 minutes x 3 daily" or "up in chair for meals." If a nurse can't supervise such a patient while he's sitting up, at least make sure another member of the health care team is available.

Restraints

Usually prescribed to ensure a patient's safety, restraints unfortunately can also endanger the patient. When a physician prescribes a restraining device, keep in mind that such devices don't remove a nurse's responsibility for the patient's safety. In fact, they increase it.

For example, when a patient wears a restraining belt, the nurse needs to make sure he doesn't undo it or inadvertently readjust it; if he does, it could choke or otherwise injure him. The nurse also has to make sure the belt fits properly; if it's too tight, it could restrict the patient's breathing or irritate his skin. The nurse may have to decide when the belt is no longer necessary. Check the governing laws and protocols for an automatic expiration of restriction orders. If a nurse fails to handle patient restraints properly, she may be accused of false imprisonment. (See *Caring for a patient in restraints or seclusion.*)

Consider this example. In *Rhode v. Lawrence General Hospital (1993),* police brought the patient into the hospital at 1 a.m. following an auto accident. The patient assaulted a clinician in the ED and was diagnosed as having an "acute psychotic episode." The physician ordered leather restraints.

Around 6 a.m., the patient escaped from four-point restraints, went into a parking lot, found a car that had been left running, and drove off. He crashed the car and was seriously injured.

The patient sued the hospital, the ED physician, and two nurses for medical malpractice, claiming that the staff didn't supervise him properly and that his restraints weren't securely fastened.

To ensure proper use of restraints, follow these guidelines:

Caring for a patient in restraints or seclusion

Before you can keep a patient in restraints or in seclusion, you must get an order from the patient's physician authorizing it. Joint Commission standards are specific regarding restraint and seclusion.

GUIDELINES
The Joint Commission requires that before restraints or seclusion are used:
• documentation shows that such interventions are clinically justified
• less-restrictive interventions have been attempted
• the patient's current condition is considered.

Orders are to be time limited and written for a specific episode, with start and end times, rather than for an unspecified time in the future. Established policy should specify the maximum length of time that each intervention may be used.

In an emergency, specially trained staff may initiate the use of restraints or seclusion and obtain the physician's order within a specified time (as established by the facility's policy).

CARE REQUIREMENTS
When you're caring for a patient in restraints or seclusion, frequent face-to-face monitoring and observation is essential (as required by your facility's policy).

For patients who require frequent or prolonged restraint or seclusion, the treatment team should meet to consider alternatives and changes in the care plan. Generally, 72 hours of continuous restraint or more than four episodes in 7 days is considered prolonged or frequent.

Document such items as the patient's hydration, feeding, toileting, and range of motion and condition of limbs. The facility should have policies or procedures for addressing these concerns; they should be followed and documented accurately.

▶ Restraint is a form of imprisonment, so it should only be used as a last resort. Before restraining a patient, consider alternatives, such as constant observation or walking with the patient.

▶ Take care to avoid undue force; otherwise, you may invite a lawsuit for battery. Even threatening to use force may be sufficient cause for legal action.

▶ When a physician isn't immediately available, you're responsible to see that restraints and seclusion are used only to the extent necessary to prevent injury. Make sure the staff contacts the physician as soon as possible.

▶ Most states follow the *least restrictive principle,* which holds that no more restraint should be used than necessary. For example, a restraining vest shouldn't be used when simple wrist restraints will suffice.

▶ To avoid allegations of false imprisonment, document carefully the decision-making process that led to the use of restraints, and review the continuing need for restraints on a regular basis.

▶ Bedside rails are a form of restraint, and shouldn't be raised indiscriminately. The patient's age alone isn't a justification for raising the side rails.

▶ Sedating drugs may provide an alternative to restraints. However, use them sparingly, with caution, and only with a physician's order. The patient's right to the least restrictive treatment or to an open-door policy that allows patients to move about "freely" means little if accompanied by indiscriminate drug use as a substitute for restraints.

Suicide prevention

Suicide prevention is another important aspect of patient safety. Keep in mind that self-destructive, suicidal patients are found in medical as well as psychiatric wards.

A nurse's first obligation is to provide close supervision. A suicidal patient may require one-on-one, 24-hour-per-day supervision until the immediate threat of self-harm is over. Take from him all potentially dangerous objects, which may include belts, bed linens, glassware, and eating utensils. Make sure he swallows pills when given; otherwise, he may retain them in his mouth, to save them for later.

Assess the hospital environment carefully for possible dangers. If he can easily open or break his room windows, or if escape from the unit would be easy, the patient may need to be transferred to a safer, more secure place—if necessary, to a seclusion room.

Remember, whether working on a psychiatric unit or a medical unit, the nurse will be held responsible for the decisions made about a suicidal patient's care. If a nurse is sued because he's harmed himself while in the nurse's care, the court will judge the nurse based on whether the nurse:

▶ knew (or should have known) that the patient was likely to harm himself

▶ exercised reasonable care in helping him avoid injury or death, knowing he was likely to harm himself.

In *Woodword v. Myers, Dean, and Correctional Medical Services of Illinois (2001),* a nurse evaluated a jail detainee and documented "yes" to an intake question asking him if he had expressed thoughts about killing himself. Despite the affirmative answer, the nurse didn't obtain suicide precautions. Later, the man committed suicide while in custody. The nurse was sued on a claim that she deprived the detainee of his right to due process under the Fourteenth Amendment.

Equipment safety

Nurses are responsible for making sure that the equipment used for patient care is free from defects. They also need to exercise reasonable care in selecting equipment for a specific procedure and patient and then helping to maintain the equipment. Here again, the patient care must reflect what the reasonably well-qualified and prudent nurse would do in the same or similar circumstances. This means that if the nurse knows that a specific piece of equipment isn't functioning properly, she must take steps to correct the defects and document the steps taken. If the nurse doesn't do this and a patient is injured because of the defective equipment, she may be sued for malpractice.

Selecting proper equipment and maintaining it also means making sure it isn't contaminated. When cleaning equipment, always follow hospital procedures strictly, and document actions carefully. This will decrease the possibility that you could be held liable for using contaminated equipment.

A nurse can also be held liable for improper use of equipment that's functioning properly. This liability frequently occurs with equipment that can cause burns—for example, diathermy machines, electrosurgical equipment, and hot-water bottles. When using such equipment, carry out the procedure or therapy carefully, observe the patient continually until finished, and ask the patient frequently (if awake) whether he's experiencing pain or discomfort.

Several court cases illustrate how nurses can become involved in negligence claims based on safety or use of equipment. One high-risk area is the operating room, where highly specialized equipment and materials are used for patients who are commonly under anesthesia. In *Chin v. St. Barnabas Medical Center (1998)*, a patient was awarded $2 million dollars as a result of misuse of equipment during a hysterectomy operation. The pump used for the procedure was incorrectly connected to a gas line instead of an exhaust line and resulted in the patient's death. Even though it couldn't be proven whether the physician or nurses had made the error, the defendant hospital was found negligent for the acts of these employees. Part of the evidence included was the fact that two of the nurses assisting in the procedure hadn't been properly trained, hadn't attended any inservice training sessions about the use of the device, and that the supervising nurse wasn't aware that they were inexperienced. For these reasons the court concluded that negligence had occurred that resulted in the patient's death.[16]

Proper insertion of a urinary catheter was at issue in the case of *Pearce v. Feinstein (1990)*. A disposable indwelling urinary catheter was inserted to alleviate a stricture during surgery. Several days later a tiny hole was found in the patient's catheter that had allowed urine to leak and damage his suture line. This resulted in injury, further surgery, and treatment. As part of the evidence presented at trial to establish the standard of care, a nursing textbook was used that stated that the retention balloon should be pretested for leaks before insertion into the patient. The jury awarded damages to the patient based on the failure of the staff to follow the standard of care in using this equipment.

As a response to a growing concern for the safety of medical devices and equipment, the federal government enacted the Safe Medical Devices Act of 1990. The Act requires health care agencies to report any device-related adverse events to the manufacturer and to the Food and Drug Administration if a patient death results. This reporting allows documentation and tracking of incidents in order to promote public safety and risk management.

Disease transmission

Be careful not to cause contamination or cross-infection of patients. In *Widman v. Paoli Memorial Hospital (1989)*, the hospital was found negligent because a preoperative patient was assigned to the same room as a patient infected with the *Klebsiella* organism. The court found that the hospital didn't make sure that personnel assigned to care for the patient followed established infection control procedures.

Responsibilities of the facility for patient safety

The facility shares responsibility for the patient's safety. This institutional responsibility for patient safety rests on the two most commonly used doctrines of malpractice liability.

The first doctrine, *corporate liability,* holds the hospital liable for its own wrongful conduct—for breach of its duties as mandated by statutory law, common law, and applicable rules and regulations. The hospital's duty to keep patients safe includes the duty to provide, inspect, repair, and maintain reasonably adequate equipment for diagnosis and treatment. The hospital also has a duty to keep the facility reasonably safe. Thus,

if a patient is injured because the hospital alone breached one of its duties, the hospital is responsible for the injury.

Over time, the courts have expanded the concept of an institution's liability for breaching its duties. In a landmark case, *Darling v. Charleston Community Memorial Hospital (1965),* the Illinois Supreme Court expanded the concept of hospital corporate liability to include the hospital's responsibility to supervise the quality of care given to its patients.

In *Thompson v. The Nason Hospital (1991),* the courts went even further and discussed four general areas of corporate liability. These include:
▶ a duty to use reasonable care to maintain safe facilities and equipment
▶ a duty to staff the hospital with only competent physicians
▶ a duty to oversee all individuals practicing medicine within the hospital
▶ a duty to develop and enforce policies and procedures designed to ensure quality patient care.

The second doctrine of institutional malpractice liability is *respondeat superior.* Under this doctrine, the facility is liable for an employee's wrongful conduct. This means that both the employee and the health care facility can be found liable for a breach of duty to the patient, including the duty of ensuring his safety.

Liability

In a lawsuit involving failure to ensure patient safety, the hospital alone may be held liable or the nurse may share in the liability. The outcome depends on the facts involved.

If, for example, a court can determine that the duty to monitor patient care equipment and to repair any discovered defects rests with the hospital and the nurse, then both could be held liable for a breach of that duty.

The case of *Story v. McCurtain Memorial Management, Inc. (1981)* involved the delivery of one twin by the mother herself when she was left unattended in a shower room. The patient continuously called for help, but her calls went unanswered and the baby the mother delivered herself died.

The mother sued the hospital and the nurse on duty at the time. The court found the nurse not liable, but it held the hospital liable (under the doctrine of corporate liability) for failing to provide safeguards in the shower room and adequate supervision on the unit. Here, then, the hospital alone was liable for breaching its duty to protect patients from harm.

Nurses have an important duty to ensure a patient's safety. Remember, all actions directed toward patient safety must be in line with the hospital's policies and procedures. If no policies exist, or if they're outdated or poorly drafted, bring this to the supervisor's or nurse manager's attention. Consider volunteering to help write or rewrite the policies. By getting involved in efforts to improve patients' safety, nurses may decrease their potential liability and, at the same time, improve the quality of patient care.

Drug administration

Giving drugs to patients continues to be one of the most important—and, legally, one of the most risky—tasks that nurses perform.

Over time, nurses' responsibilities with regard to drug administration have increased. For many years, U.S. and Canadian nurses were permitted to give drugs only orally or rectally. Today, nurses give subcutaneous and I.M. injections, induce anesthesia, and give I.V. therapy. In some states, nurses may even prescribe drugs, within certain limitations.

U.S. and Canadian laws continue to strictly guard the nurse's role in drug administration. Within this limited scope, however, the law imposes exceptionally high standards.

The easiest way to guard against malpractice liability when giving drugs is to adhere to the five rights:
▶ the right drug
▶ to the right patient
▶ at the right time
▶ in the right dosage
▶ by the right route
Some also include the right reason and the right documentation.

Drug-control laws

Legally, a drug is any substance listed in an official state, jurisdictional, or national formulary. A drug may also be defined as any substance (other than food) "intended to affect the structure or any function of the body...(or) for use in the diagnosis, cure, mitigation, treatment, or prevention of disease." N.Y. Educ. Law.

A *prescription drug* is any drug restricted from regular commercial purchase and sale. A state, jurisdictional, or national government has determined that this drug is, or might be, unsafe unless used under a qualified medical practitioner's supervision.

Federal laws

Two important federal laws governing the use of drugs in the United States are the Comprehensive Drug Abuse Prevention and Control Act and the Food, Drug, and Cosmetic Act. The Comprehensive Drug Abuse Prevention and Control Act (incorporating the Controlled Substances Act) seeks to categorize drugs by how dangerous they are and regulates drugs thought to be most subject to abuse. The Food, Drug, and Cosmetic Act restricts interstate shipment of drugs not approved for human use and outlines the process for testing and approving new drugs.

State laws

At the state and jurisdictional level, pharmacy practice acts are the main laws affecting the distribution of drugs. These are state and jurisdictional laws that mirror federal laws. Through these, criminal penalties attach under state or jurisdictional law for similar violations. These laws give pharmacists (in Canada, sometimes physicians as well) the sole legal authority to prepare, compound, preserve, and dispense drugs. *Dispense* refers to taking a drug from the pharmacy supply and giving or selling it to another person. This contrasts with giving drugs—actually getting the drug into the patient. A nurse's state nurse practice act is the law that most directly affects how a nurse administers drugs.

Most nursing, medical, and pharmacy practice acts include:
▶ a definition of the tasks that belong uniquely to the profession
▶ a statement saying that anyone who performs such tasks without being a licensed or registered member of the defined profession is breaking the law.

In some states and jurisdictions, certain tasks overlap. For example, both nurses and physicians can provide bedside care for the sick and patient teaching.

In many states, a nurse prescribing a drug would be practicing medicine without a license; if the nurse goes into the pharmacy or drug supply cabinet, measures out doses of a drug, and puts the powder into capsules, she's considered to be practicing pharmacy without a license. For either action, the nurse can be prosecuted, even if no harm results. In most states and Canadian jurisdictions, to practice a licensed profession without a license is, at the very least, a misdemeanor. In *Stefanik v. Nursing Education Committee (1944)*, a Rhode Island nurse lost her nursing license in part because she had been practicing medicine illegally: She had changed a physician's drug order for a patient because she didn't agree with what had been prescribed. No one claimed she had harmed the patient. However, to change a prescription is the same as writing a new prescription, and Rhode Island's nurse practice act didn't consider that to be part of nursing practice.

Another case involved nurses altering the patient's medication plan without first consulting the physician. In *Estate of Henry James v. Hillhaven Corporation (1995)*, nurses substituted their own goals for pain management when they determined at a nursing care planning conference that the patient must be addicted to opioid medications.[17] Mr. James had entered a long-term care facility in the terminal stages of cancer with bone metastasis. The physician had ordered large doses of the opioid Robaxonal every 3 to 4 hours around the clock, but the nurses determined that the goal should be to "reduce the patient's dependence on this drug." As a result, the patient's pain was ineffectively treated, resulting in prolonged pain and suffering for several months. The decedent's estate was awarded a large amount of damages in part because of the nurses' failure to implement these orders properly. In addition, it's noted that nurses need to be aware of current pain management strategies for intractable pain and to practice according to current standards.

Medication errors and lawsuits

Unfortunately, lawsuits involving nurses' drug errors are common. The court determines liability based on the standard of care required of nurses when administering drugs. In many instances, if the nurse had known more about the proper dose, administration route, or procedure connected with giving the drug, she might have avoided the mistake that resulted in the lawsuit.

The 1999 Institute of Medicine report *To Err is Human: Building a Safer Health Care System* emphasized the need for greater safety in medication administration to reduce errors and preventable patient deaths. Nurses spend up to 60% to 75% of their time giving medications, which represents a large area of potential liability in nursing practice. In addition to civil damages for patient injury resulting from a medication error, nurses are increasingly at risk for criminal charges related to these errors, especially if a patient death occurs.

In a 1997 Colorado case, nurses who participated in a medication error that resulted in an infant's death were charged with negligent homicide.[18] The physician had written an illegible order for penicillin that was misinterpreted by the pharmacist so that ten times the normal dose for an infant was provided to the nurses. Instead of questioning this dose with the prescribing physician, the nurses

on duty checked with an advanced nurse practitioner who changed the route of administration to the I.V. route rather than the ordered I.M. route, due to the large dosage. The incorrect ten times normal dose was given and the infant died as a result. In addition to damages awarded to the family, the criminal charges were filed as a result of this "gross deviation of the standard of care." In addition to disciplinary action by the state nursing license board, the nurses faced criminal charges, which resulted in plea bargains or other agreements by the defendants.

Similarly criminal charges were filed against several nurses following a chemotherapy overdose at the Dana-Farber Cancer Center in Boston, Massachusetts in 1995. Another case resulting in criminal charges in 2006 involved a nurse who gave the wrong medication I.V. to a patient. The patient subsequently died from the medication error. Failure to follow hospital policies and the standard of care resulted in the error, including failure to properly identify the patient with the bar coding system. The nurse, an experienced nurse in the labor and delivery area, anticipated that the epidural medication would be ordered and prepared it without following proper procedures. The epidural medication (which hadn't even been ordered by the physician) was given I.V. instead of an ordered antibiotic. This recent case illustrates that even when protections are in place to prevent errors; it's still up to the nurse to be vigilant about following all standards.[19] It was also noted that the nurse was working the second part of two 8-hour shifts and was fatigued when she made this error.

In *Dessauer v. Memorial General Hospital (1981),* an ED physician ordered 50 mg of lidocaine for a patient.

However, the nurse, who usually worked in the hospital's obstetrics ward, gave the patient 800 mg. The patient died, the family sued, and the hospital was found liable.

When reviewing these cases, one point becomes clear: the courts won't permit carelessness that harms the patient.

Emergency doses

Some hospitals and extended care facilities have written policies that permit a nurse under special circumstances to go into the pharmacy and dispense an emergency drug dose. In the ED, physicians typically write emergency orders for one to three doses—just enough to hold the patient until he can go to the pharmacy and have his prescription filled. If there's no pharmacist on duty, hospital policy may allow the nurse to obtain the required drug, bottle it, and label it.

Regardless of whether the employer has such a policy, a nurse who dispenses drugs is doing so unlawfully, unless the state's pharmacy practice act specifically authorizes these actions. If the nurse makes an error in dispensing the drug and the patient later sues, the fact that the nurse was practicing as an unlicensed pharmacist can be used as evidence against her.

When needing to dispense an emergency drug dose, a nurse may choose to disregard the laws that govern nursing practice for the benefit of the patient's well-being. However, the nurse does so at her own risk. Even if no harm comes to the patient, the nurse can still be prosecuted and lose her license. When ethics and the law conflict and the nurse has to weigh concern for the patient's life or health against concern for her license, the nurse must decide what action to take.

If hospital policy requires the nurse to dispense emergency medications and is in clear violation of the state's nurse practice act, consider taking steps to have the hospital policy changed. Start by approaching the nurse-manager with a copy of the nurse practice act and relevant hospital policies. Point out the inconsistencies and the professional risk nurses in the ED are taking. Then offer to accompany the nurse-manager when approaching nursing administrators and the policy and procedure committee. Hospital administrators may designate an ED pharmacist, hire additional pharmacy staff, or prevail upon pharmacists or staff to take greater responsibility for distribution of ED medications.

Drug experimentation

At times, a nurse may participate in giving experimental drugs to patients or giving established drugs in new ways or at experimental dosage levels. A nurse's legal duties don't change, but if there are any questions, she should obtain the answers from the experimental protocol, not the usual sources (such as books and package inserts). Also, an institutional review board probably reviewed and accepted the protocol before it was instituted. This is another resource for the nurse, especially if ethical concerns regarding the treatment develop. Nurses need to ensure that no drug is given to a patient who hasn't consented to participate. (Note that if it's a federally funded experiment, consent should be in writing.)

Responsibilities and drugs

The law expects nurses to know about any drug they'll administer. An LPN or LVN assumes the same legal responsibility as an RN once she has taken a pharmaceutical course or obtained authorization to give drugs. More specifically, the law expects nurses to:

▶ know a drug's safe dosage limits, toxicity, potential adverse reactions, and indications and contraindications for use

▶ refuse to accept an illegible, confusing, or otherwise unclear drug order

▶ seek clarification of a confusing order from the physician and not to try to interpret it themselves.

Increasingly, judges and juries expect nurses to know what the appropriate observation intervals are for a patient receiving medication. They expect nurses to know this even if the physician doesn't know or if he doesn't write an order stating how often to check on the newly medicated patient. A case that was decided on this basis is *Brown v. State (1977)*. After a patient was given 200 mg of chlorpromazine, the nurses on duty left him largely unobserved for several hours. When someone finally checked on the patient, he was dead. The hospital and the nurses lost the resulting lawsuit.

Drug orders
If there's any doubt about a drug order, it must be questioned. Always follow the hospital's policies. Usually, these policies will guide the nurse to try each of the following actions until she receives a satisfactory answer:

▶ Look up the answer in a reliable drug reference.

▶ Ask the charge nurse.

▶ Ask the hospital pharmacist.

▶ Ask the nursing supervisor or the prescribing physician.

▶ Ask the chief nursing administrator

▶ Ask the prescribing physician's supervisor (service chief).

▶ Get in touch with the hospital administration and explain your problem.

Refusal to administer a drug
All nurses have the legal right not to give drugs they think will harm patients, but the nurse must always be sure to have followed the above recommendations. A nurse may choose to exercise this right in various situations, including when she thinks:

▶ the dosage prescribed is too high

▶ the drug is contraindicated because of possible dangerous interactions with other drugs, or with substances such as alcohol

▶ the patient's physical condition contraindicates using the drug.

In limited circumstances, nurses may also legally refuse to give a drug on grounds of conscience. Some states and Canadian jurisdictions have enacted right-of-conscience laws. These laws excuse medical personnel from the requirement to participate in an abortion or sterilization procedure. Under such laws, a nurse may, for example, refuse to give a drug believed to be intended to induce abortion.

When refusing to carry out a drug order, the nurse must be sure to:

▶ Notify the immediate supervisor so that alternative arrangements (assigning a new nurse, clarifying the order) can be made.

▶ Notify the prescribing physician if the supervisor hasn't done so already.

▶ If required by the employer, document that the drug wasn't given, and explain why.

Drug errors
If a nurse makes an error in giving a drug, or if the patient reacts negatively to

a properly administered drug, immediately inform the patient's physician, and protect yourself by documenting the incident thoroughly. Besides normal drug-charting information, include information on the patient's reaction and medical or nursing interventions taken. Always ensure that the patient's needs are met first.

In the event of error, also file an incident report. Identify what happened, the names and functions of all personnel involved, and what actions were taken to protect the patient after the error was discovered, including any follow up.

Roles of LPNs and LVNs

Most nurse practice acts now permit LPNs and LVNs *with the appropriate educational background or on-the-job training* to give drugs under the supervision of an RN, physician, or dentist. What constitutes appropriate training or educational background? No clear-cut definitions exist, but most courts probably would be satisfied if an LPN or LVN could prove that the supervising RN or physician had watched the LPN or LVN give drugs and had judged the nurse as competent based on supervised observation and skills testing. For tasks that require instruction and experience beyond the nurse's academic training, health care facilities usually develop didactic training with goals and competency tests. Additionally, skills testing should be documented through proficiency checklists. This provides objective documentation in case of a lawsuit. (Note, however, that some states prohibit LPNs and LVNs from inserting I.V. lines.)

Telephone triage

Telephonic medical advice traditionally has been a part of most primary care practices. This type of service, which has become known as telephone triage, generally operates with a clinician taking calls and processing requests for medical advice. As health care costs continue to rise, more managed care organizations, HMOs, and EDs are using these systems as a cost-saving and case management measure.

Most telephone triage systems are staffed with fully trained nurses who use computerized algorithms and their clinical judgment to analyze a patient's complaints and give advice. The algorithms, which are designed in a systematic, question-and-answer format, indicate what advice the nurse should give. The nurse may provide self-care instructions, or she may tell the caller to come to the ED or make an appointment with his primary care physician or a specialist.

If a nurse dispenses advice over the phone, keep in mind that a legal duty arises the minutes she says, "OK, let me tell you what to do." This indicates a nurse-patient relationship, and the nurse is responsible for advice given. After a nurse starts to give advice by telephone, she can't decide midway through that she's overwhelmed and simply hang up; that could be considered abandonment. The nurse must give appropriate advice or a referral—for example, "After listening to you, I suggest that you go to the emergency department."

Nurses also need to complete the proper documentation for every call taken. Every telephone call that the unit receives should be logged in. The log should include the date and time of the call, the caller's name and address, the caller's chief complaint or request, the disposition of the call, and the name of the person who made the disposition. This information must be documented properly. Take thorough notes during the call, and complete the call log immediately after the call has been completed, while the information is still fresh. Doing so ensures completeness and accuracy.

Telephone triage nurses run into challenges that don't exist on other units of a facility. A telephone call doesn't allow the nurse to visually assess the caller. In addition, a caller may be reluctant to provide personal details over the phone. Language and cultural differences can also make evaluating a caller's symptoms difficult. Finally, processes to follow up with the caller's physician may not be adequate.

Standards

The Emergency Nurses Association (ENA) and the American Accreditation HealthCare Commission (URAC) have established guidelines and standards for telephone triage programs. ENA guidelines require telephone triage nurses to be experienced professional RNs with specialized education in triage, telephone assessment, and communication and documentation skills. Included in the ENA guidelines are mandatory continuing education requirements; defined protocols, policies, and procedures; and a continuous quality improvement program.

URAC's Health Call Center Standards apply to managed care organizations providing triage and health information services to the public when conducted by telephone, via Web site, or other electronic means. The standards assure that RNs, physicians, or other validly licensed individuals perform the clinical aspects of triage and other health information services in a manner that's timely, confidential, and medically appropriate. URAC also mandates that each telephone triage unit must have a continuous staff management program, including orientation and training, written job descriptions, performance evaluations, and verification of licenses.

HIPAA

The Health Insurance Portability and Accountability Act (HIPAA), passed by Congress in 1996, was designed to provide safeguards against the inappropriate use and release of personal medical information, including all medical records and identifiable health information in all forms (electronic, on paper, or oral). The telephone triage nurse needs to follow HIPAA's policies and procedures and inform callers of the scope of confidentiality that exists within the telephone triage program. Although the telephone triage nurse isn't likely to be in a position to violate HIPAA regulations, she must be aware that protecting personal health information is a serious duty.

Liability

In *Shannon v. McNulty and HealthAmerica Pennsylvania (1998),* the court held HealthAmerica, an HMO, vicariously liable for the negligence of its nursing telephone triage staff when it failed to quickly refer Mrs. Shannon to her physician or hospital when she called complaining of signs and symptoms of preterm labor. Mrs. Shannon lost her child. The Shannons also alleged that HealthAmerica was liable for its lack of appropriate procedures and protocols when dispensing telephonic medical advice to its subscribers.

In a Texas case, *Norman v. Good Shepard Medical Center (2001),* the court held the hospital liable for the actions of one of its LVNs who improperly performed telephone triage when Mrs. Norman called the ED looking for medical advice regarding her 10-year-old daughter's rash. The evidence established that the LVN disobeyed a hospital policy stating that LVNs weren't to give medical advice in non–life-threatening situations. The LVN gave incorrect medical advice, which caused a delay in diagnosis and forced the child to undergo several limb amputations.

To avoid liability while working as a telephone triage nurse, nurses need to know the policies and procedures of the telephone triage unit and uphold the privacy of protected health information. Proper training that includes orientation to protocols, proper documentation and follow-up communication, continuing education, and quality improvement monitoring is paramount for the nurse's—and your patient's—protection.

Patient teaching

Anytime a patient receives information about his care or treatment, the nurse is involved in patient teaching—a professional nursing responsibility and a potential source of liability.

Patient teaching has taken on increased significance, largely because patients are routinely discharged much earlier from hospitals. Patients and their families need more understanding of patients' illnesses and how to manage them at home.

Patient teaching may be formal or informal. Formal teaching includes, for example, preparing instructions on stoma care for a colostomy patient. When giv-

ing the patient this detailed information, follow these steps:
▶ Assess what the patient wants or needs to know.
▶ Identify mutual goals to reach.
▶ Choose teaching strategies that will help reach the goals, including consideration for cultural implications.
▶ Evaluate the achievement of the goals.

Teaching *informally* occurs when, for example, a nurse calms a patient's fears by explaining an upcoming diagnostic test or when he answers a friend's questions about how to treat a child's fever.

For best results, patient teaching should include the family and others involved in the patient's care. If family members understand the reason for a patient's treatment, they'll be more willing to provide emotional support.

Standards

Most nurse practice acts in the United States and Canada contain wording about promoting patient health and preventing disease or injury. However, they don't specify a nurse's responsibility for patient teaching. Nurses can find this information in the practice standards developed by professional organizations, in nursing job descriptions, and in statements about nursing practice from national commissions.

The Joint Commission requires that the "patient and his or her family be provided with appropriate education and training to increase the knowledge of the patient's illness and treatment needs and to learn skills and behaviors that promote recovery and improve function." The Joint Commission requires that patient teaching be done in an interdisciplinary manner, considering the patient's ability to learn and any cultural or emotional factors or any cognitive or physical limitations that would affect his ability to learn.

Patient teaching should be a dynamic process that changes to meet the patient's and his family's needs. It should include instruction in how to adapt to the illness, as well as how to prevent future problems.

Patient's right to health care information

Both statutory law and common law support the patient's right to have information about his condition and treatment. In fact, when a patient is admitted to a hospital, he may be handed a patient's bill of rights that clearly outlines his rights. The doctrine of informed consent further supports the patient's right to know. (See Chapter 2 for a more in-depth discussion on patients' rights.)

Liability

Despite RNs' deep involvement in patient teaching, the courts have rarely addressed nurses' liability in this area of patient care. The issue typically arises in litigation when a patient sues and the defendant health care provider attempts to prove patient responsibility for the bad outcome. For example, a patient is seen in the ED for an infection, is prescribed an antibiotic, is told to follow up with a specialist, and is discharged. The patient doesn't follow instructions and his infection worsens. To rebut his own negligence, the patient will argue that he wasn't told the risks if he didn't follow the physician's advice. However, some legal experts believe that as nurses take on greater patient-teaching responsibilities, they'll increasingly become the target of lawsuits dealing with the patient's right to information.

If a nurse is sued for malpractice, and the alleged wrongful act involves patient teaching, the court will consider whether patient teaching was the nurse's legal duty to the patient and whether the nurse met or breached it.

The court in *Kyslinger v. United States (1975)* addressed the nurse's liability for patient teaching. In this case, a veteran's administration (VA) hospital sent a hemodialysis patient home with an artificial kidney.

He eventually died (apparently while on the machine), and his wife sued the federal government—because a VA hospital was involved—alleging that the hospital and its staff had failed to teach either her or her late husband how to properly use and maintain a home hemodialysis unit.

After examining the evidence, the court ruled against the patient's wife, as follows: "During those 10 months that plaintiff's decedent underwent biweekly hemodialysis treatment on the unit (at the VA hospital), both plaintiff and decedent were instructed as to the operation, maintenance, and supervision of said treatment. The Court can find no basis to conclude that the plaintiff or plaintiff's decedent weren't properly informed on the use of the hemodialysis unit."

Another case that involved an issue of patient teaching was *Bass v. Barksdale (1983)* where the patient developed adverse effects from medication that she says she wasn't informed about.[20] The patient, Mrs. Bass, was being treated for tuberculosis by the public health department. Nurse Barksdale was one of the public health nurses who visited her home to deliver a monthly supply of medications, one of which was ethambutol. According to her testimony, nurse Barksdale stated that she told the patient about possible adverse effects of this medication during her initial visit, including decreased visual acuity. However, Mrs. Bass testified that nurse Barksdale only told her to watch the whites of her eyes and to notify her physician if they became yellow, but that she didn't tell her about other symptoms such as blurred vision, or to have monthly vision checks. The patient's sister was present during the nurse's visit and confirmed that the nurse didn't leave any pamphlets or other material for her to review.

During the next 2 months other nurses from the health department didn't check the patient's vision when they delivered the monthly medications. After several months of treatment the patient experienced a vision decline and blurred vision. A neurologist later diagnosed her irreversible vision problems as an adverse effect of ethambutol. Expert testimony validated that if vision checks had been preformed, the loss of vision could have been detected, and the vision loss possibly could have been reversed.

In upholding the plaintiff's jury award on appeal, the court found that health department employees, including the nurse, were negligent. Apparently there was no documentation of the patient teaching in the patient care record, and no teaching materials were given to Mrs. Bass. In this case, it's clear that doing so would have greatly strengthened nurse Barksdale's assertion that she completed the appropriate patient teaching. It's recommended that all patient teaching be documented in the patient record, adverse effects of all medications should be clearly specified, and the nursing care

plan should state what assessments should be ongoing for patients. It may also be helpful to have patients sign a statement of what they've received in terms of teaching materials, and to document that they have a clear understanding of any teaching materials. All teaching materials should consider the learner's literacy level, age, medical and social condition, culture, and any language barriers.

Patient refusal

Suppose a nurse begins teaching a patient about the medications he's taking, only to hear him say, "Oh, just tell my wife; she gives me all my pills." When something like this happens, be sure to document the incident. Include the patient's exact words; then describe what was taught to the wife, and how.

Roles of LPNs and LVNs

Unlike RNs, LPNs and LVNs aren't typically taught the fundamentals of patient teaching as part of their school curriculum, nor is patient teaching included in their scope of practice. RNs are primarily responsible for patient teaching and may delegate to LPNs or LVNs only the responsibility to reinforce what has already been taught. For example, if an RN is preparing a patient for a barium enema, she could ask an LPN or LVN to tell the patient about the X-ray room and what to expect. The RN could add to the information as necessary.

Cooperation with colleagues

Physicians, nurses, and other health care team members sometimes disagree about how patient teaching should be done and who should do it. To avoid conflict, always consult physicians and other appropriate health care team members when preparing routine patient-teaching protocols. A team approach to patient teaching not only decreases conflicts, but also ensures continuity in teaching—and a better-educated patient.

Also avoid conflicts by listening to the instructions that physicians, respiratory therapists, dietitians, and others give the patient. Doing so provides the nurse with knowledge about what has already been said to him, allowing the nurse to structure teaching accordingly.

Candor and diplomacy, of course, also help reduce conflict. Everyone profits when health care team members share their patient-teaching approaches and work together to achieve patient-teaching goals.

Incident reports

An *incident* is an event that's inconsistent with the hospital's ordinary routine, regardless of whether injury occurs. In most health care facilities, an injury to a patient requires an incident report. Patient complaints, medication errors, and injuries to employees and visitors require incident reports as well.

The Joint Commission defines an incident report as "the documentation for any unusual problem, incident, or other situation that's likely to lead to undesirable effects or that varies from established policies and procedures or practices."[21] This isn't to be confused with a sentinel event, which is an unexpected occurrence that involves death or serious physical or psychological injury or possible risk of the same.[22] Incident reports may be involved with notifying The Joint Commission about sentinel events, but they aren't sentinel events. For example, tubing misconnection is an area being

identified as a sentinel event by The Joint Commission because of nine cases reported, eight of which resulted in patient deaths and one that resulted in permanent loss of function.[23]

An incident report serves two main purposes:
▶ to inform hospital administration of the incident so that it can monitor patterns and trends, thereby helping to prevent future similar incidents (risk management)
▶ to alert the administration and the hospital's insurance company to the possibility of liability claims and the need for further investigation (claims management).

Even when the incident isn't investigated, the report serves as a contemporary, factual statement of it. The report also helps identify witnesses if a lawsuit is started months or even years later.

To be useful, an incident report must be filed promptly and must be thorough and factual.

Incident reporting

Whether you're an APN, an RN, an LPN or LVN, a nursing assistant, a staff nurse, or a nurse-manager, you have a duty to report an incident of which you have firsthand knowledge. Not only can failure to report an incident lead to your being fired, it can also expose you to claims of malpractice, especially if your failure to report the incident causes injury to a patient.

If you're the staff member who knows the most about the incident at the time of its discovery, you should complete the incident report. When you do so, include only the facts: what you saw when you came upon the incident or what you heard that led you to believe an incident had taken place. If information is second-hand, place it within quotation marks and identify the source. After completing the incident report, sign and date it. You should complete it during the same shift the incident occurred or was discovered.

An incident report is an administrative report, and therefore doesn't become part of the patient's medical record. In fact, the record shouldn't even mention that an incident report has been filed because this serves only to deflect the medical record's focus. The record should include only factual clinical observations relating to the incident. (Again, avoid value judgments.)

Entering observations in the nurses' notes section of the patient's record doesn't take the place of completing an incident report. Nor does completing an incident report take the place of proper documentation in the patient's chart.

After an incident report has been filed, the nursing supervisor, the physician called to examine the patient, appropriate department heads and administrators, the hospital attorney, and the hospital's insurance company may review it. (See *Filing an incident report: Chain of events.*) The report may be filed under the involved patient's name or by the type of injury, depending on the hospital's policy and the insurance company's regulations. Reports are rarely placed in the reporting nurse's employment file.

If asked to talk with the hospital's insurance adjuster or attorney about an incident, be cooperative, honest, and factual. Fully disclosing what you know early on will help the hospital decide how to handle legal consequences of an incident and will also preserve your testimony in case you're ever called to testify in court.

Information to include

An incident report should include only the following information:
▶ the names of the persons involved and witnesses
▶ factual information about what happened and the consequences to the person involved (supply enough information so the hospital administration can decide whether the matter needs further investigation)
▶ other relevant facts (such as the nurse's immediate actions in response to the incident; for example, notifying the patient's physician).

Information not to include

Never include the following types of statements in an incident report:
▶ opinions (such as a reporter's opinion of the patient's prognosis or who's at fault)
▶ conclusions or assumptions (such as what caused the incident)
▶ suggestions of who was responsible for causing the incident
▶ suggestions to prevent the incident from happening again.

Including this type of information in an incident report could seriously hinder the defense in a lawsuit arising from the incident.

Remember, the incident report serves only to notify the administration that an incident has occurred. In effect, it says, "Administration: Note that this incident happened, and decide whether you want to investigate it further." Items such as detailed statements from witnesses and descriptions of remedial action are usually part of an investigative follow up; don't include them in the incident report itself.

Filing an incident report: Chain of events

This chart provides a comprehensive overview of incident report routing in most facilities.

```
                    ┌─────────────────────────────────┐
                    │     Patient incident occurs.     │
                    └─────────────────────────────────┘
                                    ↓
┌───────────────────────────────────────────────────────────────────┐
│   Record significant medical and nursing facts in patient's charts. │
└───────────────────────────────────────────────────────────────────┘
                                    ↓
┌───────────────────────────────────────────────────────────────────┐
│ Write incident report during the shift on which the incident took   │
│                  place or is discovered.                            │
└───────────────────────────────────────────────────────────────────┘
                                    ↓
┌───────────────────────────────────────────────────────────────────┐
│              Give incident report to supervisor.                    │
└───────────────────────────────────────────────────────────────────┘
                                    ↓
┌───────────────────────────────────────────────────────────────────┐
│ Unit supervisor forwards report to appropriate administrator within │
│                        24 hours.                                    │
└───────────────────────────────────────────────────────────────────┘
                                    ↓
┌───────────────────────────────────────────────────────────────────┐
│                 Administrator reviews report.                       │
└───────────────────────────────────────────────────────────────────┘
                                    ↓
┌───────────────────────────────────────────────────────────────────┐
│  Administrator forwards pertinent information from the report       │
│     to the appropriate department for follow-up action.            │
└───────────────────────────────────────────────────────────────────┘
                                    ↓
┌───────────────────────────────────────────────────────────────────┐
│ Incident reports are collected and summarized to detect patterns    │
│     and trends and to highlight trouble spots.                      │
└───────────────────────────────────────────────────────────────────┘
                                    ↓
┌───────────────────────────────────────────────────────────────────┐
│ Administrator reviews patterns and trends, using this information   │
│ in continuous quality improvement projects                          │
│ for a single nursing unit or a multidisciplinary committee.         │
└───────────────────────────────────────────────────────────────────┘
              ↓                                      ↓
┌──────────────────────────────┐    ┌──────────────────────────────────┐
│ Refer information to existing │    │ Use information as the basis for  │
│ quality improvement teams.    │    │ establishing new quality          │
│                               │    │ improvement projects.             │
└──────────────────────────────┘    └──────────────────────────────────┘
```

Potential pitfalls

Be especially careful that the hospital's reporting system doesn't lead to improper incident reporting. For example, some hospitals require nursing supervisors to correlate reports from witnesses and then file a single report. Also, some incident report forms invite inappropriate conclusions and assumptions by asking, "How can this incident be prevented in the future?" If your hospital's reporting system or forms contain such potential pitfalls, alert the administration to them.

Error reporting

If an incident results from your error, you still have the duty to file an incident report immediately. Making a mistake is serious and may invite corrective action by your hospital, but the potential consequences of attempting to cover it up are worse.

For one thing, the likelihood that an incident report will be used against you is slight. A hospital wants its nurses to report incidents and to keep proper records. Nurses may not do this consistently if they're always reprimanded for even small errors. Most hospitals, in fact, will reprimand a nurse for not filing an incident report if injury is done to the patient.

If an incident results from your act of gross negligence or irresponsibility or is one of a series of incidents in which you've been involved, then the hospital may take action against you; that possibility increases if the patient sustains injury because of your error.

If a fellow employee's error causes a reportable incident, the safest course is to be factual and objective in reporting what you observed. This allows institutional review to be unbiased in its investigation. Remember, the truth isn't libel. If corrective action is taken, remember that the person who made the error is responsible, not the person who made the report. By properly fulfilling your duty to your patient and your hospital, you'll also minimize potential liability if the employee files a lawsuit against you.

Here's another point to remember: Most states have laws granting "qualified privilege" to those who have a duty to discuss or to evaluate coworkers, employees, or fellow citizens. This privilege means that no liability for libel exists unless the person giving the information knows it's false or has acted with a reckless disregard for the truth.

Incident reports as courtroom evidence

Controversy exists over whether a patient's attorney may "discover" (request and receive a copy of) an incident report and introduce it into evidence in a malpractice lawsuit. The law on this issue varies from state to state. To avoid discovery, the hospital may send copies of the incident report to its attorney, or the hospital attorney may write a letter stating that the report is being made for his use and benefit only, or the hospital may make the incident report an integral part of the quality assurance process and label it as such.

Concern about incident report discovery should be minimal if an incident report contains only properly reportable material. The information in a properly completed incident report is readily available to the patient's attorney through many other sources. Only when an incident report contains inaccurate, second-hand information, opinions, conclusions, accusations, or suggestions for preventing such incidents in the future does discovery of the incident report become an important issue for attorneys and the courts.

Risk management strategy

How can a nurse minimize the chances that a patient will sue after an incident? And how can nurses protect themselves and the hospital in case he does? The best way is to follow the "three Rs" of risk management strategy: rapport, record, and report.

Rapport

Answer his questions honestly. Don't offer an explanation if you weren't personally involved in the incident; instead, refer the patient to someone who can supply answers. If you try to answer his questions without direct knowledge of the incident, inconsistencies could arise and the patient could interpret these as a cover-up.

If you feel uncomfortable talking to the patient or family, ask your supervisor, hospital patient-relations specialist, or an administrator for advice on how to answer questions or to participate and help you provide answers. Remember that patients usually respond favorably if they know you're being honest and show that you care about their well-being and are doing everything you can to alleviate any consequences of the error.

Don't blame anyone for the incident. If you feel someone was at fault, tell your charge nurse or supervisor, not the patient.

If an incident changes the patient's care plan (such as medication orders), tell him about it and clearly explain the reasons for the change.

Record

Be sure to note the facts of the incident in the medical record. Remember, truthfulness is the best protection against lawsuits. If you try to cover up or play down an incident, you could end up in far more serious trouble than if you had reported it objectively. Never write in the medical record that an incident report has been completed. An incident report isn't clinical information but rather an administrative tool.

Report

Some nurses think incident reports are more trouble than they're worth and, furthermore, that they're a dangerous admission of guilt. That's false. Here's why incident reports are important:

▶ Incident reports jog our memories. The medical chart is client-focused, and facts pertinent to the incident, but not the patient, may be left out. Much time may pass between an incident and when it comes to court. We simply can't trust our memories, but we can trust an incident report. Therefore it must be completely accurate.

▶ Incident reports help administrators act quickly to change the policy or procedure that seems to be responsible for the incident. An administrator can also act quickly to talk with patients' families and offer assistance, explanation, or other appropriate support. Sometimes helpful communication with an injured patient and his family can calm a family's anger and prevent a lawsuit.

▶ Incident reports provide the information hospitals need to decide whether restitution should be made. One example is tracking "lost" belongings or compensating the patient for medical care resulting from the incident.

The patient who's a minor

A minor is a person under the age of majority, which is usually 18 or 21, depending on state or jurisdictional law. When caring for a minor, nurses need to keep in mind the way minors' legal rights are structured. What legal rights a minor has depends largely on his age. He may also have special legal status.

Minor's rights

A minor's rights fall into three categories:

▶ *Personal rights that belong to everyone from birth*. Examples include the right to privacy and the right to protection against crimes.

▶ *Rights that can be exercised as a minor matures*. These fall into two groups. The first includes the right to drive a car, to work at a paying job, and to have sexual relations—as long as both partners are of legal age. These rights are granted at certain ages, according to state laws, whether or not the minor is mature enough to exercise the right intelligently.

The second group includes rights granted by the courts rather than by statutory law. These are given to a minor who shows the mental and emotional ability to handle them.

▶ *Rights that belong to adults and can be exercised only by adults and by emancipated minors*. Examples include many financial and contractual rights, such as the right to consent to medical treatment.

The law provides special protection for minors so that they may exercise certain rights after reaching the age of majority. For example, because a minor can't sue in court, most states give minors a grace period after they reach the age of majority to bring any lawsuit relating to when they were minors. This includes suing persons their parents could have sued earlier on the minor's behalf but chose not to. Because this can include a lawsuit for medical malpractice, the law generally requires that hospitals keep the records of pediatric patients longer than the records of adults.

Mature minor

A mature minor is a nonemancipated minor in his middle to late teens who shows clear signs of intellectual and emotional maturity. A mature minor may be able to exercise certain adult rights, depending on laws in his state.

Emancipated minor

Emancipation is the legal process whereby children may obtain freedom from the custody, care, and control of their parents before the age of majority. Under most state statutes, an emancipated minor loses his right to financial support from his parents in exchange for the ability to govern his own affairs. Emancipation may also enable a minor to enter into binding contracts and to sue and be sued in his own name. Some statutes also give an emancipated minor the ability to consent to medical, dental, or psychiatric care without parental consent.

Depending on the jurisdiction, emancipation may be addressed by common law or statutory law. Most state statutes require a hearing in emancipation cases.

Standards for emancipation may include:

▶ *best interests of the minor* (Many state statutes contain a provision allowing judges to use the best interests of the child as a standard for emancipation.)

▶ *ability to manage financial affairs* (Many state statutes have a provision requiring that a minor demonstrate the ability to manage financial affairs before becoming emancipated.)

▶ *living separate and apart from parents* (Many statutes require that minors who wish to be emancipated live separate and apart from their parents. Some require parental consent for separate living arrangements.)

▶ *parental consent* (Many states require parental consent for an emancipation petition; others ignore this requirement altogether.)

▶ *age.* (Most states require that children be at least age 16 before initiating emancipation proceedings. A few states don't have an age requirement.)

Under most circumstances, treat an emancipated minor the same as if he were an adult.

Rights' restrictions

Note that even an emancipated minor may not exercise some rights. If he's 18 and the drinking age in his state is 21, he can't legally buy an alcoholic beverage. Some states set a minimum age for making a will (usually the age of majority). In those states, even if the minor is married or has a child, a will he draws up won't be valid.

Guardians ad litem

A *guardian ad litem* is a person appointed by the court to protect the interest of a minor in a legal proceeding. The court may appoint a *guardian ad litem* when these conditions coexist:
▶ A decision is needed for the minor.
▶ A "diversion of interest" exists. (The court possesses evidence that the interest of the minor's parents or legal guardians probably doesn't coincide with the minor's welfare.)

The court may appoint a *guardian ad litem* even if one or both parents are still living and interested in the minor's welfare or if the minor already has a guardian.

Consent

By far the most common problem with minors is obtaining proper consent for their medical care. Although the physician bears the legal responsibility for this, nurses will commonly be involved in the process. Here are several different situa-

tions that nurses may face in helping to obtain a minor's consent.

Nonemancipated minor

If the minor isn't emancipated, his mother, father, or legal guardian has the right to refuse or consent to treatment for him. Whenever possible, consent should be obtained from both parents or both guardians when joint guardians have custody of the minor.

If the parents are divorced or separated, the policy is to obtain consent from the parent who has custody. If the minor's parents are incompetent or dead and he has no legal guardian, the court will usually appoint a legal guardian. The guardian can consent or refuse, just as if he were a parent.

Mature, nonemancipated minor

In some Canadian jurisdictions under certain circumstances, mature, nonemancipated minors may consent to certain types of medical treatment themselves. Where legislation exists, common law provides that if nonemancipated minors understand the nature and consequences of treatment, they may give their own consent. In the United States, nonemancipated but mature minors' rights aren't as broad. However, in some jurisdictions, parental consent is no longer necessary for various types of medical and psychiatric care. In California, for example, nonemancipated minors age 15 and older, who live separate from their parents and manage their own finances, may consent to their own medical care. Ask the hospital attorney about the state's statutes in this area.

Emancipated minor

An emancipated minor can usually refuse or consent to treatment himself. However, if he can't do so (for example, he's unconscious after an accident), the nurse needs to try to find someone who can give consent for him. Talk to the hospital attorney to determine if there are state laws that designate surrogate decision makers when the patient becomes incompetent. Possibilities, in descending order of preference, include his spouse, parents or guardians, and nearest living relative. You may waive this requirement for consent only in an emergency situation when your failure to treat a minor immediately could result in further injury or death.

Disagreement between parents or joint guardians

Problems can arise when parents (whether married, divorced, or separated) or joint guardians disagree about consenting to treatment for a nonemancipated minor. The hospital's only recourse may be to go to court, where a judge either decides or assigns responsibility to one parent or guardian. If you find yourself in a situation in which a minor's parents or guardians can't agree on consenting to his treatment, tell the hospital administrators immediately so they can talk to the parents or guardians and, if necessary, alert the hospital's attorney.

Emergency care

The legal rule to follow when a minor needs emergency care is the same as that for adults: treat first and get consent later. Some courts have held that a mature minor, emancipated or not, may give valid and binding consent to emergency treatment. For example, in *Younts v. St. Francis Hospital and School of Nursing*

(1970), a nonemancipated but mature 17-year-old was held able to consent to surgical repair of a severed fingertip.

Request for an abortion

U.S. Supreme Court rulings, including *Ohio v. Akron Center for Reproductive Health (1990)* and *Hodgson v. Minnesota (1990),* indicate that state laws can't prevent a minor from seeking and obtaining a legal abortion; however, states can impose conditions on consent. The law in some states (such as Virginia, in which abortion-consent laws have been upheld by the Supreme Court) may require a minor seeking an abortion to notify her parents or to bypass this consent requirement by going before a judge, a procedure called *judicial bypass*.

Check with the facility's attorney for state rules to be followed when verifying consent for a minor's abortion.

Request for contraception

In *Carey v. Population Services International (1977),* the U.S. Supreme Court ruled unconstitutional a state law prohibiting the sale of contraceptives to anyone younger than age 16. The court held that the decision to bear a child is a fundamental right and that state interference can be justified only if it protects a compelling state interest. As a result, a minor can obtain contraceptives without parental consent.

Again, consult the hospital's attorney about questions regarding restrictions on distributing contraceptives to minors. For example, your state may require you to notify a parent or guardian about the matter.

Treatment for a communicable disease

Most states and Canadian jurisdictions have laws that permit minors to consent to treatment for serious communicable diseases, including sexually transmitted diseases, without parental approval.

If you must deal with a minor who's refusing diagnosis or treatment for a communicable disease, check your state's laws. Most states permit public health authorities to deal with a nonconsenting minor as an adult, including deciding whether he should be quarantined.

Treatment for substance abuse

State and federal laws generally permit minors to consent to take part in drug-abuse treatment and rehabilitation programs just as though they were adults. Like adults, minor patients in drug treatment programs are entitled to have their records kept confidential.

Conflicts of religious beliefs

If a patient or his parents or guardians are Jehovah's Witnesses or Christian Scientists, you may have special problems getting consent to treatment.

Although competent adults or emancipated minors may refuse treatment for religious reasons, nonemancipated minors may not. In most states in which the question has come before the courts, judges have ruled that parents and guardians can't stop a hospital from treating their child solely on religious grounds if a reasonable chance exists that the treatment will help the patient.

Note, however, that in this situation a court will have to appoint a *guardian ad litem* for the sick minor. This may take some time, so to avoid delaying the minor's treatment unnecessarily, notify the hospital administration as quickly as possible.

Mental health care

Minors, like adults, may be treated at private and state-run mental health facilities. When the minor and his parents agree to seek such treatment for the minor, the facility will follow its normal medical guidelines and procedures in deciding whether to admit him. This usually involves informing the patient and his parents or guardian of their rights and then obtaining their informed consent for admission.

In many states, however, the rules controlling admission of minors to inpatient mental health facilities are more rigorous. The rules may call for a full-scale hearing, with attorneys present, within a set time after admission (if not concurrent with admission).

The patient who's a victim of abuse

In the course of her nursing career, it's likely that the nurse will encounter victims of abuse. Sometimes abuse is physical battering, such as when a son regularly beats his aging father. At other times, abuse involves verbal, sexual, or emotional attack, or neglect and abandonment.

People who abuse others come from all socioeconomic levels and all ethnic groups. No specific psychiatric diagnosis encompasses the abuser's personality and behavior. However, many abusers have a history of being abused themselves when young or of having witnessed abuse of parents or siblings. Such childhood experiences are usually profound and can influence a person's behavior throughout his adult life. In many cases, abusive persons lack self-esteem and the security of being loved—qualities that help nonabusive persons cope with stress.

In times of crisis, abusers resort to the behavior learned in childhood. They abuse just as they were abused—all in an attempt to restore their own feelings of self-control and self-esteem. After all, if abuse was an acceptable behavior for their parents, why can't it be the same for them now?

Abusers usually can't tolerate personal failure or disapproval from spouses, children, or friends. When an abuser's self-esteem is low, he expects rejection and will act in ways that cause others to reject him. Rejection in turn provokes the abuser to commit further verbal or emotional abuse.

Abusers commonly have unrealistic expectations of the people they abuse. When an individual fails to live up to those expectations, the abuser feels a stronger compulsion to control, mortify, reject and, if necessary, physically injure that individual.

Cycle of abuse

Low self-esteem may prompt an abuser to choose a partner much like himself. Each will then feed into the other's forms of abuse. If the couple has children, in many cases they become targets of their parents' abusive behavior. What the children witness and suffer usually begins another cycle of abused child-to-child abuser.

Child abuse

U.S. government studies indicate that abused children who die from their injuries are most likely to die before age 4. Approximately four children die every day as a result of child abuse and 75% of these children are younger than age 4.[24] Studies have indicated that the majority of maltreatment fatalities occur in children younger than age 5. (See *Responding to suspected child abuse.*)

Children with behavior problems are particularly vulnerable to abuse, as are malformed or developmentally disabled children and children born prematurely or to unmarried parents. From the abusive parent's perspective, such a child represents an unplanned disruption or a stress-producing crisis. If the child has mental or physical defects, the parent may see this as reaffirming his own inadequacy and weakness. If the child has severe defects, the parent may be unable to accept that the child is his: he may pour on abuse in an effort to be rid of the child.

Parents may also view children as extensions of persons they hate. Sometimes this results from similarities in physical appearance or similarities in behavior. If a child resembles a spouse who deserted the family, he may be blamed for the spouse's failures and abused accordingly.

Adult abuse

Spouses, disabled persons, and elderly parents or relatives are the most common victims of adult abuse.

The abused spouse in many cases suffers from lack of self-esteem. An abused spouse's parents may have abused each other, or one parent may have abused the other. Having witnessed these attacks as a child, the present-day abused spouse accepts that she too will be abused. By behaving passively, spouses make it easy for their partners to abuse them repeatedly without fear of retaliation.

Like children, adults can become abuse victims if they're viewed as too depend-

Responding to suspected child abuse

Suppose you're on duty in the emergency department when Mrs. Firth comes in with her son Billy, age 4. She tells you, "Billy was riding in a friend's car and they had an accident. I didn't think he was hurt at first, but later on his knee swelled up. I decided I'd better have a doctor look at it."

You examine Billy closely for head and neck injuries. You don't see any, but you do notice some bruises on his left arm and on his legs that look several weeks old. You question Mrs. Firth about the accident, but she offers few details. Then, when you ask her about Billy's injuries, she gets defensive. Although his injuries look painful, Billy sits quietly while you examine him.

HOW TO RESPOND

You suspect Billy has been abused. What should you do next? Follow these guidelines:
• Tell the physician your reasons for suspecting child abuse and ask him to order a total-body X-ray, especially if you detect multiple old and new fractures or suspicious-for-age fractures. Also, inform your supervisor of the situation.
• If you suspect the child has been forced to ingest drugs or alcohol, get an order for toxicology studies of the child's blood and urine.
• Document the location, size, and appearance of all bruises and wounds (old or fresh) on an intake form with a body profile, being sure to sign and date it. Pictures may be taken, but proper identification of the patient, date, and time needs to be included in the photograph.

• If the child is severely bruised, get an order for a blood coagulation profile.
• If X-rays or other studies suggest the child has been abused, talk with the physician about confronting the parents. Ask how you might help him do this.
• If a parent admits to abusing the child and appears to want help, give the address and telephone number of a local group, such as a local chapter of Parents Anonymous, and encourage the parent to call.
• Whether or not the parent admits to abusing the child, report all suspected abuse to the state-designated agency empowered to investigate the situation. Keep in mind that in many states, failure to report suspected abuse is a crime.

---

ent, too sickly, or too much like a hated person. Ill or elderly persons who make financial, emotional, or personal demands in many cases will end up injured when the stress they create becomes intolerable for their abusers. (See *Elder abuse,* page 240.)

Among abusers of adults, men who abuse women predominate, but sometimes the opposite happens. Abused men, married or not, in most cases show the same low self-esteem and passivity as abused women. Sometimes an abused man is the less aggressive and more subservient member of the relationship and accepts a certain level of abuse in the hope that it won't get worse. At other times, he may be so ashamed by his in-

ability to provide adequately that he invites abuse to give himself a feeling of atonement.

Also be aware that abuse occurs in same-sex relationships, but the abused person may fail to report it out of fear of homophobia.

Abuse and the law

In 1874, grossly battered "Mary Ellen," age 9, was found chained to her bed in a New York City tenement. Etta Wheeler, a church worker, tried to find help for Mary Ellen, but she quickly discovered that New York had no laws to protect children. Her only recourse was the American Society for the Prevention of

Elder abuse

Elder abuse has reached alarming proportions, having increased 150% between 1986 and 1996. Estimates range from 700,000 to 2 million annual cases of mistreatment in the United States alone. A study by the Administration on Aging and the Administration for Children and Families estimates that more than 500,000 older people in domestic settings were abused or neglected during 1996 and that for every reported incident, about five went unreported.

The greater an elderly person's disabilities, the more vulnerable he is to abuse or neglect by caregivers—usually his relatives. Family members provide about 80% of all care given to older people, and about 85% of all reported abuse involves a family member's behavior.

DEFINING ABUSE AND NEGLECT

Nearly every state has laws mandating that suspected elder abuse be reported to the authorities. However, not all states define elder abuse. Instead, they leave its diagnosis to health care professionals. One definition of abuse and neglect goes as follows:
• *Elder abuse* is destructive behavior that's directed at an older adult, carried out in a context or relationship of trust, and occurring intensely or frequently enough to produce harmful physical, psychological, social, or financial suffering and a decreased quality of life.
• *Elder neglect* is harm caused by failure to provide prudently adequate and reasonable assistance to meet the elderly person's basic physical, psychological, social, and financial needs.

DETECTING ABUSE

As a nurse—especially if you're in an outpatient or acute care setting—you have more contact with patients than most other members of the health care team. You may be the first to notice or suspect mistreatment of an elderly patient. In fact, in hospitals with special Elder Assessment Teams, most abuse referrals are generated by nurses, especially those in the emergency department. If you suspect elder abuse, report it according to hospital or agency policy or as mandated by state law.

SIGNS AND SYMPTOMS

Detecting abuse in a frail, elderly person with multiple health problems can challenge your assessment skills. A situation or condition that suggests mistreatment may actually represent the progression of disease. For example, you may suspect that an elderly woman covered with bruises is battered when in fact she has a coagulation disorder caused by the medication she takes for heart disease.

The following signs and symptoms, although not definitive for abuse, call for further investigation and reporting:
• unexplained bruises, fractures, or burns
• poor hygiene or nutritional status
• pressure ulcers or other evidence of skin breakdown or infection
• dehydration
• fear of a family member or a caregiver
• indications of overmedication or undermedication, such as grogginess or decreased level of consciousness
• unusual listlessness or withdrawal
• signs and symptoms of sexually transmitted disease.

Cruelty to Animals, which agreed to intervene on Mary Ellen's behalf.

One year after Mary Ellen's case reached the courts, New York state adopted the country's first child-protection legislation. This gave child-protection agencies a legal base, and it proved a breakthrough for other disadvantaged groups as well.

Since then, child abuse has gained increasing attention from the public, from legislators, and from concerned health care professionals. In 1946, for example, radiologists reported that subdural hematomas and abnormal X-ray findings in the long bones were commonly associated with early childhood traumatic injuries. In 1961, an American Academy of Pediatrics symposium on child abuse introduced the term "battered child."

The first statutes requiring mandatory reporting of child abuse resulted from a 1963 report by the Children's Bureau of the U.S. Department of Health, Education, and Welfare (now the Department of Health and Human Services). Most states, using the model in the report, developed protective legislation by the early 1970s. Unfortunately, the diversity of these laws made uniform interpretation impossible.

To help remedy this, Congress passed the Child Abuse Prevention and Treatment Act in 1973. This Act requires states to meet certain uniform standards to be eligible for federal assistance in setting up programs to identify, prevent, and treat the problems caused by child abuse. The Act also established a national center on child abuse and child neglect.

The Act was amended in 1984 in response to "Baby Doe" cases. These cases involved parents who refused life-saving treatment for mentally and physically handicapped infants. The amendments require the states to respond to reports of a child's medical neglect. States must respond to reports that medically indicated treatment (including appropriate nutrition, hydration, and medication) has been withheld from an infant. The law allows three exceptions under which treatment may be withheld:
▶ when the infant is chronically ill and irreversibly comatose
▶ when treatment would only prolong dying

▶ when treatment itself would be inhumane and futile in terms of survival.

According to interpretive guidelines to the regulations (which don't have the force of law), even when one of these exceptions is present, the infant must still receive appropriate nutrition, hydration, and medication.

Most state child abuse legislation shares two common features:
▶ empowering of a social welfare or law enforcement bureau to receive and investigate reports of actual or suspected abuse
▶ granting of legal immunity from liability, for defamation or invasion of privacy, to a person reporting an incident of actual or suspected abuse in good faith.

Laws protecting abused spouses are still being written. Although many domestic relations laws exist, additional legislation is required to help protect victims of domestic violence.

Duty to report abuse

Nurses play a crucial role in recognizing and reporting incidents of suspected abuse. While caring for patients, you can readily note evidence of apparent abuse. When you do, you must pass the information along to the appropriate authorities. In many states, failure to report actual or suspected abuse constitutes a crime.

Abuse recognition

Learn to recognize the events that trigger abuse and the signs and symptoms that mark the abused and the abuser. Early in your relationship with an abused patient, you'll need to be adept at spotting the subtle behavioral and interactional clues that signal an abusive situation.

Examine the patient's relationship with the suspected abuser. For example, abused people tend to be passive and fearful. An abused child usually fails to protest if his parent is asked to leave the examining area. An abused adult, on the other hand, usually wants his abuser to stay with him.

Abused persons may react to procedures by crying helplessly and incessantly. They tend to be wary of physical contacts, including physical examinations.

Many facilities have a policy, procedure, or protocol that establishes criteria to help nurses and other health care providers make observations that will help identify possible victims of abuse. Learning these criteria will make spotting victims of abuse more objective and prevent cases from going unrecognized.

Assessment of the abuser

Sometimes the abuser will appear overly agitated when dealing with health care personnel; for example, he'll get impatient if they don't carry out procedures instantly. At other times, he may exhibit the opposite behavior: a total lack of interest in the patient's problems.

Assessment of the victim

When an abuse victim is reporting his history, he may be vague about how he was injured and tell different stories to different people. When you ask directly about specific injuries, he may answer evasively or not at all. Sometimes he'll minimize or try to hide his injuries.

Look for characteristic signs of abuse. In most cases of abuse, you'll find old bruises, scars, or deformities the patient can't or won't explain. X-ray examinations may show the presence of many old fractures.

Documentation of findings

Always document findings objectively; try to keep emotions out of the documentation charting. One way to do this is to use the SOAP technique, which calls for these steps:

▶ In the subjective (S) part of the note, record information in the patient's own words.

▶ In the objective (O) part, record your personal observations.

▶ Under assessment (A), record your evaluations and conclusions.

▶ Under plan (P), list sources of hospital and community support available to the patient after discharge.

Liability protection

If you've ever hesitated to file an abuse report because you fear repercussions, remember that the Child Abuse Prevention and Treatment Act protects you against liability. If your report is bona fide (that is, if you file it in good faith), the law will protect you from a suit filed by an alleged abuser.

Filing of a report

Make the report as complete and accurate as possible. Be careful not to let personal feelings affect either the way the report is made out or the decision to file the report.

Abuse cases can raise many difficult emotional issues. Remember, however, that not filing a report can have more serious consequences than filing one that contains an unintentional error. It's better to risk error than to risk breaching the child abuse reporting laws—and, in effect, perpetuating the abuse.

Support services

Many support services have become available for both abusers and their victims. For example, if a female victim is afraid to return to the scene of her abuse, she may find temporary housing in a women's shelter. If no such shelter is available, she may be able to stay with a friend or family member.

Social workers or community liaison workers may also be able to offer suggestions for shelter. Another possibility is a church, synagogue, or mosque, which may have members willing to take the patient in. If no shelter can be found, the patient may have to stay at the hospital for her safety.

Alert the patient to state, county, or city agencies that can offer protection. The police department should be called to collect evidence if the patient wants to press charges against the abuser. If the patient is a child, the law will probably require filing a report with a government family-service agency.

Evaluate the abuser's ability to handle stress. He'll probably pose a continued threat to others until he gets help in understanding his behavior and how to change it. In such a situation, you may attempt to refer him to an appropriate local or state agency that can offer help.

For abusive fathers or mothers, a local chapter of Parents Anonymous (PA) may be helpful. (See *Help for the abused and the abuser.*) PA, a self-help group made up of former abusers, attempts to help abusing parents by teaching them how to deal with their anger.

Besides helping short-circuit abusive behavior, a self-help group takes abusing parents out of their isolation and introduces them to individuals who can empathize with their feelings. It also pro-

---

Help for the abused and the abuser

Organizations offer support and counseling for the abuse victim and the abuser. Also check the "Guide to Human Services" section of the telephone directory under "Abuse" and "Child and Youth" for local or state agencies.

National Child Abuse Hotline
ChildHelp USA
1-800-4-A-CHILD
www.childhelp.org

National Court Appointed Special Advocate Association
1-800-628-3233
www.nationalcasa.org

National Domestic Violence Hotline
1-800-799-SAFE
www.ndvh.org

Rape, Abuse, and Incest National Network
1-800-656-HOPE
www.rainn.org

---

vides help in a crisis, when members may be able to prevent an abusive incident.

Telephone hot lines to crisis intervention services also give abusers someone to talk with in times of stress and crisis and may help prevent abuse. Typically staffed by volunteers, telephone hot lines provide a link between those who seek help and trained counselors.

These and other kinds of help are also available through family-service agencies and hospitals. By becoming familiar with national and local resources, you'll be able to respond quickly and authoritatively when an abuser or his victim needs your help.

Public education

Besides your duty to report abuse, you also have the opportunity to teach the public about abuse. The Child Abuse Prevention and Treatment Act encourages health care facilities to develop programs to identify, report, and ultimately prevent abuse. You can help reduce the incidence of abuse by teaching people about its signs and symptoms, diagnosis, and treatment, not just in the workplace, but in health fairs, at school presentations, or other interactions with the public.

The patient who's mentally ill or developmentally disabled

Despite his usually dependent condition, a mentally ill or developmentally disabled patient has most of the same rights as other members of society. In fact, usually the law covers such a patient's rights in extra detail to ensure that he receives proper care and treatment. If you violate these rights, even unwittingly, you could face serious legal complications.

Much of today's concern for the rights of the mentally ill and developmentally disabled stems from attempts to correct past abuses. Under the U.S. Constitution, a person's rights can't be limited or denied merely because of his mental status. The courts have generally interpreted the Constitution to mean that mentally ill and developmentally disabled persons have a right to fair and humane treatment, including during hospitalization. Under most circumstances, such a patient can't be kept in a hospital against his will, for example. Nor can he be denied the right to refuse treatment or to receive information, so he can give informed consent to proposed surgery.

Legislation

State governments have tried to ensure the rights of this special population by enacting legislation specifically addressing the problems of the mentally ill and developmentally disabled. This legislation describes and authorizes specific services and provides the necessary funding.

The federal government also provides for the mentally ill and developmentally disabled. The Rehabilitation Act of 1973, for example, earmarked funds specifically for rehabilitative programs. It provides cash assistance for persons who, because of their disabilities, can't provide adequately for themselves or their families. The Act also outlines 14 patient's rights to ensure high standards of health care. Facilities that participate in Medicare must comply with these 14 rights and make sure that the patient, his guardian, next of kin, or sponsoring agency knows about them, too.

The Americans with Disabilities Act of 1990 (P.L. 101-336) further ensures a disabled citizen's rights by providing a "national mandate for the elimination of discrimination against individuals with disabilities." This Act addresses discrimination in employment, public accommodations, and public services, programs, and activities.

Canada makes similar provisions for mentally ill and developmentally disabled persons. As in the United States, Canadian legislation seeks to prevent maltreatment and to fund programs that help these persons to function successfully in society.

Legal responsibility for a patient

When a mentally ill or developmentally disabled child is admitted to a hospital, legal responsibility for him must be established immediately. If a parent accompanies the patient, usually the parent will be legally responsible.

If the child has been institutionalized before entering the hospital, the institution may have responsibility. However, this is true only if the parents have waived responsibility and the institution has written evidence to prove it.

If the courts have found the parents unfit or unable to care for the child, a legal guardian will have been appointed. This person has the legal right to assume responsibility for the child.

When no guardian has been appointed for the child, the state may act as a guardian under the doctrine of *parens patriae*. This doctrine also applies to mentally ill or developmentally disabled adults, who must have guardians.

If the mentally ill or developmentally disabled patient is an adult, check his chart to see if he requires a legal guardian and to establish who it is. It may be a parent. Or if the patient is married, it may be the patient's spouse.

Sometimes an adult patient and his guardian will seriously disagree about the patient's care. When this happens, get clarification by going through proper hospital channels.

Remember, you have no right to control the life of a mentally ill or developmentally disabled patient. Restricting his liberty for any reason is almost never legally permissible, except when he may otherwise harm himself or others. You must analyze each situation carefully to determine at what point the patient needs help in making health care decisions.

Informed consent

When consent is required from a patient who's mentally ill or developmentally disabled, consider these three questions:

▶ Can consent for treatment or a special procedure be obtained the same way it is from any other patient?

▶ Does the patient fully understand the procedure that he's to undergo, including the risks and alternatives?

▶ Does the patient have the authority to give his own consent, or must someone else give it?

The answers to these questions will vary with each patient. Clearly, if the patient is of unsound mind and can't understand the nature, purpose, alternatives, and risks of the proposed treatment, he can't legally consent. In such a case, consent must be obtained from the patient's legal guardian.

If the legal guardian is unavailable, a court authorized to handle such matters may authorize treatment.

Patient's ability in question

Sometimes a physician or nurse may doubt a patient's capacity to consent, even though he hasn't been judged incompetent. This commonly happens during an illness that causes temporary mental incompetence. In such a situation, you must follow your state laws to determine who can make health care decisions for the patient. Typically, the nearest relative's consent is often obtained or, if none can be found, the court must authorize treatment.

In the New York case of *Collins v. Davis (1964)*, a hospital administrator sought a court order to permit surgery on an irrational adult whose life was considered to be in danger. The patient's wife had previously refused to give consent, allegedly for reasons she felt served the patient's best interest. The court, after considering the entire situation—especially the patient's prognosis if surgery wasn't performed—agreed that the hospital and the physician had only two choices: Either let the patient die, or perform the operation against his wife's wishes. The court overruled the wife's refusal, holding that the patient had sought medical attention and that treatment normally given to a patient with a similar condition should be provided.

Nurse's role

A nurse can best protect the mentally ill or developmentally disabled patient's legal rights to informed consent by making sure that a physician has provided him or his guardian with information. Find out if the patient's and guardian's questions have been answered to their satisfaction.

Unless a nurse's absence would place the patient in danger, she should refuse to assist with procedures on a patient whose informed consent hasn't been obtained. If you do participate, you can be held liable along with the physician and the hospital. In fact, if your patient is a minor, you could face double liability: his parents could sue you now, and he could sue you when he comes of age.

Forced hospitalization and use of restraints

Mentally ill or developmentally disabled persons may be involuntarily kept in hospitals if they're at risk for taking their own lives or if they pose a threat to other people's property or lives. However, mental illness alone isn't a sufficient legal basis for detaining a patient.

Similar restrictions apply to physical restraint of patients. Most states require

a physician to write the restraint order and place it in the patient's medical record before applying restraints.

Restraint (or seclusion) may be used only to prevent a patient from seriously injuring himself or others, and only when all other less-restrictive physical and psychological therapies would likely fail to prevent such injuries. Whenever possible, use minimal restraint—only that amount necessary to protect the patient and safeguard the staff and others. Restraint should never be used for punishment, for the convenience of staff, or as a substitute for treatment programs. Use of restraints is usually limited to a specific period.

Nurse's role

If you make a decision to apply restraints, you should immediately request that a physician examine the patient and write an order to restrain him. In an emergency situation, such as a violent outburst with actual or potential harm to persons or property, a person may apply restraints to the patient. However, obtain an order for the restraint as soon as possible, and document the incident carefully. (See discussion of restraints earlier in this chapter.)

Potential liability

As a nurse, you may be held liable in a lawsuit if you can't verify that, in your judgment, a patient needed to be restrained and that he was restrained only as long as necessary. If you restrain or seclude a patient simply for shouting obscenities, for example, you risk a lawsuit for false imprisonment.

You should also make sure you know how to use restraining devices safely and effectively. You may be held liable if your restraints don't prove effective and the patient is injured as a result.

If a competent patient makes an informed decision to refuse restraint, the facility may require the patient to sign a release that would absolve the facility of liability should injury result from the patient's refusal to be restrained.

Right to privacy

The law has tried to protect all citizens from unwarranted intrusion into their private lives. Unfortunately, mentally ill and developmentally disabled patients' rights to privacy are easily violated. A good definition of privacy, first presented at the International Commission of Justice in 1970, reads: "Privacy is the ability to lead one's life without anyone:
▶ interfering with family or home life
▶ interfering with physical or mental integrity or moral and intellectual freedom
▶ attacking honor and reputation
▶ placing one in a false light
▶ censoring or restricting communication and correspondence, written or oral
▶ disclosing irrelevant or embarrassing information
▶ disclosing information given or received in circumstances of professional confidence."

Keep this definition in mind as you work with mentally ill and developmentally disabled patients, and do all you can to protect their right to privacy.

Right to writ of *habeas corpus*

Institutionalization may, at times, breach a patient's rights, giving him cause to petition for a writ of *habeas corpus*. This writ seeks to ensure the timely release of a person who claims that he's being detained illegally and deprived of his liberty.

Right to treatment

In *Wyatt v. Stickney (1972),* the court upheld the legal right of a mentally ill person hospitalized in a public institution to receive adequate psychiatric treatment. This decision suggests that when a patient is involuntarily committed because he needs treatment, his rights are violated if he doesn't receive proper care. Furthermore, if the underlying reason for a patient's commitment is that he's dangerous to himself or others, treatment must be provided to make him less so.

In the Wyatt decision, the court outlined a complete bill of rights for the mentally ill patient. Among the key points, the court said treatment should be given:
▶ by adequate staff
▶ in the least restrictive setting
▶ in privacy
▶ in a facility that ensures the patient a comfortable bed, adequate diet, and recreational facilities
▶ with the patient's informed consent before unusual treatment
▶ with payment for work done in the facility, outside of program activities
▶ according to an individual treatment plan.

If possible, ensure that a mentally ill or developmentally disabled patient knows what treatment he needs and how he'll get it. You must know what his major problems are and what he can do for himself, or what others must do for him, to help him get ready for discharge. You should also involve him in formulating his treatment plan, unless you have a documented reason why he can't or won't be involved.

Sexual rights

Many questions remain regarding the sexual rights of mentally ill and developmentally disabled patients. For example, should developmentally disabled persons be given sex education? Should they be allowed to reproduce, practice contraception, or undergo voluntary sterilization?

Although the general inclination is to let guardians make these decisions, the issue of the individual's right to make his own decisions won't go away. If good care can be given to both the developmentally disabled and their offspring, who's to say that they should be denied the opportunity to enjoy the same satisfactions others do?

The U.S. Supreme Court has upheld the rights of mentally ill or developmentally disabled patients:
▶ to marry
▶ to have children
▶ to use contraception, abortion, or sterilization, if desired
▶ to follow a lifestyle of their own choosing.

Several cases, such as *Sengstack v. Sengstack (1958)*, *Wyatt v. Stickney (1972)*, and *O'Connor v. Donaldson (1975)*, have used the U.S. Supreme Court decisions as a basis for their rulings.

Involuntary sterilization

Involuntary sterilization of developmentally disabled patients isn't used today as in the past. Although the U.S. Supreme Court upheld the constitutionality of involuntary sterilization in *Buck v. Bell (1927)*, if a similar case were to come before the Supreme Court today, the precedent would likely be overturned.

In *Buck*, the court held that the state has the right to sterilize a developmentally disabled or mentally ill person, provided that:
▶ the sterilization isn't prescribed as punishment
▶ the policy is applied equally to all
▶ a potential child's interest is sufficient to warrant the sterilization.

Courts today can authorize such a procedure, but only within specific guidelines. Generally, it must be shown that sterilization is the only workable means of contraception. In some cases, the court orders a separate, independent presterilization review of the case. (In New York state, unlike California, for example, an independent medical review board must review and approve every planned involuntary sterilization before it can be performed.) Even though the patient's guardian has requested sterilization, if the patient refuses to submit to surgery, the court may call for use of a less permanent birth control method.

Participation in research

Another troublesome area involves using mentally ill and developmentally disabled persons as subjects for medical or other research, especially if risks are involved. Guidelines for consent to experimentation and drastic, questionable, or extreme forms of treatment are complicated and raise many unresolved questions. The so-called Willowbrook decision, *N.Y. State Association for Retarded Children, Inc. v. Carey (1977)*, however, decreed that both voluntary and involuntary residents of a mental health facility have the constitutional right to be protected from harm. The proper authority (usually an institutional review board) should allow the patient to participate in the research only if it's relevant to his needs and the needs of others like him, and its potential benefits outweigh its potential risks. For example, a depressed patient shouldn't be asked to participate in research involving anxiety and schizophrenia.

Strict federal regulations guide how experimental treatment can be carried out. Such treatment must be given with extreme caution to mentally ill or developmentally disabled patients.

Responses to patient requests

"Ordinary" requests made by mentally ill or developmentally disabled patients may require special consideration. For example, a patient may demand to smoke a cigarette. His physician hasn't written an order for the request. If the patient should smoke only under supervision because of the danger of fire, you may decide to stay with him while he does so. If you have a duty to be elsewhere, you should refuse his request, explaining why and telling him when he'll be able to smoke. If you know a refusal will agitate and anger him, you can also ask another nurse or caregiver to supervise the patient while he smokes.

Perhaps the patient is well aware that he's violating the hospital's no-smoking policy and his request is really a challenge to authority. If so, you may decide to refuse the request, explaining the need to follow the hospital's social and safety policies.

If the patient's behavior is part of a pattern that includes, for example, refusing to shower, refusing to go to bed by a certain time, and demanding to make an immediate phone call, then you need to refer the situation to the treatment team for a well-thought-out decision—one that serves the best interests of both the patient and the hospital. After it's made,

ask all the health care team members to enforce this decision consistently.

The patient who's a suspected criminal

Suppose you're asked to care for an injured suspect who's accompanied by police. Because the police need evidence, they ask you to give them the patient's belongings and a sample of his blood. Should you comply? The answer to this question isn't simple. Evidence turned over to law enforcement may not be admissible in court if the nurse is ignorant of the law and fails to follow proper protocol. Worse still, later on, the patient may be able to sue you for invasion of privacy.

Constitutional rights

The Fourth Amendment to the U.S. Constitution provides that "the right of the people to be secure in their persons, houses, papers and effects, against unreasonable searches and seizures shall not be violated, and no warrants shall issue, but upon probable cause." This means that every individual, even a suspected criminal, has a right to privacy, including a right to be free from intrusions that are made without search warrants. However, the Fourth Amendment doesn't absolutely prohibit all searches and seizures, only unreasonable ones.

Further, under constitutional law, when a magistrate issues a warrant authorizing a police officer to conduct a search, the warrant must be specific about the places to be searched and the items to be seized.

Probably the exclusionary rule is the most common rule affecting nurses in relation to suspected criminals and their victims. This rule stems from the Fourth

Amendment's prohibition of unreasonable searches and seizures. In the landmark case of *Mapp v. Ohio (1961)*, the U.S. Supreme Court held that evidence obtained through an unreasonable or unlawful search can't be used against the person whose rights the search violated.

Searches without a warrant

Under certain circumstances, a police officer may lawfully conduct a search and obtain evidence without a warrant:
▶ If an accused person consents to a search, any evidence found is considered admissible in court (*Schneckloth v. Bustamonte [1973]*).
▶ A search incidental to an arrest may be conducted without a warrant. Usually, such a search shouldn't extend beyond the accused person's body or an immediate area where he could reach for a weapon. However, in *Maryland v. Buie (1990)*, the U.S. Supreme Court ruled that a search incidental to an arrest could extend to adjoining rooms and closets of a private residence from which an accomplice could attack. Police may even conduct a sweep of an entire area if they have reason to think they may be in danger. Although this Supreme Court case dealt with searches in a private home, the ruling could apply to searches conducted in a hospital.
▶ Police may search an area, even out of arm's reach, to recover a weapon that could pose a threat to their safety (*New York v. Class [1985]*).
▶ Police may enter a private area and seize items in plain view if they're in "hot pursuit" of a criminal suspect (*Warden v. Hayden [1967]*).

The laws of search and seizure are complex and subject to change by new legal decisions. Consult with the administration or an attorney before complying with a police request to turn over a patient's personal property. Some state laws require that police obtain a warrant before they're legally entitled to this evidence.

Evidence obtained as part of a blood test

Opinions differ as to whether a blood test, such as a blood alcohol test, is admissible in court if the person refused consent for the test. In *Schmerber v. California (1966)*, the U.S. Supreme Court said that a blood extraction obtained without a warrant, incidental to a lawful arrest, isn't an unconstitutional search and seizure and is admissible evidence. Many courts have held this to mean that a blood sample must be drawn *after* the arrest to be admissible.

Further, the blood sample must be drawn in a medically reasonable manner. In *People v. Kraft (1970)*, a suspect was pinned to the floor by two police officers while a physician drew a blood sample. In *State v. Riggins (1977)*, a suspect's broken arm was twisted while a policeman sat on him to force consent to a blood test. In both cases, the courts ruled the test results inadmissible. The courts have also ruled as inadmissible—and as violative of due process rights—evidence gained by the forcible and unconsented insertion of a nasogastric tube into a suspect to remove stomach contents (*Rochin v. California [1952]*).

Courts have admitted blood tests as evidence when the tests weren't drawn at police request but for medically necessary purposes such as blood typing (*Commonwealth v. Gordon [1968]*). Some courts have also allowed blood work to be admitted as evidence when it was drawn for nontherapeutic reasons and voluntarily turned over to police.

Be careful, though. A physician or nurse who does blood work without the patient's consent may be liable for committing battery, even if the patient is a suspected criminal and the blood work is medically necessary.

Blood alcohol testing

Many states have enacted so-called implied consent laws as part of their motor vehicle laws. These laws hold that by applying for a driver's license, a person implies his consent to submit to a blood alcohol test if he's arrested for drunken driving. Many of these laws state specifically that if an individual refuses to submit to the chemical test, it may not be given, but the driver then forfeits his license. Check to see whether such laws exist in your state.

Evidence obtained during a surgical procedure

A Massachusetts case, *Commonwealth v. Storella (1978),* involved a bullet that a physician removed during a medically necessary operation. After the operation, the physician turned the bullet over to the police. The court allowed the bullet to be admitted as evidence because the physician was acting according to good medical practice, and not as a state agent, in removing the bullet.

In 1985, the U.S. Supreme Court ruled that the constitutionality of such court-ordered surgery to acquire evidence must be decided on a case-by-case basis. The interest in individual privacy and security must be weighed against the societal interest in collecting evidence. Therefore, be wary if asked to assist in a highly invasive procedure to help the state obtain

evidence if the suspect doesn't consent. If necessary, consult an attorney.

Swallowed contraband

Drug couriers have been known to carry contraband by swallowing it in small balloons, which can be recovered after elimination. As a nurse, you may become involved in efforts to detect and recover swallowed contraband. In *United States v. Montoya de Hernandez (1985),* the U.S. Supreme Court ruled that the police could lawfully detain drug couriers until swallowed items could be recovered and seized.

Private party searches

In *Burdeau v. McDowell (1921),* the U.S. Supreme Court said that the Fourth Amendment protections applied only to governmental (such as police) action and not to searches conducted by private parties. Although several courts have criticized this rule, it has been repeatedly upheld.

In *State v. Perea (1981),* a nurse took a suspect's shirt for safekeeping, then turned it over to the police even though they hadn't requested it. A New Mexico court allowed the shirt to be admitted as evidence. The reason: because no governmental intrusion was involved, the suspect's Fourth Amendment right wasn't violated.

The case of *United States v. Winbush (1970)* produced a similar result. In this case, the court ruled that evidence found during a routine search of an unconscious patient's pockets was admissible because the purpose of the search was to obtain necessary identification and medical information.

Conducting a drug search

If you suspect your patient is abusing drugs or alcohol, you have a duty to do something about it. If such a patient harms himself or anyone else, resulting in a lawsuit, the court may hold you liable for his actions.

WHEN YOU KNOW ABOUT DRUG ABUSE

Suppose you know for certain that a patient is abusing drugs—if you're an emergency department nurse, you may find drugs in a patient's clothes or handbag while looking for identification. Your hospital policy may obligate you to confiscate the drugs and take steps to ensure that the patient doesn't acquire more.

WHEN YOU SUSPECT DRUG ABUSE

When a patient's erratic or threatening behavior makes you suspect he's abusing drugs or alcohol, your hospital's policy may require that you conduct a search. Is your search legal? As a rule of thumb, if you strongly believe the patient poses a threat to himself or others and you can document your reasons for searching his possessions, you're probably safe legally.

GUIDELINES FOR SEARCHES

Before you conduct a search, review your hospital's guidelines on the matter. Then follow these guidelines carefully. Most hospital guidelines will first direct you to contact your supervisor and explain why you have legitimate cause for a search. If she gives you her approval, ask a security guard to help you. Besides protecting you, he'll serve as a witness if you do find drugs. When you're ready, confront the patient, tell him you intend to conduct a search, and tell him why.

Depending on your hospital's guidelines, you can search a patient's belongings as well as his room. If you find illegal drugs during your search, confiscate them. Depending on your hospital's guidelines, you may be obligated to report the patient to the police.

If you find alcoholic beverages during your search, hospital guidelines may require you to take them from the patient. Explain to the patient that you'll return them when he leaves the hospital.

MAINTAINING WRITTEN RECORDS

After you've completed your search, record your findings in your nurses' notes and in an incident report. Your written records will be an important part of your defense (and your hospital's) if the patient decides to sue.

Evidence in plain view

As a nurse, if you find a gun, knife, drug, or other item that the suspect could use to harm himself or others, you have a right to remove it. You should, however, notify the administration immediately and maintain control over the evidence until you can give it to an administrator or law enforcement official. The facility should have specific policies and procedures to follow if this situation occurs.

Ability of suspect to sue

In general, searches that occur as part of medical care don't violate a suspect's rights. However, searches made for the sole purpose of gathering evidence—especially if done at police request—very well may. Several courts have said that a suspect subjected to an illegal private search has a right to seek remedy against the unlawful searcher in a civil lawsuit. One such case was *Stone v. Commonwealth (1967)*. (See *Conducting a drug search*.)

Canadian law

The major difference between U.S. and Canadian law regarding searches is that, in Canada, evidence obtained during an illegal search may still be admissible in court. However, a police officer should have a search warrant before searching a suspected criminal to protect his rights.

Nursing responsibilities

Over the years, nurses have become increasingly involved as witnesses in criminal trials, either as expert witnesses or in providing firsthand knowledge of a situation.[25] Nurses need to be knowledgeable about what evidence can be admissible in court.

One area that may be problematic is statements made by the victim or the suspect. Evidentiary rules on the state and federal level don't permit statements the nurse heard "secondhand" (considered *hearsay*) as admissible. This hearsay rule also applies to statements made to the nurse by the victim, for example, "my husband shot me."

There are exceptions to the hearsay rule. These include statements made by a patient who's near death or who's aware that death is imminent. Statements are admissible as a dying declaration.

Two other exceptions used are residual hearsay and excited utterance. Residual hearsay is used for testimony that's undeniably truthful. For example, the nurse documents information in the medical record using the patient's exact words in quotation marks. This information would be admissible under the residual hearsay rule. Excited utterance refers to statements said by a person in the heat of the moment at the same time or immediately after the heightened event.[26]

Overall, the relationship between a patient and nurse is considered confidential and, as such, usually not admissible. However, in criminal court, particularly involving cases of felony and homicide, these statements may be admissible.

Documentation

Be careful and precise in documenting all medical and nursing procedures when caring for a patient who's a criminal suspect. Note blood work done and list all treatments and the patient's response to them.

If the nurse turns anything over to the police or administration, she needs to record what it was and the name of the person to whom it was given. Record a suspect's statements that are directly related to his care. If a suspect says, "I shot a cop in the arm tonight," that isn't related to his care. However, if he says, "I think I was shot in the leg by a cop," that relates directly to his medical care.

Evidence protection

Before any evidence can be admissible in court, the court must have some guarantee of where—and how—it was gathered. Someone must account for the evidence from the moment you collect it until it appears in court, a continuum known as the *chain of custody*. Evidence can't be left unattended because it might be tampered with.

If you discover evidence, use your facility's chain of custody form. First used when evidence is taken from the patient, this form should remain with the evidence until the trial. It documents the identity of each person handling the evidence, as well as the date and time it was in their possession. In effect, the form should serve as an uninterrupted log of the evidence's whereabouts.

If the facility doesn't have a chain of custody form, keep a careful note as to exactly what was taken, by whom, and when. Give this information to the administrator upon delivering the evidence. Until such time as the evidence can be turned over, it should be kept in a locked area.

When a suspect dies, most states provide that the coroner can claim the body. Police are free to gather any evidence that won't mutilate the body. A dead body has no constitutional rights, so no rights are violated by a search.

Incarceration

Even after conviction, an individual doesn't forfeit all constitutional rights. Among those retained is the Eighth Amendment's proscription against cruel and unusual punishment. This implies that prison officials and health care workers must not deliberately ignore a prisoner's medical needs.

The U.S. Supreme Court, in *Estelle v. Gamble (1976),* stated that the Eighth Amendment prohibits more than physically barbarous punishment. The amendment embodies "broad and idealistic concepts of dignity, civilized standards, humanity, and decency against which we must evaluate penal measures."

Right to medical care

The state has an obligation to provide medical care for those it imprisons. The Supreme Court has concluded that "deliberate indifference to serious medical needs of prisoners constitutes the unnecessary and wanton infliction of pain proscribed by the Eighth Amendment. This is true whether the indifference is manifested by prison physicians in response to a prisoner's needs or by prison personnel in intentionally denying or delaying access to medical care or intentionally interfering with the treatment once prescribed."

In *Ramos v. Lamm (1980),* the court outlined several ways in which prison officials show deliberate indifference to prisoners' medical needs:
▶ preventing an inmate from receiving recommended treatment
▶ denying access to medical personnel capable of evaluating the need for treatment
▶ allowing repeated acts of negligence that disclose a pattern of conduct by prison health care staff
▶ allowing such severe deficiencies in staffing, facilities, equipment, or procedures to exist that inmates are effectively denied access to adequate medical care.

Provision of care

Working daily with prisoners is difficult and demanding, both professionally and emotionally. Along with exhibiting a host of other unpleasant behaviors, prisoners can be abusive, manipulative, and angry. In spite of this, health care professionals can't forget their ethical and legal duty to provide quality care.

Nurses working in a prison setting should be aware that the doctrine of *respondeat superior* doesn't apply to prison cases when the prisoner sues for violations of his constitutional rights. The nurse supervisor or manager can't be held responsible for accusations of "cruel and unusual punishment" unless he has personally acted to deprive the prisoner of medical care. *Vinnedge v. Gibbs (1977).*

Refusal of treatment

Several courts have stated that individuals have a constitutional right to privacy based on a high regard for human dignity and self-determination. That means any competent adult may refuse medical care, even lifesaving treatments. For instance, in *Lane v. Candura (1978),* an appellate court upheld the right of a competent adult to refuse a leg amputation that would have saved her life.

A suspected criminal may refuse unwarranted bodily invasions. However, an arrested suspect or convicted criminal doesn't have the same right to refuse lifesaving measures. In *Commissioner of Correction v. Myers (1979),* a prisoner with renal failure refused hemodialysis unless he was moved to a minimum security prison. The court disagreed, saying that although the defendant's imprisonment didn't divest him of his right to privacy or his interest in maintaining his bodily integrity, it did impose limitations on those constitutional rights.

As a practical matter, anytime a patient refuses lifesaving treatments, inform the facility's administration. In the case of a suspect or prisoner, notify law enforcement authorities as well.

The patient with a living will

When a legally competent person draws up a living will, he declares the steps he wants or doesn't want taken when he's terminally ill, incompetent, or no longer able to express his wishes. (A durable power of attorney allows a competent patient to delegate the authority for consent to or refuse health care treatment.) Generally, a living will authorizes the attending physician to withhold or stop certain lifesaving procedures under specific circumstances.

The will is called *living* because its provisions take effect before death. By clearly stating his wishes regarding lifesaving procedures, the patient also helps relieve guilt his family and the health care team might otherwise feel for discontinuing life support.

A living will is considered a legal statement of the patient's wishes. State laws vary in their requirements. For example, Arizona requires one witness and notarization for a living will. In Connecticut, the document requires two witnesses whose signatures are notarized and this document isn't considered valid if the patient is pregnant. Massachusetts and Michigan state law have no provisions for a living will. However, they require two witnesses for the designation of a health care agent (durable power of attorney for health care).[27]

A patient may also choose to execute a durable power of attorney for health care. Should the patient become incompetent, this document designates a surrogate decision maker with authority to carry out the patient's wishes regarding health care decisions. Most states have laws authorizing only durable power of attorney for the purpose of initiating or terminating life-sustaining medical treatment.

Content of living will laws

Living will laws usually include provisions, such as:
▶ who may execute a living will
▶ witness and testator requirements
▶ immunity from liability for following a living will's directives
▶ documentation requirements
▶ instructions on when and how the living will should be executed
▶ under what circumstances the living will takes effect.

When living wills don't apply

When the patient's condition is such that the living will isn't applicable, or in cases in which the patient hasn't executed a living will, the patient's surrogate will need to make decisions regarding the removal of life support systems and treatment.

The Supreme Court's ruling in *Cruzan v. Director, Mo. Dept. of Health (1990)* has influenced court rulings in this area. The U.S. Supreme Court held that the state of Missouri has the constitutional right to refuse termination of life-sustaining treatment unless "clear and convincing evidence" exists about a patient's wishes, implying that the patient's wishes will be honored. Because states differ on what they consider "clear and convincing evidence," consult the facility's ethics committee or attorney in cases of this type.

Interpretation

A physician may also face real difficulties in determining when a living will should apply. Wording in many living wills is vague. What, for example, is a "reasonable expectation of recovery?" And what's a "heroic" or an "extraordinary" measure? When a patient actually enters into a coma, it may be difficult to precisely interpret the intentions expressed in his living will. That's one reason why legislatures have been slow to make living wills binding.

States have tried to relieve patients and families from the burden of judicial involvement in medical decisions, encouraging decision making by the patient, family, and physician. Unfortunately, the more latitude provided for decision makers, the less protection for the patient. For instance, the original Illinois Health Care Surrogate Act, effective January 1, 1998, expanded the boundaries of surrogate decision-making legislation to include general medical decisions, permitting the patient to remain uninformed about his loss of decision-making status and subsequent decisions. It's important to note that the Act applies to those who lack a living will or a chosen health care agent as well as to those with a living will that doesn't address the specific condition of the patient. This Act would allow a surrogate decision maker to refuse an abortion for a pregnant minor, for instance. The surrogate decision maker, a close family member, could be an abusive spouse, a child abuser, or another person whom the patient would deem unacceptable, if he were informed. Because of the uncertainty in the judicial system today, it's important that a patient clearly state in his living will exactly what medical treatments he'd choose to receive and which he'd forgo to ensure that his wishes are honored.

Patients should be encouraged to review their living wills with their families and physicians so that unclear areas can be discussed. Living wills also need to be reviewed periodically to keep pace with changes in technology. Some living wills are detailed, multipage documents; some, a simple paragraph.

If physicians, nurses, and other health care providers follow the wishes expressed in a living will authorized by law, they're generally immune from civil and criminal liability. Regardless of the state of employment, check the facility's policy and procedures manual and seek advice from the legal department as needed.

Children and living wills

Although minors can't make valid testamentary wills, and adults can't make such wills for them, living wills are another matter. In a few states, adults are authorized to make living wills for their minor children.

Parents don't normally plan for their child to die, so most are unlikely to make a living will before a child's terminal illness is diagnosed. Even then, a living will is usually legally unnecessary. If the parents and the child agree that no extraordinary means should be used to prolong life, or if the child is too young to understand, the parents have the legal right to act for the child. They can require that the health care team not use extraordinary means to prolong the child's life. The same principle also applies in reverse: if the child wants to die but his parents want him treated, the parents' wishes prevail.

If a terminally ill adolescent doesn't want extraordinary treatment but his parents do, and the adolescent has written a living will, a physician or health care facility may use the will to petition a court on his behalf. Even though the will itself is legally invalid because it was written by a minor, its existence may prompt the court to consult the adolescent and, in its ruling, grant the patient his wishes.

Living will from another state or country

U.S. law applies to foreign citizens treated in the United States. That means a foreign citizen may execute a living will while in the United States, and it must be honored if executed in a state with a living will law.

What if a patient produces a living will executed in a foreign country? What about a patient who executes a living will in one state and later finds himself terminally ill in another? The law of the state where the living will decision will be carried out prevails. Therefore, if a patient has an out-of-state living will, determine whether it matches the criteria required by the laws of the current state. When dealing with an out-of-state living will, consult the facility's legal counsel.

The same general legal principle applies to U.S. citizens in Canada or in another foreign country. A foreign country's law applies to all persons, whether citizens of that country or not, and determines the extent to which a living will must be honored. Check with the facility's attorney.

Invalidation

A living will need not be honored if it has been revoked or is out of date. State law may mandate that a living will is valid only for a limited number of years. If the patient's family and attending medical personnel find that the patient made the living will many years ago and his life circumstances have changed substantially since then, they may have legal justification for disregarding the will. For this reason, publishers of living will forms suggest reviewing the living will yearly, revising it if necessary, and re-dating and re-signing it.

If the patient asks that the will be disregarded, or if a patient tells his physician to proceed with treatment that contradicts the will, such action effectively revokes the will.

Contradictions between the living will and family wishes

The patient's family can't revoke a patient's living will unless they can prove the will is invalid. Some states provide penalties for concealing a patient's living will or for falsely reporting that it has been revoked.

Creation of a living will

Like all legal documents, a living will must be written, signed, and witnessed. State laws specify the execution requirements. If the patient asks for help drafting a living will, refer him to the facility's legal department or the local legal aid agency.

Although it isn't required, a patient should be encouraged to file copies of his living will with his physician and with family members who would attend him in the event of a terminal illness.

A nurse may be asked to witness a living will. Check to see if the state law allows this. If it doesn't, ask the nursing supervisor for the procedure to follow.

If the patient drafts a living will while under your care, document this in your nurses' notes, describing factually the circumstances under which the will was drawn up and signed.

Oral statements

Patients may make oral statements expressing their wishes about further medical treatment before or during a terminal illness.

When a patient has made his treatment wishes known to his family and physician in advance, they'll usually respect his wishes, even if he later becomes comatose or otherwise incompetent. If the physician and the family disagree about what's best for the patient, they may have to settle the dispute in court.

Every competent adult has the right to refuse medical treatment for himself, including the use of extraordinary means. If a competent terminally ill patient tells a physician or nurse to stop extraordinary efforts, his wishes are binding.

If a patient tells you his wishes about dying, first write what he says in your nurses' notes, using his exact words as much as possible. Next, describe the context of the discussion—for example, was the patient in pain, or had he just been informed of a terminal illness? Make sure you also tell the patient's physician about the discussion. Remember, *oral statements aren't legally enforceable,* although a patient's stated refusal of treatment is binding. Oral statements *should* be respected, however, as guidelines to how the patient feels about his treatment.

Responsibilities

Federal legislation, the Patient Self-Determination Act of 1990, requires hospitals, extended care facilities, HMOs, hospices, and home health care agencies that participate in Medicare and Medicaid to provide patients with written information about their rights under state law regarding living wills and durable power of attorney (together called *advance directives*) as well as about the facility's procedure for implementing them. The law also requires the health care facility or agency to document whether the patient has a living will or durable power of attorney.

If a patient has a living will, review the nursing or facility manual for directions on what steps to take. For instance, you may need to inform the patient's physician about it. Or you may need to ask your nursing supervisor to inform the administration and the legal affairs department. With the patient's permission, make sure that the family knows about the will; if they don't, show them a copy.

If the patient can talk, discuss the will with him, especially if it contains terms that need further definition. As always, objectively document your actions and findings in the patient's record.

Beyond these actions, your responsibilities for a patient's living will are determined by the circumstances involved, including the family's and physician's responses to the will. If there's conflict among the parties, work with family members and colleagues to come up with a unified care plan.

If implementing a living will conflicts with a nurse's personal ethics or beliefs, she may wish to discuss the matter with a clinical nurse specialist, nursing supervisor, a nursing administrator, a chaplain, an administrator at the facility, or an ethics committee member. If the nurse still can't accept the idea after talking over her feelings with one of them, she can ask for reassignment to another patient. Chances are the request will be honored and no disciplinary action will be taken. In all instances, the patient must receive care from another qualified caregiver, otherwise patient abandonment could be alleged.

REFERENCES

1. *Davis v. Allen Parish Service District.* WL 3780540, 2006 US. App. LEXIS 3119 (5th Cir. December 18, 2006).
2. *Starkey v. St. Rita's Medical Center.* 117 Ohio App.3d 164; 690 N.E.2d 57; 1997 Ohio App. LEXIS 137.
3. Houser, A., et al. "Across the States Profiles of Long-Term Care and Independent Living." AARP Public Policy Institute, 2006. [Online] Available at *www.aarp.org/research/longtermcare/trends/d18763_2006_ats.html*
4. Houser, et al, 2006.
5. Houser, et al, 2006.
6. Houser, et al, 2006.
7. Schumann, M.J. (2006) "ANA Coming to You." [Online] Available at *www.nursingworld.org/.*
8. The National Association for Home Care & Hospice. *Basic Statistics About Home Care,* 2007. Available at *www.nahc.org/facts/07HC_Stats.pdf.*
9. *Lama v. Borras.* 16 F.3d 473, 1994.
10. Schumann, M.J. (2006). "ANA Coming to You 2006." [Online] Available at *http://www.nursingworld.org/MainMenuCategories/ThePracticeofProfessionalNursing/workplace/Workforce/ShortageStaffing/UtilizationGuide.aspx.*
11. Mueller, C., and Karon, S.L. "ANA Nurse Sensitive Quality Indicators for Long-term Care Facilities," *Journal of Nursing Care Quality* 19(1):39-47, January-March, 2004.
12. American Nurses Association (1999). "Nursing-Sensitive Quality Indicators for Acute Care Settings and ANA's Safety and Quality Initiative." [Online] Available at *http://nursingworld.org/MainMenuCategories/ThePracticeofProfessionalNursing/PatientSafetyQuality/NDNQI/Research/QIforAcuteCareSettings.aspx.*
13. United American Nurses, AFL-CIO (2007). "Legislative Summary. The Safe Nurse Staffing for Patient Safety and Quality Care Act of 2007 (H.R. 2123)." [Online] Available at *www.uannurse.org/legislative/pdfs/RNratioIssueBrief110Congress.pdf.*
14. *Francis v. Memorial General Hospital.* 104 N.M. 698; 726 P.2d 852: 1986 N.M. LEXIS 3070.
15. The Joint Commission (2008). "2008 National Patient Safety Goals Hospital

Program." [Online] Available at *www.jointcommission.org/PatientSafety/NationalPatientSafetyGoals/08_hap_npsgs.htm.*

16. Fiesta, J. "Who's Liable for Equipment Cases?" *Nursing Management* 30(4): 12-13, 15, April 1999.

17. Cushing, M. "Pain Management on Trial," *AJN* 92(2):21, 23, February 1992.

18. Smelzer, J. "Lessons from Colorado. Beyond Blaming Individuals," *Nursing Management* 29(6):49-51, June 1998.

19. Dennik-Champion, G., and Dawson, L. "The Criminalization of Medical Error: A Wisconsin Case Study." Teleconference Presentation, sponsored by The American Association of Nurse Attorneys (TAANA), 2007.

20. Killon, S.W. "Case Commentary—*Bass v. Barksdale*: Implications for Public Health and Home Care Nurses," *Public Health Nursing* 10(2):129-133, 1993.

21. The Joint Commission (2007). "Sentinel Event Glossary of Term." [Online]. Available at *www.jointcommission.org/SentinelEvents/se_glossary.htm.*

22. The Joint Commission (2007). "Sentinel Event Policy and Procedures." [Online]. Available at *www.jointcommission.org/SentinelEvents/PolicyandProcedures/.*

23. The Joint Commission (2006). "Sentinel Event Alert. Tubing Misconnections—A Persistent and Potentially Deadly Occurrence." [Online] Available at *http://www.jointcommission.org/SentinelEvents/SentinelEventAlert/sea_36.htm.*

24. National Child Abuse Statistics (2006). "Childhelp: Prevention and Treatment of Child Abuse." [Online] Available at *http://www.childhelp.org/resources/learning-center/statistics.*

25. Frascogna, L. "Nurse Testimony in Criminal Court," *AJN* 102(5):65-66, May 2002.

26. Frascogna, 2002.

27. "State Laws: Living Wills." [Online] Available at *http://estate.findlaw.com/estate-planning-living-wills/estate-planning-law-state-living-wills.html.*

ADDITIONAL RESOURCES

The American Association of Nurse Attorneys. "TAANA Position Paper on Expert Testimony in Nursing Malpractice Actions," *Journal of Nursing Law* 9(4):18-25, 2004.

Grace, P. "Patient Safety and the Limits of Confidentiality," *AJN* 104(11):33, 35, 37, November 2004.

Green, M. "Nursing Error and Human Nature," *Journal of Nursing Law* 9(4):37-44, 2004.

Institute of Medicine. *Keeping Patients Safe: Transforming the Work Environment of Nurses.* Washington, D.C., 2004.

Rogers, A.E., et al. "The Working Hours of Hospital Staff Nurses and Patient Safety," *Health Affairs* 23(4):202-12, July-August 2004.

6

Legal rights off duty

Numerous guidelines define the legal limits of nursing practice during work hours. They include hospital policies, standards issued by nursing organizations, and state or jurisdictional nurse practice acts. Statutory law and common law provide additional direction. When a nurse isn't working, few specific guidelines exist, blurring the boundaries of the nurse's legal responsibilities. For example, a nurse probably wouldn't hesitate to perform an abdominal thrust maneuver to save a choking victim. However, what if that nurse panics, makes a mistake, and injures the patient? Can the nurse be sued by the victim or his estate? Can her nursing license be suspended or revoked? Does the law protect the nurse because of her good intentions?

Fortunately, thus far, lawsuits resulting from off-duty nursing actions have been extremely rare. However, whether a nurse frequently provides off-duty care or just gives free advice occasionally to her neighbor, it's important to act on sound legal footing.

This chapter discusses legal issues related to off-duty nursing. These issues include:

▶ acting as a Good Samaritan—liability when giving emergency care at an accident scene or in a disaster
▶ giving free health care advice—legal ramifications of giving advice to family members and friends
▶ donating nursing services—protecting one's self legally when volunteering nursing skills
▶ acting during disasters—legal aspects of providing nursing services during emergencies and declared disasters.

Nurses need to be able to distinguish between what the law requires and what the law allows. In addition, nurses also need information about how their nurse practice act and other state laws apply to off-duty actions.

ACTIONS AS A GOOD SAMARITAN

Imagine driving in heavy traffic and not far ahead, you see an automobile accident and a bloodied motorist gesturing for help. Nearby, another victim lies sprawled at curbside. What should you do? Your conscience and compassion prompt you to help the victim in any health care emergency. Your common sense prompts you to ask if helping out means courting legal trouble.

You have three options:
▶ Help the accident victim at the scene.
▶ Leave the scene, stop at the nearest phone, and call for an ambulance or other rescue service.
▶ Pass the scene and make no attempt to call for help.

In almost every state, nurses have the legal right to choose any of these options. In most cases, off-duty nurses in the United States and Canada have no legal duty to rescue anyone.

In general, the only people with a legal duty to rescue others are individuals who perform rescues as part of their jobs—firefighters, police officers, emergency medical technicians, and a few others such as public transportation workers. However, in a few states, such as Vermont, Rhode Island, Minnesota, and Wisconsin, "duty to rescue" laws may apply to nurses. Unless a nurse is covered by a duty-to-rescue law, the decision to help remains voluntary and personal.

Common law protection

When choosing to help the accident victim, two kinds of laws protect nurses: common law and statutory law, specifically the Good Samaritan acts.

Common law, also known as *case law*, is the cumulative result of court decisions over the years. These decisions may provide guidelines for acting in a similar situation.

Good Samaritan act protection

Good Samaritan acts were enacted to encourage people to voluntarily help someone in need without the fear of being sued for any reasonable care rendered—even if some mistake in treatment might occur. Every state has enacted a Good Samaritan act, but each state's statute varies. Some may apply specifically to nurses or other health care professionals, while others may apply to anyone who offers assistance. Always verify the law applicable to your state of practice.

Good Samaritan acts limit a person's liability for any service rendered at an accident or emergency scene unless it's proved that his or her care was grossly negligent or intentionally harmful or that the individual was the person who initially caused the emergency situation. Most states require these services to be performed in good faith, meaning that the person sincerely intended to help. In addition, the act must be voluntary, such that there's no duty to care and there's no expectation of compensation.[1] Also, a few states specifically require consent for the services rendered. If someone is unconscious or can't communicate, implied consent is assumed. However, Good Samaritan acts don't prevent an accident victim from filing a malpractice suit.

Proof of malpractice

Usually, to bring a malpractice suit to a jury trial, the patient must establish the following:
▶ the nurse owed a duty, based on a nurse-patient relationship
▶ the nurse breached that duty
▶ the patient was harmed
▶ breach of duty caused the harm or how foreseeable it is that the nurse's actions will cause harm.

Legal duty

As long as a nurse passes the accident scene, even if she stops down the road to call for help, the nurse owes the victim no legal duty unless she resides in a state that has a duty-to-rescue law. The victim isn't the nurse's patient, and he has no legal claim to the nurse's professional services.

However, just by stopping her car at the scene, the nurse incurs a legal duty. From that point on, the nurse can't leave the victim until he's being cared for by another health care professional with at least as much training as the nurse has or until the police order the nurse from the scene. Otherwise the nurse could be charged with abandonment.

When stopping her car at the scene, the nurse gives the appearance to other potential rescuers that she'll take care of the victim. At that point, a nurse-patient relationship is established for that particular emergency. The nurse owes the victim the normal duty owed to any patient—treatment that meets the standard of care of a reasonably prudent nurse in a similar situation.

Breach of duty

After a nurse stops to help, she can avoid breaching duty by using the same good judgment used every day on the job. However, what if the nurse *does* breach her duty in this unusual situation?

If the nurse's performance falls below the standard of care expected of a reasonably prudent nurse in a similar situation, the court will decide whether her act worsened the victim's condition. In most states the nurse's action or inaction has to be grossly negligent, intentional, or reckless for there to be a cause of action. If the act didn't make the victim measurably worse, the court may find that the harm committed doesn't warrant damages. The act must cause measurable

harm for the court to consider the nurse legally responsible.

Causation

Some states consider the fact that a person has difficulty in proving causation and will allow an "increased risk of harm standard"; that is, the nurse's action or inaction increased the risk of harm and was a substantial factor in causing damages. The victim must prove that the probability is better than 50% that the nurse's error (whether an act of commission or omission) caused his injuries. Historically, the courts have recognized the 50% figure as the standard. Because the typical victim already has suffered injuries from the accident, he's likely to have a hard time proving that the nurse's error caused or worsened his injuries.

In making it hard for the accident victim to prove the nurse negligent, the courts must balance the victim's right to justice with society's need to encourage trained professionals to assist in emergencies.

Gross negligence

No law can protect the nurse if she commits an act of gross negligence—an extremely careless act or omission that seriously violates the applicable standard of care.

In court, jury members decide whether the nurse's negligent error constitutes "ordinary" negligence or "gross" negligence. To make this distinction, they measure the error against the local standard of care, which may vary from place to place. For example, what may qualify as ordinary negligence in rural Georgia may be gross negligence in metropolitan New York. However, as more nurses take certification examinations that are na-

Care tips for Good Samaritans

When you stop at an emergency scene to offer assistance, always observe professional standards of nursing care, regardless of the setting. To reduce your malpractice risk, follow these guidelines:

• Call 911 for assistance.
• Ask the injured person, or family member, if available, for permission to help.
• Care for the victim in the vehicle or at the exact site, if you can do so safely.
• Assess the possibility of fractures.
• Move the victim if he's in danger and if conditions permit. Avoid moving him needlessly, and don't try to straighten his arms and legs.
• Let him lie or sit quietly. Don't carry him or force him to walk.
• Keep his airway open.
• Stop his bleeding.
• Keep the victim warm.
• Determine his level of consciousness.
• Ask the victim where he feels pain.
• Avoid speculating about who or what caused the accident.
• Allow only skilled personnel to attend or treat the victim.
• Stay at the accident site until skilled personnel arrive to assume care of the victim.
• Provide a complete picture of the care given.
• Guard the injured person's personal property. Release it to the police or members of his family.

tional in scope, members of the profession are held increasingly accountable to a national standard, like physicians.

Additionally, the court considers the nurse's training and experience to decide whether she has breached the standard of care and, if so, to what degree. This means that the court holds registered nurses (RNs)—even as Good Samar-

itans—to a higher standard than it holds licensed practical nurses (LPNs). (See *Care tips for Good Samaritans.*)

Legal discrepancies

Good Samaritan protection varies. For example, some acts specifically include nurses, whereas other acts—those in Florida and Alaska, for example—protect any person who offers help to a victim. Some acts protect out-of-state nurses only if they're trained in cardiopulmonary resuscitation. In some jurisdictions, Good Samaritan acts include only "practitioners of the healing arts." The courts usually interpret this terminology to mean physicians and dentists. (See *Understanding Good Samaritan acts.*)

Compensation for care

Keep in mind that most Good Samaritan acts apply only to uncompensated emergency care. If a nurse charges or accepts money for services, the law usually says that the nurse forfeits the special protections afforded by such acts.

Application of Good Samaritan law

Regardless of the kind of Good Samaritan act that's established in the nurse's state or jurisdiction, accident victims rarely sue "Good Samaritans." Although nurses have been sued, when the Good Samaritan defense has been raised, no nurse has been found responsible. In addition, common law so far has served as a deterrent.

Ironically, though, auto accident victims sometimes claim that a Good Samaritan act *requires* a nurse or physician to respond at an accident scene. To date, the courts have accepted this argu-

Understanding Good Samaritan acts

Am I covered by a Good Samaritan act if I respond to an emergency outside the hospital while I'm officially on duty?
That depends on two things: the wording of the act in your state and court decisions, if any, interpreting that act. All Good Samaritan acts cover aid at the scene of an emergency, accident, or disaster. If an emergency occurs just outside the hospital and you provide care while on duty, most likely this would be considered providing care in an emergency setting and, therefore, would be covered under Good Samaritan law. Note that some states' Good Samaritan statutes specifically cover emergencies outside of the hospital, physician's office, and other places that have medical equipment.

I live and work in Kansas. Every year, I go skiing in a different state. What if I help an accident victim while I'm vacationing? Does the Good Samaritan act of the state I'm in apply to me?
It does if that state's act says it applies to "any person." It may not, however, if the act specifically states that it applies only to "nurses." The designation "nurses" in a law or act may mean

a registered nurse, licensed practical nurse, or licensed vocational nurse licensed in that state.

Does the Good Samaritan Act apply if I accept money from the person I've helped?
Not usually. By accepting money in such a situation, you establish a professional relationship with the person you've helped.

For how long am I responsible to the person I've helped?
Statutory law doesn't address this subject, but common law does. The courts say your responsibility ends:
• when the emergency ends (when you're certain that the victim is no longer in danger)
• when an authorized rescuer or other qualified medical service takes over for you
• when the victim is pronounced dead.
If a physician and I respond to the same emergency, does the Good Samaritan act cover us equally?
Not necessarily. In some states, the Good Samaritan act for nurses differs completely from the Good Samaritan act for physicians. Contact your state nursing board to find out what's true for your state.

ment only in those states that have enacted duty-to-rescue laws.

In some states, physicians have invoked a Good Samaritan act as a defense against malpractice suits, claiming that the act protects them from liability for emergency services they provided in a hospital. In Illinois, a physician responded to an in-hospital emergency in which both parties (mother and fetus) later died, and the estate brought suit. The physician successfully invoked, as part of his defense, the Illinois Good Samaritan Act. The appellate court found that the Act protected the physician from liability for a true hospital emergency in which

the service was provided in good faith and without fee. Using this argument in California, physicians have met with mixed results. The same argument won't hold for nurses in California because the Good Samaritan act specifically covers nurses only during emergencies "outside both the place and course" of employment.

Only a few states and one Canadian jurisdiction (Quebec) have taken the Good Samaritan principle a step further by requiring potential rescuers to help a victim. Vermont's law, the first of its type in the United States, defines a *rescuer* as a person who knows another is exposed to grave physical harm. The Vermont law requires that anyone (Vermont resident or not) who can help a victim must do so, provided he won't be endangering himself or interfering with important duties he owes to others. Minnesota has a similar law, as do Rhode Island and Wisconsin (which has a "duty to rescue crime victims" law).

These duty-to-rescue statutes provide penalties for failure to comply. For example, the Rhode Island and Wisconsin statutes set fines of up to $500 and possible imprisonment for up to 6 months; the Vermont statute provides for a fine of up to $100; Minnesota doesn't set out specific penalties, but it does consider the violation a petty misdemeanor.

In Quebec, the duty to act is derived from the Quebec Charter of Human Rights and Freedoms (1975) and the Civil Code. According to the Charter, a person is "obligated to render aid if it can be accomplished without serious risk to the Good Samaritan or a third person."[2] The Civil Code requires that every person act as a reasonably prudent person ("bon père de famille").[3]

In contrast, some other states have duty-to-rescue statutes that apply specifically to criminal events causing injury. They generally provide for liability if someone on the scene fails to report the crime or call for assistance, but they don't specifically address the requirement to render aid to the victim.

How a duty-to-rescue law would apply to nurses remains uncertain. For example, if a nurse passes an accident scene on the way to the dentist, the duty-to-rescue law requires the nurse to stop and try to help. However, what if the nurse is on her way to work? Would the nursing job be considered an important duty owed to others? The answer to this question eventually will come from the courts.

FREE HEALTH CARE ADVICE

Most likely, friends and family members rely on individuals who are nurses for advice on health matters. Respond cautiously, even though this may seem unnatural when speaking with individuals you know well. Keep in mind that nurses can be sued for giving inappropriate advice. If you decide not to give advice at all, be reassured: the law doesn't require it.

If you choose to offer advice, be aware of positions on the issue taken by the state's nurse practice act, common law, professional organizations, and the nurse's malpractice insurance coverage. (See *Minimizing legal risks when giving advice*.)

Legal implication of free advice

In a hospital setting, giving health care advice may be considered part of patient teaching, a recognized nursing function. Outside of this setting, giving advice may subject the nurse to liability if, in giving the advice, she doesn't act as a reasonably prudent nurse.

The person suing the nurse for harm caused by inappropriate advice must prove that the nurse owed him a specific duty, that the nurse breached that duty, that he was harmed, and that the harm was a result of the breach of duty.

Breach of duty

For a duty to exist, the nurse must have a nurse-patient relationship with the person asking for advice. This rarely occurs in everyday, short-lived conversations with other people. Suppose, for example, that a nurse is a guest at a cocktail party. Another guest finds out that the person is a nurse and bombards the nurse with questions about his health. If the nurse decides to answer, she has a duty to answer as correctly as a reasonably prudent nurse would, but the nurse doesn't have a duty to follow up after the party is over or to monitor the outcome of the advice. The person who's asking for advice hasn't established (or clearly indicated to the nurse that he intends to establish) an ongoing nurse-patient relationship with the nurse.

Probable reliance

The situation may be different if a nurse decides to give advice to a neighbor. For instance, imagine that a neighbor calls across the yard and asks the nurse about her child's fretfulness. The nurse observes honestly that the child's activity doesn't appear to warrant a call to the physician. A day later, the nurse sees the mother and child together outdoors, and the child appears particularly listless. If the nurse discovers that the child has a fever or other signs and symptoms of illness, the nurse is legally and professionally responsible for telling the mother to take the child to a physician as soon as possible. This holds true regardless of the nurse's original advice.

A nurse must respond to the mother's probable reliance for further advice, even though the nurse's original intention

---

Minimizing legal risks when giving advice

Here are some steps to minimize your risk when giving health care advice to friends or family.

WHAT TO DO

- Make sure that your advice reflects accepted professional and community standards.
- Check whether your (or your employer's) professional liability insurance covers such off-the-job nursing activities as giving advice.
- Remember that Good Samaritan acts exclude gratuitous actions not associated with an emergency. However, keep in mind that some state statutes specifically include illnesses.
- Know what, if anything, your state's nurse practice act says about giving advice to friends.
- Give advice only within the confines of your nurse practice act, education, and experience.
- Make sure that the advice you give is up-to-date. You'll be judged on current nursing standards if your advice results in a lawsuit.

WHAT NOT TO DO

- Don't charge a fee or accept money for your advice.
- Avoid speculating about your friends' illnesses or ailments.
- Never suggest that friends change or ignore their physicians' orders.
- Steer clear of giving a medical diagnosis, medical opinion, or advice about medical care.
- Avoid giving directions that, if wrong or misinterpreted, could result in serious or permanent injury.

---

wasn't to form a nurse-patient relationship with her and her child.

Again, if the nurse realizes that the neighbor now relies on the nurse for further advice, the nurse has an obligation—

Neighborly advice: Some legal safeguards

My best friend Sara and I have babies the same age. Sara isn't a nurse, and I know she relies on my judgment a lot. How should I answer her when she asks questions? For instance, yesterday, she asked, "If your Richie had a rash like Tommy's, would you take him to the doctor?"

If you answer "yes," no harm will result from your advice, and you'll be on safe legal ground. If you answer "no," and if following your advice results in harm to the child, you may be liable. In such situations—best friend or not—conservative advice is legally safer, especially if you have doubts.

I seem to be the neighborhood ear-piercer. Of course, with children I require a parent's permission, and I warn everyone about the risks of infection and how to reduce them. Still, I'm worried: If someone got an infection and sued me, would this verbal warning protect me from malpractice liability?

Some states have legislation or regulations governing ear piercing, so check with your state licensing board. If your state doesn't have regulations on ear piercing, your warnings about

possible infection protect you only if infection results from piercing done according to accepted standards. The warning doesn't protect you if the infection results from your negligence. Written confirmation of the warning provides a little better protection.

One of my neighbors comes to see me whenever one of her family members gets sick or enters the hospital. She's a good friend and I'm glad to help, but I think she's making a habit of asking for my advice. I feel especially uncomfortable when she asks me to explain everything the physician tells her. Once she said, "The doctor says my husband might have adhesions from a previous operation. What does that mean? Is that common?" How can I answer her questions and protect myself too? Should I say, "I can tell you only what I know from my own experience?"

You'd be better off saying, "I can tell you what those terms usually mean, but not what they mean in your husband's case." You can best serve your neighbor, though, by encouraging her to ask the physician to explain anything she doesn't understand.

a legal and professional duty—to keep the advice current as the situation changes. Or the nurse may opt to take formal steps to break off the relationship by telling the mother to look elsewhere for help.

Keep in mind that the principles that apply to a nurse's on-duty work also apply to off-duty advice. The help and advice given to a patient Monday morning may have to be changed by Tuesday afternoon. Furthermore, if a patient's questions reveal that his problem may be beyond the scope of nursing practice, the nurse has a clear duty to advise the individual to seek a physician's care. (See

Neighborly advice: Some legal safeguards.)

Professional standards

Whenever a nurse establishes a professional relationship with an individual seeking advice, she must provide an answer as good as any reasonably prudent nurse would give in similar circumstances.

Do this by applying the same standards that are expected when in a regular work situation. If a nurse feels confident that she knows the answer—and her education and experience support her—she's legally free to give it. Naturally, she must make sure the answer is correct and that giving it falls within her scope of nursing practice.

To protect herself, a nurse might say something such as, "I think your problem sounds like arthritis, but it could be something more serious, and I'm not sure. You should ask a physician."

Remember, a nurse is legally protected if she refers the questioner to her physician. However, the law doesn't require the nurse to make that suggestion if she's honestly convinced that it isn't necessary and that a reasonably prudent nurse wouldn't make it either.

Guard against the temptation to say, "Don't worry," when family members or friends ask for advice. Reassure them only if you're certain that nothing is seriously wrong. The law requires a nurse to apply this standard: "If I were at work and one of my patients asked the same question, what would I tell him?" Try to imagine that an inquiring family member or friend is a complete stranger. Then give the best professionally considered answer.

Medical advice

Giving health care advice can lead to legal problems if the advice can be interpreted as medical advice. Then the nurse may be at risk for practicing medicine without a license. Instead, urge the person seeking medical advice to seek medical attention, either at a hospital or with a physician.

ACTIONS DURING A DISASTER

Think back to the horrors of September 11, 2001. Then fast forward to 2005 and the effects of Hurricane Katrina. Imagine a tornado levels a part of a local community. Spring floods take life and property at the south end of town. A freight train derails, blanketing the community with toxic vapor. The brakes fail on an airplane carrying 137 passengers, and the craft careens off the runway. Any of these disastrous events can overload local medical and nursing resources. In situations such as these, nurses have special responsibilities and legal rights.

Contract duties

When providing nursing care during a disaster, professional, ethical, and legal concerns figure heavily in every decision a nurse makes. In general, with the exception of declared emergencies, a nurse's responsibilities in a disaster don't differ legally from her everyday responsibilities. The fundamental principle of the American Nurses Association (ANA) Code of Ethics for Nurses is that the patient's interests are the nurse's utmost concern. This principle applies to any situation including disaster conditions.[4]

Nurses may have specific duties to perform in specific kinds of disasters, and they may be legally bound to perform those duties, but that's likely to be based on the nurse's employment contract and not on laws or precedent-setting legal cases. The nurse also is responsible for adhering to the Scope and Standards of Practice established by the ANA that identifies the nurse's professional respon-

Adapting the standards of care

Recent disasters such as the attack on the World Trade Center in 2001 and Hurricane Katrina in 2005 have prompted the American Nurses Association (ANA) to address the issue of standards of care during major natural or man-made disasters. The ANA recognizes that nurses working under these conditions are faced with patient care issues and decision making that may question or oppose the established standards of care. As a result, the ANA convened a multidisciplinary expert panel and held a policy conference in June 2007, which led to creation of a document titled, "Adapting Standards of Care Under Extreme Conditions."[5] This document is available for review and comment by the public.

Source: American Nurses Association (2008). "Adapting Standards of Care Under Extreme Conditions" [Online]. Available at http://nursingworld.org/MainMenuCategories/HealthcareandPolicyIssues/DPR/ TheLawEthicsofDisasterResponse/AdaptingStandardsofCare.aspx

sibilities. (See *Adapting the standards of care*.)

For example, when working in a city hospital, the employment contract may contain a provision that the nurse can be called to work whenever a government official declares a state of emergency. If the nurse refuses to come in, she can be disciplined, suspended, or fired. This rule applies even if the work the nurse is assigned to do isn't normally part of her job description.

If a nurse is already on the job when a disaster occurs, the same contractual provisions may be invoked to keep the nurse from going home at the end of the shift. And the same penalties apply if the nurse refuses to cooperate.

Similarly, if a nurse is an unpaid volunteer for a community service, such as the Red Cross or an ambulance unit, she may be expected to report for duty in any local disaster as long as this reporting doesn't conflict with the nurse's regular employment. If the nurse refuses, the service can drop her from its roster; if a nurse is a paid, part-time worker for such an organization, she can be dismissed.

These duties apply even if work arrangements are unwritten but are part of an oral agreement.

Contract defenses

Because reporting for work in an emergency, including a disaster, is usually a contract matter, specific contract defenses apply if a nurse is disciplined for failing to fulfill her duties. One such contract defense is that of impossibility. If reporting is impossible for the nurse and she can prove it—even if she's contractually required to do so and would be paid for the work—she can't be disciplined or prosecuted. For example, if a blizzard absolutely prohibits travel from the nurse's home to the job or disastrous flooding causes the governor to ban all travel in the area, what the contract says doesn't matter much. In addition, if the nurse is disciplined, she has a legal defense. However, watch for exceptions to travel bans—for example, a ban may be announced for all but "required personnel" or "persons with medical or nursing training." In those situations, obviously the nurse must report for duty.

Volunteering of services

No law prevents a nurse from voluntarily donating services, and specific statutory or common laws may provide protection. If a nurse wants to volunteer help in a disaster, she should do so, even if no one in authority has asked. (See *Minimizing legal risks during a disaster.*)

Suppose a facility doesn't have a policy mandating that health care personnel report to work when a disaster occurs. A nurse can still volunteer to stay for extra shifts or to perform services outside the normal scope of employment. The hospital will almost certainly accept the offer, if they haven't already asked for help. That's especially likely if emergency conditions prevent other staff nurses from reporting to work.

A nurse can't necessarily expect her pay to reflect the extra work performed during a disaster. Most facilities will try to pay for the overtime, but some may not. If curious, find out what the facility's policy is before a disaster occurs. The policy may depend on union rules, state fair labor employment laws or, if the nurse works in a city or state hospital, on city ordinances or state regulations.

Decision to volunteer

When deciding whether to help out in a disaster, assess your actual ability to help. Caring for the disaster victims may require particular skills—for example, knowledge of a special area, such as toxicology. Alternatively, the skill required may be as simple as rowing a boat in a flood.

Also, consider whether you can get to the disaster site or to the place where care will be provided. If an airliner crashes, for example, and emergency departments throughout the city are treating victims, your ability to get to your hospital or another hospital quickly may figure in whether you decide to volunteer. What if, for example, the disaster involves a riot occurring during a total blackout in your city, and the mayor decrees, "Don't travel to work unless you're within walking distance"? If you try to drive into the city from your suburban home, you'll only complicate driving conditions—and you probably won't get to your hospital in time to be helpful.

You may also consider whether volunteering in the disaster will keep you from

Minimizing legal risks during a disaster

By taking a few precautions, you can help assure protection from liability when working under disaster conditions.

BE PREPARED
Don't wait for a disaster to happen before you ask your charge nurse what you'll be required to do during a disaster. Keep equipment you're likely to need available and in working condition.

FOLLOW INSTRUCTIONS
In any disaster, public officials and other authorities, such as medical personnel, public health workers, or municipal staff, will probably issue orders. Even if these people aren't normally your superiors, follow their directions as much as possible. Offer advice only when you think necessary.

KNOW YOUR LIMITS
Don't work beyond the point of effectiveness. If you're so tired that you can't make correct decisions, no one will benefit from your care. Describe your fatigue to the person in charge, and ask for a break.

working and earning your regular salary. Find out, too, whether your professional liability insurance covers services provided in a disaster or other off-the-job activities.

Out-of-state volunteering

Nurse practice acts don't legally restrict a nurse from volunteering during a disaster in an out-of-state location. For instance, suppose a nurse is licensed in California and while on vacation in Oregon, a disaster occurs. The nurse can provide nursing services during the disaster without concern that she's breaching California's or Oregon's nurse practice act. That's because most nurse practice acts have a special exemption for care given in emergencies that usually includes disasters. Some state statutes specifically address nurses with out-of-state licenses.

Refusal to volunteer

If a nurse doesn't want to volunteer, and hospital policy or contract doesn't require it—or, as happens rarely, if the nurse doesn't have a contract—in most states a nurse has the right to refuse. Most nurse practice acts don't require nurses to provide emergency care in disasters, any more than they require nurses to perform care. They only permit such care. Similarly, Good Samaritan acts provide some legal immunity for giving emergency care but don't require nurses to provide that care, except in states with duty-to-rescue laws.

Civil defense laws, also known as *disaster relief laws*, don't apply in most states to nurses who aren't already involved in civil defense work—although in a declared national emergency, nurses (like anyone else) can be drafted. Alter-

natively, martial law may be imposed, which makes all citizens subject to public authority. Many civil defense laws authorize state or federal governing bodies to enforce special regulations dealing with the duties of medical and nursing personnel in a declared emergency. Some states already have such plans ready for use in a sufficiently serious disaster.

Working outside your scope of practice

In a disaster, nurses may find themselves performing duties outside the usual scope of practice. For example, an LPN or licensed vocational nurse (LVN) may be asked to perform duties that ordinarily would be restricted to RNs, and nursing assistants may be asked to do work an LPN or LVN would usually do. An RN may find herself doing tasks usually reserved for medical residents. Either the nurse or a resident may be asked to do work a nursing assistant would normally do. Provided the person has the knowledge and skill to meet minimum safety requirements, she may be permitted to give such substitute care in disasters based on the same exemption in nurse practice acts that lets an out-of-state nurse volunteer her services in a disaster. This exemption may be construed as letting the nurse expand the scope of practice in a disaster. Check the state's nurse practice act to determine such exemption. Even if it can't be construed this way, statutory or common laws usually permit regulatory authorities to place the public welfare above strict enforcement of the letter of the law.

Emergency preparedness

Throughout history nurses have been a major group of individuals responding to emergency and disaster situations. However, "few nurses have had practical experience in providing care during an epidemic or other large scale disaster, that may involve hundreds of individuals requiring care" under highly unusual circumstances.[6] As a result, current efforts are focusing on integrating nurses as a major component of disaster response teams to ensure that their skills can be used most effectively.

The emphasis of these efforts involves preparation in advance with the development of a personal and professional plan. A personal plan addresses issues involving the family, such as food and supplies and communication methods. A personal plan addresses employment issues. The ANA has developed two sets of guidelines to assist nurses and their employers in dealing with this topic.

In addition, a nurse interested in responding to a disaster is encouraged to preregister with a disaster registry or response organization. By doing so, the nurse can receive appropriate training, have her license validated before the disaster, and then be deployed through a recognizable system.[7] Although this system is helpful in reducing the legal ramifications of disaster response, nurses still need to know the legal limits of their practice in such a situation.

DONATION OF NURSING SERVICES

Many health care professionals, including nurses, donate their professional services to community organizations or activities. Usually, when volunteering nursing services, no pay is involved. At times, a nurse may "volunteer" services for pay by providing nursing care outside of her usual paid work. In such situations, the nurse is volunteering personal time while being paid for her nursing services.

A nurse might donate nursing services to family members, friends, or such community organizations and activities as:
▶ a community ambulance service
▶ a bloodmobile or hypertension outreach program
▶ a home and school association panel discussion on child health issues
▶ a community or sporting event.

As a nurse, responsibilities to patients don't change when you donate your services. However, the nurse's legal status does. It becomes less defined than when an individual is paid. In most states, nurse practice acts specify only the legal limits of paid nursing practice.

Legal implications

Being exempt from the state's nurse practice act if a nurse donates nursing services doesn't mean the nurse will be exempt from a lawsuit. In such a situation, the court can use the provisions of the state nurse practice act—together with expert witness testimony and applicable standards of nursing care—to determine if the nurse acted as a prudent nurse would have acted in similar patient care circumstances. If the court finds that the nurse's

Minimizing legal risks when donating services

When offering your time and skills for free, observe the same standards of care that you observe in your paid job. Consider these guidelines:

HAVE NECESSARY ORDERS
Obtain a physician's order or a standing order before giving any treatment or medication that requires such an order.

DOCUMENT YOUR ACTIONS
Document your donated care as carefully as you document the care you give on the job. Keep a copy of your nurses' notes so you have a permanent record of your actions should a question ever arise.

CHECK YOUR COVERAGE
Check your professional liability insurance and its limitations from every angle before agreeing to donate your services to any organization. Also check the coverage provided by the organization that receives your volunteer services. Does your or the organization's coverage include the volunteer nursing duty that you're considering? Is the coverage adequate in light of the potential damages and legal fees that you might have to pay if sued?

care. In such a situation, the board may suspend or even revoke the nurse's license.

If a nurse travels to a state in which she isn't licensed to practice, she isn't prohibited from donating nursing services as long as that state's nurse practice act covers only paid nursing care. However, if the nurse is sued, the court will probably evaluate her actions and their consequences against whatever standard of nursing care would apply in that state rather than the nurse's home state.

Good Samaritan acts won't cover a nurse in day-to-day situations involving the donation of nursing services. These acts apply only to accidents or other emergency situations. In addition, not all state Good Samaritan acts extend coverage to all nurses.

REFERENCES

1. American Medical Association (2007). "Emergency Care: Responsibilities and Alternatives" [Online]. Available at *http://medi-smart.com/gsama.htm*.
2. Canadian Law (2007). "Good Samaritan Law: Obligation to Help Someone in Trouble" [Online]. Available at *www.canadianlawsite.ca/goodsamaritan.htm*.
3. Canadian Law (2007).
4. American Nurses Association (2007). "ANA Comments on Nursing Care during Hurricane Katrina" [Online]. Available at *http://nursingworld.org/DocumentVault/Ethics/ANAonKatrina.aspx*.
5. American Nurses Association (2008). "Adapting Standards of Care Under Extreme Conditions" [Online]. Available at *http://nursingworld.org/MainMenuCategories/HealthcareandPolicyIssues/DPR/TheLawEthicsofDisasterResponse/AdaptingStandardsofCare.aspx*

care didn't conform to the requirements of the state's nurse practice act, the nurse may face a malpractice suit. In addition, the nurse's malpractice insurance may not cover voluntary services. Because insurance is a contract, review the insurance policy's language to determine its application and coverage. (See *Minimizing legal risks when donating services.*)

Even if no lawsuit results, a nurse may be subject to discipline by the state nursing board if the board finds that her services fall below the accepted standard of

6. Gebbe, K. and Qureshi, K (2006). "A Historical Challenge: Nurses and Emergencies" [Online]. Available at *http://nursingworld.org.MainMenu Categories/ANAMarketplace/ANAPerio dicals/OJIN/TableofContents/Volume11 2006/Number3/NURSESANDEMER-GENCIES.aspx.*

7. Peterson, C.A. (2006) "Be Safe, Be Prepared: Emergency System for Advance Registration of Volunteer Health Professionals in Disaster Response" [Online]. Available at *http://nursingworld.org/MainMenu Categories/ANAMarketplace/ANAPerio dicals/OJIN/TableofContents/Volume11 2006/Number3/tpc31_216083.aspx.*

ADDITIONAL RESOURCES

Kennedy, M.S. "On the Road to Disaster—and Back: AJN's News Director Visited Health Officials and Rescuers Immediately after Hurricane Katrina," *AJN* 105(11):24-26, November 2005.

Thompson, J. "Katrina's Aftermath: How Our Disaster Plan Was Tested," *RN* 70(8):36-42, August 2007.

Documentation and the law

The need for accurate complete documentation by nurses is absolute. Consider Lauren Ball, RN, a nurse at the Good Samaritan Hospital in West Islip, N.Y. In 1987, Ms. Ball failed to document in her nurses' notes that a patient, Gerolamo Kucich, reported seeing a bearded man in a white laboratory coat put "something" in his I.V. line. The bearded man, Richard Angelo, was subsequently convicted of assaulting Kucich and killing four others by injecting the drug pancuronium to paralyze their breathing. Ms. Ball saved Kucich's life and was a key witness in the trial against Angelo. Nevertheless, in 1991, she was charged with negligence and professional misconduct and faced possible revocation of her license and a $10,000 fine simply for failing to document the patient's observation.

Thankfully, incidents such as this are rare. Nevertheless, the fact that the state pressed charges against Ms. Ball underscores the seriousness of the nurse's responsibility to document in the eyes of the law. Nursing documentation has become increasingly scientific and complex, and its quality has taken on greater legal significance than ever before.

This chapter describes the legal significance of the patient's medical record—the principal tool used by the health care team to plan, coordinate, and document the care given to each patient. The chapter also emphasizes the importance of good nursing documentation, examines several court cases in which documentation quality affected the patient's outcome, and reviews guidelines for avoiding documentation errors. Computerized medical records and their legal implications, as well as new documentation systems prompted by health care reform initiatives and the pressure to reduce costs are addressed.

ACCURATE DOCUMENTATION

The trend toward increasing specialization means that patients are being assessed, cared for, and treated by more health care professionals than ever before. Complete, accurate, and timely documentation is crucial to the continuity of each patient's care.

Documentation systems

Various types of documentation systems are in use today. Each has its own advantages and disadvantages (See *Advantages and disadvantages of documentation systems.*) Regardless of the system used, accuracy, completeness, and timeliness are crucial.

Source-oriented system

Health care facilities have been using the source-oriented system since record keeping began. Under this system, each professional group keeps a separate record. This system was widely practiced until recently, with physicians charting the progress notes and nurses charting the nurses' notes. The drawback is that a person must consult several sources to get an accurate picture of the patient's condition. Also, failure to consult all the individual records carries potentially serious consequences for the patient and staff. For example, in a case from Louisiana, *Villetto v. Weilbaecher, 377 So. 2d 132 (La. Ct. App. 1979),* nurses observed that a patient had developed several blisters 8 days after knee surgery. They recorded their observation in the nurses' notes and reported the problem to the physician. However, the physician didn't mention the blisters in his notes until 6 days later. The patient sued, and was awarded damages for pain and scarring; the physician was found liable for failure to treat the blisters. The nurses were found not liable because the record showed that they had met their standard of care.

Problem-oriented system

Facilities may use problem-oriented records, which give a comprehensive picture of the patient's clinical status and response to therapy. All members of the health care team combine their data into a format known by the acronym SOAP. *S* stands for subjective patient data. *O* is for objective findings on observation, assessment, and examination. *A* is for assessment of the subjective complaints and objective findings. *P* is for plan for present and future therapy.

For instance, if the problem is pain on ambulation, the nurse might record:

S — The patient says, "My side hurts when I walk."

O — Patient favoring left side, appendectomy performed 01/11/08. About 2 cm erythematous area surrounding stitches.

A — Local inflammation of appendectomy stitches causing pain.

P — Report to physician. Assist when walking.

Traditional narrative format

In this approach, the nurse documents ongoing assessment data, nursing interventions, and patient responses in chronological order. Although writing narrative notes is time-consuming and repetitive, the nurse will have a detailed record to refresh her memory if a lawsuit is filed years later. Also, tracking problems and trends can be difficult because an individual must read the entire record to arrive at the patient outcome. Today this system, when used, is typically combined with the source-oriented system, using an integrated record where all professionals document their care consecutively as care is given.

FOCUS CHARTING

This technique makes patient care problems the focus of concern. A focus may be a nursing diagnosis, a sign or symp-

Advantages and disadvantages of documentation systems

DOCUMENTATION SYSTEM	ADVANTAGES	DISADVANTAGES
Source-oriented system	• Discipline-specific sections for charting data; easy for discipline to find other team member data	• Time-consuming in that one needs to review several sources to obtain accurate patient picture • Data fragmented, making it difficult to track trends
Problem-oriented system	• Interdisciplinary approach: all disciplines working together to develop problem list • Collaborative approach: all disciplines recording information on same form	• Lengthy and time-consuming to review • Possible difficulty in determining discipline recording information
FOCUS CHARTING	• Highlights patient concerns • Provides structure for progress notes • Enhances documentation of nursing process • Promotes analytical thinking • Can be adapted to all clinical settings	• Required regular monitoring to ensure compliance with response component • Possible need for in-depth training to use • Many checklists and flow sheets • Possible difficulty for some nurses to write accurate, logical notes using this system
Problem, Intervention, and Evaluation (PIE) charting	• Encourages use of nursing diagnoses • Simplifies charting by incorporating care plan in progress notes • Calls for evaluation of each identified problem at least once every shift	• Time-consuming; may lead to repetitive entries by requiring reevaluation of each problem on every shift • Eliminates planning step of nursing process • No opportunity to document expected outcomes • Elimination of care plan or protocol to guide care • Not well suited to long-term care
Charting by exception	• Elimination of need to document routine care through use of nursing standards • Decreased charting time and report time • Patient data directly to permanent record • Risk reduction in transcription errors • Available access of other caregivers to most current patient data • Standardized assessments so that all caregivers evaluate and document findings consistently • Easy to identify trends in patient's care status • Marked reduction in chart size	• Need for large time commitment by the institution to develop clear guidelines and standards of care • Need for major teaching effort for implementation • Thorough understanding and correct use necessary by all staff members to be effective • Questionable legal basis • Need for well-formatted flow sheet

tom, a patient behavior, a special need, or an acute change in the patient's condition. It could also include therapies, responses, and significant events such as teaching, consultation, monitoring, and management of activities of daily living or functional health patterns.[1] The focus is identified by reviewing assessment data. Then the focus is documented precisely by filling out a progress sheet. This usually takes the form of *data*, *action*, and *response*, or DAR.

PIE charting

In this system, information is grouped into three categories: *problem*, *intervention*, and *evaluation* (PIE). PIE charting integrates the care plan into the nurses' progress notes, omitting the need for a separate care plan. Each problem is identified by a number. The nurse keeps a daily patient assessment flow sheet and progress notes.

Charting by exception

Charting by exception (CBE) requires documentation of only abnormal or significant findings. It relies on written standards of practice that identify nurses' basic responsibilities to patients and protocols for interventions. The CBE format includes a standardized care plan based on nursing diagnoses, as well as several types of flow sheets, which allow for easy tracking of trends. It's important to continue to document specific patient information when needed. Generalized nursing care charts won't assist nurses in refreshing their memory years later, nor does this format always convince a jury that care was provided if it wasn't specifically noted by the nurse in the record. Many computerized documentation systems use the same principles as CBE and

should also allow the nurse to document the specifics of care provided. CBE doesn't assist the provider in refreshing his memory of patient care provided and may result in neglect or oversight of individualized care needed or provided.

Uses for documentation

In addition to documentation providing evidence for the continuity of patient care, the medical record is a legal and business record with many uses. A well-documented medical record:

▶ reflects the patient care given
▶ demonstrates the results of treatment
▶ helps to plan and coordinate the care contributed by each professional
▶ allows interdisciplinary exchange of information about the patient
▶ provides evidence of the nurse's legal responsibilities toward the patient
▶ demonstrates standards, rules, regulations, and laws of nursing practice
▶ supplies information for analysis of cost-to-benefit reduction
▶ reflects professional and ethical conduct and responsibility
▶ furnishes data for various uses—continuing education, risk management, diagnosis-related group assignment and reimbursement, continuous quality improvement, case management monitoring, and research.

MEDICAL RECORD AND THE LAW

The medical record provides legal proof of the nature and quality of care the patient received. The weight it carries in legal proceedings can't be overemphasized. The record may be the focus of inquiry in personal injury,

Legal risks of charting by exception

Charting by exception (CBE) omits all charting related to routine nursing care. Instead, it relies on written standards of practice that identify the nurse's basic patient responsibilities. Of course, care must be consistently provided even though it isn't documented.

Because this charting system requires the nurse to document only information that deviates from the expected, it can raise legal concerns. To ensure a legally sound patient record, well-defined guidelines and standards of care for its use must be understood by all nursing staff members and used consistently.

WHEN CBE VIOLATES THE LAW

Lama v. Boras (1994) illustrates what can go wrong when nurses don't follow accepted standards of care when using CBE. On May 15, 1985, Roberto Romero Lama had surgery for a herniated disk. Two days later, a nurse wrote in his chart that the bandage covering the surgical wound was "very bloody." An entry the next day indicated he had pain at the incision site.

On May 19, a nurse documented the bandage as "soiled again." The next day, Mr. Romero began to complain of severe back discomfort; he passed the night screaming in pain. On May 21, the physician diagnosed an infection in the space between the vertebral disks, and ordered antibiotics. The patient was hospitalized for several months to treat the infection.

Mr. Romero sued the hospital and the physicians who treated him, alleging that they failed to prepare and monitor proper medical records. The hospital didn't dispute the charge that nurses didn't supply the required notes; instead, it pointed out that they followed the hospital's official CBE policy.

The court ruled against the hospital on the grounds that Puerto Rico law requires qualitative nurses' notes for each nursing shift, and that violation of this regulation had caused Mr. Romero's injury. The court reasoned that a more complete picture of his evolving condition was unavailable because the hospital's CBE policy called for nurses to note qualitative observations only when needed to chronicle important clinical changes. Although objective aspects of the patient's care and condition (temperature, vital signs, medications) were charted regularly, important details, such as the changing condition of the surgical wound and the patient's reports of pain, weren't.

PLAYING IT SAFE

Although CBE complies with legal principles, the system may be questioned in court until it becomes more widely known. If you believe your facility's CBE policy is unsafe or ambiguous, confer with your colleagues and supervisors, and then approach an administrator about clarifying it.

professional malpractice, or product liability claims, as well as in workers' compensation, child custody, and employment disputes.

A factual, consistent, timely, and complete record defends the nurse against allegations of negligence, improper treatment, and omissions in care. Health care professionals have a legal duty to maintain the medical record in sufficient detail, and inadequate documentation of care may result in liability or nonreimbursement by third-party payers.

In fact, documentation of care has become synonymous with care itself, and failure to document implies failure to provide care.[2] Despite the recent introduction of CBE—a system that implies all standards have been met with a normal or expected response unless otherwise documented—the prevailing rule is: "If it isn't documented, it hasn't been done." (See *Legal risks of charting by exception*.)

In *Collins v. Westlake Community Hospital,* 57 Ill. 2d 388, 312 N.E. 2d

Using flow sheets

Flow sheets are record-keeping forms used for tracking information about the repetitive tasks you perform through the day, such as giving medication or monitoring your patient's vital signs or fluid balance. Using a flow sheet enables you to keep all routine measurements in one place and to compare data quickly. Flow sheets come in various styles, including blank-ruled paper and graph paper, to suit various documenting needs.

ADVANTAGES

A flow sheet offers these advantages:
● It displays a specific aspect of your patient's condition, such as his temperature, at a glance. You don't have to search through pages of notes to determine his temperature pattern during the past 48 hours.
● It saves you time. You can note the vital signs or medication given without having to write a full descriptive entry every time. You can use your nurses' notes to describe how the patient is responding to treatment.
● It documents that you're giving the patient continuous care.
● It provides a mechanism for nonlicensed personnel to record their care and observations. Because nonlicensed personnel usually aren't permitted to chart in the nurses' notes, information they have about patient care may be lost. Instead, you can ask them to describe their care and initial each entry on a flow sheet. Then if you have a question about the status of your patient's skin, for example, you can check the flow sheet to identify the nursing assistant who gave that day's bed bath.

COMMON ERRORS

Flow sheets can create a legal tangle if you don't avoid two common mistakes:
● The first mistake is to treat flow sheets casually. For instance, some nurses will routinely check off whatever the previous shift checked off on the flow sheet, or made checks at the beginning of the shift before the care is provided regardless of the care given, and then carefully chart the actual care in the nurses' notes. This creates an inconsistency. As part of the legal medical record, the flow sheet must accurately reflect the care provided.
● The second mistake is to depend too heavily on flow sheets. Flow sheets can help you document, quickly and accurately, what care was given and who provided it. However, don't neglect to record the patient's response to care in your nurses' notes. Like other chart forms, retain the flow sheet as part of the permanent chart so that you have a progressive picture of the patient's status and a record of your care.

---

614 (1974), a boy was hospitalized with a fractured leg, which was put in a cast and placed in traction. The evening nurse recorded the condition of the boy's toes several times during her shift. The night nurse, however, didn't record the condition of his toes until 6 a.m., when she noted that they were dusky and cold, and that his physician had been contacted. The leg required partial amputation, and the boy's family sued the hospital, claiming that the amputation was necessary because the night nurse had negligently failed to observe the condition of the toes in a timely fashion.

In her defense, the nurse testified that she had observed the toes periodically and that they were normal. Experts for the defense testified that only abnormal findings required documentation. However, the jury disagreed, concluding that failure to document implied failure to observe, and held the nurse liable for malpractice.

Contents of the medical record

Federal regulations, such as those governing Medicare and Medicaid reimbursement, partially determine the form and content of the medical record. Although state laws vary in their stringency and specificity, all states require health care facilities to maintain the medical record in sufficient detail.

These documents are usually included in the medical record:
▶ patient admission form and history
▶ physician's order form and progress notes
▶ nursing assessment and nursing diagnoses
▶ patient's medication record
▶ nurses' notes and progress notes
▶ diagnostic and laboratory test results
▶ X-ray and other radiologic reports
▶ operative and other treatment reports
▶ flow sheets, checklists, and graphic sheets (see *Using flow sheets.*)
▶ discharge summary
▶ referral summaries
▶ consent forms, such as advance directives, living wills, do-not-resuscitate orders, name of health care proxy or legal guardian, and patient privacy consent forms such as the Health Insurance Portability and Accountability Act (HIPAA) form
▶ home care instruction sheet.

Failure to properly maintain the medical record

As a general rule, the medical record is presumed to be accurate if there's no evidence of fraud or tampering. Evidence of tampering can cause the record to be ruled inadmissible as evidence in court and harm the nurse's credibility. Medical records may be corrected if the portion in error remains legible; deleting or rendering the entry illegible can impose liability.

Late entries are usually acceptable if they're clearly marked "late entry" when made. Loss of the medical record raises a presumption of negligence (which may be overcome by contrary evidence).

NURSING DOCUMENTATION

With a large number of health care professionals involved in each patient's care, nursing documentation must be complete, accurate, and timely to foster continuity of care. It should cover:
▶ initial assessment using the nursing process and applicable nursing diagnoses
▶ nursing actions, particularly reports to the physician
▶ ongoing assessment, including the frequency of assessment
▶ variations from the assessment and plan
▶ accountability information, including forms signed by the patient, location of patient valuables, and patient education
▶ notation of care by other disciplines, including physician visits, if practical
▶ health teaching, including content and response
▶ procedures and diagnostic tests
▶ patient response to therapy, particularly to nursing interventions, drugs, and diagnostic tests
▶ statements made by the patient
▶ patient comfort and safety measures
▶ evidence of supervision of assistive personnel related to care that they've been delegated to perform.

Sources of documentation duties and standards

Factors that influence nursing documentation standards include:
▶ federal statutes and regulations

"Do not use" list

In 2004, The Joint Commission developed a list of abbreviations that shouldn't be used in documentation. This list was created in response to meeting the National Patient Safety Goal addressing a standardized list of abbreviations, acronyms, and symbols that aren't to be used throughout an organization. The list was published for public comment. The overwhelming response supported the creation and adoption of this list. The list shown below applies to all hand-written orders and medication-related documentation (including free-text computer entry or entry on preprinted forms).

DO NOT USE	POTENTIAL PROBLEM	USE INSTEAD
U (unit)	Mistaken for "0" (zero), the number "4" (four), or "cc"	Write out "unit"
IU (International Unit)	Mistaken for IV (intravenous) or the number "10" (ten)	Write out "International Unit"
Q.D., QD, q.d., qd (daily) Q.O.D, QOD, q.o.d., qod (every other day)	Mistaken for each other Period after the Q mistaken for "I" and the "O" mistaken for "I"	Write "daily" or write "every other day"
Trailing zero (X.0 mg)* Lack of leading zero (.Xmg)	Decimal point is missed	Write X mg Write 0.X mg
MS MSO$_4$ or MgSO$_4$	Can mean morphine sulfate or magnesium sulfate Confused for one another	Write "morphine sulfate" Write "magnesium sulfate"

*Exception: A "trailing zero" may be used only where required to demonstrate the level of precision of the value being reported, such as laboratory results, imaging studies that report size of lesions, or catheter/tube sizes. It may not be used in medication orders or other medication-related documentation.

The Joint Commission also has identified additional abbreviations, acronyms, and symbols that may be included in future "do not use" lists. These are shown below.

DO NOT USE	POTENTIAL PROBLEM	USE INSTEAD
> (greater than) < (less than)	Misinterpreted as the number "7" (seven) or the letter "L" Confused with one another	Write "greater than" Write "less than"
Abbreviations for drug names	Misinterpreted due to similar abbreviations for multiple drugs	Write drug names in full
Apothecary units	Unfamiliar to many practitioners Confusion with metric units	Use metric units
@	Mistaken for the number "2" (two)	Write "at"
cc	Mistaken for U (units) when poorly written	Write "ml" or "milliliters"

"Do not use" list *(continued)*

DO NOT USE	POTENTIAL PROBLEM	USE INSTEAD
µg	Mistaken for mg (milligrams) resulting in one thousand-fold overdose	Write "mcg" or "micrograms"

According to 2006 Joint Commission surveys, almost one-fourth of noncompliance issues were related to failure to implement the "do not use" list in medication orders.

Source: The Joint Commission. *Official "Do Not Use" List.* Available at http://www.jointcommission.org/NR/rdonlyres/2329F8F5-6EC5-4E21-B932-54B2B7D53F00/0/06_dnu_list.pdf.

The Joint Commission. *"Do Not Use" List. Facts about the Official "Do Not Use" List.* Available at http://www.jointcommission.org/PatientSafety/DoNotUseList/fact_dnu.htm.

▶ state regulations and statutes, including licensing statutes and nurse practice acts
▶ accrediting bodies
▶ standards of practice issued by professional organizations
▶ institutional policies and procedures.

Professional organizations and accrediting bodies have developed and refined recommendations and standards of practice for nursing documentation. Sometimes these standards are more stringent than those required by state law.

The American Nurses Association (ANA) has included documentation in its Standards of Nursing Practice. The ANA says documentation must be systematic, continuous, accessible, communicated, recorded, and readily available to all health care team members. In addition, the ANA has developed principles for documentation using the organization's Code of Ethics for Nurses with Interpretative Statements and Nursing: Scope and Standards of Practice.[3] The ANA principles demonstrate the legal status of documentation and provide general rec-

ommendations that can be applied to any documentation system. The ultimate outcome is accurate and complete documentation of the care given to patients and their response to care.[4,5]

The Joint Commission also sets standards. Current standards stress a change from source-oriented documentation to a fully integrated, multidisciplinary approach.

Documentation should reflect the collaborative planning and provision of care and treatment. The Joint Commission doesn't specify a format for medical record documentation. Thus, patient care, treatment, and rehabilitation may involve many forms, from preprinted forms to handwritten reports to electronic formats, which may include decision algorithms and care maps.

The Joint Commission also has developed a list of abbreviations that shouldn't be used in documentation. This list was created as a means of meeting one of the National Patient Safety Goals.[6,7] (See *Do not use list*.)

Managed care: Implications for documentation

Because managed care balances the importance of a medical procedure or treatment against its cost, it requires greater standardization of care plans as well as continuous monitoring of health care outcomes. To improve outcomes, several tools have been developed.

Clinical practice guidelines are standards developed to help practitioners and patients make decisions regarding appropriate care in specific clinical circumstances.

Practice parameters are educational tools that enable physicians to obtain the advice of clinical experts, keep abreast of the latest clinical research, and assess the clinical significance of conflicting research findings.

Clinical pathways and *critical paths* are clinical management tools that help to organize, sequence, price, and time the major interventions of nurses, physicians, and other health care providers for a particular case type, subset, or condition.

Care maps are elaborate critical pathways that show the relationships of sets of interventions to sets of intermediate outcomes along a timeline. They merge standards of care with standards of practice in a cause-and-effect relationship.

Many of the professional specialty societies, such as the American Association of Critical-Care Nurses, the Association of Operating Room Nurses, and the Emergency Department Nurses Association, have developed guidelines, standards, or recommendations concerning content and technique of nursing documentation.

Institution policy

Typically, a health care facility has integrated the appropriate laws, regulations, and standards into its own policy and procedure manual. The best assurance of following the law may be to adhere to the facility's policy, which usually describes who's to maintain each portion of a patient's record and by which technique. The nurse must comply with the employer's or facility's documentation policies, even if she has a preference for another documentation format. Deviation from the accepted norm can provide an attorney with means to portray a negative picture to a jury.[8] (See *Managed care: Implications for documentation*.)

In a dispute, the law will frequently support a health care facility's policies and procedures with regard to documentation. Consider the following case (*Stack v. Wapner, 368A.2d 292, 244 [Pa. Super. Ct. 278, 1976.]*).

The plaintiff was admitted to the hospital to give birth. At 2:45 a.m., according to her chart, I.V. oxytocin was started to induce labor. Accepted medical practice requires continuous monitoring of patients receiving oxytocin to prevent complications of excessive uterine contractions, such as subsequent fetal distress or uterine rupture. However, the labor room record didn't document monitoring of her clinical status until 5:15 a.m.

After delivery, the patient developed heavy uterine bleeding. Unable to stop the bleeding, the physician performed a total hysterectomy. The patient later sued, claiming that her complications resulted from improper administration and monitoring of oxytocin.

Both the attending physicians testified that they had monitored the administration of the drug. However, they had no defense against evidence that hospital policy required them to document on the patient's chart all information that supported diagnosis and treatment, as well as the patient's response to treatment. The patient was awarded damages.

Nurses must document the baseline assessment and clinically significant changes thereafter. The health care facility's policy will provide a guide for what strips need to be saved. Fetal monitoring strips are usually part of the record. Document the time started on the strip as well as clinically significant activity that would correlate with changes in the strip.

Hazards of improper documentation

Nurses need to know how to document and what to document to make sure that the record reflects an accurate and complete picture of the patient. (See *Documentation tips,* page 288.) When involved in legal action, jurors can't assume a patient received care if a nurse failed to document care. Therefore, a nurse must record the facts, including those related to any adverse event to provide supportive evidence that the nurse acted within the standards of care.[9]

Nurses or other health care providers make documentation errors that contribute substantially to the legal outcome. The cases reviewed here include faulty record keeping, failure to include information, charting after the fact, misplaced records, and failure to follow set standards of care when using charting by exception. All these cases contain important lessons about the courts' determination to uphold standards of documentation.

Faulty record keeping
Rogers v. Kasdan (612 S.W.2d 133 [Ky. 1981]) involved a woman who died of

brain damage 7 days after admission for injuries sustained in an accident. The Supreme Court of Kentucky ruled against the physician and the hospital, based on the patient's medical record: the emergency department records were incomplete, fluid intake and output was incorrectly tallied, and other records contained discrepancies or were illegible or incomplete.

Absence of information
St. Paul Fire and Marine Insurance Co. v. Prothro (266 Ark. 1020, 590 S.W.2d 35 [Ark. Ct. App. 1979]) involved a claim in which the patient, after undergoing a total hip replacement, was injured while being lowered into a Hubbard tank by a nursing assistant. The metal basket holding him collapsed, struck his hip, and reopened the wound. The nursing assistant stopped the bleeding and took the plaintiff to his room, where a nurse treated the wound. However, the nurse failed to document the incident. The wound subsequently became infected, necessitating removal of the prosthesis and leaving the patient with a permanent limp. The court ruled in the patient's favor and noted that a determining factor was the absence of critical information on the patient's chart, which would have helped the physician and staff provide proper care.

Gaps in the record provide opportunities for speculation.[10]

Charting after the fact
In *Thor v. Boska (38 Cal. App. 3d 558, 113 Cal Rptr. 296 [1974])*, a rewritten copy of a patient's record was suspected of being an altered record. This lawsuit involved a woman who had seen her physician several times because of a breast lump. Each time, the physician ex-

Documentation tips

If you're ever involved in a malpractice lawsuit, how you documented, what you documented, and what you didn't document will heavily influence the jury and the outcome of the trial. Following these tips can ensure that your records don't tip the scales of justice against you.

HOW TO DOCUMENT

● Use the appropriate form, and document in ink.
● Record the patient's name and identification number on every page of his chart.
● Record the complete date and time of each entry.
● Document the care given in a timely manner.
● Include patient statements in quotations when significant.
● Be specific. Avoid general terms and vague expressions.
● Use standard abbreviations only.
● Use a medical term only if you're sure of its meaning.
● Document symptoms by using the patient's own words.
● Document objectively.

WHAT TO DOCUMENT

● Document all nursing actions you take in response to a patient's problem. For example: "8 p.m. medicated for incision pain." Be sure to include the medication name, dose, route, and site.
● Document the patient's response to medications and other treatment.
● Document safeguards you use to protect the patient. For example: "raised side rails" or "applied safety belts."
● Document the incident in two places: in your progress notes and in an incident report. Don't mention the incident report in the patient's record, unless your facility or state requires it.
● If the incident report is mentioned in the nursing notes, it becomes part of the patient record (termed *incorporation by reference*) and is available to the patient's attorney if a lawsuit is filed. Otherwise, the incident or occurrence report is a protected risk management tool that isn't available to the patient or plaintiff.

● Document each observation. Failure to document observations will produce gaps in the patient's records. These gaps will suggest that you neglected the patient.
● Document procedures after you perform them, never in advance.
● If a treatment or medication isn't given because of a change in patient status, document notification to the physician and justification for withholding care that may harm the patient. Otherwise the lack of care or missing documentation may appear to be a negligent oversight.
● Write on every line. Don't insert notes between lines or leave empty spaces for someone else to insert a note.
● If you have empty spaces, place a line through them so that someone else can't insert information in the middle of your notes.
● Sign every entry.
● Chart an omission as a new entry. Never backdate or add to previously written entries. Within the body of the note, reference the time and date of omission.
● Correct errors according to your facility's policies and procedures.
● Draw a thin line through an error and mark "error" above it, with the date and your initials. Never erase or obliterate an erroneous entry.
● Document only the care you provide. Never document for someone else.
● Understand and follow the documentation standards of your facility and your state or province. These standards are usually defined in the facility's policy and procedure manuals, state or provincial nurse practice acts (the statutes governing nursing practice), and in state or provincial administrative codes (the rules and regulations governing nursing practice).

amined her and made a record of her visit. After 2 years, the woman sought a second opinion and learned that she had breast cancer. She sued her first physician. Rather than producing his records in court, the physician brought copies of the records and said he had copied the originals for legibility. The court reasoned that he was withholding incriminating evidence, and held in favor of the plaintiff.

In a suspected case of notes written after litigation, handwriting experts are retained by the plaintiff's attorney to determine when portions were written. An alteration in the record can make a defensible case indefensible. Attempting to fit information into space available on the record can lead to questions about why the information was documented after the fact. It also can suggest that something is being covered up.

Missing records

The case of *Battocchi v. Washington Hosp. Center (581 A.2d 759 [D.C. App. 1990])* underscores the significance of missing records. In this case, parents brought a medical malpractice suit against the hospital and a physician for injury to their son during forceps delivery. The nurse had immediately documented the delivery and posted the record in the chart.

Later, the hospital's risk management personnel apparently lost the nurse's record. The court ruled in favor of the hospital and physician, saying the jury couldn't presume negligence and causation simply because the hospital lost the nurse's notes. The appeals court sent the case back to the trial court to determine whether loss of the record stemmed from negligence or impropriety.

Poor communication

Although thorough documentation is crucial, it isn't always enough. Unless a nurse reports significant findings that he documents, exemplary charting can be worthless. In a 1995 Nebraska case, a couple sued a hospital, claiming that the staff's negligence caused brain damage to their newborn son. Jeffrey Critchfield was born at 7:30 a.m., weighing 4 lb, 10 oz. According to the admission assessment, Jeffrey had chest wall retractions, cyanosis, pallor, weak cry, and flaccid muscles. He was admitted to the neonatal intensive care unit, where nurses documented his grunting, pallor, and chest retractions. At about 7:45 p.m., a nurse documented that Jeffrey was lethargic.

At the trial, a pediatric neurologist testifying for the Critchfields stated that lethargy was a sign of neurologic changes, and that nursing observations recorded throughout the night indicated that Jeffrey had signs of acute brain damage from lack of oxygen and blood to the brain. He also said that the nurses should have reported these findings to the attending physician during the night and the early morning hours. Another expert testified that the hospital should have had a policy requiring expert consultation, and that if nurses had reported Jeffrey's problems, his brain damage could have been ameliorated. The court ruled in favor of the Critchfields, reasoning that the hospital had a duty, through its nursing staff, to report medically significant changes in a patient's condition to the treating physician without delay.

Bias

Comments written in a patient's medical record must be specific and nonjudgmental. Inappropriate comments or terms that label the patient, such as rude, obnoxious, demanding, or hostile, are to be avoided. Use of such terms implies bias and can be interpreted later on in a lawsuit as interfering with the nurse's ability to provide an appropriate level of care, such that the labeled patient received less than appropriate care when compared to a patient who was considered compliant or agreeable. In addition to professional negligence, the nurse may be sued for defamation of character because of the labeling.

Documentation errors

In addition to their potential impact on patient care, charting errors or omissions, even if seemingly harmless, will undermine your credibility in court. Especially avoid the following issues. Relevant court cases are listed where appropriate.

Omissions

All significant facts that other nurses will need to assess the patient must be included. Otherwise, a court may conclude that the nurse failed to perform an action missing from the record or tried to hide evidence.

Change in treatment

When an ordered treatment is no longer appropriate, which may occur after a change in the patient's condition, document why the treatment wasn't given and any communications with the patient's physician regarding the need for new orders.

Personal opinions

Never enter personal opinions. These may be construed as bias. (See *Distinguishing between subjective and objective*

charting.) Record only factual and objective observations and the patient's statements. (*Brookover v. Mary Hitchcock Memorial Hospital 893 F.2d 411 [1st Cir. 1990].*)

Vague entries

Vague entries are open to interpretation and suspicion. Generalities don't provide a clear picture of the patient or the patient's status. For example, instead of "Patient had a good day," state why: "Patient didn't complain of pain."

Late entries

If a late entry is necessary, identify it as such, sign, and date it. Reference the date and time you're relating back to. Also adhere to the facility's policy related to adding a late entry. When an entry is made a few days later, provide a reason for the entry.[11]

Improper corrections

Never erase or obliterate an error. Instead, draw a single line through it, label it "error," and sign and date it. Follow the facility's policy for correcting errors. Some facilities believe the word "error" raises red flags unnecessarily, but that it's appropriate to document "correction."

Unauthorized entries

Only you should be keeping your records. (*Henry By Henry v. St. John's Hospital 512 N.E.2d 1044 [Ill. App. 4 Dist. 1987].*)

Erroneous or vague abbreviations

Use only standard abbreviations, and follow your facility's policies. In addition, follow the Joint Commission "do not

Distinguishing between subjective and objective charting

The most common error most nurses make when they chart is writing value judgments and opinions—subjective information—rather than factual, or objective, information. Subjective information reflects how the nurse *feels* about the patient's condition, not the patient's condition itself. Here are some subjective entries, with their objective alternatives.

SUBJECTIVE CHARTING	OBJECTIVE CHARTING
She's drinking well.	Drank 1,500 ml liquids between 7 a.m. and noon.
She reported good relief from Demerol.	Pain in R hip decreasing, now described as "like a dull toothache."
Dorsalis pedis pulse present. Good pedal pulses.	Peripheral pulses in legs 2+/4+ bilaterally.
Moves legs and feet well.	Leg strength 5+/5+ bilaterally all major muscle groups. Sensation intact to light touch, pin; denies numbness or tingling. Skin warm and dry. No edema.
Voiding qs.	Voided 350 ml clear yellow urine in bedpan.
Patient is nervous.	Patient repeatedly asks about length of hospitalization, expected discomfort, and time off from work.
Breath sounds normal.	Breath sounds clear to auscultation all lobes. Chest expansion symmetrical—no cough. Nail beds pink.
Bowel sounds normal.	Bowel sound present in all quadrants—abdomen flat. NPO since 12:01 a.m.
Ate well.	Ate all of soft diet.

use" recommendations for documentation.

Illegibility and lack of clarity

Always write clearly and legibly so that others can read the entry. Use correct grammar and spelling. In addition, use a dictionary when unsure of spelling or usage. Poorly written or misspelled words suggest a lack of professionalism and can undermine one's credibility.

Documentation of physician's orders

Physician's orders fall into three groups: correct as written, ambiguous, and apparently erroneous. Follow the health care facility's policy for clarification of orders that are vague or possibly in error. If the facility lacks a policy, contact the prescribing physician, and always document your actions. Then ask your nursing administrator for a step-by-step policy to follow in this situation, so that if it happens again, you'll know what to do.

An order may be correct when issued but improper later because of changes in the patient's status. When this occurs, delay the treatment until contacting the physician and clarifying the situation. Always follow the facility's policy for clarifying an order. In *Poor Sisters of St. Francis Seraph of the Perpetual Adoration et al. v. Catron 435 N.E.2d 305 [Ind. Ct. App. 1982])*, a hospital was held liable for negligence because a nurse failed to question the physician's use of an endotracheal tube for an excessively long period. The patient's voice box was irreparably damaged.

If the order is correct as written, initial and checkmark each line. Below the physician's signature, sign your name, the date, and the time.

Ambiguous or erroneous orders
Ambiguous orders must be clarified with the physician. Document efforts to clarify the order and whether the order was carried out.

If a nurse believes that a physician's order is in error, the nurse should refuse to carry it out. Make a record of the refusal together with the reasons and an account of all communication with the physician.

Verbal and telephone orders
As a general rule, verbal and telephone orders are acceptable only under acute or emergency circumstances, when the physician can't promptly attend to the patient, or according to facility policy. If possible, have another nurse listen to the verbal order with you to avoid miscommunication and to ensure accurate interpretation. Read the documented order back to the physician to verify its correct-

ness and document this process of verification. Communication errors can be avoided, and proof or evidence of the verbal order is more easily established. Record the order on the physician's order sheet, note the date and time of the order, and record the order verbatim. On the following line, write "v.o." for verbal order or "t.o." for telephone order and record the physician's name, followed by your signature and the time. To avoid liability, be certain the physician countersigns the order within the time specified by your facility's policy.

Preprinted standing orders or protocols and standing order admission sheets are usually checkmarked and signed by the physician, cosigned by the nurse, and retained in the chart according to the facility's policy. (See *Documenting spoken orders.*)

Documentation of controlled substances
Nurses are responsible for proper storage of controlled substances on the nursing unit as well as for maintaining detailed records of each dose dispensed and the remaining quantities. The legal consequences of improper charting are especially significant when giving opioids and other controlled substances and maintaining controlled substance records. Be familiar with the facility's policy when dispensing and giving these drugs. Also be aware of *controlled substance acts*— federal and state laws that control the distribution, classification, sale, and use of drugs. Consult the facility's policies or contact the state board of nursing for information about these laws. For a specific question about the propriety of a policy or procedure in the facility, talk to the facility's attorney or write to the state

board of nursing and request a formal board opinion or a declaratory ruling.

Opioid administration

For proper, accurate documentation of opioids, use the special opioids records—the control sheet and the check sheet—provided by the pharmacy and follow the procedure described below.

Before you give a controlled substance:
▶ Verify the count in the opioids drawer.
▶ Sign the control sheet to indicate you removed the drug.
▶ Get another nurse to sign the control sheet if you waste or discard all or part of a dose. A second nurse must act as a witness anytime an opioid is discarded, wasted, or a portion isn't used. The signature of the witness nurse confirms the discarding or wasting of the drug.

At the end of the shift or designated time:
▶ Record the amount of each opioid in the drawer on the control sheet while the nurse beginning her shift counts the opioids out loud.
▶ Sign the check sheet only if the count is correct. Have the other nurse countersign.
▶ Identify and correct discrepancies before nurses leave the unit.

In some facilities, a computerized system for dispensing opioids is used. In such situations, the nurse uses a secure identification code to enter the system. The patient's identity is confirmed via name or identification number. The count is verified for each drug as it's removed. The identification code used to enter the system is equivalent to the nurse's signature. This process eliminates the need for checking the opioid count at a specified interval such as the end of shift. However, any time a opioid count

is inaccurate, the nurse is responsible for reporting it immediately.

For your own protection, conform to all facility, nursing department, and pharmacy policies and procedures if an ordered dose of a controlled substance isn't given, or if it's wasted or discarded.

Documentation of discharge planning

Discharge planning and summary are an important component of the patient's

---

Documenting spoken orders

When a physician writes an order for the patient and signs it—or when another health care professional writes an order and the physician countersigns it—the courts usually won't question the legality of the order. However, if a physician gives you a verbal order, either in person or by telephone, protect yourself legally, as follows:
• Write down the order exactly as he gives it, the date, and the time.
• Repeat the order back to him so that you're sure you heard correctly.
• Follow up to ensure that the physician signs the order.

THE DANGER OF POOR DOCUMENTATION

Here's what can happen if you don't document verbal orders:
• You could face disciplinary measures by your employer and state board of nursing for failing to document or charges of practicing medicine without a license.
• You could damage your defense or your hospital's in a malpractice suit.
• Other nurses, not knowing what orders have been given, may follow prior orders that result in harm to the patient.
• If controlled substances are given, suspicions could be raised that you're diverting drugs for your own use.

Documenting discharge planning

The final document in each patient's record, the discharge summary highlights the patient's condition, treatment, status at discharge, discharge nursing diagnoses, and all medications. It should also include a home care instruction sheet, the name of an escort, the patient's discharge address, and his transportation mode.

Document the names of family members or other caregivers who are present for discharge instructions, especially if competency issues are of concern. Also document their understanding of the discharge orders and instructions.

Make appropriate referrals for follow-up care and document the patient's status, discharge instructions, and other instructions or special considerations verbalized to the patient, family, or medical team.

TAKING IT STEP-BY-STEP

When preparing a discharge summary, take these steps:
● First, review the patient's nursing diagnoses or problem list, care plan, flow sheets, and progress notes to develop an overall impression of his hospital stay.
● Follow your facility's policies regarding the format and content of the summary.
● Include any exceptional details or unusual findings.
● Outline all patient teaching and provide, as a record, written instructions in a language the patient understands.

REVIEWING THE SUMMARY

Make sure that the discharge summary:
● summarizes the patient's care
● provides useful information for further teaching, evaluation, and readmission
● shows that the patient has information needed for self-care or to get further help
● shows that you've met Joint Commission documentation requirements for collaboration with other disciplines and for patient teaching
● helps safeguard you and your employer against malpractice charges.

medical record. When planning a patient's discharge, be sure to document in the medical record that he or his family is aware that treatment and care will be stopped on a specific date. Also document the alternative resources and specific plans that must be organized to ensure continuity of care. (See *Documenting discharge planning*.)

The Joint Commission requires that all patients receive discharge instructions when they're to be released from the facility. These instructions should include:
▶ assessment of the patient's continuing health needs
▶ a realistic plan of care for the patient to meet these needs
▶ patient's responsibilities for his continuing health care

▶ teaching provided to the patient and family so that they can fulfill the responsibilities and meet these needs.[12]

Written instructions are essential for teaching to minimize the risk of confusion. These instructions should include information about exactly what teaching was done, such as that related to any restrictions in diet or activity, medications, treatments or procedures, skills taught, possible complications, and follow up. If English isn't the patient's primary language, provide written instructions in the patient's primary language and use an interpreter to confirm that the patient has understood what was taught. Document the steps taken to ensure that any language barriers were addressed.

Upon completion of the discharge instructions, have the patient sign a copy of the instructions. This copy then becomes part of the patient's record.

Documentation signature

Sign all notes with your first initial, full last name, and title. Place your signature on the right side of the page as proof that you entered all the information between the previous nurse's signature and your own. If the last entry is unsigned, request that the nurse who made the entry sign it. Never sign for procedures completed by another care provider. (In rare instances, you may need to sign for another health care provider to maintain and update the record; in this situation, explain why you're signing and for whom.) Draw lines through empty or remaining spaces to prevent subsequent amendments or additions. (See *Signing your notes*.)

Registered nurses (RNs) need to be aware of the legality of countersigning notes made by licensed practical nurses (LPNs), licensed vocational nurses, or nursing assistants when they haven't supervised their actions. If a nurse is delegating nursing care to assistive personnel, the nurse is responsible for supervising the care provided.

For protection, find out what the facility's policy says. Does the facility interpret countersigning to mean that the LPN or nursing assistant performed the nursing actions in the countersigning RN's presence? If so, don't countersign unless you were there when the actions occurred.

If your facility acknowledges that you don't necessarily have time to witness your coworkers' actions, then your countersignature implies that:
▶ the notes describe care that the LPN or nursing assistant had the authority and competence to perform

Signing your notes

To discourage other nurses from adding information to your nurse's notes, draw a line through a blank space after your entry and sign your name on the far right side of the column.

> p: will continue plan and request
> diabetic nurse specialist to assess
> patient's knowledge of diabetes
> mellitus 3rd or 4th post-op day.
> ————————— L. Fallon, R.N.

If you don't have enough room to sign your name after the last word in the entry, draw a line from the last word to the end of the line. Then drop down to the next line, draw a line from the left margin almost to the right margin, and sign your name on the far right side.

> and hyperglycemia.
> a: excellent knowledge of disease
> and management. p: see no need
> for additional follow-up ———
> ——————————— L. Fallon, R.N.

If you have a lot of information to record and you anticipate running out of room on a page, leave room on the right side of the page for your signature. Sign the page, continue your notes on the next page, and then sign that page as usual.

> pt. drowsy and relaxed on
> (continued) ——— L. Fallon, R.N.

> departure for O.R. —————
> ——————————— L. Fallon, R.N.

▶ you verified that all required patient care was actually carried out (and that you were performing your supervisory responsibilities).

What should a nurse do if another nurse asks her to document her care or sign notes? In a word, "Don't!" Unless the facility policy authorizes or requires a nurse to witness someone else's notes, the nurse's signature will make that nurse responsible for anything put in the notes above it.

Potential legal traps

In the event of a legal challenge, or if the medical record has been requested for examination in a trial, avoid making changes, corrections, or additions. To do so could raise suspicion, even if the nurse has legitimate reasons and the best intentions.

In addition, many lawyers advise against keeping personal notes and journals about a questionable patient care incident. Commonly those notes are written when the nurse is less than objective and may convey a far different message than was intended. Personal notes and journals are considered to be part of "discovery." Discovery is a process that occurs before a trial in which both sides of the lawsuit examine the strengths and weaknesses of the other side to determine if a trial is in their best interest.[13] In addition, a plaintiff's attorney can obtain personal notes the nurse used as part of the discovery process to prepare for a deposition or trial; in a trial, if a nurse denies using them—or a source of information other than the patient's record—to refresh his or her memory, the nurse is committing perjury. If a nurse admits that she did use personal notes, they may be used to incriminate the nurse or other defendants. Simply put, avoid written or oral statements without first consulting your attorney.

When reviewing the medical record of a potential plaintiff, certain areas are considered red flags to a lawyer. These include:

▶ lack of patient identification information on pages
▶ use of incorrect dates or times or dates or times that don't correlate with the rest of the medical record
▶ inappropriate sequencing of entries, especially when the entries are long narrative notes
▶ irregularities in handwriting, such as changes in the slant or uniformity of the writing or changes in ink color on the same entry
▶ erasures or "white out" of information
▶ results of laboratory or diagnostic tests that don't appear to relate to the patient's assessment findings or complaints.[14]

Be alert to these red flags and ensure that documentation is clear, complete, timely, and accurate.

COMPUTERIZED MEDICAL RECORDS

As with the manual record system, the computerized medical record provides a detailed account of the patient's clinical status, diagnostic tests, treatments, and medical history. However, unlike the manual system, the computerized record stores all the patient's medical data in a single, easily accessible source.

Using computers to maintain and access records dramatically increases efficiency and precision. Computerization improves the quality and accuracy of the documentation, improves clarity and legibility, makes the patient record more complete, and keeps patient information more current. The computerized record also allows practitioners to rely less on human recall, which helps to increase accuracy. Computers prove especially useful in areas that benefit from automated patient monitoring, such as the intensive care unit and the coronary care unit.

Nurses must receive comprehensive training on the correct use of computerized documentation systems being used in their facility. Correction of errors, late entries, and other documentation issues are affected by the computerized system. Delays in treatment can occur if the nurse isn't prepared to effectively use a new method of documenting the care provided on numerous patients. Feedback on the computerized system should be provided to the facility administration if nurses believe improvements in the system are needed to improve patient care.

Hospital computer systems

Senior hospital officials usually introduce computers for the sake of controlling health care costs. A hospital's computer system typically consists of a large, centralized computer to store information, linked to smaller video display terminals in each work area. In some instances there's a computer for each patient room or a mobile laptop computer that can be easily transported from one patient room to another. Alternatively, there may be several computer terminals placed strategically on the unit for nurses to access.

To use the system, a nurse signs in by typing onto the keyboard a signature code, or password, that provides access to a patient's records. The nurse must protect the privacy of her self-identifier and never allow another person to enter a patient's record using this personal information. Only staff with a need to

know about a patient have the legal right to access a patient's medical record.

The computer recognizes by the signature code that the nurse has authorized access to the information stored in its memory. After a patient's code number is entered, the computer displays the patient's records on the screen. The nurse may access care plans, vital signs, medication records, general progress notes, laboratory and diagnostic test results, assessment findings, discharge plans, and other information. The nurse can also order a printed copy of the patient's record.

Benefits

Just how computer technology will change the nursing profession remains to be seen. Some experts predict a paperless chart. Health care reform may further transform the documentation process, with the creation of a universal medical record that follows a patient throughout his life. At best, integrating computers into nursing practice will free nurses to spend more time meeting the needs of patients. The computerized medical record can save time spent filing, searching for, and retrieving information about a patient. By improving legibility, computers reduce the risk of misinterpretation. Computers also reduce misinterpretation by offering standardized, structured input formats and mandatory charting fields for assessment reports, flowcharts, and care plans. Time-stamping minimizes scheduling errors. Correct spelling and legibility are major advantages of computerized systems. (See *Faxing medical orders,* page 298.)

Drawbacks

Many critics fear that computers will diminish the personal satisfaction that

Faxing medical orders

Question: *Is the process of faxing or document imaging technology a feasible venue for communicating medication orders from the nursing station to the pharmacy?*

Research: A system consisting of existing fax machines and document-imaging software that could capture images of written orders and send them from nursing stations to a central database server was evaluated. The pharmacists would receive the faxed order images and then enter the orders in an electronic medical record system. A 30-day trial of the order imaging system was successfully conducted at one of the larger institutions of a seven-hospital group. The new system was then implemented at the remaining six hospitals over a period of 60 days. The transition from a paper-order system to electronic communication via a standardized pharmacy document management application tailored to the specific needs of this health system was accomplished.

Conclusion: Medication order entry can be successfully accomplished using an imaging system and fax to communicate the original medical orders to the pharmacy where it can be entered into the electronic medication system. This standardized application eliminated the problems that had previously been associated with the hand delivery of paper orders, the use of the pneumatic tube system for order delivery, and the printing of traditional faxes.

Application: The use of imaging technology and fax transmission is useful to prevent medication order entry errors and improve patient safety through the reduction of medication errors.

Source: Simonian, A.I. "Medication order communication using fax and document-imaging technologies," *American Journal of Health-System Pharmacy* 65(6):570-73, March 15, 2008.

nurses derive from practicing their profession. They argue that technical advances tend to have a dehumanizing effect on the workplace. Relying on computers may mean less opportunity for interaction and communication with coworkers and patients. In addition, patients may be less truthful in providing medical histories and details about illnesses if they know that the information is going into a computer, which could be used to improperly divulge their medical information. HIPAA laws were established to protect the privacy of the patient record. (See Chapter 2 for more information; also see *Computerized order entry*.)

Some systems provide nurses with a selection of words and phrases from which they can quickly create a complete narrative note. Use of an incorrect descriptive prompt or phrase can give a misleading assessment. If the prompts aren't exactly descriptive, then it's important to type or write out the assessment.

Another disadvantage of a computerized medical record system is the need for backup records in case computers break down, making information unavailable. Ensuring completeness and continuity in charting requires a backup system. Poorly designed computer systems or human error can also scramble entries and spread flawed data. Obviously, the key to avoiding these problems is for all members of the health care team to know how to use the system.

Computerized order entry

Question: *Does computerized order entry prevent medication errors in hospitalized children?*

Research: It has always been assumed that computerized order entry system was a successful method of reducing medication errors in the pediatric population. Despite initial research, no comprehensive error surveillance studies had ever been conducted to evaluate the effect of the computerized medication order entry system and the reduction of medication errors in children.

This study used interrupted time-series regression analysis to review all of the orders, chart and incident reports on 40 hospital admission per month specifically to the neonatal intensive care units and the pediatric intensive care units. Inpatient pediatric wards were also evaluated. The areas were evaluated for 7 months before and 9 months after the implementation of a computerized physician order entry system.

Conclusion: In 627 pediatric admissions, with 12,672 medication orders written over 3,234

patient-days, 156 medication errors were detected, including 70 nonintercepted serious medication errors. Twenty-three errors resulted in patient injury. In time-series analysis, there was a 7% decrease in level of the rates of nonintercepted serious medication errors. There was no change in the rate of injuries as a result of error after computerized physician order entry implementation.

Application: The rate of nonintercepted serious medication errors in this pediatric population was reduced by 7% after the introduction of a computerized physician order entry system making it a valid tool to protect patients and reduce errors in the pediatric population.

Source: Walsh, K.E., et al. "Effect of computer order entry on prevention of serious medication errors in hospitalized children," *Pediatrics* 121(3):e421-27, March 2008.

Verification

Verification is one way of reducing errors in the computerized record. It serves the same purpose as signing off on the manual record of a physician's order. To use verification, the unit secretary enters the physician's order into the computer. The order is held in a "suspense file" until a nurse reviews the entry, verifies the order, and adds it to the active record file.

Legal implications

The legal implications of computerized medical records are ever-changing. (See *Computer charting: Minimizing your legal risks,* page 300.) Most computer records are legitimate substitutes for manual records. However, some state laws require written records as well.

The most pressing legal questions concern the threat to patient privacy and confidentiality. With traditional records, information is restricted simply by keeping the record on the unit; computer records can be called up at any terminal in the facility. The primary safeguard is the signature code, limiting access to the records. For example, a nurse's code would call up a patient's entire record, but a technician's code would produce only part.

Various laws protect the privacy of a patient's medical records. The Federal Privacy Act of 1974 protects the confidential medical information of patients in veterans' hospitals. The HIPAA of 2003 protects the privacy, confidentiality, and security of medical information.

Computer charting: Minimizing your legal risks

Your liability when working with computer documentation is exactly the same as when working with a manual system. You may be liable for any patient injuries associated with charting errors. The American Nurses Association, American Medical Record Association, and the Canadian Nurses Association have developed guidelines to ensure safe computerized charting. In maintaining safety, legal risks are minimized. Therefore, to minimize your legal risks:

- Receive detailed training on how to use the computerized documentation system.
- Always double-check all patient information.
- Keep your password or signature code private; never share or give your password or code to anyone, including other nurses on the unit and physicians.
- Inform your supervisor if you suspect that someone is using your password or code.
- Document your information and then log off; never leave the computer terminal unattended after you've logged on.
- Indicate whether the physician's order is written, verbal (in person), or verbal (by telephone), and when the entry is made.
- Follow the facility's policy and procedures if an error is made. If the information has already been saved and you note the error, indicate the entered information as erroneous by inserting "mistaken entry"; then add the correct information, date and initial the information. If the in-

formation was recorded in the wrong chart, use the same procedure but add "wrong chart" after noting the mistaken entry.
- Never leave patient information displayed on the computer screen where it could be seen by others. If printouts have been generated, keep these secure and out of the view of others.
- Be knowledgeable about the state's rules and regulations and facility's policies and procedures regarding privileged data, confidentiality, and disclosure. To learn about state rules and regulations, consult the facility's policy and procedure manual, check with the facility's attorney, or consult the state board of nursing or the state statutory and administrative codes.
- Know the requirements of the Health Insurance Portability and Accountability Act concerning privacy, confidentiality, and security of medical information.

(Under HIPAA, only those who have a need to know patient information for the care of the patient and those authorized by the patient to have access to his medical information can lawfully enter a patient's medical record.) Some state practice acts impose an ethical duty to guard patients' privacy. However, no one can fully guarantee that unauthorized persons won't gain access to computerized records.

Care also must be taken to safeguard patient information sent by fax machine. In particular, policies and procedures should be established to prevent confidential patient information such as a positive result on a human immunodeficien-

cy virus test from being transmitted by fax machine—especially one that's centrally located and easily seen by staff members or the general public. HIPAA requires that procedures be in place to reduce the exposure of patient information to anyone who doesn't have a need to know the patient's private information.

In addition, hospitals must show that their computer systems are trustworthy enough to be used in court. For example, they should use software that automatically records the date and time of each entry and each correction, as well as the name of the author or anyone who modifies a record. When an error is corrected, the software should preserve both the original and corrected versions and identify each author.

Computerized records in court

In 1977, a patient in New York charged that a computerized record system was an invasion of his privacy. In *Whalen v. Roe (429 U.S. 589, 97 S. Ct. 869 [1977]),* the patient challenged the constitutionality of a state law that required patients buying certain prescription drugs to list their name, address, age, the drug, dosage, and prescribing physician's name for a state database. The state then entered all the information into a computer. The Supreme Court upheld the law but acknowledged the threat to privacy implicit in the system. The Court reasoned that central storage and easy accessibility of computerized data vastly increase the potential for abuse of that information.

DOCUMENT WITNESSING AND SIGNING

A nurse may be asked to witness the signing of documents, such as deeds, bills of sale, powers of attorney, contracts, and wills. Nurses may also participate in witnessing oral statements made by patients and others that may have legal significance. The nurse's actions at these times can influence whether what she witnessed has the force of law, and they can also expose the nurse to legal consequences. Later, a nurse may be called to testify in court about the signing and the circumstances surrounding it.

Significance of the signature

When signing as a witness, a nurse is usually certifying only that she saw the person, known to the nurse by a certain name, place his signature on the document. The nurse isn't necessarily certifying the presence or absence of duress, undue influence, fraud, or error. Also, keep in mind that the nurse isn't validating that the patient has been told the significant risks, benefits, and options for treatment, which constitute informed consent. When a nurse witnesses consent forms in a nursing capacity, her signature merely attests to the signer's:
▶ authenticity
▶ voluntariness
▶ capacity.

If a nurse is called to testify about the signing, don't underestimate the importance of this testimony. A court looking into charges of fraud or undue influence used in executing a document will usually give great weight to a nurse's perception. The nurse may be asked about the patient's physical and mental condition at the time of the signing, and the court may ask the nurse to describe her interactions with the patient's family, his attorney, and others.

Legal implications

In the United States and Canada, nurse practice acts establish nurses' scope of professional and legal accountability. When a nurse witnesses a document, other laws also apply. For example, all states have laws setting out the legal requirements for written and oral wills, dying declarations, living wills, powers of attorney, and gifts in expectation of death.

State laws establish requirements for wills, including:
▶ format requirements
▶ the number of witnesses needed
▶ who can be a witness
▶ what makes a will valid or invalid

- how to make a will inoperative
- how to contest a will.

Usually, an individual must be age 18 or older and have two witnesses present to make a valid will. In about two-thirds of all states, the will may be handwritten—such a document is called a *holographic will.*

In many states, a nurse's signature on a will certifies that:

- she witnessed the will signing
- she heard the maker of the will declare it to be his will
- all witnesses and the maker of the will were actually present during the signing.

By attesting to the last two facts, the nurse helps to ensure the authenticity of the will and the signatures. The signature doesn't certify, however, that the maker of the will is competent.

Certain precautions are necessary if a patient asks a nurse to serve as a witness when drawing up a will:

- Always notify the patient's physician and nursing supervisor before acting as a witness.
- Don't give the patient any legal advice.
- Don't offer to assist him in phrasing the document's wording.
- Don't allow yourself to be named as a recipient in the will.
- Don't comment on the nature of his choices.
- Document all actions in the nurses' notes.

The laws also cover dying declarations and gifts in expectation of death, specifying when they're valid and when they aren't.

In the case of a living will, state law may prohibit a nurse from acting as a witness because of her role in executing the instructions in a living will.

Liability

A nurse can be held liable and in violation of the prevailing standard of care if the signature witnessed is false or if the nurse signs knowing the patient is incompetent or has given uninformed consent. Nurses can also be held liable if they knowingly allow a minor, nonguardian, or other ineligible person to sign a document.

If the nurse is the only person who informs a patient about a planned medical procedure and then the same nurse witnesses his signature, the nurse can be liable for practicing outside the nurse practice act, for practicing medicine without a license, or both. The facility may be liable for negligence under the doctrine of *respondeat superior.* If the nurse gives the patient false information in an attempt to deceive him, she may be guilty of fraud or misrepresentation.

Self-protection

Before signing any document, the nurse should always examine the document's title and first page and give careful attention to what's written immediately above the place for the signature. (The place for the witnessing signature should be clearly labeled.) She should read at least enough of the document to make sure it's the type of document the primary signer represents it to be. Usually, a nurse won't have to read all the text, and legally that isn't necessary for a signature to be valid as a witness only.

A legible signature with the full legal name is essential when signing a document. When signing as a witness on hospital forms, the nurse should add her title. On other documents, the title is optional, but adding it will establish why the nurse is in the facility.

When asked to sign as a witness, do so only if you believe the patient to be mentally and physically competent. Legally, the nurse doesn't need to have knowledge of exactly what's contained in the documents being witnessed. However, professionally the nurse should be aware of the content, just as she should be aware of the content when witnessing the patient's signature to an informed consent form.

There are instances when a nurse shouldn't witness a document. These include:

▶ when the patient can't legally give consent—for example, when he's a minor or a nonguardian

▶ when the patient isn't who he says he is, or the nurse can't be sure

▶ when the patient has no power of free choice—for example, when he's being blackmailed or otherwise pressured into signing

▶ when the patient is uninformed about what he's consenting to because he has been given misleading information, doesn't understand the information given, or hasn't been told of the risks involved. (Clarify with the physician why known risks haven't been disclosed.)

▶ when a patient is obviously incompetent—for example, when he's suffering from advanced dementia and is being pressured to sign a deed transferring a real estate title to someone else or if he's on medication

▶ when the nurse feels uncomfortable about signing.

Keep in mind that nurses have no legal obligation to witness a will or other document. In such situations, simply explain the choice of not acting as a witness. Then record the incident in the nurses' notes, using a chronological format.

Chart the setting, the patient's mental and physical condition, the reason for the refusal, what you saw and heard, and what happened after your refusal (for instance, that someone else witnessed or someone else gave consent).

Finally, report the incident to other concerned staff members—for example, the nursing supervisor and the patient's physician.

Documentation

When documenting that a nurse has witnessed a patient's signature on a document, always include something about apparent perceptions of the patient's health and general circumstances.

When witnessing a written will, document that it was signed and witnessed, who signed it, who else was present, what was done with it after signing, and the patient's condition at the time.

When witnessing oral statements, such as dying declarations and oral wills, document the names of other witnesses, the patient's physical and mental condition at the time, and the patient's reaction to the statements afterward. Make notations carefully: remember, they could be used in court for probating the will, for resolving creditors' claims, or for prosecuting alleged criminals. The notes will also refresh the nurse's memory if she's called to testify in court.

Canadian procedures

Formalities of signing and witnessing documents in the United States and Canada may differ. Both countries, however, have legal systems based primarily on English common law, and both have essentially the same rules governing how a witness should sign legal documents.

REFERENCES

1. Taylor, C., et al. *Fundamentals of Nursing,* 5th ed. Philadelphia: Lippincott Williams & Wilkins, p. 346, 2005.
2. Ferrel, K.G. "Documentation, Part 2: The Best Evidence of Care. Complete and Accurate Charting can be Crucial to Exonerating Nurses in Civil Lawsuits," *AJN* 107(7):61-64, July 2007.
3. American Nurses Association (2005). "Principles for documentation" [Online]. Available at *http://www.nursingworld. org/staffing/lawsuit/principlesdocumen tation.pdf.*
4. Monarch, K. "Documentation, Part 1: Principles for Self-Protection. Preserve the Medical Record—and Defend Yourself," *AJN* 107(7):58-60, July 2007.
5. Ferrel, K.G., 2007.
6. The Joint Commission. "Official 'Do Not Use' List" [Online]. Available at *http://www.jointcommission.org/NR/ rdonlyres/2329F8F5-6EC5-4E21-B932- 54B2B7D53F00/0/06_dnu_list.pdf.*
7. The Joint Commission. 'Do Not Use' List. Facts about the Official 'Do Not Use' List" [Online]. Available at *http://www.jointcommission.org/Patient Safety/DoNotUseList/fact_dnu.htm.*
8. Austin, S. "Ladies & Gentlemen of the Jury, I Present...the Nursing Documentation," *Nursing* 36(1):56-62, January 2006.
9. Ferrel, K.G., 2007.
10. Austin, S., 2006.
11. Austin, S., 2006.
12. Austin, S., 2006.
13. Brooke, P.S. "So You've Been Named in a Lawsuit? What Happens Next?" *Nursing* 36(7):44-48, July 2006.
14. Austin, S., 2006.

ADDITIONAL RESOURCES

Ashley, R.C. "Weighing the Evidence in your Favor," *Critical Care Nurse* 25(1):60-61, February 2005.

Clayton, M.F. "Communication: An Important Part of Nursing Care," *AJN* 106(11):70-71, November 2006.

Iyer, P.W., and Camp, N.H. *Nursing Documentation: A Nursing Process Approach,* 4th ed. Flemington, N.J.: Med League Support Services, 2005.

PART II

Ethics and nursing practice

8

Ethics versus the law

Every day, nurses make ethical decisions in their nursing practice. These decisions may involve patient care, actions related to coworkers, or nurse-physician relations. At times nurses may find themselves trapped in the middle of an ethical dilemma, pulled in every direction by their duties and responsibilities to the patient, to the employer, and to themselves. Even after making the decision, the nurse may ask, "Did I do the right thing?"

There are no automatic guidelines for solving all ethical conflicts. Although such conflicts may be painful and confusing, particularly in nursing, a nurse need not be a philosopher to act ethically or to make decisions that fall within nursing's ethical codes. Nonetheless, nurses need to understand the principles of ethics that guide nursing practice. Legally, nurses are responsible for using their knowledge and skills to protect the comfort and safety of their patients. Ethically, nurses are responsible, as patient advocates, for safeguarding their patients' rights.

Although a nurse isn't legally responsible, for example, for obtaining a patient's informed consent, she's ethically responsible, as the patient's advocate, for reporting to the physician a patient's mis-

understandings about treatment or withdrawal of consent. To be an effective advocate, a nurse must understand the ethical and legal principles of informed consent and that the patient's consent isn't valid unless he understands his condition, the proposed treatment, treatment alternatives, potential risks and benefits, and relative chances of success or failure.

OVERVIEW OF ETHICS

Ethics is the area of philosophic study that examines values, actions, and choices to determine right and wrong. It's defined as a system of valued behaviors and beliefs that govern conduct appropriate for all members of a group to ensure the rights of an individual. Ethics involves reasoning, analysis, questions, and judgments that help to differentiate right from wrong or how things ought to be.

Ethics versus the law

Laws are binding rules of conduct enforced by authority. In many situations, laws and ethics overlap. When they diverge, you have to identify and examine the fine lines that separate them.

When a law is challenged as unjust or unfair, the challenge usually reflects some underlying ethical principle. That's because, ideally, laws are based on what's right and good. Realistically, however, the relationship between law and ethics is complex. Most nurses realize that most malpractice suits result from patients' dissatisfaction with care they received. When patients believe they haven't been treated with respect and dignity or that their needs and rights have been ignored or violated, they're more likely to initiate legal action. Patients must suffer harm to challenge care legally. Many ethical dilemmas become the subject of laws when health care providers need guidance dealing with difficult decisions that must be made. Once a law states how care must be provided, the nurse and the patient lose the ability to deal with the situation on an individual basis. There's a strong connection between ethics and law regarding the nurse's role as patient advocate. (See *Nursing ethics and the law*.)

Values and ethics

Values are strongly held personal and professional beliefs about worth and importance. (The word *value* comes from the Latin *valere*—to be strong.) They give meaning to one's life and provide a framework for an individual's decisions and actions. Values are key to developing ethical consciousness. They're highly individualized but subject to outside influences.

The remarks that follow are examples of value statements:
▶ "Nursing is a meaningful profession."
▶ "Nurses make a difference to their patients by comforting, caring, and teaching."

▶ "Nurses should be paid more for what they do."
▶ "The nursing profession must change radically to survive in today's health care system."
▶ "HMOs put too much pressure on professional health care employees."
▶ "Physicians, not hospital administrators, should make important health care decisions."
▶ "A new emphasis on preventive medicine will make nursing a more valuable and respected profession."

Not all nurses would agree with every one of these value statements. Value conflicts arise when events or situations arise that could force one to act against one's beliefs. Value conflicts are common among nurses, physicians, patients, families, and health care facility administrators. Resolution of value conflicts requires awareness of one's values and the values of others along with values clarification. Clarifying personal values is an important part of developing a professional ethic.

Values awareness

People may become more aware of their personal values by consciously examining their statements and behavior. (See *Developing value awareness*, pages 310 and 311.)

In addition to personal values, there are professional values that are the foundation for practice and that guide interactions with patients, colleagues, other professionals, and the public. The American Association of Colleges of Nursing have identified five values that exemplify professional nurses. These are:
▶ altruism (concern for the welfare and well-being of others, such as patients, staff, or others)

Nursing ethics and the law

When you make decisions, your choices and actions ideally should fulfill three criteria:
- They should be the best practice clinically.
- They should be within the scope of policies, procedures, and practice acts legally.
- They should be the right things to do morally.

Sometimes ethics, law, and best practices don't agree. Certain actions may be considered by some people to be morally or legally ambiguous. Each type of situation shown below can present potential moral dilemmas for nurses.

NURSING CHOICES, DECISIONS, AND ACTIONS

	Ethical	*Unethical*
Legal	Type 1: Actions of this type are the ideal—they're ethical and legal, although not always without complications and inconveniences. *Example:* While prepping and medicating a patient for surgery, a nurse realizes that the patient doesn't want the operation but has given consent only because her husband insisted. Because this isn't a valid consent, the nurse contacts the patient's physician, even though this action will alter surgical schedules and planned outcomes.	Type 2: Actions of this type might be considered unethical but are, nevertheless, legal. *Example:* A nurse caring for a 12-year-old boy with cancer learns that he has accepted the fact that he's dying and wants to stop chemotherapy. His parents have consented to try a new, aggressive course of chemotherapy. The nurse goes ahead and gives the chemotherapy as ordered by the physician.
Illegal	Type 3: Actions of this type might be considered ethical by some but are, nevertheless, illegal. *Example:* A nurse is caring for an elderly patient with dementia and cancer. The patient's husband asks for information about "terminal sedation"—what type and how much medication could be used to bring about a peaceful death. The nurse gives him this information and arranges for the patient to be discharged home in her husband's care.	Type 4: Actions of this type are neither legal nor ethical. *Example:* A physician informs a nurse that he routinely prescribes antidepressants for every new resident admitted to a nursing home. If residents ask about the medication, he instructs the nurse to say, "This is just a pill your physician ordered," because telling them more might upset them. The nurse follows the physician's orders because he's politically powerful and she doesn't want to cross him. A physician asks a nurse to witness the making of a new will for a patient in which the physician is identified as the main beneficiary of the patient's belongings. The physician tells the nurse that he'll share the proceeds of the patient's will with her for this support.

▶ autonomy (respect for the patient's right to make decisions)
▶ human dignity (respect for all others as unique and worthy individuals)
▶ integrity (actions that reflect the accepted standards of practice and ethical codes)

▶ social justice (actions to assure equal treatment and access to care under the law).[1]

Nurses must develop self-awareness to avoid unconsciously imposing their own personal values into patient decisions, especially when the patient's values differ

Developing value awareness

Nurses, like all people, sometimes tend to rely on hearsay, opinions, or prejudice, instead of developing a strong sense of their own values. Only infrequently do they stop to reflect on the values that are mirrored in their conversation and behavior.

Consider the following dialogue, in which three nurses express various value judgments. As you read, ask yourself, "What values does each nurse express? Do the values of the three conflict? Are individual nurses expressing consistent values? Do they show a high regard for patient autonomy?"

SHOP TALK

Kate: I can't believe it. I have to float to the ICU—and it's only my second week on the job. I hate floating, especially to intensive care.

Dean: So do I. The last time I floated to ICU, I was assigned to a 300-lb patient who had been driving drunk and wasn't wearing a seat belt. The guy was badly hurt, and I had to do all the positioning myself because the unit was so short-staffed. I just about killed my back. It isn't fair that they always assign male nurses to obese patients.

Pat: Floating is really a tough issue. I try to see it from the patient's side, though. I mean, maybe you were assigned to care for this patient because you're a good nurse and could give him the best care.

Kate: What bugs me is having to care for patients such as that drunk driver, who obviously don't care how they live. They don't watch their weight, they drive drunk, they don't use seat belts—and we get pulled from the work we're comfortable with to care for them. I can't even find time for a cigarette break.

Pat: Don't forget, Kate, we're supposed to take care of patients, regardless of their health habits or lifestyle. No one's perfect, after all.

Kate: Yeah, I guess you're right, but floating makes me nervous anyway. I'm scared I'll really mess up because everything's so unfamiliar.

Dean: Let me give you some advice. No matter what you think about floating, don't say anything. If you're pegged as a complainer around here, your career is over.

Pat: You sound like you think nurses shouldn't ever speak out if something is wrong with the system. I think nurses do have the power to change things for the better, but that won't happen if we aren't willing to take some risks.

Dean: You're an idealist. I'm a realist. I ask, what's worth risking your job?

Pat: I think being a nurse means not being willing to compromise your standards of care just to keep a job.

Kate: What happened to the 300-lb patient? Is he still in ICU? Do you think I might get assigned to him?

Dean: Well, no. It's the craziest thing. He was a quadriplegic after the accident. So we put all this time and effort into stabilizing his condition and

from what the nurse believes the patient should decide.

Values clarification

Each nurse and patient brings values to the health care system. These values include beliefs about such concepts as life, death, a higher power, and who should and shouldn't receive health care, as well as other complex issues such as organ transplantation and the right to die. The patient's values may change when he's faced with illness, injury, and possible death. So, too, may the nurse's values change.

Values clarification refers to the process of raising unconscious values to the consciousness so that value conflicts can be resolved. Nurses are likely to encounter many conflicting sets of values in the course of their professional careers. To provide optimal support to the patient, nurses must undergo a personal values clarification process.

keeping him infection-free, and one day he decides it isn't worth it, so the physician just turned everything off. Now I ask you, is that right?

EXAMINING VALUES

The nurses in this scenario make various moral judgments. By analyzing their attitudes, you can come to a better understanding of your own values.

• Kate criticizes the health habits of an obese trauma patient but insists on her own right to have time for a cigarette break. What values are guiding her opinions? Do you think her outlook is consistent?

• Dean thinks that Kate should take an assignment for which she isn't prepared rather than risk losing favor with the administration. Do you think this attitude is irresponsible or merely realistic?

• Pat is accused of being an idealist. Is that a fair judgment?

• What values are mirrored in each nurse's attitude about floating?

• At the end of the conversation, Dean mentions that the physician decided to withdraw treatment from the quadriplegic patient. If the three nurses were to discuss the ethical questions raised by the physician's decision, how do you think each nurse would respond?

• Would these three nurses have similar or conflicting views about what it means to be a patient advocate?

Exercises such as analyzing conversations between coworkers offer one way to clarify values. Reflecting on one's own statements and actions is another way.

Nurses need to choose among competing values to establish their own values. Then they need to incorporate these chosen values into everyday thoughts and actions. Doing so allows them to be better prepared to act on chosen values when confronted with difficult choices.

Making values decisions need not be haphazard. By clarifying personal values and checking to see if they're consistent with the established standards of the nursing profession, nurses can enhance their ability to make responsible judgments.

Morals and ethics

Morals is a term commonly used interchangeably with ethics. However, a slight distinction should be made. Morals are the standards of right and wrong that one learns through socialization. They determine what's good or bad, right or wrong in a situation and are commonplace, such that most individuals are in agreement with them. Morals usually are based on customs, traditions, culture, and religious beliefs. Morals are typically highly personal.

ETHICAL PRINCIPLES

Several principles are at the heart of ethics for nurses. These principles provide a basis for action and decision making in a nurse-patient relationship.

Autonomy

Autonomy refers to the right to make decisions about one's life. It's the personal choice or control that an individual has as he goes through life. In nursing, autonomy typically involves the person's right to make decisions about his health care.

Key components of autonomy include:

▶ an intention to choose actions
▶ understanding of the choices
▶ action without interference or control.

A person who's autonomous acts intentionally or unintentionally and his actions are clear and deliberate.[2] However, the person's understanding of the choices and action without interference or control may not be realistic. For autonomy, "the person doesn't have to be fully understanding nor fully independent and free from controlling influences."[3]

The principle of autonomy is demonstrated by the use of informed consent. The patient receives information about the condition, treatment, or plan. He then demonstrates an understanding of this information, ultimately arriving at a decision to accept or reject the plan. Nurses as well as other health care providers must respect the patient's decision, even if they don't agree with the decision.

Consider this example. A patient receives a placebo but is led to believe that the placebo is aimed at relieving his symptoms. Such an action is deception and can outweigh the good that might be derived from the effect of the placebo.[4] Additionally, trust in the caregiver can be destroyed if the deception is discovered. Deception involves failure to respect a patient's right to make an informed decision[5] and thus undermines the principle of autonomy.

Certain situations may limit autonomy. Two examples include: when the rights of one person interfere with the rights of another and when there's a high probability that a person may injure himself or others.

Justice

Justice refers to fairness or the obligation to be fair to all people. It's reflected by equal and fair treatment of others regardless of race, sex, marital status, economic level, religion, diagnosis, or sexual orientation. All patients are to be treated equally. However, justice doesn't imply that all patients are treated the same or identically.[6] Health care providers apply the principle of justice when care is given based on the person's needs.

Beneficence

Beneficence refers to the obligation to do good and not harm. It involves five rules:

1. Protecting and defending the rights of others.

2. Preventing harm from occurring to others.

3. Removing conditions that will cause harm to others.

4. Helping persons with disabilities.

5. Rescuing persons in danger.[7, 8]

Typically, health care providers apply the principle of beneficence by providing care to achieve optimal outcomes. Sometimes, however, health care providers must balance the "good," or benefits against the "harm," or risks. For example, a temporary harm to a patient, such as debridement of scar tissue that results in pain and discomfort, ultimately restores the patient's health and functioning

Nonmaleficence

Along the same lines as beneficence, nonmaleficence refers to the obligation to inflict no harm on others. This "do no harm" obligation involves both intentional and unintentional harm. It encompasses protecting individuals who can't protect themselves from harm. Health care providers apply the principle of nonmaleficence with actions to promote a patient's safety. For example, a nurse might report a coworker who's abusing drugs to the supervisor, who then suspends the coworker's employment. The

Ethical principles in conflict

Nurses commonly identify ethical principles, such as beneficence, nonmaleficence, autonomy, justice, and fidelity, and strive to honor them in making ethical decisions and choosing courses of action. This way of making ethical decisions, called *principlism*, deductively uses general ethical principles to logically determine the best resolution of an issue. It's effective only as long as ethical principles aren't in conflict. In the reality of a nurse's daily responsibilities, ethical principles can—and commonly do—conflict with each other.

ETHICAL PRINCIPLES	ETHICAL ISSUE
The principle of beneficence	A 45-year-old patient is brought by ambulance to the emergency department. He's anxious, pale, and diaphoretic, and complaining of severe substernal pain. An assessment, electrocardiogram, and other initial tests are inconclusive to rule out a myocardial infarction. The patient receives medication for pain and is admitted to the cardiac care unit for further observation. After 30 minutes, the patient tells the nurse that he's pain-free.
The principle of autonomy	This patient insists that because he's now feeling fine again, he's leaving the hospital because he absolutely has to be at an important business meeting. He says that he has already called a taxi.
Beneficence and autonomy conflict	The nurse tells the physician, who orders her to convince the patient to stay in the hospital for his safety and well-being. How should the nurse interpret and carry out the physician's order while respecting her patient's autonomy? Does "convince" mean "coerce"? Even if the patient is willing to leave against medical advice, is letting him go the right thing to do?

nurse safeguards the patients from potential harm that might result from a coworker's care while under the influence of the drug.

Fidelity

Fidelity refers to an individual's faithfulness or loyalty to agreements and responsibilities that he has accepted. It's one of the key elements of accountability. Nurses demonstrate the principle of fidelity by providing safe, up-to-date, current care that's appropriate to the patient's needs. In addition, nurses demonstrate fidelity by maintaining competence in nursing practice.

Fidelity involves *confidentiality*—respecting privileged information; a pa-

tient's right to privacy must be balanced against society's right to be informed of potential threats to public health.

Fidelity also involves a commitment to *veracity*—telling the truth; fully informing a patient of his medical condition. Truth is vital to the nurse-patient relationship. Honest, open, therapeutic communication is essential so that the patient receives accurate, nonjudgmental information in terms that he can understand to ensure his right to self-determination. Unfortunately this principle isn't absolute. Various factors such as culture, or situations in which truth telling may harm the patient, can cause deviation from this principle. (See *Ethical principles in conflict*.)

ETHICAL THEORIES

Ethical theories attempt to provide a system of principles and rules for resolving questions about ethics. Ethical theories consist of fundamental beliefs about what's morally right or wrong, and propose reasons for maintaining those beliefs. These theories provide the basis for professional codes of ethics. A code of ethics is a group of fundamental beliefs about what's morally right or wrong, along with reasons for maintaining these beliefs. The American Nurses Association has established a code of ethics to guide the practicing nurse in using professional skills to provide the most effective holistic care possible, such as serving as a patient advocate and striving to protect the health, safety, and rights of each patient.[9] Other organizations have also developed codes of ethics.[10,11] (See *Ethical codes for nurses*.)

Two major ethical theories commonly used by health care providers, including nurses, are teleology and deontology. Another ethical theory, moral relativism, also is described.

Teleology

Teleologic ethical theories determine what's right or wrong based on an action's consequences. Teleology is sometimes called *situation ethics* or *calculus morality*. One such teleologic theory, called *utilitarian ethics* or *utilitarianism*, requires decision makers to determine and choose those actions that will result in maximized good—that is, the greatest good for the greatest number of people. It judges acts based on their usefulness. Useful acts bring about good and useless acts bring about harm.

Key elements

According to teleology, good is defined as happiness or pleasure; right is defined as the greatest amount of good and the least amount of harm for the greatest number of people. Teleology has no strict principles, moral codes, duties, or rules to determine conduct in particular situations.

A basic assumption of teleology is that good and harm can be quantified, as in a mathematical formula, so that one can evaluate the degree of good and harm in a specific case. In teleologic theories, ethical decisions are usually made through a process called *risk-benefit analysis*. For example, you may help patients and their families evaluate several courses of treatment to decide which one will produce the greatest amount of relief (benefit) with the least danger of suffering (risk). Applying teleology, the decision maker judges actions in terms of their consequences for the general welfare if all people acted in a similar manner in the same situation.

Limitations

The fact that teleologic theory assumes that good and harm can be quantified and evaluated can make it a less than ideal approach to resolving health care issues. Determining the "greatest good" is highly subjective and can result in inconsistent decisions. Some contend that teleology advocates the maximum good or happiness of a few rather than the average good or happiness of all. Teleology tends to ignore the individual's rights and needs. Moreover, quantifying the relative good and harm of actions, especially in health care, is usually difficult, if not impossible.

Ethical codes for nurses

Two of the most important ethical codes for registered nurses are the American Nurses Association (ANA) code and the Canadian Nurses Association (CNA) code. Licensed practical nurses (LPNs) also have an ethical code. The International Council of Nurses (ICN), an organization based in Geneva, Switzerland that seeks to improve the standards and status of nursing worldwide, has also published a code of ethics.

ANA CODE OF ETHICS

The ANA views nurses and patients as individuals who possess basic rights and responsibilities and whose values and circumstances should command respect at all times. The ANA code provides guidance for carrying out nursing responsibilities consistent with the ethical obligations of the profession.

According to ANA code, the nurse:
• provides services with respect for human dignity and the uniqueness of the patient, unrestricted by considerations of social or economic status, personal attributes, or the nature of health problems
• safeguards the patient's right to privacy by judiciously protecting information of a confidential nature
• acts to safeguard the patient and the public when health and safety are affected by incompetent, unethical, or illegal practice of any person
• assumes responsibility and accountability for individual nursing judgments and actions
• maintains competence in nursing
• exercises informed judgment and uses individual competence and qualifications as criteria in seeking consultation, accepting responsibilities, and delegating nursing activities to others
• participates in activities that contribute to the ongoing development of the profession's body of knowledge
• participates in the profession's efforts to implement and improve standards of nursing
• participates in the profession's efforts to establish and maintain conditions of employment conducive to high-quality nursing care
• collaborates with members of the health professions and other citizens in promoting community and national efforts to meet the health needs of the public.

CNA CODE OF ETHICS

The CNA code consists of eight primary values that form the basis of nursing obligations:

Safe, competent, and ethical care
Nurses value the ability to provide safe, competent, and ethical care that allows them to fulfill their ethical and professional obligations to the people they serve.

Health and well-being
Nurses value health promotion and well-being and assisting persons to achieve their optimum level of health in situations of normal health, illness, injury, or disability, or at the end of life.

Choice
Nurses respect and promote the autonomy of persons and help them to express their health needs and values and to obtain desired information and services so they can make informed decisions.

Dignity
Nurses recognize and respect the inherent worth of each person and advocate the respectful treatment of all persons.

Confidentiality
Nurses safeguard information learned in the context of a professional relationship and ensure that it's shared outside the health care team only with the person's informed consent, as may be legally required, or where the failure to disclose would cause significant harm.

Justice
Nurses uphold principles of equity and fairness to assist persons in receiving a share of health services and resources proportionate to their needs and in promoting social justice.

(continued)

Ethical codes for nurses *(continued)*

Accountability
Nurses are answerable for their practice, and they act in a manner consistent with their professional responsibilities and standards of practice.

Quality practice environments
Nurses value and advocate for practice environments that have the organizational structures and resources to ensure safety, support, and respect for all persons in the work setting.

CODE FOR LPNS
The code for LPNs seeks to provide a motivation for establishing, maintaining, and elevating professional standards. This code requires these nurses to:
- regard conservation of life and disease prevention as a basic obligation
- promote and protect the physical, mental, emotional, and spiritual well-being of the patient and his family
- fulfill all duties faithfully and efficiently
- function within established legal guidelines
- take personal responsibility for actions and seek to earn the respect and confidence of all members of the health care team
- keep confidential all information about the patient obtained from any source
- give conscientious service and charge reasonable fees
- learn about and respect the religious and cultural beliefs of all patients
- meet obligations to patients by staying abreast of health care trends through reading and continuing education
- uphold the laws of the land and promote legislation to meet the health needs of its people.

ICN CODE OF ETHICS
According to the ICN, the fundamental responsibility of the nurse is fourfold: to promote health, to prevent illness, to restore health, and to alleviate suffering.

    The ICN further states that the need for nursing is universal. Inherent in nursing is respect for life, dignity, and the rights of man. It's unrestricted by considerations of nationality, race, color, age, gender, politics, or social status.

Nurses and people
- The nurse's primary responsibility is to people who require nursing care.
- The nurse, in providing care, respects the beliefs, values, and customs of the individual.
- The nurse holds in confidence personal information and uses judgment in sharing this information.

Nurses and practice
- The nurse carries personal responsibility for nursing practice and for maintaining competence by continual learning.
- The nurse maintains the highest standards of nursing possible within the reality of a specific situation.
- The nurse uses good judgment in relation to individual competence when accepting and delegating responsibilities.
- The nurse, when acting in a professional capacity, should at all times maintain standards of personal conduct that would reflect credit upon the profession.

Nurses and society
- The nurse shares with other citizens the responsibility for initiating and supporting actions to meet the health and social needs of the public.

Nurses and coworkers
- The nurse sustains a cooperative relationship with coworkers in nursing and other fields.
- The nurse takes appropriate actions to safeguard the patient when his care is endangered by a coworker or another person.

Nurses and the profession
- The nurse plays a major role in determining and implementing desirable standards of nursing practice and nursing education.
- The nurse is active in developing a core of professional knowledge.
- The nurse, acting through the professional organization, participates in establishing and maintaining equitable social and economic working conditions in nursing.

Use of utility as the guiding concept to determine whether an action is right or wrong usually leads to many conflicts going unresolved. In addition, questions arise about which is better, that is, to produce the greatest amount of good or the least amount of harm for all.

Deontology

Deontologic ethical theories emphasize moral obligation or commitment. Deontology is a theory of ethical decision making based on the discovery and confirmation of a set of morals or rules that govern the resolution of ethical dilemmas. Deontology attempts to determine what's right or wrong based on one's duty or obligation to act rather than on the action's consequences.

Deontologic theories give most weight to obeying moral laws, such as "Always tell the truth" and "Never harm a patient." According to deontologic theories, honoring ethical obligations ensures the greatest good, even though actions may be difficult and consequences painful. Due to the theory's emphasis on duty or obligation to another, it's commonly the only accepted theory for ethical decision making in health care.

Key elements

Deontology is based on unchanging and absolute principles that are derived from universal values at the heart of all major religions. Its basic principle is to ensure the survival of the species by fulfilling one's duty or obligation to another. Any act in agreement with one's duty or obligation is right and any act not in agreement is wrong.

Limitations

Because deontology centers on duty or obligation to others, many experts consider it the only acceptable theory for ethical decision making in health care. Nevertheless, deontology is inflexible and complications can arise when duties conflict with one another and you have to decide which duty takes precedence.

For example, suppose someone proposes keeping a brain-dead patient on a ventilator while recipients for a kidney transplant are found. Several staff members object because the patient had expressed a wish to die naturally, without artificial support.

On the one hand, you may favor maintaining the patient on a ventilator because you recognize how useful his kidneys will be to others. On the other hand, if you resolve this dilemma by deciding which course of action best supports the patient's rights, you would probably give more weight to his right of self-determination. This would lead you to oppose maintaining the patient on a ventilator. So, as you can see from this example, duties can conflict, and you'll have to determine which duty takes precedence.

Moral relativism

The question arises: Are certain values intrinsically best, or are values always a matter of personal interpretation? A theory of ethics known as *moral relativism* holds that there are no ethical absolutes, that whatever a person believes is right is right for him or her at that moment.

Consider what would happen if everyone practiced moral relativism.
▶ There would be no objective way to resolve moral dilemmas.

▶ A person could never question or disapprove of another's moral judgment.
▶ Professional standards, such as nursing standards, would become meaningless.
▶ Law and order in society would disappear.
▶ People and cultures would be unable to grow morally.

Although different people and cultures have different values, moral relativism doesn't provide an adequate basis for ethical decision making. Because nurses will probably face numerous moral conflicts in the course of their careers, they need to develop consistent ethical standards to guide behavior.

Other ethical theories
Numerous ethical theories exist that may not be relevant to health care but can be of help in ethical decision making. Like teleology and deontology, these alternative theories also have limitations. (See *Alternative ethical theories*.)

Ethical decision making
Nurses usually combine aspects of both teleologic and deontologic theories when making ethical decisions. To avoid becoming confused, develop orderly, systematic, objective decision-making methods. Otherwise, decision making becomes subjective and arbitrary, and results in moral relativism.

Equally important is the process of self-reflection. This involves uncovering, sharing, and discussing:
▶ personal and professional values relevant to the situation (values clarification)
▶ cultural considerations (ethnic groups may have different perceptions as to what constitutes acceptable treatment; however, this must be balanced with notions of moral relativism)

▶ prejudices or biases that affect objectivity
▶ previous experiences with similar situations and decisions
▶ limitations that affect skills or understanding
▶ motives and intentions, particularly those of self-interest and convenience.

Ethical and moral dilemmas
A nurse who must decide whether to follow a physician's orders to give an unusually high dose of an opioid faces a *moral dilemma*—an ethical problem caused by a conflict of rights, responsibilities, and values.

Such a dilemma carries with it a great deal of stress. As a nurse grapples with the situation, trying to decide what to do, she'll probably experience internal psychological and emotional stress, such as fear or guilt. The nurse may also experience stress caused by external factors that are political or interpersonal—for example, the nurse may be nervous about confronting the physician with her doubts because she fears his anger.

Ethical and moral dilemmas call for ethical choices in the face of profound uncertainty. At times, the nurse may not know what the right or ethical course of action should be. At other times, she may believe completely that a particular action is morally right and yet, for various reasons, find it difficult to act.

An ethical or moral dilemma may be further complicated by psychological pressures and personal emotions, especially when a choice is a forced one at best and, in many cases, results in an uncomfortable compromise. Many dilemmas in nursing involve choices about justice or fairness, when scant resources (such as bed space or limited staffing)

Alternative ethical theories

In addition to deontology and teleology, other ethical theories may guide decision making, but each has its limitations.

EGOISM

Egoism considers self-interest and self-preservation as the only proper goals of all human actions, insisting that the only right decision is the one that maximizes the autonomy of the decision maker.

Limitations
- Egoism ignores moral principles or rules outside the individual's point of view.
- Inconsistencies arise from one decision to the next, even in similar situations.
- Social chaos can result when individuals act solely in their own interests.
- Because it ignores the rights of others, egoism is unacceptable for most ethical decisions in health care.

OBLIGATIONISM

Obligationism attempts to resolve ethical dilemmas by balancing distributive justice (dividing equally among all) with beneficence (doing good and not harm). This theory holds that benefits and burdens should be distributed equally, according to merits and needs.

Limitations
- The two basic principles of obligationism—justice and beneficence—may conflict in certain situations.
- The theory can be useful in determining public policy, but it's impractical for decisions that affect one person.

SOCIAL CONTRACT THEORY

Social contract theory is based on the concept of original position. The least advantaged people (such as children and the disabled) are considered the norm. Whether an act is right or wrong is determined from the norm's point of view.

Limitations
- Without specific guidelines, the theory is useless in day-to-day health care decisions.
- Social inequalities are persistent.

THEOLOGICAL ETHICS

Ethical theories and moral-legal principles can be based in religious traditions—for example, Good Samaritan acts are based on the biblical concept of altruism and selflessness.

Limitations
- It may be difficult for someone who doesn't share a particular religious faith to understand its beliefs or to apply its teachings to health care situations.

VIRTUE ETHICS

Virtue ethics encourages and focuses on character traits, such as trustworthiness, loyalty, helpfulness, friendliness, kindness, bravery, generosity, cleanliness, reverence, and the like.

Limitations
- Virtue ethics tends to neglect conduct and outcome. It also doesn't provide a formula for resolving conflict cases.

must be divided among patients with equal needs. In other cases, a choice must be made quickly because the patient's condition is fluctuating or rapidly deteriorating. Typically, nurses who are compelled to make ethical decisions don't have the luxury of time.

Factors contributing to ethical dilemmas

Ethical dilemmas can result from various situations. Numerous factors have contributed to the development of ethical dilemmas which in turn necessitate the need for ethical decision making in health care. These factors include socio-cultural changes, scientific and techno-logical advances, legal issues, changes in occupational status of health care work-ers, and consumer involvement in care. (See *Factors influencing ethical decision making*.)

Types of dilemmas

Ethical dilemmas can arise from various situations. Many involve issues of tech-nological advances affecting options re-lated to treatment, financial constraints that may limit access to care, and cultur-al differences due to the increasing diver-sity of patient populations. Common themes involve informed consent, confi-dentiality, effective communication, futil-ity, death with dignity, and patient safety.

Most dilemmas in nursing can be iden-tified according to the ethical principle involved using these classifications:
▶ Dilemmas of beneficence—dilemmas that involve deciding what's good as op-posed to what's harmful. Dilemmas com-monly occur when health care providers, patients, or family members disagree about what course of action is "in the patient's best interest."
▶ Dilemmas of nonmaleficence—dilem-mas that involve the avoidance of harm. These issues typically involve a nurse's responsibility to "blow the whistle" if he sees others compromising the patient's safety.
▶ Dilemmas of autonomy—dilemmas that involve deciding what course of ac-tion maximizes the patient's right of self-determination. The patient's decision should be honored even if it contradicts what the staff or family of the patient be-lieve. Autonomy issues are usually closely

related to beneficence issues, especially when individuals other than the patient must determine (or attempt to determine) what's best for the patient. (See *Ethical dilemmas in telephone nursing*, page 322.)
▶ Dilemmas of justice—ethical issues of fairness and equality, such as dilemmas that involve dividing limited health care resources fairly.
▶ Dilemmas of fidelity—those that in-volve honoring promises. These may in-clude the extent and limits of a nurse's role and duties to a patient that might conflict with other duties, such as duties to the physician.

Types of decisions

When dealing with an ethical or moral dilemma, the types of decisions facing nurses usually can be grouped into four categories:
▶ Active decisions—ethical decisions and moral judgments that lead directly to ac-tions and bring about change
▶ Passive decisions—decisions that deny, delay, or avoid action and maintain the status quo by denying or shifting respon-sibility to avoid change
▶ Programmed decisions—decisions that use precedents, established guidelines, procedures, and rules to resolve antici-pated, routine, and expected types of moral dilemmas
▶ Nonprogrammed decisions—decisions that require a unique response to com-plex and unexpected moral dilemmas.

Most commonly, a nurse's pro-grammed decisions are also active ones. For example, when a physician tells a pa-tient what to expect in surgery and then asks the patient to sign a consent form,

Factors influencing ethical decision making

Decisions about ethical dilemmas are influenced by numerous and wide-ranging factors. As the world changes, new ethical dilemmas will arise and older ones may take on new significance. Some of the factors affecting decision making are highlighted below.

FACTOR	EXAMPLES
Sociocultural factors	• Changes in attitudes about women and women's roles • Beliefs and practices related to marriage and the family • Family structure changes • Increased emphasis on individual rights • Religious values • Values that society places on life and the right to die with dignity • Demographic changes (increase in poverty and number of older adults) • Increasing cultural diversity • Government funding for health care (changes in reimbursement practices, emphasis on cost containment)
Scientific and technological factors	• Intensive care units (including neonatal intensive care units) and specialized care units • Sophisticated patient monitoring and treatment devices • Life-sustaining medications • Artificial life-support systems and devices • Organ transplantation, donors, and artificial organs; stem cell research • Computerized diagnostic equipment and treatment devices
Legal issues	• Abortion • Adoption and baby selling • In vitro fertilization • Surrogacy • Right to die • Right to refuse care • Violence • Substance abuse
Occupational status of health care workers	• Nursing shortage • Advanced practice • Changes in roles and responsibilities • Educational preparation • Unionization, collective bargaining
Consumer involvement	• Consumer demand for increased voice in health care decisions • Demand for more personalized health care delivery • Increased knowledge of patient as a consumer of health care • Patient advocacy

EVIDENCE-BASED PRACTICE

 Ethical dilemma in telephone nursing

Question: *What ethical dilemmas do nurses experience when performing telephone nursing?*

Research: Telephone nursing has an important place in patient care; however, it hasn't been studied to determine if nurses face ethical dilemmas such as conflicts in their values, norms, and interests with those patients with whom they interact. Telephone nurses assess patient care needs; provide advice, support, and information to patients; and recommend and coordinate healthcare resources. However, when ethical dilemmas arise between the nurses and their patients, the nurses need an open dialogue to help sort out these ethical dilemmas. In Sweden, 12 telephone nurses were interviewed twice between 2004 and 2005. Their interviews were then analyzed according to common themes.

Conclusion: Questions of autonomy, integrity, and prioritizing are highlighted by the participating nurses and five common themes arose:
  – talking through a third party

  – discussing personal and sensitive problems over the phone
  – insufficient resources and the organization of health care
  – balancing callers' information needs with professional responsibility
  – judging the caller's credibility.

Application: Any organization that utilizes telephone nursing as a means of providing patient care and follow-up should make available to their nurses opportunities for building ethical competence. These facilities should provide their nurses with a means for discussing these dilemmas with peers to enhance competence and decrease moral uncertainty.
Source: Holmström, I., and Höglund, A.T. "The faceless encounter: ethical dilemmas in telephone nursing," *Journal of Clinical Nursing* 16(10):1865-71, October 2007.

he's participating in a programmed decision process that involves ethical and legal practices (such as truth telling) as well as patients' rights (such as self-determination).

The patient facing surgery—feeling unprepared to make a complex decision—may respond passively, saying, "I don't know what's best. Should I risk the complications of having surgery or the danger of not having it? I'll do whatever you tell me."

In such a situation, the physician must make a choice. He must either relieve the patient's stress by telling him what's "best" for him or ensure the patient's autonomy by removing himself from the decision-making process. By providing

education and clarification to the patient throughout the process of informed consent (or refusal of consent), the health care provider can balance the principles of autonomy and beneficence without "taking over" the decision for the patient. (See *Principles yardstick*.)

Whenever a nurse is faced with an ethical or moral dilemma, she must make judgments that lead to decisions about right and wrong courses of action. Even passive decisions—for example, deciding to protect herself by remaining silent or not taking a stand on an issue—are based on moral judgments.

Principles yardstick

In situations involving conflicting ethical principles, it's helpful to avoid the trap of "either/or" thinking. Instead, think of ethical principles as yardsticks, and strive for compromise rather than sacrificing one principle for another. For example, the principles yardstick would look like this:

Abandonment of patient	◄◄ AUTONOMY-BENEFICENCE ►►	Paternalism

If we move too far toward emphasizing autonomy without balancing it with beneficence, the result is abandoning the patient. If we move too far in the other direction by emphasizing doing good without balancing it with respect for the patient's autonomy, the result is paternalism.

Frameworks for decision making

Ethical conflicts have no automatic solutions. Although these conflicts may be painful and confusing, nurses don't need to be philosophers to act ethically or to make decisions that fall within nursing's ethical codes. Legally, nurses are responsible for using knowledge and skills to protect the comfort and safety of patients. Ethically, nurses in their role as patient advocates are responsible for safeguarding their patients' rights.

Ethical decision making most commonly involves reflection on:
▶ options or courses of action available
▶ options that seem unavailable
▶ consequences, both good and bad, of all possible options (teleology)
▶ rules, obligations, and values that should direct choices (deontology)
▶ who should make the choices
▶ desired goal or outcome.

All these elements should come together when making an ethical decision.

Various frameworks are available to nurses to aid in ethical decision making. Most frameworks involve identifying the problem and the relevant facts, evaluating the ethical problem, identifying and analyzing possible alternatives for action, choosing an action and then acting on it, and lastly, evaluating and modifying the plan as necessary. Regardless of the framework used, nurses need to ask themselves important questions to facilitate the process. (See *Approaching ethical decisions*, page 324.)

Ethical decision making and the nursing process

Every nurse is familiar with the nursing process. This method can be a helpful framework to apply for use in ethical decision making.

The nursing process is a continuous, interdependent, systematic organization of cognitive behaviors designed to resolve problems and promote well-being. The essential steps of the nursing process include assessment, planning, implementation, and evaluation.

Assessment begins with the nurse's initial contact with a patient. It involves collecting systematic data, and identifying the patient's needs.

Approaching ethical decisions

When faced with an ethical dilemma, consider these questions:

- What health issues are involved?
- What ethical issues are involved?
- What further information is necessary before a judgment can be made?
- Does a law exist that directs what must happen?
- Who will be affected by this decision? (Include the decision maker and other caregivers if they'll be affected emotionally or professionally.)
- What are the values and opinions of the people involved?
- What conflicts exist between the values and ethical standards of the people involved?
- Must a decision be made and, if so, who should make it?
- Is the patient legally competent to decide?
- What alternatives are available?
- For each alternative, what are the ethical justifications?
- For each alternative, what are the possible outcomes?

Nursing diagnosis is based on the clustering of significant assessment data and analyzing the patterns to determine the patient's actual or potential health problems. These problems are then prioritized based on acuity.

Outcome identification and planning includes determining goals and outcomes of nursing actions, identifying appropriate nursing actions necessary to attain the outcomes and goals, establishing indicators to determine if the outcomes were met, and developing a nursing care plan.

Implementation involves coordinating, performing, or delegating activities speci-

fied in the nursing care plan and recording results.

Evaluation includes collecting data, measuring outcomes against outcome indicators, and altering the nursing care plan by continuation of the nursing process.

Nurses can effectively use the same type of continuous, systematic, rational approach when making ethical decisions.

Assessment

▶ Gather facts, perceptions, and opinions about the ethical problem. Read the patient's chart. Talk with the patient and his family, other health care providers, and anyone who may be familiar with the patient's values.

▶ Identify the people involved in the problem, and assess their roles, responsibilities, authority, and decision-making abilities.

▶ Identify available resources. These may include the ethics committee, chaplain, nurse ethicist, counselors, and facilitators. Resources may also include institution policies, as well as literature on similar cases.

▶ Help decision makers participate in values clarification.

Nursing diagnosis, outcome identification and planning

▶ Determine the priority problems.

▶ Identify the types of moral dilemmas involved—beneficence, autonomy, justice, fidelity, nonmaleficence, confidentiality, or veracity. Identify the specific issues involved by examining the rights, duties, and values that are in conflict.

▶ Identify possible courses of action, along with their probable and possible risks and benefits (teleology).

▶ Formulate and assign priorities to the ethical goals or outcomes desired by the people involved.

▶ Determine the ethical obligations of those involved and the ethical principles that shape their actions (deontology).

Implementation

▶ Develop an ethical goal that maximizes the greatest good; work with others involved, as appropriate.

▶ Determine the course of action that will produce results closest to those of the ethical ideal.

▶ Determine if that course of action violates legal or moral principles. (If so, modify or change the course of action until it doesn't do so.)

▶ Carry out the agreed-on course of action.

Evaluation

▶ Determine if the results approximate the ethical ideal.

▶ If the results fall short of the ideal, determine what new moral dilemmas have been created.

▶ Reenter the decision process in the assessment phase to resolve additional moral dilemmas.

Although this process imposes the structure and objectivity necessary for resolving a moral dilemma, it doesn't provide all the answers. Because human beings are fallible, it's impossible for anyone to gather all the facts or to be completely without bias. Psychological and emotional factors can wreak havoc on fairness and impartiality.

Ethics committee

Most facilities have ethics committees that review ethical dilemmas. All members of the ethics committee hold equal standing. No one person or professional opinion dominates the discussion. The information that advocates for the patient's best interests and desires is the focus of the work of the ethics committee. (See *The ethics committee,* page 326.)

Nurses may consider consulting the ethics committee if:

▶ the physician disagrees with the patient or family regarding treatment

▶ health care providers disagree among themselves about treatment options

▶ family members disagree about what should be done.

Skillful communication

When it comes to making fair and ethical decisions, personality conflicts, political forces, and power plays can sabotage even the best intentions. For this reason, the nurse should use communication skills and management techniques to help promote collaboration and prevent divisiveness. In addition, nurses need to observe the following rules of behavior:

▶ Act within professional bounds, following the appropriate laws and codes of ethics.

▶ Don't make ethical decisions alone. Seek counsel and advice from other professionals.

▶ Validate information. Don't base ethical decisions on rumors, innuendo, hearsay, first impressions, or snap judgments.

▶ If religious faith and spiritual values are important to you or others involved in the ethical dilemma, respect these values in the decision-making process.

The ethics committee

The ethics committee addresses ethical issues regarding the clinical aspects of patient care. It provides a forum for the patient, his family, and health care providers to resolve conflicts.

The functions of an ethics committee include:
• policy development (such as developing policies to guide deliberations over individual cases)
• education (such as inviting guest speakers to visit your health care facility and discuss ethical concerns)
• case consultation (such as debating the prognosis of a patient who's in a persistent vegetative state)
• addressing a single issue (such as reviewing all cases that involve a no-code, or do-not-resuscitate [DNR], order)
• addressing problems of a specific population group (for example, the American Academy of Pediatrics recommending that hospitals have a standing committee called the "infant bioethical review committee")
• addressing issues of organization ethics (such as business practice, marketing, admission, and reimbursement).

PROS AND CONS

Properly run, an ethics committee provides a safe outlet for venting opposing views on emotionally charged ethical conflicts. The committee process can help lessen the bias that interferes with rational decision making. It enables members of disparate disciplines, including physicians, nurses, clergy, social workers, hospital administrators, and ethicists, to express their views on treatment decisions.

Critics of the ethics committee think that committee decision making is too bureaucratic and slow to be useful in clinical crises. They also point out that one dominating committee member may intimidate others with opposing views. Furthermore, they contend that physicians may view the committee as a threat to their autonomy in patient-care decisions. For these reasons, many ethics committees use a "rapid response team" of committee members who are on call

to respond quickly in emergency ethical dilemmas. The rapid-response team usually consists of three or four committee members, including a physician, who have had special training in negotiation and mediation. The entire committee will then review each case.

SELECTION OF COMMITTEE MEMBERS

Committee members should be selected for their ability to work cooperatively in a group. The American Hospital Association recommends the following ratio of committee members: one-third physicians, one-third nurses, and one-third others, including lay persons, clergy, and other health care professionals. Joint Commission regulations require that nursing staff members participate in the hospital ethics committee.

THE NURSE'S ROLE ON A HOSPITAL ETHICS COMMITTEE

Because of the nurse's close contact with the patient, his family, and other members of the health care team, the nurse is commonly in a position to identify ethical dilemmas, such as when a family is considering a DNR order for a relative. In many cases, the nurse is the first to recognize conflicts among family members or between the physician and the patient or his family.

Before ethics committees were widely used, nurses had no official outlet for voicing their opinions in ethical debates. In many situations, physicians made ethical decisions about patient care behind closed doors. Nursing supervisors would commonly call meetings to alert nursing staff about treatment decisions and discourage protest. Now, ethics committees provide nurses with an avenue to express their views, hear the opinions of others, and understand more deeply the rationale behind ethical decisions.

Patient advocacy

One of the nurse's most important moral obligations is the role of patient advocate. When a patient must make an ethical decision, the nurse should help him resolve his moral dilemma in ways that enhance personal values, priorities, freedom, dignity, and the quality of life.

As an advocate, nurses must never impose personal agendas or values on a patient. By listening carefully to the patient and asking thoughtful questions, nurses may be able to help the patient and his family make ethical decisions with which they're most comfortable. Consider asking the patient to describe the problem and then ask him these questions to help him clarify his thoughts:

▶ What has the physician told you about the situation?

▶ What options are you considering?

▶ Have you considered making a list of the best and worst things for each option you're considering?

▶ What else would it help you to know as you're making the decision?

▶ Is there anyone you'd like to speak with about this decision (for example, clergy, counselor, social worker, trusted friend, or lawyer)?

▶ What's the hardest part about coping with this decision?

▶ What things in the past have helped you cope with difficult decisions or situations?

▶ What would make it easier for you and your family to talk about this situation?

▶ What do you think is the best thing to do?

Learn as much as possible to help the decision-making process for the patient, his family, his physician, and yourself.

REFERENCES

1. American Association of Colleges of Nursing. *The Essentials of Baccalaureate Education for Professional Nursing Practice.* Washington, D.C.: AACN, 1998.
2. Zindler, L. "Ethical Decision Making in First Trimester Pregnancy Screening," *Journal of Perinatal Neonatal Nursing* 19(2):122-131, April-June 2005.
3. Zindler, 2005.
4. Grace, P.J. "The Clinical Use of Placebos. Is it ethical? Not when it involves deceiving patients," *AJN* 106(2):58-61, February 2006.
5. Grace, 2006.
6. Zindler, 2005.
7. Zindler, 2005.
8. Beauchamp, T., and Childress, J. *Principles of Biomedical Ethics,* 5th ed. New York: Oxford University Press, 2001.
9. American Nurses Association. "ANA Code of Ethics for Nurses, 2002." [Online.] Available at *http://www.nursingworld.org/MainMenuCategories/ThePracticeofProfessionalNursing/EthicsStandards/CodeofEthics/Aboutthecode.aspx.*
10. Canadian Nurses Association. "Code of Ethics for Registered Nurses, 2002." [Online.] Available at *http://www.cna-nurses.ca/cna/documents/pdf/publications/PS71_Code_of_Ethics_RN_June2004_e.pdf.*
11. International Council of Nurses. "The ICN Code of Ethics for Nurses, 2006." [Online.] Available at *http://www.icn.ch/icncode.pdf.*

ADDITIONAL RESOURCES

Bosek, M.S. "Refusal of Brain Death Diagnosis," *JONA'S Healthcare Law, Ethics and Regulation* 9(3): 87-94, July-September 2007.

Butler, K.A. "Ethics Paramount When Patient Lacks Capacity," *Nursing Management* 35(11):18-20, November 2004.

Crawford, G.W. "A Commentary: A Practical Application for a Framework for Ethical Decision Making," *Dimensions of Critical Care Nursing* 24(2):80-81, March-April 2005.

Phillips, S. "Ethical Decision-Making When Caring for the Noncompliant Patient," *Journal of Infusion Nursing* 29(5):266-71, September-October 2006.

Ethical conflicts in nursing practice

Rapid advances in medical research have outpaced society's ability to solve the ethical problems associated with new health care technology. For nurses, ethical decision making in clinical practice is complicated by sociocultural factors, legal controversies, growing professional autonomy, and consumer involvement in health care.

This chapter describes ethical issues common to all areas of practice, such as the right to die and life-sustaining interventions, end-of-life care, human immunodeficiency virus (HIV) and acquired immunodeficiency syndrome (AIDS), substance abuse among coworkers, and organ donation and transplantation. It also addresses ethical issues that may be encountered when working in specialty care areas, such as the intensive care unit, maternal-neonatal nursing, child health, and mental health and psychiatric nursing. Regardless of the area of practice, nurses will probably encounter at least one of these conflicts during their career.

Ethical dilemmas resist easy resolution. The choice is typically between two desirable or two undesirable alternatives. By learning as much as possible about the underlying ethical principles, nurses will be better equipped to participate in the decision-making process. The more nurses practice ethical thinking, the more confident they'll become in their ability to make decisions.

When ethical problems arise, discuss them candidly with other members of the health care team, especially the patient's physician. Also, consider calling on social workers, psychologists, the clergy, and ethics committee members to help resolve difficult ethical problems. Learn as much as possible to facilitate the decision-making process for the patient, his family, and his physician, as well as for yourself. Remember, facilities typically have ethics committees to address ethical problems. (See *The nurse's role on the ethics committee,* page 330.)

COMMON ETHICAL CONFLICTS

Ethical conflicts can affect any nurse and may arise in any situation or practice setting. As in any profession, nursing is expected to maintain high ethical standards. Many current ethical issues weren't a concern 10 to 15 years ago. However, rapid advances in technology and science, as well as

The nurse's role on the ethics committee

If your organization *doesn't* have an ethics committee, you may be able to help start one. If one already exists, you may be able to play a vital role as a committee member or by educating patients, residents, or clients and their families about the existence and work of the ethics committee.

It's of no value for an organization to have an ethics committee if patients, residents, or clients and their families don't know how the committee can help them.

Make sure that when your organization informs those it serves about their rights as patients, residents, or clients, it also tells them about their right to access an ethics committee for help in making difficult choices about care and treatment. All patients, residents, or clients should receive written information about their rights that includes at least a simple paragraph such as this:

The ethics committee is available to help you and your family as you deal with difficult decisions about your care and what's right and fair. There's no charge for this service. To find out more about the ethics committee, ask your nurse.

COMMITTEE MAKEUP

The ethics committee is usually multidisciplinary. Membership includes nurses, physicians, allied health care professionals, and other key members of the care team (respiratory therapists, registered dietitians, licensed clinical social workers, chaplains), administrators, ethics experts such as a nurse ethicist, and a community representative familiar with the role of the ethics committee who's a strong patient advocate. Nurse members should include staff, advance practice nurses or clinical experts, and nurse administrators.

KEY COMMITTEE FUNCTIONS

The ethics committee has three key functions:
- Develop and revise policies and procedures relevant to ethics (such as policies and procedures on patient rights, advance directives, confidentiality, informed consent, and forgoing treatment and resuscitation).
- Educate committee members to develop a level of competency consistent with the guidelines of the American Society for Bioethics and Humanities Core Competencies for Health Care Ethics Consultation, and then educate staff, administration, trustees, patients, families, and the community about issues of importance in health care ethics.
- Develop a team to do case consultation through facilitation, discussion, research, negotiation, resolution, and documentation of difficult cases and evaluation of outcomes to monitor and improve quality.

---

changes in legislation and a growing emphasis on patients' rights, have led to an increased emphasis on certain issues, resulting in ethical conflicts. These ethical conflicts commonly involve critical points in a person's life, such as birth and death. Many of the conflicts have no clear-cut solutions. Nurses are challenged to think about the issues, to clarify their values and ethical beliefs, and to make the best possible choices about resolving the conflict. Ethical issues are further complicated by the laws involved and the legal questions that arise.

Right to die and life-sustaining measures

The most difficult ethical decisions in health care involve whether to initiate or to withhold life-sustaining treatment for a patient who's irreversibly comatose or vegetative or suffering with end-stage terminal illness. Treatment decisions for this type of patient can be morally troubling. The patient, his family, and the health

EVIDENCE-BASED PRACTICE

Ethical decision-making

Question: *What involvement do nurses have in the ethical decision of initiating or withdrawing of artificial nutritional support?*

Research: Nurses do not actively participate in the decision making process of initiation or withdrawal of nutritional support in seriously ill patients.

Using qualitative methods to obtain the data, 15 health care professionals were involved from a nutritional unit in the United Kingdom. Information was gathered regarding who was involved in the decision making process regarding the initiation as well as the withdrawal of nutritional support.

Conclusion: The study determined that the physicians and clinical nurse specialists were more involved in the decision making. The nurses felt that the ethical decision making was out of their

hands as they did not have the knowledge to make those kinds of ethical decisions.

Application: Nurses must become more knowledgeable about nutritional support in terminally ill patients and that they should become more knowledgeable about making these types of difficult ethical decisions. They can become more knowledgeable through experience and research into ethical decision making.

Source: Tsaloglidou, A., et al. "Nurses' ethical decision-making role in artificial nutritional support," *British Journal of Nursing* 16(16):996-1001, September, 2007.

care team may be asked to choose between a potentially painful extension of life and immediate death. Surrogate decision makers—people who are designated to act when a patient can no longer decide his own fate—also face tremendous moral and emotional pressures.

Sometimes, the patient's expressed wishes to withhold life-sustaining treatment are ignored or overridden by physicians and family members. Nurses may feel that they're caught in the middle, frustrated and demoralized by the demands of caring for an unresponsive patient who had expressly wished to withhold life-sustaining treatment. (See *Ethical decision-making.*)

Definition of death

Part of the problem stems from a lack of consensus about what constitutes death.

Some people define *death* as the loss of all vital functions, whereas others define it by neurologic criteria, such as *brain death*—the irreversible cessation of brain functioning accompanied by ongoing biological functioning in all other parts of the body that's only maintained by life-support measures. All 50 states have recognized the Uniform Determination of Brain Death Act since its passage in 1981. According to this act, brain death is indicated by loss of all brain function as determined by accepted medical standards.[1] (See *Determining brain death*, page 332.)

People view death from different perspectives. Some think of death as the ending of all vital functions, whereas others may view it as life without dignity. Additionally, some people maintain a strong ethical belief in the absolute sanc-

Determining brain death

Facilities usually develop their own criteria for determining brain death. However, three cardinal signs must be evident:

- Coma
- Absence of brain stem reflexes
- Apnea
  To substantiate these cardinal signs, the following are typically used:
- Patient is unresponsive to all stimuli
- Pupillary responses are absent
- All brain function ceases
- No eye movements are noted when cold water is instilled into the ears (caloric test)
- Corneal reflex is absent
- Gag reflex is absent
- Eyes remain fixed when the patient's head is quickly rotated from left to right (doll's eye reflex)
- Response to painful stimuli is absent
- No spontaneous breathing occurs (apnea test)
- EEG shows no brain activity or response

tity of life. Others argue that it's wrong and wasteful to continue life support when a patient's life is devoid of dignity. To function effectively when caring for patients, nurses need to be aware of personal feelings about death and quality-of-life issues.

Ordinary versus extraordinary treatment

Ordinary means of medical treatment are medications, procedures, and surgeries that offer the patient some hope of benefit without incurring excessive pain or expense. In contrast, extraordinary means, sometimes called *heroic measures,* merely maintain or prolong a patient's life, usually at great expense and suffering for the patient and his family.

Because of continuing advances in medicine and technology, the distinction between "ordinary" and "extraordinary" treatments is becoming blurred, leading to much controversy and debate.

In 1983, the President's Commission for the Study of Ethical Problems in Medicine and Biomedical and Behavioral Research defined *ordinary* and *extraordinary* treatments: The Commission believes that extraordinary treatment is that which, in the patient's view, entails significantly greater burdens than benefits and is therefore undesirable and not obligatory, whereas ordinary treatment is that which, in the patient's view, produces greater benefits than burdens."[2] The Commission further stated that health care professionals aren't obligated to provide treatment that's considered useless or futile.

Do-not-resuscitate orders

Cardiopulmonary resuscitation (CPR) is widely used to treat victims who experience cardiac arrest. Questions arise about its usefulness in prolonging life. Most facilities require CPR unless a specific medical order, known as a *do-not-resuscitate (DNR) order* (also called a *no-code situation*), is written to prevent this. This order states that no attempts are to be made to resuscitate a patient who has stopped breathing or whose heart has stopped. Before writing a DNR order, the physician usually must notify and discuss this issue with the patient and family.

Historically, physicians who wanted to issue a DNR order but couldn't obtain the patient's or family's agreement for such an order sometimes asked the staff to perform a "slow code." Slow codes are considered unethical and most likely illegal. Health care providers are obligated to adhere to the standard of care and attempt resuscitation if there's no DNR order.

Discontinuation of treatment

Despite the Commission's recommendations, countless terminally ill patients continue to receive treatment that's unlikely to benefit them. Determining whether a particular treatment is futile is highly subjective. Futility refers to treatment that offers no hope or interventions that aren't likely to benefit the patient, even though they may appear to be effective. For example, a patient with a terminal illness who's expected to die experiences a cardiac arrest. CPR may be effective in restoring a heartbeat but may still be deemed futile because it doesn't change the patient's outcome.

Many such decisions are based on incomplete information and are further complicated by value judgments about the quality of life. Various methods have attempted to quantify outcomes to minimize the use of subjective value judgments. One example is the Acute Physiology and Chronic Health Evaluation System (APACHE). This device, created in 1981, has undergone several changes since its inception. APACHE is a scoring system that measures physiologic variables, along with other variables such as age, chronic health status, and disease groups. Then using sophisticated equations and computerized information, a patient's mortality and prognosis can be determined.[3]

When deciding whether to terminate life-sustaining treatment, health care providers face incredible emotional pressure; a patient can't be brought back after he stops treatment. Nurses do have one ethically sound option: helping patients determine their own fate by educating them about their right to refuse extraordinary treatment.

Refusal of treatment

The right to refuse treatment, a fundamental patient right, and a legal issue based on the 14th Amendment to the U.S. Constitution, is grounded in the ethical principle of respect for the autonomy of the individual (*Norwood Hospital v. Munoz* 564, N.E.2nd 1017 Mass., 1991).[4] This principle of autonomy has led to the concept of informed consent—the obligation of health care providers to inform the patient of the risks and benefits of a procedure and to obtain permission before the procedure is carried out. Terminally ill patients who receive life-sustaining treatment have an equal right to informed consent.

Because the nursing profession is oriented to saving and prolonging lives, nurses may find it difficult to go along with a patient's decision to withhold life-sustaining treatment. Keep in mind that limiting treatment doesn't mean abandoning the patient. Supportive measures aren't considered extraordinary treatment. A patient who has chosen to forgo life-sustaining treatment still has the right to receive care that preserves his comfort, hygiene, and dignity. In particular, he has the right to adequate pain control.

Withholding and withdrawing of treatment

The issue of withholding or withdrawing treatment also presents some ethical dilemmas. When withdrawing treatment from a patient, even at the patient's request, controversy over the principle of nonmaleficence (to prevent harm) may arise.

Some controversy revolves around the definition of harm. For example, some feel that removing a patient from a ventilator or from nutritional support and allowing death is an intentional infliction of harm. Others argue that keeping a person on a ventilator or maintaining nutritional support against the patient's will, and thus prolonging death, is an intentional infliction of harm.

Euthanasia

Euthanasia, also known as *mercy killing,* and assisted suicide further confuse the right-to-die issue. Although DNR orders and other decisions to limit treatment are sometimes referred to as *passive euthanasia,* euthanasia usually refers to active intervention such as lethal injection to bring about death. The issue of whether nurses or other health care professionals can ever ethically assist in taking a life is hotly debated in professional journals and the mass media.

In 1994, Oregon voters legalized physician-assisted suicide. Enactment of the law was delayed in the courts, but similar bills were introduced in other states. The Oregon law states (with qualifying safeguards) that a terminally ill person can ask a physician to prescribe a lethal dose of oral medication, which the patient will take when he deems it appropriate. Although assisted suicide laws remain on the books in Oregon and several other states, the federal Assisted Suicide Funding Restriction Act of 1997 has, to a large extent, negated the effects of these laws. This act forbids the use of federal funds to cause or assist suicide or mercy killing. Several states considering assisted suicide legislation have dropped it, and other states that had passed assisted suicide laws have since withdrawn them.

Consider the following case, *Dennis Vacco, Attorney General of New York , et al. Petitioners v. Timothy E. Quill, et al.* This case alleges that because New York permits a competent person to refuse life-sustaining medical treatment, and because the refusal of such treatment is "essentially the same thing" as physician-assisted suicide, New York's assisted suicide ban violates the Equal Protection Clause of the 14th Amendment.[5] The U. S. Supreme Court held that refusal of life-sustaining treatment and assisted suicide are different and thus determined that New York's law doesn't violate the Equal Protection Clause (all persons have equal protection under the law and states can't deny this protection). Other states also have grappled with the issue of assisted suicide (see *Gonzales v. Oregon,* available at *http://www.law.cornell.edu/ supct/html/04-623.ZS.html* and *Washington, et al. Petitioners v. Harold Glucksber et al.* available at *http://supct. law.cornell.edu/supct/html/96-110.ZO. html*). Check with the state board of nursing about the legal status of assisted suicide for that state.

Proponents of euthanasia and assisted suicide base their argument on the right to self-determination. They argue that if a terminally ill patient is in unendurable pain that can't be controlled, physician-assisted suicide might be seen as a more humane alternative. (See *Compassion and Choices: End-of-life care advocates.*)

Public reaction to highly publicized cases of assisted suicide indicates that many people support a patient's right to control his own fate. Dr. Jack Kevorkian, who has assisted the suicides of more than 130 terminally ill persons, has numerous supporters, including jurors who have acquitted him of criminal charges brought by the state of Michigan in 1995. However, in fall 1998, Dr. Kevorkian raised the legal and ethical stakes.

On the nationally broadcast network news show 60 Minutes, Dr. Kevorkian not only admitted to giving a lethal drug to a patient without the patient's assistance but also made and played a videotape that showed the incident. The patient, who had amyotrophic lateral sclerosis (Lou Gehrig's disease), had requested that Dr. Kevorkian kill him and had signed a consent form and release. Dr. Kevorkian admitted that his motivation for the act was to be tried in a test case for active euthanasia. He was convicted of second-degree murder, sentenced in 1999 to up to 25 years in prison, and was released from prison on June 1, 2007. Numerous articles are available at *http://topics.nytimes. com/top/reference/timestopics/people/k/ja ck_kevorkian/index.html?8qa.*

Many critics, however, find the mercy killing concept repugnant. Although many nurses would agree with allowing the family of a comatose patient to withdraw food and fluids, most oppose more active forms of euthanasia. Allowing euthanasia, many argue, would eventually lead to patients selectively being put to death without consent. The potential object of mercy killing—a patient with Alzheimer's disease or a patient in a persistent vegetative state, for example—has lost the capacity to express his wishes. Family members and health care providers don't know if the patient truly desires to die and don't have the moral right to make the decision for him.

All major professional nursing and medical organizations have taken positions against assisted suicide. The American Nurses Association (ANA) has

Compassion and Choices: End-of-life care advocates

Compassion and Choices is an organization that advocates for choice in dying. It was developed in 2005, when two other organizations, Compassion in Dying and End-of-Life Choices (originally known as the *Hemlock Society*) joined forces.

This organization is active in the legislatures and courts, working to reform laws that limit a patient's right to appropriate end-of-life care and personal control. Their mission is to make aid to dying legally available for terminally ill, mentally competent adults.

Compassion and Choices focuses on four areas of end-of-life practice:
- defending and expanding choice at the end of life
- enforcement of living wills/advance directives for health care
- ensuring appropriate pain and symptom management for dying patients
- guarding the rights of physicians to adequately treat dying patients' pain.

Source: Compassion and Choices. Available at: *http://www.compassionandchoices.org.*

reaffirmed this position repeatedly through its publications. American Medical Association (AMA) policy contains the following: "It is understandable, though tragic, that some patients in extreme duress—such as those suffering from a terminal, painful, debilitating illness—may come to decide that death is preferable to life. However, allowing physicians to participate in assisted suicide would cause more harm than good. Physician-assisted suicide is fundamentally incompatible with the physician's role as healer, would be difficult or impossible to control, and would pose serious societal risks."

Health care workers' rights

Although patients have the right to decide whether to accept or forgo heroic measures, they don't have the right to insist on treatments that provide no medical benefit. If a nurse believes that she'll violate personal values by implementing a certain treatment, she has the obligation to arrange for the transfer of the patient's care to another provider. Likewise, if a nurse believes that she'll violate personal values by withholding treatment, she should request the transfer. This right, also known as *the conscience clause* or *conscientious objection,* applies to assisting in abortions, as well as to noninitiation or withdrawal of life-sustaining treatment or euthanasia. (See discussion later in this chapter.)

Patient's wishes

A patient who has a strong desire to request or reject aggressive treatment measures should document his wishes. He should also designate a surrogate decision maker to speak for him if he can no longer make his own health care decisions. Statements that indicate a patient's wishes in the event he loses his decision-making capability are known as *advance directives,* the patient's best means of ensuring that his wishes will be respected. The advance directive includes a living will, which goes into effect when the patient can't make decisions, and the durable power of attorney for health care, which authorizes another person to make those decisions. If a patient has a living will and a durable power of attorney for health care, the person with durable power should be in complete support of the patient's wishes. No family member or health care provider can then override the person with the durable power of attorney.

Although specific treatments can be requested in an advance directive, most people execute a living will to make sure that no extraordinary procedures are used to sustain or prolong life. A durable power of attorney designates a surrogate decision maker, who will have full authority to carry out the patient's wishes regarding health care decisions. The authority of this surrogate decision maker is based on the principle of substituted judgment, allowing the surrogate to make the same decisions the patient would, if he could. (See chapter 2 for an in-depth discussion of advance directives.)

Advance directives, although useful, haven't ended the controversy over a patient's right to limit treatment. Critics contend that they represent the first step toward active euthanasia, or mercy killing. These people believe that advance directives, such as living wills, should be restricted to a narrow range of circumstances. (See *When family members contest a living will.*)

Although many states have enacted so-called natural death acts to encourage practitioners to abide by a living will by granting statutory enforcement, these laws vary from state to state. Several require a "reasonable effort by the physician" to transfer the patient to a physician who will abide by the living will.

Preparation planning

Of the many professionals who care for patients, nurses probably have the best chance to act as true patient advocates. The patient will probably look to both the nurse and the physician for guidance.

When family members contest a living will

A living will isn't a guarantee that the patient's expressed wishes will be honored. The language in many living wills is vague and unclear. Patients who have added specific requests to a standardized form (for example, requesting termination of tube feedings) may not realize that such requests may conflict with state law. Nurses and physicians sometimes find it difficult to carry out wishes expressed years before current treatment options became available.

The family's response to the living will can also create problems. Family members may not know about the living will or may choose to ignore it in their turmoil over "letting go." As the following case history demonstrates, health care workers, including nurses, can be caught in the crossfire.

CONFLICTING DEMANDS

Esther Summerson was brought to the emergency department (ED) in respiratory distress after a long history of chronic obstructive pulmonary disease (COPD). The ED staff asked Mrs. Summerson if she wanted help breathing, but they couldn't get a clear response before she lost consciousness. She was intubated and transferred to the intensive care unit.

When Mrs. Summerson's older daughter, Jean, arrived at the hospital, she was upset to find that her mother had been placed on a ventilator. She showed the staff a copy of her mother's living will, specifying that her mother not be placed on a ventilator or receive supplementary nutrition. Miss Summerson also produced a form giving her durable power of attorney. As her mother's designated decision maker, she

demanded that her mother be removed from the ventilator.

Susan Johnson, Mrs. Summerson's younger daughter, reached the hospital about an hour after her sister. Although her mother was still unresponsive, Mrs. Johnson didn't want her removed from the ventilator. "I don't know what I'd do without Mom," she sobbed. "I want you to do everything you can for her."

IMPLEMENTING HOSPITAL POLICY

Fortunately, the hospital had developed procedures for resolving this sort of conflict. Mrs. Summerson's physician, her primary nurse, her priest, and a representative of the hospital's ethics committee called a meeting with Miss Summerson, Mrs. Johnson, and Mrs. Johnson's husband. They explained the living will and Miss Summerson's role as the surrogate decision maker, emphasizing that Mrs. Summerson's living will clearly specified her opposition to the ventilator. Mrs. Johnson and Miss Summerson were informed that without the ventilator their mother might breathe on her own or she might die. If she did die, however, it would be from lung damage caused by her long-standing COPD. Each step of the procedure was carefully reviewed.

As a result of this discussion, Mrs. Johnson changed her mind and agreed to removal of the ventilator. All three family members decided to be present when this occurred. After they had a chance to talk to Mrs. Summerson and express their love for her, the balloon was deflated and the tube removed. Mrs. Summerson died quietly 2 days later, with her daughters and her son-in-law by her side.

Nurses can't make the ultimate medical decisions to initiate or limit treatment, but they can help the patient express his wishes about his health care and guide him in translating these desires into advance directives.

When discussing limiting treatment with a patient, consider these suggestions:
▶ Present options, such as DNR orders, in a realistic but positive context. Reassure the patient that he'll continue

to receive supportive care and pain medication.

▶ Pay attention to the patient's questions and misunderstandings. Be especially alert for unexpressed fears.

▶ During your discussions with the patient, note his nonverbal cues and emotional responses.

Despite best efforts to provide objective advice, the patient may not be able to reach a decision about initiating or terminating care. Remember that a nurse must respect the patient's explicit refusal to participate in health care decisions.

Determination of decision-making ability

Commonly used standards for judging decision-making capability include:

▶ the ability to indicate a choice

▶ a clear understanding of the issues at hand

▶ the ability to reason based on the information given

▶ an appreciation of the true nature of the situation.

These standards are similar to those used to obtain informed consent from a patient. "The determination of whether patients are competent is critical to striking a proper balance between respecting the autonomy of patients who are capable...and protecting those with cognitive impairment."[6] If a patient can't make a decision, it becomes the duty of a surrogate decision maker or the health care team to act in his best interest.

Nurses may question whether a particular patient should be allowed to decide to refuse life-sustaining treatment. Consider whether the patients described at right are capable of making life-and-death decisions.

▶ Joe Ryan suffered a stroke 2 years ago that left him paralyzed on the right side and unable to speak. He was admitted to the hospital with sepsis caused by infected stasis ulcers of his lower legs. Mr. Ryan's physician recommended bilateral above-the-knee amputations. As he was being prepared for the surgery, Mr. Ryan became visibly agitated.

▶ Mary Kane suffered a severe head injury in a traffic accident that also left her a quadriplegic and dependent on a ventilator. About 3 months after the accident, she insisted that the ventilator be removed. A hospital psychiatrist determined that Mrs. Kane was seriously depressed.

▶ George Bowen has Alzheimer's disease. He can't remember a recent conversation, the names of his three children, or how to find his bedroom, although he's still continent and responsive. When Mr. Bowen was admitted to the hospital with his third heart attack, his wife told the physician he had begged to be allowed to "meet his maker."

The concept of informed consent creates ethical dilemmas in situations in which the patient's ability to make an informed judgment about his treatment options is questionable. If the patient is nonverbal, depressed, demented, or semiconscious, can he truly consent to or refuse life-sustaining treatment?

Legal concepts applied for decision-making capacity typically include these abilities:

▶ communicate a choice

▶ understand relevant information

▶ appreciate consequences of the situation

▶ reason about choices.[7]

Although these concepts apply to consent to treatment, they also can be used to determine whether a patient has the capacity to decide about end-of-life care issues and treatment. Ethical issues arise because there are no clear-cut standards or formal practice guidelines to determine a patient's capacity to consent.[8]

It's important to remember that some patients may remain capable of expressing health care preferences even when they can't manage in other areas, such as personal care, eating, or speaking.

Decision making for the patient

Two ethical principles can be used in making decisions for an incapacitated patient. The *substituted judgment* test professes to make the same decision the patient would, if he were capable (the principle of autonomy). Alternatively, the decision may be based on the best interest standard, or deciding what's best for the patient, given his current circumstances (the principle of beneficence). Both principles are ethically valid. If the two are at odds, they can create dilemmas for family members, physicians, and nurses.

Cost considerations

The mention of cost considerations in the context of limiting treatment for the terminally ill may be thought of as offensive. Such considerations, however, are ethically legitimate. The necessity of conserving resources eventually will force the public to consider this issue. Health care resources—including organs available for transplants, beds in the intensive care unit (ICU), and experimental drugs—are limited in quantity and are costly. Some individuals have begun to debate the equity of giving a disproportionate share of the most expensive medical treatments and procedures to elderly patients who

are gravely ill. Medicare pays out $21 billion, or 28% of its budget, for bills incurred in the final year of life. Some policymakers believe that the patient's age should be a valid ethical consideration in the delivery of medical care, especially when so much money is spent to achieve relatively small gains in life expectancy.

Health care in the United States is already rationed to a degree through policies that discourage the poor from seeking medical attention. Unaffordably high insurance rates, underfinanced state medical programs, and crowded clinics, in effect, ration care.

Deciding how to ration lifesaving technology is an ethical dilemma of huge proportions. It ultimately will have to be resolved by society at large using the ethical principle of justice.

Communication

Effective communication is essential when helping families decide whether to limit or withhold treatment. If a nurse is helping family members or surrogates while they're making life-and-death decisions, the following guidelines can improve communication.

▶ Create a quiet, private, and unhurried environment—keep all communication simple, factual, and direct.
▶ Encourage decision makers to ask questions.
▶ Express medical information in simple, clear language.
▶ Ask decision makers to summarize and check their responses.
▶ Clarify missing or misunderstood information.

Keep in mind that this may be the most heartrending decision family members or surrogates will ever be asked to

Terminally ill and health care decisions

Question: *Do the terminally ill desire others (loved ones and physicians) to make health care decisions for them in the event of decisional incapacity?*

Research: The research was designed to determine a terminally ill patient's desire to have their loved one or physicians make health care decisions for them when they no longer could make these decisions for themselves.

One hundred forty-seven patients with amyotrophic lateral sclerosis, cancer, or heart failure were surveyed at baseline, 3 months and again in 6 months. At the baseline survey, most participants opted for shared decision-making but leaned slightly toward making independent decisions. This did not change at the 3- or 6-month surveys. The survey also revealed that more independent decision-making was associated with college education and being female.

The wishes of the terminally ill varied but most opted for shared decision-making with loved ones and their physicians. However, the longer they lived with their terminal illness; they became less reliant on their physicians.

Conclusion: Terminally ill patients do not want their physicians or their loved ones to be the sole decision makers if they become unable to make their own decisions but prefer to still have a say in their care along with their loved ones and physicians.

Application: The results of this study will help health care workers be advocates for their patients by better understanding their wishes for decision making to be shared between loved ones and the physician.

Source: Sulmasy, D.P., et al. "How would terminally ill patients have others make decisions for them in the event of decisional incapacity? A longitudinal study," *Journal of the American Geriatrics Society* 55(12):1981-88, December 2007.

make. They need plenty of time, care, and understanding.

(See *Terminally ill and health care decisions.*)

HIV and AIDS

Nurses have always honored their professional responsibility to care for all patients, regardless of personal attributes, lifestyle, or the nature of the illness. Today, HIV and AIDS challenge this long-standing professional ethic. No other infectious disorder incites such emotionally charged ethical debate.

HIV and AIDS touch on two highly controversial social issues: sexuality and drug use. It isn't surprising that many nurses experience value conflicts when working to meet their professional obli-

gations. (See *Ethical issues and AIDS: Where do you stand?*)

Prejudice, fear, and misunderstanding surround HIV and AIDS. An HIV-positive test result may mean the loss of a job, medical insurance, financial security, and even housing. Family, friends, and even the public may shun the HIV or AIDS patient. As a result, maintaining confidentiality is a serious concern for people with HIV and AIDS.

Mandatory testing

Although there has been a major effort at education about HIV transmission, the Centers for Disease Control and Prevention (CDC) estimates that most of the 1.5 million Americans infected with HIV don't know about it. Lack of awareness can seriously undermine both pa-

ETHICAL DILEMMA

 Ethical issues and AIDS: Where do you stand?

Acquired immunodeficiency syndrome (AIDS) raises numerous ethical issues for nurses and other health care professionals. These issues range from personal safety to societal obligations. Read and answer the questions below to help you articulate your ethical position on AIDS.

- Should all health care professionals have the right to refuse to treat patients who are HIV-positive?
- Should patients with AIDS receive "heroic" life-sustaining treatments?
- Should patients who are pregnant and who are also HIV-positive have abortions rather than risk the chance of passing the virus to their unborn children?
- Should health departments obtain lists of all sexual contacts of people diagnosed as HIV-positive and notify those on the lists of their risk of exposure?
- Should the U.S. government provide free medical insurance to patients who are HIV-positive and who can no longer buy health insurance?

- Should pregnant drug abusers who acquire HIV and infect their infants be charged with child abuse?
- Should costly, limited intensive care unit (ICU), neonatal ICU, and pediatric ICU resources be tied up in the care of patients with AIDS if other patients with better prognoses for survival are being deprived?
- Should health care facilities test all current and new employees for HIV infection?
- Should states and jurisdictions enact special laws allowing terminally ill patients with AIDS to request and receive a lethal, painless injection?

tient care and prevention efforts.[9] (See *HIV transmission: Facts versus fiction,* page 342.)

Testing for HIV isn't the same as testing for other infectious diseases. The patient with a positive gonorrhea culture doesn't face the same likelihood of discrimination and stigmatization as the patient who's HIV-positive.

Some organizations, including the military and correctional facilities, and many insurance companies insist on mandatory testing. Several states attempted to institute mandatory testing to obtain a marriage license and then abandoned the policy because of high costs and the low percentage of positive results. Most states now mandate written consent for testing and mandate pretest and posttest counseling.

Does mandatory testing violate the ethical principles of autonomy (the patient's right to control his own fate) and justice (his right to be treated fairly)? Does it violate his right to privacy? Many nurses believe that it doesn't. Health care workers, they argue, have a right to protect themselves and need a complete picture of the patient's health status to deliver quality care.

Public health officials contend that mandatory testing would improve our understanding of the spread of the disease and aid in prevention. Hospital administrators say that knowing a patient's HIV status could lower health care costs by pinpointing those who require extra precautions.

Opponents of mandatory testing emphasize the risk of discrimination and the

HIV transmission: Facts versus fiction

Human immunodeficiency virus (HIV) is a fragile virus. It can't live for very long outside the body. As a result, the virus is *not* transmitted through day-to-day contact and activities, such as shaking hands, hugging, or a casual kiss. You can't become infected from a toilet seat, drinking fountain, doorknob, dishes, drinking glasses, food, or pets. You also can't get HIV from mosquitoes.

HIV is primarily found in the blood, semen, or vaginal fluid of an infected person. HIV is transmitted in three major ways:
• having unprotected sex (anal, vaginal, or oral) with someone infected with HIV
• sharing needles and syringes with someone infected with HIV
• being exposed (fetus or infant) to HIV before or during birth or through breast-feeding.

Source: Centers for Disease Control and Prevention. *HIV and Its Transmission.* Available at http://www.cdc.gov/hiv/resources/factsheets/transmission.htm.

high cost of screening all patients. They also believe that testing drives away patients who need care because many people fear being tested. (See *Mandatory testing: A case in point.*)

Mandatory testing can also backfire. An exposed person can take 12 weeks or longer to develop HIV antibodies. During this time, he's contagious but seronegative.

Public's right to know
Many people believe that all health care providers should be routinely tested for HIV. The public, they argue, has the right to know a nurse's or physician's HIV status.

After at least three patients contracted HIV from a Florida dentist, the AMA and the American Dental Association recommended that physicians and dentists who are HIV-positive perform no invasive procedures and tell their patients that they're infected.

State and federal lawmakers have considered proposals to prevent physicians who are HIV-positive from performing surgery and other risky procedures. Such proposals are highly controversial. In April 1991, a New Jersey court upheld the right of a Princeton hospital to prohibit a surgeon with AIDS from performing surgery.

Some people question the need for restrictions based on status alone. Rules about impaired health care workers, whether based on addiction, mental status, or physical illness, seem fairer and minimize the chance of HIV-based discrimination.

Testing guidelines
Following the guidelines below can help to ensure that HIV testing is carried out in an ethically responsible manner.
▶ The sole purpose of any screening program should be to prevent the spread of HIV.
▶ The confidentiality of the test results must be ensured. If it's necessary to disclose the results (when a blood donor tests positive), the affected person should be notified.
▶ The patient should receive adequate pretest and posttest counseling.
▶ The diagnostic laboratory must be reliable.
▶ Informed consent should be obtained before a patient is allowed to participate in a voluntary screening program. (See

Mandatory testing: A case in point

The following example illustrates some of the ethical problems raised by mandatory testing.

Karen Owen, a trauma nurse, was accidentally exposed to a patient's blood during emergency surgery to treat a gunshot wound. Many patients with acquired immunodeficiency syndrome (AIDS) are treated at Ms. Owen's inner-city hospital. Although, as a precautionary measure, hospital policy dictated HIV testing of the patient because the hospital employee was exposed to blood or body fluids, Ms. Owen's patient strongly objected. She argued that she was equally likely to have contracted AIDS from Ms. Owen. She demanded that Ms. Owen be tested as well.

Is this a legitimate request and must the hospital honor it? What about Ms. Owen's right to privacy? If she proved to be HIV-positive, would she lose her job? If she was HIV-negative, would she have to consent to be retested at a later date?

Out of concern for her own health, Ms. Owen agreed to be tested. To provide further reassurance, the hospital noted on the patient's consent form that the test was necessary because of worker exposure, not because that patient was part of a high-risk group.

Correcting a flawed HIV-testing policy, page 344.)

Standard precautions
The CDC contends that mandatory testing isn't necessary to protect nurses if health care workers follow standard precautions for all patients. This means using gloves, gowns, and goggles to prevent contact with a patient's blood or body fluids and strictly adhering to safety measures when handling needles, scalpels, and other sharp instruments.

Unfortunately, nurses fail to follow these precautions all the time. Some hospitals fail to provide enough supplies. Some nurses complain that gloves and gowns make it more difficult to perform certain procedures. Nurses working in the emergency department may not have time to adhere meticulously to standard precautions. Furthermore, many white, middle-class patients are automatically assumed to be seronegative.

Standard precautions are time-consuming, expensive, and obstructive. Nonetheless, following these precautions means that nurses can protect themselves without forcing patients to undergo mandatory testing.

Refusal to provide care
Dorothy Smith, an intensive care nurse, struggled for many months with her prejudices against AIDS patients. Although she was deeply committed to her career, her religion taught that homosexuality and drug use were sins. She also was apprehensive about the danger of contracting AIDS. Finally, she begged her supervisor to avoid assigning her to AIDS patients.

Marie James, who worked on the surgical floor of a large teaching hospital, also wanted to avoid AIDS patients, but for a different reason. She had just learned that she was pregnant, and she wanted to avoid exposure to cytomegalovirus (CMV), a common opportunistic infection associated with AIDS. The infection causes severe and overt disease in fetuses.

The ANA Code for Nurses states that "the nurse provides services unrestricted

Correcting a flawed HIV-testing policy

Regardless of whether human immunodeficiency virus (HIV) testing is voluntary or mandatory, careless procedures can ruin lives and increase liability. Consider this sample case scenario.

SURGEON'S REQUEST

Mike Robertson, a robust, athletic 25-year-old, suffered a herniated disk in a bicycling accident. When bed rest and anti-inflammatories didn't relieve his pain, he was referred to an orthopedic surgeon. The physician recommended surgery but insisted that Mr. Robertson undergo HIV testing before the operation.

"I don't understand why I need an HIV test," Mr. Robertson told Sherry Water, the nurse-counselor who performed his preadmission counseling.

She explained that the physician's request was legal and that it was probably a routine practice. She reviewed the details of the test procedure, emphasizing that a positive result didn't mean that he had acquired immunodeficiency syndrome, although it would mean that he faced a high risk of developing the disease and could infect others. Finally, she pointed out that his test results would remain confidential but, if he preferred, she could refer him to an anonymous testing site.

"No, that's OK," Mr. Robertson replied. "I want to get this done and get my back fixed next week. It's really been killing me."

DEVASTATING RESULTS

Mr. Robertson's surgery was scheduled for the following Tuesday. Ms. Water set up an appointment for Monday afternoon to give him the test results. To her dismay, he was HIV-positive. Then, making things worse, he didn't keep his appointment. Later that day, he called to reschedule the appointment for the morning of the surgery.

Ms. Water became frantic. Should she tell Mr. Robertson the test results just before sur-

gery, when the information could be dangerously upsetting? Should she wait until after surgery, when he would still be somewhat sedated and might not really understand?

Ms. Water finally reached Mr. Robertson's surgeon just an hour before the operation. Even though Mr. Robertson had already received preoperative sedation, the physician immediately canceled surgery. He recommended that Ms. Water explain Mr. Robertson's test results as soon as he woke up. She agreed, knowing that Mr. Robertson would need an explanation for the cancellation.

Mr. Robertson was disappointed and angry that the surgery hadn't taken place and horrified to learn that he was HIV-positive. He felt that his physician had abandoned him, leaving him with two untreated medical problems: his back and his HIV status.

CHANGING HOSPITAL POLICY

Ms. Water also was disappointed and angry. Fortunately, she capitalized on her feelings to improve her hospital's HIV-testing program. She discussed Mr. Robertson's case with the director of nursing and stressed that, in the future, she would refuse to carry out a test unless ample time was provided for posttest counseling. In response, the hospital established new guidelines. Physicians who requested the HIV antibody test before any medical procedure had to verify that posttest counseling had taken place before the procedure could be performed. In addition, the physician was required to specify whether he would continue to care for a patient who tested positive. If not, he would need to designate another physician who would do so.

---

by considerations of social or economic status, personal attributes, or the nature of health problems." Thus, Ms. Smith's refusal to care for AIDS patients because this duty conflicts with her religious be-

liefs isn't ethically viable. No matter how strong a nurse's personal feelings, she can't allow them to interfere with the moral obligation to provide care.

This obligation isn't absolute, however. If the risk to the nurse is greater than the potential benefit to the patient, she can ethically refuse to take that risk. Mrs. James, for example, was justified in refusing to care for patients with CMV infection because of the risk to her unborn child. However, she couldn't avoid caring for patients with *Pneumocystis carinii* pneumonia, where subclinical infection is common and antibodies are present in 75% of 4-year-olds in the United States, or patients with Kaposi's sarcoma, which is a cancer and not infectious.

Nurses may also refuse to perform procedures on a patient who deliberately puts the nurse at risk. For example, if a patient with HIV deliberately moves his arm while the nurse is drawing blood, the nurse has the right to refuse to carry out the procedure. The nurse may even be justified in refusing altogether to care for this patient, but she can't abandon the patient. Ethically and legally, the nurse is required to find someone else to care for him.

What if a patient with AIDS becomes violent or threatens to bite the nurse? If the patient's decisional capability is in doubt, the use of chemical or physical restraints may be justified. If the patient makes threats because of anger, warn him that his aggressive behavior must stop or treatment can't continue. You and the physician should document the patient's behavior, stating, if necessary, that because treatment can't be administered at this time, the patient is being discharged.

Contact notification

The patient's right to privacy may conflict with the nurse's duty to prevent the spread of the disease. Although the patient may balk when the nurse requests that he inform his partner of the HIV-positive status, the nurse should attempt to impress on the patient how crucial it is for the other person to know about exposure to the AIDS virus. Anonymous contact notification programs may provide assistance. Should the patient refuse to cooperate in notifying intimate partners, the nurse would discuss this with the patient's physician and determine that the appropriate state public health agency has been notified of the HIV-positive test results. Certain sexually transmitted infections, such as syphilis, gonorrhea, chlamydia, chancroid, HIV infection, and AIDS are reportable diseases in every state.[10]

Many married patients are reluctant to notify their spouses, especially if the infection can be traced to sexual contact outside the marriage. Legally, nurses can't compel the patient to tell the spouse, but the nurse can explore options that may make it easier for him to do so. For example, ask the patient if he would feel more comfortable if a family physician gave her the news. A counselor could also work with the patient to reduce his anxiety about informing his wife, as well as to support him when he tells her.

Laws dealing with contact notification are ever-changing. For example, in 1998, New York lawmakers passed a law requiring medical personnel to report identifying information of those patients with HIV infection, HIV-related illness, and AIDS to the state health department for the purposes of monitoring, tracking, and notifying sexual partners whom the patient may have infected. Since then, other state legislatures have passed similar laws. This was the basis for the 1998 H.R. 4431 HIV Partner's Protection Act.

As of May 1, 2003, Canadian law requires public health officials to be notified when a person tests positive for HIV, but it doesn't require HIV-positive persons to divulge the names of sexual partners or notify others of a positive test result.

Many states charge HIV-infected individuals with murder when they have unprotected sex with partners whom they didn't inform of their infection. In 1991, a man in Oakland, California, was sentenced to 3 years in prison for this offense. In Florida, a 22-year-old man was convicted of attempted second-degree murder for knowingly engaging in intercourse while infected with HIV. He was sentenced to 4 to 5 years in jail and 13 years of probation.

AIDS and the pregnant patient

Mandatory testing of pregnant women gained support when it was learned that giving a woman zidovudine (Retrovir) significantly lessened the chance of HIV transmission to her fetus. Giving zidovudine to the neonate of an HIV-positive woman also helps the at-risk baby.

Those who favor mandatory testing say the potential reduction in transmission is so important that the woman's autonomy should be set aside. Others condemn forced testing or forced medication and, again, raise the specter of women who fear the test and who then avoid seeking prenatal care and harm more babies in the long run.

Economic impact of AIDS

With the AIDS population rapidly growing, the cost of providing care will cause society to rethink questions about whether health care is a right or a privilege. Nurses must provide care regardless of the patient's ability to pay for it. But what about the rest of the health care system? Must hospitals and government agencies bear the burden of AIDS patients who can't handle the financial burdens imposed by their illness?

The right to health care is, at best, a tentative and unenforceable right with no legal foundation, although most agree that a patient who enters the health care system has a right to receive treatment appropriate to his illness. Still, health care resources are limited, especially for lower- and middle-income and uninsured patients. With such limitations, the best nurses can do is to refer patients to the appropriate social service agencies and support legislation that guarantees equal access to health care.

Substance abuse among coworkers

The ANA estimates that 6% to 8% of nurses in the United States are addicted to alcohol or drugs. In one state study, researchers found that more than 90% of disciplinary hearings for nurses in the state were related to alcohol and drug abuse. These statistics aren't surprising in light of the high stress levels in nursing today. Nurses can experience frustration and feelings of powerlessness when trying to act as patient advocates. Frequent floating to unfamiliar units, unrealistic workloads, and long or double shifts may bring on fatigue and loneliness. Many nurses today must shoulder tremendous family and financial obligations while trying to meet professional demands. And, of course, nurses aren't immune to the harsh social realities of modern life. Combined with the avail-

Substance abuse and healthcare professionals

Question: *What are the risk factors for healthcare professionals and substance abuse?*

Research: Current nursing shortages and increased workload in hospitals can be a risk factor for substance abuse in nurses. Few studies examined risk factors or predictors for alcohol and other substance abuse by health care professionals.

This study examined a stratified randomized sample of 697 dentists, nurses, physicians and pharmacists in a northeastern state. A survey was sent to the participants. The participants were surveyed on lifetime, past year and past month prevalence of alcohol and other substance use. They were also asked the frequency of use and any drug related dysfunctions, misuse or potential misuse.

Conclusion: Despite their admission of past year use, the health care professionals felt that the risk factors included being in situations where they were offered alcohol or other substances, feeling immune to the addictive effects of the drugs and socializing with individuals who

were known substance abusers. Also there was a great risk factor in those healthcare professionals with a younger practice license and a moderate pattern of alcohol use and not socializing with know substance abusers.

Application: Policies need to be instituted by state and national organizations to develop policies that concentrate on prevention, treatment and rehabilitation of healthcare professionals that abuse alcohol and other substances. The study revealed the characteristics of those at risk for substance abuse which will help the organizations develop better policies to protect the public as well as more specific interventions for the healthcare professionals.

Source: Kenna, G.A., and Lewis, D.C. "Risk factors for alcohol and other drug use by healthcare professionals," *Substance Abuse Treatment Prevention and Policy,* 3:3, January 29, 2008.

ability of controlled substances, such stressors can lead a nurse to substance abuse. (See *Substance abuse and health care professionals.*)

Attitudes toward substance abuse

In the past, nurses who were caught abusing drugs or alcohol were punished. The prevailing ethic held that a nurse who abused drugs violated the public trust and the standards of her profession and deserved to be subject to strong disciplinary action.

Nursing administrators were expected to report suspected substance abusers to their state nursing board. The board would then investigate the allegation,

and if it found the nurse guilty, it would impose punishment such as revocation of her license.

In practice, though, many administrators didn't report substance abuse but chose instead to fire the offending nurse. Furthermore, colleagues of a suspected substance abuser commonly didn't report their suspicions because they knew the nurse's job would be in jeopardy. Aware of the harsh treatment that awaited them, nurses who abused drugs or alcohol switched jobs frequently, rather than endure the repercussions that would follow an admission of abuse.

Ethical viewpoint

From an ethical viewpoint, this punitive approach to substance abuse left much to be desired. Administrators who simply fired a substance abuser abnegated their ethical responsibility to help nurses in need and to prevent qualified nurses from dropping out of their profession. Colleagues who didn't report substance abuse abandoned the best interests of both the addicted nurse and her patients. The substance abuser usually switched jobs rather than ask for help. She had little motivation to change, knowing that she was unlikely to receive understanding or rehabilitation.

Current perspectives

Fortunately, society is learning to view substance abuse as a treatable disorder, and the emphasis is on rehabilitating chemically dependent nurses. Within the nursing profession, there's a greater understanding of the importance of peer support for the nurse struggling with addiction. In 2002, the ANA adopted a resolution that called attention to the widespread prevalence of impaired nurses in practice. The resolution addressed ways to help nurses who abuse or are addicted to substances to seek out recovery and get back their careers.[11] The goal of this resolution was to provide support for alternatives to discipline. (See *ANA's resolution for the problem of addiction.*) These alternative programs would provide comprehensive monitoring and support for the impaired nurse so that she could receive treatment and rehabilitation services and eventually return to the workforce. Not all states have adopted this alternative approach model.

Nurse practice acts may include provisions that encourage chemically dependent nurses to complete a treatment program. Many facilities now have policies for dealing with substance abuse among employees, from initial reporting through rehabilitation and returning to work. Also, treatment programs have become commonplace, and associations for recovering nurses are available to provide needed support.

Suspicion of substance abuse

Because of the high rate of chemical dependency among nurses, chances are you'll encounter this problem sometime during your career. Like many nurses, you may experience confusion, guilt, anger, and remorse if faced with the responsibility of confronting and reporting a nurse-addict. Numerous potential ethical conflicts may arise from this situation.

▶ You may resent the increased workload, risk to patients, and stress created by the nurse's drug or alcohol problem.
▶ You may be torn between your obligation to protect patients and your loyalty to a fellow nurse.
▶ You may think that you contributed to the addiction by not acting sooner.
▶ If you aren't entirely certain your suspicions are correct, you may fear the damage you could do to an innocent nurse's reputation and career.
▶ You may have difficulty accepting the addict's self-destructive behavior as part of her addiction.
▶ You may think that you're betraying a friendship.

Though the decision to report a coworker is never an easy one, nurses have an ethical obligation to intervene if they suspect that a colleague is abusing drugs or alcohol. Intervening enables the nurse to fulfill a moral obligation to the

POLICY & POLITICS

ANA's resolution for the problem of addiction

Impaired nursing practice is reflected in the American Nursing Association's (ANA's) Code of Ethics for Nurses in Provision 3: The nurse promotes, advocates for, and strives to protect the health, safety, and rights of patients.

Nurses who are impaired pose a threat to patient safety. In addition, they've failed to care for themselves, which the ANA believes is a part of the nurse's duty for compassion and caring. As a result, in 2002, the ANA House of Delegates resolved the following:

- Support the efforts to educate the public and professional nurses on the prevalence of addiction and psychiatric disorders as diseases for which society and registered nurses are at risk.
- Seek to preserve the current and future workforce by promoting awareness of impaired practice, its prevalence, treatment monitoring, and implications for public safety.
- Increase awareness of the health and patient safety risks associated with untreated addiction and psychiatric illness.
- Renew its commitment to the support of activities that improve nurses' access to alternative-to-discipline programs and promote member

and affiliate actions that encourage the development and use of alternatives to discipline for health professionals in those states where they currently don't exist.
- Support extension of peer assistance to include professional nursing.
- Support efforts by the United American Nurses and the Commission on Workplace Advocacy to advocate for the rehabilitation and retention of nurses who are living with the disease of addiction and psychiatric disorders.
- Support RN regulatory boards in developing alternative-to-discipline programs for recovering nurses deemed appropriate for such programs.

Source: ANA House of Delegates. *The Profession's Response to the Problem of Addiction and Psychiatric Disorders in Nursing*, 2002. Available at *http://www.nursingworld.org/MainMenuCategories/ThePracticeofProfessionalNursing/workplace/ImpairedNurse/Response.aspx.*

colleague: by reporting abuse, the nurse is compelling the coworker to take the first step toward regaining control over her life and undergoing rehabilitation. The nurse also fulfills her obligation to patients by protecting them from a nurse whose judgment and care don't meet professional standards. Reporting a coworker for substance abuse isn't whistleblowing. The ANA's Code of Ethics for Nurses requires that a "nurse's duty is to take action designed to protect patients and to assure that the impaired individual receives assistance in regaining optimal function. Nurses must be vigilant to protect the patient, the public, and the profession from potential harm when a

colleague's practice in any setting appears to be impaired. If impaired practice poses a threat or danger to self or others, regardless of whether the individual has sought help, the nurse must take action to report the individual to persons authorized to address the problem. Nurses who advocate for others whose job performance creates a risk for harm should be protected from negative consequences."[12]

Identification of substance abuse

Be aware that allegations of substance abuse are serious and potentially damaging. To make an accurate assessment, be familiar with the signs of substance abuse. These may include:

▶ rapid mood swings, usually from irritability or depression to elation
▶ frequent absences, lateness, and use of private quarters, such as bathrooms
▶ frequent volunteering to give medications
▶ excessive errors or problems with controlled substances, such as reports of broken vials or spilled drugs
▶ illogical or sloppy charting
▶ inability to meet deadlines or minimum job requirements
▶ avoidance of new and challenging assignments
▶ increased errors in treatment, particularly in dosage computation
▶ poor personal hygiene and appearance
▶ inability to concentrate or remember details
▶ alcohol on the breath
▶ slurred speech, unsteady gait, flushed face, or red eyes
▶ discrepancies in opioid supplies detected at the end of the nurse's shift
▶ opioids signed out to patients only on the nurse's shift
▶ patient complaints of no relief from opioids supposedly given when the nurse is on duty
▶ preference for working alone or on the night shift, when supervision is minimal
▶ social withdrawal
▶ memory loss
▶ alcohol-induced complications, including jaundice, bruises (from falls), and delirium.

Reporting of substance abuse

If a nurse detects signs of substance abuse, the first step is to document them. Include the time, date, and place of the incident; a description of what happened; and the names of any witnesses. Be sure to leave out personal opinions and judgments. For example, "At about 9 p.m. on November 15, 2003, Mrs. Fox in room 501 told me that my injections of morphine were much better than those the other nurse gives. I asked what she meant. She told me that June Barrett's injections never seemed to take away her pain but that mine always did. Two nights later, at 10:15 p.m., I went to the restroom. When I opened the door, I saw June Barrett injecting some solution into her thigh using a hospital syringe. She told me to get out. I did. We didn't talk about it afterward."

Never confront or accuse the suspected nurse on your own. After documenting the incident, discuss it with the nurse-manager. She'll need to gather additional information by examining patient charts, medication records (especially for opioids), and reports from patients and other nurses. After the nurse-manager completes this review, she'll try to determine if the evidence corroborates the incident report.

Confrontation of the coworker

If the nurse-manager concludes that substance abuse is likely, she'll need to confront the nurse with the facts and explain the options. It's hoped that these options will include treatment and perhaps eventual reinstatement in her position. (See *Steps to helping an impaired colleague.*) If you're asked to be present for this confrontation, keep in mind that you best fulfill your moral obligation to the substance abuser by being honest, compassionate, and nonjudgmental and by expressing your willingness to help. Expect that she'll feel threatened and may at-

Steps to helping an impaired colleague

Colleagues can take steps to put a stop to a nurse-addict's self-destructive behavior. By using an effective, nonpunitive, group-oriented approach, they can break the cycle of addiction. In this approach, group members confront the nurse-addict, help her to acknowledge her condition, and motivate her to seek rehabilitation before she harms a patient or herself.

INTERVENTION TEAM

The team includes two to ten carefully selected persons who are personal and professional associates of the nurse-addict. If possible, the team also includes a colleague who has successfully entered rehabilitation and a nurse who possesses experience in treating drug and alcohol addiction.

Team members must share a nonjudgmental attitude. Each must accept that the nurse's self-destructive behavior represents an aspect of her illness and doesn't indicate that she's morally deficient. Furthermore, each should avoid expressing judgments about her.

CONFRONTING THE COLLEAGUE

- Team members document all evidence of the nurse's chemical dependence, including the date, time, and place of relevant incidents.
- They should be careful not to include any judgmental remarks in their documentation.
- The team leader reviews all important documentation, including patient charts, nurses' notes, physician's orders, medication administration and opioid records, and the impaired nurse's personnel file.
- Team members meet with the impaired nurse in a private room away from the nurses' station. The group leader explains why the team has gathered. Participants present their evidence, always prefacing their testimony with positive remarks.
- The impaired nurse is given a chance to respond.
- The team leader makes clear the options available to the impaired nurse. The impaired nurse is given an opportunity to voluntarily enter a treatment program; otherwise, she may lose her job and be reported to the state board of nursing.
- Arrangements are made for the team leader to monitor how the nurse is progressing in therapy.
- Events of the meeting are documented.
- To ease the tension stirred up by the confrontation, the team leader may arrange for follow-up discussions.

tempt to deny her condition, even if the facts are fully substantiated.

In most substance abuse cases, if the nurse is willing to enter a treatment program and successfully completes it, no disciplinary action is taken against her. If the nurse refuses to enter treatment, she may be reported to the state board of nursing, suspended, or dismissed.

Recovery

In most instances, the recovering nurse can return to work. She may be placed under a special contract that stipulates conditions for continued employment. These conditions may include:

▶ attending weekly meetings with a counselor
▶ participating in a 12-step program and meetings with other recovering nurses
▶ submitting to random blood and urine screenings
▶ remaining drug-free.

The nurse-manager who's responsible for the recovering nurse should carefully document all meetings and keep a copy of all contracts.

The chemically dependent nurse's colleagues must use their professional train-

National Organ Transplant Act

In response to widespread public interest in organ transplantation, Congress enacted the National Organ Transplant Act of 1984 (PL 98-507). This act:
• prohibits the sale of organs
• provides funding for grants to organ procurement agencies
• establishes a national organ-sharing system.

TASK FORCE ON ORGAN TRANSPLANTATION
This act also convened the 25-member Task Force on Organ Transplantation, with members representing medicine, law, theology, ethics, allied health, the health insurance industry, and the general public. Representatives from the Office of the Surgeon General, the National Institutes of Health, the Food and Drug Administration, and the Health Care Financing Administration also were appointed to the task force. This task force examined the medical, legal, ethical, economic, and social issues created by organ transplantation.

In its final report, the task force concluded that the best way to close the gap between the small number of organ donors and the large number of potential transplant recipients was to actively solicit donations from bereaved families. As a result, the task force recommended that all state legislatures introduce and enact legislation requiring health care professionals to present organ donation as an option to families ("required request").

ASSERTIVE APPROACH
Required request policies are legally mandated in many states. This assertive approach to organ procurement has proved highly successful; as many as 80% of families given the option to become donor families ultimately do so. Significantly, studies show that organ donation can facilitate the grieving process and speed recovery for the bereaved family.

ing to try to understand the nurse's condition. Coworkers play a crucial role in the recovering nurse's ultimate success or failure. When recovering from addiction, a person's needs include:
▶ finding ways to improve self-esteem, including assertiveness training
▶ developing a stronger support system
▶ developing stress management and coping techniques
▶ learning to come to terms with past traumatic experiences, such as physical or sexual abuse.

Welcoming a recovering nurse back to the work setting and offering support during the critical transition period is as important as detecting and reporting signs of abuse. From an ethical point of view, working with a colleague who's a substance abuser can be frustrating and uncomfortable, but helping a nurse recognize her problem and begin the process of recovery is an act of significant moral courage and humanity. It's a prime example of advocacy.

Organ donation and transplantation
When asked, most people say that they support organ donation. However, only a small percentage of qualified organs are ever donated. Tens of thousands of names are on waiting lists for organs in the United States alone.

The benefits of organ transplantation are widely recognized by health care professionals and the general public. Nevertheless, organ transplantation poses serious ethical concerns. Transplant procedures affect families of the donor and the recipient, nurses, physicians, and even emergency medical personnel at the deepest emotional level. In such a highly

IN THE NEWS

Revised Uniform Anatomical Gift Act, 2006

According to the Uniform Anatomical Gift Act, a person becomes a donor only if the donor or someone acting on the donor's behalf specifically indicates the desire to make the anatomical gift. This is the underlying rule for the revised Act and all previous Acts, indicating that the choice for organ donation is done freely.

The revised Act of 2006 is limited specifically to anatomical gifts from deceased donors based on the choice to donate made before or after their deaths. Donations by living donors aren't addressed in this Act. For an anatomical gift under this act, the prospective donor must be declared dead.

Some of the important changes associated with the revised act include:
• Expansion of the list of those who may make anatomical gifts
• Permission for minors eligible to apply for a driver's license to be a donor
• Establishment of standards for donor registries
• Recognition of anatomical gifts made under the laws of other jurisdictions
• Allowance for use of electronic records and signatures.

Source: The National Conference of Commissioners on Uniform State Laws. *Uniform Anatomical Gift Act.* Available at *http://www.anatomicalgiftact.org/*.

charged atmosphere, conflicts of rights easily can develop.

▶ If the potential donor is a child, questions may arise as to the validity of informed consent.

▶ Controversy may occur over when to declare a potential donor dead.

▶ The wishes of a potential donor's family may conflict with the needs of a transplant patient.

▶ Because the number of available donor organs is limited, difficult choices must be made about which patients should receive transplants.

▶ Many transplants are prohibitively expensive; questions arise as to whether subsidizing the procedure is a just allocation of health care resources.

▶ In light of the limited number of available donor organs and the high cost of the procedure, questions arise as to the patient's right to multiple transplants.

Even if nurses don't make the ultimate medical decisions about an organ transplant, they may play a critical role in resolving ethical conflicts.

Legislation

Several pieces of legislation have been passed related to organ donation. In 1984, the U.S. Congress passed the National Organ Transplant Act. This Act was designed to address the shortage of organs available for donation. It established the Organ Procurement and Transplantation Network to create a national registry for organ matching. (See *National Organ Transplant Act.*)

In addition, the Uniform Anatomical Gift Act was passed originally in 1968 and revised in 1987. It was further revised and amended in July of 2006.[13] This act governs the donation of organs and tissues. (See *Revised Uniform Anatomical Gift Act, 2006.*)

Protection of donor rights

Some transplantation procedures pose few ethical problems. An autograft, in which tissue is transplanted from one part of the patient's body to another (such as a skin graft to treat a third-degree burn) is a good example. Certain types of transplants from one person to another (allograft), including blood transfusions and cornea or bone marrow transplants, also are widely accepted and ethically untainted.

The most difficult ethical issues surround the procurement of essential organs, such as hearts, kidneys, livers, and lungs. In these instances, organ procurement remains ethical only if steps are taken to ensure that the donor's life and functional integrity aren't compromised.

Nonmaleficence

At first glance, removing an organ from a healthy person who has nothing to gain from the procedure seems to violate the ethical principle of *nonmaleficence*—the obligation to "do no harm." However, when providing care, there are many instances in which the principle of nonmaleficence can't be strictly applied. Some harm, in the form of an invasive or a potentially risky procedure, must be incurred in diagnosing and treating many diseases.

When a living person donates the organ, the key issue is informed consent. From both an ethical and a legal standpoint, informed consent requires the donor to be fully aware of all risks and benefits that can result from the transplant procedure. Because relatives, particularly identical twins or full siblings, typically provide the closest match for a transplanted organ, a great deal of emotional pressure can be exerted on a po-

tential donor. Extreme guilt feelings and emotional distress may disturb a potential donor's ability to render informed consent.

Children as donors

Special problems arise when the potential donor is a child. Because, in most cases, a minor's consent is legally invalid, the parents or legal guardians must give substitute consent. The revised Uniform Anatomical Gift Act allows a minor who can obtain a driver's license to identify himself as an organ donor.[14]

Sometimes the wishes of the child and the parents are clearly the same. A 13-year-old girl whose parents support her wish to donate a kidney to her 5-year-old brother can probably give valid informed consent. But what about a 3-year-old child who can't express his opinion? Can his parents ethically "volunteer" this child to donate a kidney? Parents have a moral obligation to protect the life and well-being of all their children. Sometimes it's unclear how to best uphold this obligation. Which are more important—the rights of the healthy child or the rights of the child who needs the kidney?

In a widely publicized 1991 case, physicians at the City of Hope Medical Center in Duarte, California, transplanted bone marrow into Anissa Ayala, a 19-year-old woman with potentially fatal leukemia. The marrow came from her infant sister, Marissa. The parents said that they conceived Marissa to provide bone marrow to save Anissa's life. This marked the first time a family publicly admitted to conceiving a child to serve as an organ or a tissue donor.

The case raised troubling ethical questions. Does conceiving a child as a source of donated organs violate the principle that children should be brought into the world and cherished for their own sake and no other motive? If prenatal tests indicate that the fetus has the wrong tissue type to serve as a donor, is an abortion justifiable? Selling organs is both unethical and illegal in many countries, but the legal and ethical status of conceiving potential donors remains unclear.

Deceased donors

Harvesting organs from a deceased donor poses a different set of ethical problems. Perhaps the most fundamental issue involves the actual definition of *death*. Although some organs and tissues, such as bone, skin, corneas, and even kidneys, can be transplanted after complete cardiac arrest, other organs, including the heart, lungs, liver, and pancreas, aren't viable unless they're taken from a brain-dead, or "beating heart," cadaver.

Most states recognize the definition of brain death set forth by the Uniform Determination of Death Act as the legal definition of death. In general terms, a patient is pronounced brain dead when all functional activity in every area of the brain, including the brain stem, stops. Significantly, this definition isn't universally accepted by health care workers, ethicists, or lay persons. Many find it difficult to declare death when other aspects of bodily function continue, even if by artificial support.

The issue of declaring brain death must be approached cautiously. The determination that a person is brain dead should be made by neurologic consult and never by a physician who's involved in organ removal. No request for organ donation should be made until the potential donor's family understands what brain death is as well as the finality of its state.

Informed consent

The Uniform Anatomical Gift Act allows a person to donate specific organs or even his entire body for organ transplantation. A patient who, before death, indicated his willingness to be an organ donor could be considered to have given informed consent. True informed consent, however, requires that the patient have the option to withdraw consent at any time before a medical procedure. Therefore, the final decision is left up to the potential donor's family, even if it results in the loss of an organ donation.

In the United States, the "opt-in" principle is used as the rule. According to this principle, a person becomes a donor only if he or someone acting on his behalf "affirmatively makes the anatomical gift."[15] This is in contrast to other countries, such as Europe, who adhere to an "opt-out" policy. Here, the person is considered to be a donor unless he or another person acting on his behalf states otherwise. This policy is commonly referred to as "presumed consent." (See *Organ donation and the concept of consent*, page 356.)

The donor and family

All states have enacted required request acts. These laws require hospitals to ask families of potential organ donors to permit donation. The required request laws are intended to increase organ availability.

Most required request laws are fair to the families of potential donors. Family members are under no compulsion to grant permission to donate organs. Most required request acts grant an exclusion

Organ donation and the concept of consent

Recent legislative initiatives to increase the supply of organs available for donation have sought to broaden the definition of consent. One recent proposal is based on the concept of presumed consent—the assumption that all sane and rational people would consent to donate organs if they had the chance to do so.

Under this legislation, each person would be considered an organ donor unless he carried a card stating that he didn't want to donate his organs. Rather than being asked if they wanted to have their loved one's organs transplanted, family members would be asked if they had any objections to transplantation.

A VIOLATION OF INFORMED CONSENT?

Although the doctrine of presumed consent is applied to other aspects of health care law, when applied to organ donation, it's a controversial idea. Opponents argue that it's coercive and violates the right to informed consent. It contradicts the widely held belief that a person should have free choice in all decisions related to his own body.

For additional information about this topic, see Gundle, K. "Presumed consent for organ donation. Perspectives of Health Policy Specialists 2004. [Online.] Available at http://surj.stanford.edu/2004/pdfs/gundle.pdf.

if the request will cause the family severe emotional distress.

These laws may create serious ethical conflicts, however, for a nurse who opposes organ transplantation or who finds the idea of approaching a grieving family offensive. Should a nurse be forced to request organ donation regardless of her feelings? One solution to this dilemma is assigning the job of approaching the donor's family to an organ procurement team whose members have been specially trained to deal with emotional situations.

If a nurse is making the request for an organ donation from a patient's family, she should approach family members tactfully and be sufficiently informed to answer their questions. The nurse should be able to explain the potential good to others, while remembering that the decision of the family must be respected.

Use of fetal tissue

Because the mother and the health care team carrying out an abortion are responsible for the death of the fetus, the transplantation of fetal tissue is far more controversial than transplantation where the donor is a cadaver. (See Fetal tissue and stem cell research, discussed later in this chapter.)

Use of organs from anencephalic infants

Anencephaly is the congenital absence of most or all of the cerebral hemispheres. Many anencephalic infants are stillborn, but others have a functional brain stem and live for a short time after birth.

Anencephalic infants might seem to be ideal organ donors. Their immune systems are still immature, reducing the chance of rejection. Also, their small organs can be readily used in children, who commonly encounter the most trouble locating a suitable donor.

The anencephalic infant, however, isn't a "beating heart" cadaver. Although severely debilitated, an infant with a functioning brain stem must be considered to be in a persistent vegetative state or a coma, not brain dead. Until an anencephalic infant meets the clinical criteria for brain death, his organs can't ethically be used for transplantation.

Laws have been proposed that would increase the supply of organs available for donation from anencephalic infants by broadening the definition of brain death (to discount brain stem function). Another option, called *presumed consent,* would presume every person would donate unless they carried a card stating otherwise.

Care of a potential donor

If a nurse is caring for a patient who's a potential donor, her ethical responsibility includes maintaining the patient's dignity as a human being until he's declared legally dead. Follow normal cleaning and skin maintenance procedures and keep the body properly covered. Also adhere to the physician's instructions for stopping medication and avoiding procedures that could damage the organ.

Maintaining a brain-dead patient until preparations for the transplant are complete raises additional ethical questions. If *death* is defined as "brain death," doesn't the patient have the right to die when this determination is made? If not, how long can he be ethically maintained on a life-support system? One day? One week? Is this a justifiable allocation of resources? The effort and money spent to maintain a brain-dead organ donor for any appreciable period might be better spent helping living patients.

Selection of transplant recipients

The number of potential transplant recipients far exceeds the number of available donors. How should one determine who receives a transplant and who's turned down?

Medical and physical factors rule out some matches. For example, the donor and the recipient must have compatible blood and tissue types and be fairly close in size and age (it would be impossible to place a 30-year-old accident victim's heart in the chest cavity of a 5-year-old patient). Beyond these limitations, the selection of transplant recipients depends on value judgments. As a result, the potential for serious value conflicts and unethical behavior is tremendous. For example, the high cost of transplantation raises questions about the fair distribution of organs. Should a wealthy or well-insured patient be given priority over an indigent patient with a similar need? (See *Choosing between potential transplant recipients,* page 358.)

Another concern is transplanting organs into people whose unhealthy lifestyles have destroyed their health. Mickey Mantle's 1995 liver transplant is a case in point. He had admitted causing damage through years of alcohol and drug abuse. When he died quickly of lung cancer, his long-term smoking became an issue as well. Considering his lifestyle, should he have been a successful transplant candidate?

Ethically, the principle of distributive justice could work both ways in lifestyle cases. Underlying the principle is the belief in equal treatment, which suggests that Mr. Mantle should have had an even chance at a new liver. In the other view, distributive justice applied to scarce resources says the organs should go to people more likely to sustain them with a healthy lifestyle.

To ensure that transplant recipients are selected as fairly as possible, most medical centers have adopted certain guidelines, which are discussed on the next pages.

Choosing between potential transplant recipients

One concern about organ transplantation is the potential for elitism when choosing one recipient over another. Consider the following situation, in which the committee on organ donation and transplantation at a major teaching hospital had to choose between two potential liver recipients.

PATRON'S DAUGHTER

Jodi Morgan, a 5-year-old girl, received a liver transplant 18 months ago. Although her initial response was promising, she has recently been hospitalized again with signs of irreversible hepatic failure.

Jodi was born with multiple birth defects. In addition to biliary atresia, which led to her need for a transplant, she has only one functioning kidney and a cyanotic heart defect. She's mildly retarded and can't speak and has only recently mastered toilet training.

Jodi's father, Jack, is a prominent local businessman, politician, and patron of the hospital. He wants Jodi placed at the head of the registry for a second liver transplant. She spent 4 months on the registry before her first transplant. Nonetheless, rumors spread that Mr. Morgan had "bought" Jodi's first transplant by making a sizable donation to the hospital's new cardiology wing.

MOTHER OF THREE

Brenda DeStefano, a 22-year-old mother of three young children, heads the list of potential liver recipients. In chronic hepatic failure for nearly 2 years, she has been on the transplant list most of that time and is now near death. She's unemployed and has no health insurance. Because the federal government won't reimburse for a liver transplant, the hospital stands little chance of being paid for her surgery.

COMMITTEE DECISION

According to state law, Jodi couldn't receive a second transplant unless she was returned to the registry. But should she be placed at the head of the list?

The committee struggled with many ethical questions:
• Mr. Morgan would probably exert a great deal of political and financial pressure on the hospital. Could committee members realistically ignore this factor?
• How might past rumors that Mr. Morgan bought Jodi's first transplant influence the present thinking of committee members?
• Mrs. DeStefano's inability to pay would probably create a financial hardship for the hospital. Should this influence its decision?
• Do risk-benefit calculations justify another procedure for Jodi Morgan? Because of her underlying cardiac pathology and renal dysfunction, even if the transplant is successful, her prognosis is poor. The potential for success of the transplant is less than it would be for healthier patients.
• Should a child such as Jodi be given automatic preference over an adult? What about Mrs. DeStefano's children? Should their right to have a mother be an overriding consideration?

After much debate, the committee decided to return Jodi to the transplant list, behind Mrs. DeStefano. After a donor was found for Mrs. DeStefano, Jodi could have a second chance at life.

Transplant coordination

A regional organ donation center is expected to coordinate the matching of transplant recipients and potential donors. The principle of "first come, first served" should form one criterion for selection.

All transplant decisions are expected to be made by a committee under the auspices of an impartial organization such as the American Red Cross that includes a physician, nurse, lawyer, religious leader, and well-informed lay person. The committee should take every precaution, including the institution of policies and procedures, to prevent transplanting the wrong organ or other deleterious events.

Neither the donor nor his family ought to play a role in the selection procedure. Because of the potential for manipulation (a payoff by the recipient), such participation isn't compatible with an ethical selection procedure.

Determination of need

The selection procedure should be based on need as well as the potential for survival. Patients with the greatest need (those closest to death) and best survival potential are assigned the highest priority.

Determination of potential for survival

Survival is a more complex issue than need. For example, the potential for survival doesn't necessarily decrease as a patient ages. A health-conscious elderly patient may represent a better transplant risk than a younger patient who has neglected his health.

A patient's willingness to comply with lifestyle changes, drug regimens, and dietary restrictions can also influence survival. Lifestyle factors may raise questions about a patient's suitability as a transplant recipient. Should a heavy smoker who refuses to quit be given a heart-lung transplant? Because of the controversy created by Mickey Mantle's liver transplant and subsequent debate over the fairness of organ donation, the United Network for Organ Sharing (UNOS) began, in 1998, to develop a new system, including a way to make donor livers available on a nationwide basis.

UNOS has moved from a local to a regional allocation system. In 1998, categories of potential recipients were revised: status 4, the least serious, was eliminated, and status 2 was divided into 2A and 2B. The 1999 naturalistic data on regional and state sharing reveal that:
▶ sharing increases the most serious status 1 transplantation rates
▶ sharing decreases status 2B pretransplantation mortality
▶ sharing decreases transplantation rates of status 3 patients, thereby providing more organs for seriously ill patients
▶ sharing, which decreased transplantation rates for status 3 patients, didn't provide a concomitant increase in mortality of status 3 patients.

Determination of potential value to community

The selection procedure can also take into account a potential recipient's value to the community. A good case could be made for assigning a higher priority to a mother of two young children than to a convicted drug dealer. Note that value is the last criterion, to be used only if a decision can't be made based on need or potential for survival.

Last resort

When other criteria fail to establish priority, the final selection should be made by lot. Although imperfect, this method is unbiased.

Cost considerations

Organ transplants can be prohibitively expensive. Considering the costs for organ procurement, hospital, physician, evaluation, follow-up and immunosuppressant therapy, a kidney transplant costs about $226,000; a heart transplant may exceed $500,000. A liver transplant can cost close to $450,000 while a pancreatic transplant can cost over $300,000.[16] Third party reimbursement for the services vary across the country and with the individual payor.

Along the same line, one might pose an even more challenging question: Is it fair for one person to receive that great a share of the limited funds available for health care? The cost of a heart transplant would finance inoculations for several thousand children or prenatal care for hundreds of women. Utilitarian ethical theory would claim that the rights of hundreds of potential patients to a quality life exceed the right of one person to a heart transplant.

Additional considerations

The issue of multiple transplants is closely related to the concept of distributive justice. At first glance, it might seem unethical, or at least unfair, for the same person to receive three or four transplants. The nurses and physicians caring for a transplant recipient, however, may believe that everything possible must be done to keep the patient alive, including another transplant.

Perhaps the most equitable course of action is to place a repeat-transplant patient back on the regional transplant center register for a fair evaluation.

An additional wrinkle has been added to the debate over transplant ethics. In January 1999, a man in the United States had a hand transplant to replace the one he lost some 13 years before in a firecracker accident; a man in Italy underwent a testicular transplant in the spring of the same year. Although the initial procedures were successful, the long-term outcome of these transplants is still uncertain.

The ethical issues involved revolve around beneficence and maleficence. Before the procedures, these transplant recipients were healthy. It's accepted that all surgeries have risks, but transplant surgeries are riskier than most because of the length of time they take and the possible damage they may cause to the vascular system. Also, there are many possible complications, including embolus formation in the attached appendage, the possibility of infection due to the use of antirejection drugs posttransplant, and the transmission of diseases, such as hepatitis and HIV.

The fundamental question becomes, "Does the health care provider violate the principle of beneficence by changing an otherwise healthy person (who's missing a hand or other body part) into an immunocompromised patient who will need to take antirejection drugs for the rest of his life?" We justify the dangers of transplantation and antirejection drugs in kidney, heart, and liver transplants because these transplants are performed for life-threatening conditions. However, missing a hand or set of testes, although inconvenient, definitely isn't life-threatening.

ETHICAL CONFLICTS IN SPECIALTY AREAS OF PRACTICE

Nurses practice in all different areas interacting with a variety of patients with wide-ranging needs. Subsequently they may be faced with unique ethical dilemmas owing to the nature of the practice area. Several specialty practice areas are addressed here.

Intensive care and emergency nursing

Nurses working in intensive care or the emergency department routinely deal with ethical dilemmas. These dilemmas commonly revolve around quality-of-life issues, especially as they relate to end-of-life decisions, such as DNR orders, life support, and patients' requests for no heroic measures. When considering quality of life, nurses must ensure that others don't impose their own value systems on the patient. Each person has a set of personal values that are influenced by environment and culture. Nurses also have a set of professional values.

Common ethical dilemmas

The threat of death is common in intensive care and emergency departments. Perhaps at no other time is the holistic care of patients and their families as important as it is during this time.

End-of-life decisions are almost always difficult for patients, families, and health care professionals. Intensive care and emergency nurses are in a unique position as advocates to assist patients and their families through this process.

The nurse's primary role as patient advocate is to promote the patient's wishes. In many instances, however, the patient's wishes may not be known. Decisions aren't always easy to make and answers aren't usually clear cut.

Sometimes it's difficult to determine what can be done to achieve good quality of life and what can simply be achieved technologically.

Historically, death was considered a natural part of life and most people died

at home surrounded by their families. Today, most people die in hospitals, and death is commonly regarded as a medical failure rather than a natural event. Sometimes it may be difficult to determine if the nurse is assisting in extending a patient's life or delaying his death.

Medical futility of interventions is another area leading to ethical dilemmas for intensive care and emergency nurses. Even though the interventions appear to be effective, how much of a benefit are they, especially when the situation is hopeless.

The issue of withholding and withdrawing treatment in the intensive care unit or emergency department presents some ethical dilemmas. Treatment withdrawal, even when requested by the patient, seems to contradict the ethical principle of nonmaleficence.

The use of advance directives may be helpful in resolving some of the ethical issues surrounding end-of-life care. Although the Patient Self-Determination Act requires hospitals and other institutions to make information available for patients, it isn't mandatory for patients to have advance directives. Thus the nurse may be faced with a patient who hasn't discussed his wishes with his family and subsequently must rely on uninformed members to make important health care decisions.

Organ donation is another area that intensive care and emergency nurses face. Family members may be dealing with a sudden unexpected tragedy and loss, such as in the case of a trauma victim, or grieving for the patient who's approaching death. Regardless of the situation, nurses are faced with dealing with families at a very difficult time in their lives, and questioning them about their wishes for organ donation. (See Organ donation and transplantation, discussed earlier in this chapter.)

Mental health and psychiatric nursing

Nurses working in the mental health and psychiatric fields face ethical dilemmas commonly involving the patient's rights, including the right to treatment, right to refuse treatment, right to informed consent, and the right to privacy.

Ethical principles commonly involved with mental health and psychiatric nursing include autonomy, beneficence, veracity and fidelity, and justice. For the mental health and psychiatric nurse, ethics and the law go hand-in-hand.

One common area of ethical conflict involves behavior control. Behavior control can involve psychotherapy, aversion therapy, desensitization, psychopharmacology, seclusion and restraints, and electroconvulsive therapy. The ultimate goal is to help the person achieve socially acceptable behavior.

Ethical concerns arise due to the conflict between the individual's right to freedom, including the right to self-determination and the right to refuse treatment and society's obligation to maintain order. Misuse of behavior control measures suppresses personal freedom. In addition, these measures may deprive the individual with mental health problems the right to choose his course of treatment without coercion. Moreover, behavioral changes that meet society's needs may contradict the patient's wishes and needs.

The patient's right to confidentiality and privacy also is an area in which conflict can arise. Disclosure of confidential information is appropriate only in the following situations: suspected child abuse, criminal cases, government requests, and potential threat to the public or an individual. (For additional information, see Chapter 5, Legal risks on the job.)

Perinatal and child health nursing

Some of the most difficult decisions made in the health care setting are those involving children and their families. Maternal-neonatal nursing and child health nursing are family centered. Conflicts commonly arise because family members may not agree on how a situation should be handled. In addition, the values of the health care provider may conflict with those of the family.

Critically ill and preterm neonates

Twenty years ago, a neonate born at 26 weeks' gestation had almost no chance of surviving, yet today such neonates can survive. Thanks to spectacular advances in neonatology, such as intrauterine surgery, synthetic lung surfactant, and new antibiotics, physicians can save increasingly smaller and sicker infants.

Many people argue that this lifesaving technology has gone too far. Physicians and nurses who treat critically ill neonates, they say, act too aggressively, commonly overriding the wishes of the neonate's parents. Treatment leads to even greater suffering for the neonate and places an enormous financial burden on society. Ethical questions are complicated by lack of knowledge about the long-term outcome of heroic measures.

Sanctity of life versus quality of life
Without life, other values are irrelevant. As a result, society holds the sanctity of

life in high regard. The belief that all human lives have meaning and ought to be respected supports the notion that a critically ill infant should be kept alive at any cost.

But what about the quality of life? A utilitarian ethic would support a decision to withhold treatment for a severely disabled neonate when the prospect for an acceptable quality of life is poor. But what's an "acceptable quality of life?"

One measure of the value of a person's life is his ability to achieve certain goals. Thus, if a neonate has little hope of achieving anything but sheer survival, it may be ethically acceptable to terminate treatment.

The best-interest criterion is another measure of the quality of life. Unfortunately, not everyone agrees on its exact meaning. Is death ever in anyone's best interest?

Still another definition considers the patient's potential to establish some type of human relationship. According to this view, an infant who has little chance of recognizing and relating to his family has such a poor quality of life that withholding treatment is both compassionate and ethical. There are two objections to the human-relationship standard. First, the standard suggests that medical treatment be withheld from adults who have a limited capacity for human relationships. You would almost certainly find it morally unacceptable to refuse to perform an emergency appendectomy on a psychotic patient or to withhold medication from a comatose automobile accident victim.

Some experts argue that the infant isn't the only one with a right to an acceptable quality of life. The financial and emotional cost of sophisticated perinatal technology places an enormous burden on the infant's family and on society in general. Is this too great a price for a few extra months or years of life?

Decision making

The best-qualified person to make a quality-of-life decision is the patient himself. But who's best qualified to give proxy consent for a premature neonate born at 25 weeks' gestation?

Parents

Although no one knows the neonate's true desires, legal and ethical precedent suggests that his parents ought to be the chief decision makers. Others argue that the parents' ability to make a wise and rational decision on short notice in such an emotionally charged atmosphere is limited. Furthermore, few parents have the necessary medical knowledge to make an informed decision. The combination of time pressures, ignorance, prejudice, and religious or moral beliefs can force parents into a decision that's at odds with the opinions of the medical team caring for their neonate.

Health care team

Members of the health care team are more objective and better informed about the potential outcomes of the various treatment options. Ethically, however, this paternalistic approach is unacceptable. After all, the health care team won't bear the burden of raising the child.

Ethics committee

Unfortunately, the slow pace of most committee decisions is incompatible with the rapid decisions required when treating seriously ill neonates. Also, using this approach might simply substitute the biases of the committee members for the biases of the parents, physicians, and nurses.

Courts

As the designated protector of individual rights, the legal system typically takes a narrow view of the issues. For example, up to the time of birth, greater weight is given to the rights of the mother. However, during or after birth, the courts usually have decided that the rights of the neonate supersede those of the parents.

"Baby, Doe" regulations

Court-mandated settlements to perinatal ethical conflicts have created significant debate. The best-known case involved a neonate born with Down syndrome and a tracheoesophageal fistula. The family opted to forgo surgical treatment of the fistula and withhold supplemental nutrition, reasoning that the child's quality of life was too severely compromised. A nurse caring for the child disagreed. She contacted the authorities, but during the ensuing legal battle, the neonate died.

On the basis of this and similar cases, the federal government instituted regulations standardizing the care of critically ill or severely disabled neonates. Enacted under the umbrella of the Child Abuse Protection and Treatment Act, these "Baby Doe" regulations prohibited physicians and nurses from denying treatment to disabled infants. The only exceptions were infants in an irreversible coma; those for whom treatment would prolong dying, not life; and those for whom treatment would be futile or even inhumane. Violators could be prosecuted for negligence or malpractice.

Some lawmakers opposed the constitutionality of the Baby Doe regulations. The Supreme Court agreed and, in June 1986, struck down federal laws requiring the treatment of all disabled neonates. Furthermore, it reinforced the right to privacy by denying access to Baby Doe's medical records. Because many states backed up the federal laws with their own Baby Doe regulations, it's still possible to be prosecuted for withholding treatment.

The major ethical problem with these regulations is their failure to address the quality-of-life issue. Also, they're based on the mistaken assumption that a set of rigid laws can take the place of the ethical decision-making process. The American Academy of Pediatrics (AAP) "supports individualized decision making about life-sustaining medical treatment for all children, regardless of age."[17] The AAP recommends a joint decision-making process that involves the parents and health care providers.

Implications for nurses

The repeal of federal Baby Doe regulations hasn't clarified the ethical issues surrounding the care of critically ill infants. If anything, by creating a conflict between the federal government and state and local laws, it has made the situation even more complicated.

To help the parents of an extremely premature or critically ill neonate reach ethically sound decisions, nurses need to present all available options in a compassionate, unbiased manner using simple terms. By carefully considering the pros and cons of both initiating and withholding treatment, nurses can help family members come to terms with their child's condition and reach a decision with

Critically ill neonate

If you care for extremely premature or severely disabled infants or their mothers, family members will look to you to assist them in life-and-death decisions. Consider the nurse's role in this case study.

GRIM PROGNOSIS

Matthew Klein, a microcephalic infant with transposition of the great arteries, was born more than 6 weeks prematurely. He also had spina bifida. The news of his condition was devastating to his parents, an older professional couple who had eagerly anticipated their first child.

The attending pediatrician asked a noted neurosurgeon and a pediatric cardiologist to consult on Matthew's case. These experts concurred that without immediate corrective surgery, he might live as long as 1 month on life support. Even with surgery, he probably wouldn't live past age 20. During that time, physicians explained to Mr. and Mrs. Klein that Matthew could be expected to suffer from seizure disorders, paralysis, and episodes of heart failure. He would be highly susceptible to infection and severely retarded. In fact, he faced a grave risk just from the surgery.

TREATMENT OPTIONS

Mr. and Mrs. Klein were given two options. They could choose aggressive surgical intervention for their child. If Matthew survived, he would need additional surgery at age 4 and again at age 10. Alternatively, the Kleins could elect a conservative treatment plan, which included antibiotics, nutrition, and comfort measures but no heroic treatment.

Angelica Perez, a registered nurse with more than 3 years of experience in caring for seriously ill neonates, was assigned as Matthew's primary nurse. Ms. Perez soon realized that

Matthew's parents were overwhelmed. She knew that, as a result, their decision-making ability was compromised.

Ms. Perez strongly believed in the sanctity of life, but her practical experience gave her an appreciation for quality-of-life issues. In her professional opinion, the quality of Matthew's life was likely to be poor, and the conservative treatment option would be the best.

She carefully reviewed both treatment plans with Matthew's parents, analyzing the possible outcomes and explaining unfamiliar medical terms. She pointed out that even with surgical intervention, Matthew might be too severely brain damaged to ever recognize or interact with them. Mrs. Klein would have to quit her job to care for Matthew, and his medical expenses would pose an enormous financial burden. Eventually, he was almost certain to require institutional care.

Ms. Perez recognized that the conservative option presented problems for the Kleins as well. Deeply religious, both husband and wife strongly opposed mercy killing. They had difficulty seeing the distinction between allowing their son to die and actually causing his death.

Even after extensive counseling, the Kleins couldn't reach a decision. At this point, Ms. Perez suggested that the couple discuss their feelings with the physician, a social worker, and their minister. As a result of these discussions, Mr. and Mrs. Klein accepted the conclusion that conservative treatment was best for Matthew. The baby survived 2 weeks and died in his mother's arms.

---

which they can live. (See *Critically ill neonate.*)

Abortion

Abortion poses a complex and painful ethical dilemma for nurses and their pa-

tients. Consider the cases described here.

▶ Ashley Adams, a pregnant 14-year-old, quietly wept with her mother sitting next to her. They were waiting in the short procedure unit for Ashley's turn in the operating room. When the nurse took her aside to talk privately, Ashley began to cry harder. She told the nurse that she didn't really want an abortion but her parents had placed so much pressure on her that she had no real choice.

▶ Loretta Hofmann was pregnant with her fourth child. Recently fired from his job, her husband had begun drinking heavily and on more than one occasion had become emotionally abusive. One of her three children was hyperactive and having trouble in school. Mrs. Hofmann believed that she couldn't handle another child or cope with going through a pregnancy and placing the child for adoption. To get to the abortion clinic, she had to pass through a picket line of pro-life protesters, who harassed and taunted her. During her initial interview with the nurse, she was visibly shaken and said that she could no longer cope with the stress in her life.

▶ Lynnette Mack worked in a women's health center that provided general family planning, treatment for vaginal infections, counseling, health care for adolescents, and abortion services. Although she was fervently pro-choice when she took the job, over the months her feelings about abortion changed. She wanted to continue working at the center but without participating in abortions. She feared that this would create tension as well as extra work for her colleagues. Mrs. Mack, who was the primary wage earner for her family, considered resigning for ethical reasons.

The U.S. Supreme Court has handed down more than 20 decisions related to the abortion issue. Court rulings, however, can't answer the ethical questions about abortion that nurses encounter in their daily practice.

Fetus as a human being?

The status of the fetus as a human life is an important element in the abortion controversy. Should the fetus be considered a human being or a potential human being? Even if the early embryo isn't considered a human being (at least not in the same sense as a neonate), does its potential to become a human being guarantee a right to life?

This confusion is complicated by the fact that the age of fetal viability—the age at which a fetus can survive outside the womb—has decreased to between 20 and 24 weeks.

Many bioethicists use measurable criteria of human body development, such as fetal movement and the existence of a heart and nervous system, to determine when the fetus is alive, but this hasn't ended the debate.

Pro-life position

The pro-life position cuts across all religions and philosophies. Opponents of legal abortion argue that human life begins at conception and, therefore, abortion is murder. In 1869, Pope Pius IX of the Roman Catholic Church condemned all abortions as a form of murder. Before then, the church had imposed no penalties for abortions within the first 40 days of pregnancy.

Antiabortion groups also contend that tolerance for the murder of unborn children implies tolerance for assisted suicide, death by neglect, and murder of other categories of "undesirable" people, such as the mentally disabled, seriously ill, and deformed.

Pro-choice position

Those who support legal abortion argue that an embryo or a young fetus represents the potential for human life but shouldn't be considered a human being at the time. They view abortion as a type of surgery necessary for the physical and psychological well-being of certain women. Abortion, they point out, will always be part of human society, regardless of whether it's legal. Legal abortions reduce the number of mutilations and deaths associated with illegal abortions. Further, they argue that legal abortions help reduce the number of unwanted children and forced marriages as well as the economic stress on some families.

Some take a third position: Abortions should be allowed only when the life of the pregnant woman is in danger or when the woman is a victim of incest or rape.

Continued debate

The furor over abortion is unlikely to go away anytime soon. An abortion-inducing pill, mifepristone (RU-486; Mifeprex) has sparked new controversy. Taken in the first 7 weeks of pregnancy, mifepristone blocks progesterone receptors, allowing prostaglandins to stimulate uterine contractions and detach the conceptus. Mifepristone has been marketed in France since 1989 and is used in Britain and Sweden. In the United States, the drug obtained Food and Drug Administration (FDA) approval for use on July 19, 1996.

In 1995, two more drugs were found to induce abortion safely and effectively. They're common prescription drugs to fight cancer (methotrexate) and ulcers (misoprostol). Methotrexate is injected and stops the division of cells, either malignant or fetal. Then, 5 to 7 days later, a misoprostol suppository is given to induce contractions and expel the fetus.

One researcher suggests that the procedure could be administered by a nurse practitioner under a physician's supervision, increasing availability and lowering costs of abortion. This treatment regimen received FDA approval in 1997.

Although many manufacturers may not supply mifepristone for fear of reprisals from pro-life organizations, the cancer- and ulcer-fighting drugs are too valuable to be forced off the market. Antiabortion leaders, meanwhile, have made mifepristone a prime target and won't ignore the newest method.

The ethical principle of autonomy (self-determination) is an important part of the abortion debate. This principle upholds a woman's right to control her own body. From the mother's point of view, that right includes choosing whether to have an abortion. Many women may think that they shouldn't be forced into the physical, emotional, and financial hardships of pregnancy.

Opponents of abortion maintain that pregnancy involves two persons with a right to autonomy—the mother and the fetus.

Personal views and resolution

A nurse who's ethically or morally opposed to abortion can't be forced to participate in the procedure. On the other hand, a nurse's employer can insist that she provide nursing to all in her care.

To reach a personal ethical resolution to the abortion issue, examine your views honestly and carefully. You'll also want to periodically reevaluate your position in light of new medical information and your own experience. If you feel strongly one way or the other, you should work for a facility that matches your views on abortion.

Postabortion care

Every nurse has an ethical obligation to provide competent, compassionate care. Even nurses who strongly oppose abortion shouldn't allow their personal feelings to interfere when caring for a postabortion patient. Nor is it appropriate to impose your values on the patient. If the patient expresses guilt or regret over her decision, an appropriate therapeutic response might be, "You made a decision that you believed was best for you. I want to help you live with your decision and rebuild your life. What can I do to help you." Providing a referral to social services or a mental health counselor and offering to find a clergy member are other helpful measures.

Prenatal screening

Because of diagnostic procedures, such as amniocentesis, ultrasound, alpha-feto-protein screening, and chorionic villus sampling, it's now possible to detect genetic disorders and congenital abnormalities well before birth. In a few cases, the diagnosis has paved the way for repair of the defect in utero. However, because it's easier to detect genetic disorders than to treat them, prenatal screening may force a patient to choose between having an abortion and taking on the emotional and financial burden of raising a severely disabled child.

Even those who are opposed to abortion may waver after seeing a child afflicted with Tay-Sachs disease or Duchenne muscular dystrophy. Is the quality of these children's lives so poor that it would be more compassionate to prevent their births? Is death ever more beneficial than life?

Some ethicists worry that this line of reasoning could cater to a desire for "perfect" children. How would this affect attitudes toward the disabled? How severe must a defect be for abortion to be considered an ethically acceptable option? For example, should a fetus with cleft palate, a surgically correctable defect, be aborted because of the disability? What about a girl conceived by parents who desperately want a boy?

The diagnostic procedures themselves involve some risk to the fetus. Amniocentesis, for example, causes serious complications or death about 0.5% of the time. This risk creates a conflict between the rights of the fetus and the parents' rights. If testing is to be conducted ethically, patients must understand the associated risks before the procedure. Health care providers must provide full information to patients regardless of whether the information is pleasant. In addition, the couple needs to have the risks, benefits, and alternatives explained to them in terms they can understand. At all times, the health care provider must remain nonjudgmental and unbiased.[18]

Patients must also comprehend what the test can and can't tell them, as well as all the available options. Thus, just as in HIV testing, effective pretest and posttest counseling are essential parts of an ethical prenatal screening program.

In vitro fertilization

Infertility can have devastating effects on the emotional well-being of a couple who yearns for children. As a result, many couples will spend a great deal of time and money trying to conceive or adopt a child. When medical procedures (such as fertility drugs, hysterosalpingostomy [opening blocked fallopian tubes], and artificial insemination) fail and adoption is impossible, infertile couples may turn to assisted reproductive techniques, including in vitro fertilization (IVF).

IVF refers to the process of removing ova from a woman's ovaries, placing them in a Petri dish filled with a sterilized growth medium, and covering them with healthy motile spermatozoa for fertilization. Three to five ova are implanted in the woman's uterus 10 to 14 days after fertilization, and the remaining fertilized ova are frozen for future use or discarded. IVF can use the partner's sperm (homologous) or a donor's sperm (heterologous) to fertilize the ova.

Complicated and expensive, IVF has resulted in the birth of thousands of healthy test-tube babies since the first successful attempt in 1978. The parents of these babies have no doubts about the procedure; they're thankful for the opportunity to have children.

Some people hail scientific manipulation of the ova and sperm as a medical miracle. However, others denounce it as circumvention of the natural process of procreation.

Sperm and egg banks

One of the results of the widespread use of IVF is an increased number of sperm and egg banks in which to store semen and ova until they're ready for use in the IVF procedure. Sperm banks have existed for many years. In the past, stored semen was primarily used for artificial insemination of women whose husbands were infertile and couldn't make adequate quality or amounts of semen to produce fertilization.

To obtain ova, a woman is given a hormone preparation that hyperstimulates the ovaries to produce 30 times the usual number of mature ova. The ova are then removed by laparoscopy or vaginal ultrasound-guided aspiration. The ova can be fertilized immediately or frozen and stored in an egg bank for later use.

With the increase of IVF procedures, egg banks are experiencing shortages and couples desiring IVF have to wait from weeks to a year.

The ethical and legal issues involved with stored semen and ova are similar to those in the storage of in vitro–fertilized ova. One obvious ethical-legal question is, "Who owns the ova and semen after they're deposited for storage in the bank?" Traditionally, after semen was donated and the donor paid for his services, the semen was considered the property of the storage facility to be sold at a later date to an appropriate customer. The donor couldn't find out the names of the women who used the semen for fertilization.

By similar logic, it would seem that women who donate ova to an egg bank and are paid for their services would also lose their possession rights to the ova. But most women undergo the ova stimulation and harvesting procedure for their own IVF, thus retaining ownership of their ova.

Several complicated legal and ethical dilemmas have surfaced from the storage of semen and ova. In a landmark case, a man who knew he was dying donated semen to a sperm bank. After his death, his wife wanted to be fertilized with his semen to have his children. But the husband's family, who didn't like the wife, sued to prevent her from becoming pregnant using his semen. The decedent's parents claimed that the semen belonged to them because the man was their son and that the wife had no legal right to use it for insemination. The court held that the wife had ownership rights to her husband's semen because he intended for her to use it after his death.

Consider this issue: how long can the semen and ova be stored? Almost indefinitely, with current cryotechnology, but no one knows how long-term storage affects semen and ova. Would it be ethical to fertilize ova that have been stored for a decade or two only to produce children who have major birth defects?

Another question that arises from the procedure raises additional issues: Who do the children of stored semen and ova belong to? Obviously, they belong to the couple if their semen and ova are used in IVF. However, what about the couple who benefits from semen and ova donated by strangers? If the child has a birth defect, is mentally disabled, or is of the wrong sex, the couple could claim that the child really wasn't theirs anyway. What happens to the child? Can they give it back? Does it become a ward of the state, like an abandoned child? Where do we apply the principles of distributive justice in this case?

Although nurses aren't usually responsible for the technical process of obtaining semen and ova, you may have to teach and counsel patients about the risks and complications involved in the procedures. Assess their awareness and understanding of the ethical and legal issues involved in the process. Equally critical are their feelings about sexuality and reproduction. If they're to receive ova that don't belong to them, how will they feel about the resulting child? Even though the IVF procedure is technical and artificial, the result of the process is hardly so. Producing a child is a human event, not a manufacturing process.

Disposition of embryos

IVF would pose fewer ethical problems if only one embryo were needed to guarantee a successful pregnancy. Unfortunately, it doesn't work that way. About 15 to 20 embryos may result from a single fertilization effort, but only 3 to 5 are implanted in the mother's uterus. The question arises: What should be done with the leftover embryos? Is it ethical to discard them, destroy them, or perform experiments on them?

In practice, leftover embryos usually are frozen. This raises questions with regard to parental responsibility for the frozen embryos. In 1989, for example, a divorcing Tennessee couple fought a custody battle over seven fertilized eggs that were frozen at an IVF clinic in Knoxville. Mary Sue Davis wanted custody for future implantation; her estranged husband, Junior Davis, insisted on having a joint say in the future of the embryos. In a controversial decision, a circuit court judge ruled that the embryos are people, not property, and should go to the mother.

Possible effects on child development

Parents may feel less responsible for IVF children born with congenital defects or conceived with donor sperm. Test-tube babies themselves may develop identity or adjustment problems after they learn the facts surrounding their conception.

Government regulation

Although the federal government has several proposals for legislation to regulate the use of IVF, none have become law. Several states have regulations. Information about these regulations can be found at *http://www.ncsl.org/programs/health/embryodisposition.htm.*

Court decisions made on actual cases involving IVF and reproductive controversies have produced a small amount of case law. However, the cases are dissimilar and the decisions tend to be inconsistent. In some situations, the courts support the property rights of self-determination and choice of the mother or patients. In other cases, the courts uphold the child's right to life and nurturing.

In practice, most decisions about IVF and sperm and egg banks are made outside the legal system by the couples and their lawyers. Some facilities have developed internal guidelines to determine who would be acceptable candidates for IVF. If you work in a facility that performs IVF or maintains a sperm or an egg bank, it's important that, as a nurse, you become involved in the development of policies and guidelines based on your knowledge of ethical standards. (See *What would you do?* page 372.)

Conversely, if IVF becomes a medically essential procedure, the ethical principle of distributive justice holds that everyone, regardless of socioeconomic status, should have access to it.

Surrogate motherhood

A surrogate mother is a woman who gives birth after carrying the fertilized ovum of another woman or, more commonly, after being artificially inseminated with sperm from the biological father. In this case, the infant is then legally adopted by the wife of the biological father. Since the first surrogate birth in England in 1976, thousands of babies have been born through this arrangement.

Surrogate motherhood offers hope to the 60% to 70% of infertile couples in which the woman is the infertile partner.

It's also an option for women whose age or health makes pregnancy risky. A surrogate birth poses no greater risk to the fetus (or the surrogate mother) than does a normal birth.

Surrogate motherhood versus conventional motherhood
One concern about surrogate motherhood involves the true nature of mothering. Is "motherhood" merely the biological act of bearing children? Many people believe that motherhood also implies a long-term commitment to the care and nurture of the child. By agreeing to give the baby to the contracting couple, is a surrogate mother defaulting on a moral commitment? The advertising of services by potential surrogate mothers involving huge fees may suggest to some that surrogate motherhood represents a form of baby selling.

Conflicts of rights
Surrogate motherhood can also produce conflicts among the rights of the surrogate mother, the infertile couple, the fetus, and society.

The basic dispute revolves around who has the strongest claim to the child. Is it the surrogate mother by virtue of her biological connection? Or does the surrogate contract guarantee the infertile couple the right to the child? Courts of law usually have ruled in favor of the couple.

Surrogate mother contracts seemingly violate adoption laws, which prohibit a mother from surrendering parental rights before the infant is born. Such laws, enacted to protect a biological mother from undue pressure, typically specify an initial waiting period of a few days. In many cases, she can't terminate all

What would you do?

Marjie May, RN, has worked at the Reproductive Sciences Center (RSC) of the University Research Hospital in a large city for 6 years. The RSC has a reputation for using cutting-edge technology and has received many public and privately funded grants for developing innovative procedures and techniques to help couples with infertility problems. The RSC has sperm and egg banks that provide semen and ova for the artificial inseminations and in vitro fertilization (IVF) procedures conducted at the center. As a circulating nurse at RSC, she's exposed to routine IVF procedures. Although initially she had ethical issues regarding IVF and artificial insemination, she resolved those concerns and now feels comfortable with most of the activities at the center.

One day, Ms. May's closest friend, a technician in the IVF laboratory where the eggs are fertilized, tells her that Dr. Floral, head of RSC and the person most responsible for its funding, has been experimenting with somatic cell nuclear transfer technique, and that he's planning to use cloned embryos for one of the IVF procedures that Ms. May is to assist the next morning. The woman to be implanted with the cloned embryo thinks that she's getting an IVF embryo from one of her own eggs harvested earlier and fertilized by the sperm of an unknown donor. The woman is an admitted lesbian but wants to have a child without having intercourse with a man.

Ms. May hasn't resolved the ethics of cloning humans but generally believes it's unethical and probably immoral. She also believes that not telling the truth to the woman is a violation of the principle of veracity and informed consent. Before the center closes for the day, Ms. May expresses her concerns about the ethics of the procedure to the nurse-manager. The nurse-manager states her belief that all forms of unnatural reproduction are basically the same and, if IVF is OK, so is cloning. Because the woman didn't know the semen donor, not knowing it was a cloned embryo was basically the same thing, she reasoned.

The nurse-manager also reminds Ms. May that Dr. Floral is the main authority at the center and that questioning him and going against his wishes by telling the woman the truth might result in Ms. May losing her job. Furthermore, revealing the cloning technique's use at RSC might jeopardize the center's funding and close it permanently because the government has banned human cloning. The nurse-manager reasons: "If the center shuts down, we won't be able to help those sad couples who come here with infertility problems. Do you want that to happen?"

What's the basis of Ms. May's ethical dilemma? Are her concerns legitimate? What action can she take? What ethical system seems to guide the nurse-manager's reasoning? Are Dr. Floral's actions ethical? What would you do if you were Ms. May?

parental rights until 6 months after the birth.

What if no one wants the child? This can become an issue if the infant is born with a disability. Can the infertile couple or the surrogate mother refuse to take responsibility for such a child? What if the defect isn't apparent until the child is 4 years old? Can the infertile couple return the child to his biological mother?

Clearly, the rights of the child to a normal family life must not be lost in the debate over custody. (See *Orphaned ova*, pages 374 and 375.)

Exploitation

The infertile couple and the surrogate mother are highly vulnerable to exploitation. The couple, blinded by a longing for a child, are easy victims for financial and emotional blackmail. On the other hand, surrogate motherhood can be used to exploit poor women, who have few marketable skills other than their ability

? Orphaned ova

ed questions about in vitro fertilization (IVF) and surrogate motherhood may soon come to
ety. Consider this case study, which explores what could happen if a surrogate motherhood
nt doesn't go as planned.

ED BEFORE BIRTH

lmont, age 39, owned a successful
ng company. He and his wife,
e 35, had been trying to have a
ears without success. After the
derwent a battery of infertility tests,
an concluded that Mrs. Belmont
e and produce mature ova but
ceive or bear children. On the physi-
stion, the couple began to explore
y of IVF and surrogate motherhood.
ny consideration, Mrs. Belmont had
zed in vitro using her husband's
some of the fertilized ova were
blantation, the Belmonts located a
her, Hazel Towers. Ms. Towers
a long-term contract saying that
r three children for Mr. and Mrs.
ontract stated that Ms. Towers
$100,000 for the first child and
ady placed in trust) for the subse-
dren. Ms. Towers was successfully
Mr. and Mrs. Belmont's fertilized
. Towers was near the end of the
pregnancy, Mr. and Mrs.
illed in an automobile accident.

OFFER

vo brothers and one sister stood
mpany and assets worth $15 mil-
ccording to the will of the de-
f Ms. Towers had the baby, the

child would inherit the estate.

Mr. Belmont's brothers and sister offered Ms.
Towers $500,000 if she would abort the fetus
and refuse to be implanted with any more fertilized ova. In addition, the brothers and sister offered to make a $1 million donation for the con-
struction of a new pediatric wing to the hospital
where the fertilized ova were stored if the administrator agreed to have the ova destroyed.

MS. TOWERS' DILEMMA

Ms. Towers was placed under a great deal of
stress. She realized that she could base her actions only on her own ethical principles. The
$500,000 offer was a temptation she would
have to ignore; she didn't think that financial
gain justified an abortion. According to the contract, she was to surrender the child to Mr. and
Mrs. Belmont at its birth. She had serious misgivings, however, about surrendering it to the brothers or sister in light of the offer they made for her
to have an abortion.

When they learned that Ms. Towers refused to
surrender the child, the brothers and sister accused her of having the child for financial gain.
They pointed out that the child would be heir to
a large fortune; Ms. Towers would probably benefit from the estate in caring for the child.

PREBORN SIBLINGS

Questions remained about production of the two
other children agreed on in the contract. Was

ecessary to produce a
and have fully active
s essentially a zygote.
e divided and separated,
anted into several appro-
d will continue to divide
identical twins, or
Also, when the embryo

is in the four- to eight-cell stage, the cells
can be separated, the DNA material removed from them, and new genetic material inserted. The cell with the new DNA
will then grow into a twin of the animal
from which the DNA was taken. It appears that by using the embryo-splitting
technique, scientists could produce an

to bear children. "Womb renting" is as ethically unacceptable as baby selling.

Implications for nurses

A nurse is unlikely to be directly involved in the IVF procedure or in drawing up a surrogate mother contract, but you may be called on to care for patients who choose these options. Before you can do so effectively, you'll need to examine your views on these controversial procedures and become familiar with the legal and ethical pitfalls they present.

Nurses can't be forced to participate in procedures they find ethically and morally objectionable. But according to the ANA Code for Nurses, nurses are obligated to care for all patients assigned, regardless of their beliefs or feelings. In any event, nurses have an ethical obligation to be aware of and report abuses of IVF and surrogate motherhood.

Cloning

With the successful birth of Dolly, the sheep, in 1996 in Scotland, the world has awakened to the reality of cloning as a viable reproductive method. The concept of cloning, however, has existed since the discovery of deoxyribonucleic acid (DNA) by Watson and Crick. It's based on the fact that every cell in an animal's body contains all the genetic information needed to reproduce every other cell in the body. In the strict scientific meaning of the word, the cloning process occurs when a cell in the animal's body is removed and placed in an appropriate growth environment, where it develops into an identical reproduction of the animal from which the cell came. However, scientists still don't know what triggers some parts of the DNA strand to become active and reproduce and others to re-

main dorma[...]
moved and [...]
it will grow[...]
person.

Althoug[...]
cloning, th[...]
cess used t[...]
identical a[...]
monkeys)[...]
technique[...]
ing unfer[...]
then rem[...]
from the[...]
the DN[...]
wish to[...]
tilized,[...]
new D[...]
of an a[...]
into a[...]
In the[...]
her m[...]
she w[...]
ident[...]
she's[...]

A[...]
ferre[...]
ting[...]
spe[...]
(ca[...]
co[...]
ha[...]
al[...]
ev[...]
w[...]
o[...]
t[...]
z[...]

netic material n[...]
new individual,[...]
DNA, each cell [...]
After the cells a[...]
they can be impl[...]
priate females a[...]
and develop into[...]
triplets, or more.

ETHICAL [...]

Unanswere[...]
haunt soci[...]
arrangeme[...]

ORPHAN[...]
Howard Be[...]
manufactur[...]
Marsha, ag[...]
baby for 2 [...]
Belmonts un[...]
their physici[...]
could ovula[...]
couldn't con[...]
cian's sugge[...]
the possibilit[...]
After lengt[...]
her ova fertil[...]
sperm. Wher[...]
frozen for im[...]
surrogate mo[...]
agreed to sig[...]
she would be[...]
Belmont. The [...]
would be paid[...]
$75,000 (alre[...]
quent two chil[...]
implanted with[...]
ova. When M[...]
first trimester o[...]
Belmont were [...]

MAKING AN[...]
Mr. Belmont's t[...]
to inherit his co[...]
lion. However, [...]
ceased couple,[...]

the contract binding after the death of Mr. and Mrs. Belmont? Because the money had already been set aside, could Ms. Towers be implanted with the ova, bear the children, and expect to be paid?

What about the hospital administrator and his role in the destruction of fertilized ova? If he believed that the ova weren't human, he probably wouldn't hesitate to carry out this request. However, what if he believed that human life started at the moment of conception? Then it would be betraying his ethical beliefs to destroy the ova.

OUTCOME

Over time, Ms. Towers began to think of the child in her womb as her own. She realized that her child would need to be loved and cherished for its own sake. She accepted the fact that she would probably lose her surrogate mother's fee because the contract stipulated that she must turn the child over to the Belmonts. She decided to raise the child, regardless of the financial consequences.

Because of the severe emotional stress she experienced, Ms. Towers decided to forgo having more fertilized ova implanted. The Belmont family immediately initiated a legal action contesting her child's inheritance; eventually, an out-of-court settlement was reached.

Ms. Towers experienced a bitter lesson in the moral uncertainty that surrounds IVF and surrogate motherhood. Existing laws aren't sufficient to answer the many questions raised by reproductive technology; future court rulings may provide better.

unlimited supply of ova for the somatic cell nuclear transfer procedure.

With the IVF procedure, embryo splitting, and DNA transfer, the fertilization and early development process occurs in a Petri dish in the laboratory. After the cells begin to develop, they're implanted into an appropriate female for the re-

mainder of the pregnancy. Although the cloning or embryo-splitting process is relatively simple, its success rate is at best marginal. For instance, to produce Dolly, more than 1,000 ova were genetically created. Of these, only 29 began to develop and only one actually produced Dolly. Although it's theoretically possible to reproduce humans using this technique, so far it has been used to produce only animals.

Legal and ethical issues

Shortly after the news of Dolly reached the United States, a crucial debate developed over whether cloning of humans was ethical or even legal. The three most troubling ethical issues were the loss of uniqueness of the individual, the potential misuse of the technology by diabolical scientists, and degeneration of society as it now exists. Other, more traditional ethical concerns, such as medical risks to the mother or child (beneficence and nonmaleficence), life status of the embryo produced by the procedure, distributive justice issues of cost and availability of technology, and autonomy issues of using humans as incubators or sources of organs for donation, are also part of the debate.

The concern for loss of individuality and uniqueness stems from the fact that clones are exact copies of their DNA donors. For many people, it conjures up an Orwellian image of rows of tanks in which identical babies are being grown and incubated, giving rise to genetic determinism and the production of inferior humans through mass photocopying.

The belief that genetic determinism will produce individuals who not only look the same but also act identically is flawed. Although every cell in one twin body is genetically identical to that of the other twin body, experience shows that twins develop individual personalities and character traits. Personality development is influenced by a wide range of environmental and experiential elements—not just genetic composition. If and when it happens, cloned human babies born to mothers who live in different situations, although they may look the same, will probably have different personalities.

Similarly, experience doesn't support the belief that each time an individual is cloned, quality is lost. In many cases, photocopies may be of higher quality than the original. However, cloning is more than making photocopies because the process is quite different. The danger of "bad copies" from cloning that may result in inferior quality offspring or offspring with congenital defects arises from the mechanical collection and transfer of the fragile DNA strands. Damaging even one gene sequence can produce birth defects.

In most ethical dilemmas, motivation is an important element in determining if the act was right or wrong. There are several possible motivations to clone human beings, ranging from egoism to helping an infertile couple have a child.

The egoistic motivation conjures up images of the diabolical scientist or a political leader who wants to create a "super race" by the repeated cloning of physically and mentally superior individuals. It isn't hard to imagine what Hitler might have done with this technology. How about cloning genius inventors, brilliant leaders, and superb athletes? Could embryo factories be far behind?

A somewhat more altruistic, although no less diabolical motive, is cloning humans for organ donation. In theory, a person who needs a heart transplant could donate his DNA and, after some time, have an individual who has a heart with a perfect genetic match. Most people, however, detest the idea of using cloned children as a means to an end, especially if harvesting the organ (as in a heart transplant) would result in the child's death. Scientists in Texas have cloned mice without heads whose organs were then transplanted into DNA donor mice. What if human clones could be created without heads? Would these headless beings truly be human? Or would they just be biological storage units for organs to be used for donation when the need arose? At first glance, this practice might seem abhorrent. However, is it any different from the sperm, egg, embryo, or organ banks that exist today?

In the past few years, parents who have children with leukemia have gone on to have more children for the primary purpose of providing bone marrow for the sick child. In many cases, the younger children were identical six-antigen matches, and the bone marrow was harvested from the infant and transplanted into the sick child who recovered from the disease. Is having children for this purpose different from cloning children for organ transplantation? What if scientists can clone one organ or a specific tissue? If a person needed a liver, the DNA from his liver could be transferred to an ovum and then a new liver grown in the laboratory. A similar procedure is being used already, without ethical objections, for growing new skin to graft onto burn patients.

Some parents might be tempted to clone a replacement child for one who's dead or dying. These parents could "set aside" a clone through the embryo-splitting technique that could be stored in an embryo bank to be implanted and grown if the child died. The underlying motivation would seem to be selfish and self-serving, to create a replacement child for the relief of grieving patients. However, is the cloned child really a replacement for the child who died? Physical appearance may be identical, but experience has shown that the child's personality and temperament could be radically different.

Similarly, an infertile couple who had tried all other methods and couldn't have a child might seek a cloned embryo as a last resort. Perhaps this motivation could pose the fewest ethical objections. Rather than using semen or ova from strangers, they might provide their own DNA, either from the father or the mother, to produce a child.

In 1997, President Clinton issued an executive order banning any federal funding for cloning involving humans. He also proposed legislation that would outlaw human cloning for at least 5 years, but Congress defeated the legislation in February 1998. As a result, human cloning remains banned in all publicly funded institutions in the United States but remains legal in privately funded institutions.

Fetal tissue and stem cell research

Fetal tissue from aborted fetuses offers new hope for treating Parkinson's disease, Alzheimer's disease, diabetes, and other degenerative disorders. The immaturity of the fetal immune system reduces the chances of rejection, making transplantation of fetal tissue ideal. However, from an ethical standpoint, fetal tissue research is a cause for concern.

Along similar lines, embryonic stem cells are being investigated as an alternative therapy for treating disease. Stem cells differ from other types of cells in the body. They're unspecialized cells that can divide and renew themselves for long periods. They also can be triggered to produce specialized cells, such as those of the heart or pancreas. Researchers are proposing that stem cells can be studied to determine the underlying problems in cell division that lead to certain disease processes. Additionally, they're suggesting that stem cells could be used to test new drugs. The most important indication, however, would be to develop cell-based therapies, providing a "renewable source of replacement cells and tissues to treat diseases including Parkinson's and Alzheimer's diseases, spinal cord injury, stroke, burns, heart disease, diabetes, osteoarthritis, and rheumatoid arthritis.[19]

Early research obtained embryonic stem cells from embryos via IVF from couples undergoing infertility treatments that were being discarded by these couples. Another reported source for embryonic stem cells was from cadaver fetal tissue after an elective abortion. Currently embryonic stem cells are derived from donated embryos via in vitro fertilization for research purposes with the consent of the donor.

Regardless of the source of the stem cells, ethical questions arise as to the status of the embryo.

"For those who believe that the embryo has the moral status of a person from the moment of conception, research or any activity that would destroy it is wrong. For those who believe the human embryo deserves some measure of respect, but disagree that the respect due should equal that given to a fully formed

The President's stem cell executive order

In 2007, President George W. Bush signed an executive order for stem cell research. In this order, President Bush recommended the exploration of ways to increase the number of available stem cell lines without the need to produce an embryo for obtaining such cells. As a result of this order, the National Institutes of Health (NIH) announced that they'll conduct and support research that takes advantage of other methods to produce stem cells, such as somatic cells or cells found in amniotic fluid.

Source: National Institutes of Health. "NIH Announces Plan to Implement President's Stem Cell Executive Order," *NIH News*, September 18, 2007. Available at *http://www.nih.gov/news/pr/sep2007/od-18.htm*.

human, it could be considered immoral not to use embryos that would otherwise be destroyed."[20]

At the center of this controversy is the ongoing question, do the ends justify the means? Do the benefits to be derived from stem cell research, such as the potential for cellular therapies to treat diseases override the issue of destruction of the embryos during research? Others might argue that because the embryos were most likely going to be destroyed, wouldn't it make more sense to use them practically to gain knowledge? Moreover, questions about funding arise, such as, should federal funds be used for research that some find unethical? (See *The President's stem cell executive order*.)

Another aspect involved with fetal tissue and stem cell research is the destruction of the tissue. In other words, is it moral or ethical to conduct research that destroys the welfare of the donor (embryo)?

Nurses need to be aware of their beliefs and values related to this issue. In addition, nurses need to stay informed about developing research so that they can provide their patients with the most current information.

Eugenics and gene manipulation

Eugenics is the science of improving a species through control of hereditary factors—in other words, by manipulating the gene pool. In the past, medical research has been limited to efforts to repair or halt the damage caused by disease and injury. Today, however, genetic manipulation and engineering have tremendous potential for altering the course of human development

Genetic engineering, also known as *genetic manipulation*, continues to contribute significantly to medical progress. Scientists are discovering new ways to identify and manipulate the genetic material of everything from single-celled organisms to human beings.

Each cell of an animal or a plant carries a genetic blueprint for the entire organism. This information is encoded by the DNA in its nucleus. By removing or adding DNA, scientists can program the cell or the entire organism to carry out new functions. Such manipulation can be highly beneficial. For example, it has yielded new antibiotics and hormones (such as human insulin) and increased our understanding of cancer cells. But genetic manipulation also gives researchers the potential to alter the gene pool in unethical ways and to create terrifying biological weapons.

Each of the estimated 100,000 genes found in nearly every human cell contains a set of signals for a single protein involved in a specific body function. Even a small error in the gene produces a defective protein that can result in disease or deformity. More than 4,000 inherited disorders result from such genetic mistakes. Gene therapy, the introduction of healthy genes to overcome an inherited defect, may some day provide cures for such diseases as cystic fibrosis, muscular dystrophy, and hemophilia.

The identification of the genes responsible for inherited diseases and congenital malformations has spurred the development of screening tests. Genetic testing is now a fairly common component of prenatal care, facilitating the identification of fetuses with disorders, such as Down syndrome and Tay-Sachs disease. The screening of neonates for phenylketonuria is legally required by most states.

Potential for discrimination
Researchers have also identified the genes responsible for adult-onset disorders, such as Huntington's disease, polycystic kidney disease, and some forms of cancer. Ideally, the results of genetic screening could encourage patients to make lifestyle changes that reduce their risk of developing the disease. At the least, the knowledge can help them prepare to deal with the disease. Unfortunately, this information can also lead to genetic discrimination, preventing people from obtaining health or life insurance or jobs and adopting children.

Language of genetic manipulation

The following terms are associated with the science of genetic manipulation.

Cloning: production of an entire organism from a single cell
Eugenics: science of improving a species through control of hereditary factors by manipulation of the gene pool
Gene: fragment of deoxyribonucleic acid (DNA) that encodes a single protein
Gene splicing: technique by which recombinant DNA is produced and made to function in an organism
Gene therapy: insertion of a normal gene into the nucleus of a cell to compensate for a defective one
Genetic marker: dominant gene or trait that serves to identify genes or traits linked with it
Germ cell alteration: changes in DNA structure during the earliest stages of cell growth (before differentiation)
Recombinant DNA synthesis: insertion of DNA segments from one species into the DNA of another species
Restriction fragment length polymorphism: genetically variable DNA fragments usually used as markers for a nearby disease gene
Somatic alteration: in vitro isolation of a specific gene that's then synthetically reproduced in the laboratory

Ethics of genetic engineering
Genetic engineering has tremendous potential for altering the course of human development. By themselves, genetic engineering techniques, including cloning, somatic alteration, germ cell alteration, recombinant DNA synthesis, and gene therapy, are ethically neutral. It's the application of these techniques that creates ethical problems. (See *Language of genetic manipulation*.)

Control over future generations

Do researchers have a greater obligation to help those currently alive or, alternatively, to protect the interests of future generations? It would appear that the most ethical applications of genetic engineering should do both, and research should concentrate on solving long-term medical and environmental problems, such as hereditary disease, cancer, pollution, and hunger.

Safety

Genetic researchers have a moral obligation to take all necessary precautions to recognize and prevent harmful consequences of their work, such as the accidental release of new pathogens. Patients who participate in gene therapy trials must be fully informed of the potential risks as well as the benefits. For example, the retroviral vectors used to introduce new genes may also increase a patient's risk of developing cancer.

Dehumanization

In the past, medical research has been limited to efforts to repair or halt the damage caused by disease and injury. But genetic engineering gives science the ability to recreate the human body. Is this unethical? If genetic engineering techniques are used to cure disease and improve the quality of life, society stands to benefit. Imagine a society, however, in which genetically "perfect" children or genetically inferior servants could be created in the laboratory. Such unethical applications clearly violate human dignity and integrity.

Voluntary versus mandatory genetic screening

Screening for genetic disorders isn't new. Progress in mapping defective genes to particular chromosomes has led to more sophisticated tests that probe directly for the faulty gene or a nearby "marker" gene. Moreover, scientists are learning more about the genetic basis of such diseases as diabetes, cancer, and hypertension.

Like genetic engineering, genetic screening is ethically neutral. Applications of this technology, however, may be acceptable. Prenatal, neonatal, and adult screening can be used to improve treatment, guide personal decisions, and initiate prevention programs. Other applications are an ethical Pandora's box.

Mandatory screening

The ethical principle of beneficence requires that a procedure help the patient. Mandatory genetic screening can be beneficial, such as in the case of neonatal screening for phenylketonuria, in which early detection prevents mental retardation. But what about mandatory testing for incurable diseases such as Huntington's disease? Although some patients want to know this information for constructive reasons, others could be seriously harmed psychologically. In this instance, voluntary screening is ethically acceptable, and mandatory screening isn't.

Creation of a "biological underclass"

Insurance companies have been among the first to be charged with genetic discrimination. From the company's point of view, it's a sound business decision to increase premiums or deny coverage to anyone with a serious medical condition or at high risk for developing such a condition. Unfortunately, predictive tests don't always tell the whole story. A single faulty gene may not cause trouble unless other related genes are also defective, or the gene may never be expressed unless it's set off by an environmental trigger. A patient who's seen as "certain to become disabled" rather than "at risk" could easily join the ranks of the uninsured—with little legal recourse.

Employers represent another source of potential genetic discrimination. In times of increasing health care costs, employers may avoid hiring someone who's likely to incur large medical bills. Industry officials also argue that genetic screening can identify workers who might be especially sensitive to industrial toxins. A more ethical approach would be to clean up the workplace so that all workers face a decreased risk.

Patient confidentiality

Preserving patient confidentiality may help to guard against abuses of genetic information. However, confidentiality isn't an absolute right. The confidentiality of health-related information, in particular, is protected by law only when the health and well-being of others aren't threatened. For example, the law requires a physician or nurse to report sexually transmitted diseases, gunshot wounds, and suspected child abuse.

It's unclear whether the disclosure of genetic information represents a breach of confidentiality. Certainly, the right to treatment of a child with phenylketonuria supersedes the parents' right to confidentiality. But what about a patient who has a positive test result for the Huntington's disease gene? Here, confidentiality should be preserved, but the widespread use of computerized records makes this task increasingly difficult.

Justice and genetic screening

Justice, as an ethical principle in health care, requires equal sharing of the risks and benefits of diagnostic tests and treatments offered to patients. Genetic screening programs haven't always adhered to this principle. When large-scale screening programs for sickle cell carriers were initiated in the 1970s, for example, participants received little or no posttest counseling or follow-up care. In contrast, similar programs set up to screen for Tay-Sachs disease included teaching programs, support groups, and financial aid. All genetic screening programs need to incorporate this sort of thorough follow-up care.

The justice principle also impinges on the issue of health insurance coverage. Because serious chronic diseases raise everyone's premiums, it would seem that justice is best served by asking those who pose a greater risk to bear more than the average share of the cost. The danger is that these people may never develop the disease. If so, they've been unfairly overcharged.

Right to know versus right to safety

Seeking new knowledge is an essential part of human nature. Yet society tends to oppose the scientist's right to uncontrolled experimentation. This is particularly true with regard to genetic research. Many people believe in the sanctity of life and view genetic screening and manipulation as violations of that principle, especially when human beings are involved. The public also has a right to protection and personal safety. It seems likely that the federal government will be involved in regulating genetic research.

Scientists will remain suspicious of attempts to control their work, and a large segment of the public will oppose unregulated tinkering with the building blocks of life. Our hope is that both sides will remember that the dignity, value, and worth of human life must be preserved at all costs.

Implications for nurses

Genetic manipulation, including gene therapy, is still experimental. As a result, few nurses are directly involved in this aspect of genetic research. Nonetheless, you have an ethical obligation to stay informed and to support efforts to establish legal and technological safeguards.

If you're more likely to be involved in genetic screening, you have an important role to play in dealing with the related ethical conflicts. Your ethical responsibilities may involve:

▶ making sure that the patient understands the procedure and gives informed consent before the test
▶ thoroughly reviewing options for treatment or prevention of a genetic disease during posttest counseling
▶ refusing to take part in compulsory screening programs
▶ refusing to disclose test results to unauthorized people
▶ actively supporting legislation to prevent genetic discrimination by employers and insurance companies.

REFERENCES

1. Henneman, E.A., and Karras, G.E. "Determining Brain Death in Adults: A Guideline for Use in Critical Care," *Critical Care Nurse* 24(5):50-56, 2004.

2. "President's Commission for the Study of Ethical Problems in Medicine and Biomedical and Behavioral Research, July, 1981." [Online.] Available at *http://www.bioethics.gov/reports/past_co mmissions/defining_death.pdf*.

3. Cerner Corporation. "The APACHE® IV Equations: Benchmarks for Mortality and Resource Use White Paper, 2005." [Online.] Available at *http://www.cern-er.com/public/Cerner_3.asp?id=27300*.

4. *Norwood Hospital v. Munoz*, 564 N.E.2d 1017 Mass., 1991. [Online.] Available at *http://www.jehovah.to/gen/legal/blood/munoz.htm*.

5. *Dennis Vacco, Attorney General of New York, et al. "Petitioners v. Timothy E. Quill, et al.* Supreme Court of the United States No. 95-1858." [Online.] Available at *http://supct.law.cornell.edu/supct/html/95-1858.ZO.html*.

6. Appelbaum, P.S. "Assessment of Patients' Competence to Consent to Treatment," *New England Journal of Medicine* 18(357): 1834-40, 2007.

7. Appelbaum, 2007.

8. Appelbaum, 2007.

9. Centers for Disease Control and Prevention. *HIV and Its Transmission*, July 1999. [Online.] Available at *http://www.cdc.gov/hiv/resources/factsheets/transmission.htm*.

10. Centers for Disease Control and Prevention. *Sexually Transmitted Diseases Treatment Guidelines 2006. Clinical Prevention Guidance.* [Online.] Available at *http://www.cdc.gov/std/treatment/2006/clinical.htm*.

11. ANA House of Delegates. *The Profession's Response to the Problem of Addiction and Psychiatric Disorders in Nursing,* 2002. [Online.] Available at *http://www.nursingworld.org/MainMenu Categories/ThePracticeofProfessionalNu rsing/workplace/ImpairedNurse/Respons e.aspx*.

12. *ANA Code of Ethics for Nurses with Interpretive Statements Provision 3.6 Addressing impaired practice.* [Online.]

Available at *http://nursingworld.org/ ethics/code/protected_nwcoe813.htm#3. 6.*

13. The National Conference of Commissioners on Uniform State Laws. *Uniform Anatomical Gift Act.* [Online.] Available at *http://www. anatomicalgiftact.org.*

14. The National Conference of Commissioners on Uniform State Laws.

15. The National Conference of Commissioners on Uniform State Laws.

16. UNOS. *Estimated U.S. Average Billed Charges Per Transplant as of July 1, 2005.* [Online.] Available at *http://www.transplantliving.org/before-thetransplant/finance/costs.aspx.*

17. American Academy of Pediatrics Committee on Bioethics. *Ethics and the Care of Critically Ill Infants and Children, 1996.* [Online.] Available at *http://aap-policy.aappublications.org/cgi/content/ab stract/pediatrics;98/1/149?fulltext=ethics %2Bthe%2Bcare%2Bof%2Bcritically% 2Bill%2Bin.*

18. Zindler, L. "Ethical Decision Making in First Trimester Pregnancy Screening," *Journal of Perinatal Neonatal Nursing* 19(2):122-131, 2005.

19. National Institutes of Health. *Stem Cell Information, 2008.* [Online.] Available at *http://stemcells.nih.gov/info/basics/ basics6.asp.*

20. National Human Genome Research Institute. *Cloning/Embryonic Stem Cells, 2006.* [Online.] Available at *http://www.genome.gov/10004765.*

National Institutes of Health. "NIH Announces Plan to Implement President's Stem Cell Executive Order," *NIH News* September 18, 2007. [Online.] Available at *http://www.nih.gov/news/pr/ sep2007/od-18.htm.*

Stanford University. *Competency to Make Medical Decisions.* [Online.] Available at *http://www.stanford.edu/group/psy-lawseminar/Competency.htm.*

ADDITIONAL RESOURCES

Callister, L.C. "Perinatal Ethics: State of the Science," *Journal of Perinatal and Neonatal Nursing* 20(1):37-39, January-March 2006.

Gundle, K. *Presumed Consent for Organ Donation. Perspectives of Health Policy Specialists, 2004.* [Online.] Available at *http://surj.stanford.edu/2004/pdfs/ gundle.pdf.*

Appendices and index

ADVANCED PRACTICE NURSING AND THE LAW

Advanced practice nurses (APNs) are those nurses who are prepared at the graduate degree level. These include clinical nurse specialist (CNS), nurse practitioner (NP), nurse-anesthetist, and nurse-midwife. APNs have received specialized education, including supervised clinical practice and demonstrate advanced clinical knowledge and skills, which allows for independent judgment, the ability to integrate and synthesize complex assessment data, and plan and initiate care.[1]

A major legal issue involving APNs is prescriptive authority. The ability of an APN, specifically NPs and CNSs, to prescribe medications, including controlled substances, varies widely from state to state. Further complicating the issue is the state's definition of an APN. In some states, such as Maine, New York, Pennsylvania, and California, APNs include only NPs; other states, such as Alabama, Arizona, New Jersey, and South Carolina, include NPs and CNSs in their definition of advanced practice.

There are, however, several general guiding principles that apply to all 50 states and the District of Columbia regarding prescriptive authority:

▶ A collaborating physician's signature is *not* required in any state on any prescription that an NP is authorized to write.

▶ Any prescription written for a controlled substance will include the prescribing NP's federal U.S. Drug Enforcement Administration (DEA) number, identifying the NP's independent or plenary authority to prescribe according to the state's scope of practice.

▶ It's presumed that all prescriptions include the standard information expected from all authorized prescribers: the prescriber's name, title, license or specialty, ID or prescription number as appropriate, practice address, and phone number; patient's name; date of prescription; drug name, dose, strength, route, specific directions, quantity, number of refills, and instructions regarding generic substitution.[2]

The table on the next page identifies the state-by-state definition of advanced practice, specifics related to medication prescriptions, and prescriptive authority for controlled substances. Nurses are urged to check with their state's board of nursing for continuing updates in this area.

STATE	DEFINITION OF ADVANCED PRACTICE	MEDICATION PRESCRIPTIONS	PRESCRIPTION OF CONTROLLED SUBSTANCES
Alabama	NP and CNS	• General authority • Collaborating physician's name and address on prescription	• No authority
Alaska	NP	• General authority	• Schedules II–V
Arizona	NP and CNS	• General authority	• Schedules II–V based on collaborative practice agreement with physician
Arkansas	NP and CNS	• General authority	• Schedules III–V based on collaborative practice agreement with physician and written guidelines and protocols
California	NP	• General authority • Prescription label showing collaborating physician's name	• Schedules II–V based on collaborative practice agreement with physician
Colorado	NP and CNS	• General authority as outlined in prescriber's collaborative practice agreement	• Schedules II–V
Connecticut	NP and CNS	• General authority as outlined in prescriber's collaborative practice agreement	• Schedules IV–V with required state registration in addition to DEA registration • Possibly schedules II-III if allowed by prescriber's collaborative agreement
Delaware	NP and CNS	• General authority	• Schedules II–V
District of Columbia	NP and CNS	• General authority	• Schedules II–V with required district registration in addition to DEA registration
Florida	NP	• General authority	• No authority
Georgia	NP	• General authority • Collaborating physician's name required on prescription	• Schedules III–V except as excluded by state formulary
Hawaii	NP and CNS	• General authority based on documentation filed with state Department of Commerce and Consumer Affairs • Limitation to state-issued exclusionary formulary unless otherwise specified by collaborative practice protocols	• No authority

STATE	DEFINITION OF ADVANCED PRACTICE	MEDICATION PRESCRIPTIONS	PRESCRIPTION OF CONTROLLED SUBSTANCES
Idaho	NP and CNS	• General authority	• Schedules II–V with required state registration in addition to DEA registration
Illinois	NP and CNS	• General authority based on collaborative practice agreement • Collaborating physician's name on all prescriptions	• Schedules III–V with required state registration in addition to DEA registration
Indiana	NP and CNS	• General authority	• Schedules II–V unless explicitly prohibited in prescriber's collaborative prescriptive agreement; required state registration in addition to DEA registration • No extension of controlled substances for purposes of weight management
Iowa	NP and CNS	• General authority	• Schedules II–V with required state registration in addition to DEA registration
Kansas	NP and CNS	• General authority as outlined in state Board of Pharmacy statute • Collaborating physician's name, address, and phone number required on prescription	• Schedules II–V as per Board of Pharmacy statute
Kentucky	NP and CNS	• General authority	• Schedules II–V
Louisiana	NP and CNS	• General authority • Collaborating physician's name on all prescriptions	• Schedules III–V with required state registration in addition to DEA registration • Possible schedule II if relevant to practice • No extension to prescriptions for purposes of weight management or control of chronic, intractable pain
Maine	NP	• General authority	• Schedules II–V (consistent with practice specialty) • Extension through off-label prescribing if in accordance with common and established practice standards
Maryland	NP	• General authority	• Schedules II–V unless expressly limited by collaborative prescriptive agreement; required state registration in addition to DEA registration
Massachusetts	NP	• General authority • Collaborating physician's name on prescription	• Schedules II–V with required state registration in addition to DEA registration • No refill for Schedule II drugs • Schedules II–III drugs limited to 30-day supply except attention deficit hyperactivity disorder drugs, which can be written for 60 days

STATE	DEFINITION OF ADVANCED PRACTICE	MEDICATION PRESCRIPTIONS	PRESCRIPTION OF CONTROLLED SUBSTANCES
Michigan	NP and CNS	• General authority	• Schedules III–V as per prescriber's collaborative prescriptive agreement • Schedule II drugs only if practice within a hospital, surgicenter, or hospice • Schedule II drugs limited to 7-day post-discharge supply • Prescriptions showing name and DEA number of prescriber and collaborating physician
Minnesota	NP and CNS	• General authority based on prescriber's collaborative prescriptive agreement	• Schedules II–V
Mississippi	NP	• General authority based on prescriber's collaborative prescriptive agreement	• Schedules II–V subject to a two-step approval process
Missouri	NP and CNS	• General authority based on prescriber's collaborative prescriptive agreement • Collaborating physician's name, practice address, and phone number on prescription	• No authority
Montana	NP and CNS	• General authority based on prescriber's collaborative prescriptive agreement	• Schedules II–V; limited to 3-month supply; refills in writing if ordered
Nebraska	NP	• General authority	• Schedules II–V
Nevada	NP	• General authority as per state Board of Pharmacy regulations	• Schedules II–V as per practice specialty; schedule I if related to practice • Refills for up to 6 months; noncontrolled substances refill for up to 1 year
New Hampshire	NP	• General authority as stated in state formulary	• Schedules II–V except as excluded in state formulary
New Jersey	NP and CNS	• General authority based on prescriber's collaborative prescriptive agreement • Prescriber's and collaborating physician's name, address, and phone number on prescription	• Schedules II–V with required state registration in addition to DEA registration • Prescriptions written on official prescription forms; state license number and federal DEA number of prescriber and collaborating physician required
New Mexico	NP and CNS	• General authority	• Schedules II–V as per individualized formulary for practice specialty and setting and with required state registration in addition to DEA registration

STATE	DEFINITION OF ADVANCED PRACTICE	MEDICATION PRESCRIPTIONS	PRESCRIPTION OF CONTROLLED SUBSTANCES
New York	NP	• General authority with prescriber's title and prescription number on prescription	• Schedules II–V with required state registration in addition to DEA registration • Schedule II drugs (including anabolic steroids) and benzodiazepines written on official prescription form
North Carolina	NP	• General authority with prescription showing collaborating physician's name	• Schedule II–V as per collaborative practice agreement • Schedules II–III prescriptions limited to 30-day supply without refill
North Dakota	NP and CNS	• General authority based on prescriber's collaborative prescriptive agreement	• Schedules II–V
Ohio	NP and CNS	• General authority	• Schedule III-V as per state formulary • Schedule II in emergency situations for terminally ill patients and limited to 24-hour supply • Extension through off-label prescribing if specified in collaborative practice agreement
Oklahoma	NP and CNS	• General authority • Collaborating physician's name on prescription	• Schedules III–V with required state registration in addition to DEA registration except as excluded by state formulary • 7-day supply limit
Oregon	NP and CNS	• General authority	• Schedules II–V as per state formulary; no prescriptions for treatment of narcotics addiction or schedule II drugs for weight management
Pennsylvania	NP	• General authority based on prescriber's collaborative prescriptive agreement • Collaborating physician's name on prescription	• Schedules III–V • Schedule II possibly but limited to 72-hour supply if specified in prescriber's collaborative prescriptive agreement
Rhode Island	NP	• General authority	• Schedules II–V as per prescriber's collaborative prescriptive agreement and specified in state formulary with required state registration in addition to DEA registration
South Carolina	NP and CNS	• General authority • Prescriber's and collaborating physician's name, address, and phone number	• Schedules III–V as per prescriber's collaborative prescriptive agreement
South Dakota	NP	• General authority	• Schedules II–V with required state registration in addition to DEA registration
Tennessee	NP and CNS	• General authority with collaborating physician's name on prescription	• Schedules II–V as per prescriber's collaborative prescriptive agreement

STATE	DEFINITION OF ADVANCED PRACTICE	MEDICATION PRESCRIPTIONS	PRESCRIPTION OF CONTROLLED SUBSTANCES
Texas	NP and CNS	• General authority with collaborating physician's name, address, and phone number on prescription	• Schedules II–V as per prescriber's practice protocols with required state registration in addition to DEA registration • Limit of 30 days with no refills
Utah	NP and CNS	• General authority	• Schedules IV–V with required state registration in addition to DEA registration • Schedules II–III in accordance with consultation and referral plan but not for weight management • Cocaine HCl limited to topical preparation
Vermont	NP	• General authority	• Schedules II–V
Virginia	NP	• General authority	• Schedules II–VI as per prescriber's collaborative practice agreement
Washington	NP	• General authority	• Schedules II-V
West Virginia	NP and CNS	• General authority	• Schedules II–VI except as excluded by state formulary
Wisconsin	NP and CNS	• General authority	• Schedules II–V with restrictions on amphetamines and anabolic steroids
Wyoming	NP and CNS	• General authority	• Schedules II–V

REFERENCES

1. Berry, P.H., and Dahl, J.L. "Advanced Practice Nurse Controlled Substance Prescriptive Authority: A Review of the Regulations and Implications for Effective Pain Management at End-of-Life," *Journal of Hospice and Palliative Nursing* 9(5):238-245, 2007.
2. Byrne, W. (2008 March 21). "U.S. Nurse Practitioner Prescribing Law: A State-by-State Summary" [Online]. Available at *www.medscape.com/viewarticle/440315.*

EVIDENCE-BASED NURSING PRACTICE

Evidence-based practice is nursing practice built on information obtained from research. The basic steps involved in evidence-based nursing practice include:
▶ formulating the clinical question
▶ searching for peer-reviewed evidence-based articles on the clinical question
▶ analyzing and comparing data—critically evaluating and comparing the articles
▶ applying the information from the studies.

Step 1: Formulating the clinical question
Follow these steps to help you formulate the clinical question:
▶ Start with a specific and concrete question.
▶ Formulate the question in terms of a relationship between:
 – a patient or patient population
 – an intervention (typically a treatment, diagnostic test, or nursing procedure)
 – the result of the intervention
 – what else could be done instead.

Step 2: Searching for evidence
Your goal in doing this database search is to find published reports of the results of research projects. First and foremost is to use only articles that are published in peer-reviewed journals. These journals require outside experts to review articles submitted for publication. If the title of the article leaves you unsure whether the article is a report of a research project, read the abstract carefully. Look for evidences from these resources:
▶ Library
▶ Web sites
▶ Electronic databases: Web-based tools, such as CINAHL, MEDLINE, and PubMed (see Evidence-based resources, page 395).

A standard format for research reports contains these sections:
▶ abstract
▶ introduction or review of the literature (a brief summary of past related research)
▶ methods
▶ results
▶ discussion section.

Step 3: Analyzing and comparing data
Evaluating the quality of a research report can be difficult if you haven't had some training in research methodology. In fact, even seasoned researchers debate the quality of studies and how to interpret and apply the results. However, if

you follow a few basic rules, you can be sure that the study you read has met a baseline standard of quality.

▶ *Validity* refers to whether the research project actually measures what it claims to measure.

▶ *Reliability* refers to whether the results of the study will be repeatable. Ideally, you shouldn't accept the results of any study as true without finding at least one attempt to repeat it with the same results.

▶ *Randomizing* is a hallmark of high-quality research. Ideally, researchers assign people randomly to either a study or control group.

▶ *Group size* is important. Research on large numbers of subjects produces more reliable results than smaller studies.

However, not all types of research can use randomization, double-blinding, control groups, and large populations. Understanding the acceptable alternatives requires training and experience.

Comparing the studies you have gathered is the next step, and this can be challenging. You must weigh variables, such as patient population characteristics and quality of the study design. Final decisions usually require discussion and compromise.

Levels of evidence

Weighing and leveling the degree of evidence that study has can be a daunting task. A systematic approach to leveling the evidence can be found below. (See *Leveling the evidence.*)

Leveling the evidence is based on these questions:

▶ Was the study randomized?
▶ What was the study population?
▶ What criteria needed to be met by participants?
▶ Was the intervention described properly?
▶ Was the study blinded?

Leveling the evidence

LEVEL AND QUALITY OF EVIDENCE	TYPE OF EVIDENCE
Level I	Evidence from a systematic review or meta-analysis of all relevant randomized clinical trials (RCTs), or evidence-based clinical practice guidelines based on systematic reviews of RCTs or three or more RCTs of good quality that have similar results.
Level II	Evidence obtained from at least one well-designed RCT
Level III	Evidence obtained from well-designed controlled trials without randomization
Level IV	Evidence from well-designed case-control or cohort studies
Level V	Evidence from systematic reviews of descriptive and qualitative studies
Level VI	Evidence from a single descriptive or qualitative study
Level VII	Evidence from the opinion of authorities and/or reports of expert committees

Adapted from Melnyk, B.M. and Fineout-Overholt, E. (2005) *Evidence-Based Practice in Nursing & Healthcare: A Guide to Best Practice.* Philadelphia: Lippincott, Williams & Wilkins; modified from Guyatt, G., and Rennie, D. (2002). *Users' Guides to the Medical Literature.* American Medical Association: AMA Press; and Harris, R.P., et al. (2001). "Current methods of the U.S. Preventive Services Task Force: A review of the process." *American Journal of Preventive Medicine* 20:21-35.

▶ How was the data was collected?
▶ How was the data analyzed?
▶ What were the end results?
▶ What conclusions were achieved?
▶ Did the study have any limits?

Step 4: Applying the data

After the evidence has been evaluated, the next step is to determine whether the evidence supports rejecting the intervention or implementing it. If the evidence supports a change, procedures or policies can be changed or created to implement the new evidence.

EVIDENCE-BASED RESOURCES

Here is a list of Web sites to search for evidence-based articles.

Academic Center for Evidence-Based Practice: *www.acestar.uthscsa.edu/About.htm*

American Academy of Pediatrics: *www.aap.org/policy/paramtoc.html*

American Association of Clinical Endocrinologists: *www.aace.com*

American Association of Critical-Care Nurses: *www.aacn.org/AACN/practiceAlert.nsf/vwdoc/pa2?opendocument*

American Association of Respiratory Care: *www.rcjournal.com/cpgs/*

American Cancer Society: *www.cancer.org/docroot/ped/content/ped_2_3x_acs_cancer_detection_guidelines_36.asp?sitearea=ped*

American College of Cardiology: *www.acc.org/qualityandscience/clinical/statements.htm*

American College of Physicians: *www.acponline.org/clinical_information/guidelines/*

American Medical Directors Association: *www.amda.com/publications/index.cfm*

American Psychiatric Association: *www.psych.org/MainMenu/Psychiatric Practice/PracticeGuidelines_1.aspx*

Association of Women's Health, Obstetric and Neonatal Nurses: *http://awhonn.org*

Clinical Trials: *www.clinicaltrials.gov*

CMA InfoBase: *http://mdm.ca/cpgsnew/cpgs/index.asp*

Cochrane Library: *www.cochrane.org/*

Educational Resources Information Center: *www.eric.ed.gov*

Guidelines Advisory Committee: *www.gacguidelines.ca*

Guidelines International Network: *www.G-I-N.net*

Health Services/Technology Assessment Text: *http://hstat.nlm.nih.gov*

Healthlinks at University of Washington: *http://healthlinks.washington.edu*

Infusion Nursing Society: *www.ins1.org*

Institute for Clinical Systems
Improvement:
www.icsi.org/guidelines_and_more/

Joanna Briggs Institute:
http://www.joannabriggs.edu.au/about/
home.php

Ministry of Health Services, British
Columbia, Canada:
www.healthservices.gov.bc.ca/msp/
protoguides

National Association of Neonatal
Nurses: *www.nann.org*

National Cancer Institute:
www.cancer.gov/search/cancer_literature/

National Guideline Clearinghouse:
www.guideline.gov

National Institute for Health and Clinical
Excellence:
www.nice.org.uk/catcg2.asp?c=20034

National Kidney Foundation:
www.kidney.org/professionals/doqi/
guidelineindex/cfm

New York Academy of Medicine:
www.ebmny.org/cpg.html

NLM Gateway:
http://gateway.nlm.nih.gov/gw/Cmd

Oncology Nursing Society:
www.ons.org

Ovid MEDLINE:
www.ovid.com/site/products/ovidguide/
nursing.htm

Primary Care Clinical Practice
Guidelines:
http:/medicine.ucsf.edu/resources/
guidelines/

PubMed:
www.pubmed.gov

Registered Nurses' Association of
Ontario:
www.rnao.org/bestpractices

Resources for Evidence-Based Nursing
at McMaster University:
http://hsl.lib.mcmaster.ca/education/
nursing/ebn/index.htm

Scottish Intercollegiate Guidelines
Network:
www.sign.ac.uk/guidelines/index.html

Teaching/Learning Resources for
Evidence-Based Practice:
www.mdx.ac.uk/www/rctsh/ebp/
main.htm

Thomson Scientific: *http://scientific.*
thomson.com/isi/

University of Iowa Gerontological
Nursing Interventions Research Center:
http:/www.nursing.viowa.edu/
excellence/nursing_interventions

Veterans Administration:
www.oqp.med.va.gov/cpg/cpg.htm

Virginia Henderson International
Nursing Library:
www.nursinglibrary.org/portal/main.aspx

Wound, Ostomy and Continence Nurses
Society:
www.wocn.org/WOCN_Library/
Position_Statements

COURT CASE CITATIONS

A

American Hospital Association v. NLRB, *111 S. Ct. 1539, 59 U.S.L.W. 4331 (1991)*

Application of the President and Directors of Georgetown College, Inc., *331 F.2d 1000 (D.C. Cir. 1964); cert. denied, 377 U.S. 978 (1964)*

Ashley v. Nyack Hospital, *412 N.Y.S.2d 388, 67 A.D.2d 671 (1979)*

B

Babits v. Vassar Brothers Hospital, *732 N.Y.S. 2nd 46 (N.Y. App. 2001)*

Bailie v. Miami Valley Hospital, *8 Ohio Misc. 193, 221 N.E.2d 217 (1966)*

Barber v. Reinking, *68 Wash. 2d 139, 411 P. 2d 861 (1966)*

Barber v. Time, Inc., *348 Mo. 1199, 159 S.W.2d 291 (1942)*

Battocchi v. Washington Hosp. Center, *581 A.2d 759 (D.C. App. 1990)*

Bellotti v. Baird II, *443 U.S. 622, 99 S. Ct. 3035 (1979)*

Big Town Nursing Home v. Newman, *461 S.W.2d 195 (Tex. Civ. App. 1970)*

Brookover v. Mary Hitchcock Memorial Hospital *893 F. 2d 411 (1st Cir. 1990)*

Brown v. State, *391 N.Y.S.2d 204, 56 A.D.2d 672 (1977)*

Burdreau v. McDowell, *256 U.S. 465, 41 S. Ct. 574 (1921)*

Butler v. South Fulton Medical Center, Inc., *215 Ga. App. 809, 452 S.E.2d 768 (1994)*

Byrne v. Boadle, *159 Eng. Rep. 299 (1863)*

C

Cannell v. Medical and Surgical Clinic S.C., *21 Ill. App. 3d 383, 315 N.E.2d 278 (1974)*

Canterbury v. Spence *464 F.2d 772 (D.C. Cir. 1972)*

Carey v. Population Services International, *431 U.S. 678, 97 S. Ct. 2010 (1977)*

Carr v. St. Paul Fire and Marine Insurance Co., *384 F. Supp. 821 (W.D. Ark. 1974)*

Cline v. Lund, *31 Cal. App.3d 755, 107 Cal. Rptr. 629 (1973)*

Claypool v. Levin, *Wis. 562 N.W.2d 584, 209 Wis. 2d 284 (1997) No. 942457*

Collins v. Davis, *254 N.Y.S.2d 666, 44 Misc. 2d 622 (1964)*

Collins v. Westlake Community Hospital, *57 Ill. 2d 388, 312 N.E.2d 614 (1974)*

Colorado State Board of Nurse Examiners v. Hohu, *129 Colo. 195, 268 P.2d 401 (1954)*

Commissioner of Correction v. Myers, *379 Mass. 255, 399 N.E.2d 452 (1979)*

Commonwealth v. Gordon, *431 Pa. 512, 246 A.2d 325 (1968)*

Commonwealth v. Porn, *196 Mass. 326, 82 N.E. 31 (1907)*

Commonwealth v. Storella, *6 Mass. App. 310, 375 N.E.2d 348 (1978)*

Cooper v. National Motor Bearing Co., *136 Cal. App. 2d 229, 288 P.2d 581 (1955)*

Crowe v. Provost, *52 Tenn. App. 397, 374 S.W.2d 645 (1963)*

Cruzan v. Director, Mo. Dept. of Health, *110 S. Ct. 2841, 111 L. Ed. 2d 224 (1990)*

D

D. v. D., *108 N.J. Super. 149, 260 A.2d 255 (1969)*

Darling v. Charleston Community Memorial Hospital, *33 Ill. 2d 326, 211 N.E.2d 253 (1965)*

Dembie, *21 RFL 46 (1963)*

Derrick v. Portland Eye, Ear, Nose and Throat Hospital, *105 Ore. 90, 209 P.2d 344 (1922)*

Dessauer v. Memorial General Hospital, *96 N.M. 92, 628 P.2d 337 (N.M. Ct. App. 1981)*

Doe v. Roe, *400 N.Y.S.2d 668, 93 Misc. 2d 201 (Sup. Ct. 1977)*

In re Doe Children, *402 N.Y.S.2d 958, 93 Misc. 2d 479 (1978)*

Dowey v. Rothwell, *[1974] 5 W.W.R. 311 (Alberta)*

E

Eastern Maine Medical Center v. NLRB, *658 F.2d 1 (1st Cir. 1981)*

Edith Anderson Nursing Homes, Inc. v. Bettie Walker, *232 Md. 442, 194 A.2d 85 (1963)*

Eisenstadt v. Baird, *405 U.S. 438, 92 S. Ct. 1029 (1972)*

Emory University v. Shadburn, *47 Ga. App. 643, 171 S.E. 192 (Ct. App. 1933)*

Estelle v. Gamble, *429 U.S. 97, 97 S. Ct. 285 (1976)*

F

Farrell v. Snell, *2 S.C.R. (Ct. App., New Brunswick, 1990)*

Feeney v. Young, *181 N.Y.S. 481, 191 A.D. 501 (1920)*

G

Garcia v. Bronx Lebanon Hospital, *731 N.Y.S. 2nd 702 (N.Y. App., 2001)*

Garcia v. Presbyterian Hospital Center, *92 N.M. 652, 593 P.2d 487 (1979)*

Geransy, *13 R.F.L.2d 202 (1977)*

Griswold v. Connecticut, *381 U.S. 479, 85 S. Ct. 1678 (1965)*

Gugino v. Harvard Community Health Plan, *380 Mass. 464, 403 N.E.2d 1166 (1980)*

HI

Hammonds v. Aetna Casualty and Surety Co., *237 F. Supp. 96 (D.C. Ohio 1965)*

Harrell v. Louis Smith Memorial Hospital, *3975 E.2d 746 (Ga. 1990)*

Henry By Henry v. St. John's Hospital, *512 N.E.2d 1044 (Ill. App. 4 Dist. 1987)*

Hernicz v. Fla. Dept. of Professional Regulation, *390 So. 2d 194 (Dist. Ct. App. 1980)*

Hiatt v. Groce, *215 Kan. 14, 523 P. 2d 320 (1974)*

H.L. v. Matheson, *450 U.S. 398, 101 S. Ct. 1164 (1981)*

Hodges v. Effingham County Hospital, *355 S.E.2d 104 (Ga. 1987)*

Hodgson v. Minnesota, *110 S. Ct. 2926, 111 L. Ed. 2d 344 (1990)*

Horton v. Niagara Falls Memorial Medical Center, *380 N.Y.S 2d 116, 51 A.D.2d 152 (1976)*

Hudock v. Children's Hospital of Philadelphia, *Civil Action No. 98-929, 1999 U.S. Dist. LEXIS 19269 (3d Cir. 1999)*

Hunt v. Palms Springs General Hospital, *352 So. 2d 582 (Fla. Dist. Ct. App. 1977)*

Hunter v. Hunter, *65 O.L.R. 586 (1930)*

J

Jefferson v. Griffin Spalding County Hospital Authority, *247 Ga. 86, 274 S.E.2d 457 (1981)*

Jones v. Hawkes Hospital, *175 Ohio 503, 196 N.E.2d 592 (1964)*

Justice v. Natvig, *178, 381 S.E.2d 8 (Va. 1989)*

K

Kansas State Board of Nursing v. Burkman, *216 Kan. 187, 531 P. 2d 122 (1975)*

Karp v. Cooley, et al., *493 F.2d 408, 419 (1974)*

Keyes v. Humana Hospital, Alaska, Inc., *750 P.2d 343 (Alaska 1988)*

Kyslinger v. United States, *406 F. Supp. 800 (W.D. Pa. 1975)*

L

Laidlaw v. Lions Gate Hospital, *[1969] 70 W.W.R. 727 (B.C. 1969)*

Lama v. Boras, *16 F.2d 473 PR (1994)*

Lane v. Candura, *6 Mass. App. 377, 376 N.E.2d 1232 (1978)*

Larrimore v. Homeopathic Hospital Association, *176 A.2d 362, aff'd, 54 Del. 449, 181 A.2d 573 (1962)*

Leib v. Board of Examiners for Nursing, *177 Conn. 78, 411 A.2d 42 (1979)*

Leigh v. Board of Registration in Nursing, *395 Mass. 670, 481 N.E.2d 1347 (1985)*

Lopez v. Swyer, *115 N.J. Super. 237, 279 A.2d 116 (1971)*

Loton v. Massachusetts Paramedical, Inc., *Mass. Sup. Ct. 1987, 4 National Jury Verdict Review and Analysis 5 (1989)*

Lott v. State, *225 N.Y.S.2d 434, 32 Misc. 2d 296 (1962)*

Lovato v. Colorado, *198 Colo. 419, 601 P.2d 1072 (1979)*

M

Manning v. Twin Falls Clinic and Hospital, *830 P. 2nd 1185 (Idaho, 1992)*

Mapp v. Ohio, *367 U.S. 643, 81 S. Ct. 1684 (1961)*

Maryland v. Buie, *494 U.S. 325, 110 S. Ct. 1093 (1990)*

Mathias v. St. Catherine's Hospital, *212 Wis. 2d 540, 569 N.W.2d 330 (1997)*

May v. Broun, *261 Ore. 28, 492 P.2d 776 (1972)*

McCarl v. State Board of Nurse Examiners, *39 Pa. Cmwlth. 628, 396 A.2d 866 (1979)*

McCutchon v. Mutual of Omaha Insurance Co., *354 So. 2d 759 (La. Ct. App. 1978)*

McInnes v. Dillard Department Stores, Inc., *736 So. 2d 1190; 1999 Fla. App. LEXIS 6322*

McIntosh v. Milano, *168 N.J. Super. 466, 403 A.2d 500 (1979)*

In re Melideo, *390 N.Y.S. 2d 523, 88 Misc. 2d 974 (Sup. Ct. 1976)*

Methodist Hospital v. Ball, *50 Tenn. App. 460, 362 S.W.2d 475 (1961)*

Misericordia Hospital Medical Center v. NLRB, *623 F.2d 808 (2d Cir. 1980)*

Mohr v. Jenkins, *393 So. 2d 245 (La. Ct. App. 1980)*

Mohr v. Williams, *95 Minn. 261, 104 N.W. 12 (1905)*

Moore v. Guthrie Hospital, *403 F.2d 366 (4th Cir. 1968)*

Moore v. Willis-Knighton Medical Center, *720 So. 2nd 425 (La. App. 1998)*

In re Mount Sinai Hospital and Ontario Nurses Association, *17 L.A.C.2d 242 (1978)*

Mutual Insurance of Arizona v. American Casualty Co. of Reading, PA, *189 Ariz. 22, 938 P.2d 71 (1997)*

N

Nathanson v. Kline, *186 Kan. 393, 350 P.2d 1093 (1960)*

Nelson v. Trinity Medical Center, *419 N.W.2d 886 (S. Ct. N.D. 1988)*

New York v. Class, *475 U.S. 106, 106 S. Ct. 960 (1985)*

NLRB v. Baptist Hospital, *442 U.S. 773, 99 S. Ct. 2598 (1979)*

NLRB v. Health Care & Retirement Corporation, *114 S. Ct. 1778 (1994)*

NLRB v. Health Care & Retirement Corp., *511 U.S. 571 (1994)*

NLRB v. Kentucky River Community Care, Inc., *532 U.S. 706 (2001)*

Norman v. Good Shepard Medical Center, *2001 Tex. App. LEXIS 5571, August 17, 2001. Filed.*

Norton v. Argonaut Insurance Co., *144 So. 2d 249 (La. Ct. App. 1962)*

N.Y.C. Health and Hospitals Corporation v. Sulsona, *367 N.Y.S.2d 686, 81 Misc. 2d 1002 (1975)*

N.Y. State Association for Retarded Children, Inc. v. Carey, *438 F. Supp. 440 (E.D. N.Y. 1977)*

O

O'Connor v. Donaldson, *422 U.S. 563, 95 S. Ct. 2486 (1975)*

Ohio v. Akron Center for Reproductive Health, *110 S. Ct. 2972, 111 L. Ed. 2d 405 (1990)*

Oliff v. Florida State Board of Nursing, *374 So. 2d 1054 (Fla. Dist. Ct. App. 1979)*

O'Neill v. Montefiore Hospital, *202 N.Y.S.2d 436, 11 A.D. 2d 132 (1960)*

In re Osborne, *294 A.2d 372 (D.C. 1972)*

P

Pedersen v. Zielski, *Adv 3785, 822 P.2d 903 (Ak. 1991)*

People v. Doe, *410 N.Y.S.2d 233, 96 Misc. 2d 975 (1978)*

People v. Kraft, *3 Cal. App. 3d 890, 84 Cal. Rptr. 280 (1970)*

Planned Parenthood of Central Missouri v. Danforth, *428 U.S. 52, 96 S. Ct. 2831 (1976)*

Planned Parenthood of Northwest Ind. v. Vines, *543 N.E.2d 654 (Ind. App. 1989)*

Planned Parenthood of S.E. Pennsylvania v. Casey, *127 L.E.2d 352, 114 S. Ct. 909 (1992)*

Pommier v. ABC Insurance Co., et al., *715 So. 2d 1270 (La. App. 3d Cir. 1998)*

Poor Sisters of St. Francis Seraph of the Perpetual Adoration, et al. v. Catron, *435 N.E.2d 305 (Ind. Ct. App. 1982)*

Pounders v. Trinity Court Nursing Home, *265 Ark. 1, 576 S.W.2d 934 (1979)*

Powell v. Columbia-Presbyterian Medical Center, *267 N.Y.S.2d 450, 49 Misc. 2d 215 (Sup. Ct. 1965)*

Prairie v. University of Chicago Hospitals, *298 Ill. App. 3d 316, 327 (1998)*

Q

In re Quinlan, 137 N.J. Super. 227, 348
A. 2d 801 (Ch. Div. 1975); modified,
70 N.J. 10, 355 A.2d 647 (1976)

R

Ramos v. Lamm, 639 F.2d 559 (10th Cir.
1980)

Richardson v. Brunelle, 119 N.H. 104,
398 A.2d 838 (1979)

Roach v. Springfield Clinic, Ill. App. 4
Dist., 166 Ill. Dec. 48, 585 N.E.2d
1070, 223 Ill. App.3d 597, appeal allowed 173 Ill. Dec. 13, 596 N.E.2d
637, 145 Ill. 2d 644, aff'd in part,
rev'd in part 191 Ill. Dec. 1, 623
N.E.2d 246, 157 Ill. 2d 29 (1992)

Rochin v. California, 342 U.S. 165, 72 S.
Ct. 205 (1952)

Roe v. Wade, 410 U.S. 113, 93 S. Ct. 705
(1973)

Rogers v. Kasdan, 612 S.W.2d 133 (Ky.
1981)

Rohde v. Lawrence General Hospital, 34
Mass. App. Ct. 584, 614 N.E.2d 686
(1993)

Rust v. Sullivan, 59 U.S.L.W. 4451
(1991)

S

Salgo v. Leland Stanford Jr. Univ. Board
of Trustees, 154 Cal. App. 2d 560, 317
P.2d 170 (1957)

In re Sampson, 328 N.Y.S.2d 686, 278
N.E.2d 918 (1972)

Sanchez v. Bay General Hospital, 116
Ca. App. 3d 776, 172 Cal. Rptr. 342,
Cal. App. 4 Dist., (1981)

In re SAS, 1 LMQ 139 (1977)

Schloendorff v. Society of New York
Hospitals, 211 N.Y. 125, 105 N.E. 92
(1914)

Schmerber v. California, 384 U.S. 757,
86 S. Ct. 1826 (1966)

Schneckloth v. Bustamonte, 412 U.S.
218, 93 S. Ct. 2041 (1973)

Sengstack v. Sengstack, 4 N.Y.2d 502,
176 N.Y.S.2d 337; 151 N.E.2d 887
(1958)

Shannon v. McNulty and HealthAmerica
Pennsylvania, 718 A.2d 828; 1998 Pa.
Super LEXIS 2383, filed October 5,
1998

Simonsen v. Swenson, 104 Neb. 224, 177
N.W. 831 (1920)

Snelson v. Culton, 141 Me. 242, 42 A.2d
505 (1949)

Stack v. Wapner, 368 A.2d 292, 244 (Pa.
Super. Ct. 278, 1976)

Stahlin v. Hilton Hotels Corp., 484 F.2d
580 (7th Cir. 1973)

State v. Brown, 8 Ore. App. 72, 491 P.2d
1193 (1971)

State v. Perea, 95 N.M. 777, 626 P.2d
851 (1981)

State v. Riggins, 348 So. 2d 1209 (Fla.
Dist. Ct. App. 1977)

Stefanik v. Nursing Education Committee,
70 R.I. 136, 37 A.2d 661 (1944)

Stevenson v. Alta Bates, 20 Cal. App. 2d
303, 66 P.2d 1265 (1937)

Stone v. Commonwealth, 418 S.W.2d
646 (Ky. 1967); cert. denied, 390 U.S.
1010

Story v. McCurtain Memorial Management, Inc., 634 P.2d 778 (Okla. Ct.
App. 1981)

Story v. St. Mary Parish Service District,
La. No. 77, 471C (January 17, 1987)

St. Paul Fire and Marine Insurance Co. v.
Prothro, 266 Ark. 1020, 590 S.W.2d
35 (Ark. Ct. App. 1979)

St. Germain v. Pfeifer, 637 N.E.2d 848
(Mass. 1994)

Sweet v. Providence Hospital, 881 P.2d
304, Alaska (1995)

T

Tarasoff v. Regents of the University of California, *131 Cal. Rptr. 14, 551 P.2d 334 (1976)*

Thompson v. The Nason Hospital, *527 Pa. 330, 591 A.2d 703 (1991)*

Thor v. Boska, *38 Cal. App. 3d 558, 113 Cal. Rptr. 296 (1974)*

Tighe v. State Board of Nurse Examiners, *40 Pa. Cmwlth. 367, 397 A.2d 1261 (1979)*

Tuma v. Board of Nursing, *100 Idaho 74, 593 P.2d 711 (1979)*

U

Ullo v. State Board of Examiners, *41 Pa. Cmwlth. 204, 398 A.2d 764 (1979)*

United States v. Montoya de Hernandez, *473 U.S. 531, 105 S. Ct. 3304 (1985)*

United States v. Winbush, *428 F.2d 357 (6th Cir. 1970)*

Utter v. United Health Center, *160 W. Va. 703, 236 S.E.2d 213 (1977)*

V

Viletto v. Weilbaecher, *377 So. 2d 132 (La. Ct. App. 1979)*

Vinnedge v. Gibbs, *550 F.2d 926 (CA 4 VA 1977)*

WX

Warden v. Hayden, *387 U.S. 294, 87 S. Ct. 1642 (1967)*

Washington State Nurses Ass'n v. Board of Medical Examiners, *93 Wash. 2d 117, 605 P.2d 1269 (1980)*

Webster v. Reproductive Health Services, *492 U.S. 490, 109 S. Ct. 3040 (1989)*

Whalen v. Roe, *429 U.S. 589, 97 S. Ct. 869 (1977)*

Whitney v. Day, *100 Mich. App. 707, 300 N.W.2d 380 (Ct. App. 1980)*

Widman v. Paoli Memorial Hospital, *No. 851034 Pa 1989*

Winters v. Miller, *446 F.2d 65 (2nd Cir. 1971)*

Woodward v. Myres, Dean, and Correctional Medical Services of Illinois, *2001 WL 506863 (N.D.Ill. 2001)*

Wyatt v. Stickney, *325 F. Supp. 781 (M.D. Ala. 1971); 344 F. Supp. 387 (M.D. Ala. 1972)*

YZ

Ybarra v. Spangard, *154 2nd 687 (California, 1994)*

Younts v. St. Francis Hospital and School of Nursing, *205 Kan. 292, 469 P.2d 330 (1970)*

Young v. Board of Hospital Directors, Lee County, *#82429 (Fl. 1984)*

INTERPRETING LEGAL CITATIONS

You may obtain information on a specific court case or law (statute or regulation) from your county courthouse law library or local law school library. If you're looking for an overview or summary of a court case or law, look up the citation in a standard legal reference, such as a legal encyclopedia *(Corpus Juris Secundum)* and a legal text *(Restatements of Law)*.

If you have a full citation, you can locate the complete text of a court case. A full citation includes the name of the court case and a series of identifying numbers and letters. If you're missing some or all of the identifying information, you can look up the case name in the index of a legal reference.

Most of the court cases on the state level will have two complete series of identifying numbers. The first series is the *official citation,* indicating where the case can be found in that state's set of court case decisions. The second series is the *unofficial citation,* indicating where the case can be found in a commercially published set of court case decisions grouped by region. Keep in mind that an "unofficial" legal reference doesn't have any less authority than an "official" legal reference.

Each citation includes an abbreviation for the legal reference that contains the law or case. For example, "U.S.L.W." stands for *United States Law Week.* For more information on legal citations, see *The Bluebook: A Uniform System of Citation,* 17th Edition. (The Harvard Law Review Association, 2000).

The number that precedes the abbreviation indicates either a volume number or title classification within the legal reference. A title classification is a body of laws or cases on a particular subject such as malpractice. A title can be one book or many books, depending on the amount of cases that bear on the titles.

Two sets of numbers follow the abbreviation. The first set indicates the page where you'll find the case. The second set, in parentheses, indicates the year of the decision.

GLOSSARY

A

AA abbr Alcoholics Anonymous

abuse of process A civil action in which it's alleged that the legal process has been used in an improper manner. For example, an abuse of process action might be brought by a physician attempting to countersue a patient or by a psychiatric patient attempting to demonstrate wrongful confinement.

ad hoc committee A committee commissioned for a specific purpose.

adjudicated incompetent Declared incompetent by exercise of judicial authority. Note that a patient who has been adjudicated incompetent may still have the mental capacity to make an informed decision about his medical care. Compare incompetence and mental incompetence.

administrative review An investigation conducted by the state board of nursing when a nurse is accused of professional misconduct. The board first reviews the complaint and then may hold a formal hearing at which evidence is presented and witnesses examined and cross-examined. Court proceedings—and possibly legal penalties—may result from the board's findings.

admissible evidence Authentic, relevant, reliable information that's present during a trial and may be used to reach a decision.

ADN abbr associate degree in nursing

adult 1. One who's fully developed and mature and who has attained the intellectual capacity and the emotional and psychological stability characteristic of a mature person. 2. A person who has reached legal age (in most states, age 18 or 21).

advance directive A document (or documentation) allowing a person to give directions about future medical care or to designate another person(s) to make medical decisions if and when the individual patient loses decision-making capacity.

advance directive system A system implemented by health care institutions (including hospitals, extended-care facilities, and hospices) to ensure that every patient, at admission, is informed of his right to execute a living will or durable power of attorney for health care decisions.

advanced practice nurse (APN) An individual whose education and certification meet criteria established by each state's board of nursing, including current licensure as a registered nurse and a master's degree or postbasic program certificate in a clinical nursing specialty with national certification.

adverse reaction A harmful, unintended reaction to a drug administered at normal dosage.

affidavit A written statement sworn to before a notary public or an officer of the court.

affirmative defense A denial of guilt or wrongdoing based on new evidence rather than simple denial of a charge. For example, a nurse who pleads immunity under the Good Samaritan law is making an affirmative defense. The defendant bears the burden of proof in an affirmative defense.

against medical advice A patient's decision to leave a health care facility against his physician's advice.

age of majority 18 or 21 years, depending on the laws of each state or Canadian province.

agency A relationship between two parties in which the first party authorizes the second to act as an agent on behalf of the first.

agent A party authorized to act on behalf of another and to give the other an account of such actions.

AHA abbr American Hospital Association

Alcoholics Anonymous (AA) An international nonprofit organization founded in 1935 that consists of abstinent alcoholics whose purpose is to help other alcoholics stop drinking and maintain sobriety through group support, shared experiences, and faith in a power greater than themselves.

alcoholism The extreme dependence on excessive amounts of alcohol, associated with a cumulative pattern of deviant behaviors. Alcoholism is a chronic illness with a slow, insidious onset, which may occur at any age. The cause is unknown, but cultural and psychosocial factors are suspect. Also, families of alcoholics have a higher incidence of alcoholism. See also drug addiction.

AMA abbr against medical advice; American Medical Association

amendment An alteration to an existing law or complaint.

American Hospital Association (AHA) Founded in 1898, the AHA is a national association comprised of individuals and health care institutions, including hospitals, health care systems, and preacute and postacute health care delivery organizations. The AHA is dedicated to promoting the welfare of the public through its leadership and assistance to its members in the provision of better health services for all people.

American Medical Association (AMA) A professional association including practitioners in all recognized medical specialties as well as general primary care physicians. The AMA is governed by a Board of Trustees and House of Delegates. Trustees and delegates represent various state and local medical associations as well as such government agencies as the Public Health Service and medical departments of the Army, Navy, and Air Force.

American Nurses Association (ANA) The national professional association of registered nurses in the United States. It was founded in 1896 to improve standards of health and the availability of health care given in order to foster high standards for nursing, to promote the professional development of nurses, and to advance the economic and general welfare of nurses. The ANA is made up of 53 constituent associations from 50 states, the District of Columbia, Guam, and the U.S. Virgin Islands, representing more than 900 district associations. Members may join one or more of the five Divisions on Nursing Practice: Community Health, Gerontological, Maternal and Child, Medical-Surgical, and Psychiatric and Mental Health Nursing. These divisions are coordinated by the Congress for Nursing Practice. The Congress evaluates changes in the scope of practice, monitors scientific and educational developments, encourages research, and develops statements that describe ANA policies regarding legislation that affects nursing practice. Other commissions within the association include the Commission on Nursing Education, the Commission on Nursing Services, the Commission on Nursing Research, and the Economic and General Welfare Commission.

American Red Cross A nationwide organization that seeks to reduce human suffering through various health, safety, and disaster relief programs in affiliation with the International Committee of the Red Cross. The Committee and all Red Cross organizations evolved from the Geneva Convention of 1864, following the example and urging of Swiss humanitarian Jean-Henri Dunant, who aided wounded French and Austrian soldiers at the Battle of Solferino in 1859. The American Red Cross (one of more than 120 national Red Cross organizations) has more than 130 million members in about 3,100 chapters throughout the United States. Volunteers constitute the entire staffs of about 1,700 chapters. Other chapters maintain small paid staffs and some

professionals but depend largely on volunteers. See also International Red Cross Society.

ANA abbr American Nurses Association

answer The response of a defendant to the claims of a plaintiff. The answer contains a denial of the plaintiff's allegations and may also contain an affirmative defense or a counterclaim. It's the principal pleading on the part of the defense and is prepared in writing, usually by the defense attorney, and submitted to the court.

APN abbr advanced practice nurse

appellant The party who lost the case in lower court and is appealing the appellate court to change the lower court's decision.

appellate court A court of law that has the power to review the decision of a lower court. An appellate court doesn't make a new determination of the facts of the case; instead, it reviews the way in which the law was applied to the case.

appellee The party in an appeal who won the case in a lower court. The appellee argues that the decision of the lower court shouldn't be modified by the appellate court.

arbitration The settlement of a dispute by an impartial person chosen by the disputing parties.

arbitrator An impartial person appointed to resolve a dispute between parties. The arbitrator listens to the evidence as presented by the parties in an informal hearing and attempts to arrive at a resolution acceptable to both parties.

assault An attempt or threat by a person to physically injure another person.

associate degree in nursing (ADN) An academic degree obtained after satisfactory completion of a 2-year course of study, usually at a community or junior college. The recipient is eligible to take the national licensing examination to become a registered nurse. An associate degree in nursing isn't available in Canada. Compare bachelor of science in nursing.

attending physician The physician who's responsible for a specific patient. In a university setting, an attending physician usually also has teaching responsibilities and holds a faculty appointment. Also called the attending (informal), physician of record.

attorney of record The attorney whose name appears on the legal records for a specific case as the agent of a specific client.

audit A methodical examination; to examine with intent to verify. Nursing audits examine standards of nursing care.

authorization cards Cards employees sign to authorize a union election.

autonomy The principle of self-determination. The right to make decisions about one's own health care.

autopsy A postmortem examination of a body to determine the cause of death.

B

bachelor of science in nursing (BSN) An academic degree awarded upon satisfactory completion of a 4-year course of study in an institution of higher learning. The recipient is eligible to take the national licensing examination to become a registered nurse. A BSN degree is prerequisite to advancement in most systems and institutions that employ nurses. Compare associate degree in nursing.

bargaining agent A person or group selected by members of a bargaining unit to represent them in negotiations.

bargaining unit A group of employees who participate in collective bargaining as representatives of all employees.

BASIC abbr Beginners' All-purpose Symbolic Instruction Code, a programming language widely used on personal computers and small business systems.

battered woman syndrome (BWS) This syndrome is the "learned helplessness" that results from repeated but failed attempts to escape a batterer's violence. Eventually, the woman stops trying to escape the violence. Such violence tends to follow a predictable pattern. The first phase is characterized by the abuser's increased irritability, edginess, and tension. These feelings are expressed in the form of verbal criticism and abuse as well as physical shoves and slaps. The second phase is the time of acute, violent activity. As tension mounts, the woman becomes unable to placate the male abuser and she may argue or defend herself. The man uses this as justification for his anger and assaults her, usually saying that he's "teaching her a lesson." The third stage is characterized by apology and remorse with promises of change on the part of the abuser. The calm continues until tension builds again. BWS occurs at all socioeconomic levels and one-half to three-quarters of female assault victims are the victims of an attack by a lover or husband. It's estimated that up to 2 million women are beaten by their husbands each year.

battery The unauthorized touching of a person by another person. For example, a physician who has treated a patient beyond what the patient has consented to has committed battery.

beneficence The promotion of good and prevention of harm.

benefits Nonsalary forms of compensation an employer provides for employees—for example, medical and dental insurance.

binding arbitration A process of settling disputes in which all parties agree to be bound by the determination of an arbitrator.

block charting A method of charting in which procedures carried out during a block of time are detailed in paragraph form.

BMA abbr British Medical Association

board of health An administrative body acting on a municipal, county, state, province, or national level. The functions, powers, and responsibilities of boards of health vary with the locale. Each board is generally concerned with the recognition of the health needs of the people and the coordination of projects and resources to meet and identify those needs. Among the tasks of most boards of health are prevention of disease, health education, and implementation of laws pertaining to health.

borrowed-servant doctrine A legal doctrine that courts may apply in cases in which an employer "lends" his employee's services to another employer who, under this doctrine, becomes solely liable for the employee's wrongful conduct. Also called ostensible agent doctrine. Compare captain-of-the ship doctrine and dual agency doctrine.

brain death Final cessation of activity in the central nervous system, especially as indicated by a flat electroencephalogram for a predetermined length of time. The cessation of all measurable function or activity in every area of the brain, including the brain stem. Compare death.

breach of contract Failure to perform all or part of a contracted duty without justification.

breach of duty Neglect or failure to fulfill in a proper manner the duties of an office, job, or position.

British Medical Association (BMA) A national professional organization of physicians in the United Kingdom.

BSN abbr bachelor of science in nursing

BWS abbr battered woman syndrome

C

Canadian Association of University Schools of Nursing (CAUSN) A national Canadian organization of nursing schools affiliated with institutions of higher learning.

Canadian Nurses Association (CNA) This official national organization is a federation of professional nurses associations from 11 jurisdictions and territories. It represents more than 110,000 members and is the national voice of the profession in Canada.

capitation A per-member, monthly payment to a provider that covers contracted services and is paid in advance of delivery. In essence, a provider agrees to provide specified services to enrollees for this fixed payment for a specified term, regardless of how many times the member uses the service.

captain-of-the-ship doctrine A legal doctrine that considers a surgeon responsible for the actions of his assistants when those assistants are under the surgeon's supervision. Compare borrowed-servant doctrine.

care plans A charting format that shows the relationships of sets of interventions to sets of intermediate outcomes along a time line.

case management The process by which a designated health care professional, usually a nurse, manages all health-related matters of a patient. Case managers coordinate and ensure continuity of care. They develop a plan to use health care resources efficiently and achieve the optimum patient outcome in the most cost-effective manner. They also match the appropriate intensity of services to the patient's needs.

causa mortis Latin phrase meaning "in anticipation of approaching death." The state of mind of a person approaching death.

CAUSN abbr Canadian Association of University Schools of Nursing

CCU abbr coronary care unit; critical care unit

CDC abbr Centers for Disease Control and Prevention

Centers for Disease Control and Prevention (CDC) An agency of the U.S. government that provides facilities and services for the investigation, identification, prevention, and control of disease.

central processing unit (CPU) In data processing, the group of physical components of a computer system containing the logical, arithmetical, and control circuits for the system. Also called hardware.

certification A statement recognizing that a nurse is specially qualified, based on predetermined standards, to provide nursing care in a particular area of nursing practice.

CGFNS abbr Commission on Graduates of Foreign Nursing Schools

certified nurse-midwife See midwife.

chain of custody An evidentiary rule requiring that each individual having custody of a piece of evidence be identified and that the transfer of evidence from one custodian to another be documented so that all evidence is

accounted for. Also called chain of evidence.

challenge An objection by a party (or his lawyer) to the inclusion of a particular prospective juror as a member of the jury that's to hear the party's cause or trial, with the result that the prospective juror is disqualified.

challenge for cause A challenge based on a particular reason (such as bias) specified by law or procedure as a reason that a party (or his lawyer) may use to disqualify a prospective juror.

charting by exception A shorthand method for documenting normal findings, based on clearly defined standards of practice and predetermined criteria for nursing assessments and interventions.

child abuse The physical, sexual, or emotional mistreatment of a child. It may be overt or covert and commonly results in physical or psychological injury, mental impairment or, sometimes, death. Child abuse results from complex factors involving both parents and child, compounded by various stressful environmental circumstances, such as poor socioeconomic conditions; inadequate physical and emotional support within the family; any major life change or crisis, especially those crises arising from marital strife; or a combination of these factors. Also called battered child syndrome for children younger than age 3. Compare child neglect.

child neglect Failure by parents or guardians to provide for the basic needs of a child by physical or emotional deprivation that interferes with normal growth and development or that places the child in jeopardy. Compare child abuse.

child welfare Any service sponsored by the community or special organizations that provides physical, social, or psychological care for children in need of that service.

chronic care A pattern of medical and nursing care that focuses on the long-term care of people with chronic diseases or conditions, either at home or in a medical facility. It includes care specific to the problem and measures to encourage self-care, promote health, and prevent loss of function.

circumstantial evidence Testimony based on inference or hearsay rather than actual personal knowledge or observation of the facts in question.

civil defense laws The body of statutory law that's invoked when the jurisdiction is under attack—for example, during a war.

civil penalty Fines or money damages imposed as punishment for a certain activity.

claims-made policy A professional liability insurance policy that covers the insured only for a claim of malpractice made while the policy is in effect.

claims review agency An agency that investigates claims for payment made to an insurance company. It determines whether the claim is legitimate, assesses how severe the loss is, and determines the amount the insurance company is required to pay.

clinical nurse specialist (CNS) A registered nurse who holds a master of science degree in nursing (MSN) and who has acquired advanced knowledge and clinical skills in a specific area of nursing and health care.

clinical pathways A clinical tool used by case managers to achieve better quality and cost outcomes by outlining and sequencing the usual and desired care for particular groups of patients. Clinical pathways incorporate care

requirements from preadmission through postdischarge. Also called critical paths.

clinical practice guidelines A decision-making tool used to help practitioners determine how diseases or disorders can most effectively and appropriately be prevented, diagnosed, treated, and managed clinically. These guidelines include advice and information from recognized clinical experts.

closed shop See union shop.

CNA abbr Canadian Nurses Association

CNM abbr certified nurse-midwife; see midwife.

CNS abbr clinical nurse specialist

code 1. A published body of statutes, such as a civil code. 2. A collection of standards and rules of behavior, such as a dress code. 3. A symbolic means of representing information for communication or transfer, such as a genetic code. 4. Informal. A discreet signal used to summon a special team to resuscitate a patient without alarming patients or visitors. See also no-code order.

codes A system of assigned terms designed by a medical institution for quick and accurate communication during emergencies or for patient identification.

collective bargaining A legal process in which representatives of unionized employees negotiate with employers about such matters as wages, hours, and conditions.

collectively bargained contract A contract negotiated by a labor organization or union. Also called a collective contract.

Commission on Graduates of Foreign Nursing Schools (CGFNS) An organization established in 1977 to ensure safe nursing care for the American public and to protect graduates of foreign nursing schools from employment exploitation.

commitment 1. The placement or confinement of an individual in a specialized hospital or other institutional facility. 2. The legal procedure of admitting a mentally ill person to an institution for psychiatric treatment. The process varies from state to state but usually involves judicial or court action based on medical evidence certifying that the person is mentally ill. 3. A pledge or contract to fulfill some obligation or agreement, used especially in some forms of psychotherapy or marriage counseling.

common law Law derived from previous court decisions as opposed to law based on legislative enactment (statutes). Also called case law. In the absence of statutory law regarding a subject, the judge-made rules of common law are the law on that subject.

comparative negligence Determination of liability in which damages may be apportioned among multiple defendants. The extent of liability depends on each defendant's relative contribution to the harm done as determined by the jury.

complaint 1. In a civil case, a pleading by a plaintiff made under oath to initiate a suit. It's a statement of the formal charge and the cause for action against the defendant. In a criminal case, a serious felony prosecution requires an indictment with evidence presented by a state's attorney. 2. Informal. Any ailment, problem, or symptom identified by the patient, member of the patient's family, or other knowledgeable person. The chief complaint is usually the reason the patient has sought health care.

computerized medical record system A system that stores medical records in the memory bank of a computer.

confidentiality A professional responsibility to keep all privileged information private. In some instances, confidentiality is mandated by state or federal statutes and case law.

consent form A document that's prepared for a patient's signature, disclosing his proposed treatment in general terms.

consequential damages See special damages.

consumer A person who buys goods or services for his own needs and not for resale or to use in the production of other goods or services for resale.

continuum of care The full range of health care services, from health promotion and disease prevention through delivery of primary care, acute care, home health care, and long-term care.

contract defense An answer to an allegation that a breach of contract has occurred. Compare impossibility defense.

contract duties Duties defined in a contract such as an employment contract.

contract violations Actions that break mutually accepted contract provisions such as those of an employment contract.

controlled substance Any substance that's strictly regulated or outlawed because of its potential for abuse or addiction. Controlled substances include cannabis, depressants, hallucinogens, opioids, and stimulants. Compare prescription drug.

convalescent home See extended-care facility.

cooperation strategy A plan for bringing about change in which the person who initiates change influences others to adapt to the change, using open communication and interpersonal skills.

coronary care unit (CCU) A specially equipped hospital area designed for the treatment of patients with sudden, life-threatening cardiac conditions. Such units contain resuscitation and monitoring equipment and are staffed by personnel specially trained and skilled in recognizing and immediately responding to cardiac emergencies with cardiopulmonary resuscitation techniques, administration of antiarrhythmics, and other appropriate therapeutic measures.

coroner A public official who investigates the causes and circumstances of a death occurring within a specific legal jurisdiction or territory, especially a death that may have resulted from unnatural causes. Also called medical examiner.

corporate liability The legal responsibility of a corporation and its officers. A corporation's liability is normally limited to its assets; the shareholders are thus protected against personal liability for the corporation.

counterclaim A claim made by a defendant establishing a cause for action in his favor against the plaintiff. The purpose of a counterclaim is to oppose or detract from the plaintiff's claim or complaint.

countersignature A signature obtained from another health care professional to verify that information is correct and is within the verifier's personal knowledge.

CPU abbr central processing unit

critical care unit (CCU) A hospital unit in which patients requiring close monitoring and intensive care are housed for as long as needed. A critical care unit contains highly technical and sophisticated monitoring devices and equipment, and the staff in the unit is educated to provide intensive care, as needed by the patients. See also intensive care unit.

critical paths See clinical pathways.

CRNA abbr certified registered nurse anesthetist; see nurse anesthetist.

cross-examination The questioning of a witness by the attorney for the opposing party.

custodial care Services and care of an unskilled nature provided on a long-term basis, usually for convalescent and chronically ill individuals. Custodial care may include providing board and personal assistance.

D

damages The amount of money a court orders a defendant to pay the plaintiff when the case is decided in favor of the plaintiff.

DEA abbr Drug Enforcement Administration

death 1. The final and irreversible cessation of life as indicated by the absence of heartbeat or respiration. 2. The total absence of meaningful activity in the brain and the central nervous, cardiovascular, and respiratory systems, as observed and declared by a physician. Also called legal death. Compare brain death.

declared emergency Situation in which a government official formally identifies a state of emergency.

decree of educational equivalency An official decision stating that a person's experience is of equal value to an academic degree.

default judgment A judgment rendered against a defendant because of the defendant's failure to appear in court or to answer the plaintiff's claim within the proper time.

defendant The party that's named in a plaintiff's complaint and against whom the plaintiff's allegations are made. The defendant must respond to the allegations. See also answer and litigant.

defense independent medical examination In malpractice litigation, a medical examination of the injured party by a physician selected by the defendant's attorney or insurance company. Compare discovery device.

delinquency 1. Negligence or failure to fulfill a duty or obligation. 2. An offense, fault, misdemeanor, or misdeed; a tendency to commit such acts.

delinquent 1. Characterized by neglect of duty or violation of law. 2. Behavior characterized by persistent antisocial, illegal, violent, or criminal activity; a juvenile delinquent.

deontology An ethical theory based on moral obligation or commitment to others.

dependent nursing function A function the nurse performs following another health care professional's written order on the basis of that professional's judgment and for which that professional is accountable.

deposition A sworn pretrial testimony given by a witness in response to oral or written questions and cross-examination. The deposition is transcribed and may be used for further pretrial investigation. It may also be presented at the trial if the witness can't be present or changes his testimony. Compare discovery device and interrogatories.

direct access The right of a health care provider and a patient to interact on a professional basis without interference.

direct contract model HMO A managed-care organization that contracts direct-

ly with individual physicians to provide services to its members.

directed verdict A verdict given by a jury at the direction of the trial judge.

direct examination The first examination of a witness called to the stand by the attorney for the party the witness is representing.

direct patient care Care of a patient provided in person by a member of the staff. Direct patient care may involve any aspect of the health care of a patient, including treatments, counseling, self-care, patient education, and administration of medication.

disclosure laws Legislation requiring that potentially confidential information be reported—for example, laws that mandate nurses report suspected child abuse or neglect.

discovery device A pretrial procedure that allows the plaintiff's and defendant's attorneys to examine relevant materials and question all parties to the case. Compare deposition, defense independent medical examination, and interrogatories.

discovery rule A rule stating that the time period for a statute of limitation begins when a patient discovers the injury. This may take place many years after the injury occurred and after the applicable statute of limitation has formally run out.

discretionary powers The freedom of a public officer to choose courses of action within the limits of his authority.

disease state management An effort to provide cost-effective care for a chronic condition by emphasizing treatment protocols and changes in personal habits. It's a comprehensive approach to lowering costs and improving patient outcomes that's applied on a disease-by-disease basis.

dismiss To discharge or dispose of an action, suit, or motion trial.

dispense To take a drug from the pharmacy and give or sell it to another person.

distributive justice The principle that advocates equal allocation of benefits and burdens to all members of society.

DO abbr Doctor of Osteopathy; see physician.

Doctor of Medicine (MD) See physician.

Doctor of Osteopathy (DO) See physician.

documentation The preparation or assembly of written records.

drug abuse The use of a drug for a nontherapeutic effect, especially one for which it wasn't prescribed or intended. Some of the most commonly abused substances are amphetamines, barbiturates, tranquilizers, and cocaine. Drug abuse may lead to organ damage, addiction, and disturbed patterns of behavior. Some illicit drugs, such as lysergic acid diethylamide, phencyclidine hydrochloride, and heroin, have no recognized therapeutic effect. Use of these drugs can incur criminal penalties in addition to the potential for physical, social, and psychological harm. See also drug addiction.

drug addiction A condition characterized by an overwhelming desire to continue taking a drug to which one has become habituated through repeated consumption because it produces a particular effect, usually an alteration of mental activity, attitude, or outlook. Addiction is usually accompanied by a compulsion to obtain the drug, a tendency to increase the dose, a psychological or physical dependence, and detrimental consequences for the individual and society. Common addictive drugs are barbiturates, cocaine, crack, and morphine and other opioids, especially heroin, which has slightly greater euphorigenic properties than other opium derivatives. See also alcoholism and drug abuse.

Drug Enforcement Administration (DEA) An agency of the federal government empowered to enforce regulations regarding the import or export of narcotic drugs and certain other substances or the traffic of these substances across state lines.

dual agency doctrine A legal doctrine stating that both the agency and the "borrowing" party may be held liable for the actions of the agent. Under this doctrine, a nurse from a nurses' registry may be held to be the agent of both the registry and the hospital. Compare borrowed-servant doctrine.

due process rights Personal rights based on the principle that the government may not deprive an individual of life, liberty, or property unless certain rules and procedures required by law are followed.

durable power of attorney A legal document enabling an individual to designate another person, called an attorney-in-fact, to act on the individual's behalf, even if the principal person becomes disabled or incapacitated. This power is revoked when the principal person dies. Compare power of attorney.

duty A legal obligation owed by one party to another. Duty may be established by statute or another legal process, such as by contract or oath supported by statute, or it may be voluntarily undertaken. Every person has a duty to avoid causing harm or injury to others by negligence.

duty-to-rescue laws Legislation that requires certain people—those who perform rescues as part of their jobs—to rescue people in need. These people include firefighters, police officers, and emergency medical technicians. Only a few states apply duty-to-rescue laws to nurses.

E

egoism An ethical theory that considers self-interest to be the goal of all human actions.

emancipated minor A minor who's legally considered free from the custody, care, and control of his parents before the age of majority. To be considered emancipated, a minor must meet one of three conditions: be living separate from parents or guardian and managing his or her own financial affairs for any length of time (with or without permission), be married, or be the birth mother of a child. Emancipated minors lose the right to parental support but may gain certain other rights, such as the right to consent to their own medical care and the right to enter into binding contracts.

Emergency Medical Service (EMS) A network of services coordinated to provide aid and medical assistance from primary response to definitive care, involving personnel trained in the rescue, stabilization, transportation, and advanced treatment of trauma or medical emergency patients. Linked by a communications system that operates on both a local and regional level, EMS is usually initiated by a citizen calling an emergency number. Stages include the first medical response; involvement of ambulance personnel, medium and heavy rescue equipment, and paramedic units, if necessary; and continued care in the hospital with emergency department nurses and physicians, specialists, and critical care nurses and physicians.

EMS abbr Emergency Medical Service

endorsement 1. The act of giving approval, support, or sanction. 2. A policy whereby the state board of nursing will accept an out-of-state license to practice nursing.

EPO abbr exclusive provider organization

ethical diagnosis The determination that a moral dilemma exists, followed by classification of the dilemma by type.

ethics An area of philosophy that examines values, actions, and choices to determine right and wrong. The study of standards of conduct and moral judgments.

euthanasia Deliberately bringing about the death of a person who's suffering from an incurable disease or condition, either actively (for example, by administering a lethal drug) or passively (for example, by withholding treatment).

evaluation Determining the extent to which nursing care has achieved its goals.

exclusionary rule A constitutional rule of law that states that otherwise admissible evidence may not be used in a criminal trial if it was obtained as a result of an illegal search and seizure.

exclusive provider organization (EPO) EPOs limit health care benefits to participating providers. EPOs are regulated under insurance laws.

executing a contract Carrying out all the terms of a contract.

exemplary damages See punitive damages.

expert witness A person who has special knowledge of a subject about which a court requests testimony. Special knowledge may be acquired by experience, education, observation, or study and isn't possessed by the average person. An expert witness gives expert testimony or expert evidence. This evidence usually serves to educate the court and the jury about the subject under consideration. Compare witness.

express contract A verbal or written agreement between two or more people to do or not do something.

extended-care facility An institution devoted to providing medical, nursing, or custodial care for an individual over a prolonged period of time, such as during the course of a chronic disease or during the rehabilitation phase after an acute illness. Kinds of extended-care facilities are intermediate care facilities and skilled nursing facilities. Also called convalescent home and nursing home.

extraordinary life-support measures Resuscitative efforts and therapies that maintain or prolong a patient's life, usually at great expense and suffering.

F

false imprisonment The act of confining or restraining a person without his consent for no clinical or legal reason.

family nurse practitioner (FNP) A nurse practitioner possessing skills necessary for the detection and management of acute self-limiting conditions and the management of chronic stable conditions. An FNP provides primary ambulatory care for families in collaboration with primary care physicians.

FDA abbr Food and Drug Administration

Federal Tort Claims Act (FTCA) A federal law that regulates how and under what circumstances the U.S. government can be sued. Sections of the law include the statute of limitations for

filing suits, the procedure for filing suits, and causes of action that may be alleged against the government.

fee-for-service 1. A charge made for a professional activity such as a physical examination. 2. A system for the payment of professional services in which the practitioner is paid for the particular service rendered rather than receiving a salary for providing professional services as needed during scheduled hours of work or time on call.

fidelity Faithfulness to agreements that one has accepted.

fiduciary A person having a duty, created by his undertaking, to act primarily for the benefit of another in matters connected with that undertaking.

fiduciary relationship A legal relationship of trust and confidence that exists whenever one person relies on another, as in a physician-patient relationship.

first aid The immediate care given to an injured or ill person. It includes self-help and home care measures.

flexible staffing patterns Work schedules that vary—for example, 10- and 12-hour shifts, shorter work weeks, and special weekend schedules.

flextime, flexitime A system of staffing that allows flexible work schedules. A person who works 7 hours daily might choose to work from 7 to 3, 10 to 5, or other hours. Use of this system tends to improve morale and decrease turnover.

FNP abbr family nurse practitioner

Food and Drug Administration (FDA) The federal agency responsible for the enforcement of federal regulations regarding the manufacture and distribution of food, drugs, and cosmetics.

forensic medicine The application of medical science to legal problems and issues.

fraud Intentional deception resulting in damage to another, whether to his person, rights, property, or reputation. Fraud usually consists of a misrepresentation, concealment, or nondisclosure of a material fact, or at least misleading conduct, devices, or contrivance.

FTCA abbr Federal Claims Tort Act

G

gatekeeper Usually a physician or nurse who screens people seeking medical care and eliminates costly and sometimes needless medical intervention and referrals to specialists for diagnosis and management.

general damages Compensation for losses that are directly referable to a legal wrong but abstract in nature, such as pain and suffering and a worsening change in lifestyle. Compare punitive damages and special damages.

gerontologic nursing Nursing care that provides for the physical, intellectual, and emotional needs of elderly people. As defined by the American Nurses Association, gerontologic nursing is the care and treatment of an older adult holistically, not just as a diseased or sick person. Nurses may choose gerontologic nursing as an area of clinical specialty.

good faith Total absence of intention to seek unfair advantage or to defraud another party; an intention to fulfill one's obligations.

Good Samaritan acts State or provincial laws that provide civil immunity from negligence lawsuits for individuals who stop and render care in an emergency.

grace period In general, any period specified in a contract during which payment is permitted, without penalty, beyond the due date of the debt.

grandfather clause A provision permitting persons engaged in an activity before passage of a law affecting that activity to receive a license without having to meet the new requirements.

grievance A complaint about working conditions or contract violations brought by an employee or union against an employer.

grievance procedure Steps agreed upon by employees and their employer to settle disputes in an orderly fashion. A labor contract may outline grievance procedures.

gross negligence The flagrant and inexcusable failure to perform a legal duty in reckless disregard for the consequences.

ground rules Rules governing a particular situation that describe legitimate behavior.

group model HMO A managed-care organization that contracts with a multispecialty group of physicians to provide all physician services to its members. The physicians are employed by the group practice—not the HMO—and may treat other patients.

guardian ad litem A person appointed by the court to safeguard a minor's or other incompetent person's legal interest during certain kinds of litigation.

H

health care consumer Any actual or potential recipient of health care, such as a patient in a hospital, a client in a community mental health center, and a member of a prepaid health maintenance organization.

health care industry The complex of preventive, remedial, and therapeutic services provided by hospitals and other institutions, nurses, physicians, dentists, government agencies, voluntary agencies, noninstitutional care facilities, pharmaceutical and medical equipment manufacturers, and health insurance companies.

health care professional Any person who has completed a course of study in a field of health care—for example, a nurse. The person is usually licensed by a government agency, such as a board of nursing, and becomes registered or licensed in that health care field. In some instances, as in a certified nursing assistant, the person is certified by a state regulatory body.

Health Insurance Portability and Accountability Act (HIPAA) A federal law that requires the Department of Health and Human Services to adopt national standards for electronic health care transactions and code set compliance.

health maintenance organization (HMO) An organization that provides basic and supplemental health maintenance and treatment services to voluntary enrollees who prepay a fixed periodic fee that's set without regard to the amount or kind of services received. Individuals and families who belong to an HMO are cared for by member physicians with limited referral to outside specialists.

health provider Any individual who provides health services to health care consumers.

HIPAA abbr Health Insurance Portability and Accountability Act

HIS abbr hospital information system

HMO abbr health maintenance organization

homestead laws Laws protecting any property designated as a homestead (any house, outbuildings, and surrounding land owned and used as a dwelling by the head of a family) from seizure and sale by creditors.

hospice A system of family-centered care designed to assist the chronically ill person to maintain a satisfactory lifestyle through the terminal phases of dying. Hospice care is multidisciplinary and includes home visits, professional medical help available on call, teaching and emotional support of the family, and physical care of the patient. Some hospice programs provide care in a center as well as in the home.

hospital information system (HIS) A computer-based information system with multiple access units to collect, organize, store, and make available data for problem solving and decision making.

hospital quality assurance program A program, developed by a hospital committee, that monitors the quality of the hospital's diagnostic, therapeutic, prognostic, and other health care activities.

hospital quality improvement program An approach to continuous study and improvement of the processes of providing health care services.

human investigations committee A committee established in a hospital, school, or university to review applications for research involving human subjects in order to protect the rights of the people to be studied. Also called human subjects investigation committee.

human subjects investigation committee See human investigations committee.

I

ICN abbr International Council of Nurses

ICU abbr intensive care unit

illegal abortion Induced termination of a pregnancy under circumstances or at a gestational time prohibited by law. Many illegal abortions are performed under medically unsafe conditions. Also called criminal abortion. Compare legal abortion and therapeutic abortion.

immunity from liability Exemption by law of a person or institution from a legally imposed penalty.

immunity from suit Exemption by law of a person or institution from being sued.

implementation 1. A deliberate action performed to achieve a goal, as in carrying out a plan in caring for a patient. 2. In the nursing process, a category of nursing behavior in which the actions necessary for accomplishing the health care plan are initiated and completed.

implied conditions Elements of a contract that aren't stated but are assumed to be part of the contract.

implied contract A contract manifested by conduct rather than words. An implied contract is based on an obligation created by law for reasons of justice and fairness. Also called quasicontract.

implied-in-law contract Obligations imposed upon a person by the law without his agreement and against his will or design because the circumstances between the parties render it just that the one should have a right and the other a corresponding liability similar to those that would arise from a contract between them.

impossibility defense A contract defense that says circumstances rendered the violation of a contract (such as not showing up for work) impossible to avoid. Compare contract defense.

incident An event that's inconsistent with ordinary routine, regardless of whether injury occurs.

incident report A formal, written report that informs a health care facility's administration (and its insurance company) about an incident and serves as a contemporary, factual statement of the incident in the event of a lawsuit.

incompetence The inability or lack of legal qualification or fitness to discharge the required duty. Compare adjudicated incompetent and mental incompetence.

indemnification Repayment or compensation for a loss. A person who has compensated another for injury, loss, or damage caused by a third party may file a suit seeking indemnification from the third party.

independent contractor A self-employed person who renders services to clients and independently determines how the work will be done.

independent practice association (IPA) model HMO A managed-care organization that contracts with an association of physicians to provide physician services to its members. The physicians maintain their independent practices.

independent provider organization (IPO) A hybrid form of managed-care organization with characteristics of both IPAs and medical associations. They're commonly organized by community physicians to provide a mechanism for evaluating and negotiating participation in HMOs.

individual contract A contract negotiated with an employer by an individual employee.

informed consent Permission obtained from a patient to perform a specific test or procedure after the patient has been fully informed about the test or procedure.

injunction A court order restraining a person from committing a specific act or requiring the individual to do something.

in loco parentis Latin phrase meaning "in the place of the parent." The assumption by a person or institution of the parental obligations of caring for a child without adoption.

inpatient 1. A patient who has been admitted to a hospital or other health care facility for at least an overnight stay. 2. Pertaining to the treatment of such a patient or to a health care facility to which a patient may be admitted for 24-hour care.

interrogatories A series of written questions submitted to a witness or other person having information of interest to the court. The answers are transcribed and are sworn to under oath. Compare deposition and discovery device.

invalid contract Any contract concerning illegal or impossible actions; no legal obligation exists.

JK

job description A written statement describing responsibilities of a specific job and the qualifications an applicant for that job should have.

Joint Commission A private, nongovernmental agency that establishes guidelines for the operation of hospitals and other health care facilities, conducts accreditation programs and surveys, and encourages the attainment of high standards of institutional medical care. Members include representatives from the American Medical Association,

American College of Physicians, and American College of Surgeons.

joint practice 1. The (usually private) practice of a physician and a nurse practitioner who work as a team, sharing responsibility for a group of patients. 2. In inpatient nursing, the practice of making joint decisions about patient care by committees of physicians and nurses working in a division.

joint statement A statement, opinion, or recommendation issued jointly by two or more organizations or committees.

judicial bypass statutes Statutes that allow a minor to go before a judge to avoid a strict requirement of parental notification or consent to obtain an abortion.

just cause A lawful, rightful, proper reason to act. A defendant establishes a cause for action in his favor.

L

law 1. In a field of study: a rule, standard, or principle that states a fact or a relationship between factors, such as Dalton's law regarding partial pressures of gas and Koch's law regarding the specificity of a pathogen. 2. a. A rule, principle, or regulation established and promulgated by a government to protect or to restrict the people affected. b. The field of study concerned with such laws. c. The collected body of the laws of a people derived from custom or from legislation.

lay jury A jury made up of people who aren't from a particular profession. For example, a lay jury in a medical malpractice trial wouldn't include physicians, nurses, or other members of the medical profession.

liability Legal responsibility for failure to act or action that fails to meet standards of care that causes another person harm.

liable Legally bound or obligated to make good any loss or damage; responsible.

liaison nurse A nurse who acts as an agent between a patient, the hospital, and the patient's family and who speaks for the entire health care team.

libel A tort consisting of a false, malicious, or unprivileged written publication aiming to defame a living person or to damage the memory of a deceased person. Compare slander.

licensed practical nurse (LPN) A person trained in basic nursing techniques and direct patient care who practices under the supervision of a registered nurse or other health care provider. An LPN must complete a course of training that usually lasts 1 to 2 years, pass the NCLEX-PN examination, and meet the requirements set forth by the board of nursing for licensure in her state. In Canada, an LPN is called a nursing assistant. In the United States, an LPN is also called a licensed vocational nurse.

licensed vocational nurse (LVN) See licensed practical nurse.

licensure Permission granted by a competent authority (usually a government agency) to an organization or person to engage in a practice or activity that would otherwise be illegal. Kinds of licensure include the issuing of licenses for general hospitals or nursing homes, for health care professionals such as physicians, and for the production or distribution of biological products. Licensure is usually granted on the basis of education and examination rather than performance. It's usually permanent but a periodic fee, demonstration of competence, or continuing education may be required. Licensure may be revoked by the granting agency for incompetence, criminal acts, or other reasons stipulated in the rules governing the specific area of licensure.

litigant A party to a lawsuit. See also defendant and plaintiff.

litigate To carry on a suit or to contest a suit.

living will A witnessed document indicating a patient's desire to be allowed to die a natural death, rather than be kept alive by heroic, life-sustaining measures. The will applies to decisions that will be made after a terminally ill patient is incompetent and has no reasonable possibility of recovery. Compare testamentary will.

living will laws Laws that help to guarantee that a patient's documented wishes regarding terminal illness procedures will be carried out. Living will laws may set forth testator and witness requirements for executing a living will and medical requirements for terminating treatment. Living will laws may also address other issues, such as authorization of a proxy for health care decisions, immunity from liability for following a living will's directives, and the withholding or withdrawal of life-sustaining treatment. Also called natural death laws and right-to-die.

locality rule Allowance made, when considering evidence in a trial, for the type of community in which the defendant practices his profession and the standards of that community.

LPN abbr licensed practical nurse

LVN abbr licensed vocational nurse; see licensed practical nurse.

M

malfeasance Performance of an unlawful, wrongful act. Compare misfeasance and nonfeasance.

malpractice A professional person's wrongful conduct, improper discharge of professional duties, or failure to meet standards of care that results in harm to another person.

managed-care organization (MCO) A system that integrates the financing and delivery of appropriate health care services to covered individuals by means of contracts with selected providers.

mandatory bargaining issues Issues, such as wages and working conditions, that an employer must address during collective bargaining.

medical directive A comprehensive advance care document that covers preferred treatment goals and specific scenarios of patient incompetence. It also includes the option to designate a proxy decision maker or power of attorney for the event of incompetence, the option to record a personal statement, and a place to designate wishes for organ donation. Also called physician's directive.

medical record A written, legal document that includes every aspect of the patient's care. A record of a person's illnesses and treatment.

medical release form The form an institution asks a patient to sign when he refuses a medical treatment. The form protects both the institution and the health care professional from liability if the patient's condition worsens because of his refusal.

Medicare Federally funded national health insurance authorized by the Social Security Act for persons age 65 and older.

medicolegal Of or pertaining to both medicine and law. Medicolegal considerations are a significant part of the process of making many patient care decisions and in setting policies about the treatment of mentally incompetent people and minors, the performance of sterilization or therapeutic abortion, and the care of terminally ill patients. Medicolegal considerations, decisions, definitions, and policies provide the framework for informed consent, professional liability, and many other aspects of health care practice.

mental competence The ability to understand information and act reasonably. A mentally competent person is capable of understanding explanations and is able to comprehend the results of his decisions.

mental incompetence The inability to understand the nature and effect of the action a person is engaged in. A mentally incompetent person is incapable of understanding explanations and is unable to comprehend the results of his decisions. Compare adjudicated incompetent and incompetence.

minor A person not of legal age; below the age of majority. Minors may not be able to consent to their own medical treatment unless they are legally emancipated. However, in many jurisdictions, parental consent is no longer necessary for certain types of medical and psychiatric treatment.

misdemeanor An offense that's considered less serious than a felony and carries with it a lesser penalty, usually a fine or imprisonment for less than 1 year.

misfeasance An improper performance of a lawful act, especially in a way that might cause damage or injury. Compare malfeasance and nonfeasance.

misrepresentation The statutory crime of giving false or misleading information, usually with the intent to deceive or be unfair.

moral dilemma An ethical problem caused by conflicts of rights, responsibilities, and values.

moral relativism An ethical theory that holds there are no ethical absolutes and whatever an individual feels is right for him at that moment is indeed right.

moral turpitude Vileness, intentional violence, deceit, fraud, or dishonesty of a high degree. A crime of moral turpitude demonstrates depravity in the private and social duties a person owes to others, contrary to what's accepted and customary. The act is considered intentionally evil.

MSN abbr Master of Science in Nursing; see master's degree program in nursing.

N

natural death laws See living will laws.

negligence Failure to act as an ordinary prudent person would under similar circumstances. Conduct that falls below the standard established by law for the protection of others under the same circumstances.

negligent nondisclosure The failure to completely inform a patient about his treatment.

negotiation A meeting at which an employer and employees confer, discuss, and bargain to reach an agreement.

nonfeasance Failure to perform a task, duty, or undertaking that one has agreed to perform or that one has a legal duty to perform. Compare malfeasance and misfeasance.

nonmaleficence An ethical principle based on the obligation to do no harm.

NP abbr nurse practitioner

nurse 1. A person educated and licensed in the practice of nursing. The nurse acts to promote, maintain, or restore the health of the patient. The American Nurses Association defines nursing as the "diagnosis and treatment of human responses to actual and potential health problems." The nurse may be a generalist or a specialist and, as a professional, is ethically and legally accountable for the nursing activities performed and for the actions of others to whom the nurse has delegated responsibility. 2. To provide nursing care. 3. To breast-feed an infant. See also nursing and registered nurse.

nurse anesthetist A registered nurse qualified by advanced training in an accredited program in the specialty of nurse anesthetist to manage the anesthetic care of the patient in certain surgical situations.

nurse practice act A law enacted by a state's legislature outlining the legal scope of nursing practice within that state.

nurse practitioner (NP) A nurse who, by advanced training and clinical experience in a branch of nursing (as in a master's degree program in nursing or a certification program), has acquired expert knowledge in a specialized branch of practice.

nursing 1. The professional practice of a nurse. 2. The process of acting as a nurse and providing care that encourages and promotes the health of the person being served. 3. According to the American Nurses Association, the "diagnosis and treatment of human responses to actual and potential health problems." 4. Breast-feeding an infant. See also nurse and registered nurse.

nursing administrator A nurse who's responsible for overseeing the efficient management of nursing services.

nursing diagnosis Descriptive interpretations of collected and categorized information indicating the problems or needs of a patient that nursing care can affect. According to the North American Nursing Diagnosis Association, "a clinical judgment about individual, community, or family responses to actual or potential health problems or to life processes. Nursing diagnoses provide the basis of selection of nursing interventions for which the nurse is accountable."

nursing process An organizational framework for nursing practice, encompassing all the major steps a nurse takes when caring for a patient. These steps are assessment, diagnosis, planning, implementation, and evaluation.

O

obligationism An ethical theory that attempts to resolve ethical dilemmas by balancing distributive justice with beneficence.

occurrence policy A professional liability insurance policy that protects against an error of omission occurring during a policy period, regardless of when the claim is made.

ombudsman A person who investigates complaints, reports findings, and helps to achieve equitable settlements.

open shop A place of employment where employees may choose whether to join a union.

oral contract Any contract that isn't in writing or isn't signed by the parties involved.

ordinary negligence The inadvertent omission of the care that a reasonably prudent nurse would ordinarily provide under similar circumstances.

original position The underlying principle of the social contract theory, which states that people in a society determine the principles of justice by which all members are bound to live.

ostensible agent doctrine See borrowed-servant doctrine.

outcomes management A process of systematically tracking a patient's clinical treatment and responses. The system encourages caregivers to follow a set of guidelines (practice guidelines or clinical pathways) that research has shown to be the "one best way" to treat a medical condition.

P

parens patriae A doctrine that appoints the state as the legal guardian of a child or incompetent adult when a person hasn't been appointed as guardian.

patient advocate A person (typically a nurse) who seeks to protect a patient's rights from infringement by institutional policies.

patient antidumping laws Amendments to the Social Security Act intended to prevent hospitals from turning away patients who are uninsured or unable to pay. They require that hospitals participating in Medicare provide medical screening and stabilizing treatment for any patient who has an emergency condition or is in labor and provide guidelines and require documentation for transfers to other facilities or for hospital discharge.

patient classification systems Ways of grouping patients so that the size of the staff needed to care for them can be estimated accurately.

patient's bill of rights Documents that define a person's rights while receiving health care. Bills of rights for patients are designed to protect such basic rights as human dignity, privacy, confidentiality, informed consent, and refusal of treatment. The American Hospital Association, the National League for Nursing, the American Civil Liberties Union, and other organizations and health care institutions have prepared patient's bills of rights. Concepts expressed in these documents may be incorporated into law. Although bills of rights issued by health care institutions and professional organizations don't have the force of law, nurses should regard them as professionally binding.

peremptory challenge A right given to attorneys at trial to dismiss a prospective juror for no particular reason; the number of times an attorney can invoke this right is usually limited.

persistent vegetative state A state of severe mental impairment in which only involuntary bodily functions are sustained.

physician 1. A health professional who has earned a degree of Doctor of Medicine (MD) after completion of an approved course of study at an approved medical school and satisfactory completion of the National Board Examinations. 2. A health professional who has earned a degree of Doctor of Osteopathy (DO) by satisfactorily completing a course of education in an approved college of osteopathy.

physician of record See attending physician.

physician assistant (PA) A health care professional licensed to practice medicine with physician supervision. PAs conduct physical examinations, diagnose and treat illnesses, order and interpret tests, counsel on preventive health care, assist in surgery, and write prescriptions. PAs are trained in intensive education programs accredited by the Accreditation Review Commission on Education for the Physician Assistant. PAs are educated in the medical model designed to compliment physician training. Upon graduation, physician assistants take a national certification examination developed by the National Commission on Certification of PAs in conjunction with the National Board of Medical Examiners. Graduation from an accredited physician assistant program and passage of the national certifying examination are required for state licensure.

plaintiff A person who files a civil lawsuit initiating a legal action. In criminal actions, the prosecution is the plaintiff, acting on behalf of the people in the jurisdiction. See also litigant.

policy defense Rationale for denying coverage given by professional liability insurance carriers when a client submits a claim. Reasons for denial may include failure to pay a premium on time or failure to renew the policy.

power of attorney A legal document enabling an individual to designate another person, called an attorney-in-fact, to act on the individual's behalf as long as the individual doesn't become disabled or incapacitated. Power of attorney continues to operate only with the continued consent of the person who granted it. If the grantor of the power should become incompetent, the power of attorney is automatically revoked. It's also revoked when the grantor dies. Compare durable power of attorney.

PPO abbr preferred provider organization

practicing medicine without a license Practicing activities defined under state or provincial law in the Medical Practice Act without medical supervision, direction, or control.

practicing pharmacy without a license
Practicing activities defined under state or provincial law in the Pharmacy Practice Act without pharmacist supervision, direction, or control. These laws give pharmacists the sole legal authority to prepare, compound, preserve, and dispense drugs.

presumed consent A legal principle based on the belief that a rational and prudent person would consent in the same situation, if able to. Applies primarily to emergency care of unconscious patients but may be expanded to cadaver organ donors.

privacy One's private life or personal affairs. The right to privacy refers to the right to be left alone and to be free from unwanted publicity.

privileged communication A conversation in which the speaker intends the information given to remain private between himself and the listener.

privilege doctrine A doctrine that protects the privacy of persons within a fiduciary relationship, such as a husband and wife, a physician and patient, or a nurse and patient. During legal proceedings, a court can't force either party to reveal communications between them unless the party who would benefit from the protection agrees.

probate 1. The act of proving that a purported will was signed and executed in accordance with the law and of determining its validity. 2. The combined result of all procedures necessary to establish the validity of a will.

probation period A period of time during which an individual is observed and evaluated to ascertain fitness for a particular job or duty.

professional liability A legal concept describing the obligation of a professional person to pay a patient or client for damages caused by the professional's act of omission, commission, or negligence, after a court determines that the professional was negligent. Professional liability better describes the responsibility of all professionals to their clients than does the concept of malpractice, but the idea of professional liability is central to malpractice.

professional liability insurance A type of liability insurance that protects professional persons against malpractice claims.

proviso A condition or stipulation. Its general function is to except something from the basic provision, to qualify or restrain its general scope, or to prevent misinterpretation.

proximate cause A legal concept of cause and effect, which says a sequence of natural and continuous events produces an injury that wouldn't have otherwise occurred.

proxy The recipient of a grant of authority to act or speak for another.

psychiatric nurse practitioner A nurse practitioner who, by advanced study and clinical practice, has gained expert knowledge in the care and prevention of mental disorders.

PTNA abbr Provincial Territorial Nurses Association

punitive damages Compensation in excess of actual damages that are a form of punishment to the wrongdoer and reparation to the injured. These damages are awarded only in rare instances of malicious and willful misconduct. Also called exemplary damages. Compare general damages and special damages.

Q

qualified privilege A conditional right or immunity granted to the defendant because of the circumstances of a legal case.

quality of life A legal and ethical standard that's determined by relative suffering or pain, not by the degree of disability.

R

reasonably prudent nurse The standard a court uses to judge a nurse being sued for negligence. The court considers whether another nurse would have acted similarly to the defendant under similar circumstances.

rebuttable presumption A presumption that may be overcome or disputed by contrary evidence.

redefinition A rewriting of the fundamental provision of a nurse practice act. This changes the basic premise of the entire act without amending or repealing it.

registered nurse (RN) 1. In the United States: A professional nurse who has completed a course of study at an approved school of nursing, passed the NCLEX-RN, and met the requirements for licensure set forth by the board of nursing in her state. A registered nurse may use the initials RN following her signature. RNs are licensed to practice by individual states. 2. In Canada: A professional nurse who has completed a course of study at an approved school of nursing and who has taken and passed an examination administered by the Canadian Nurses Association Testing Service. See also nurse and nursing.

remand To send back. An appellate court may send a case back to the lower court that considered the case, ordering that further action be taken there.

res ipsa loquitur Latin phrase meaning "the thing speaks for itself." A legal doctrine that applies when the defendant was solely and exclusively in control at the time the plaintiff's injury occurred, so that the injury wouldn't have occurred if the defendant had exercised due care. In addition, the injured party couldn't have contributed to his own injury. When a court applies this doctrine to a case, the defendant bears the burden of proving that he wasn't negligent.

respondeat superior Latin phrase meaning "let the master answer." A legal doctrine that makes an employer indirectly liable for the consequences of his employee's wrongful conduct while the employee is acting within the scope of his employment.

right-of-conscience laws Based on freedom of thought or of religion, these laws allow a health care provider to refuse to care for a patient when an objection to the care or lack of care exists.

right-to-access laws Laws that grant a patient the right to see his medical records.

right-to-die law Law that upholds a patient's right to choose death by refusing extraordinary treatment. Also called living will law and natural death law.

right to notice 1. A due process right requiring that the accused receive timely notification of both the pending charges and the hearing date. 2. An employee's right to receive sufficient notification or warning before termination. This allows the employee time to protest or appeal the termination and to seek employment elsewhere.

risk management The identification, analysis, evaluation, and elimination or reduction—to the extent possible of risks to an organization's patients, visitors, or employees. Risk management programs are involved with both loss prevention and loss control and handle all incidents, claims, and other insurance- and litigation-related tasks.

rule A guide for conduct that describes the actions that should or shouldn't be taken in specific situations. Compare policy.

S

school nurse practitioner (SNP) A registered nurse qualified by postgraduate study to act as a nurse practitioner in a school.

scope of practice In nursing, the professional nursing activities defined under state or province law in each state's (or Canadian province's) nurse practice act.

service of process The delivery of a writ, summons, or complaint to a defendant. The original document is shown; a copy is served. Service of process gives reasonable notice to allow the person to appear, testify, and be heard in court. See also summons.

settlement An agreement made between parties to a suit before a judgment is rendered by a court.

slander Spoken words that may damage another person's reputation. Compare libel.

slippery slope principle An ethical principle based on the belief that, when an ethical or legal barrier has been lowered, desensitization to the ethical or legal principle occurs.

sovereign immunity doctrine A privilege granted to the elected government and its appointed agents—government employees—giving them immunity from lawsuits.

special damages Compensation for indirect loss or injury, such as present and future medical expenses, past and future loss of earnings, and decreased earning capacity. Also called consequential damages. Compare general damages and punitive damages.

specialty standard The standard of care that applies to a given nursing specialty.

standard 1. A criterion that serves as a basis for comparison for evaluating similar phenomena or substances, such as a standard for the practice of a profession. 2. A pharmaceutical preparation or a chemical substance of known quantity, ingredients, and strength that's used to determine the constituents or the strength of another preparation. 3. Of known value, strength, quality, or ingredients.

standards of care Criteria that serve as a basis of comparison when evaluating the quality of nursing practice. In a malpractice lawsuit, a measure by which the defendant's alleged wrongful conduct is compared—acts performed or omitted that an ordinary, reasonably prudent nurse, in the defendant's position, would have done or not done.

statute of limitation Law that sets forth the length of time within which a person may file a specific type of lawsuit.

statutory law A law passed by a federal or state legislature.

statutory rape Sexual intercourse with a person below the age of consent. (Age of consent varies from state to state; usually age 18.)

steward A union representative.

subpoena A writ issued under authority of a court to compel the appearance of a witness at a judicial proceeding; disobedience may be punishable as contempt of court.

substantive laws Laws that define and regulate a person's rights.

substitute consent Permission obtained from a parent or legal guardian of a patient who's a minor or who has been declared incompetent by the court.

substitute judgment A legal term indicating the court's substitution of its own judgment for that of a person the court considers unable to make an informed decision such as an incompetent adult.

sudden emergency exception Defense used by hospitals in liability cases involving understaffing when staffing shortages couldn't have been anticipated, as opposed to chronic understaffing.

summary judgment A judgment requested by any party to a civil action to end the action when it's believed that there's no genuine issue or material fact in dispute.

summons A document issued by a clerk of the court upon the filing of a complaint. A sheriff, marshal, or other appointed person serves the summons, notifying a person that an action has been begun against him. See also service of process.

T

terminate In contract law, to fulfill all contractual obligations or to absolve oneself of the obligation to fulfill them.

termination The procedure an employer follows to fire an employee.

testamentary Any document, such as a will, that doesn't take effect until after the death of the person who wrote it.

testamentary will A will whose provisions take effect after death. Compare living will.

testator One who makes and executes a testament or will.

therapeutic privilege A legal doctrine that permits a physician to withhold information from the patient if he can prove that disclosing it would adversely affect the patient's health.

third-party reimbursement Reimbursement for services rendered to a person in which an entity other than the giver or receiver of the service is responsible for the payment. Insurance plans commonly pay third-party reimbursement for the cost of a subscriber's health care.

tort A civil wrong outside of a contractual relationship.

trial de novo A proceeding in which both issues of law and issues of fact are reconsidered as if the original trial had never taken place. New testimony may be introduced, or the matter may be determined a second time on the basis of the evidence already produced.

U

unfair labor practices Actions taken by an employer that are prohibited by state and federal labor laws. This term commonly refers to tactics used by an employer to discourage employees from participating in union activities. For example, under the National Labor Relations Act, unfair labor practices include interfering with, restraining, or coercing employees who exercise their right to organize.

Uniform Anatomical Gift Act A law in all 50 states that allows anyone older than age 18 to sign a donor card, donating some or all of his organs after death.

V

values Strongly held personal and professional beliefs about worth and importance. The social principles, goals, or standards held by an individual or society.

verbal order A spoken order given directly and in person by a physician to a nurse.

voluntary bargaining issues Issues such as noneconomic fringe benefits that an employer or union may or may not address during collective bargaining.

WXYZ

witness 1. One who gives evidence in a case before a court and who attests or swears to facts or gives testimony under oath. 2. To observe the execution of an act, such as the signing of a document, or to sign one's name to authenticate the observation.

writ of habeas corpus Literally means "you have the body"; a process whereby an individual detained or imprisoned asks the court to rule on the validity of the detainment or imprisonment. If the person is granted the writ, he must be released immediately.

wrongful death statute A statute existing in all states that provides that the death of a person can give rise to a cause of legal action brought by the person's beneficiaries in a civil suit against the person whose willful or negligent acts caused the death. Prior to the existence of these statutes, a suit could be brought only if the injured person survived.

wrongful life action A civil suit usually brought against a physician or health care facility on the basis of negligence that resulted in the wrongful birth or life of an infant. The parents of the unwanted child seek to obtain payment from the defendant for the medical expenses of pregnancy and delivery, for pain and suffering, and for the education and upbringing of the child. Wrongful life actions have been brought and won in several situations, including unsuccessful tubal ligations and vasectomies. Failure to diagnose pregnancy in time for abortion and incorrect medical advice leading to the birth of a defective child have also led to malpractice suits for a wrongful life.

INDEX

i refers to an illustration; t refers to a table.

i refers to an illustration; t refers to a table.

i refers to an illustration; t refers to a table.

i refers to an illustration; t refers to a table.